BELLAMY & CHILD

EUROPEAN COMMUNITY
LAW OF COMPETITION

BELLAMY & CHILD

EUROPEAN COMMUNITY LAW OF COMPETITION

SECOND CUMULATIVE SUPPLEMENT

by

VIVIEN ROSE

Chairman of the Competition Appeal Tribunal

OXFORD
UNIVERSITY PRESS

OXFORD
UNIVERSITY PRESS

Great Clarendon Street, Oxford ox2 6dp

Oxford University Press is a department of the University of Oxford.
It furthers the University's objective of excellence in research, scholarship,
and education by publishing worldwide in

Oxford New York

Auckland Cape Town Dar es Salaam Hong Kong Karachi
Kuala Lumpur Madrid Melbourne Mexico City Nairobi
New Delhi Shanghai Taipei Toronto

With offices in

Argentina Austria Brazil Chile Czech Republic France Greece
Guatemala Hungary Italy Japan Poland Portugal Singapore
South Korea Switzerland Thailand Turkey Ukraine Vietnam

Oxford is a registered trade mark of Oxford University Press
in the UK and in certain other countries

Published in the United States
by Oxford University Press Inc., New York

© Oxford University Press, 2012

British Library Cataloguing-in-Publication Data
Data available

Library of Congress Cataloging-in-Publication Data
Data available

Typeset by Cenveo, Bangalore, India
Printed in Great Britain
on acid-free paper by
CPI Group (UK) Ltd, Croydon, CR0 4YY

ISBN 978–0–19–963969–4

1 3 5 7 9 10 8 6 4 2

OVERSEAS CASE REPORTS FOR THE FIRST SUPPLEMENT

GENERAL EDITOR

Peter Roth

A Justice of the High Court and Chairman of the Competition Appeal Tribunal

CORRESPONDENT EDITORS

CONTENTS

Preface and Highlights of the Second Supplement to the 6th Edition ix
Note on the Lisbon Treaty xxiii
Alphabetical Table of EU Cases and Decisions xxv
Tables of European Court of Human Rights, EFTA Court and
 National Cases xli
Cases Published since the 6th Edition xlvii
Tables of Equivalences: Treaty on European Union and Treaty on the
 Functioning of the European Union xlix

1. The Treaty and its Territorial Reach 1
2. Article 81(1) 15
3. Article 81(3) 43
4. Market Definition 51
5. Common Horizontal Agreements 69
6. Vertical Agreements Affecting Distribution or Supply 97
7. Joint Ventures and Similar Collaborative Arrangements 125
8. Merger Control 137
9. Intellectual Property Rights 173
10. Article 82 183
11. The Competition Rules and the Acts of Member States 219
12. Sectoral Regimes 227
13. Enforcement and Procedure 253
14. The Enforcement of the Competition Rules in the Member States 329
15. State Aids 353

PREFACE AND HIGHLIGHTS OF THE SECOND SUPPLEMENT TO THE 6TH EDITION

This second supplement to the 6th edition of *Bellamy & Child*, combined with the 2012 edition of the Materials Volume, covers the substantial changes that have occurred in the years since the main work was published. It incorporates the material included in the first Supplement and so effectively replaces that volume. The 18 months since the first Supplement have brought revisions of the block exemptions relating to vertical restraints and motor vehicle distribution, research & development and specialisation agreements. The Commission has also published important guidance and 'best practice' covering both substantive and procedural matters. The General Court has determined a multitude of appeals from cartel decisions, each one developing the law on procedure and fining practice, including the first appeals considering the provisions of the 2006 Guidelines on Fines.

My thanks go to Andrew Macnab for his excellent work in ensuring that the Materials volume continues to be a comprehensive and user-friendly source book for the materials considered in both the main work and this Supplement.

Other important developments are highlighted in the following paragraphs.

Chapter 1. The Treaty and its Territorial Reach

The Lisbon Treaty was ratified by the 27 Member States and came into effect on 1 December 2009. This brings about various changes to nomenclature including the replacement of the EC Treaty with the Treaty on the Functioning of the European Union; the renumbering of the Treaty articles; the disappearance of the term 'European Community' in favour of 'European Union'; and the renaming of the Court of First Instance as the General Court.

The Court of Justice has laid down the rules as to the appropriate regime under which the Commission can sanction anti-competitive conduct in the sectors which used to be covered by the ECSC Treaty: Case C-352/09P *ThyssenKrupp Nirosta v Commission*, judgment of 29 March 2011 and Cases C-201&216/09P *ArcelorMittal v Commission*, judgment of 29 March 2011.

Chapter 2. Article 81(1)

The fundamental concepts of Article 101 TFEU continue to develop with clarification of the circumstances in which a shareholder is to be treated as part of the undertaking in which the shares are held: Case C-222/04 *Ministero dell'Economia e delle Finanze v Cassa di Risparmio di Firenze SpA* [2006] ECR I-289, [2008] 1 CMLR 705 subsequently applied in Cases T-208&209/08 *Gosselin Group v Commission*, judgment of 16 June 2011. The vexed question of when a State entity is carrying on economic activity caught by the competition rules was the subject of an important judgment of the Court of Justice in Case C-113/07P *SELEX Sistemi Integrati SpA v Commission* [2009] ECR I-2207, holding that the range of activities which are to be treated as connected with the exercise of public functions (and hence beyond the scope of the competition rules) is wider than the General Court had indicated in its judgment in the case. The relationship between a regulatory body and the State was also examined by the Commission in COMP/39510 *Ordre National des Pharmaciens en France (ONP)*, decn of 8 December 2010. Some of the same issues have been tackled by the Irish High Court in *Hemat v The Medical Council* [2010] IESC 24; and *Neurendale Ltd t/a Panda Waste Services v Dublin City Council* [2009] IEHC 588.

The occupation and use of publicly owned facilities was the subject of an important judgment in Case T-196/04 *Ryanair v Commission* [2008] ECR II-3643, a State aid case where the General Court held that the fixing of the amount of landing charges at Charleroi airport and an indemnity granted to Ryanair by the Walloon Region amounted to an economic activity.

The law relating to when social insurance schemes linked with collective labour relations constitute 'undertakings' for the purposes of the competition rules has also been revisited by the Luxembourg Courts in Case C-437/09 *AG2R Prevoyance v Beaudout*, judgment of 3 March 2011.

There have been several important cases on the elements required to establish a concerted practice: Case C-8/08 *T-Mobile Netherlands BV v Raad van bestuur van de Nederlandse Mededingingsautoriteit*, judgment of 4 June 2009 where the Court held that the presumption of an effect on the market arising from continued presence of the undertakings on the market is an integral part of applicable EU law and therefore prevails when the national court is applying Article 101. Further, the Court held, the presumption applies even if the concerted action is the result of a meeting held by the participating undertakings on a single occasion rather than of a course of conduct. The circumstances in which a plausible alternative explanation for apparent parallel conduct is relevant to the existence of a concerted practice were considered in COMP/38698 *CISAC*, 16 July 2008, [2009] 4 CMLR 577; and Case T-36/05 *Coats Holdings Ltd v Commission* [2007] ECR II-110, [2008] 4 CMLR 45. There have been several cases concerning when a series of meetings can be characterised as a 'single continuous infringement' with the General Court overturning part of the Commission's decision in *Choline Chloride*: see Cases T-101&111/05 *BASF AG and UCB SA v Commission* [2007] ECR II-4949, [2008] 4 CMLR 347.

The issue of when a complex set of anti-competitive meetings can be treated as a single continuous infringement has continued to generate much case law: see, eg Cases T-204&212/08 *Team Relocations v Commission*, judgment of 16 June 2011 and the appeals from the *Butadiene Rubber, Gas Insulated Switchgear* and *Industrial Thread* cartel decisions. Appeals from cartel decisions have also generated more case law on the question of how far a participant in one branch of a cartel can be held responsible for the larger infringement of which that branch formed a part: see, eg Case T-21/05 *Chalkor v Commission*, judgment of 19 May 2010, [2010] 5 CMLR 1295; Case T-385/06 *Aalberts Industries NV v Commission*, judgment of 24 March 2011; and also Case T-18/05 *IMI plc v Commission*, judgment of 19 May 2010. The General Court has continued to uphold the Commission's reliance on evidence from one cartel participant to prove the infringement of other participants, provided the necessary corroboration is present: Case T-377/06 *Comap v Commission*, judgment of 24 March 2011; and Case T-133/07 *Mitsubishi Electric v Commission*, judgment of 12 July 2011. In the latter case the General Court rejected an argument that the heavy fines now imposed on cartel participants meant that the traditionally permissive attitude towards the admissibility of evidence was no longer justified. However, there have been some cases where the General Court found that the Commission's case was 'not proven' against a participant or a parent found jointly and severally liable: see Cases T-235/07 *Bavaria v Commission*, judgment of 16 June 2011; and Case T-53/07 *Trade-Stomil v Commission*, judgment of 13 July 2011.

Some of the discussion in the 6th edition of the main work of the conceptual issues surrounding competition and consumer detriment must now be read in the light of the Court of Justice's judgment in Cases C-501/06P, etc, *GlaxoSmithKline Services Unlimited v Commission*, judgment of 6 October 2009, [2010] CMLR 50. The Court of Justice overturned the General Court's analysis insofar as it held that it was necessary to prove that an agreement entails disadvantages for final consumers as a prerequisite for a finding of anti-competitive object. There have been other important cases on how to define the 'object' of an agreement for the purposes of Article 101(1), particularly Case C-209/07 *Beef Industry Development Society Ltd v Barry Brothers (Carrigmore) Meats Ltd* [2008] ECR I-8637, [2009] 4 CMLR 310, [2009] All ER (EC) 367; and *Bookmakers' Afternoon Greyhound Services v Amalgamated Racing Ltd* [2009] EWCA Civ 750 in the English Court of Appeal.

Chapter 3. Article 81(3)

The relationship between the two paragraphs of Article 101 in the post-Modernisation world has been considered by the Commission in some important decisions concerning payment card systems: COMP/37860 *Morgan Stanley/Visa International and Visa Europe*, decn of 3 October 2007; and COMP/34579 *MasterCard MIF charges*, decn of 19 December 2007, para 690. The Chapter also notes a number of new block exemptions for vertical agreements, motor vehicle distribution agreements, insurance agreements, research and development agreements and specialisation/production agreements and their accompanying guidelines.

Chapter 4. Market Definition

Cases under the Merger Regulation continue to provide illustrations of a wide variety of issues arising from market definition such as critical loss analysis (Case M.5141 *KLM/Martinair* (17 December 2008); and Case M.4734 *INEOS/Kerling* (30 January 2008)); shock analysis or event evidence (Case M.5046 *Friesland/Campina* (17 December 2008) and Case M.4734 *INEOS/Kerling* (30 January 2008)); and the relevance of in-house production (Case M.4731 *Google/DoubleClick* (11 March 2008) and Case M.4781 *Norddeutsche Affinerie/Cumerio* (23 January 2008)).

The payment card system decisions have also clarified the Commission's approach to analysing 'two-sided markets' with the General Court upholding the Commission's analysis in Case T-461/07 *Visa v Commission*, judgment of 14 April 2011; see also COMP/38606 *Groupement des Cartes Bancaires*, decn of 17 October 2007; and Case M.4523 *Travelport/Worldspan* (21 August 2007).

The case concerning spare parts for luxury Swiss watches provides a useful illustration of the General Court's analysis of ancillary and systems markets: Case T-427/08 *Confédération européenne des associations d'horlogers-réparateurs (CEAHR) v Commission*, judgment of 15 December 2010 and the General Court's ruling in the *AstraZeneca* Article 102 case also showed how markets can develop in the rapidly evolving sector of pharmaceutical products: Case T-321/05 *AstraZeneca v Commission*, judgment of 1 July 2010, [2010] 5 CMLR 1575.

The Chapter also highlights a number of merger cases in which the Commission has considered whether internet retail distribution forms part of the same relevant market as bricks-and-mortar shops.

Chapter 5. Common Horizontal Agreements

The Commission has continued to impose substantial fines on cartels in recent years. The General Court upheld the Commission's finding that a trade association which provides administrative and secretarial assistance to a cartel can be regarded as a party to the cartel even if it is not itself a producer of the relevant product: Case T-99/04 *AC-Treuhand AG v Commission* [2008] ECR II-1501, [2008] 5 CMLR 962. Important decisions have been published in particular sectors: credit cards and payments systems (COMP/34579 *MasterCard MIF charges*, decn of 19 December 2007; COMP/34579 *MasterCard MIF charges*, decn of 19 December 2007; and COMP/38606 *Groupement des Cartes Bancaires*, decn of 17 October 2007) and the collective licensing of music rights (COMP/38698 *CISAC*, 16 July 2008, [2009] 4 CMLR 577).

The Commission's Horizontal Cooperation Guidelines (OJ 2011 C11/1) set out the Commission's approach to a range of non-covert horizontal agreements in particular information exchange where the Commission explains the different factors that make an agreement more or less likely to fall foul of Article 101. The Guidelines also cover agreements on commercialisation which involve cooperation between competitors in the selling, distribution or promotion of their products. The Guidelines indicate the importance of assessing the impact of the arrangement on neighbouring markets as well as on the market to which the products directly covered by the arrangements belong.

The practice of cover bidding has been the subject of scrutiny both at the European and national level: see Case T-210/08 *Verhuizingen Coppens v Commission*, judgment of 16 June 2011; and *Kier Group plc v Office of Fair Trading* [2011] CAT 3 in the United Kingdom Competition Appeal Tribunal.

The *Ship Classification* decision by the Commission (decision of 14 October 2009) provided an opportunity to revisit the law governing membership rules of an important trade association concerned with standard setting. Standard setting more generally has been considered in the Horizontal Cooperation Guidelines and in the important decision in COMP/38636 *RAMBUS*, decn of 9 December 2009 where the Commission accepted commitments to remove the adverse effects of an alleged 'patent ambush' in relation to essential computer components.

Chapter 6. Vertical Agreements Affecting Distribution or Supply

This Chapter explores the new Vertical Restraints block exemption (Regulation 330/2010) and Motor Vehicle Distribution Agreements block exemption (Regulation 461/2010) together with their respective accompanying new guidelines. One point to highlight in relation to Regulation 330/2010 is the introduction of a market share threshold for the buyer whose business must also not exceed 30 per cent of the relevant market on which it purchases the contract goods or services. The Vertical Restraints Guidelines are notable for their discussion of how the concepts of active and passive sales apply to internet and email marketing. The Chapter describes the interaction of Regulation 330/2010 with the new block exemption for motor vehicle agreements. The latter category of agreements are now treated differently depending on whether they relate to new cars (in which case they will be governed by the general block exemption after 31 May 2013) or aftersales service (in which case they are governed by a slimmed down special regime as from 1 June 2010).

The provisions of the new Guidelines relating to other categories of vertical agreement are also discussed in the Chapter.

Chapter 7. Joint Ventures and Similar Collaborative Arrangements

Although there continues to be little case law arising from joint venture arrangements, this Chapter now explores the two new block exemptions for research and development agreements (Regulation 1217/2010) and specialisation agreements (Regulation 1218/2010). Both kinds of agreements are also considered in the Commission's new Horizontal Cooperation Guidelines.

Chapter 8. Merger Control

As always, I am pleased to be able to express my warm thanks to John Boyce and Marzena Rembowski at the Brussels office of Slaughter and May for providing the updates for the tables in the Mergers chapter and for helping me to identify the decisions under the Merger Regulation which need to be included.

The Commission has issued a revised Notice on Remedies (OJ 2008 C267/1). The Notice provides guidance on different commitments that can be offered at any stage of the process, focusing particularly on divestiture. A new Form RM has been incorporated into the Implementing Regulation as Annex IV specifying the information and documents that undertakings should submit when offering commitments. The Commission has also issued Non-Horizontal Merger Guidelines setting out how it will analyse the competitive effects in vertical and conglomerate mergers. There have been a number of important decisions analysing vertical mergers (Case M.5121 *News Corp/Premiere* (26 June 2008); Case M.4854 *Tom Tom/Tele Atlas* (14 May 2008); Case M.4942 *Nokia/Navteq* (2 July 2008); and Case M.4523 *Travelport/Worldspan* (21 August 2007)) and conglomerate mergers (Case M.4731 *Google/DoubleClick* (11 March 2008)).

The discussion in this chapter of oligopolistic markets must now be read in the light of the Court of Justice's judgment in Case C-413/06P *Bertelsmann AG and Sony Corporation of America v Impala and Commission* [2008] ECR I-4951. The test for characterising a market as oligopolistic has been applied in a number of subsequent decisions, for example Case M.4980 *ABF/GBI Business* (23 September 2008); and Case M.5114 *Pernod Ricard/V&S Vin & Sprit* (17 July 2008). A number of decisions have discussed the role of a target company which operated as a 'maverick' constraint (Case M.4919 *Statoil/ConocoPhillips (Jet)* (21 October 2008); and Case M.4844 *Fortis/ABN Amro Assets* (3 October 2007)).

The distinction between dominance or strengthening of dominance on the one hand and a significant impediment to effective competition on the other was analysed in Case M.5529 *Oracle Corporation/Sun Microsystems* (21 January 2010). That decision was also notable for the Commission's reliance on public 'pledges' made by Oracle to the software using community as allaying concerns about possible downgrading of the competing Sun Microsystems product post-merger. Conglomerate effects were analysed in Case M.5984 *Intel/McAfee* (26 January 2011) where the

Commission also considered the ability and incentive of the entity post-merger to downgrade interoperability and foreclose the market. In the latter decision the Commission also noted that behavioural rather than structural remedies are often more appropriate in conglomerate cases.

The ongoing litigation concerning Ryanair's minority interest in Aer Lingus is also covered in the Chapter.

Chapter 9. Intellectual Property Rights

The conflict between the Court of Justice's judgments in *Silhouette* and *Sebago* and the EFTA Court's judgment in *Mag Instrument* has now been resolved in favour of a consistent interpretation of Article 7 of Directive 89/104 and a prohibition on international exhaustion within the EEA: Cases E-9&10/07 *L'Oréal Norge v Per Aarskog AS*, decision of the EFTA Court 8 July 2008. The Court's judgment in C-275/06 *Promusicae* [2008] ECR I-276, [2008] All ER (EC) 809 considered the obligations imposed on an internet service provider to assist a rights holder by disclosing the identities of those using file sharing internet sites. The Court also upheld the General Court's analysis of the application of Article 102 to the licensing fees set for the use of the Green Dot logo on recyclable packaging: Case C-385/07P *Der Grüne Punkt—Duales System Deutschland v Commission*, judgment of 16 July 2009, [2009] 5 CMLR 2215.

At time of writing, the Advocate General had delivered her opinion in the Greek decoder cards case: Cases C-403&429/08 *Football Association Premier League v QC Leisure/ Murphy v Media Protection Services* but the Court of Justice has not delivered its judgment. Advocate General Kokott suggested a strict stance to the segregation of national markets, considering that allowing rights-holders to prohibit third parties from watching and showing those football matches in Member States other than those intended constituted a serious restriction on the freedom to use services from another Member State. Further she considers that the restriction was not justified by the need to safeguard the specific subject matter of these rights. Her opinion contains an interesting analysis of the much older *Coditel I* judgment.

Chapter 10. Article 82

The Commission's Guidance on Enforcement Priorities in applying Article 82 to exclusionary conduct contains much useful guidance on how the Commission will approach issues such as defining anti-competitive foreclosure generally, and in relation to particular abuses such as exclusive dealing, tying and bundling, and predation. The Commission has also adopted the decision in COMP/37990 *Intel*, decn of 13 May 2009 imposing substantial fines for exclusionary conduct.

The discussion of collective dominance focuses on the judgment of the Court of Justice in Case C-413/06P *Bertelsmann AG and Sony Corporation of America v*

Impala and Commission [2008] ECR I-4951. The Court describes the conditions in which collective dominance will arise. The Court emphasised the importance of avoiding a mechanical approach involving the separate verification of each of those criteria taken in isolation and emphasised that one must take account of the overall economic mechanism of a hypothetical tacit coordination.

There has been a series of decisions clarifying the law on margin squeeze: Case C-280/08P *Deutsche Telekom v Commission*, judgment of 14 October 2010, [2010] 5 CMLR 1485; Case C-52/09 *Konkurrensverket v TeliaSonera Sverige AB*, judgment of 17 February 2011; and, in the English Court of Appeal *Dŵr Cymru Cyfyngedig v Albion Water Limited* [2008] EWCA Civ 536 on appeal from the Competition Appeal Tribunal. It is now clear that the correct test is the 'equally efficient competitor' rather than the 'reasonably efficient competitor' and that there is no need to establish that the dominant undertaking's wholesale price was excessive.

There have been other important decisions on Article 102 in national courts: see *Neurendale Ltd t/a Panda Waste Services v Dublin City Council* [2009] IEHC 588 (Irish High Court); *SEL-Imperial Ltd v British Standards Institution* [2010] EWHC 854 (Ch) (English High Court); and *Purple Parking Ltd v Heathrow Airport Ltd* [2011] EWHC 987 (Ch) (English High Court).

The question of objective justification for alleged abusive behaviour was discussed by the Court of Justice in Cases C-468/06, etc, *Sot Lelos kai Sia EE v GlaxoSmithKline* [2008] ECR I-7139, [2008] 5 CMLR 1382, [2009] All ER (EC) 1 and there have been some interesting decisions on pricing issues: COMP/37792 *Microsoft*, decn of 27 February 2008; and Case C-52/07 *Kanal 5 Ltd and TV 4 AB v Föreningen Svenska Tonsättares Internationella Musikbyrå (STIM) upa* [2008] ECR I-9275, [2009] 5 CMLR 2175.

The implications of the General Court's judgment upholding the decision fining AstraZeneca are also discussed: Case T-321/05 *AstraZeneca v Commission*, judgment of 1 July 2010, [2010] 5 CMLR 1575.

Chapter 11. The Competition Rules and the Acts of Member States

The Court of Justice's reiteration of the strictness of the test for when national legislation absolves an undertaking of responsibility for allegedly abusive conduct in Case C-280/08P *Deutsche Telekom v Commission*, judgment of 14 October 2010, [2010] 5 CMLR 1485 is discussed in the Chapter.

The Commission's decision in COMP/39562 *Slovakian postal legislation relating to hybrid mail services*, 7 October 2008, [2009] 4 CMLR 663 was an interesting application of the prohibition in Article 106(1) to the extension of a postal monopoly to a previously liberalised service. In two recent cases, the creation of an 'inequality of opportunity' in favour of the undertaking granted special or exclusive rights has been condemned: Case C-462/99 *Connect Austria* [2003] ECR I-5197, [2005]

5 CMLR 302; and COMP/38700 *Greek Lignite and Electricity generation*, decn of 5 March 2008, [2009] 4 CMLR 495.

Chapter 12. Sectoral Regimes

There have been several legislative developments in the transport sectors with a new enabling regulation (Regulation 246/2009) and a new block exemption regulation (Regulation 906/2009) for liner consortia. There is also a new Code of Conduct for airline computer reservation systems (Regulation 2299/89) and a new enabling regulation in the air transport sector (Regulation 487/2009). The Commission has also issued guidance on the application of Article 101 to maritime transport services. In the insurance sector, a new block exemption has been adopted (Regulation 267/2010).

New directives which replace the Electricity and Gas Directives referred to in the section dealing with energy matters have been adopted and there have been some interesting cases on the application of the competition rules in the energy sector, notably COMP/38700 *Greek Lignite and Electricity generation,* decn of 5 March 2008, [2009] 4 CMLR 495 concerning exclusive access to lignite deposits in Greece. Other cases concern conduct in the energy sector that has been modified following the Commission's intervention, for example COMP/39386 *Long term contracts—France*, decn of 17 March 2010 (commitments accepted from EDF to allay concerns arising from the long term exclusive supply contracts which also prevented customers from reselling the electricity); COMP/39351 *Swedish Interconnectors*, decn of 14 April 2010 (commitments accepted to prevent congestion in domestic transmission services); and COMP/39315 *ENI*, decn of 29 September 2010 (divestiture commitments accepted to open up transmission capacity to third party suppliers).

In the field of electronic communications, the new package of measures adopted at the end of 2009 is described. The 2003 Recommendation on relevant markets has been replaced by a new Recommendation which reduces the number of markets in which *ex ante* regulation is warranted to seven, and the Postal Directive has been amended to require Member States to abolish any remaining reserved monopolies granted to the universal service provider.

Chapter 13. Enforcement and Procedure

There have been many cases concerning procedural matters—the Commission's fine for the breach of a seal affixed during an investigation at an undertaking's premises was upheld by the General Court: Case T-141/08 *E.ON Energie v Commission*, judgment of 15 December 2010 and there have been several judgments concerning the content of the statement of objections (see for example Case C-413/06P *Bertelsmann AG and Sony Corporation of America v Impala and Commission* [2008] ECR I-4951; Cases C-322/07P, etc, *Papierfabrik August Koehler*

AG and Bolloré SA v Commission, judgment of 3 September 2009, [2009] 5 CMLR 2301; and Cases C-101&110/07P *Coop de France bétail et viande and FNSEA v Commission* [2008] ECR I-10193, [2009] 4 CMLR 743).

The Commission has introduced a new settlement procedure to complement the existing Leniency Notice (see Regulation 622/2008 amending Regulation 773/2004) and has published a Notice explaining how the procedure will apply. The Chapter also considers the Best Practice guidance relating to proceedings for infringements of Articles 101 and 102, the Best Practice Guidance relating to the submission of economic evidence and the recent guidance about the role of the Hearing Office.

On fines, the General Court has recently analysed cases where the fines were calculated using the 2006 Guidance and has commented on the comparison between these Guidelines and the previous versions: Cases T-204&212/08 *Team Relocations v Commission*, judgment of 16 June 2011; and Case T-211/08 *Putters International v Commission*, judgment of 16 June 2011.

A number of cases have considered the effect on the time limit for appealing to the General Court of the Commission's practice of publishing the text of a decision on the web before or instead of publishing the full text in the Official Journal (Case T-48/04 *Qualcomm Wireless Business Solutions v Commission* [2009] ECR II-202; and Case T-388/02 *Kronoply and Kronotex v Commission*, judgment of 10 December 2008, [2008] ECR II-305*).

The Court of Justice has handed down its judgment concerning the liability of the Commission for loss caused by a defective decision in Case C-440/07P *Commission v Schneider Electric*, judgment of 16 July 2009 and there have been other cases in which claims for damages have been dismissed by the General Court, such as Case T-344/04 *Bouychou v Commission*, judgment of 17 July 2007, [2007] ECR II-91*.

A table unravelling the decisions, adopted and readopted, and appeals in the *Soda ash* cases is set out for the convenience of the reader in the context of the procedure to be adopted by the Commission when readopting a decision annulled for procedural irregularity.

There have been a plethora of cases concerning the attribution of liability to a parent for a subsidiary's infringing conduct, with the Court of Justice confirming the importance of the presumption of decisive influence arising from 100 per cent share ownership but finding in some instances that the Commission had erred in imposing joint and several liability: see, eg Cases T-122/07, etc *Siemens AG Österreich v Commission*, judgment of 3 March 2011. The consequences for the parent of a successful appeal by the subsidiary and the scope of the parent's obligations have also been considered in a number of cases: see, eg Case T-382/06 *Tomkins plc v Commission*, judgment of 24 March 2011.

Continuing developments in the disclosure of documents to assist claimants in follow-on damages proceedings are explored in the Chapter: Case C-506/08P

MyTravel Group v Commission, judgment of 21 July 2011; Case 28/08P *Bavarian Lager Co v Commission*, judgment of 29 June 2010; Case T-237/05 *Éditions Odile Jacob SAS v Commission*, judgment of 9 June 2010; Case T-111/07 *Agrofert Holding v Commission*, judgment of 7 July 2010; and Case C-360/09 *Pfleiderer v Bundeskartellamt*, judgment of 14 June 2011.

Chapter 14. The Enforcement of the Competition Rules in the Member States

The Court of Justice has clarified the scope of the Commission's power to intervene in proceedings in national courts under Article 15 of Regulation 1/2003, holding that the power can be exercised even if the proceedings concerned do not pertain directly to the application of Articles 101 and 102: Case C-429/07 *Inspecteur van de Belastingdienst v X BV*, judgment of 11 June 2009. More generally, instances of the Regulation 1/2003 powers being used and the relationship between the Commission and the national competition authorities are described in the Chapter, see for example Case C-439/08 *VEBIC*, judgment of 7 December 2010; Case C-375/09 *Tele 2 Polska*, judgment of 3 May 2011; and *National Grid Electricity Transmission plc v ABB Ltd* [2009] EWHC 1326 (Ch) (English High Court).

On the question of jurisdiction, the ratification of the Lugano Convention and the ongoing litigation between the tyre manufacturers and the participants in the *Butadiene Rubber and Emulsion Styrene Butadiene Rubber* cartels are explored in relation to *Cooper Tire & Rubber Company Europe v Dow Deutschland Inc* [2010] EWCA Civ 864.

The Commission's White Paper on actions for damages published in April 2008 recommends various procedural steps that the Member States could take to facilitate follow-on claims and the English Courts have considered a number of issues arising in such claims such as the availability of restitutionary remedies: *Devenish Nutrition v Sanofi-Aventis* [2008] EWCA Civ 1086 and the point at which proceedings should be stayed in the event of a challenge to the infringement decision on which the claimant relies: *National Grid Electricity Transmission plc v ABB Ltd* [2009] EWHC 1326 (Ch).

The Table of National Enforcement Regimes has not been updated for the Second Supplement. The Reader is referred to the Commission's ECN Briefs available on the website; in particular the special issue published in December 2010 provides information and contact details for each NCA in the Union. Subsequent legislative developments are noted in the Briefs and will provide more up-to-date information than this Supplement can attempt.

Chapter 15. State Aids

There has been a substantial volume of legislation on State aids since the 6th edition, some of which was planned as part of the State Aid Action Plan and some of which was a response to the banking crisis and the subsequent economic downturn. As to the former category, the General Block Exemption Regulation has replaced the three previous block exemptions. The new block exemption increases the aid intensities and notification ceilings allowed by the previous exemptions. It also introduces additional exemptions for various kinds of aid measures. Guidance on the application of the State aid rules to environmental protection measures and to aid in the form of guarantees has also been issued. Finally, the Simplification Package has introduced a simplified procedure for the notification of certain kinds of State aid. The Commission has responded to the banking crisis by issuing guidance about aid schemes aimed at stabilising individual financial institutions and taking a large number of individual decisions approving aid. It has also introduced a temporary EU framework for measures aimed at helping the real economy to recover. These measures were extended to apply throughout 2011, though some only in modified form.

There continues to be a great deal of litigation on the different elements which make up a State aid, including the application of the *Altmark* criteria (Cases T-309/04, etc, *TV2/Danmark v Commission* [2008] ECR II-2935; and Case T-266/02 *Deutsche Post v Commission* [2008] ECR II-1233); and concerning the 'market economy investor principle', Case C-140/09 *Fallimento Traghetti del Mediterraneo v Presidenza del Consiglio dei Ministri*, judgment of 10 June 2010).

Significant developments as regards the role of the Member State in recovering unlawful aids have been made in the jurisprudence of the Court of Justice. The Court has clarified the effect of the final sentence of Article 88(3) EC in national courts (Case C-199/06 *CELF v SIDE* [2008] ECR I-469, [2008] 2 CMLR 561; and Case C-384/07 *Wienstrom v Bundesminister für Wirtschaft und Arbeit* [2008] ECR I-10393). The Court has also considered when damages ordered to be paid by a Member State to a recipient of unlawful aid can be set off against the aid that the State is bound to recover: Case C-369/07 *Commission v Greece (Olympic Airways)*, judgment of 7 July 2009. The extent to which the conduct of the national court applying domestic rules is regarded as incompatible with the State's obligations to recover the aid was considered in Case C-305/09 *Commission v Italy*, judgment of 5 May 2011; Case C-507/08 *Commission v The Slovak Republic*, judgment of 22 December 2010; and Case C-305/09 *Commission v Italy*, judgment of 5 May 2011. The Commission has also focused on the role of the Member State in this area of the law, issuing a new Notice on the enforcement of State aid law by national courts and a Notice towards an effective implementation of Commission decisions ordering a Member State to recover unlawful aid.

The vexed question of when an undertaking is directly and individually affected by a Commission refusal to open the formal procedure and a Commission decision on the compatibility of an aid with the common market has continued to generate much case law, see for example Cases C-71/09P, etc *Comitato 'Venezia vuole vivere' v Commission*, judgment of 9 June 2011; Case C-487/06P *British Aggregates Association v Commission* [2008] ECR I-10505; Case T-193/06 *Télévision française 1 SA (TF1) v Commission*, judgment of 13 September 2010; and Case T-189/08 *Forum 187 v Commission*, judgment of 18 March 2010.

I have attempted to ensure that the book is up-to-date to 31 August 2011. All remaining errors and omissions are my responsibility. For the sake of good order I should again make clear that any views expressed in this Supplement should not be taken to indicate how the Competition Appeal Tribunal may decide any issue that falls for determination in the future.

May I thank the team at Oxford University Press for their continued support and patience and Sophie Barham for her help with the updating of the case tables. The preparation of this second supplement has coincided with the early stages of preparing the 7th edition of the main work. I am delighted that David Bailey has agreed to be the co-editor of that edition. A large team of practitioner contributors is in place to work with us on the revision the main text. As this supplement proves, competition law continues to expand and develop both in the Court of Justice and in the Member States—in ways both expected and unexpected. Recording and analysing its evolution is likely to remain an important and enjoyable task.

Vivien Rose
31 August 2011

NOTE ON THE LISBON TREATY

The Treaty of Lisbon came into force on 1 December 2009 and replaced the Treaty on European Union and the EC Treaty with a new Treaty on European Union ('TEU') and a Treaty on the Functioning of the European Union ('TFEU'). Although the term 'European Community' has now passed into history, the title of this volume still reflects the name of the main work *European Community Law of Competition* to which it is the Supplement.

The Lisbon Treaty also resulted in a renumbering of the articles of the former EC Treaty, most of which are now incorporated into the TFEU. In the text of this Supplement I have used the new numbering throughout. But where a paragraph or footnote in the main work needs updating only because of the changes of the numbering, this has not merited an update paragraph in the Supplement. The wording of the chapter headings and sub-headings and the bold lead-in sentences of the paragraphs have not been changed since the aim of these is to enable the reader to orient themselves from the text of the main work to the relevant paragraphs of the Supplement. The Tables of Equivalences published in the *Official Journal* are reproduced in this Supplement for the readers' convenience.

Under the Lisbon Treaty the whole court system of the European Union will be known as the Court of Justice of the European Union, currently comprising three courts: the Court of Justice, the General Court (that is, the former Court of First Instance) and the Civil Service Tribunal. I have used the abbreviations 'CJ' and 'GC' to refer to the courts throughout, even in relation to pre-Lisbon judgments.

ALPHABETICAL TABLE OF EU CASES
AND DECISIONS

1. garantovaná a.s. v Commission (T-392/09R) Order of 2 March 2011 . . . . .13.248
3F v Commission (C-319/07P) judgment of 9 July 2009 . . . . .2.034, 15.115, 15.116

Aalberts Industries NV v Commission (T-385/06) judgment of 24 March 2011 . . . . . 2.053, 2.055
Abbott/Solvay Pharmaceuticals (M.5661) (11 February 2010) 4.092
Abertis Infraestructuras v Commission (T-200/09) Order of 18 May 2010 . . . . .13.071
ABF/GBI Business (M.4980) (23 September 2008) 4.074, 8.044, 8.211, 10.055
AC Treuhand v Commission (T-99/04) [2008]
    ECR II-1501, [2008] 5 CMLR 962 . . . . 1.016, 1.091, 2.053, 5.014, 13.028, 13.032,
                                    13.082, 13.170
Acciona/Enel/Endesa (M.4685) (5 July 2007), OJ 2007 C130/19. .8.104
AceaElectrabel Produzione v Commission (C-480/09P)
    judgment of 16 December 2010 . . . . .2.019, 15.086, 15.099
Activision Blizzard v Commission (C-260/09P)
    judgment of 10 February 2011 . . . . .2.110, 6.053,
                        6.061, 13.065, 13.076, 13.161, 13.166, 13.173, 13.226
AEE/Lentjes (M.4647) (5 December 2007) 4.029, 8.207, 10.022
AEPI v Commission (C-425/07P) [2009] ECR I-3205, [2009] 5 CMLR 1337 . . . . . 1.132, 13.072
Aer Lingus v Commission (T-411/07R) [2008] ECR II-411, [2008] 5 CMLR 538 . . . . 8.160,
                                            13.249, 13.250
Aer Lingus Group plc v Commission (T-411/07) judgment of 6 July 2010,
    [2011] 4 CMLR 358 . . . . 8.160, 8.273
Aeroporia Aigaiou Aeroporiki v Commission (T-202/11) not yet decided 4.097, 8.207
AG2R Prevoyance v Beaudout (C-437/09)
    judgment of 3 March 2011 . . . . .2.012, 2.034, 11.011, 11.017, 11.030, 11.053
Agrofert Holding v Commission (T-111/07) judgment of 7 July 2010. . . . . 13.100, 13.241
Airfreight (COMP/39258) decn of 9 November 2010 . . . . 13.113A
Aker Warnow Werft GmbH, & Kvaerner ASA v Commission (T-68/05)
    judgment of 10 March 2009. . . . . .15.122
Akzo Nobel v Commission (C-97/08P) judgment of 10 September 2009,
    [2009] 5 CMLR 2633 . . . . 2.018, 2.052, 5.083, 13.181, 13.205
Akzo Nobel Chemicals v Commission (C-550/07P) judgment of
    14 September 2010, [2010] 5 CMLR 1143. . . . . .1.015, 13.056, 13.075
Akzo Nobel (monochloroacetic acid) (T-175/05) judgment of 30 September 2009,
    [2009] 5 CMLR 2774 . . . . .13.205
Alcoa Trasformazioni v Commission (T-332/06) judgment of 25 March 2009,
    [2009] ECR II-29*. 15.030, 15.074, 15.112, 15.122, 15.123
Alfa Acciai v Commission (T-98/03) [2007] ECR II-4331, [2008] 4 CMLR 176 . . . . .1.004
Algerian gas imports (COMP/37811) Press Release IP/07/1074 (11 July 2007). 6.056, 12.079
Alitalia v Commission (T-301/01) [2008] ECR II-1753 . . . . 13.240, 15.013,
                                     15.086, 15.120, 15.122

Alliance One v Commission, Standard Commercial Tobacco and Trans-Continental
     Leaf Tobacco v Commission (T-24/05) judgment of 27 October 2010. . . . 5.027, 13.162, 13.205
Alliance One International v Commission (T-25/06) judgment of
     9 September 2011. . . . . 5.027, 5.063, 13.137, 13.171, 13.205, 13.205A, 13.206
Allianz Hungária Biztosító v Gazdasági Versenyhivatal (C-32/11) not yet decided 12.179
Almamet GmbH Handel mit Spänen und Pulvern aus Metall v Commission
     (T-410/09R) Order of the President 7 May 2010, [2010] 5 CMLR 219 . . . . .13.248
Alrosa v Commission (C-441/07P) judgment of 29 June 2010 . . . . 10.098, 13.114, 13.115,
                                                                13.116, 13.126, 13.221, 13.227, 13.228
Altstoff Recycling Austria AG v Commission (T-419/03) judgment of
     22 March 2011. . . . . 1.131, 3.064, 6.198, 6.199
Aluminium Fluoride (COMP/39180) decn of 25 June 2008. .13.149
Amann & Söhne GmbH v Commission (T-446/05) judgment of
     28 April 2010, [2010] 5 CMLR 789 . . . . 1.066, 2.052, 4.016, 4.034, 4.052,
                                                                13.124, 13.137, 13.181, 13.203, 13.227
Amcor/Alcan (M.5599) (15 December 2009). 4.052, 8.200
Apple and iTunes (COMP/39154) Press Release IP/08/22 (9 January 2008) 5.113
Arcelor v Commission (T-405/06) [2009] ECR II-771, [2010] 4 CMLR 787 . . . . . . .1.004, 5.028,
                                                                13.084, 13.208, 13.223
ArcelorMittal v Commission (C-201&216/09P)
     judgment of 29 March 2011. 1.004, 5.028, 13.084, 13.208, 13.223
ArcelorMittal/Noble European Holding (M.5545) (17 July 2009) 8.032, 8.181
Archer Daniels Midland v Commission (C-510/06P) (sodium gluconate)
     [2009] ECR I-1843, [2009] 4 CMLR 889 . . . . .13.147, 13.148, 13.164
Archer Daniels Midland v Commission (C-511/06P) (citric acid) judgment of
     9 July 2009. . . . . .5.009, 13.084, 13.154, 13.164, 13.173, 13.197
Areva v Commission (T-117&121/07) judgment of 3 March 2011. . . . . 13.162, 13.206
Arjowiggins/M-Real Zanders' Reflect paper mill (M.4513) (4 June 2008) 4.052, 8.085,
                                                                8.196, 10.022
Arkema France v Commission (methacrylates) (T-217/06) judgment of 7 June 2011. . . . . . .13.177
Arkema France v Commission (sodium chlorate) (T-343/08) judgment of
     17 May 2011 . . . . .13.160
Arsenal/DSP (M.5153) (9 January 2009) 8.167
Artijus Magyar v Commission (T-411/08R) Order of 14 November 2008,
     [2008] ECR II-270*, [2009] 4 CMLR 353. . . . . .2.046, 5.112, 13.249
Artijus Magyar v Commission (C-32/09P(R)) Order of 31 August 2010, [2010]
     5 CMLR 1208 . . . . .2.046, 5.112, 13.249
ASM Brescia v Comune de Rodengo (C-347/06) [2008] ECR I-5641, [2008]
     3 CMLR 1024 . . . . 12.075
ASM Brescia SpA v Commission (T-189/03) [2009] ECR II-1831 . . . . . . .15.026, 15.074, 15.115
Association Belge des Consommateurs Tests-Achats v Commission (T-224/10),
     not yet decided. 8.093, 12.059
Associazione italiana del risparmio gestito v Commission (T-445/05)
     [2009] ECR II-289. . . . . .15.02, 15.031, 15.115
AstraZeneca v Commission (T-321/05) judgment of 1 July 2010, [2010]
     5 CMLR 1575 . . . . 2.052, 4.022, 4.023, 4.092, 9.028, 9.072, 9.074, 10.025, 10.030,
                                                  10.036, 10.041, 10.047, 10.058, 10.063, 10.064,
                                                  10.103, 10.129, 10.153, 10.154, 13.076, 13.139,
                                                  13.169, 13.225,13.226, 13.227, 14.140
AstraZeneca v Commission (C-457/10P) not yet decided 2.052, 4.022, 4.023, 4.092, 9.028,
                                                  9.072, 9.074, 10.025, 10.030, 10.036, 10.041, 10.047, 10.058,
                                                  10.063, 10.064, 10.103, 10.129, 10.153, 10.154, 13.076, 13.139,
                                                  13.169, 13.225, 13.226, 13.227, 14.140

Athens International Airport (COMP/38469) decn of 2 May 2005 . . . . .2.007, 12.050, 13.072
Athinaïki Teckniki v Commission (C-521/06P) [2008] ECR I-5829,
    [2008] 3 CMLR 979 . . . . 13.220, 15.112
Athinaïki Teckniki v Commission (C-362/09P) judgment of
    16 December 2010 . . . . 13.071, 13.220, 15.112, 15.121
Atlantic Container Line AB v Commission (T-113/04) [2007] ECR II-171*,
    [2008] 4 CMLR 1357 . . . . .13.209, 13.242, 13.248
Auto 24 SARL v Jaguar Land Rover France (C-158/11), not yet decided 6.134

BA/AA/IB (COMP/39596) decn of 14 July 2010 . . . . 4.097, 7.133
Bananas (COMP/39188) decn of 15 October 2008,
    [2009] 5 CMLR 2949 . . . . 1.086, 2.052, 5.016, 5.085, 13.171, 13.205B
La Banque Postale, Caisses d'Epargne and Crédit Mutuel (C(2007) 2110 final)
    decn of 10 May 2007 . . . . 11.015, 11.050
BASF Ludwigshafen v Commission (T-101&111/05) [2007] ECR II-4949,
    [2008] 4 CMLR 347 . . . . 2.052, 5.008, 5.011, 5.083, 13.160,
                                                 13.165, 13.174, 13.177
Bathroom fittings and fixtures (COMP/39092) decn of 23 June 2010 . . . . .13.179
Bavaria v Commission (T-235/07) judgment of 16 June 2011 . . . . 2.055, 13.180
Bavarian Lager Co v Commission (C-28/08P), judgment of 29 June 2010 . . . . .13.100
Beef Industry Development and Barry Brothers (C-209/07) [2008] ECR I-8637,
    [2009] 4 CMLR 310, [2009] All ER (EC) 367 . . . . 2.096, 5.054
Belgian Sewing Thread v Commission (T-452/05) judgment of 28 April 2010,
    [2010] 5 CMLR 889 . . . . 2.052, 13.054, 13.134, 13.149, 13.150, 13.152,
                                                 13.167, 13.179, 13.203
Bertelsmann and Sony Corp v Impala (C-413/06P)
    [2008] ECR I-4951 . . . . .8.137, 8.145, 8.146, 8.147, 8.156, 8.210, 8.212, 8.214, 8.236,
                       8.247, 8.252, 8.255, 10.053, 10.057, 13.083, 13.234, 13.254
Bertelsmann/KRR/JV (M.5533) (8 September 2009) 5.111, 8.033, 8.044, 8.054
Bertelsmann/Planeta/Circulo (M.5838) (5 July 2010) 4.034, 4.076
BNP Paribas v Commission (T-335/08) judgment of 1 July 2010 . . . . .13.221, 15.031, 15.115
BNP Paribas/Fortis (M.5384) (3 December 2008) 5.045
Boehringer Ingelheim v Swingward (C-348/04) [2007] ECR I-3391, [2007]
    2 CMLR 1445, [2008] All ER (EC) 411 . . . . .9.039
Boliden AB v Commission (T-19/05) judgment of 19 May 2010, [2010]
    5 CMLR 1251 . . . . .2.053
Bouychou v Commission (T-344/04) judgment of 17 July 2007, [2007]
    ECR II-91* 13.241, 15.021
Bouygues SA v Commission (C-431/07P) [2009] ECR I-2665 . . . . .11.004, 15.010,
                                                          15.020, 15.024
BPB plc v Commission (T-53/03) [2008] ECR II-1333,
    [2008] 5 CMLR 1201 . . . . 2.023, 2.052, 2.058, 2.097, 2.121, 5.088, 5.089, 5.090,
                       13.076, 13.086, 13.088, 13.091, 13.096, 13.145, 13.153,
                                 13.160, 13.164, 13.174, 13.226, 13.240
British Aggregates Association v Commission (C-487/06P) [2008] ECR I-10505 . . . . 15.033,
                                                          15.116, 15.122
British Aggregates Association v Commission (T-359/04) judgment of
    9 September 2010 . . . . .15.033, 15.116, 15.122
Buczek Automotive v Commission (T-1/08) judgment of 17 May 2011 . . . . 15.013, 15.120
Bundesverband deutscher Banken v Commission (T-163/05) judgment of
    3 March 2010 . . . . 15.013, 15.122
Bundesverband deutscher Banken v Commission (T-36/06) judgment of
    3 March 2010 . . . . .15.116

BUPA v Commission (T-289/03) [2008] ECR II-81 . . . . .11.050, 15.012, 15.116
Business case Norrköping (Case N791/2006) decn of 10 July 2007 . . . . .15.021
Butadiene Rubber and Emulsion Styrene Butadiene Rubber (COMP/38638) decn
    of 29 November 2006, [2009] 4 CMLR 421 . . . . .2.052, 5.012, 13.160, 13.205C, 13.206

Caffaro v Commission (T-192/06) judgment of 16 June 2011 . . . . .13.170, 13.172, 13.178
Calcium carbide and magnesium based reagents (COMP/39396) decn of
    22 July 2009 . . . . 13.160, 13.179, 13.181, 13.206
Cañas v Commission (T-508/09) not yet decided 5.161
Candle Waxes (COMP/39181) decn of 1 October 2008,
    [2009] 5 CMLR 2441 . . . . 1.110, 2.055, 4.021, 5.014
Cantiere Navale De Polic v Commission (T-584/08) judgment of 3 February 2011 . . . . .15.065
Cantieri Navali Termoli v Commission (T-70/07) judgment of 12 November 2008,
    [2008] ECR II-250* 15.039
Cap Gemini/BAS (M.5301) (13 October 2008) 4.090
Car glass (COMP/39125) decn of 12 November 2008 . . . . 5.059, 13.149
Carlsberg/Scottish & Newcastle assets (M.4952) (7 March 2008) .8.046
Carphone Warehouse/Tiscali UK (M.5532) (30 June 2009) 12.146
Cartesio Okato (C-210/06) [2008] ECR I-9641, [2009] All ER (EC) 296 . . . . .14.090
CD-Contact Data v Commission (T-18/03)
    [2009] ECR II-1021 . . . . 2.024, 2.027, 2.055, 2.110, 6.053, 6.061, 13.065, 13.161,
                                  13.166, 13.173, 13.203
CEAHR (Confédération européenne des associations d'horlogers-réparateurs)
    v Commission (T-427/08) judgment of 15 December 2010 . . . . 4.009, 4.037, 4.059,
                                    4.060, 13.072, 13.227
CELF v SIDE (C-199/06) [2008] ECR I-469, [2008] 2 CMLR 561 . . . . . .15.092, 15.105, 15.109
Cementbouw Handel & Industrie BV v Commission (C-202/06P) [2007]
    ECR I-12129, [2008] 4 CMLR 1324 . . . . .8.024, 8.036, 8.044, 8.060,
                                    8.165, 8.246, 8.252
Centre de coordination Carrefour v Commission (T-94/08) judgment of
    18 March 2010 . . . . .15.106
Centrica/Venture Production (M.5585) (21 August 2009) 8.218, 12.073
Centro Europa 7 v Ministero delle Comunicazioni (C-380/05) [2008] ECR I-349,
    [2008] 2 CMLR 512 . . . . .12.112
CEPSA v Tobar (C-279/06) [2008] ECR I-6681 . . . . .2.020, 6.030, 6.054
Certain joueur de tennis professionnel/Agence mondiale antidopage (COMP/39471)
    decn of 13 October 2009 . . . . .5.161
Cetarsa v Commission (T-33/05) judgment of 3 February 2011 . . . . 5.027, 13.162
Chalkor AE Epexergasias Metallon v Commission (T-21/05) judgment of 19 May 2010,
    [2010] 5 CMLR 1295 . . . . 1.066, 2.053, 13.145, 13.172, 13.216
Chalkor AE Epexergasias Metallon v Commission (C-386/10P) not yet decided 2.053,
                                        13.172, 13.216
Chronopost and La Poste v UFEX (C-341&342/06P) [2008] ECR I-4777,
    [2008] 3 CMLR 568 . . . . .13.029, 15.014, 15.120
CIRFS and others v Commission (C-313/90) [1993] ECR I-1125 . . . . .13.221
CISAC (COMP/38698) decn of 16 July 2008, [2009] 4 CMLR 577 . . . . 1.037, 1.091, 2.027,
                              2.032, 2.046, 2.060, 4.096, 5.111,
                      5.112, 5.113, 5.114, 11.050, 13.011, 13.249
Cisco/Tandberg (M.5669) (29 March 2010) 10.022
Clearstream v Commission (T-301/04) judgment of 9 September 2009,
    [2009] 5 CMLR 2677 . . . . 10.060, 10.141, 13.170
CNOP and CCG v Commission (T-23/09) Order of 26 October 2010 . . . . 2.059, 13.043

Coats Holdings and Coats v Commission (T-36/05) [2007] ECR II-110,
    [2008] 4 CMLR 45 . . . . .2.046, 2.052. 2.055, 5.062, 13.076

Comap v Commission (T-377/06) judgment of 24 March 2011 . . . . .2.055

Comitato 'Venezia vuole vivere' v Commission (C-71/09P, etc) judgment of
    9 June 2011 . . . . 15.010, 15.026, 15.102, 15.115

Commission v Alrosa (C-441/07P) judgment of 29 June 2010,
    [2010] 5 CMLR 643 . . . . .10.098, 13.114, 13.115, 13.116, 13.126, 13.221, 13.227, 13.228

Commission v Département du Loiret (C-295/07P) [2008] ECR I-9363 . . . . .15.100

Commission v Deutsche Post (C-399/08P) judgment of 2 September 2010 . . . . .15.012

Commission v France (C-441/06) [2007] ECR I-8887. . . . . .1.030

Commission v Freistaat Sachsen (C-334/07P) [2008] ECR I-9465 . . . . .1.004, 15.001,
                                  15.064, 15.067, 15.078, 15.085

Commission v Germany: Re Supply of Medicines by Pharmacies
    to nearby Hospitals (C-141/07) [2008] ECR I-6935, [2008] 3 CMLR 1479. . . . . .1.033

Commission v Greece (Olympic Airways) (C-369/07) judgment of July 2009. . . . . 15.098,
                                                15.102, 15.113

Commission v Infront WM (C-125/06P) [2008] ECR I-1451, [2008] 2 CMLR 785 . . . . . . .5.116

Commission v Italy (C-494/06P) [2009] ECR I-3639 . . . . 15.026, 15.120

Commission v Italy (C-304/09) judgment of 22 December 2010 .15.102

Commission v Italy (C-305/09) judgment of 5 May 2011. 15.102, 15.110

Commission v Koninklijke FrieslandCampina NV (C-519/07P) judgment of
    17 September 2009. . . . . .15.106

Commission v Poland (C-331/09) judgment of 14 April 2011 . . . . .15.103

Commission v Scott (C-290/07P) judgment of 2 September 2010 . . . . . . 15.036, 15.083, 15.094,
                                                15.119, 15.122

Commission v Schneider Electric (C-440/07P) judgment of 16 July 2009. . . . . .8.011, 8.198,
                                                 13.083, 13.241

Commission v Slovak Republic (C-507/08) judgment of 22 December 2010 . . . . .15.103

Commission v Spain (C-177/06) [2007] ECR I-7689. . . . . .15.113

Commission v Spain (C-196/07) judgment of 6 March 2008, [2008] ECR I-41* 8.104

Compagnie Maritime Belge (T-276/04) [2008] ECR II-1277 . . . . 10.082, 10.101, 13.180,
                                              13.204, 13.208, 13.238

Compañía Española de Comercialización de Aceite (C-505/07) judgment of
    1 October 2009, [2010] 4 CMLR 11 . . . . .12.195

Compass-Datenbank GmbH v Republik Österreich (C-138/11) not yet decided 2.009

Componenta v Commission (T-455/05) judgment of 18 December 2008,
    [2008] ECR II-336*. 15.013

Consumer detergents (COMP/39579) decn of 13 April 2010,
    OJ 2011 C193/14 . . . . 3.044, 5.013, 5.016, 13.113A

Copad SA v Christian Dior couture SA and SIL (C-59/08) [2009] ECR I-3421 . . . . 6.093,
                                                    9.045, 9.172

Coopération de France Bétail et Viande v Commission (C-101&110/07P) [2008]
    ECR I-10193, [2009] 4 CMLR 743 . . . . 2.059, 5.019, 5.027, 5.058, 11.004,
                          12.202, 12.203, 13.084, 13.164, 13.168, 13.181, 13.204, 13.207

Corus UK v Commission (T-48/00) [2004] ECR II-2325. . . . . .13.240

DaimlerChrysler and others (COMP/39140–39143) Press Release IP/07/1332
    (14 September 2007) 6.131

Danone/Numico (M.4842) (31 October 2007) 4.064, 8.166, 8.207

Degussa v Commission (C-266/06P) judgment of 22 May 2008, [2008] ECR I-81*. 13.145

Deltafina v Commission (T-29/05) judgment of 8 September 2010. . . . . 2.052, 2.053, 5.027,
                                                    5.063, 13.162

Deltafina v Commission (T-12/06) judgment of 9 September 2011. . . . . .5.027, 5.063, 13.137, 13.171, 13.182, 13.186, 13.205C

Deltafina v Commission (C-537/10P) not yet decided 2.053, 5.027, 13.162

Département du Loiret v Commission (T-369/00) [2007] ECR II-851. . . . . .15.100

Der Grüne Punkt—Duales System Deutschland v Commission (C-385/07P)
  judgment of 16 July 2009, [2009] 5 CMLR 2215 . . . . 1.131, 1.132, 3.060, 6.198, 9.178, 10.028, 10.129, 10.150, 13.128

Deutsche Bank /ABN AMRO Assets (M.5296) (1 October 2008). 8.044

Deutsche Post v Commission (T-266/02) [2008] ECR II-1233. . . . . .15.012

Deutsche Post et DHL International v Commission (T-388/03)
  [2009] ECR II-199. . . . . 15.012, 15.117

Deutsche Telekom v Commission (C-280/08P) judgment of 14 October 2010,
  [2010] 5 CMLR 1485 . . . . .1.076, 10.067, 10.112, 10.113, 11.004, 11.050, 12.164, 13.168, 13.169, 13.170, 14.078

Deutsche Telekom/OTE (M.5148) (2 October 2008). 4.094, 8.032, 12.101

Deutsche Telekom v Bundesrepublik Deutschland (C-262/06) [2007]
  ECR I-10057, [2008] 4 CMLR 240 . . . . .12.090

Deutsche Telekom v Commission (T-271/03) [2008] ECR II-477, [2008]
  CMLR 631 . . . . 1.076, 10.067, 10.112, 10.113, 11.004, 11.050, 12.164, 13.168, 13.169, 13.170, 14.078

DHL Aviation v Commission (T-452/08) judgment of 7 October 2010 . . . . 15.038, 15.098

Diputación Foral de Álava and Comunidad autónoma del País Vasco—Gobierno
  Vasco v Commission (T-227/01, etc) judgment of 9 September 2009 . . . . 15.027, 15.031

Distrigas (COMP/37966) decn of 11 October 2007. . . . . .12.080

Doulamis (C-446/05) [2008] ECR I-1377 . . . . 5.040, 11.033

Dow Chemical v Commission (T-42/07) judgment of 13 July 2011 . . . . .13.156

DRAMS (COMP/38511) decn of 19 May 2010. . . . . 13.113A

Duales System Deutschland v Commission (Der Grüne Punkt) (C-385/07P)
  judgment of 16 July 2009 . . . . 1.131, 1.132, 3.060, 6.198, 9.178, 10.028, 10.129, 10.150, 13.128

EARL Salvat père & fils v Commission (T-136/05) [2007] ECR II-4063. . . . . 15.019, 15.115

easyJet v Commission (T-300/04) removed from the register 6 September 2007 . . . . 3.055, 4.097, 7.026, 7.134, 12.047

EdF/British Energy (M.5224) (22 December 2008) 4.061, 4.067

EDF/Exeltium (COMP/39386) MEMO/08/533 of 31 July 2008. .12.066

EDF/Segebel (M.5549) (12 November 2009). 8.200, 8.212, 12.059, 12.073

Edison v Commission (T-196/06) judgment of 16 June 2011 . . . . 13.205A

Éditions Odile Jacob SAS v Commission (T-279/04) judgment of
  13 September 2010 (compatibility of Lagardère acquisition) 8.049, 8.170

Éditions Odile Jacob SAS v Commission (T-452/04) judgment of
  13 September 2010 (approval of purchaser of divested assets) 8.049, 8.170

Éditions Odile Jacob SAS v Commission (T-237/05) judgment of 9 June 2010
  (access to Commission documents). 13.100

Electrabel/Compagnie Nationale du Rhône (M.4994) (10 June 2009) 8.181

Elf Aquitaine v Commission (sodium chlorate) (T-299/08) judgment of
  17 May 2011 . . . . 13.205, 13.205A

EMC Development AB v Commission (T-432/05) judgment of 12 May 2010,
  [2010] 5 CMLR 757 . . . . 5.140, 13.067

ENI (COMP/39315) decn of 29 September 2010 . . . . 10.143, 12.081

ENI v Commission (T-39/07) judgment of 13 July 2011 . . . . .13.160

ENI/Distrigaz (M.5220) (15 October 2008). 8.167

E.ON (breach of seal) (COMP/39326) decn of 30 January 2008, [2009] 4 CMLR 371. . . . 13.048

E.ON Energie v Commission (T-141/08) (breach of seal) judgment of
 15 December 2010 . . . . 13.048, 13.050
E.ON Energie v Commission (C-89/11P) not yet decided 13.048, 13.050
E.ON gas foreclosure (COMP/39317) decn of 4 May 2010 . . . . .10.143, 12.073, 12.081
E.ON—GDF (COMP/39401) decn of 8 July 2009 . . . . 2.032, 5.060, 5.065, 12.079
E.ON—GdF collusion (COMP/39401) decn of 8 July 2009 . . . . 5.065, 12.079
E.ON German electricity markets (COMP/39388&39389) decn of
 26 November 2008 . . . . .10.048, 10.054, 10.097, 10.151,
 12.066A, 12.067, 12.069, 14.072
E.ON/Electrabel Acquired Assets (M.5519) (13 September 2009) .8.167
Ericsson/STM/JV (M.5332) (25 November 2008) 8.232
Erste Bank der österreichischen Sparkassen v Commission (C-125/07P, etc)
 judgment of 24 September 2009, [2010] 5 CMLR 443 . . . . 1.029, 1.115
Essent Netwerk Noord v Aluminium Delfzijl (C-206/06) [2008] ECR I-5497,
 [2008] 3 CMLR 895 . . . . 15.012, 15.019, 15.031, 15.135
Estaser El Mareny v Commission (T-274/06) [2007] ECR II-143*
 (dismissed as inadmissible) 1.068, 6.052, 6.152, 13.232

FAB Fernsehen aus Berlin GmbH v Commission (T-8/06) judgment of 6 October 2009 . . . . .15.012
Fachverband der Buch- und Medienwirtschaft v LIBRO Handelsgesellschaft
 mbH (C-531/07) [2009] ECR I-3717 . . . . 1.033, 1.037, 5.025, 11.033
Fachvereinigung Mineralfaserindustrie v Commission (T-254/05&375/03)
 judgment of 20 September 2007, [2007] ECR II-124* 15.115
Fallimento Traghetti del Mediterraneo v Presidenza del Consiglio dei Ministri
 (C-140/09) judgment of 10 June 2010 . . . . .15.012
Feralpi Siderurgica v Commission (T-77/03) [2007] ECR II-139* .1.004
Ferriera Valsabbia and Valsabbia Investimenti v Commission (T-97/03) [2007]
 ECR II-4331, [2008] 4 CMLR 176 . . . . .1.004
Ferriere Nord v Commission (T-94/03) judgment of 25 October 2007, [2007]
 ECR II-141* 1.004
Ferriere Nord v Commission (C-49/05P) judgment of 8 May 2008, [2008]
 ECR I-68* 15.060, 15.083
Fiat/Chrysler (M.5518) (24 July 2009) 8.029
FMC Foret v Commission (T-191/06) judgment of 16 June 2011 .2.055
Football Association Premier League v QC Leisure/Murphy v Media Protection
 Services (C-403&429/08) Opinion of 3 February 2011 . . . . .2.068, 9.061, 9.064
Fortis ABN Amro Assets (M.4844) (3 October 2007) 8.046, 8.207
Forum 187 v Commission (T-189/08) judgment of 18 March 2010 . . . . 15.106, 15.115
FRA.BO SpA v Commission (T-381/06) judgment of 24 March 2011 . . . . 13.182, 13.199
France Télécom v Commission (C-202/07P) [2009] ECR I-2369 . . . . 4.018, 10.030, 10.071,
 10.076, 10.078, 10.079, 12.157
Friesland/Campina (M.5046) (17 December 2008) 4.057
Frucona Košice v Commission (T-11/07) judgment of 7 December 2010 . . . . 15.013, 15.122
Fuji v Commission (T-132/07) judgment of 12 July 2011 . . . . 2.055, 13.205B

Gaz de France (GDF Suez) (COMP/39316) decn of 8 July 2009 . . . . .2.054, 12.073, 12.080
GDF Suez/International Power (M.5978) (26 January 2011) 8.216
General Química v Commission (T-85/06, etc) judgment of 18 December 2008,
 [2008] ECR II-338* 13.138, 13.205
General Química v Commission (C-90/09P) judgment of 20 January 2011 . . . . . . 13.138, 13.205
General Technic-Otis v Commission (T-141/07, etc) judgment of 13 July 2011 . . . . 13.174,
 13.199, 13.205 13.205A
Germany v Commission (C-156/98) [2000] ECR I-6857 . . . . .15.023

Germany v Commission (T-490/04) removed from register 7 May 2008 . . . . .10.084, 11.010,
11.013, 11.050, 12.183
Germany and Glunz v Kronofrance SA (C-75&80/05P) [2008] ECR I-6619 . . . . .15.122
Gibraltar v Commission (T-211&215/04) [2008] ECR II-3745 . . . . 15.031, 15.034
Gibtelcom v Commission (T-433/03, etc) Order of 26 June 2008, [2009]
4 CMLR 344 . . . . .12.168
GlaxoSmithKline Services Unlimited v Commission (C-501/06P, etc) judgment
of 6 October 2009, [2010] CMLR 50 . . . . 1.029, 1.072, 1.074, 1.075, 1.115, 2.026,
2.064, 2.077, 2.094, 2.096, 2.097, 2.015, 2.110, 3.009, 3.015, 3.020,
3.021, 4.092, 6.053, 6.058, 10.086, 11.006, 13.227, 13.242
González y Díez v Commission (T-25/04) [2007] ECR II-31231 . . . . 1.004, 15.001
Google/DoubleClick (M.4731) (11 March 2008) 4.035, 4.065, 8.085, 8.202,
8.216, 8.219
Gosselin Group v Commission (T-208&209/08) judgment of 16 June 2011 . . . . . . 1.117, 2.004A,
13.108, 13.150, 13.163, 13.205, 13.205A
Greece v Commission (T-415/05, etc) judgment of 13 September 2010 . . . . .15.013, 15.020,
15.099, 15.102, 15.120
Greek Lignite and Electricity generation (COMP/38700) decn of 5 March 2008,
[2009] 4 CMLR 495 . . . . 1.117, 4.059A, 4.072, 11.001, 11.020A, 12.066A, 12.067A
Groupement des Cartes Bancaires (COMP/38606) decn of 17 October 2007 . . . . . . .2.067, 2.095,
2.096, 4.022A,5.047
Groupe Partouche v Commission (T-315/10) not yet decided 8.093
Grúas Abril Asistencia v Commission (T-386/09) Order of 24 August 2010 . . . . .13.220
Gütermann AG and Zwicky v Commission (T-456&457/05) judgment of
28 April 2010, [2010] 5 CMLR 930 . . . . 1.091, 2.052, 13.124,
13.127, 13.179, 13.181

Heineken Nederland v Commission (T-240/07) judgment of 16 June 2011 . . . . 2.055, 13.180
Heineken/Scottish & Newcastle (M.4999) (3 April 2008) 8.046, 8.091, 8.207
Hitachi v Commission (T-112/07) judgment of 12 July 2011 . . . . .2.055
Hoechst v Commission (T-410/03) [2008] ECR II-881, [2008] 5 CMLR 839 . . . . 5.012,
5.083, 5.085, 13.028, 13.084, 13.091, 13.093, 13.094,
13.095, 13.127, 13.145, 13.160, 13.162, 13.177,
13.182, 13.188, 13.207, 13.216
Holland Malt v Commission (T-369/06) judgment of 9 September 2009 . . . . .15.026
Holland Malt v Commission (C-464/09P) judgment of 2 December 2010 . . . . 15.026, 15.075
Hospital Consulting v Esaote SpA, (C-386/07) Order of 5 May 2008,
[2008] ECR I-67* 11.033
Hotel Cipriani v Commission (T-254/00, etc) [2008] ECR II-3269 . . . . . .15.010, 15.026, 15.115
Hynix Conductor v Commission (T-149/10) not yet decided 5.139A

IACS (Ship Classification) (COMP/39416) decn of 14 October 2009 . . . . 5.135, 12.020
Iberia/British Airways (M.5747) (14 July 2010) 4.097, 4.098, 7.133, 8.200
Iberia/Clickair/Vueling (M.5364) (9 January 2009) 8.166
IBP Ltd v Commission (T-384/06) judgment of 24 March 2011 . . . . 5.016, 13.161
ICI v Commission (T-66/01) judgment of 25 June 2010 . . . . 4.075, 10.024, 10.092,
13.109A, 13.160, 13.178, 13.208
IMI plc v Commission (T-18/05) judgment of 19 May 2010, [2010]
5 CMLR 1215 . . . . .2.052, 2.053, 2.056, 13.086, 13.145, 13.155
INEOS/Kerling (M.4734) (30 January 2008) 4.044, 4.071, 4.079
Inspecteur van de Belastingdienst v X BV (C-429/07) judgment of
11 June 2009 . . . . 13.209, 14.070

Intel (COMP/37990) decn of 13 May 2009 . . . . 10.005, 10.029, 10.034,
                                         10.036, 10.0 38, 10.091, 10.096, 13.075
Intel Corp v Commission (T-457/08R) Order of 27 January 2009, [2009]
    ECR II-12* 13.246
Intel/McAfee (M.5984) (26 January 2011) 8.166, 8.219
Internationale Fruchtimport Gesellschaft Weichert v Commission (T-2/09) order of
    30 November 2009. . . . . .13.232
International Mail Spain SL v Administración del Estado (C-162/06) [2007]
    ECR I-9911, [2008] 4 CMLR 18 . . . . .12.183
International Removal Services (COMP/38543) decn of 11 March 2008 . . . . .13.179
International Transport Workers Federation v Viking Line ABP (C-438/05)
    [2007] ECR I-10779, [2008] 1 CMLR 1372 . . . . .2.034
IPIC/MAN Ferrostaal (M.5406) (13 March 2009) 8.163
Ireland v Commission (T-50/06, etc) judgment of 12 December 2007, [2007]
    ECR II-172* 15.120
Iride SpA v Commission (T-25/07) [2009] ECR II-245 . . . . .15.010, 15.019, 15.086
IRO v Commission (T-79/03) [2007] ECR II-4331, [2008] 4 CMLR 176 . . . . .1.004
ISD Polska v Commission (T-273&297/06) [2009] ECR II-2185 . . . . .1.082, 13.221,
                                         13.232, 15.099, 15.100, 15.115
Italy v Commission (T-424/05) judgment of 4 March 2009, [2009] ECR II-23* 15.023
Italy v Commission (T-211/05) judgment of 4 September 2009 . . . . .15.026, 15.033, 15.043
Italy v Commission (T-53/08) judgment of 1 July 2010 . . . . .15.010
Italy v Commission (T-3/09) judgment of 3 February 2011 . . . . .15.065
Italy v Commission (T-202/11) not yet decided 8.093
Itema/BarcoVision (M.4874) (4 August 2008) 8.218
Itochu Corporation v Commission (T-12/03) [2009] ECR II-883, [2009]
    5 CMLR 1375 . . . . 2.110, 6.053, 6.061, 13.065, 13.161,
                                         13.173, 13.181, 13.203, 13.205

Jan Rudolf Maas (KG Holding) v Commission (T-81/07, etc) [2009] ECR II-2411 . . . . . . 15.026,
                                         15.030, 15.103
Jungbunzlauer v Commission (T-492/04) appeal withdrawn 10 July 2008 . . . . .13.162

Kahla/Thüringen Porzellan v Commission (T-20/03) [2008] ECR II-2305 . . . . .15.070
Kahla/Thüringen Porzellan v Commission (C-537/08P) judgment of
    16 December 2010. . . . . .15.070
Kaimer v Commission (T-379/06) judgment of 24 March 2011 .13.091
Kanal 5 Ltd and TV 4 AB v Föreningen Svenska Tonsättares Internationella
    Musikbyrå (STIM) upa (C-52/07) [2008] ECR I-9275, [2009] 5 CMLR 2175. . . . . . 10.090,
                                         10.109, 10.134
Kattner Stahlbau GmbH v Maschinenbau-und Metall-Berufsgenossenschaft
    (C-350/07) [2009] ECR I-1513. . . . . .2.012
Kaučuk v Commission (T-44/07) judgment of 13 July 2011 . . . . .13.205C, 13.226
Kempter v Haupzollamt Hamburg-Jonas (C-2/06) [2008] ECR I-411, [2008]
    2 CMLR 586 . . . . 1.049, 14.090
KLM/Martinair (M.5141) (17 December 2008). 4.018, 4.040, 4.044, 4.097, 4.098,
                                    7.133, 8.041, 8.207, 8.229, 8.230
KME Germany v Commission (T-25/05) judgment of 19 May 2010,
    [2010] 5 CMLR 1329 . . . . .13.149, 13.160A, 13.163, 13.179,
                                         13.203, 13.215, 13.216
KME Germany v Commission (C-389/10P) not yet decided 13.160A, 13.163, 13.179,
                                         13.203, 13.216

KM Europa Metal v Commission (T-127/04) [2009] ECR II-1167 . . . . .5.015, 5.085,
13.149, 13.154, 13.158, 13.164, 13.167, 13.193, 13.203
Knauf Gips KG v Commission (C-407/08P) judgment of 1 July 2010,
[2010] 5 CMLR 708 . . . . 13.086, 13.091, 13.205B, 13.242
Kone Oyj v Commission (T-151/07) judgment of 13 July 2011 .13.167
Konkurrensverket v TeliaSonera Sverige (C-52/09) judgment of 17 February 2011 . . . . 10.059,
10.068, 10.112
Konsum Jämtland Ekonomisk Förening (C35/06 (ex NN 37/06)) OJ 2008 L126/3 . . . . . . .15.110
Kraft Goods/Cadbury (M.5644) (6 January 2010) 4.037
Kronoply v Commission (T-162/06) [2009] ECR II-1 . . . . .15.042
Kronoply and Kronotex v Commission (T-388/02) judgment of
10 December 2008, [2008] ECR II-305* 13.232, 15.042, 15.116
Kronospan/Constantia (M.4525) (19 July 2007) 4.052, 4.073
Kühne & Heitz (C-453/00) [2004] ECR I-837, [2006] 2 CMLR 17. . . . . .14.090

Lafarge v Commission (T-54/03) [2008] ECR II-120* 2.055, 13.081
Lafarge v Commission (C-413/08) judgment of 17 June 2010, [2010]
5 CMLR 586 . . . . .2.055, 13.076, 13.081, 13.160, 13.226, 13.253
L'Air Liquide v Commission (T-185/06) judgment of 16 June 2011 . . . . 13.205A
Le Carbone-Lorraine v Commission (T-73/04) [2008] ECR II-2661,
[2010] 5 CMLR 81 . . . . .2.052, 13.086, 13.163
Le Carbone-Lorraine v Commission (C-554/08P) judgment of 12 November 2009 . . . . 2.052,
13.086, 13.163
Leali v Commission (T-46/03) [2007] ECR II-4331, [2008] 4 CMLR 176. . . . . .1.004
Legris Industries v Commission (T-376/06) judgment of 24 March 2011 . . . . 13.205A
Lesaffre/GBI UK (M.5020) (11 July 2008). 8.211
Linea Gig v Commission (T-398/02R) [2003] ECR II-1139. . . . . .13.248
Linea Gig (in liquidation) v Commission (T-398/02) removed from the register
2 May 2005 . . . . 2.110, 6.053, 6.061, 13.065, 13.161, 13.173, 13.248
Lubricantes y Carburantes Galaicos ('Lubricarga') v GALP Energía España
(C-506/07) Order of 3 September 2009 . . . . 2.121, 6.050
Lucchini v Commission (T-80/03) [2007] ECR II-4331, [2008] 4 CMLR 176. . . . . .1.004
Long term contracts—France (COMP/39386) decn of 17 March 2010 . . . . 12.066, 12.066A
Lucchini Siderurgia (C-119/05) [2007] ECR I-6199 . . . . .1.004
Lufthansa/British Midland (M.5403) (14 May 2009) .4.097, 4.098, 7.133

Marine Hoses (COMP/39406) decn of 28 January 2009. . . . . 5.059, 13.149
Maas (Jan Rudolf) v Commission (T-81/07, etc) [2009] ECR II-2411 . . . .15.026, 15.030, 15.103
MasterCard MIF charges (COMP/34579) decn of 19 December 2007 . . . . . . 2.059, 2.060, 2.093,
3.021, 4.022A, 4.030, 4.037, 5.045, 5.046, 13.128, 13.201
Mediaset v Commission (T-177/07) judgment of 15 June 2010 . . . . .15.023, 15.105, 15.120
Mediaset v Commission (C-403/10P) judgment of 28 July 2011. . . . . .15.023, 15.105, 15.120
Microsoft (COMP/37792) decn of 27 February 2008. . . . . .4.042, 10.106, 13.202
Microsoft (T-167/08R) Order of 20 November 2008, [2009] 4 CMLR 775,. 13.202
Microsoft Corp v Commission (T-271/06) (appeal from periodic penalty) appeal
withdrawn 6 December 2007 . . . . 10.122, 13.130, 13.134, 13.202
Microsoft (Tying) (COMP/39530) decn of 16 December 2009 .10.122
Microsoft/Yahoo! Search business (M.5727) (18 February 2010). 8.026, 8.058, 8.207
Ministero dell'Economia e delle Finanze v Cassa di Risparmio di Firenze SpA
(C-222/04) [2006] ECR I-289, [2008] 1 CMLR 705 . . . . 2.004A, 15.026, 15.031
Mitsubishi Electric v Commission (T-133/07) judgment of 12 July 2011. . . . . 2.055,
13.084, 13.149A
Monsanto v Commission (T-112/97) [1999] ECR II-1277. . . . . .15.115

Monty Program v Commission (T-292/10) not yet decided. 8.166, 8.196, 8.207
Morgan Stanley/Visa International and Visa Europe (COMP/37860)
    decn of 3 October 2007 .2.067, 2.087, 2.091, 3.009, 3.011, 4.022A,
                            5.047, 13.073, 13.124, 13.156
Motosykletistiki Omospondia Ellados NPID (MOTOE) v Elliniko Dimosio
    (C-49/07) [2008] ECR I-4863, [2008] 5 CMLR 790, [2009] All ER (EC) 150. . . . . . . 2.003,
                      2.009, 5.156, 11.016, 11.019
MTU Friedrichshafen v Commission (T-196/02) [2007] ECR II-2889. . . . . .15.094
MyTravel Group v Commission (T-403/05) [2008] ECR II-2027, [2008]
    3 CMLR 1517 . . . . 13.100, 13.221

NDSHT v Commission (T-152/06) [2009] ECR II-1517. . . . . 15.071, 15.112
Nederlandse Vakbond Varkenshouders (NVV) v Commission (T-151/05) [2009]
    ECR II-1219, [2009] 5 CMLR 1613 . . . . .4.067, 4.070, 4.073, 4.076,
                      8.133, 13.103, 13.225
Netherlands v Commission (C-382/99) [2002] ECR I-5163. . . . . .15.023
Netherlands v Commission (emission trading scheme) (T-233/04) [2008]
    ECR II-591 . . . . .15.017, 15.023, 15.114
News Corp/Premiere (M.5121) (26 June 2008) 4.096, 8.029, 8.216
Nintendo Corp and Nintendo of Europe v Commission (T-13/03) [2009]
    5 CMLR 1421 . . . . 2.110, 6.053, 6.061, 13.065, 13.161, 13.162 13.164,
                  13.173, 13.177, 13.182, 13.203
Nitrile Butadiene Rubber (COMP/38628) decn of 23 January 2008. . . . . .13.167
Nokia/Navteq (M.4942) (2 July 2008) 8.085, 8.211, 8.216, 8.218, 8.229
Nokia Siemens Networks/Motorola Network Business (M.6007) (15 December 2010). 10.022
Norddeutsche Affinerie/Cumerio (M.4781) (23 January 2008). 4.065, 8.211
Novartis/Alcon (M.5778) (9 August 2010) 4.092
Nuova Agricast v Commission (T-362&363/05) judgment of 2 December 2008,
    [2008] ECR II-297* 13.241
Nuova Agricast v Commission (C-67/09P) judgment of 14 October 2010 . . . . 13.241, 15.106
Nuove Industrie Molisane v Commission (T-212/00) [2002] ECR II-347, [2003]
    1 CMLR 257 . . . . .15.115

O$_2$ Holdings v Hutchison 3G UK Ltd (C-533/06) [2008] ECR I-4231, [2008]
    3 CMLR 397 . . . . 9.033, 9.042
Olympiaki Aeroporia Ypiresies v Commission (T-268/06) [2008] ECR II-1091 . . . 15.039, 15.120
Olympic Air/Aegean Airlines (M.5830) (26 January 2011) 4.097, 8.207
Omnis Group v Commission (T-74/11) not yet decided 10.122
Omnis/Microsoft (COMP/39784) decn of 1 December 2010. . . . . .10.122
Omya v Commission (T-145/06) [2009] ECR II-145, [2009] 4 CMLR 827. . . . . . . 8.155, 8.172,
                  8.175, 13.230, 13.241
ONP and others v Commission (T-90/11) not yet decided 2.013, 2.059, 2.092, 13.204
Oracle Corporation/Sun Microsystems (M.5529) (21 January 2010) 8.166, 8.196, 8.207
Ordre National des Pharmaciens en France (ONP) (COMP/39510) decn of
    8 December 2010. . . . . .2.004, 2.013, 2.029, 2.059,
                2.060, 2.092, 5.016, 5.049, 13.204
Orifarm v Paranova Danmark (C-400/09&207/10) judgment of 28 July 2011 . . . . .9.039
Otto/Primondo Assets (M.5721) (16 February 2010) .4.034, 8.026, 8.204
Outokumpu v Commission (T-122/04) [2009] ECR II-1135, [2009]
    5 CMLR 1553 . . . . 1.004, 5.015, 5.085, 13.160
Outokumpu v Commission (copper plumbing tubes) (T-20/05) judgment of
    19 May 2010, [2010] 5 CMLR 1276 . . . . 13.149, 13.160
Owens Corning/Saint Gobain Vetrotex (M.4828) (26 October 2007). 8.207

Oxley Threads v Commission (T-448/05) judgment of 28 April 2010,
  [2010] 5 CMLR 864 . . . . .13.152

Papierfabrik August Koehler AG and Bolloré SA v Commission (C-322/07P, etc)
  judgment of 3 September 2009, [2009] 5 CMLR 2301 . . . . .13.032, 13.084, 13.205
Pedro IV Servicios Sl v Total España (C-260/07) [2009] ECR I-2437, [2009]
  5 CMLR 1291 . . . . 6.152
Pegler v Commission (T-386/06) judgment of 24 March 2011 . . . . .2.005, 13.177, 13.209
Pergan Hilfsstoffe für industrielle Prozesse GmbH v Commission
  (T-474/04) [2007] ECR II-4225, [2008] 4 CMLR 148 . . . . .1.068, 13.076, 13.112
Pernod Ricard/V&S Vin & Sprit (M.5114) (17 July 2008) 4.037, 8.211, 8.221
Peugeot SA and Peugeot Nederland NV (T-450/05) [2009] ECR II-2533 . . . . .13.154
Pfizer/Wyeth (M.5476) (17 July 2009) 4.092
Pfleiderer v Bundeskartellamt (C-360/09) judgment of 14 June 2011 . . . . .13.198, 14.020,
                                                                                      14.028, 14.031

Pierre Fabre Dermo-Cosmétique SAS v Competition Authority (C-439/09)
  not yet decided 6.095
Polimeri Europa v Commission (T-59/07) judgment of 13 July 2011 . . . . .13.160
Post Danmark v Konkurrencerådet (C-209/10) not yet decided 10.075, 12.191
Posten AB/Post Danmark A/S (M.5152) (21 April 2009) 8.163
Power transformers (COMP/39129) decn of 7 October 2009 . . . . 5.060, 13.149, 13.149A
Prestressing Steel (COMP/38344) decn of 30 June 2010. . . . . .13.179
Printers (EFIM complaint) (COMP/39391) decn of 20 May 2009 . . . . .4.060
Professional Videotape (COMP/38432) [2008] 5 CMLR 702 . . . . 5.015, 13.161, 13.205,
                                                                                      13.206, 13.208
Prokent-Tomra (COMP/38113) [2009] 4 CMLR 101 . . . . .1.091, 4.004, 4.076, 4.089,
                                                    6.196, 8.259, 10.022, 10.027, 10.031, 10.041,
                                                    10.062, 10.091, 10.093, 10.094, 10.098, 13.156
Promusicae (C-275/06) [2008] ECR I-276, [2008] All ER (EC) 809 . . . . .9.052
Provincia di Ascoli Piceno and Comune di Monte Urano v Sun Sang Kong Yuen
  Shoes Factory (C-461/07P(I)) [2008] ECR I-11*, [2008] 2 CMLR 425 . . . . .13.221
Prym and Prym Consumer v Commission (T-30/05) [2007] ECR II-107* 2.052, 2.055, 5.062
Prym and Prym Consumer v Commission (C-534/07) judgment of 3 September 2009,
  [2009] 5 CMLR 2377 . . . . 2.052, 2.055, 5.062, 13.154
Putters International v Commission (T-211/08) judgment of 16 June 2011. . . . . . . 13.149, 13.155

Qualcomm Wireless Business Solutions v Commission (T-48/04) [2009]
  ECR II-2029 . . . . 8.058, 8.218, 8.240, 13.232
Quimitécnica.com and de Mello v Commission (T-574/10) not yet decided 13.209

Rambus (COMP/38636) decn of 9 December 2009 . . . . 5.139A, 9.072A, 10.153
Rambus (COMP/38636) decn of 15 January 2010 . . . . 5.139A
RCA/MAV Cargo (M.5096) (25 November 2008) 8.207
Reagens SpA v Commission (T-30/10R) Order of 12 May 2010, [2010] 5 CMLR 237 . . . . .13.248
Région Nord-Pas-de-Calais v Commission (T-267&279/08) judgment of
  12 May 2011 . . . . 15.013, 15.018
Republic of Poland v Commission (T-41/06) appeal withdrawn 10 April 2008 . . . . .8.104
Rewe/Plus Discount (M.5112) (3 July 2008) 8.091
Rexel/Hagemeyer (M.4963) (22 February 2008). 8.046, 8.207
Riva Acciaio v Commission (T-45/03) judgment of 25 October 2007,
  [2007] ECR II-138* 1.004
Romana Tabacchi SpA v Commission (T-11/06R) [2006] ECR II-2491 . . . . .13.248

RWE Gas Foreclosure (COMP/39402) decn of 18 March 2009, [2009]
  5 CMLR 1667 . . . . 12.081
Ryanair v Commission (T-196/04) [2008] ECR II-3643. . . . . .2.010, 15.013, 15.109
Ryanair v Commission (T-342/07) judgment of 6 July 2010 . . . . 4.037, 4.097, 4.098, 8.160,
                                                        8.189, 8.204, 8.207, 10.038
Ryanair v Commission (T-423/07) judgment of 19 May 2011 . . . . .13.242, 13.244, 15.116
Ryanair (T-411/07) (*see* Aer Lingus Group v Commission)

Sbarigia v Azienda USL RM/A, Comune di Roma (C-393/08) judgment of 1 July 2010 . . . .11.033
Sanofi-Aventis/Zentiva (M.5253) (4 February 2009). 4.091
SCA/ P&G (European tissue business) (M.4533) (5 September 2008) 4.064, 8.204
Schering-Plough/Organon Biosciences (M.4691) (11 October 2007) 4.012, 4.091, 8.166
Schunk GmbH v Commission (T-69/04) [2008] ECR II-2567, [2009]
  4 CMLR 2 . . . . 1.016, 13.026, 13.086,
                                                        13.144, 13.145, 13.205, 13.215
Scippacercola and Terezakis v Commission (T-306/05) [2008] ECR II-4*,
  [2008] 4 CMLR 1418 (further appeal dismissed Case C-159/08P,
  Order of 25 March 2009) 2.007, 10.106, 12.050, 13.067, 13.072, 13.221
Scott v Ville d'Orléans (C-210/09) judgment of 20 May 2010. . . . . .15.110
SELEX Sistemi Integrati v Commission (C-113/07P) [2009] ECR I-2207 . . . . 2.003, 2.005,
                                                        2.007, 2.014, 13.225, 13.242
SELEX Sistemi Integrati SpA v Commission (C-481/07P) judgment of
  16 July 2009 (damages claim) 2.007, 13.241
Seydaland Vereinigte Agrarbetriebe v BVVG Bodenverwertungs- und -verwaltungs
  (C-239/09) judgment of 16 December 2010. . . . . .15.036
SGAE v Commission (C-112/09P) Order of 14 January 2010. .13.232
SGL Carbon v Commission (T-68/04, etc) [2008] ECR II-2511, [2009]
  4 CMLR 7 . . . . 2.052, 5.013, 5.016, 13.145, 13.152,
                                                        13.181, 13.203, 13.209, 13.216
SGL Carbon AG v Commission (C-564/08P) judgment of 12 November 2009 . . . . .2.052, 5.013,
                                                        5.016, 13.145, 13.152, 13.181, 13.203, 13.209, 13.216
Shell Petroleum v Commission (T-38/07) judgment of 13 July 2011 . . . . 13.205A
Ship Classification (IACS) (COMP/39416) decn of 14 October 2009 . . . . 5.135, 12.020
SIC v Commission (T-442/03) [2008] ECR II-1161. . . . . .11.048, 11.050,
                                                        15.021, 15.031, 15.033, 15.038, 15.068, 15.116
SIDE v Commission (T-348/04) [2008] ECR II-625 . . . . .15.064
Si.mobil/Mobitel (COMP/39707) decn of 24 January 2011 . . . . 13.072, 14.017
Si.mobil v Commission (T-201/11) not yet decided 13.021, 13.072, 14.017
Siemens v Commission (T-110/07) judgment of 3 March 2011 . . . . . .2.046, 2.051, 2.052, 2.055,
                                                        5.066, 13.076, 13.109, 13.162, 13.199, 13.208
Siemens AG Österreich v Commission (T-122/07 etc)
  judgment of 3 March 2011 . . . . 2.051, 13.103, 13.149A, 13.205, 13.205D
Skoma-Lux sro v Celiní Editelství Olomouc (C-161/06) [2007] ECR I-10841,
  [2008] 1 CMLR 1336 . . . . .1.039
SkyTeam (COMP/37984) [2008] 4 CMLR 228. . . . . .7.133
Slovakian postal legislation relating to hybrid mail services (COMP/39562)
  decn of 7 October 2008, [2009] 4 CMLR 663 . . . . 11.017, 11.018, 11.028,
                                                        11.052, 12.184, 12.188
Slovak Telekom v Commission (T-171/10) not yet decided. 1.110, 13.033
SNCF/LCR/Eurostar (M.5655) (17 June 2010) 4.097, 8.054
SNCF-P/CDPQ/ Keolis/EFFIA (M.5557) (30 October 2009) 8.091
SNIA v Commission (T-194/06) judgment of 16 June 2011 . . . . .13.206

Sniace v Commission (T-141/03) [2005] ECR II 1197, [2006] 2 CMLR 621 . . . . .15.115

Sniace v Commission (C-260/05P) [2007] ECR I-10005, [2008] 1 CMLR 1035 . . . . .15.117

Société Régie Networks v Direction de contrôle fiscal Rhône-Alpes
    Bourgogne (C-333/07) [2008] ECR I-10807 . . . . 15.042, 15.107, 15.109, 15.120

Socratec v Commission (T-269/03) judgment of 19 June 2009, [2009] ECR II-88* 8.240

Solvay v Commission (T-57/01: Soda ash, Article 102 appeal) judgment of
    17 December 2009. . . . . 1.121, 4.075, 13.109A

Solvay v Commission (T-58/01: Soda ash, Article 101 appeal) judgment of
    17 December 2009. . . . . 1.119, 1.131, 5.059, 13.078, 13.091,
                                                                    13.108, 13.109, 13.109A, 13.208

Solvay v Commission (hydrogen peroxide and perborate) (T-186/06)
    judgment of 16 June 2011 . . . . .13.197

Solvay v Commission (C-110/10P: appeal from T-58/01) not yet decided. 1.131, 13.078,
                                                                    13.091, 13.108, 13.109, 13.208

Solvay Solexis v Commission (hydrogen peroxide and perborate) (T-195/06)
    judgment of 16 June 2011 . . . . .13.093

Sot Lélos kai Sia v GlaxoSmithKline (C-468/06, etc) [2008] ECR I-7139,
    [2008] 5 CMLR 1382, [2009] All ER (EC) 1 . . . . 1.031, 1.075, 2.064, 2.110, 10.128

SP v Commission (T-27/03) [2007] ECR II-4331, [2008] 4 CMLR 176 . . . . .1.004

Spain v Commission (C-207/07) judgment of 17 July 2008, [2008] ECR I-111* 8.104

Spain v Commission (T-65/08R) Order of 30 April 2008, [2008] ECR II-69*. 8.104

Spain v Lenzing (C-525/04P) [2007] ECR I-9947, [2008] 1 CMLR 1068 . . . . 15.013,
                                                                    15.117, 15.122

Stadtwerke Schwäbisch Hall v Commission (C-176/06P) judgment of
    29 November 2007, [2007] ECR I-170*. 15.116

Standard Commercial Tobacco, Alliance One v Commission and
    Trans-Continental Leaf Tobacco v Commission (T-24/05) judgment of
    27 October 2010 . . . . .5.027, 13.162, 13.205

Statoil/ConocoPhillips (Jet) (M.4919) (21 October 2008) 8.207

STX/Aker Yards (M.4956) (5 May 2008) 4.098, 8.029, 8.204, 8.207, 10.022

Sun Chemical Group v Commission (T-282/06) [2007] ECR- II 2149. . . . . 8.207, 13.221

Syniverse/BSG Wireless Business (M.4662) (4 December 2007) 4.029, 10.022, 10.041

Suez Environnement—breach of seal, decn of 24 May 2011 . . . . 13.048, 13.050

Sweden v Commission (C-506/08P) (appeal from *Mytravel v Commission*) judgment
    of 21 July 2011. . . . . 13.100, 13.221

Swedish Interconnectors (COMP/39351) decn of 14 April 2010 . . . . 2.007, 10.097, 12.059,
                                                                    12.066A, 12.072

Syngenta/Monsanto sunflower seed business (M.5675) (17 November 2010) 4.068, 8.207, 8.218

Team Relocations (T-204&212/08) judgment of 16 June 2011. . . . . 2.052, 13.145, 13.148,
                                                                    13.149, 13.150, 13.152, 13.153, 13.155, 13.157, 13.168, 13.179

Tele 2 Polska (C-375/09) judgment of 3 May 2011 . . . . . . 13.124, 14.007, 14.056, 14.081, 14.087

Telekomunikacja Polska (COMP/39525) decn of 22 June 2011 . . . . .12.152

Télévision française 1 SA (TF1) v Commission (T-193/06) judgment of
    13 September 2010. . . . . .15.116

Territorio Histórico de Álava—Diputación Foral de Álava v Commission (T-30/01, etc)
    judgment of 9 September 2009 . . . . 15.043, 15.070

Teva/Barr (M.5295) (19 December 2008). 4.091

Teva/Ratiopharm (M.5865) (3 August 2010) 4.092, 8.200

TF1 v Commission (T-354/05) [2009] ECR II-471 . . . . 13.232, 15.030, 15.073, 15.112

Thomas Cook/travel business of Co-operative Group/travel business of Midlands
    Co-operative Society (M.5996) (6 January 2010) 4.034, 8.035

ThyssenKrupp Stainless AG v Commission (T-24/07) [2009] ECR II-2309 . . . . .1.004
ThyssenKrupp Acciai Speciali Terni v Commission (T-62/08) judgment of
    1 July 2010. . . . . 15.010, 15.105
ThyssenKrupp Liften Ascenseurs v Commission (T-144/07, etc) judgment of
    13 July 2011. . . . . .13.160
ThyssenKrupp Nirosta v Commission (C-352/09P) judgment of 29 March 2011 . . . . .1.004
Tirrenia di Navigazione v Commission (T-265/04, etc) judgment of 4 March 2009,
    [2009] ECR II-21* 15.068, 15.070, 15.120
T-Mobile Netherlands BV v Raad van bestuur van de Nederlandse
    Mededingingsautoriteit (C-8/08) judgment of 4 June 2009. . . . . .2.038, 2.042,
                                           2.045, 5.016, 5.087
T-Mobile/Orange (M.5650) (1 March 2010) 8.200
Tomkins plc v Commission (T-382/06) judgment of 24 March 2011 . . . . .13.205C, 13.240
Tomra Systems v Commission (T-155/06) judgment of 9 September 2010 . . . . .1.091, 4.004,
                4.076, 4.089, 6.196, 8.259, 10.022, 10.027, 10.031,
                10.041, 10.062, 10.091, 10.092, 10.093,
                10.094, 10.098, 13.154, 13.156, 13.203A
TomTom/Tele Atlas (M.4854) (14 May 2008) 8.085, 8.211, 8.216, 8.218
Toshiba Corp v Commission (T-113/07) judgment of 12 July 2011 . . . . 13.149A
Toshiba Corp v Czech Competition Authority (C-17/10) not yet decided 1.110,
                14.015, 14.042
Total and Elf Aquitaine v Commission (methacrylates) (T-206/06) judgment of
    7 June 2011 . . . . .13.176
Towers Perrin/Watson Wyatt (M.5597) (3 December 2009) 8.200
Trade-Stomil v Commission (T-53/07) judgment of 13 July 2011 . . . . 2.055, 13.205C, 13.226
Transportes Evaristo Molina SA v Commission (T-45/08) Order of
    14 November 2008, [2008] ECR II-265* 13.232
Travelport/Worldspan (M.4523) (21 August 2007). 4.022A, 4.059, 8.207, 8.211,
                8.216, 10.041, 12.048
Treuhand v Commission (T-99/04) [2008] ECR II-1501, [2008] 5 CMLR 962 . . . . .1.016, 1.091,
                2.053, 5.014, 13.028, 13.032, 13.082, 13.170
Trioplast Wittenheim v Commission (T-26/06) judgment of 13 September 2010 . . . . 2.052,
                13.149A, 13.155, 13.205, 13.305D
Trioplast Industrier v Commission (T-40/06) judgment of 13 September 2010 . . . . 2.056,
                13.149A 13.155, 13.205, 13.205D
TV2/Danmark v Commission (T-309/04, etc) [2008] ECR II-2935. . . . . 15.011,
                15.012, 15.019, 15.030, 15.068, 15.115, 15.120
Tyco Electronics /ADC Telecommunications (M.5983) (7 December 2010) 10.022

UCB (T-111/05) [2007] ECR II-4949, [2008] 4 CMLR 347 . . . . 2.052, 5.008, 5.011,
                5.083, 13.165, 13.174, 13.177
UGT Rioja v Juntas Generales de Territorio Histórico de Vizcaya (C-428/06, etc)
    [2008] ECR I-6747, [2008] 3 CMLR 1397 . . . . .15.034
Unibet (London) Ltd v Justitiekanslern (C-432/05) [2007] ECR I-2271. . . . . .14.095
Union française de l'express (UFEX) v Commission (T-60/05) [2007]
    ECR II-3397, [2008] 5 CMLR 580 . . . . 11.023, 13.067, 13.072, 13.078, 13.079
Unipetrol v Commission (T-45/07) judgment of 13 July 2011 . . . . 13.205C
United Airlines/Continental (M.5889) (27 July 2010) 7.133, 8.200
Universal v Commission (T-42/11) not yet decided. 13.205C

VEBIC (C-439/08) judgment of 7 December 2010 . . . . 14.013, 14.070A
Verhuizingen Coppens v Commission (T-210/08) judgment of 16 June 2011 . . . . 2.052, 5.122

Viega v Commission (T-375/06) judgment of 24 March 2011 . . . . .13.149

Vienna Insurance Group/Erste Bank (M.5075) (17 June 2008). 12.169

Visa v Commission (T-461/07) judgment of 14 April 2011. . . . . .2.064, 2.067, 2.087, 2.091,
2.099, 2.102, 3.009, 3.011, 4.020, 4.022A, 5.047,
13.073, 13.110, 13.124, 13.156, 13.169, 13.180, 13.227

Visa MIF (COMP/39398) decn of 8 December 2010. . . . . .5.046

Vivendi, Iliad/France Télécom (COMP/39653) decn of 2 July 2010 . . . . .11.020

Vivendi v Commission (T-568/10) not yet decided. 11.020

Vodafone España v Commission (T-109/06) [2007] ECR II-5151, [2008]
4 CMLR 1378 . . . . 12.104

Votorantim/Fischer (M.5907) (4 May 2011). 8.207, 8.210

Wanadoo España/Telefónica (COMP/38784) decn of 4 July 2007 . . . . 10.112, 10.113

Westfälische Drahtindustrie v Commission (T-393/10R) Order of 13 April 2010 . . . . .13.248

Wieland Werke v Commission (T-116/04) [2009] ECR II-1087, [2009]
5 CMLR 1517 . . . . 5.015, 5.085

Wieland-Werke AG v Commission (T-11/05) judgment of 19 May 2010 . . . . 13.145, 13.207

Wienstrom v Bundesminister für Wirtschaft und Arbeit (C-384/07) [2008]
ECR I-10393 . . . . 15.092, 15.109

World Wide Tobacco España v Commission (T-37/05) judgment of
8 March 2011. . . . . 5.027, 13.162, 13.167, 13.177

Yellow Cab Verkehrsbetriebs v Landeshauptmann von Wien (C-338/09) judgment of
22 December 2010. . . . . .11.033

X BV v Inspecteur van de Belastingdienst (C-429/07) judgment of
11 June 2009 . . . . 13.209, 14.070

Ziegler SA v Commission (T-199/08) judgment of 16 June 2011 . . . . .1.124, 4.006,
13.029, 13.228

TABLES OF EUROPEAN COURT OF HUMAN RIGHTS, EFTA COURT AND NATIONAL CASES

EUROPEAN COURT OF HUMAN RIGHTS

Behrami v France (Application No. 71412/01) judgment of 2 May 2007. . . . . .1.017
Menarini Diagnostics v Italy (No. 43509/08) judgment of 27 September 2011 . . . . .13.030

EFTA COURT

L'Oréal Norge v Per Aarskog AS (E-9&10/07) decn of 8 July 2008 . . . . 1.089, 9.044
Private Barnehagers Landsforbund v EFTA Surveillance Authority (E-5/07)
    decn of 8 February 2008, [2008] 2 CMLR 818 . . . . . . 2.012, 15.004, 15.080, 15.116, 15.117
Reassur Aktiengesellschaft v EFTA Surveillance Authority (E-4/10 etc)
    judgment of 10 May 2011 . . . . 2.017, 12.179

NATIONAL CASES

Austria

Deutsches Amtshilfeersuchen (16 Ok 7/09) judgment of the Supreme Court,
    15 July 2009. . . . . .14.021
Elevator Cartel (I) (16 Ok 5/08) judgment of the Supreme Court, 18 October 2008 . . . . . . .13.196
Europay (Case GZ 27 Kt 20, 24, 27/06) judgment of the Cartel Court,
    22 December 2006; on appeal, (16 Ok 4/07) judgment of the Supreme Court,
    12 September 2007. . . . . .5.045, 10.107, 10.108

Belgium

Bima NV v Sodrepe NV (Case 2002/AR/2580) judgment of the Brussels Court of
    Appeal, 10 October 2008 . . . . .14.058
Brouwerij Haacht v BM (Case C.08.0029.N) judgment of the Supreme Court,
    15 May 2009 . . . . .14.058
CT v Orde de Architecten (D.06.0010.N) judgment of the Cour de Cassation,
    27 April 2007. . . . . 2.092
FBIAC v WEX (2006/AR/2392), [2008] ECC 9 judgment of the Brussels Court
    of Appeal, 15 June 2007 . . . . 5.153
L'Ordre des Pharmaciens (2007/MR/5) judgment of Brussels Court of Appeal,
    7 April 2009. . . . . 2.092

Denmark

Dansk Transport og Logistik, decn of the Competition Council, 17 December 2008. . . . . . . 5.090
International Transport Danmark, decn of the Competition Council, 25 February 2009 . . . . 5.090
Post Danmark, decn of the Competition Council, 24 June 2009 . . . . 10.096, 12.193
Post Danmark v Competition Council (Ø'LR (13 Afd) B 2656/05) judgment of
    the High Court of Eastern Denmark, 21 December 2007 . . . . 12.193

Schneider Electric Danmark A/S v Competition Council (U.2008.851/1H) judgment
of the Supreme Court, 7 January 2008 . . . . 10.096
Viasat Broadcasting UK Ltd v Competition Council (Ø´LR B-3926-06) judgment
of the High Court of Eastern Denmark. 10.096
Viasat judgment of Danish Competition Appeal Tribunal (ECN 4/2010, p2) 7.119, 10.096

France

Apple Sales International v Bouygues Télécom, judgment of 4 February 2009,
BOCCRF No. 4 of 8 April 2009. . . . . .6.081
Arrow Génériques (Pourvoi No. P 08-12.510) judgment of the Cour de Cassation,
13 January 2009. . . . . .10.154
Bouygues Télécom, SFR, Orange, judgment of 11 March 2009, BOCCRF No. 7 of
17 July 2009. . . . . .5.091
CELF v Ministre de la culture et de la communication, decn of the Conseil d'État,
19 December 2008. . . . . .15.109
Chambre de commerce et d'industrie de Strasbourg v Brit Air, decn of the
Conseil d'État, 27 February 2006 . . . . .15.109
CNIM v Electricité de France [2008] ECC 208 judgment of the Cour de Cassation
(Commercial Chamber) 10.146
ETNA v France Télécom and SFR judgment of the Paris Court of Appeal,
2 April 2008, BOCCRF No. 7 of 15 September 2008 . . . . .12.164
ETNA v France Télécom and SFR judgment of the Cour de Cassation, judgment
of 3 March 2009. . . . . .12.164
France Télécom (prices in la Réunion) decn of the Competition Authority,
Decision No. 09-D-24 of 28 July 2009 . . . . 10.108, 10.114, 12.151, 12.162
Laboratoire GlaxoSmithKline (France) v Competition Council, judgment of the
Paris Court of Appeal, 14 March 2007, BOCCRF No. 7 of 15 September 2008 . . . . . .10.004
Laboratoire GlaxoSmithKline (France) v Competition Council (Case No. E08-14.503)
judgment No. 259 of the Cour de Cassation, 17 March 2009 . . . . .10.004
Léonidas Network (Decn No. 07-D-24) [2008] ECC 190. . . . . .6.101
MLP v NMPP judgment of the Cour de Cassation, 20 February 2007, BOCCRF No. 4
of 7 June 2007 . . . . .10.138
Régie départmentale des passages d'eau de la Vendée (Case Cass. Com., 05-17.566)
judgment of the Cour de Cassation, 17 June 2008 [2009] ECC 63 . . . . .10.075
Régie départmentale des passages d'eau de la Vendée judgment of the Cour de Cassation,
9 June 2009, BOCCRF No. 8 of 3 August 2009 . . . . .10.075

Germany

Cartel Damage Claims v Dyckerhoff AG (Case KZR42/08) judgment of the
Federal Supreme Court, 7 April 2009, Bundesgerichtshof press release No. 80/2009
of 17 April 2009 . . . . .14.112
Cement Cartel II (Case 2 U 10/03 Kart.) judgment of the Higher Regional Court of
Berlin, 1 October 2009. . . . . .14.125
Harry Potter (WuW DE-R 2018) judgment of the Frankfurt am Main Higher
Regional Court, 17 April 2007 . . . . 9.179
Lottoblock (WuW DE-R 2408) judgment of the Federal Supreme Court of
14 August 2008 . . . . 5.100
Online lotteries (WuW DE-R 2034) judgment of the Federal Supreme Court,
8 May 2007 . . . . .11.034
Orange-Book Standard (WuW/E DE-R2613) judgment of the Federal Supreme Court,
6 May 2009 . . . . 9.073

Secondary Car Dealer (WuW DE-R 2444) judgment of the Higher Regional Court
    of Frankfurt, 13 May 2008 . . . . .6.123
SIM-Card, WuW DE-R 2427, judgment of the Oberlandesgericht Düsseldorf of
    13 March 2008. . . . . 10.128, 11.008
Soda-Club (WuW DE-R 2268) judgment of Federal Supreme Court,
    4 March 2008. . . . . 4.030, 4.060, 10.121

Hungary

Allianz Hungária, Generali-Providencia and ors, Case 2.Kf.27.129/2009, judgment
    of the Budapest Court of Appeal, 23 September 2009 . . . . 6.157, 12.179
Baucont/ÉPKER/KÉSZ Case Kfv.II.39162/2008, judgment of the Supreme Court,
    17 June 2009 . . . . .5.123
Borsodi (Case No. Vj-28/20007/42) decn of the Competition Authority, 16 May 2008 . . . . 6.026
Hungarian Bar Association (Advertising Rules) Case No. 2.K.30.863/2009,
    judgment of the Budapest Metropolitan District Court, 29 October 2009. . . . . .5.040
Magyar Államvasutak ('MÁV') (Case 2.Kf.27.165/2008/14) judgment of the
    Budapest Court of Appeal, 18 February 2009 . . . . 10.151, 12.014

Ireland

BUPA Ireland Ltd v Health Insurance Authority judgment of the Supreme Court
    [2008] IESC 42 . . . . 11.049, 11.053
Competition Authority v Beef Industry Developments Society Limited & anor
    judgment of the Supreme Court [2009] IESC 72 . . . . 2.096, 3.013, 3.028,
                                                     3.060, 5.054
Goode Concrete v Cement Roadstone Holdings [2011] IEHC 15 14.131, 14.133
Hemat v The Medical Council [2010] IESC 24. . . . . 2.013, 11.033
Medicall Ambulance Ltd v HSE [2011] IEHC 76 (Irish High Court) 2.008
Neurendale Ltd t/a Panda Waste Services v Dublin City Council [2009] IEHC 588,
    [2010] ECC 21 . . . . 2.009, 2.010, 2.016, 3.010, 10.036, 10.050,
                                               10.064, 10.152, 11.033

Italy

Fastweb SpA v Telecom Italia SpA (Giur. It. 2007, 4, 919) decn of the Milan Court of
    Appeal, 16 May 2006 . . . . 12.151
Glaxo-PRINCIPI ATTIVI (Case A363) decn of the Autorità Garante della
    Concorrenza e del Mercato, 8 February 2006 No. 15175. . . . . 10.154
Italian Motor Insurers (1) judgment of the Corte di Cassazione, 3rd section,
    No. 2305, 2 February 2007. . . . . .14.121
Italian Motor Insurers (2) judgment of the Corte di Cassazione, No. 3640, of
    13 February 2009 . . . . .14.121
O.N.I.—Cantieri del Mediterraneo (Case No. 7589) judgment of the Council of
    State, 3 April 2009 . . . . 10.151
SEA SpA and AdR SpA (ECN Brief 4/2010, p2). 10.108, 11.004

Lithuania

SE Vilnius International Airport (ECN Brief 3/2010, p2) 2.010 .10.140
UAB Schneidersöhne Baltija/UAB Libra Vitalis (ECN Brief 1/2010, p2) 14.069

Netherlands

AUV v NMA (Cases AWB 06/526, etc, LJN: BD6629 & 6635) judgment of
    the Trade and Industry Appeal Tribunal, 3 July 2008. 2.060, 13.078

Dutch shrimp producers and wholesalers agreement, judgment of the Trade and
    Industry Appeal Tribunal, Cases AWB 06/599 etc, judgment of 19 January 2009,
    LJN: BD0436 . . . . .5.155
Dutch shrimp producers and wholesalers agreement, Dutch Administrative High Court
    for Trade and Industry (ECN Brief 2/2011, p2) 5.155, 12.196
Inspecteur van de Belastingdienst v X BV (ECN Brief 2/2010, p2) .13.209
NMa v NIP, NVVP and LVE judgment of the Trade and Industry Appeal Tribunal,
    6 October 2008 LJN: BF8820 . . . . .5.040

Poland

PKP Cargo v Office of Competition, judgment of 9 May 2011 . . . . .10.084
Polish Football Association and Canał (Case III SK 16/08) judgment of the
    Supreme Court, 7 January 2009 . . . . 5.116, 6.159
Telekomunikacja Polska SA (ECN Brief 3/2010, p2). 12.160
Visa—MasterCard, Case No. XVII AmA 109/07 judgment of the Court for
    Competition and Consumer Protection, 12 November 2008 . . . . 5.046, 14.080
Visa Card—Mastercard Polish Court of Appeal (ECN Brief 3/2010, p2). 5.046, 14.080

Portugal

Association of Certified Accountants (OTOC) (ECN Brief 4/2010, p2) 5.039
PT Group/ZON Group (ECN Brief 1/2010, p2) 10.114A

Slovak Republic

Zeleznicna spolocnost Cargo Slovakia (ECN Brief 5/2010, p2). 13.206, 14.070

Spain

ADIPAV (Case 640/08) decn of the Spanish Competition Commission,
    29 December 2008. . . . . .5.162
Asefa, Mapfre Empresa, Caser (ECN Brief 1/2010, p2). 12.169
ASINEM-ENDESA (Case 606/05) decn of the Court for the Defence of Competition,
    14 December 2006. . . . . .10.151
Canarias de Explosivos (Case 626/07) decn of the Competition Authority,
    12 February 2008. . . . . .10.107
Conduit Europe v Telefónica judgment of the Madrid Provincial Court of Appeal,
    25 May 2006 . . . . .14.121
Envases Hortofruticolas (ECN Brief 3/2010, p2) 14.021
Iberdrola Generación (Case 166/07) judgment of the Spanish National High Court,
    2 July 2009 . . . . .10.107
Mediapro/Gol TV (ECN Brief 2/2011, p2) 5.115
Telefónica de España SA v Retevisión SA (Case 9174/2003) judgment of the
    Supreme Court, 20 June 2006 . . . . .10.090

Sweden

Andersson v Åre Municipality (Case No. 1715-06) judgment of the Sundsvall
    Administrative Court of Appeal, 9 April 2008. . . . . .15.110
Boliden Mineral AB v Birka Värme Stockholm AB, Case NJA 2004 s. 804,
    judgment of the Supreme Court, 23 December 2004 . . . . 14.104A
Europe Direct AB and ors v VPC AB (Case No. T-32799-05) judgment of the
    Stockholm District Court, 20 November 2008 . . . . .10.127
Scandanavian Airlines Systems (SAS) (No. 324/2008) decn of the National
    Competition Authority, 9 January 2009 . . . . .10.096

Skyways v Kristianstad Airport (Case No. Ö 916-08) judgment of the Court of
  Appeal of Skåne and Blekinge, 7 May 2007 . . . . 15.021, 15.109
Svensson v Stockholm Municipality (Case No. 4514-07) judgment of the
  Stockholm Administrative Court of Appeal, 25 May 2007 . . . . .15.013

United Kingdom

Albion Water Ltd v Water Services Regulation Authority (Dŵr Cymru/Shotton Paper)
  [2008] EWCA Civ 536. . . . . 10.112, 10.114, 10.114A
Albion Water Ltd v Dŵr Cymru [2010] CAT 30 . . . . .14.122
Arriva Scotland West Limited v Glasgow Airport Ltd [2011] CSOH 69 . . . . 4.061, 14.132
BCL Old Company Ltd v BASF [2009] EWCA Civ 434. . . . . .14.149
BCL Old Co v BASF AG [2010] EWCA Civ 1258 . . . . .14.149
Bookmakers' Afternoon Greyhound Services v Amalgamated Racing Ltd
  [2008] EWHC 1978 (Ch) 2.099, 5.116A, 14.157
Bookmakers' Afternoon Greyhound Services v Amalgamated Racing
  Ltd [2008] EWHC 2688 (Ch) 2.055
Bookmakers' Afternoon Greyhound Services v Amalgamated Racing Ltd
  [2009] EWCA Civ 750. . . . . 2.093, 2.096, 2.112, 2.116, 4.034,
                                                                5.116A, 13.076, 14.104A
British Sky Broadcasting v Virgin Media Communications [2008] EWCA Civ 612. . . . . . . 14.158
B.S.A. International S.A v Irvine [2010] CSOH 12 13.206
Chester City Council v Arriva Buses [2007] EWHC 1373 (Ch) 14.157
Conex Banninger Ltd v The European Commission [2010] EWHC 1978 (Ch). 13.206,
                                                                13.220, 14.094, 14.095
Consumers' Association v JJB Sports plc 14.123
Cooper Tire & Rubber Europe v Shell Chemicals [2009] EWHC 1529 (Comm) 14.051, 14.145
Cooper Tire & Rubber Company Europe v Dow Deutschland Inc [2010]
  EWCA Civ 864 . . . . 14.046, 14.050, 14.051, 14.117
Crest Nicholson v Office of Fair Trading [2009] EWHC 1875 (Admin) 13.113D
Deutsche Bahn AG v Morgan Crucible [2011] CAT 16 . . . . .14.149
Devenish Nutrition v Sanofi-Aventis [2007] EWHC 2394 (Ch), [2008] 2 All ER 249. . . . . .14.122
Devenish Nutrition v Sanofi-Aventis [2008] EWCA Civ 1086 .14.123
Emerald Supplies v British Airways [2009] EWHC 741 (Ch) 14.160B
Emerald Supplies v British Airways [2010] EWCA Civ 1284. 14.160B
Emerson Electric v Morgan Crucible Company Plc and others [2007] CAT 28 . . . . .14.149
Emerson Electric v Morgan Crucible Company [2011] CAT 4 . . . . 14.117, 14.145
Enron Coal Services Ltd v English Welsh and Scottish Railway [2009] EWCA Civ 647. . . . .14.145
Enron Coal Services v English, Welsh and Scottish Railways [2011]
  EWCA Civ 2 . . . . 14.145, 14.146
Fiona Trust Corporation v Primalov [2007] UKHL 40 . . . . .14.164
Football Association Premier League Limited v QC Leisure [2008] EWHC 44 (Ch) 14.161
Football Association Premier League Ltd v QC Leisure [2008] EWHC 1411 (Ch) 14.094
Hays Specialist Recruitment Ltd v Office of Fair Trading [2011] CAT 8 . . . . .13.149
Honda Motor Company v David Silver Spares Ltd [2010] EWHC 1973 (Ch). 9.046
Humber Oil Terminals v Associated British Ports [2011] EWHC 352 (Ch). 10.105, 14.152
Hutchison 3G UK Ltd v O$_2$ (UK) Ltd [2008] EWHC 55 (Comm). 14.158
Hutchison 3G UK Ltd v OFCOM [2009] EWCA Civ 683. . . . . 10.041, 12.093, 12.100
IB v The Queen [2009] EWCA Crim 2575. . . . . 14.033A, 14.056
Independent Media Support Ltd v OFCOM [2008] CAT 13 . . . . .4.065
Intecare Direct Ltd v Pfizer Ltd [2010] EWHC 600 (Ch), [2010] ECC 28 . . . . . . 10.125, 14.132
Jones v Ricoh UK Ltd [2010] EWHC 1743 (Ch) 2.090, 2.096, 14.063, 14.161
Kier Group plc v Office of Fair Trading [2011] CAT 3. . . . . .5.122

Mastercigars Direct Ltd v Hunters & Frankau Ltd [2007] EWCA Civ 176, [2007]
    RPC 24 . . . . .9.045
National Grid v The Gas and Electricity Markets Authority [2009] CAT 10 . . . . . .10.041, 10.060,
    10.091, 13.168
National Grid v Gas and Electricity Markets Authority [2010]
    EWCA Civ 114 . . . . .10.041, 10.058, 10.060, 10.061, 10.091, 13.168
National Grid Electricity Transmission plc v ABB Ltd [2009] EWHC 1326 (Ch) 14.074,
    14.145, 14.160A
National Grid Electricity Transmission v ABB Ltd [2011] EWHC 1717 (Ch) 13.198,
    14.028, 14.070
Norris v Government of the United States of America [2008] UKHL 16 . . . . 14.033A
Oracle America, Inc (Formerly Sun Microsystems, Inc) v M-Tech Data Limited
    [2010] EWCA Civ 997. . . . . .14.138
Pirtek (UK) Ltd v Joinplace Ltd [2010] EWHC 1641 (Ch). 6.175, 6.186, 14.063, 14.106
Purple Parking Ltd v Heathrow Airport Ltd [2011]
    EWHC 987 (Ch) 2.010, 4.028, 4.037, 4.061, 10.005, 10.063, 10.068,
    10.089, 10.125, 10.135
R v George, Burns, Burnett and Crawley [2010] EWCA Crim 1148 . . . . 14.033A
R v GG [2008] UKHL 17. . . . . 14.033A
Ryanair Holdings v Office of Fair Trading [2011] CAT 23. . . . . 8.012, 14.075
Safeway Stores v Twigger [2010] EWCA Civ 1472 . . . . 2.021, 14.114
SEL-Imperial Ltd v British Standards Institution [2010] EWHC 854 (Ch) 2.026, 5.139,
    10.062A, 14.151, 14.161
Software Cellular Network Ltd v T-Mobile (UK) Limited [2007] EWHC 1790 (Ch) 14.133
South Somerset District Council v Tonstate (Yeovil Leisure) Ltd [2009]
    EWHC 3308 (Ch) 14.098
The Trademark Licensing Company Ltd v Leofelis SA [2009]
    EWHC 3285 (Ch) 14.046, 14.050
Union of European Football Associations (UEFA) v Euroview Sport Limited [2010]
    EWHC 1066 (Ch) 14.094
VIP Communications v OFCOM [2009] CAT 28 . . . . 10.128, 11.008
Wheeler v The Office of the Prime Minister [2008] EWHC 1409 (Admin), [2008]
    2 CMLR 1583 . . . . .1.012

United States

Cascade Health Solutions v PeaceHealth, 515 F.3d 883 (9th Cir, 2008). 10.095, 10.120
Pacific Bell Telephone Co v Linkline Communications Inc, 129 S.Ct. 1109 (2009). 10.112
Re payment card interchange fee and merchant discount (ECN Brief 4/2010, p2). . . 1.101, 13.198
In re Rubber Chemicals Antitrust Litigation, 486 F Supp 2d (ND Ca, 2007). 14.032

CASES PUBLISHED SINCE THE 6TH EDITION

*The following cases in the Court
of Justice of the European Union have
been published in the law reports
since the 6th edition (the judgment
date is given when only a summary
has been published in the ECR)*

AEESCAM v Commission (T-95/03) [2006] ECR-II 4739
AEPI v Commission (T-229/05) judgment of 12 July 2007, [2007] ECR II-84*
Akzo Nobel Chemicals and Akcros Chemicals v Commission (T-125&253/03) [2007]
    ECR II-3523, [2008] 4 CMLR 97, [2008] All ER (EC) 1
Alrosa v Commission (T-170/06) [2007] ECR II-2601, [2007] 5 CMLR 493
Annemans v Commission (T-411/05), judgment of 12 July 2007, [2007] ECR II-87*
Asklepios Kliniken v Commission (T-167/04) [2007] ECR II-2379
Au Lys de France v Commission (T-458/04) judgment of 3 July 2007, [2007] ECR II-71*
Britannia Alloys v Commission (C-76/06P) [2007] ECR I-4405, [2007] 5 CMLR 251
British Airways v Commission (C-95/04P) [2007] ECR-I 2331, [2007] 4 CMLR 982
Boehringer Ingelheim II (C-348/04) [2007] ECR I-3391, [2007] 2 CMLR 1445
Bolloré v Commission (T-109/02, etc) [2007] ECR-II 947, [2007] 5 CMLR 66
Bouygues v Commission (T-475/04) [2007] ECR II-2097
City Motors Groep v Citroën Belux (C-421/05) [2007] ECR I-653, [2007] 4 CMLR 455
Commission v Netherlands (C-523/04) [2007] ECR I-3267, [2007] 2 CMLR 1299
Commission v Volkswagen (C-74/04P) [2006] ECR I-6585, [2008] 4 CMLR 1297,
    [2007] ICR 217
Dalmine v Commission (C-407/04P) [2007] ECR I-829
Degussa v Commission (T-279/02) [2006] ECR II-897, [2008] 5 CMLR 7
Endesa v Commission (T-417/05) (judgment) [2006] ECR II-2533, [2008] 4 CMLR 1472
FNCBV and FNSEA v Commission ('French Beef') (T-217&245/03) [2006]
    ECR II-4987, [2008] 5 CMLR 406
France Télécom v Commission (T-340/03) [2007] ECR I-107, [2007] 4 CMLR 919, [2008]
    All ER (EC) 677
France Télécom v Commission (T-339/04) [2007] ECR II-521, [2008] 5 CMLR 502
France Télécom v Commission (T-340/04) [2007] ECR II-573
Germany v Commission (C-506/03) judgment of 24 November 2005 (unpublished)
Groupe Danone v Commission (C-3/06P) [2007] ECR I-1331, [2007] 4 CMLR 701
Groupement des cartes bancaires (CB) v Commission (T-266/03) judgment of 12 July 2007,
    [2007] ECR II-83*
Grüne Punkt—Duales System Deutschland v Commission (T-151&289/01) [2007]
    ECR II-1607 (Art 82) and 1691 (Art 81), [2007] 5 CMLR 300 (Art 82) and 356 (Art 81)
Holcim (Deutschland) v Commission (C-282/05P) [2007] ECR I-2941, [2007] 4 CMLR 1090
Microsoft Corp v Commission (T-201/04) [2007] ECR II-3601, [2007] 5 CMLR 846
Ministero dell'Industria v Lucchini (C-119/05), [2007] ECR-I 6199

MyTravel v Commission (T-212/03), judgment of 11 July 2007 not yet published

Peróxidos Orgánicos v Commission (T-120/04) [2006] ECR II-4441, [2007] 4 CMLR 153

Raiffeisen Zentralbank Österreich v Commission (T-259/02) [2006] ECR II-5169, [2007] 5 CMLR 1142

Salzgitter Mannesmann v Commission (C-411/04P) [2007] ECR I-959, [2007] 4 CMLR 682

Schneider Electric v Commission (T-351/03) [2007] ECR II-2237, [2008] 4 CMLR 1533

SELEX Sistemi Integrati v Commission (T-155/04) [2006] ECR II-4797, [2007] 4 CMLR 372

SGL Carbon v Commission (C-328/05P) [2007] ECR I-3921, [2007] 5 CMLR 16

Sumitomo Metal Industries v Commission ('Seamless Steel Tubes') (C-403&405/04P) [2007] ECR I-729, [2007] 4 CMLR 650

Sun Chemical Group v Commission (T-282/06) [2007] ECR II-2149, [2007] 5 CMLR 438

Technische Glaswerke Ilmenau v Commission (C-404/04P) judgment of 11 January 2007, [2007] ECR I-1*

Ter Lembeek International v Commission (T-217/02) [2006] ECR II-4483

Tirrenia di Navigazione v Commission (T-246/99) judgment of 20 June 2007, [2007] ECR II-65*

Unibet (C-432/05) [2007] ECR I-2271, [2007] 2 CMLR 725

Westfalen Gassen Nederland v Commission (T-303/02) [2006] ECR II-4567, [2007] 4 CMLR 334

TABLES OF EQUIVALENCES (*)
(CONDENSED)

Treaty on European Union

Old numbering of the Treaty on European Union	New numbering of the Treaty on European Union
TITLE I — COMMON PROVISIONS	TITLE I — COMMON PROVISIONS
Article 1	Article 1
	Article 2
Article 2	Article 3
Article 3 (repealed)(¹)	
	Article 4
	Article 5 (²)
Article 4 (repealed) (³)	
Article 5 (repealed) (⁴)	
Article 6	Article 6
Article 7	Article 7
	Article 8
TITLE II — PROVISIONS AMENDING THE TREATY ESTABLISHING THE EUROPEAN ECONOMIC COMMUNITY WITH A VIEW TO ESTABLISHING THE EUROPEAN COMMUNITY	TITLE II — PROVISIONS ON DEMOCRATIC PRINCIPLES
Article 8 (repealed) (⁵)	Article 9
	Article 10 (⁶)

(¹) Replaced, in substance, by Article 7 of the Treaty on the Functioning of the European Union ('TFEU') and by Articles 13(1) and 21, paragraph 3, second subparagraph of the Treaty on European Union ('TEU').
(²) Replaces Article 5 of the Treaty establishing the European Community ('TEC').
(³) Replaced, in substance, by Article 15.
(⁴) Replaced, in substance, by Article 13, paragraph 2.
(⁵) Article 8 TEU, which was in force until the entry into force of the Treaty of Lisbon (hereinafter 'current'), amended the TEC. Those amendments are incorporated into the latter Treaty and Article 8 is repealed. Its number is used to insert a new provision.
(⁶) Paragraph 4 replaces, in substance, the first subparagraph of Article 191 TEC.

(*) Tables of equivalences as referred to in Article 5 of the Treaty of Lisbon. The original centre column, which set out the intermediate numbering as used in that Treaty, has been omitted.

Old numbering of the Treaty on European Union	New numbering of the Treaty on European Union
	Article 11
	Article 12
TITLE III — PROVISIONS AMENDING THE TREATY ESTABLISHING THE EUROPEAN COAL AND STEEL COMMUNITY	TITLE III — PROVISIONS ON THE INSTITUTIONS
Article 9 (repealed) [7]	Article 13
	Article 14 [8]
	Article 15 [9]
	Article 16 [10]
	Article 17 [11]
	Article 18
	Article 19 [12]
TITLE IV — PROVISIONS AMENDING THE TREATY ESTABLISHING THE EUROPEAN ATOMIC ENERGY COMMUNITY	TITLE IV — PROVISIONS ON ENHANCED COOPERATION
Article 10 (repealed) [13] Articles 27a to 27e (replaced) Articles 40 to 40b (replaced) Articles 43 to 45 (replaced)	Article 20 [14]

[7] The current Article 9 TEU amended the Treaty establishing the European Coal and Steel Community. This latter expired on 23 July 2002. Article 9 is repealed and the number thereof is used to insert another provision.

[8] — Paragraphs 1 and 2 replace, in substance, Article 189 TEC;
— paragraphs 1 to 3 replace, in substance, paragraphs 1 to 3 of Article 190 TEC;
— paragraph 1 replaces, in substance, the first subparagraph of Article 192 TEC;
— paragraph 4 replaces, in substance, the first subparagraph of Article 197 TEC.

[9] Replaces, in substance, Article 4.

[10] — Paragraph 1 replaces, in substance, the first and second indents of Article 202 TEC;
— paragraphs 2 and 9 replace, in substance, Article 203 TEC;
— paragraphs 4 and 5 replace, in substance, paragraphs 2 and 4 of Article 205 TEC.

[11] — Paragraph 1 replaces, in substance, Article 211 TEC;
— paragraphs 3 and 7 replace, in substance, Article 214 TEC;
— paragraph 6 replaces, in substance, paragraphs 1, 3 and 4 of Article 217 TEC.

[12] — Replaces, in substance, Article 220 TEC;
— the second subparagraph of paragraph 2 replaces, in substance, the first subparagraph of Article 221 TEC.

[13] The current Article 10 TEU amended the Treaty establishing the European Atomic Energy Community. Those amendments are incorporated into the Treaty of Lisbon. Article 10 is repealed and the number thereof is used to insert another provision.

[14] Also replaces Articles 11 and 11a TEC.

Treaty on the Functioning of the European Union

Old numbering of the Treaty establishing the European Community	New numbering of the Treaty on the Functioning of the European Union
PART ONE — PRINCIPLES	PART ONE — PRINCIPLES
Article 1 (repealed)	
	Article 1
Article 2 (repealed) (^{25})	
	Title I — Categories and areas of union competence
	Article 2
	Article 3
	Article 4
	Article 5
	Article 6
	Title II — Provisions having general application
	Article 7
Article 3, paragraph 1 (repealed) (^{26})	
Article 3, paragraph 2	Article 8
Article 4 (moved)	Article 119
Article 5 (replaced) (^{27})	
	Article 9
	Article 10
Article 6	Article 11
Article 153, paragraph 2 (moved)	Article 12
	Article 13 (^{28})
Article 7 (repealed) (^{29})	
Article 8 (repealed) (^{30})	
Article 9 (repealed)	
Article 10 (repealed) (^{31})	
Article 11 (replaced) (^{32})	Articles 326 to 334

(^{25}) Replaced, in substance, by Article 3 TEU.
(^{26}) Replaced, in substance, by Articles 3 to 6 TFEU.
(^{27}) Replaced, in substance, by Article 5 TEU.
(^{28}) Insertion of the operative part of the protocol on protection and welfare of animals.
(^{29}) Replaced, in substance, by Article 13 TEU.
(^{30}) Replaced, in substance, by Article 13 TEU and Article 282, paragraph 1, TFEU.
(^{31}) Replaced, in substance, by Article 4, paragraph 3, TEU.
(^{32}) Also replaced by Article 20 TEU.

Old numbering of the Treaty establishing the European Community	New numbering of the Treaty on the Functioning of the European Union
Article 11a (replaced) ([32])	Articles 326 to 334
Article 12 (repealed)	Article 18
Article 13 (moved)	Article 19
Article 14 (moved)	Article 26
Article 15 (moved)	Article 27
Article 16	Article 14
Article 255 (moved)	Article 15
Article 286 (moved)	Article 16
	Article 17
PART TWO — CITIZENSHIP OF THE UNION	PART TWO — NON-DISCRIMINATION AND CITIZENSHIP OF THE UNION
Article 12 (moved)	Article 18
Article 13 (moved)	Article 19
Article 17	Article 20
Article 18	Article 21
Article 19	Article 22
Article 20	Article 23
Article 21	Article 24
Article 22	Article 25
PART THREE — COMMUNITY POLICIES	PART THREE — POLICIES AND INTERNAL ACTIONS OF THE UNION
	Title I — The internal market
Article 14 (moved)	Article 26
Article 15 (moved)	Article 27
Title I — Free movement of goods	Title II — Free movement of goods
Article 23	Article 28
Article 24	Article 29
Chapter 1 — The customs union	Chapter 1 — The customs union
Article 25	Article 30
Article 26	Article 31
Article 27	Article 32
Part Three, Title X, Customs cooperation (moved)	Chapter 2 — Customs cooperation
Article 135 (moved)	Article 33
Chapter 2 — Prohibition of quantitative restrictions between Member States	Chapter 3 — Prohibition of quantitative restrictions between Member States

Old numbering of the Treaty establishing the European Community	New numbering of the Treaty on the Functioning of the European Union
Article 28	Article 34
Article 29	Article 35
Article 30	Article 36
Article 31	Article 37
Title II — Agriculture	Title III — Agriculture and fisheries
Article 32	Article 38
Article 33	Article 39
Article 34	Article 40
Article 35	Article 41
Article 36	Article 42
Article 37	Article 43
Article 38	Article 44
Title III — Free movement of persons, services and capital	Title IV — Free movement of persons, services and capital
Chapter 1 — Workers	Chapter 1 — Workers
Article 39	Article 45
Article 40	Article 46
Article 41	Article 47
Article 42	Article 48
Chapter 2 — Right of establishment	Chapter 2 — Right of establishment
Article 43	Article 49
Article 44	Article 50
Article 45	Article 51
Article 46	Article 52
Article 47	Article 53
Article 48	Article 54
Article 294 (moved)	Article 55
Chapter 3 — Services	Chapter 3 — Services
Article 49	Article 56
Article 50	Article 57
Article 51	Article 58
Article 52	Article 59
Article 53	Article 60
Article 54	Article 61
Article 55	Article 62
Chapter 4 — Capital and payments	Chapter 4 — Capital and payments

Old numbering of the Treaty establishing the European Community	New numbering of the Treaty on the Functioning of the European Union
Article 56	Article 63
Article 57	Article 64
Article 58	Article 65
Article 59	Article 66
Article 60 (moved)	Article 75
Title IV — Visas, asylum, immigration and other policies related to free movement of persons	Title V — Area of freedom, security and justice
	Chapter 1 — General provisions
Article 61	Article 67 (^{33})
	Article 68
	Article 69
	Article 70
	Article 71 (^{34})
Article 64, paragraph 1 (replaced)	Article 72 (^{35})
	Article 73
Article 66 (replaced)	Article 74
Article 60 (moved)	Article 75
	Article 76
	Chapter 2 — Policies on border checks, asylum and immigration
Article 62	Article 77
Article 63, points 1 et 2, and Article 64, paragraph 2 (^{36})	Article 78
Article 63, points 3 and 4	Article 79
	Article 80
Article 64, paragraph 1 (replaced)	Article 72
	Chapter 3 — Judicial cooperation in civil matters
Article 65	Article 81
Article 66 (replaced)	Article 74

(^{33}) Also replaces the current Article 29 TEU.
(^{34}) Also replaces the current Article 36 TEU.
(^{35}) Also replaces the current Article 33 TEU.
(^{36}) Points 1 and 2 of Article 63 EC are replaced by paragraphs 1 and 2 of Article 78 TFEU, and paragraph 2 of Article 64 is replaced by paragraph 3 of Article 78 TFEU.

Old numbering of the Treaty establishing the European Community	New numbering of the Treaty on the Functioning of the European Union
Article 67 (repealed)	
Article 68 (repealed)	
Article 69 (repealed)	
	Chapter 4 — Judicial cooperation in criminal matters
	Article 82 (^{37})
	Article 83 (^{37})
	Article 84
	Article 85 (^{37})
	Article 86
	Chapter 5 — Police cooperation
	Article 87 (^{38})
	Article 88 (^{38})
	Article 89 (^{39})
Title V — Transport	Title VI — Transport
Article 70	Article 90
Article 71	Article 91
Article 72	Article 92
Article 73	Article 93
Article 74	Article 94
Article 75	Article 95
Article 76	Article 96
Article 77	Article 97
Article 78	Article 98
Article 79	Article 99
Article 80	Article 100
Title VI — Common rules on competition, taxation and approximation of laws	Title VII — Common rules on competition, taxation and approximation of laws
Chapter 1 — Rules on competition	Chapter 1 — Rules on competition
Section 1 — Rules applying to undertakings	Section 1 — Rules applying to undertakings
Article 81	Article 101
Article 83	Article 103

(^{37}) Replaces the current Article 31 TEU.
(^{38}) Replaces the current Article 30 TEU.
(^{39}) Replaces the current Article 32 TEU.

Old numbering of the Treaty establishing the European Community	New numbering of the Treaty on the Functioning of the European Union
Article 84	Article 104
Article 85	Article 105
Article 86	Article 106
Section 2 — Aids granted by States	Section 2 — Aids granted by States
Article 87	Article 107
Article 88	Article 108
Article 89	Article 109
Chapter 2 — Tax provisions	Chapter 2 — Tax provisions
Article 90	Article 110
Article 91	Article 111
Article 92	Article 112
Article 93	Article 113
Chapter 3 — Approximation of laws	Chapter 3 — Approximation of laws
Article 95 (moved)	Article 114
Article 94 (moved)	Article 115
Article 96	Article 116
Article 97	Article 117
	Article 118
Title VII — Economic and monetary policy	Title VIII — Economic and monetary policy
Article 4 (moved)	Article 119
Chapter 1 — Economic policy	Chapter 1 — Economic policy
Article 98	Article 120
Article 99	Article 121
Article 100	Article 122
Article 101	Article 123
Article 102	Article 124
Article 103	Article 125
Article 104	Article 126
Chapter 2 — monetary policy	Chapter 2 — monetary policy
Article 105	Article 127
Article 106	Article 128

Old numbering of the Treaty establishing the European Community	New numbering of the Treaty on the Functioning of the European Union
Article 107	Article 129
Article 108	Article 130
Article 109	Article 131
Article 110	Article 132
Article 111, paragraphs 1 to 3 and 5 (moved)	Article 219
Article 111, paragraph 4 (moved)	Article 138
	Article 133
Chapter 3 — Institutional provisions	Chapter 3 — Institutional provisions
Article 112 (moved)	Article 283
Article 113 (moved)	Article 284
Article 114	Article 134
Article 115	Article 135
	Chapter 4 — Provisions specific to Member States whose currency is the euro
	Article 136
	Article 137
Article 111, paragraph 4 (moved)	Article 138
Chapter 4 — Transitional provisions	Chapter 5 — Transitional provisions
Article 116 (repealed)	
	Article 139
Article 117, paragraphs 1, 2, sixth indent, and 3 to 9 (repealed)	
Article 117, paragraph 2, first five indents (moved)	Article 141, paragraph 2
Article 121, paragraph 1 (moved) Article 122, paragraph 2, second sentence (moved) Article 123, paragraph 5 (moved)	Article 140 (^{40})
Article 118 (repealed)	
Article 123, paragraph 3 (moved) Article 117, paragraph 2, first five indents (moved)	Article 141 (^{41})
Article 124, paragraph 1 (moved)	Article 142
Article 119	Article 143

(^{40}) — Article 140, paragraph 1 takes over the wording of paragraph 1 of Article 121.
  — Article 140, paragraph 2 takes over the second sentence of paragraph 2 of Article 122.
  — Article 140, paragraph 3 takes over paragraph 5 of Article 123.
(^{41}) — Article 141, paragraph 1 takes over paragraph 3 of Article 123.
  — Article 141, paragraph 2 takes over the first five indents of paragraph 2 of Article 117.

Old numbering of the Treaty establishing the European Community	New numbering of the Treaty on the Functioning of the European Union
Article 120	Article 144
Article 121, paragraph 1 (moved)	Article 140, paragraph 1
Article 121, paragraphs 2 to 4 (repealed)	
Article 122, paragraphs 1, 2, first sentence, 3, 4, 5 and 6 (repealed)	
Article 122, paragraph 2, second sentence (moved)	Article 140, paragraph 2, first subparagraph
Article 123, paragraphs 1, 2 and 4 (repealed)	
Article 123, paragraph 3 (moved)	Article 141, paragraph 1
Article 123, paragraph 5 (moved)	Article 140, paragraph 3
Article 124, paragraph 1 (moved)	Article 142
Article 124, paragraph 2 (repealed)	
Title VIII — Employment	Title IX — Employment
Article 125	Article 145
Article 126	Article 146
Article 127	Article 147
Article 128	Article 148
Article 129	Article 149
Article 130	Article 150
Title IX — Common commercial policy (moved)	Part Five, Title II, common commercial policy
Article 131 (moved)	Article 206
Article 132 (repealed)	
Article 133 (moved)	Article 207
Article 134 (repealed)	
Title X — Customs cooperation (moved)	Part Three, Title II, Chapter 2, Customs cooperation
Article 135 (moved)	Article 33
Title XI — Social policy, education, vocational training and youth	Title X — Social policy
Chapter 1 — social provisions (repealed)	
Article 136	Article 151
	Article 152
Article 137	Article 153
Article 138	Article 154
Article 139	Article 155
Article 140	Article 156
Article 141	Article 157
Article 142	Article 158

Old numbering of the Treaty establishing the European Community	New numbering of the Treaty on the Functioning of the European Union
Article 143	Article 159
Article 144	Article 160
Article 145	Article 161
Chapter 2 — The European Social Fund	Title XI — The European Social Fund
Article 146	Article 162
Article 147	Article 163
Article 148	Article 164
Chapter 3 — Education, vocational training and youth	Title XII — Education, vocational training, youth and sport
Article 149	Article 165
Article 150	Article 166
Title XII — Culture	Title XIII — Culture
Article 151	Article 167
Title XIII — Public health	Title XIV — Public health
Article 152	Article 168
Title XIV — Consumer protection	Title XV — Consumer protection
Article 153, paragraphs 1, 3, 4 and 5	Article 169
Article 153, paragraph 2 (moved)	Article 12
Title XV — Trans-European networks	Title XVI — Trans-European networks
Article 154	Article 170
Article 155	Article 171
Article 156	Article 172
Title XVI — Industry	Title XVII — Industry
Article 157	Article 173
Title XVII — Economic and social cohesion	Title XVIII — Economic, social and territorial cohesion
Article 158	Article 174
Article 159	Article 175
Article 160	Article 176
Article 161	Article 177
Article 162	Article 178
Title XVIII — Research and technological development	Title XIX — Research and technological development and space
Article 163	Article 179
Article 164	Article 180
Article 165	Article 181

Old numbering of the Treaty establishing the European Community	New numbering of the Treaty on the Functioning of the European Union
Article 166	Article 182
Article 167	Article 183
Article 168	Article 184
Article 169	Article 185
Article 170	Article 186
Article 171	Article 187
Article 172	Article 188
	Article 189
Article 173	Article 190
Title XIX — Environment	Title XX — Environment
Article 174	Article 191
Article 175	Article 192
Article 176	Article 193
	Titre XXI — Energy
	Article 194
	Title XXII — Tourism
	Article 195
	Title XXIII — Civil protection
	Article 196
	Title XXIV — Administrative cooperation
	Article 197
Title XX — Development cooperation (moved)	Part Five, Title III, Chapter 1, Development cooperation
Article 177 (moved)	Article 208
Article 178 (repealed) (^{42})	
Article 179 (moved)	Article 209
Article 180 (moved)	Article 210
Article 181 (moved)	Article 211
Title XXI — Economic, financial and technical cooperation with third countries (moved)	Part Five, Title III, Chapter 2, Economic, financial and technical cooperation with third countries
Article 181a (moved)	Article 212

(^{42}) Replaced, in substance, by the second sentence of the second subparagraph of paragraph 1 of Article 208 TFEU.

Old numbering of the Treaty establishing the European Community	New numbering of the Treaty on the Functioning of the European Union
PART FOUR — ASSOCIATION OF THE OVERSEAS COUNTRIES AND TERRITORIES	PART FOUR — ASSOCIATION OF THE OVERSEAS COUNTRIES AND TERRITORIES
Article 182	Article 198
Article 183	Article 199
Article 184	Article 200
Article 185	Article 201
Article 186	Article 202
Article 187	Article 203
Article 188	Article 204
	PART FIVE — EXTERNAL ACTION BY THE UNION
	Title I — General provisions on the union's external action
	Article 205
Part Three, Title IX, Common commercial policy (moved)	Title II — Common commercial policy
Article 131 (moved)	Article 206
Article 133 (moved)	Article 207
	Title III — Cooperation with third countries and humanitarian aid
Part Three, Title XX, Development cooperation (moved)	Chapter 1 — development cooperation
Article 177 (moved)	Article 208 (43)
Article 179 (moved)	Article 209
Article 180 (moved)	Article 210
Article 181 (moved)	Article 211
Part Three, Title XXI, Economic, financial and technical cooperation with third countries (moved)	Chapter 2 — Economic, financial and technical cooperation with third countries
Article 181a (moved)	Article 212
	Article 213
	Chapter 3 — Humanitarian aid
	Article 214
	Title IV — Restrictive measures
Article 301 (replaced)	Article 215

(43) The second sentence of the second subparagraph of paragraph 1 replaces, in substance, Article 178 TEC.

Old numbering of the Treaty establishing the European Community	New numbering of the Treaty on the Functioning of the European Union
	Title V — International agreements
	Article 216
Article 310 (moved)	Article 217
Article 300 (replaced)	Article 218
Article 111, paragraphs 1 to 3 and 5 (moved)	Article 219
	Title VI — The Union's relations with international organisations and third countries and the Union delegations
Articles 302 to 304 (replaced)	Article 220
	Article 221
	Title VII — Solidarity clause
	Article 222
PART FIVE — INSTITUTIONS OF THE COMMUNITY	PART SIX — INSTITUTIONAL AND FINANCIAL PROVISIONS
Title I — Institutional provisions	Title I — Institutional provisions
Chapter 1 — The institutions	Chapter 1 — The institutions
Section 1 — The European Parliament	Section 1 — The European Parliament
Article 189 (repealed) ([44])	
Article 190, paragraphs 1 to 3 (repealed) ([45])	
Article 190, paragraphs 4 and 5	Article 223
Article 191, first paragraph (repealed) ([46])	
Article 191, second paragraph	Article 224
Article 192, first paragraph (repealed) ([47])	
Article 192, second paragraph	Article 225
Article 193	Article 226
Article 194	Article 227
Article 195	Article 228
Article 196	Article 229
Article 197, first paragraph (repealed) ([48])	

([44]) Replaced, in substance, by Article 14, paragraphs 1 and 2, TEU.
([45]) Replaced, in substance, by Article 14, paragraphs 1 to 3, TEU.
([46]) Replaced, in substance, by Article 11, paragraph 4, TEU.
([47]) Replaced, in substance, by Article 14, paragraph 1, TEU.
([48]) Replaced, in substance, by Article 14, paragraph 4, TEU.

Old numbering of the Treaty establishing the European Community	New numbering of the Treaty on the Functioning of the European Union
Article 197, second, third and fourth paragraphs	Article 230
Article 198	Article 231
Article 199	Article 232
Article 200	Article 233
Article 201	Article 234
	Section 2 — The European Council
	Article 235
	Article 236
Section 2 — The Council	Section 3 — The Council
Article 202 (repealed) (⁴⁹)	
Article 203 (repealed) (⁵⁰)	
Article 204	Article 237
Article 205, paragraphs 2 and 4 (repealed) (⁵¹)	
Article 205, paragraphs 1 and 3	Article 238
Article 206	Article 239
Article 207	Article 240
Article 208	Article 241
Article 209	Article 242
Article 210	Article 243
Section 3 — The Commission	Section 4 — The Commission
Article 211 (repealed) (⁵³)	
	Article 244
Article 212 (moved)	Article 249, paragraph 2
Article 213	Article 245
Article 214 (repealed) (⁵⁵)	
Article 215	Article 246
Article 216	Article 247
Article 217, paragraphs 1, 3 and 4 (repealed) (⁵⁶)	
Article 217, paragraph 2	Article 248
Article 218, paragraph 1 (repealed) (⁵⁷)	

(⁴⁹) Replaced, in substance, by Article 16, paragraph 1, TEU and by Articles 290 and 291 TFEU.
(⁵⁰) Replaced, in substance, by Article 16, paragraphs 2 and 9 TEU.
(⁵¹) Replaced, in substance, by Article 16, paragraphs 4 and 5 TEU.
(⁵³) Replaced, in substance, by Article 17, paragraph 1 TEU.
(⁵⁵) Replaced, in substance, by Article 17, paragraphs 3 and 7 TEU.
(⁵⁶) Replaced, in substance, by Article 17, paragraph 6, TEU.
(⁵⁷) Replaced, in substance, by Article 295 TFEU.

Old numbering of the Treaty establishing the European Community	New numbering of the Treaty on the Functioning of the European Union
Article 218, paragraph 2	Article 249
Article 219	Article 250
Section 4 — The Court of Justice	Section 5 — The Court of Justice of the European Union
Article 220 (repealed) ([58])	
Article 221, first paragraph (repealed) ([59])	
Article 221, second and third paragraphs	Article 251
Article 222	Article 252
Article 223	Article 253
Article 224 ([60])	Article 254
	Article 255
Article 225	Article 256
Article 225a	Article 257
Article 226	Article 258
Article 227	Article 259
Article 228	Article 260
Article 229	Article 261
Article 229a	Article 262
Article 230	Article 263
Article 231	Article 264
Article 232	Article 265
Article 233	Article 266
Article 234	Article 267
Article 235	Article 268
	Article 269
Article 236	Article 270
Article 237	Article 271
Article 238	Article 272
Article 239	Article 273
Article 240	Article 274
	Article 275
	Article 276

([58]) Replaced, in substance, by Article 19 TEU.
([59]) Replaced, in substance, by Article 19, paragraph 2, first subparagraph, of the TEU.
([60]) The first sentence of the first subparagraph is replaced, in substance, by Article 19, paragraph 2, second subparagraph of the TEU.

Old numbering of the Treaty establishing the European Community	New numbering of the Treaty on the Functioning of the European Union
Article 241	Article 277
Article 242	Article 278
Article 243	Article 279
Article 244	Article 280
Article 245	Article 281
	Section 6 — The European Central Bank
	Article 282
Article 112 (moved)	Article 283
Article 113 (moved)	Article 284
Section 5 — The Court of Auditors	Section 7 — The Court of Auditors
Article 246	Article 285
Article 247	Article 286
Article 248	Article 287
Chapter 2 — Provisions common to several institutions	Chapter 2 — Legal acts of the Union, adoption procedures and other provisions
	Section 1 — The legal acts of the Union
Article 249	Article 288
	Article 289
	Article 290 (^{61})
	Article 291 (^{61})
	Article 292
	Section 2 — Procedures for the adoption of acts and other provisions
Article 250	Article 293
Article 251	Article 294
Article 252 (repealed)	
	Article 295
Article 253	Article 296
Article 254	Article 297
	Article 298
Article 255 (moved)	Article 15
Article 256	Article 299

(^{61}) Replaces, in substance, the third indent of Article 202 TEC.

Old numbering of the Treaty establishing the European Community	New numbering of the Treaty on the Functioning of the European Union
	Chapter 3 — The Union's advisory bodies
	Article 300
Chapter 3 — The Economic and Social Committee	Section 1 — The Economic and Social Committee
Article 257 (repealed) ([62])	
Article 258, first, second and fourth paragraphs	Article 301
Article 258, third paragraph (repealed) ([63])	
Article 259	Article 302
Article 260	Article 303
Article 261 (repealed)	
Article 262	Article 304
Chapter 4 — The Committee of the Regions	Section 2 — The Committee of the Regions
Article 263, first and fifth paragraphs (repealed) ([64])	
Article 263, second to fourth paragraphs	Article 305
Article 264	Article 306
Article 265	Article 307
Chapter 5 — The European Investment Bank	Chapter 4 — The European Investment Bank
Article 266	Article 308
Article 267	Article 309
Title II — Financial provisions	Title II — Financial provisions
Article 268	Article 310
	Chapter 1 — The Union's own resources
Article 269	Article 311
Article 270 (repealed) ([65])	
	Chapter 2 — The multiannual financial framework
	Article 312
	Chapter 3 — The Union's annual budget
Article 272, paragraph 1 (moved)	Article 313
Article 271 (moved)	Article 316
Article 272, paragraph 1 (moved)	Article 313
Article 272, paragraphs 2 to 10	Article 314

([62]) Replaced, in substance, by Article 300, paragraph 2 of the TFEU.
([63]) Replaced, in substance, by Article 300, paragraph 4 of the TFEU.
([64]) Replaced, in substance, by Article 300, paragraphs 3 and 4, TFEU.
([65]) Replaced, in substance, by Article 310, paragraph 4, TFEU.

Old numbering of the Treaty establishing the European Community	New numbering of the Treaty on the Functioning of the European Union
Article 273	Article 315
Article 271 (moved)	Article 316
	Chapter 4 — Implementation of the budget and discharge
Article 274	Article 317
Article 275	Article 318
Article 276	Article 319
	Chapter 5 — Common provisions
Article 277	Article 320
Article 278	Article 321
Article 279	Article 322
	Article 323
	Article 324
	Chapter 6 — Combating fraud
Article 280	Article 325
	Title III — Enhanced cooperation
Articles 11 and 11a (replaced)	Article 326 ([66])
Articles 11 and 11a (replaced)	Article 327 ([66])
Articles 11 and 11a (replaced)	Article 328 ([66])
Articles 11 and 11a (replaced)	Article 329 ([66])
Articles 11 and 11a (replaced)	Article 330 ([66])
Articles 11 and 11a (replaced)	Article 331 ([66])
Articles 11 and 11a (replaced)	Article 332 ([66])
Articles 11 and 11a (replaced)	Article 333 ([66])
Articles 11 and 11a (replaced)	Article 334 ([66])
PART SIX — GENERAL AND FINAL PROVISIONS	PART SEVEN — GENERAL AND FINAL PROVISIONS
Article 281 (repealed) ([67])	
Article 282	Article 335
Article 283	Article 336
Article 284	Article 337
Article 285	Article 338
Article 286 (replaced)	Article 16
Article 287	Article 339
Article 288	Article 340
Article 289	Article 341

([66]) Also replaces the current Articles 27a to 27e, 40 to 40b, and 43 to 45 TEU.
([67]) Replaced, in substance, by Article 47 TEU.

Old numbering of the Treaty establishing the European Community	New numbering of the Treaty on the Functioning of the European Union
Article 290	Article 342
Article 291	Article 343
Article 292	Article 344
Article 293 (repealed)	
Article 294 (moved)	Article 55
Article 295	Article 345
Article 296	Article 346
Article 297	Article 347
Article 298	Article 348
Article 299, paragraph 1 (repealed) (⁶⁸)	
Article 299, paragraph 2, second, third and fourth subparagraphs	Article 349
Article 299, paragraph 2, first subparagraph, and paragraphs 3 to 6 (moved)	Article 355
Article 300 (replaced)	Article 218
Article 301 (replaced)	Article 215
Article 302 (replaced)	Article 220
Article 303 (replaced)	Article 220
Article 304 (replaced)	Article 220
Article 305 (repealed)	
Article 306	Article 350
Article 307	Article 351
Article 308	Article 352
	Article 353
Article 309	Article 354
Article 310 (moved)	Article 217
Article 311 (repealed) (⁶⁹)	
Article 299, paragraph 2, first subparagraph, and paragraphs 3 to 6 (moved)	Article 355
Article 312	Article 356
Final Provisions	
Article 313	Article 357
	Article 358
Article 314 (repealed) (⁷⁰)	

(⁶⁸)   Replaced, in substance by Article 52 TEU.
(⁶⁹)   Replaced, in substance by Article 51 TEU.
(⁷⁰)   Replaced, in substance by Article 55 TEU.

1

THE TREATY AND ITS
TERRITORIAL REACH

2. The Community Treaties

The ECSC Treaty.   Where, after the expiry of the ECSC Treaty, the Commission   **1.004**
proceeds against conduct which took place before the expiry of the Treaty, the substantive rules to be applied are the provisions of the expired Treaty, if the conduct
would have been covered by that Treaty at the time, but the procedural rules to be
applied are those in operation at the time of the proceedings. The CJ so held in two
appeals against readopted decisions relating to steel beams and stainless steel flat
products. The original *Steel beams* decision adopted in 1994 under the ECSC Treaty
was annulled on procedural grounds in 2003. The Commission readopted it in
2006 (COMP/38907 *Steel beams*, decn of 8 November 2006). The other original
decision *Alloy surcharge* adopted under the ECSC Treaty was annulled by the GC in
2005 and readopted by the Commission in 2006 (COMP/39234 *Alloy surcharge-
readoption*, decn of 20 December 2006). In those new decisions, the Commission
applied the substantive rules of the ECSC Treaty even though it had expired in July
2002 but as regards the procedural rules and its power to impose fines, the
Commission relied on Regulation 1/2003. This approach was upheld by both the
GC and the CJ: see, as regards the *Alloy surcharge* decision Case T-24/07 *ThyssenKrupp
Stainless v Commission* [2009] ECR II-230, upheld in Case C-352/09P *ThyssenKrupp
Nirosta v Commission*, judgment of 29 March 2011; and as regards the *Steel beams*
decision, Case T-405/06 *ArcelorMittal v Commission* [2009] ECR II-771, [2010] 4
CMLR 787, upheld in Cases C-201&216/09P *ArcelorMittal v Commission*, judgment of 29 March 2011. See to similar effect Cases T-27/03, etc, *SP v Commission*
[2007] ECR II-4331, [2008] 4 CMLR 176. These were the appeals from *Concrete
Reinforcing Bars* in which the Commission had purported to adopt a decision establishing a breach of Article 65(1) ECSC after the expiry of that Treaty. The GC
annulled the decision holding that the Commission did not have competence to
take a decision under the expired provisions. The GC distinguished the position of
an appellate court which could still apply the ECSC Treaty when reviewing the
legality of measures adopted by the Commission before the Treaty expired. The GC

delivered one judgment on 25 October 2007 in Cases T-27/03, T-46/03, T-58/03, T-79/03, T-80/03, T-97/03 and T-98/03 and separate judgments on the same day and to the same effect in Cases T-45/03, T-77/03 and T-94/03. The Commission has since readopted the decision using Regulation 1/2003 as the legal base: decn of 30 September 2009.

As to the application of the State aid rules to the sectors previously covered by the ECSC Treaty see Case T-25/04 *González y Díez v Commission*, judgment of 12 September 2007. The GC held that the Commission had been correct to apply Article 108(2) TFEU and the State Aids Procedural Regulation in its decision adopted *after* the ECSC Treaty expired relating to an aid granted before that expiry. But the Commission erred in deciding that a State aid put into effect without its prior approval would be subject to the provisions of Regulation 1407/2002 which was adopted after the aid was put into effect. (Note that this conclusion may need to be reconsidered in the light of Case C-334/07P *Commission v Freistaat Sachsen* [2008] ECR I-9465). However, since the relevant provisions of Regulation 1407/2002 were identical to earlier provisions which were in force at the relevant time, the GC in *González y Díez* found that the error did not affect the validity of the decision.

In Case T-122/04 *Outokumpu Oyj v Commission (industrial tubes)* [2009] ECR II-1135, [2009] 5 CMLR 1553 the GC held that the Commission was entitled to increase a fine imposed for a cartel infringement under the EC Treaty because of an earlier cartel infringement decision taken under the ECSC Treaty competition provisions.

The CJ still has jurisdiction to answer preliminary references on the interpretation of the ECSC Treaty even after its expiry: Case C-119/05 *Lucchini Siderurgia* [2007] ECR I-6199.

1.007 **The single currency.** Cyprus and Malta adopted the euro on 1 January 2008. Slovakia adopted the euro on 1 January 2009 and Estonia on 1 January 2011.

1.010 **Charter of Fundamental Rights.** Article 6 of the new TEU states that the Union recognises the rights, freedoms and principles set out in the Charter of Fundamental Rights and states that they have the 'same legal value' as the Treaties. However, the article also makes clear that the provisions of the Charter do not extend the Union's competence. Note also that the Charter cannot be invoked against the United Kingdom or Poland: Protocol 30 to the TFEU.

1.012 **The Reform Treaty.** The Reform Treaty fared somewhat better than the Constitutional Treaty. The Treaty was signed by EU leaders on 13 December 2007 in Lisbon but the people of Ireland rejected the Treaty in a referendum in June 2008. A challenge to the decision of the United Kingdom Government not to hold a referendum before ratifying the Treaty was dismissed by the English High Court: *Wheeler v The Office of the Prime Minister* [2008] EWHC 1409 (Admin), [2008]

2 CMLR 1583. Ireland held a further referendum in October 2009 and the Lisbon Treaty was approved. Following the signature of the Czech President on 4 November 2009, the Treaty came into force on 1 December 2009.

As indicated in the text the term 'European Union' has now replaced the term 'European Community' and there are now two treaties of equal status—the Treaty on European Union (TEU) and the Treaty on the Functioning of the European Union (TFEU). The TEU contains many of the provisions previously found in the old TEU (signed in Maastricht) but many provisions have been repealed or replaced. Some of the provisions that were previously in the early articles of the old EC Treaty have been replaced by provisions in the new TEU. Thus, contrary to what is stated in the text, Article 3(1) of the EC Treaty is repealed by the Lisbon Treaty but reappears in modified form as Article 3(1)(b) of the Treaty on the Functioning of the European Union. This provides that the Union has exclusive competence in 'the establishing of the competition rules necessary for the functioning of the internal market'. Note also, as referred to in fn 37, that although the proposed reference to free and undistorted competition was not included in the final version of Article 3 of the new TEU, Protocol 27 to the Treaty states that the Member States 'considering that the internal market as set out in Article 3 of the Treaty on European Union includes a system ensuring that competition is not distorted' have agreed that the Union shall, if necessary, take action under the provisions of the Treaties to that end. What effect these changes will have in future years remains to be seen.

3. The EC Treaty

(a) Generally

The structure of the EC Treaty.   The structure of the new treaties, the Treaty on   **1.014**
the European Union (TEU) and the Treaty on the Functioning of the European Union (TFEU), has overtaken the content of this paragraph as from 1 December 2009 when the Lisbon Treaty came into force. The European Union now has legal personality.

Interpretation of the Treaty.   Fn 45. In Case C-550/07P *Akzo Nobel Chemicals v*   **1.015**
Commission, judgment of 14 September 2010, [2010] 5 CMLR 1143 the CJ described the principle of legal certainty as requiring in particular that rules involving negative consequences for individuals should be clear and precise and their application predictable for those subject to them: para 100.

Fundamental human rights.   In Case T-99/04 *AC-Treuhand AG v Commission*   **1.016**
[2008] ECR II-1501, [2008] 5 CMLR 962, the GC commented that 'fundamental rights are an integral part of the general principles of law whose observance the Community judicature ensures by taking account, in particular, of the ECHR as a source of inspiration': para 138.

See also Case T-69/04 *Schunk GmbH v Commission* [2008] ECR II-2567, [2009] 4 CMLR 2 where the GC considered the case law of the Court of Human Rights on Article 7 ECHR in relation to an assertion that the wide discretion given to the Commission when imposing a fine infringed the principle of legal certainty: paras 28–50.

Article 6 of the new TEU provides that the Union shall accede to the European Convention on Human Rights but that such accession shall not affect the Union's competences as defined in the Treaties. Further, Article 6 provides that fundamental rights, as guaranteed by the Convention and as they result from the constitutional traditions common to the Member States, shall constitute general principles of the Union's law.

1.017 **A presumption of compliance: *Bosphorus Airways*.** The Court's decision in this case was distinguished in Application No. 71412/01 *Behrami v France*, judgment of 2 May 2007, see esp para 145.

(b) The main competition provisions

1.018 **Generally.** When the Treaty on the Functioning of the European Union came into effect on 1 December 2009 the Treaty provisions were renumbered in accordance with Article 5 of the Treaty of Lisbon. That Treaty has an annex containing a table of equivalences between the old and new treaties. Articles 81–89 of the EC Treaty are now Articles 101–109 of the TFEU.

(c) Other provisions of the Treaty

Note that the numbers of the Articles of the EC Treaty referred to in the paragraphs in this section have changed on the coming into force of the TFEU and, in some instances, the provisions themselves have been revised.

1.026 **Article 3: the activities of the Community.** The term 'European Community' has now been replaced by the term 'European Union'. Article 3(1) EC which listed the activities of the Community has been repealed and replaced in substance by paragraphs 3–6 TFEU. The new Article 3 TFEU list the areas in which the Union has exclusive competence, including establishing the competition rules necessary for the functioning of the internal market. Article 4 TFEU lists those areas where the Union shares competence with the Member States including the internal market, consumer protection, transport, and energy. Article 3(3) of the new TEU provides that the Union shall establish an internal market and work for the sustainable development of Europe based on, among other things 'a highly competitive social market economy . . .'.

1.027 **Article 3(1)(g).** Article 3(1) EC is repealed by the Lisbon Treaty but reappears in modified form as Article 3(1)(b) TFEU. This provides that the Union has exclusive competence in 'the establishing of the competition rules necessary for the functioning of the internal market'. Note also Protocol 27 to the TFEU states that the Member States 'considering that the internal market as set out in Article 3 of the Treaty on European Union includes a system ensuring that competition is not distorted' have agreed that the Union shall, if necessary, take action under the provisions of the Treaties to that end.

Article 5: subsidiarity.   Article 5 EC was repealed by the Lisbon Treaty and has been replaced by Article 5 of the new TEU. This provides that the use of Union competences is governed by the principles of subsidiarity and proportionality and describes those principles using similar wording to that in Article 5 EC.   **1.028**

Subsidiarity and decentralisation of competition law.   Fn 80. Both appeals referred to have now been decided: Cases C-501/06P, etc, *GlaxoSmithKline Services Unlimited v Commission*, judgment of 6 October 2009 and Cases C-125/07P, etc, *Erste Bank der österreichischen Sparkassen v Commission*, judgment of 24 September 2009. The point discussed in this paragraph is not affected.   **1.029**

Article 10: duties of Member States.   The substance of what was Article 10 EC has been incorporated into Article 4 of the new TEU. In Case C-441/06 *Commission v France* [2007] ECR I-8887, the CJ held that France was in breach of its obligations under this provision because of its failure to cooperate with the Commission in the implementation of a State aid decision.   **1.030**

Article 12: non-discrimination.   Fn 88. Article 12 EC is now Article 18 TFEU. As to national disparities in the regulation of the pharmaceuticals market see also Cases C-468/06, etc, *Sot Lelos kai Sia EE v GlaxoSmithKline* [2008] ECR I-7139, [2008] 5 CMLR 1382, [2009] All ER (EC) 1 (extent to which a dominant undertaking can refuse to fulfil orders by a wholesaler who engages in parallel trading).   **1.031**

The *Cassis de Dijon* principle and the *Keck* distinction.   Articles 28, 29 and 30 EC are now Articles 34, 35 and 36 TFEU. For a more recent decision on *Keck* see Case C-141/07 *Re Supply of Medicines by Pharmacies to nearby Hospitals: Commission v Germany* [2008] ECR I-6935, [2008] 3 CMLR 1479 (national law the effect of which was that only local pharmacies could supply medicinal products to hospitals was a selling arrangement within the meaning of *Keck*). Cf Case C-531/07 *Fachverband der Buch- und Medienwirtschaft v LIBRO Handelsgesellschaft* [2009] ECR I-3717 where the CJ held that Austrian legislation which prevented an importer of German books from selling those books at a price lower than the minimum fixed under Austrian legislation was not a selling arrangement within the *Keck* distinction and was contrary to Article 34 TFEU (formerly Article 28 EC).   **1.033**

Other relevant Treaty provisions.   Following the renumbering of the Treaty articles on 1 December 2009:   **1.037**

• Articles 32–38 EC dealing with common agricultural policy are now Articles 38–44 TFEU;

- Articles 70–80 EC dealing with a common transport policy are now Articles 90–100 TFEU;
- Article 151 EC concerning the cultural aspects of the Union is now Article 167 TFEU;
- Article 174 EC concerning environmental policy is now Article 191 TFEU;
- Article 296 EC concerning national security is now Article 346 TFEU;
- Articles 90–93 EC concerning taxation are now Articles 110–113 TFEU;
- Article 133 EC concerning the common commercial policy and anti-dumping is now Article 207;
- Articles 133(3) EC concerning treaties with third countries is now Article 207(3) TFEU; Article 300 has been replaced by Article 218 TFEU;
- Article 134 EC has been repealed;
- Articles 136–145 EC concerning social policy are now Articles 151–161 TFEU; and
- Articles 39–42 EC concerning free movement are now Articles 45–48 TFEU.

As to Article 167(4) TFEU (cultural aspects) (formerly Article 151(4) EC) see the discussion in COMP/38698 *CISAC*, decn of 16 July 2008, [2009] 4 CMLR 577, para 95 where the Commission rejected a submission that its condemnation of certain territorial delineation terms in the model contract recommended by a collecting society was likely to harm cultural diversity. The case is on appeal Cases T-398, 410, 411, 413–422, 425, 432, 434, 442, 451/08, not yet decided.

Further on the application of Article 167(4) TFEU (formerly Article 151(4) EC) see Case C-531/07 *Fachverband der Buch- und Medienwirtschaft v LIBRO Handelsgesellschaft* [2009] ECR I-3717 where the CJ noted that the protection of books as cultural objects can be considered as an overriding requirement in the public interest capable of justifying measures restricting the free movement of goods, on condition that those measures are appropriate for achieving the objective fixed and do not go beyond what is necessary to achieve it. However, the Court held in that case that the objective of the protection of books as cultural objects could be achieved by measures less restrictive than the legislation being challenged under Article 34 TFEU (formerly Article 28 EC).

Fn 108. The new Horizontal Cooperation Guidelines adopted in 2011 (OJ 2011 C11/1: Vol II, App C22) do not contain specific provisions about standards for environmental objectives. Such agreements are now covered by the general Guidelines. The Commission has stated that this does not imply any downgrading of the assessment of environmental agreements: MEMO/10/676 (14 December 2010) para 12. See also the examples given at paras 329, 331 and 332 of the Guidelines.

4. The Institutional Structure of the Community

(a) The Community institutions

The institutions of the Community. The Lisbon Treaty made some important   **1.038**
changes to the institutions mentioned in this paragraph, in particular creating
the new post of President of the Council. The Treaty also created the role of
High Representative concerned with foreign affairs and security policy. This office
is supported by a new diplomatic service called the European External Action
Service.

The official languages of the Community. In Case C-161/06 *Skoma-Lux sro v*   **1.039**
Celiní Editelství Olomouc [2007] ECR I-10841, [2008] 1 CMLR 1336, the CJ
was asked on a reference for a preliminary ruling whether EU law provisions were
binding on the citizens of a new Member State before the provisions had been published in that State's official language in the *Official Journal.* The Court held that the
provisions were not binding, even though electronic versions were available in
Czech. However, the Court stated that the requirements of legal certainty dictate
that this should not affect the validity of national decisions taken pursuant to those
provisions, with the exception of decisions which were the subject of administrative or judicial proceedings at the date of the Court's judgment.

The fact that a hearing in a Dutch case is conducted in English is not a breach of the
rights of the defence unless the parties can show that they were prejudiced by this:
Case T-151/05 *Nederlandse Vakbond Varkenshouders (NVV) v Commission* [2009]
ECR II-1219, [2009] 5 CMLR 1613, para 211.

The European Parliament. Under the Lisbon Treaty, the number of MEPs is   **1.040**
limited to 751 and each Member State will have between six and 96 members. The
Treaty expands the role of the Parliament by increasing the number of legislative
measures that are adopted using the co-decision procedure.

The Council. The Council is now headed by a permanent President of the Council   **1.041**
in accordance with Article 15(6) TEU.

(b) The Community and EFTA Courts

The Community Courts. The coming into force of the Lisbon Treaty on   **1.045**
1 December 2009 brought about a restructuring of the courts in Luxembourg.
From that date the whole court system of the European Union is known as the
Court of Justice of the European Union and comprises three courts: the Court of
Justice, the General Court (previously the Court of First Instance) and the special-
ised courts, currently the Civil Service Tribunal.

1.049 **References under Article 234.** Article 234 EC is now Article 267 TFEU. For the nature of the proceedings under Article 267 see Case C-2/06 *Kempter v Haupzollamt Hamburg-Jonas* [2008] ECR I-411, [2008] 2 CMLR 586: 'the system of references for a preliminary ruling is based on a dialogue between one court and another, the initiation of which depends entirely on the national court's assessment as to whether a reference is appropriate and necessary' (para 42).

(c) The Directorate-General for Competition

(i) Structure

1.052 **The Directorate-General for Competition ('DG Competition').** The specialist units have been reorganised: an organogram of the current structure is available on the DG Competition website.

1.056 **The Hearing Officer.** The Commission has recently published Guidance on the role of the Hearing Officer: 'Guidance on procedures of the Hearing Officers in proceedings relating to Articles 101 and 102 TFEU' (Vol II, App B22 and available on the DG Competition website and linked to Press Release IP/10/02 (6 January 2010)). The Guidance describes all the Hearing Officers' responsibilities, particularly regarding the conduct of the oral hearing.

(iii) Enforcement through legislation and guidance

1.066 **General notices and guidance.** In February 2009 the Commission issued its Guidance on the Commission's enforcement priorities in applying Article 82 to abusive exclusionary conduct by dominant undertakings: OJ 2009 C45/7: Vol II, App C19. The Guidance is not intended to be a statement of the law but aims to provide greater clarity and predictability as regards the general framework of analysis that the Commission will employ when determining whether to pursue cases (para 2). The Guidance is considered in more detail in Chapter 10.

The GC noted the importance of guidance for transparency and enhancing legal certainty for the purposes of Article 7 ECHR: Case T-446/05 *Amann & Söhne GmbH v Commission*, judgment of 28 April 2010, [2010] 5 CMLR 789, para 137.

Fn 193. See also Case T-21/05 *Chalkor v Commission*, judgment of 19 May 2010, [2010] 5 CMLR 1295, paras 60 *et seq* where the GC considered the interaction between the Guidelines and the Commission's discretion when setting fines.

1.068 **The DG Competition website.** The GC has held that putting a non-confidential version of a decision on the website constitutes a continuing publication of that decision so that the Commission can be ordered to remove confidential information which it has wrongly included in the decision: Case T-474/04 *Pergan Hilfsstoffe für industrielle Prozesse GmbH v Commission* [2007] ECR II-4225, [2008] 4 CMLR 148, para 41.

Publication of a decision on the website may not of itself start the time for lodging an appeal; but where a notification is published in the *Official Journal* that the decision can be found on the website, the time for appealing runs from that time: Case T-274/06 *Estaser El Mareny v Commission* [2007] ECR II-143*. See further the update to paragraph 13.232, below.

5. The Aims of the Community Rules on Competition

A competitive market economy.   See also Niels, Jenkins & Kavanagh, *Economics*   **1.072**
for Competition Lawyers (2011) for an analysis of the relevant economics principles, aimed specifically at competition lawyers.

Fn 207. The CJ overturned the GC's analysis on this point in Cases C-501/06P, etc, *GlaxoSmithKline Services Unlimited v Commission*, judgment of 6 October 2009. The CJ held that neither the wording of Article 101(1) nor the case law supports the contention that agreements limiting parallel trade only have the object of restricting competition if they disadvantage final consumers: para 62.

Market integration.   The final sentence of this paragraph must now be read in the   **1.074**
light of the CJ's rejection of the GC's analysis on this point: Cases C-501/06P, etc, *GlaxoSmithKline Services Unlimited v Commission*, judgment of 6 October 2009.

Importance of parallel trading.   See also Cases C-468/06, etc, *Sot Lelos kai Sia EE*   **1.075**
v GlaxoSmithKline [2008] ECR I-7139, [2008] 5 CMLR 1382, [2009] All ER (EC) 1 (application of Article 102 to dominant undertaking refusing to fulfil orders by a wholesaler who engages in parallel trading); Cases C-501/06P, etc, *GlaxoSmithKline Services Unlimited v Commission*, judgment of 6 October 2009.

Liberalisation of markets.   Fn 217. The appeal by Deutsche Telekom was dis-   **1.076**
missed by the GC: Case T-271/03 *Deutsche Telekom AG v Commission* [2008] ECR II-477, [2008] 5 CMLR 631 and by the CJ on further appeal Case C-280/08P *Deutsche Telekom v Commission*, judgment of 14 October 2010, [2010] 5 CMLR 1485.

6. Territorial Ambit of EC Competition Rules

(a) The Member States: enlargement

Becoming 27.   For the retrospective effect of the Protocol relating to the Polish   **1.082**
steel industry see Cases T-273&297/06 *ISD Polska v Commission* [2009] ECR II-2185.

(c) EFTA and the EEA

1.086   **The EEA Agreement.**   Note that according to Article 8(3) (a) and (b) of the EEA Agreement, the provisions of the EEA Agreement only apply to products falling within Chapters 25–97 of the Harmonized Commodity Description and Coding System and to products specified in Protocol 3 of the EEA Agreement. Thus, for example, the Commission did not have jurisdiction to apply Article 53 EEA to bananas: COMP/39188 *Bananas*, decn of 15 October 2008, para 210.

1.089   **Homogeneity objective in the application of EC jurisprudence in the EEA.**   For an interesting case in which the EFTA Court considered whether the principle of homogeneity was overridden by compelling reasons for a divergent interpretation as regards international exhaustion of trade mark rights: see Cases E-9&10/07 *L'Oréal Norge v Per Aarskog AS*, judgment of 8 July 2008.

1.091   **Allocation of jurisdiction under the EEA Agreement.**   For a case where the Commission had jurisdiction to apply Article 102 and Article 54 EEA where an undertaking whose parent company was Norwegian was held to be dominant in national markets in the EU and in the EEA see COMP/38113 *Prokent-Tomra*, decn of 29 March 2006, [2009] 4 CMLR 101. Tomra's appeal was dismissed and this point was not discussed: Case T-155/06 *Tomra Systems v Commission*, judgment of 9 September 2010. For a case concerning an international body with members in both the EU and the EEA see COMP/38698 *CISAC*, decn of 16 July 2008, [2009] 4 CMLR 577 (paras 84–86) (on appeal Cases T-398, 410, 411, 413–422, 425, 432, 434, 442, 451/08, not yet decided).

See Cases T-456&457/05 *Gütermann AG and Zwicky v Commission,* judgment of 28 April 2010, [2010] 5 CMLR 930, concerning a single continuous infringement covering the Benelux and Nordic countries where the GC held that it was clear from the recitals to the decision that the Commission had only treated conduct in the EEA countries as an infringement after 1 January 1994.

Fn 275. The appeals in *Video Games, Nintendo Distribution* have now been decided by a series of judgments issued on 30 April 2009. The GC did not consider the issue discussed in this paragraph. The appeal in Case T-99/04 *AC Treuhand* was dismissed on other grounds: [2008] ECR II-1501, [2008] 5 CMLR 962.

(d) Agreements between the Community and third countries

1.098   **Croatia, the FYR of Macedonia, and Albania.**   On the progress of the candidate countries (Croatia, FYR of Macedonia and Turkey) see COM(2008) 674 final (5 November 2008) Communication from the Commission to the Council and the European Parliament '*Enlargement Strategy and Main Challenges 2008-2009*'. Of the other Western Balkan countries, the SAA with Albania entered into force on

1 April 2009; Montenegro, Serbia, and Bosnia and Herzegovina have each signed an SAA with the EU (in October 2007, April 2008 and June 2008, respectively) but these are not yet in force.

Fn 303. The SAA with the former Yugoslav Republic of Macedonia entered into force on 1 April 2004 not 1 May 2004 as cited in the footnote.

Cooperation with the United States under the comity agreement. The Commission intervened successfully as *amicus* in disclosure proceedings in a New York Court to prevent the disclosure of a transcript of an oral hearing before the Commission and the Commission's statement of objections. The disclosure was initially ordered in civil proceedings brought against Visa and Mastercard for repayment of card interchange fees. On appeal the US District Court of the Eastern District of New York concluded (27 August 2010) that the order was contrary to the law of international comity and that the Commission's interests would be significantly undermined if its confidentiality rules were disregarded by American courts in cases like this: *Re payment card interchange fee and merchant discount* ECN Brief 4/2010, p2.   **1.101**

Fn 312. These Guidelines have now been replaced by the Horizontal Cooperation Guidelines 2011, OJ 2011 C11/1: Vol II, App C22.

7. The Territorial Jurisdiction of the Community Institutions

(c) Jurisdiction over undertakings outside the Community

The issue.   In COMP/39181 *Candle Waxes*, decn of 1 October 2008, [2009] 5 CMLR 2441 the Commission rejected a challenge to its jurisdiction by a Hungarian company in respect of cartel activity before Hungary joined the Union. The Commission stated that under the effects doctrine, jurisdiction can be established on the basis of economic effects within a territory, and MOL, as well as the other cartel participants, had sales in several Member States: para 190.   **1.110**

See Case C-17/10 *Toshiba Corp v Czech Competition Authority*, not yet decided (reference from Czech court asking whether Article 101 and Regulation 1/2003 must be applied (in proceedings brought after 1 May 2004) to the whole period of operation of a cartel, which commenced in the Czech Republic before that State's entry to the European Union (that is, before 1 May 2004) and continued and ended after the Czech Republic's entry to the European Union); Case T-171/10 *Slovak Telekom v Commission*, not yet decided (challenge to information request on the grounds that Commission has no jurisdiction to request information relating to a period before the Slovak Republic joined the EU).

8. Effect on Trade between Member States

(a) Generally

1.115 **Rule of jurisdiction.** Fn 377. Both appeals referred to have now been decided: Cases C-501/06P, etc, *GlaxoSmithKline Services Unlimited v Commission*, judgment of 6 October 2009 and Cases C-125/07P, etc, *Erste Bank der österreichischen Sparkassen v Commission*, judgment of 24 September 2009. The point discussed in this paragraph is not affected.

1.117 **Trade.** Fn 385. See also Cases T-208&209/08 *Gosselin Group v Commission*, judgment of 16 June 2011, para 86.

Fn 401. See also COMP/38700 *Greek Lignite and Electricity generation*, decn of 5 March 2008, [2009] 4 CMLR 495 where the Commission held, in a case under Article 106(1) TFEU, that the State measures challenged discouraged potential entrants from investing in electricity generation and supply in Greece, including those who had applied for and obtained electricity generation and electricity supply licences. These operators were not using these licences yet, and were thus not using their right of establishment in Greece. This constituted an effect on trade for the purposes of Article 106 in conjunction with Article 102: para 244. The case is on appeal: Case T-169/08 *DEI v Commission*, not yet decided.

1.119 **The basic test: alteration of the pattern of trade.** Fn 417. See also Case T-58/01 *Solvay v Commission*, judgment of 17 December 2009, para 209: 'It is of little importance in that regard that the influence of a cartel on trade is unfavourable, neutral or favourable'.

1.121 **Altering the structure of competition.** Fn 425. Following the annulment of the decision in *Soda Ash—Solvay*, the Commission readopted the decision (OJ 2003 L10/10) and an appeal against that readopted decision was dismissed save for an adjustment to penalty: Case T-57/01 *Solvay v Commission*, judgment of 17 December 2009.

1.124 **Appreciable effect.** Where the Commission applies the 2004 Effect on Trade Notice in the case of a cartel it must first define the relevant market before considering whether the 5 per cent threshold has been crossed: Case T-199/08 *Ziegler SA v Commission*, judgment of 16 June 2011.

(b) Particular aspects

1.131 **Particular kinds of domestic agreements.** An agreement whereby one producer provides a guarantee to another producer with respect to a minimum annual sales tonnage on a national market, is by definition likely to divert trade patterns from the course which they would otherwise have followed, as it has the effect of removing from the market a part of the production that might have been exported to other Member States: Case T-58/01 *Solvay v Commission*, judgment of 17 December 2009, para 215 (on further appeal, Case C-110/10P, not yet decided).

Fn 491. A further appeal in *Der Grüne Punkt* was dismissed: Case C-385/07P *Der Grüne Punkt—Duales System Deutschland v Commission*, judgment of 16 July 2009, [2009] 5 CMLR 2215. An appeal against the decision in *ARA and ARGEV, ARO* was dismissed: Case T-419/03 *Altstoff Recycling Austria AG v Commission*, judgment of 22 March 2011.

Particular kinds of domestic abuse.   **Fn 499.** Note that the CJ in the appeal from   **1.132**
Case T-229/05 *AEPI v Commission* referred to in the footnote held that the GC had confused two separate concepts—the concept of the effect on trade between Member States and the concept of whether there is a serious impediment to EU trade. The latter concept was relevant to the Commission's assessment of whether there was a sufficient EU interest in investigating a complaint. The CJ held therefore that the Commission had rejected the complaint not because of an absence of effect on trade but because there was no serious impediment to intra-EU trade: see Case C-425/07P *AEPI v Commission* [2009] ECR I-3205, [2009] 5 CMLR 1337.

A further appeal in *Der Grüne Punkt* was dismissed: Case C-385/07P *Der Grüne Punkt—Duales System Deutschland v Commission*, judgment of 16 July 2009, [2009] 5 CMLR 2215.

2

ARTICLE 81(1)

2. Undertakings

a) Generally

Note: Article 81(1) EC has now become Article 101(1) TFEU

Undertakings. In Case C-113/07P *SELEX Sistemi Integrati SpA v Commission* **2.003**
[2009] ECR I-2207, Eurocontrol's argument that, as an international organisation,
it was immune from investigation by the Commission was rejected, though primarily for procedural reasons: paras 55 *et seq*.

Fn 12. See also Case C-49/07 *Motosykletistiki Omospondia Ellados NPID (MOTOE)
v Elliniko Dimosio* [2008] ECR I-4863, [2008] 5 CMLR 790, [2009] All ER (EC)
150, paras 27 and 28 (a non-profit making entity may be competing with profit
making entities or with other non-profit making entities).

Individuals as undertakings. **Fn 17.** The proper citation for the *CNSD* case **2.004**
referred to in line 4 is OJ 1993 L203/27, [1995] 5 CMLR 495 (appeal dismissed,
Case T-513/93 *CNSD v Commission* [2000] ECR II-1807, [2000] 5 CMLR 614).
See also COMP/39510 *Ordre National des Pharmaciens en France (ONP),* decn of
8 December 2010 where the Commission held that pharmacists are undertakings
for the purposes of Article 101.

Shareholders as undertakings. The question whether a legal entity which holds **2.004A**
shares in an undertaking which carries on commercial activity is itself an undertaking was considered by the CJ in Case C-222/04 *Ministero dell'Economia e delle
Finanze v Cassa di Risparmio di Firenze SpA* [2006] ECR I-289, [2008] 1 CMLR
705. The CJ held on a reference for a preliminary ruling that the mere fact of
holding shares, even controlling shareholdings, is insufficient to characterise as
economic an activity of the entity holding those shares, when it gives rise only to the
exercise of the rights attached to the status of shareholder or member, as well as, if
appropriate, the receipt of dividends. On the other hand, an entity which actually
exercises control by involving itself directly or indirectly in the management of the
subsidiary thereof must be regarded as taking part in the economic activity carried

on by the controlled undertaking. It was for the national court to determine whether the entity concerned not only held controlling shareholdings, but also actually exercised that control by involving itself directly or indirectly in the management of the latter.

The principles in the *Cassa di Risparmio* case were applied by the GC in Cases T-208&209/08 *Gosselin Group v Commission*, judgment of 16 June 2011 where the Court annulled the Commission's decision as against the parent of an infringing company on the ground that the parent was not itself an undertaking for the purposes of competition law. The Commission had not established that the parent entity had involved itself in the business of the infringing subsidiary: paras 42 *et seq.*

2.005 **Economic or commercial activity.** A company which was a dormant company for the purposes of English company law did not carry on any economic or commercial activity and so could not have participated in a cartel during the period of its dormancy: Case T-386/06 *Pegler v Commission*, judgment of 24 March 2011.

The operation of an airport constitutes an economic activity so that financial assistance granted to enable the building of an additional runway at the airport could constitute a State aid: Cases T-443&455/08 *Freistaat Sachsen and Land Sachsen-Anhalt v Commission*, judgment of 24 March 2011, paras 93 *et seq.*

Fn 23. In Case C-113/07P *SELEX Sistemi Integrati SpA v Commission* [2009] ECR I-2207 the CJ overturned much of the GC's analysis of what does and does not constitute economic activity although it ultimately upheld the GC's decision that the Commission had been right to reject the complaint: see update to paragraph 2.007, below.

(b) The State as an undertaking

2.007 **Member States and the essential functions of the State.** See now Case C-113/07P *SELEX Sistemi Integrati SpA v Commission* [2009] ECR I-2207. The judgment makes clear first, the importance of the constitution of the entity in establishing the scope of its functions and secondly, that the range of activities which are to be treated as connected with the exercise of public functions (and hence beyond the scope of the competition rules) is wider than the GC indicated in its judgment. Having examined the instrument setting up Eurocontrol, in particular its objectives, the CJ held that the provision of advice by Eurocontrol in connection with tendering procedures carried out by the Contracting States when buying equipment and systems for air traffic management was not an economic activity. It was closely linked to the task of technical standardisation entrusted to Eurocontrol in the context of the States' cooperation in maintaining and developing the safety of air navigation. It was thus connected with the exercise of public powers: para 76. The fact that the assistance provided by Eurocontrol was optional and that only certain States have had recourse to it did not alter the nature of the activity.

Moreover, in order for there to be a connection with the exercise of public powers, it was not necessary for the activity concerned to be essential or indispensable for ensuring the safety of air navigation: para 79. The Court also held that the GC had erred in drawing a distinction between Eurocontrol's function of adopting technical standards (which the GC agreed was a legislative, sovereign function) and the function of preparing and producing those standards (which the GC held was an economic activity). Again, examining the Convention establishing Eurocontrol, the Court held that the Contracting States entrusted Eurocontrol with both the preparation and production of standards and with their adoption, without separating those functions. Moreover, the production of technical standards was an integral part of, and directly connected to, the task of technical standardisation entrusted to Eurocontrol in the context of cooperation among States with a view to maintaining and developing the safety of air navigation, which constitute public powers. See also the rejection of the damages claim: C-481/07P *SELEX Sistemi Integrati SpA v Commission*, judgment of 16 July 2009.

In COMP/39351 *Swedish Interconnectors*, decn of 14 April 2010 the Commission found that SvK, a State-owned central administrative authority which did not have separate legal personality from the Swedish State was still an undertaking since it engaged in economic activity (ie electricity transmission); it had the capacity to be an independent party to legal proceedings; it made use of specific assets and enjoyed 'considerable autonomy': para 23.

In COMP/38469 *Athens International Airport*, decn of 2 May 2005, the Commission rejected a complaint against the level of charges imposed for passenger security checks at the airport. The main ground for rejecting the complaint was lack of EU interest but the Commission stated that when carrying out such checks, the airport, or any other entity carrying out the checks on behalf of the Greek State, was not exercising an economic activity for the purposes of Article 102 TFEU (para 49). On appeal, the GC did not address this issue: Case T-306/05 *Scippacercola and Terezakis v Commission* [2008] ECR II-4*, [2008] 4 CMLR 1418, para 145 (further appeal dismissed Case C-159/08P, Order of 25 March 2009).

The Commission has also commented on this issue in its Communication on services of general interest: COM (2007) 725 and in the Staff Working Document answering frequently asked questions about Decn 2005/842.

State-owned corporation and statutory bodies. See also *Medicall Ambulance Ltd v HSE* [2011] IEHC 76 (Irish High Court) (public health service was an undertaking insofar as it intervened to prescribe the manner in which ambulance services would be performed by economic operators and by its own National Ambulance Service when providing services to private patients for which a cost-only charge is made). **2.008**

Activities of State body to be considered individually. See also Case C-138/11 *Compass-Datenbank GmbH v Republik Österreich*, not yet decided (request for **2.009**

preliminary ruling, *inter alia*, as to whether a public authority acts as an undertaking if it stores in a database (namely a business undertakings register) the information reported by undertakings pursuant to statutory reporting obligations and allows inspection and/or printouts to be made in return for payment, but prohibits any more extensive use).

For a detailed discussion of the authorities see *Neurendale Ltd t/a Panda Waste Services v Dublin City Council* [2009] IEHC 588 (local authorities were undertakings insofar as they provided refuse collection services to householders).

Fn 42. See also Case C-49/07 *Motosykletistiki Omospondia Ellados NPID (MOTOE) v Elliniko Dimosio* [2008] ECR I-4863, [2008] 5 CMLR 790, [2009] All ER (EC) 150 (the power to authorise the organisation by others of motorcycling events stems from an act of public authority and cannot be classified as an economic activity but can be separated from the economic activity of organising and commercially exploiting motorcycling events).

2.010   **Occupation and use of publicly owned facilities.**   See also Case T-196/04 *Ryanair v Commission* [2008] ECR II-3643, a State aid case concerning advantages granted to Ryanair by the Walloon Region when Ryanair established its services at Charleroi airport. The GC held that the fixing of the amount of landing charges and the indemnity granted to Ryanair was in this case an activity directly connected with the management of airport infrastructure, which is an economic activity. It did not follow from the fact that an activity represents in legal terms an exemption from a tariff scale laid down in a regulation that that activity must be described as non-economic.

See also *SE Vilnius International Airport*, where the Lithuanian Supreme Administrative Court upheld a finding that the airport abused its dominant position in the market of management and organisation services on the territory of Vilnius International Airport by refusing to provide access to its infrastructure to UAB Naftelf. The Court held that the infrastructure was an essential facility to enable UAB Naftelf to enter the downstream market for the supply of fuel to aircraft at the airport, in competition with the Airport which itself operated as a supplier of fuel. A fine of LTL 171 000 (approx. €49,525) was imposed: ECN Brief 3/2010, p2; *Neurendale Ltd t/a Panda Waste Services v Dublin City Council* [2009] IEHC 588 (local authorities providing refuse collection services were dominant undertakings).

As to the status of regulations promulgated by an undertaking, see, eg *Purple Parking Ltd v Heathrow Airport Ltd* [2011] EWHC 987 (Ch), para 240 (where an airport facility is privately owned, the fact that the operator can enforce its propriety rights by making byelaws including criminal sanctions does not prevent the use of those byelaws to exclude competitors from being an abuse of a dominant position); and *Neurendale Ltd t/a Panda Waste Services v Dublin City Council* [2009]

IEHC 588 (a regulation by which the local councils purported to exclude private undertakings from offering competing services was economic rather than administrative in nature and constituted an agreement or at least a concerted practice between them).

Insurance and social security schemes.   The earlier case law was reviewed and the   **2.012**
principles applied in Case C-350/07 *Kattner Stahlbau v Maschinenbau-und Metall-Berufsgenossenschaft* [2009] ECR I-1513.

Similar arguments were relied on by the applicant in a State aid context where the EFTA Court held that municipal kindergartens in Norway were not undertakings: Case E-5/07 *Private Barnehagers Landsforbund v EFTA Surveillance Authority*, decn of 8 February 2008, [2008] 2 CMLR 818. The fact that 80 per cent of the costs of the kindergartens were borne by the public purse and that the fee paid by the parents was not connected to the cost of providing the service indicated that the Norwegian State was not seeking to engage in gainful activity but was fulfilling its duties towards its own population in the social, cultural and educational fields.

In Case C-437/09 *AG2R Prevoyance v Beaudout*, judgment of 3 March 2011 the CJ held that although the particular health care scheme in question had a social aim, this was not enough of itself to preclude it from being an economic activity; it was necessary also to consider whether the scheme applied the principle of solidarity and to what extent it was subject to supervision by the State. The Court found that the scheme operated with a high degree of solidarity but that the facts regarding State control were inconclusive. It was for the national court to examine whether AG2R, although being non-profit-making and acting on the basis of the principle of solidarity, was nonetheless an undertaking chosen by social partners from among other undertakings with which it competed on the market in the provident services which it offered.

Regulatory bodies.   In COMP/39510 *Ordre National des Pharmaciens en France*   **2.013**
(ONP), decn of 8 December 2010 the Commission examined the relationship between the professional body for pharmacists and the French State in concluding that the ONP was an association of undertakings: paras 607 *et seq* (on appeal Case T-90/11 *ONP and others v Commission*, not yet decided).

In *Hemat v The Medical Council* [2010] IESC 24 the Irish Supreme Court upheld the finding of the High Court that the Medical Council responsible for disciplining doctors was not an association of undertakings for the purposes of Irish competition law. The Council did not display the characteristics of a professional body since it did not provide services to the profession and was bound to consider only the public interest in its conduct.

Activities ancillary to exercise of public functions.   See Case C-113/07P *SELEX*   **2.014**
Sistemi Integrati SpA v Commission [2009] ECR I-2207, discussed in the update to paragraph 2.007, above. In that judgment, the CJ also upheld the GC's application

of *FENIN* as regards purchasing activity: the fact that technical standardisation was not an economic activity meant that the acquisition of prototypes in connection with that standardisation was not an economic activity either: para 102.

2.016   **Local authorities and municipalities.**   See also *Neurendale Ltd t/a Panda Waste Services v Dublin City Council* [2009] IEHC 588 (local authorities providing refuse collection services were undertakings).

(c) Treatment of economically linked legal entities

2.017   **Groups of companies as a single undertaking.**   A 'captive' insurance company (that is an insurance company wholly owned by a non-insurance company the purpose of which is to provide reinsurance cover exclusively for the risks of the undertaking to which it belongs) is itself an undertaking for the purpose of State aid rules: Cases E-4/10 etc, *Reassur Aktiengesellschaft v EFTA Surveillance Authority*, judgment of 10 May 2011.

2.018   **Subsidiary companies and branches.**   Fn 77. The appeal in Case T-112/05 *Akzo Nobel* and a further appeal to the CJ have now been decided: see Case C-97/08P *Akzo Nobel NV v Commission*, judgment of 10 September 2009. The CJ reaffirmed the presumption of decisive influence arising from 100 per cent ownership, see the update to paragraph 13.205, below.

2.019   **Partly owned subsidiaries.**   See also Case C-480/09P *AceaElectrabel Produzione v Commission*, judgment of 16 December 2010, where the CJ held, in a State aid case, that the Commission had been entitled to regard a company which owned 30 per cent of the shares of a subsidiary (and where the other 70 per cent were held by a single other company) as part of the same economic unit as that subsidiary.

2.020   **Agents.**   Fn 90. See similarly Case C-279/06 *CEPSA v Tobar* [2008] ECR I-6681, paras 38–39.

2.021   **Employees and trade unions.**   As regards employees, see *Safeway Stores v Twigger* [2010] EWCA Civ 1472 where the English Court of Appeal held that an undertaking that had been fined for cartel activity by the NCA could not seek reimbursement from the directors and employees who had attended the cartel meetings. The claim was barred by the rule *ex turpi causa non oritur actio* because the defendants' actions were not separate from the action of the undertaking itself.

3. Agreements, Decisions and Concerted Practices

(a) Agreements

2.023   **Agreements may be informal.**   As to gentlemen's agreements see Case T-53/03 *BPB plc v Commission* [2008] ECR II-1333, [2008] 5 CMLR 1201, para 82.

Unilateral action. See also the description in the Commission's Guidelines on **2.024** Vertical Restraints, OJ 2010 C130/1: Vol II, App C20, para 25(a) of the two ways in which 'acquiescence with a particular unilateral policy can be established' for the purpose of distinguishing between unilateral action and an informal agreement. First, acquiescence can be deduced from the powers set out in the contract between the parties, and secondly there can be tacit acquiescence where one party requires explicitly or implicitly the cooperation of the other party for the implementation of its unilateral policy and the other party complies with that requirement by implementing that unilateral policy in practice.

Note also that the fact that one party to an agreement concedes that the agreement existed does not preclude the other alleged party from disputing the existence of the agreement: Case T-18/03 *CD-Contact Data v Commission* [2009] ECR II-1021, para 51 (appeal dismissed Case C-260/09P *Activision Blizzard v Commission*, judgment of 10 February 2011).

Cases applying *ADALAT*. In *SEL-Imperial Ltd v British Standards Institution* **2.026** [2010] EWHC 854 (Ch) the English High Court considered the application of *ADALAT* to a horizontal agreement relating to safety standards for vehicle parts.

Fn 121. The point made here was not affected by the CJ's judgment in Cases C-501/06P, etc, *GlaxoSmithKline Services Unlimited v Commission*, judgment of 6 October 2009.

Incorporation of terms in an agreement. Note that in its Supplementary **2.027** Guidelines on motor vehicle distribution, OJ 2010 C138/16: Vol II, App C21, para 7, the Commission advocates a 'transparent relationship' between contracting parties as a way of minimising the risk of being held responsible for using indirect means to enforce anti-competitive objectives.

Fn 123. See also COMP/38698 *CISAC*, decn of 16 July 2008, [2009] 4 CMLR 577 where the Commission held that the membership clause under consideration had the object of allocating authors according to their nationality. It was therefore not necessary to show that the clause was applied or enforced: 'The mere existence of the clause creates a "visual and psychological" background which deters collecting societies from attracting authors who are currently either members of other collecting societies or who are not nationals of their domestic territory': para 130 (on appeal Cases T-398, 410, 411, 413–422, 425, 432, 434, 442, 451/08, not yet decided).

Fn 124. The appeals in *Video Games, Nintendo Distribution* have now been decided in a series of judgments issued on 30 April 2009. As regards the point made in this paragraph, the GC upheld the finding that the agreement underlying the written agreement existed: Case T-18/03 *CD-Contact Data v Commission* [2009] ECR II-1021 (appeal dismissed Case C-260/09P *Activision Blizzard v Commission*, judgment of 10 February 2011).

2.029   **Government measures.**   **Fn 128.** See the discussion of *Arduino* in COMP/39510 *Ordre National des Pharmaciens en France (ONP)*, decn of 8 December 2010, paras 611 *et seq.*

2.032   **Terminated or 'spent' agreements.**   For a case where an infringing exclusivity term was removed from a recommended model contract issued by a collecting society but where the members continued to include the term in their bilateral contracts, see COMP/38698 *CISAC*, decn of 16 July 2008, [2009] 4 CMLR 577, para 144. The case is on appeal Cases T-398, 410, 411, 413–422, 425, 432, 434, 442, 451/08, not yet decided.

Fn 140. See also COMP/39401 *E. ON—GDF*, decn of 8 July 2009 where although the parties signed a pro forma agreement in August 2004 allegedly 'confirming' that a 1975 market sharing agreement was no longer valid, the Commission found that the market-sharing agreement continued to exist and produce effects.

2.034   **Collective labour relations agreements.**   The fact that collective agreements fall outside the scope of Article 101 TFEU does not mean that they also fall outside the scope of the Treaty provisions on free movement of persons or services: Case C-438/05 *International Transport Workers Federation v Viking Line ABP* [2007] ECR I-10779, [2008] 1 CMLR 1372. Further, a trade union may still rely on the impact on it of an alleged State aid in order to establish standing to challenge the Commission's rejection of a complaint under Article 108(2) TFEU: Case C-319/07P *3F v Commission*, judgment of 9 July 2009.

In Case C-437/09 *AG2R Prevoyance v Beaudout*, judgment of 3 March 2011 the CJ considered the nature and purpose of a decision by a body to appoint AG2R Prevoyance to manage a scheme for supplementary reimbursement of healthcare costs and to request the public authorities to make affiliation to that scheme compulsory for all employees in a particular industry sector. The agreement took the form of an addendum to a collective agreement and was therefore the result of collective bargaining between the organisation representing employers and those representing employees within the French traditional bakery and pastry-making sector. The purpose of the agreement was to establish, within a particular sector, a scheme for supplementary reimbursement of healthcare costs which contributed to improving the working conditions of employees. The fact that, unlike in *Albany*, there was no provision for exemption from affiliation did not detract from this purpose. The agreement did not therefore come within the scope of Article 101(1) and the public authorities were not in breach of Article 101 in conjunction with Article 4(3) EU by legislating to make affiliation compulsory.

(b) **Concerted practices**

2.038   **In general.**   Many of the principles set out in this paragraph were restated by the CJ in Case C-8/08 *T-Mobile Netherlands BV v Raad van bestuur van de Nederlandse*

Mededingingsautoriteit, judgment of 4 June 2009, an Article 267 reference concerning a concerted practice by mobile phone companies.

Polypropylene: **presumption as regards effect on particpants' conduct.**   Note that   **2.042**
in this paragraph, the text immediately below the quotation refers to the judgment
of the CJ on the further appeal.

In Case C-8/08 *T-Mobile Netherlands BV v Raad van bestuur van de Nederlandse
Mededingingsautoriteit*, judgment of 4 June 2009 the CJ stated that this presumption is an integral part of applicable Union law and not merely a procedural point
concerning the burden of proof. The presumption therefore prevails when the
national court is applying Article 101 TFEU (para 53). Further, the Court held, the
presumption applies even if the concerted action is the result of a meeting held by
the participating undertakings on a single occasion rather than of a course of conduct: para 62.

Concerted practices: the requisite elements.   Note that a concerted practice   **2.045**
can be proved even if the participating undertakings meet on a single occasion:
Case C-8/08 *T-Mobile Netherlands BV v Raad van bestuur van de Nederlandse
Mededingingsautoriteit*, judgment of 4 June 2009, para 62 (an Article 267 TFEU
reference concerning a concerted practice by mobile phone companies). See also
Case T-53/03 *BPB plc v Commission* [2008] ECR II-1333, [2008] 5 CMLR 1201,
para 183 (Commission was right to hold that in a highly concentrated market, the
mere disclosure by an undertaking of the fact that it does not want a larger market
share is sufficient to inform competitors of an essential element of its strategy).

Alternative explanations for parallel behaviour.   In COMP/38698 *CISAC*, decn   **2.046**
of 16 July 2008, [2009] 4 CMLR 577, the Commission analysed whether the
inclusion of a territorial delineation clause in a series of bilateral reciprocal copyright licences entered into by collecting societies who were members of CISAC was
the result of autonomous business decisions on the part of those collecting societies
or the result of coordination among them. The Commission found that the practice
of granting exclusivity could not be explained by the market conditions but was the
result of a coordinated approach to territorial restrictions. Thus each participating
collecting society had a degree of certainty that national territorial delineation will
not only be reciprocally accepted by its contracting counterparty but will also be
implemented in all the bilateral reciprocal representation agreements signed by the
EEA CISAC members (para 157). The Commission also found that even in cases
where no exclusivity clauses were inserted into the bilateral representation agreements; where such clauses had allegedly not been applied; or where they had been
removed, the practice had continued whereby collecting societies limited the
licences they granted to the exploitation in domestic territories only (para 170).
The decision is on appeal on the issue of whether the Commission was correct to
find the existence of a concerted practice as regards the limitation of the licences to

the domestic territory of the licensee: see Cases T-398, 410, 411, 413–422, 425, 432, 434, 442, 451/08, not yet decided. The GC rejected an application for interim measures to suspend parts of the Commission's order Case T-411/08R *Artijus Magyar v Commission* [2009] 4 CMLR 353. An appeal against that ruling was dismissed: Case C-32/09P(R) *Artijus Magyar v Commission*, order of 31 August 2010, [2010] 5 CMLR 1208.

Fn 201. In Case T-36/05 *Coats Holdings Ltd v Commission* [2007] ECR II-110, [2008] 4 CMLR 45 the GC repeated that the question of whether there is another 'plausible explanation' for coordinated behaviour only arises where the Commission's case is not based on documentary evidence of collusion (para 72). But the GC went on to find that the documentary evidence relied on by the Commission was ambiguous and since that evidence was 'documentary evidence' only if the Commission's, rather than the applicants', interpretation of it was accepted, it followed that there was no documentary evidence within the meaning of the case law. As far as certain alleged aspects of agreement were concerned, the applicants were thus free to put forward a 'plausible explanation' of the facts as an alternative to the one adopted by the Commission. The GC found that only some of the elements on which the Commission had relied to fix Coats with participation in the cartel stood up to scrutiny and so reduced the fine. Coats' appeal against this decision was dismissed: Case C-468/07P [2009] 4 CMLR 301. See also Case T-110/07 *Siemens v Commission*, judgment of 3 March 2011, para 52.

2.051   **Duration of concerted practice.**   See also the discussion of the shifting burden of proof in Case T-110/07 *Siemens v Commission*, judgment of 3 March 2011. The Court considered where the burden lies as regards proof of the end date of the undertaking's involvement in a cartel: paras 171 *et seq*. The Commission asserted that once it has shown that the undertaking participated in the cartel, that participation is presumed to continue until the undertaking proves that it ceased participating. The GC rejected this, holding that the end date of participation is an essential element of the infringement so that the burden of proving it lies with the Commission. However, once the Commission has established participation to a particular date, it is up to the undertaking then to adduce evidence capable of undermining the Commission's findings.

A cartel may continue after the date of the last meeting of which the Commission has evidence: Cases T-122/07, etc *Siemens AG Österreich v Commission*, judgment of 3 March 2011, para 79. The burden of proving the duration of the cartel lies with the Commission even if the undertaking is relying on this to raise a limitation period defence: ibid, para 54.

(c) **Agreements and concerted practices: other issues**

2.052   **Single overall infringement.**   The appeal in the *Choline Chloride* case mentioned in fn 225 has now been decided: Cases T-101&111/05 *BASF AG and UCB SA v*

Commission [2007] ECR II-4949, [2008] 4 CMLR 347. In the decision, the Commission held that there had been a single continuous infringement comprising a global cartel operating between October 1992 and April 1994 and a European wide cartel operating between March 1994 and October 1998. Could these be characterised as a single continuous infringement even though they overlapped only for a short period? The GC noted that the case law envisages the existence of a common objective consisting in distorting the normal development of prices as providing a basis for treating the various agreements and concerted practices as the constituent elements of a single infringement: see paras 158 *et seq*. It is not enough to say that all the conduct concerned distorts competition in a general sense. To determine whether the conduct shared a common objective it is necessary to take into account any circumstance capable of establishing or casting doubt on that link, such as the period of application and the content (including the methods used). On examination of the facts the GC held that the Commission had not shown that these two cartels were a single infringement (paras 208 *et seq*). The result of this was that the global cartel was time barred and the fine that had been imposed for the years covered only by the global cartel was quashed. Unfortunately for BASF, the reduction in fine it had been given because of its cooperation with the investigation of the global cartel was also quashed so that BASF's fine in fact increased as a result of its success on this ground of appeal: para 222.

Two appeals from the decision in COMP/38543 *International Removal Services*, decn of 11 March 2008 can be contrasted: in Cases T-204&212/08 *Team Relocations v Commission*, judgment of 16 June 2011 the GC noted that three conditions must be met in order to establish participation in a single and continuous infringement, namely the existence of an overall plan pursuing a common objective, the intentional contribution of the undertaking to that plan, and its awareness (proved or presumed) of the offending conduct of the other participants. As regards the first condition, it was necessary to take into account any circumstance capable of establishing or casting doubt on a link of complementarity, such as the period of application, the content (including the methods used) and the objective of the various instances of misconduct. The GC held that the Commission had established a common objective, namely to establish and maintain a high price level for the provision of international removal services in Belgium and to share this market. However, in Case T-210/08 *Verhuizingen Coppens v Commission*, judgment of 16 June 2011 the GC annulled the decision insofar as it applied to the applicant because the applicant had been involved only in a cover bidding agreement and not in the wider agreement relating to commissions condemned in that decision. The Commission had not discharged the burden of proving that the applicant had been aware of the wider cartel and so it could not be held liable for the same single continuous infringement as the other addressees. Note also the GC's comments as to the Commission's inconsistent decisional practice with regard to referring to a 'single continuous infringement' in the operative part of the decision as well as in the recitals: para 33.

In appeals from the decision in COMP/38337 *Industrial Thread*, decn of 14 September 2005, the GC held that cartels relating to industrial thread and to motor industry thread were separate because (i) there were different participants; (ii) the content of the agreements was different; and (iii) they were organised differently: paras 99 *et seq.* In contrast, the industrial thread cartel in the Benelux and the industrial thread cartel in the Nordic countries were a single infringement: the products were identical, the cartel members were the same, the cartel subject-matter and modus operandi were similar, the meetings were held on the same day, and the participating undertakings were represented at those meetings by the same persons: Case T-446/05 *Amann & Söhne GmbH v Commission*, judgment of 28 April 2010, [2010] 5 CMLR 789, para 107. The GC further held in that case that the concept of the 'single continuous infringement' was sufficiently defined to meet the requirements of Article 7 ECHR: para 133. In Cases T-456&457/05 *Gütermann AG and Zwicky v Commission*, judgment of 28 April 2010, [2010] 5 CMLR 930, paras 49 *et seq* the GC held that an undertaking can infringe Article 101(1) where the purpose of its conduct, as coordinated with that of other undertakings, is to restrict competition on a specific relevant market within the common market, without itself being active on that relevant market.

In COMP/38638 *Butadiene Rubber and Emulsion Styrene Butadiene Rubber*, decn of 29 November 2006, [2009] 4 CMLR 421 the Commission treated agreements relating to two kinds of rubber as part of a single infringement so that companies which produced only one kind were nevertheless held to be responsible for the whole infringement (para 297). See similarly Case T-73/04 *Le Carbone-Lorraine v Commission* [2008] ECR II-2661, [2010] 5 CMLR 81 (further appeal dismissed, Case C-554/08P, judgment of 12 November 2009).

See also Case T-53/03 *BPB plc v Commission* [2008] ECR II-1333, [2008] 5 CMLR 1201 the GC held that the appellant's participation in meetings was 'characterised by the sole purpose of putting an end to the price war and stabilising the four plasterboard markets' (para 253). The fact that not all participants took part in all aspects of the cartel did not undermine this finding. Interestingly, the Court expressly transposed the *Aalborg Portland* reference to inferring agreement from 'a number of coincidences and indicia' to the concept of a single and continuous infringement: '[w]here there is a complex, single and continuous infringement, each manifestation corroborates the actual occurrence of such an infringement': para 249.

In Case T-110/07 *Siemens v Commission*, judgment of 3 March 2011, paras 241 *et seq* the Commission had found that Siemens had participated in the gas insulated switchgear cartel for the periods from 15 April 1988 to 1 September 1999 and from 26 March 2002 to 11 May 2004. The cartel had continued uninterrupted in Siemens' absence and the GC upheld the Commission's finding, for the purposes of applying the limitation period in Regulation 1/2003 that the cartel was a single continuous infringement. This meant that the earlier period of Siemens' participation was not time barred.

The interaction of the concept of a single continuous infringement with the issue of the duration of a particular undertaking's participation in the infringement and the application of the limitation period is illustrated by Case T-18/05 *IMI plc v Commission*, judgment of 19 May 2010. The GC held that the Commission had failed to prove that IMI's participation in the cartel continued uninterrupted and so reduced the fine to reflect a shorter duration of infringement. However, since IMI accepted that the cartel it rejoined was the same as the cartel it had left, the limitation period did not preclude the imposition of a fine for the earlier period.

In COMP/39188 *Bananas*, decn of 15 October 2008, the Commission found bilateral discussions had taken place between various banana importers. These bilateral contacts constituted a single continuous concerted practice because the discussions followed a common pattern and involved the same personnel. There was no need to demonstrate that the parties were aware of all details concerning communications between the other parties (para 252) but it was established that each was aware of the bilateral discussions between the others, or at least foresaw such discussions and took the risk that there was a common objective. The decision is under appeal: Cases T-587&588/08, not yet decided.

Fn 221. The appeal in *AstraZeneca* has been decided and the Commission's finding that this was a single continuous infringement was upheld: Case T-321/05 *AstraZeneca v Commission*, judgment of 1 July 2010, [2010] 5 CMLR 28, para 895. The case is on appeal Case C-457/10P *AstraZeneca v Commission*, not yet decided.

Fn 222. Substantial parts of the Commission's decision in *Needles* were overturned as regards Coats' involvement: Case T-36/05 *Coats Holdings Ltd v Commission* [2007] ECR II-110, [2008] 4 CMLR 45, discussed in the update to paragraph 5.062, below. Prym's appeal to the GC against the same decision was also dismissed save for a small reduction in the fine: Case T-30/05 *Prym v Commission* [2007] ECR II-107* (further appeal dismissed: Case C-534/07, judgment of 3 September 2009, [2009] 5 CMLR 2377). The principles referred to here were applied in Case T-452/05 *Belgian Sewing Thread v Commission*, judgment of 28 April 2010, [2010] 5 CMLR 889, para 39.

Fn 223. In Case T-68/04 *SGL Carbon AG v Commission* [2009] 4 CMLR 7, the appellant complained that by finding four separate infringements and adopting four separate decisions imposing fines in relation to cartel activity involving graphite products, the Commission had circumvented the 10 per cent of turnover ceiling on fines. The GC rejected this and upheld the fine: paras 131 *et seq*. A further appeal was dismissed: Case C-564/08P, judgment of 12 November 2009.

Fn 225. The appeal in Case T-112/05 *Akzo Nobel* and a further appeal to the CJ have now been decided: see Case C-97/08P *Akzo Nobel NV v Commission*, judgment of 10 September 2009.

Fn 226. The appeals from the *Spanish Raw Tobacco* decision were decided in a series of judgments, see the update to paragraph 5.027, below. The appeal against the *Industrial Bags* decision was dismissed: Case T-40/06 *Trioplast Industrier v Commission*, judgment of 13 September 2010.

2.053 **Parties to the agreement/concerted practice.** The appeal by the trade association fined in the *Organic Peroxides* decision for providing administrative and secretarial services to the cartel was dismissed by the GC: Case T-99/04 *AC-Treuhand AG v Commission* [2008] ECR II-1501, [2008] 5 CMLR 962. See update to paragraph 5.014, below.

The distinction between an *Anic* type situation where a cartel participant can be held liable for all the known aspects of a cartel even if it only participated in limited aspects and the *Sigma Technologie* situation where an undertaking must not be fined for collusion for which it has not been held liable was explored in Case T-21/05 *Chalkor v Commission*, judgment of 19 May 2010, [2010] 5 CMLR 1295, paras 90 *et seq*. The Court held that the Commission should have treated those involved in only one 'branch' of the cartel less severely than those involved in several of the 'branches' since the latter contributed more to the effectiveness and the seriousness of the cartel than the former. The Commission had thereby infringed the principle of equal treatment by treating different undertakings in the same manner. The case is on appeal Case C-386/10P, not yet decided.

It is not necessary for the undertaking to be active on the relevant market for it to be party to the infringement: Case T-29/05 *Deltafina v Commission*, judgment of 8 September 2010, paras 46 *et seq* (on further appeal Case C-537/10P, not yet decided).

Fn 236. In Case T-19/05 *Boliden v Commission*, judgment of 19 May 2010, [2010] 5 CMLR 1251 the GC rejected a submission that the applicant had not been aware of the existence of the cartel: 'Having participated for a number of years [in arrangements] which consisted of the allocation of production and monitoring of the implementation of that allocation by means of frequent and detailed exchanges in relation to sales volumes, the applicants cannot claim that Mr M's departure in the middle of 1995 gave rise to acute amnesia within the undertaking as regards the existence of the cartel or its modus operandi.': para 67.

Fn 237. In Case T-385/06 *Aalberts Industries NV v Commission*, judgment of 24 March 2011 the GC held that the Commission had not proved that one of the participants could have reasonably foreseen, when participating in meetings about the French market, that these meetings were part of a wider European cartel: para 119 (case on appeal Case C-287/11P, not yet decided). See also Case T-18/05 *IMI plc v Commission*, judgment of 19 May 2010, para 163.

2.054 **Distancing oneself from the cartel: passive attendance at meetings.** **Fn 243.** See also COMP/39316 *Gaz de France (GDF Suez)*, decn of 8 July 2009, para 111.

Proof of participation.   The judgment in Case T-36/05 *Coats Holdings Ltd v*   **2.055**
Commission [2007] ECR II-110, [2008] 4 CMLR 45 provides a useful example of
the GC examining each of the planks on which the Commission's decision was
based and finding many of them had not been established to the necessary legal
standard. In particular the GC found that the mere fact that Coats had been
informed about an anti-competitive agreement between two producers, Prym and
Entaco, cannot give rise to liability for the infringement (para 105). But the GC
found that in the circumstances of the case, the fact that Coats had, by the sale of its
needles business, triggered the mechanism of the Prym/Entaco cartel did implicate
Coats in that cartel, because the sale was part of a common plan. The fact that
Coats' suppliers, Entaco and Prym, had discussed confidential issues (such as the
creation of a cartel) with Coats showed, the GC found, that Coats' intentions must
have been of an anti-competitive nature. Note also the GC's comments on the
unreliability of one of the witnesses to whose evidence the Commission had referred:
paras 165–167. Coats' fine was reduced to reflect the more limited nature of its
involvement. Coats' appeal against this decision was dismissed: Case C-468/07P
[2009] 4 CMLR 301. Prym's appeal to the GC against the same decision was also
dismissed save for a small reduction in the fine: Case T-30/05 *Prym v Commission*
[2007] ECR II-107* (further appeal dismissed: Case C-534/07, judgment of
3 September 2009, [2009] 5 CMLR 2377).

In Case T-133/07 *Mitsubishi Electric v Commission*, judgment of 12 July 2011, the
applicant argued that a lenient evidential standard was no longer justified by the
difficulties faced by the Commission when trying to prove an infringement
because (i) the level of fines imposed should affect the intensity with which the
Commission's decisions are reviewed; and (ii) given the existence of the Leniency
Notice and the parties' cooperation obtained pursuant to that Notice, it is no longer
necessary to give the Commission a broad discretion when assessing evidence: para
77. The GC rejected this argument, emphasising the prevailing principle of 'unfet-
tered evaluation of evidence' and the high probative value of incriminating evidence
from one cartel member against the others. The GC went on to uphold the
Commission's finding of an unwritten common understanding between the
European and Japanese producers not to enter each other's markets, based on
the statements of several undertakings involved in the cartel and by the witness
statements of the employees of one of those undertakings. See in similar vein
Case T-132/07 *Fuji v Commission*, judgment of 12 July 2011, paras 86 *et seq.* In
Case T-112/07 *Hitachi v Commission*, judgment of 12 July 2011 (also an appeal
from the *Gas Insulated Switchgear* decision), the GC noted that the commitment of
a group of producers not to enter a market reserved to the other group, such as was
alleged against the Japanese producers, was based on a simple concept which can be
implemented easily; its implementation does not require, in principle, interaction
between the undertakings concerned so that it is capable of existing as an unwritten
understanding, which also reduces the likelihood of its discovery: para 91.

Where the Commission relied on handwritten notes to prove that an anti-competitive agreement went beyond price fixing to include collusion on other terms of trade, the GC annulled the decision on the grounds that the notes were sporadic and brief and inadequate to support that aspect of the infringement: see Cases T-235/07 *Bavaria v Commission*, judgment of 16 June 2011, para 163; and T-240/07 *Heineken Nederland v Commission*, judgment of 16 June 2011, para 175 (both on appeal from COMP/37766 *Dutch Beer*, decn of 18 April 2007). See also Case T-53/07 *Trade-Stomil v Commission*, judgment of 13 July 2011 where the GC held that there was insufficient evidence to show that the applicant had participated in the alleged unlawful meeting so that the finding of infringement was annulled.

The fact that one party to an agreement concedes that the agreement existed does not preclude the other alleged party from disputing the existence of the agreement: Case T-18/03 *CD-Contact Data v Commission* [2009] ECR II-1021, para 51. In dismissing the appeal, the CJ confirmed that the standard of proof is no different in the case of a vertical arrangement from the case of a horizontal arrangement: Case C-260/09P *Activision Blizzard v Commission*, judgment of 10 February 2011, para 71.

For the use by the Commission of statements made by one cartel member incriminating others see Case T-54/03 *Lafarge v Commission* [2008] ECR II-120*, paras 57 *et seq*. The point was not considered in the further appeal which was dismissed: Case C-413/08 *Lafarge v Commission*, judgment of 17 June 2010, [2010] 5 CMLR 586.

In a number of appeals from cartel decisions, the GC has emphasised that leniency statements 'have a probative value that is not insignificant, since they entail considerable legal and economic risks'. However, an admission by one undertaking accused of having participated in a cartel, the accuracy of which is contested by several other undertakings similarly accused, cannot be regarded as constituting adequate proof of an infringement committed by the latter unless it is supported by other evidence: see, eg Case T-377/06 *Comap v Commission*, judgment of 24 March 2011, para 59. See similarly COMP/39181 *Candle Waxes*, decn of 1 October 2008, [2009] 5 CMLR 2441, where the Commission rejected the suggestion that corporate statements submitted by one party under the Leniency Notice might contain a distorted version of events and said, to the contrary, that such evidence is particularly reliable. The Commission also noted that 'recollection of facts does not need to be perfect in order to be credible': para 217. The decision is on appeal, Cases T-540, 541, 543, 544, 548, 550, 551, 558, 562/08, not yet decided. For a case where the GC held that the Commission had failed to establish involvement for the whole alleged duration of the cartel because statements made in a leniency application were denied and not corroborated see Case T-385/06 *Aalberts Industries NV v Commission*, judgment of 24 March 2011, para 47 (case on appeal Case C-287/11P, not yet decided).

For the approach of the English courts to this issue see *Bookmakers' Afternoon Greyhound Services v Amalgamated Racing Ltd* [2008] EWHC 2688 (Ch), para 15–18. The judge held that the evidence of collusion relied on by the claimants was 'nowhere near strong enough' to justify rejecting the sworn evidence to the contrary of the defendants' witnesses: para 140.

Fn 246. See also Case T-110/07 *Siemens v Commission*, judgment of 3 March 2011, para 54.

Fn 250. See also Case T-191/06 *FMC Foret v Commission*, judgment of 16 June 2011, para 120 (there is no general rule however that a single piece of evidence cannot support a finding of infringement: para 122).

Duration of individual members' participation.   Although the length of the **2.056** period separating two manifestations of infringing conduct is a relevant criterion in establishing the continuous nature of an infringement, the question whether or not that period is long enough to constitute an interruption of the infringement must be assessed in the context of the functioning of the cartel in question. Thus where in respect of a particular period, the only manifestation of a collusive nature which the Commission had been able to establish was a common increase in prices, the GC held that the Commission had discharged the burden of proving that the cartel continued uninterrupted: Case T-18/05 *IMI plc v Commission*, judgment of 19 May 2010. However, the Commission's finding in the decision that the applicant had participated in collusive meetings over that period was not substantiated and the appeal was allowed to the extent of reducing the fine to reflect their shorter involvement in the cartel. See similarly Case T-40/06 *Trioplast Industrier v Commission*, judgment of 13 September 2010, para 39.

Authority to enter into agreements.   The fact that the director attending meet- **2.058** ings was acting contrary to instructions does not affect the undertaking's liability: see Case T-53/03 *BPB plc v Commission* [2008] ECR II-1333, [2008] 5 CMLR 1201, paras 360 and 431: 'Thus, even if Mr [D] did in actual fact disobey the instructions of BPB's Board of Directors and continue the information exchanges without the latter's knowledge, the Commission was entitled to impose a fine on the undertaking, whilst BPB and/or its owners were free to pursue any action deemed appropriate against Mr [D]'.

(d) Decisions by associations of undertakings

Associations of undertakings.   In COMP/34579 *MasterCard MIF charges*, decn **2.059** of 19 December 2007 the Commission held that the rules of the MasterCard organisation were still decisions of an association of undertakings after MasterCard was listed on the New York Stock Exchange. The Commission held that the bank members of the organisation had agreed to the IPO and the ensuing changes in the organisation's governance 'in order to perpetuate the MIF as part of the business model in a form which they perceived to be less exposed to antitrust scrutiny' (paras 3, 99 and 338 *et seq*). The case is on appeal: Case T-111/08, not yet decided.

See also COMP/39510 *Ordre National des Pharmaciens en France (ONP)*, decn of 8 December 2010 where the Commission held that the professional body for pharmacists was an association for the purposes of Article 101 even though some of its members were employees in hospitals or universities: para 591. The fact that the association's internal organisation was divided into different sections for different kinds of pharmacist was not material in this regard. The case is on appeal Case T-90/11 *ONP and others v Commission*, not yet decided.

Fn 265. The appeal in the *French Beef* case was dismissed: Cases C-101&110/07P *Coop de France bétail et viande and FNSEA v Commission* [2008] ECR I-10193, [2009] 4 CMLR 743.

Fn 267. See also Case T-23/09 *CNOP and CCG v Commission*, Order of 26 October 2010 (challenge by professional association of pharmacists to inspection decision dismissed).

2.060 **Decisions.**   For there to be a decision it is not necessary that the members unanimously approve it or that each of them agrees on all of its aspects. It is sufficient that a decision is taken by the competent body within the association: COMP/34579 *MasterCard MIF charges*, decn of 19 December 2007, para 384. The case is on appeal: Case T-111/08, not yet decided. See also the discussion in COMP/39510 *Ordre National des Pharmaciens en France (ONP)*, decn of 8 December 2010 concerning the nature of decisions adopted by the professional body for pharmacists: paras 596 *et seq*.

As to recommendations being regarded as decisions see COMP/38698 *CISAC*, decn of 16 July 2008, [2009] 4 CMLR 577, paras 91 and 92: model contract terms adopted by the collecting society were not binding but members were encouraged to use them and did use them. Note, however, that the finding of infringement was addressed to the members and not to the collecting society itself (on appeal Cases T-398, 410, 411, 413–422, 425, 432, 434, 442, 451/08, not yet decided).

As to when non-binding acts of an association can fall within the prohibition, in *AUV v NMA*, judgment of 3 July 2008 the Dutch Trade and Industry Appeal Tribunal held that in deciding to refuse to supply veterinary medicines to members who did not comply with its rules prohibiting onward supply other than to existing clients, the Dutch cooperative association of veterinarians was acting in its capacity as an association of undertakings within the Dutch equivalent of Article 101(1) TFEU and not as an individual undertaking: the impugned conduct was carried out at the request of some members and was intended to coordinate members' conduct on the market.

4. Restriction of Competition

(a) Some conceptual issues

The competition rules and consumer detriment. The CJ overturned the GC's   **2.064**
analysis insofar as it held that it was necessary to prove that an agreement entails
disadvantages for final consumers as a prerequisite for a finding of anti-competitive
object: Cases C-501/06P, etc, *GlaxoSmithKline Services Unlimited v Commission*,
judgment of 6 October 2009. But the CJ upheld the GC's decision that the
Commission had failed properly to examine GSK's arguments for exemption under
Article 101(3): para 104. See also Cases C-468/06, etc, *Sot Lelos kai Sia EE v
GlaxoSmithKline* [2008] ECR I-7139, [2008] 5 CMLR 1382, [2009] All ER (EC) 1
(State regulation of prices does not mean that benefits of parallel trading for
consumers are minimal).

See also Case T-461/07 *Visa v Commission*, judgment of 14 April 2011 where the
GC stated that the competition rules are designed to protect not only the interests
of competitors or consumers but also to protect the structure of the market and
thus competition as such: para 126.

See also Niels, Jenkins & Kavanagh, *Economics for Competition Lawyers* (2011) for
an analysis of the relevant economics principles, written specifically for competition lawyers.

Inter-brand and intra-brand competition. This distinction was important in   **2.067**
the Commission's analysis in COMP/37860 *Morgan Stanley/Visa International
and Visa Europe*, decn of 3 October 2007 (appeal on other grounds dismissed:
Case T-461/07 *Visa v Commission*, judgment of 14 April 2011). See similarly,
COMP/38606 *Groupement des Cartes Bancaires*, decn of 17 October 2007
where the Commission stated (also as regards payment card networks) that
'[t]he weakness of intersystem competition in France increases the need for robust
intrasystem competition. In other words, the stronger the position of a system in
intersystem competition, the more serious is any weakening of competition
inside it': para 170. In *Groupement des Cartes Bancaires* the Commission described
the free-rider argument as 'confused' because Groupement's argument was really
that the new entrants to the payment system were benefiting from the investment
made in the past over a period of many years by the traditional members. This was
not a free-riding argument since there was no evidence to show how much investment had been made, whether that investment had already been recouped or
whether the traditional members would have been discouraged from making
that investment if they had known that later banks would have been able to benefit
from it: para 382. The case is on appeal Case T-491/07 *CB v Commission*, not
yet decided.

2.068   **Need to prevent absolute territorial protection.**   In Cases C-403&429/08 *Football Association Premier League v QC Leisure/ Murphy v Media Protection Services*, Opinion of 3 February 2011, Advocate General Kokott drew an analogy between contracts imposing absolute territorial protection for goods and the licences for the transmission of satellite broadcasts of football matches. She advised that a contractual obligation linked to a broadcasting licence requiring the broadcaster to prevent its satellite decoder cards from being used outside the licensed territory has the same effect as agreements to prevent or restrict parallel exports. Such an obligation is intended to prevent any competition between broadcasters through a reciprocal compartmentalisation of licensed territories. Such licences with absolute territorial protection are incompatible with the internal market and there was no reason to treat such agreements any differently from agreements intended to prevent parallel trade. They therefore constituted an infringement of Article 101(1) by object.

(b) The main decisions

(i) The two seminal cases

2.077   **The interpretation of *Consten and Grundig* in *GlaxoSmithKline*.**   This paragraph must now be read in the light of the CJ's judgment in the appeal: Cases C-501/06P, etc, *GlaxoSmithKline Services Unlimited v Commission*, judgment of 6 October 2009. The CJ firmly rejected the GC's analysis and held that neither the wording of Article 101(1) nor the case law lends support to the GC's statement that an agreement limiting parallel trade only has the object of restricting competition if it disadvantages final consumers: para 62. The Court cited both very early case law and its recent decisions in Cases C-468/06, etc, *Sot Lelos kai Sia EE v GlaxoSmithKline* and Case C-8/08 *T-Mobile Netherlands BV* to conclude that by requiring proof that the agreement entails disadvantages for final consumers and by not finding that GSK's agreement had such an object the GC had committed an error of law. But the CJ upheld the GC's decision that the Commission had failed properly to examine GSK's arguments for exemption of the notified agreement under Article 101(3): para 104.

(ii) Market analysis

2.087   ***European Night Services*: comment.**   See the application of *European Night Services* and subsequent case law in Case T-461/07 *Visa v Commission*, judgment of 14 April 2011: paras 67–70.

Fn 342. Reg 2790/1999 has been replaced by Reg 330/2010 (OJ 2010 L102/1: Vol II, App C7A) and Reg 2659/2000 has been replaced by Reg 1217/2010 (OJ 2010 L335/36: Vol II, App C7C). Both of these continue with the economics-based approach of their predecessor instruments.

(iii) Consideration of pro- and anti-competitive effects

2.090   **Other instances.**   As regards vendor non-compete covenants see, by analogy, *Jones v Ricoh UK* [2010] EWHC 1743 (Ch) (clause purporting to protect confidential information which in fact restricted one party from dealing with or seeking to deal with the other's clients was anti-competitive by object).

'Rule of reason' in Community law?   The Commission applied the *Gøttrup-Klim*, **2.091** *Métropole Télévision* line of cases in examining the objective justification of a rule of the Visa payment card network which refused membership to a competitor: COMP/37860 *Morgan Stanley/Visa International and Visa Europe*, decn of 3 October 2007. Having found, on an analysis of the market, that the rule as applied to Morgan Stanley had appreciable restrictive effects on competition (para 201) the Commission considered that, nonetheless, the rule would not fall under Article 101(1) if it was directly related to and necessary (proportionate and non-discriminatory) for the proper functioning of Visa's network. On the facts the Commission held that this was not the case, and the rule did not fulfil the conditions of Article 101(3) either. On appeal Visa did not contest the finding that the exclusion was not objectively justified: Case T-461/07 *Visa v Commission*, judgment of 14 April 2011, see para 66 (appeal dismissed).

Wouters **and** *Meca-Medina*.   The *Wouters* 'exception' was discussed by the **2.092** Commission in COMP/39510 *Ordre National des Pharmaciens en France (ONP)*, decn of 8 December 2010, paras 684 *et seq*. The Commission rejected the submission that the body's decisions hindering the development of groups of laboratories in favour of incumbent small and medium enterprises was aimed at benefiting public health. The case is on appeal Case T-90/11 *ONP and others v Commission*, not yet decided.

Fn 371. See also the Belgian Cour de Cassation in *CT v Orde de Architecten* (D.06.0010.N), judgment of 27 April 2007: decision of the Belgian Association of Architects that requires architects' fees to be determined on the basis of the nature and dimensions of the assignment has the purpose of ensuring the proper practice of the profession and accordingly does not fall within the prohibition of Belgian competition law. Cf *L'Ordre des Pharmaciens* (2007/MR/5), Brussels Court of Appeal, judgment of 7 April 2009: although the requirements on pharmacists for on-call duty served the general interest, the rule of the Belgian Pharmacists Association regarding opening hours was not proportionate in support of those requirements and therefore did not satisfy the criteria of *Wouters* so as to escape condemnation under Belgian competition law.

Article 81(1) and Article 81(3) relationship illustrated.   In COMP/34579 **2.093** *MasterCard MIF charges*, decn of 19 December 2007, paras 524 *et seq*, the Commission set out the case law from *Pronuptia* and *Metropole* to *Gøttrup-Klim* and *Wouters* when considering whether a payment card system could operate without a multilateral exchange fee such that the fee fell outside Article 101(1). The Commission accepted that the Article 101(1) test covered the question whether there was an alternative to the fee which was 'feasible' but held that the secondary question—whether that alternative was better than the MIF—was a question to be addressed under Article 101(3) not Article 101(1): para 542. To hold otherwise would be to reverse the burden of proof under Article 101(3). In the event, the Commission held that it was feasible to operate the system without an MIF: para 549. The case is on appeal: Case T-111/08, not yet decided.

See also *Bookmakers' Afternoon Greyhound Services v Amalgamated Racing Ltd* [2009] EWCA Civ 750 where the English Court of Appeal applied the principles in *Métropole Télévision (M6)* and *Wouters* in finding that an agreement among racecourses to grant exclusive media rights to a joint venture which they had set up to compete with a former monopsony owned by the bookmakers did not have the object or effect of restricting competition and so did not fall within Article 101(1). The Court discussed the *O₂ (Germany)* case and the opinion of the Advocate General in C-209/07 *Beef Industry Development Society Ltd v Barry Brothers (Carrigmore) Meats Ltd* [2008] ECR I-8637, [2009] 4 CMLR 310, [2009] All ER (EC) 367 and rejected the argument that pro-competitive aspects of the agreement fell to be considered only under Article 101(3).

(c) The present law

2.094 **In general.** **Fn 373.** Note that the CJ overturned the GC's analysis insofar as it held that it was necessary to prove that an agreement entails disadvantages for final consumers as a prerequisite for a finding of anti-competitive object: Cases C-501/06P, etc, *GlaxoSmithKline Services Unlimited v Commission*, judgment of 6 October 2009.

2.095 **The main considerations.** Note that the restriction of competition may arise in a market where the infringer is not itself active: for example in COMP/38606 *Groupement des Cartes Bancaires*, decn of 17 October 2007 the Commission found that the bankers' association's decisions restricted competition in the market for issuing payment cards, even though the Groupement did not itself issue such cards: 'it does not follow from the fact that the Groupement is not itself an issuer (it being the banks members of the Groupement that are the issuers) that the measures cannot be examined in the context of the issuance market. European Union competition law is applicable to the conduct of an undertaking or association of undertakings restricting competition in a market other than that in which it provides its services and for the benefit of undertakings other than itself': para 179.

2.096 **The object.** In Case C-209/07 *Beef Industry Development Society Ltd v Barry Brothers (Carrigmore) Meats Ltd* [2008] ECR I-8637, [2009] 4 CMLR 310, [2009] All ER (EC) 367, the CJ described the object of the agreement as 'the precise purpose of the agreement, in the economic context in which it is to be applied' (para 15). Even if the parties acted without any subjective intention of restricting competition, but with the object of remedying the effects of an overcapacity crisis in their sector, such considerations are irrelevant for the purposes of applying Article 101(1) and are only relevant for the purposes of Article 101(3). An agreement may be regarded as having a restrictive object even if it does not have the restriction of competition as its sole aim but also pursues other legitimate objectives. The arrangements which had been notified to the Irish competition authority were intended to enable undertakings in the beef and veal processing market to implement a common policy which encouraged some of them to withdraw from the market and thereby bring about a reduction of overcapacity. The CJ held that the agreement patently conflicted with the competition rules because it was intended to dissuade the undertakings which remained in the market from increasing their market share and also discouraged new entry. The CJ did not rule out the application of Article 101(3) but this was not part of the questions referred by the Irish court for the preliminary ruling. On 3 November 2009 the Irish Supreme Court referred the matter back to the trial judge to reconsider the application of Article 101(3), Kearns J commenting that 'the initiative giving rise to the BIDS scheme was as far removed as one could imagine from objectionable cartel practises': [2009] IESC 72. The case was settled by BIDS withdrawing its High Court action asserting the applicability of Article 101(3) and the Irish Competition Authority issuing a Guidance Notice to businesses considering entering into agreements to reduce capacity in specific industries in Ireland (N/11/001 issued on 16 June 2011: see ECN Brief 1/2011, p2). See similarly, Case C-8/08 *T-Mobile Netherlands BV v Raad van bestuur van de Nederlandse Mededingingsautoriteit*, judgment of 4 June 2009, paras 28 and 30; Cases C-501/06P, etc, *GlaxoSmithKline Services Unlimited v Commission*, judgment of 6 October 2009, para 55. In COMP/38606 *Groupement des Cartes Bancaires*, decn of 17 October 2007 the Commission rejected the submissions made by the parties when they notified the rules under Regulation 17 and found that the real object of the agreement was to hinder market entry: para 251.

In *Bookmakers' Afternoon Greyhound Services v Amalgamated Racing Ltd* [2009] EWCA Civ 750 the English Court of Appeal distinguished the CJ's judgment in *Irish Beef* in relation to an agreement among racecourses to grant exclusive rights to broadcast horse races to bookmakers' premises to a joint venture which they had set up to compete with a former monopsony owned by the bookmakers. The Court rejected the allegation that the agreement had the object of restricting competition as not 'reflecting in any realistic way either the economic context in which the arrangements were made, or the object of the arrangements, ascertained objectively by reference to their nature and terms in the relevant context': para 83.

A clause purporting to protect confidential information which in fact restricted one party from dealing with or seeking to deal with the other's clients was anti-competitive by object: *Jones v Ricoh UK Ltd* [2010] EWHC 1743 (Ch), para 42.

Fn 388. See also Cases C-501/06P, etc, *GlaxoSmithKline Services Unlimited v Commission*, judgment of 6 October 2009, para 58 where the CJ noted that although the parties' intention is not a necessary factor in determining whether an agreement is restrictive, there is nothing prohibiting the Commission from taking that aspect into account.

2.097 **'Hard-core' restrictions: objects restrictive *per se*.** The qualification introduced by the GC in *GlaxoSmithKline* was firmly rejected by the CJ's judgment in the appeal: Cases C-501/06P, etc, *GlaxoSmithKline Services Unlimited v Commission*, judgment of 6 October 2009. The Court cited both very early case law and its recent decisions in Cases C-468/06, etc, *Sot Lelos kai Sia EE v GlaxoSmithKline* and Case C-8/08 *T-Mobile Netherlands BV* to conclude that by requiring proof that the agreement entails disadvantages for final consumers as a prerequisite for a finding of anti-competitive object and by not finding that GSK's agreement had such an object the GC had committed an error of law. But the CJ upheld the GC's decision that the Commission had failed properly to examine GSK's arguments for exemption under Article 101(3): para 104.

As regards the penultimate sentence of this paragraph see Case T-53/03 *BPB plc v Commission* [2008] ECR II-1333, [2008] 5 CMLR 1201, para 90 where the GC said that '[u]ndertakings which conclude an agreement whose purpose is to restrict competition cannot, in principle, avoid the application of Article [101(1) TFEU] by claiming that their agreement was not intended to have an appreciable effect on competition'.

Fn 398. These Guidelines have now been replaced by the Horizontal Cooperation Guidelines 2011, OJ 2011 C11/1: Vol II, App C22.

2.099 **The effects on competition: the whole economic context.** In Case T-461/07 *Visa v Commission*, judgment of 14 April 2011 the GC stressed that the Commission's analysis must be based on the actual economic and other factors operating in the market. Thus the Commission had been right to consider whether there was a 'real concrete possibility' for Morgan Stanley to enter the market despite being excluded from the Visa network or whether the conditions in which competition took place in the market meant that that possibility was 'unrealistic or purely theoretical'.

As to the use of expert economic evidence see the comments of Morgan J in *Bookmakers' Afternoon Greyhound Services v Amalgamated Racing Ltd* [2008] EWHC 1978 (Ch), paras 287 and 288 that the expert witnesses did not confine themselves to matters of microeconomics on which they could give admissible opinion evidence for the assistance of the court but also summarised their understanding of the legal principles which fell to be applied and then offered their conclusions as to the result of applying those legal principles to this case. Although the parties did not distinguish between parts of their statements which were truly admissible expert evidence on matters of microeconomics and those parts which went beyond the proper bounds of expert evidence, the learned judge considered it important to do so.

2.102 **Effect on potential competition.** The relevance of potential as well as actual competition was stressed by the GC in Case T-461/07 *Visa v Commission*, judgment of

14 April 2011. The GC held that the examination of conditions of competition must be based not only on existing competition between undertakings already present on the relevant market but also on potential competition since the competition rules are designed to protect not only the interests of competitors or consumers but also to protect the structure of the market and thus competition as such. The Commission had not erred in deciding that the effects of the conduct at issue were restrictive of competition because of the potential competition represented by Morgan Stanley and the structure of the market in question: paras 125 *et seq.* The existence of some actual competition in the market did not mean that the exclusion of a competitor did not restrict competition: para 130.

Markets where scope for competition is limited.   **Fn 442.** In the appeal Cases   **2.105**
C-501/06P, etc, *GlaxoSmithKline Services Unlimited v Commission*, judgment of 6 October 2009 the CJ held that the agreement did have an anti-competitive object so that there was no need to consider the effect of the agreement in the context of Article 101(1).

Vertical restrictions affecting exports or imports.   The qualification introduced   **2.110**
by the GC in *GlaxoSmithKline* was firmly rejected by the CJ's judgment in the appeal: Cases C-501/06P, etc, *GlaxoSmithKline Services Unlimited v Commission*, judgment of 6 October 2009. The Court concluded that by requiring proof that the agreement entails disadvantages for final consumers as a prerequisite for a finding of anti-competitive object and by not finding that GSK's agreement had such an object the GC had committed an error of law. Since the agreement did have an anti-competitive object, there was no need to consider the effect of the agreement in the context of Article 101(1). See now also Cases C-468/06, etc, *Sot Lelos kai Sia EE v GlaxoSmithKline* [2008] ECR I-7139, [2008] 5 CMLR 1382, [2009] All ER (EC) 1 (reference for a preliminary ruling concerning the application of Article 102 TFEU to GlaxoSmithKline's refusal to fulfil orders from a wholesaler who engages in parallel trading).

Fn 447. The appeals in *Video Games, Nintendo Distribution* have now been decided: Case T-18/03 *CD-Contact Data v Commission* [2009] ECR II-1021 (fine reduced) (appeal dismissed Case C-260/09P *Activision Blizzard v Commission*, judgment of 10 February 2011); Case T-12/03 *Itochu* [2009] ECR II-883, [2009] 5 CMLR 1375 (appeal dismissed); Case T-13/03 *Nintendo* [2009] 5 CMLR 1421 (fine reduced); Case T-398/02 *Linea Gig* (removed from register 2 May 2005).

Ancillary restrictions not within Article 81(1).   See *Bookmakers' Afternoon*   **2.112**
Greyhound Services v Amalgamated Racing Ltd [2009] EWCA Civ 750 where the English Court of Appeal upheld the first instance judge's decision ([2008] EWHC 1978 (Ch)) that the exclusive grant of media rights was an ancillary restriction within the principles established in Case T-112/99 *Métropole Télévision (M6) v Commission* [2001] ECR II-2459 and Case C-309/99 *Wouters* [2002] ECR I-1577: para 121.

2.113 **Ancillary restrictions in practice.**   Fn 460. The Guidelines referred to in parentheses have now been replaced by the Horizontal Cooperation Guidelines 2011, OJ 2011 C11/1: Vol II, App C22. These also do not appear to have replaced the Subcontracting Notice, see para 154 of the Guidelines.

2.116 **Restrictions necessary and proportionate to legitimate objective.**   See also *Bookmakers' Afternoon Greyhound Services v Amalgamated Racing Ltd* [2009] EWCA Civ 750.

5. Appreciable Effect on Competition

2.121 **In general.**   As regards the application of the *de minimis* threshold to agreements which have the object of restricting competition see Case T-53/03 *BPB plc v Commission* [2008] ECR II-1333, [2008] 5 CMLR 1201, para 90 where the GC said that '[u]ndertakings which conclude an agreement whose purpose is to restrict competition cannot, in principle, avoid the application of Article [101(1) TFEU] by claiming that their agreement was not intended to have an appreciable effect on competition'.

See Case C-506/07 *Lubricantes y Carburantes Galaicos ('Lubricarga') v GALP Energía España,* Order of 3 September 2009 the CJ confirmed that a contract which fixes resale prices and which contains other hard-core clauses taking it outside Regulation 1984/83 can still fall outside Article 101(1) if it is *de minimis.*

(a) Jurisprudence of the Community Courts

2.124 **Market structure.**   Fn 508. The 2001 Guidelines have now been replaced by the Horizontal Cooperation Guidelines 2011, OJ 2011 C11/1: Vol II, App C22. The new Guidelines do not refer to the HHI.

(b) Commission guidance

2.128 **In general.**   Fn 525. These Guidelines have now been replaced by the Horizontal Cooperation Guidelines 2011, OJ 2011 C11/1: Vol II, App C22.

2.130 **Vertical restraints: markets shares of the parties to the agreement.**   The Guidelines on Vertical Restraints referred to in the text have been replaced by the 2010 Vertical Restraints Guidelines (OJ 2010 C130/1: Vol II, App C20). The 'disconnect' referred to in the text has been resolved by the new Guidelines. In para 9 of the 2010 Vertical Restraints Guidelines, the Commission states that (i) vertical agreements entered into by non-competing undertakings whose individual market share does not exceed 25 per cent are generally considered to fall outside Article 101(1); (ii) as regards hard-core restrictions listed in the *De Minimis* Notice, Article 101(1) may apply below the 15 per cent threshold; (iii) subject to cumulative effect and hard-core restrictions, vertical agreements between SMEs are rarely capable of appreciably restricting competition and therefore generally fall outside Article 101(1).

Vertical restraints: unconcentrated markets.   The 2010 Vertical Restraints   **2.131** Guidelines cover this issue in a different way from the earlier Guidelines referred to in the text: see para 97 and paras 111 *et seq*. The Commission emphasises the importance of considering the market position of the parties as an indicator of market power (para 114), the relevance of entry barriers and the nature of the product.

Horizontal cooperation agreements.   These Guidelines have now been replaced   **2.132** by the Horizontal Cooperation Guidelines 2011, OJ 2011 C11/1: Vol II, App C22. Their scope is wider than the earlier version and they now provide guidance on information exchange agreements and standardisation agreements beyond those relating to environmental objectives. The same point about low market shares is made in paras 44–47 of the new Guidelines.

3

ARTICLE 81(3)

1. Introduction

Note: Article 81(3) EC has now become Article 101(3) TFEU

Commission Guidelines. The Horizontal Cooperation Guidelines issued in **3.004** 2001 have been replaced by those issued in 2011 (OJ 2011 C11/1: Vol II, App C22). The new Guidelines accompanied new block exemption regulations for research and development agreements (Regulation 1217/2010, OJ 2010 L335/36: Vol II, App C7C) and for specialisation agreements (Regulation 1218/2010, OJ L335/43: Vol II, App C7D).

Lapse of extant notifications for exemption. In Case T-461/07 *Visa v Commission*, **3.009** judgment of 14 April 2011 (on appeal from COMP/37860 *Morgan Stanley/Visa International and Visa Europe*, decn of 3 October 2007) the GC held that immunity from fines for notified conduct terminated when Regulation 1/2003 came into force so that the Commission would have been entitled to impose a fine from that date: para 211. In fact the Commission had imposed a fine only in relation to conduct from a later date, the date in August 2004 when the SO had been served. The GC also rejected Visa's claim of discrimination based on the *Mastercard* and *Cartes Bancaires* cases (in which no fines had been imposed).

Fn 18. In the appeal Cases C-501/06P, etc, *GlaxoSmithKline Services Unlimited v Commission*, judgment of 6 October 2009 the CJ found that the agreement had an anti-competitive object but still upheld the GC's decision that the Commission had failed properly to examine GSK's arguments for exemption under Article 101(3) TFEU: para 104.

Application of Article 81(3) by national courts. For an example of a national **3.010** court applying the domestic equivalent of Article 101(3) see *Neurendale Ltd t/a Panda Waste Services v Dublin City Council* [2009] IEHC 588 (regulation issued by the local authorities by which they purported to exclude private companies from offering competing refuse collection services did not fulfil the conditions of section 4(5) of the Competition Act 2002): paras 119 *et seq*.

See also Niels, Jenkins & Kavanagh, *Economics for Competition Lawyers* (2011) for an analysis of the relevant economics principles, written specifically for competition lawyers.

3.011 **Relationship between Article 81(1) and 81(3).** See how the Commission approached this in COMP/37860 *Morgan Stanley/Visa International and Visa Europe*, decn of 3 October 2007. The Commission found, on an analysis of the market, that a rule of the Visa payment network, as applied to exclude Morgan Stanley, had appreciable restrictive effects on competition (para 201). Referring to the *Gøttrup-Klim*, *Métropole Télévision* line of cases, the Commission considered that, nonetheless, the rule would not fall under Article 101(1) if it was directly related to and necessary (proportionate and non-discriminatory) for the proper functioning of Visa's network. On the facts the Commission held that this was not the case. The Commission then went on to consider whether the conditions of Article 101(3) were fulfilled. Visa had not expressly relied on the points raised in relation to objective justification as also being relevant to the application of Article 101(3). But the Commission considered that such arguments needed to be taken into account in considering whether the exclusion of Morgan Stanley from the network was necessary to generate efficiencies that outweigh and thereby justify the restriction of competition caused by such exclusion: para 317. The Commission held that the conditions of Article 101(3) were not fulfilled. On appeal Visa did not contest the finding that the exclusion was not objectively justified: Case T-461/07 *Visa v Commission*, judgment of 14 April 2011, see para 66 (appeal dismissed).

2. Application in Individual Cases

(a) Generally

3.013 **Unlimited theoretical application of Article 81(3).** Note *Competition Authority v Beef Industry Development Society Ltd* [2009] IESC 72, where after the CJ's ruled on a reference under Article 267 TFEU that the arrangements for reducing overcapacity in the beef slaughtering industry gave rise to an infringement by object, the Irish Supreme Court referred the case back to the High Court to determine whether the conditions of Article 101(3) TFEU were satisfied. However, the case concerned an open and transparent rationalisation scheme, not a secret cartel. (For the CJ judgment, see further the update to paragraph 2.096, above). The case was settled by BIDS withdrawing its High Court action asserting the applicability of Article 101(3) and the Irish Competition Authority issuing a Guidance Notice to businesses considering entering into agreements to reduce capacity in specific industries in Ireland (N/11/001 issued on 16 June 2011, see ECN Brief 1/2011, p2).

3.015 **Burden of proof.** The burden and standard of proof for Article 101(3) TFEU was considered by the CJ in Cases C-501/06P, etc, *GlaxoSmithKline Services Unlimited* *v Commission*, judgment of 6 October 2009. First, the Court rejected an argument that attempted to draw an analogy between the appraisal of the competitive effects of a concentration with the appraisal needed under Article 101(3): para 78. Thus the CJ confirmed that it is for the undertakings concerned to demonstrate by means of convincing arguments and evidence that the conditions are fulfilled. However, the facts relied on by that undertaking 'may be such as to oblige the other party to provide an explanation or justification, failing which it is permissible to conclude that the burden of proof has been discharged': para 83. The CJ upheld the GC's finding that the Commission had failed to take into account certain aspects of the market which had been highlighted by GSK in its request for exemption: para 104. See also the Advocate General's comments on the standard of proof required: para 193 of her opinion, approved by the Court at para 93 of the judgment.

(b) The first condition: economic and other benefits

(i) Generally

Benefits must be objective.   See also Cases C-501/06P, etc, *GlaxoSmithKline*   **3.020**
Services Unlimited v Commission, judgment of 6 October 2009, para 102.

Efficiencies and other benefits.   The Commission has stressed that the existence   **3.021**
of efficiencies cannot be determined in a general manner by economic theory alone, 'as theories always rely on assumptions that may not sufficiently reflect market reality'. Claims that restrictions create efficiencies 'must be founded on detailed, robust and compelling analysis that relies in its assumptions and deductions on empirical data and facts': COMP/34579 *MasterCard MIF charges*, decn of 19 December 2007, para 690. The Commission held that MasterCard had not established that the first condition of Article 101(3) was met. The case is on appeal: Case T-111/08, not yet decided.

On appeal in the *GlaxoSmithKline* case mentioned towards the end of the paragraph, the CJ upheld the GC's analysis as regards the application of Article 101(3): Cases C-501/06P, etc, *GlaxoSmithKline Services Unlimited v Commission*, judgment of 6 October 2009. The Advocate General noted at para 193 of her opinion that Article 101(3) required a prospective analysis of the likely occurrence of the advantages said to arise from the agreement. The first condition of Article 101(3) would therefore be satisfied if the Commission was able, on the basis of the arguments and evidence submitted, to arrive at the conviction that the occurrence of the appreciable objective advantage is sufficiently likely in the light of actual experience. In her opinion, a high degree of probability must be required since losses in efficiency in the form of a restriction of competition must *ex hypothesi* exist. The Court approved this passage: see para 93 of the judgment.

Benefits in various markets.   Fn 62. The 2001 Guidelines have been replaced by   **3.022**
the Guidelines on horizontal cooperation agreements issued in 2011: OJ 2011 C11/1: Vol II, App C22, see update to paragraph 3.044, below.

3.028 **Commission's current approach.** However, in *Competition Authority v Beef Industry Development Society Ltd* [2009] IESC 72, the Irish Supreme Court, commenting on the Article 101(3) Guidelines, held that it was not necessary to establish with precision what the exact value or magnitude of the benefits resulting from the arrangements would be. Per Kearns P: 'It will suffice if BIDS can demonstrate positive gains or at least a state of neutrality from the point of view of the consumer'. These observations were expressly made in the context of the facts of the case, which concerned a rationalisation scheme in an industry facing chronic overcapacity.

The Commission has issued a document called 'Best Practices for the Submission of Economic Evidence and Data Collection in Cases Concerning the Application of Articles 101 and 102 TFEU and in Merger Cases' (Vol II, App B21, and on the DG Competition website and linked to Press Release IP/10/02 (6 January 2010)). It describes, *inter alia*, the preferred content and presentation of economic and econometric data and best practice on responding to requests for quantitative data.

(ii) Cost efficiencies

3.032 **Danger of relying on cost efficiencies.** Fn 86. See now the Horizontal Cooperation Guidelines 2011, OJ 2011 C11/1: Vol II, App C22. The new Guidelines do not contain a statement equivalent to that in para 33 of the earlier version.

(v) General public benefits

3.044 **Environmental protection.** The 2001 Guidelines have been replaced by the Guidelines on horizontal cooperation agreements issued in 2011: OJ 2011 C11/1: Vol II, App C22. The Guidelines do not contain specific provisions about standards for environmental objectives. Such agreements are now covered by the general provisions. The Commission has stated that this does not imply any downgrading of the assessment of environmental agreements: MEMO/10/676 (14 December 2010) para 12. See also the examples given at paras 329, 331, and 332 of the Guidelines.

See however, COMP/39579 *Consumer detergents*, decn of 13 April 2010, OJ 2011 C193/14 where the Commission condemned a price fixing cartel which arose in response to an environmental initiative to achieve dosage and weight reductions of detergent and restrictions on packaging material. The Commission found that the detergent producers had sought to achieve market stabilisation by ensuring that none of them would use the environmental initiative to gain competitive advantage over the others and that market positions would remain at the same level as prior to actions taken within the environmental initiative.

(d) The third condition: indispensability of restrictions

3.060 **Establishing indispensability.** The case was settled by BIDS withdrawing its High Court action asserting the applicability of Article 101(3) and the Irish

Competition Authority issuing a Guidance Notice to businesses considering entering into agreements to reduce capacity in specific industries in Ireland (N/11/001 issued on 16 June 2011, see ECN Brief 1/2011, p2).

Fn 195. As to the last sentence see now *Competition Authority v Beef Industry Development Society Ltd* [2009] IESC 72. The Irish Supreme Court first referred questions to the CJ under Article 267 TFEU and, following the preliminary ruling (Case C-209/07 [2008] ECR I-8637, [2009] 4 CMLR 310), referred the case back to the Irish High Court to assess the application of Article 101(3) TFEU. In his judgment the President of the Irish Supreme Court, Kearns P, indicated that the imposition of non-compete covenants on those paid to leave the market may be indispensable conditions of an industry rationalisation scheme if the objective of reducing capacity came within Article 101(3).

Fn 196. A further appeal in *Der Grüne Punkt* was dismissed: Case C-385/07P *Der Grüne Punkt—Duales System Deutschland v Commission*, judgment of 16 July 2009, [2009] 5 CMLR 2215.

(e) The fourth condition: no elimination of competition

Generally.   Fn 203. See now the Horizontal Cooperation Guidelines 2011, OJ 2011 C11/1: Vol II, App C22. The new Guidelines do not contain a statement equivalent to that in para 36 of the earlier version. New Guidelines on Vertical Restraints have been published (to accompany the new Vertical Restraints block exemption Reg 330/2010) replacing the 2000 Guidelines referred to. The new Guidelines are published at OJ 2010 C130/1: Vol II, App C20 and the new block exemption regulation at OJ 2010 L102/1: Vol II, App C7A. The point referred to here is expressed rather differently in para 127 of the 2010 Guidelines where the Commission says that a restrictive agreement which maintains, creates or strengthens a market position approaching that of a monopoly can normally not be justified on the grounds that it also creates efficiency gains.   **3.062**

Market shares.   Fn 209. An appeal against the decision in *ARA and ARGEV, ARO* was dismissed: Case T-419/03 *Altstoff Recycling Austria AG v Commission*, judgment of 22 March 2011.   **3.064**

3. Block Exemption

(a) Generally

Function of block exemptions.   Fn 225. New Guidelines on Vertical Restraints have been published (to accompany the new Vertical Restraints block exemption Reg 330/2010) replacing the 2000 Guidelines referred to in the text. The new Guidelines are published at OJ 2010 C130/1: Vol II, App C20 and the new block   **3.068**

exemption regulation at OJ 2010 L102/1: Vol II, App C7A. A similar point is made in para 96 of the 2010 Vertical Restraints Guidelines.

3.069   **Agreements outside a block exemption may benefit from Article 81(3).   Fn 228.** Reg 1400/2002 has been replaced by Reg 461/2010 (OJ 2010 L129/52: Vol II, App C7B). Recitals (3) and (15) of the new Reg make the point referred to in the text.

3.075   **Council enabling regulations.**   Regulation 3976/87 relating to air transport and the regulations amending it have been repealed and replaced as from the end of June 2009 by a consolidating instrument: Regulation 487/2009 on the application of Article [101(3)] to certain categories of agreements and concerted practices in the air transport sector, OJ 2009 L148/1: Vol II, App E9A.

Regulation 479/92 relating to liner consortia has been replaced as from March 2009 by Regulation 246/2009 on the application of Article [101(3)] to certain categories of agreements, decisions and concerted practices between liner shipping companies (consortia), OJ 2009 L79/1: Vol II, App E7A.

(b) Current block exemption regulations

3.076   **Specialisation/production agreements.**   Regulation 2658/2000 has been replaced by Regulation 1218/2010 (OJ 2010 L335/43: Vol II, App C7D) which came into force on 1 January 2011 and expires on 31 December 2022. Its scope is, broadly, as set out in this paragraph: see further updates to paragraphs 7.087 *et seq*, below.

3.077   **Research and development.**   Regulation 2659/2000 has been replaced by Regulation 1217/2010 (OJ 2010 L335/36: Vol II, App C7C) which came into force on 1 January 2011 and expires on 31 December 2022. Its scope is, broadly, as set out in this paragraph though it now also covers agreements whereby one party merely finances the R&D activities of the other party: see further updates to paragraphs 7.078 *et seq*, below.

3.078   **Vertical restraints.**   Regulation 2790/99 has been replaced by Regulation 330/2010 which came into force on 1 June 2010 and expires on 31 May 2022 (OJ 2010 L102/1: Vol II, App C7A). The new Regulation was accompanied by a new set of Guidelines on Vertical Restraints (OJ 2010 C130/1: Vol II, App C20).

3.079   **Motor vehicle distribution.**   Motor vehicle distribution agreements are now covered by Regulation 461/2010, OJ 2010 L129/52: Vol II, App C7B. The new Regulation extends the application of Regulation 1400/2002 until 31 May 2013 insofar as it relates to vertical agreements for the purchase, sale and resale of new motor vehicles. After that date, those agreements will be covered only by the general block exemption for vertical restraints, Regulation 330/2010 (OJ 2010 L102/1: Vol II, App C7A). This will mean that the market share threshold for agreements relating to new motor vehicles will be 30 per cent as it is for vertical agreements in general. However, for agreements relating to the after sales markets (that is to the markets for the purchase, sale or resale of spare parts and/or for the provision of repair and maintenance services) Regulation 461/2010 continues to make special provision which applies in addition to the requirements of Regulation 330/2010. This means that, as from 1 June 2010 (when Regulation 461/2010 came into force) agreements relating to after sales markets will be exempt only if they comply with Regulation 330/2010 and do not contain any of the three hard-core restrictions set out in Article 5 of Regulation 461/2010: see the Commission's Supplementary Guidelines on vertical restraints in agreements for the sale and repair of motor vehicles and for the distribution of spare parts for motor vehicles, OJ 2010 C138/16: Vol II, App C21, paras 9–16. Regulation 461/2010 came into force on 1 June 2010 and expires on 31 May 2023.

Insurance.   Regulation 358/2003 has been replaced by Regulation 267/2010   **3.081**
(OJ 2010 L83/1: Vol II, App E27A). The new block exemption covers only two of the categories of agreements previously exempted, namely collaboration between insurers in relation to joint compilations, tables and studies of risk and insurance pools. Agreements relating to standard terms and to the specification of security devices are no longer exempted and are now subject to individual assessment under Article 101: see the updates to paragraphs 12.170 *et seq*, below.

Liner consortia.   The Commission has adopted a new block exemption for liner   **3.084**
consortia, pursuant to the new enabling regulation: Regulation 906/2009, OJ 2009 L256/31: Vol II, App E7B. The Regulation came into force on 26 April 2010 when Regulation 823/2000 expired. The Regulation applies only to consortia insofar as they provide international liner shipping services from or to one or more EU ports and extends to all liner shipping cargo services, whether containerised or not. The list of exempted activities has been revised in order to reflect current market practices and hard-core restrictions such as price-fixing and market- or customer-sharing will still deprive the agreement of the benefit of the exemption. The market share threshold has been reduced from 35 per cent to 30 per cent and the method of its calculation has been clarified. The permissible restrictions on a member withdrawing from the consortium have also been revised.

(c) Withdrawal and disapplication

Withdrawal from individual agreements.   Fn 277. Reg 358/2003 has been   **3.086**
replaced by Reg 267/2010 (OJ 2010 L83/1: Vol II, App E27A). As with other block exemptions adopted after Reg 1/2003, the new Reg does not contain specific provision for withdrawal and the general provisions in Reg 1/2003 apply.

Withdrawal by Member State authorities.   Fn 283. Reg 1400/2002 has now   **3.087**
largely been replaced by Reg 461/2010, OJ L129/52: see updates to paragraphs 6.109 *et seq*, below. The new Reg does not contain provisions relating to its withdrawal either by the Commission or by the Member State authorities, since this is now provided for by Reg 1/2003: see Recitals (21) and (22) of Reg 461/2010.

3.089   **Disapplication of block exemption in respect of networks of agreements.**   For motor vehicle distribution see now Regulation 461/2010, OJ 2010 L129/52: Vol II, App C7B, Article 6. There is no time period specified before which such a withdrawal regulation can come into effect.

4. Article 53(3) of the EEA Agreement

3.093   **Current block exemptions.**   The updated details of this table are as follows:

	EU Regulation	EEA Annex XIV
Specialisation/production agreements	1218/2010	Point 6[1]
Research and development	1217/2010	Point 7[2]
Vertical restraints	330/2010	Point 2[3]
Motor vehicle distribution	461/2010	Point 4b[4]
Technology transfer	No change	Point 5
Insurance	267/2010	Point 15b[5]
Road, rail and inland waterway	169/2009	Point 10[6]
Liner conferences	Exemption abrogated	Point 11[7]
Liner consortia	906/2009	Point 11c[8]
Air passenger tariff conferences	Exemption abrogated	Point 11e[9]

[1] Text replaced by Decn 3/2011, OJ 2011 L93/32). See also the Horizontal Cooperation Guidelines.
[2] Text replaced by Decn 3/2011 (OJ 2011 L93/32).
[3] Text replaced by Decn 77/2010 (OJ 2010 L244/35).
[4] Text replaced by Decn 91/2010 (OJ 2010 L277/44).
[5] Text replaced by Decn 52/2010 (OJ 2010 L181/20).
[6] Text replaced by Decn 130/2010 (OJ 2011 L85/14).
[7] Text deleted by Decn 130/2010 (OJ 2011 L85/14).
[8] Text replaced by Decn 51/2010 (OJ 2010 L181/19).
[9] Text deleted by Decn 130/2010 (OJ 2011 L85/14).

4

MARKET DEFINITION

1. Introduction and Overview

(a) The concept of the relevant market

Risk of error in defining markets. For an example of the difficulty of conclusive **4.004** definition of the relevant market see COMP/38113 *Prokent-Tomra* [2009] 4 CMLR 101, para 46 where the Commission took a wider market definition as the basis for the decision since this favoured the undertaking alleged to be dominant. Tomra's appeal was dismissed and this point was not discussed: Case T-155/06 *Tomra Systems v Commission*, judgment of 9 September 2010.

(b) Relevance of market definition in EC competition law

Cartel cases. In Case T-199/08 *Ziegler SA v Commission*, judgment of 16 June **4.006** 2011 the GC held that although the Commission does not have to show that the agreement has an anti-competitive effect, there is an obligation to define the market where it is impossible, without such a definition, to determine whether the conduct is liable to affect trade between Member States and has as its object or effect the prevention, restriction or distortion of competition: para 45.

Anti-competitive effect under Article 81(1). Fn 25. These Guidelines have now **4.007** been replaced by the Horizontal Cooperation Guidelines 2011, OJ 2011 C11/1: Vol II, App C22. As to the relevance of market shares in this context see paras 39–47 of the Guidelines. The chapters dealing with particular kinds of agreement contain guidance about market share thresholds applied by the Commission.

Thresholds in block exemptions. See, eg Case T-427/08 *Confédération européenne* **4.009** *des associations d'horlogers-réparateurs (CEAHR) v Commission*, judgment of 15 December 2010. The GC held that the Commission had erred in its analysis of the relevant market when rejecting a complaint about the conduct of Swiss watch manufacturers refusing to supply spare parts to independent watch repairers. Further, if the Commission had analysed the market differently, it might not have concluded that the alleged agreements were likely to fall below the threshold of the vertical agreements block exemption: para 163.

Fn 28. The Motor Vehicle Block Exemption referred to in the footnote has now been largely replaced by Reg 461/2010, OJ 2010 L129/52: Vol II, App C7B although it still applies to agreements for the distribution of new motor vehicles until 31 May 2013. Apart from that, agreements in this sector are now governed by the new Vertical Restraints Block Exemption (Reg 330/2010): see the updates to paragraphs 6.109 *et seq*, below.

4.012   **Merger cases.** See, eg Case M.4691 *Schering-Plough/Organon Biosciences* (11 October 2007) where the Commission examined the competitive impact of the merger on over 200 relevant markets, noting that many animal health markets have quite a small size, sometimes as small as €10,000 (for example the market for monovalent tetanus vaccine for horses in Denmark) (para 50).

(c) Methodology for determining market definition

(i) Jurisprudence and guidelines

4.016   **The Relevant Market Notice.** Fn 47. See also the comments of the GC concerning the importance of guidance for transparency and enhancing legal certainty for the purposes of Article 7 ECHR: Case T-446/05 *Amann & Söhne GmbH v Commission*, judgment of 28 April 2010, [2010] 5 CMLR 789, para 137.

4.018   **Reconciling the various approaches to market definition.** Fn 57. The appeal referred to in the footnote was dismissed by the CJ: Case C-202/07P *France Télécom v Commission*, judgment of 2 April 2009. The CJ judgment did not consider issues concerning market definition. In Case M.5141 *KLM/Martinair* (17 December 2008) the Commission described the market survey carried out among passengers flying from Schiphol airport to the Caribbean: see paras 105 *et seq*.

(ii) Factors relevant to defining markets

4.020   **Potential competition.** See the discussion of whether Morgan Stanley was a potential competitor whose exclusion from the market by Visa's conduct was restrictive of competition in Case T-461/07 *Visa v Commission*, judgment of 14 April 2011 (on appeal from COMP/37860 *Morgan Stanley/Visa International and Visa Europe*, decn of 3 October 2007). The GC held that the Commission had to show that there had been 'real concrete possibilities' for Morgan Stanley to enter the relevant market and to compete with established undertakings. An expression of intention was relevant but not enough but it was also not necessary to show that the undertaking intended to enter the market in the near future: 'The mere fact of its existence may give rise to competitive pressure on the undertakings currently operating in that market, a pressure represented by the likelihood that a new competitor will enter the market if the market becomes more attractive': para 169. The GC rejected reliance on the definition of potential competition in the Vertical Restraints Guidelines, referring instead to the 2001 Guidelines on Horizontal Cooperation Agreements: para 171.

Market definitions are contextual.   In COMP/39181 *Candle Waxes*, decn of   **4.021**
1 October 2008, [2009] 5 CMLR 2441 the Commission stated that it is not obliged
to engage in any market definition when conducting cartel investigations. Instead,
it is the subject of the contacts between the companies involved in a cartel which
defines the products to which the infringement relates. It was therefore not surpris-
ing that such a definition may be different from a market definition used in a
merger control procedure. That the Commission may have defined a market in a
certain way in a merger decision has no relevance for a cartel decision: para 279. The
decision is on appeal, Cases T-540, 541, 543, 544, 548, 550, 551, 558, 562/08, not
yet decided.

'One-way' markets.   See Case T-321/05 *AstraZeneca v Commission*, judgment of   **4.022**
1 July 2010, [2010] 5 CMLR 1575 for an example of an asymmetrical market
analysis: para 97. The fact that a new product exercised competitive constraint on
the sales of the old product and hence was in the same relevant market as the old
product did not mean that the old product was in the same relevant market as the
new product. The judgment is on appeal: Case C-457/10P *AstraZeneca v Commission*,
not yet decided.

Analysis of two-sided demand markets.   In COMP/34579 *MasterCard MIF*   **4.022A**
charges, decn of 19 December 2007 the Commission considered how to define
markets in a case under Article 101 TFEU where there is a two-sided demand; in
that case, a demand on the part of merchants who honour the cards at their point
of sale and a demand on the part of cardholders who use the cards to make payments. There were also 'network' effects in the sense that both merchants and cardholders saw a benefit in having a larger network of users of the system. MasterCard
argued that in these circumstances there was in fact 'joint demand' on the part of
merchants and cardholders matched by a 'joint service' by acquiring and issuing
banks so that the product was in fact the whole card payment system. They argued
that the SSNIP test should thus be applied to the aggregate of the charges set for
merchants and cardholders to see how far that payment system competed with
other card payment systems, with cash and other payment methods. The
Commission rejected this analysis holding that such an approach was not appropriate for assessing the potential effect of the charge in question on competition *within*
the payment scheme and as between acquiring banks because it ignores the different levels of interaction and supply and demand within such a scheme (para 265).
Instead the Commission identified an upstream 'network market' where card
scheme owners compete to persuade financial institutions to join their scheme and
on which they provide services to such institutions. There were also the downstream
markets for acquiring merchants and issuing cards to cardholders. The downstream
acquirers market did not compete with cash or other payment methods (paras 285
and 307). On the issuing market, cash and cheques were held not to be sufficiently
substitutable on the demand side (paras 310 *et seq*). The Commission concluded
that the relevant market for assessing the MIF fees was the market for acquiring

payment cards: para 329. The case is on appeal: Case T-111/08, not yet decided. See also COMP/37860 *Morgan Stanley/Visa International and Visa Europe*, decn of 3 October 2007 where the Commission identified three relevant markets in a case under Article 101(1) about a rule excluding competitors from Visa network membership: (i) a market for network services, in which card networks (such as Visa or MasterCard) provide services to individual financial institutions; (ii) an 'issuing market' in which card issuers compete with each other to issue cards and provide card-related services to individuals; and (iii) an 'acquiring market' in which acquirers sign merchants for all of the services necessary for the merchant to accept cards: para 41. An appeal on other grounds was dismissed: Case T-461/07 *Visa v Commission*, judgment of 14 April 2011. See similarly, COMP/38606 *Groupement des Cartes Bancaires*, decn of 17 October 2007, 'the "two-sided" nature of an economic activity by no means signifies that the system concerned constitutes a single market': para 180 (on appeal Case T-491/07 *CB v Commission*, not yet decided).

On two-sided markets see also Case M.4523 *Travelport/Worldspan* (21 August 2007) (global distribution systems for travel services provide a service to airlines, hotels and other travel services providers on one side and to travel agents on the other). This case, and the theory of harm for two-sided markets are discussed in Vannini, 'Bargaining and two-sided markets: the case of Global Distribution Systems (GDS) in Travelport's acquisition of Worldspan' (2008) 2 Competition Policy Newsletter 43.

4.023 **Market definitions are not static.** For an interesting analysis of markets where a new product gradually replaces an existing product and results in a re-positioning of the old product see Case T-321/05 *AstraZeneca v Commission*, judgment of 1 July 2010, [2010] 5 CMLR 1575, paras 90 *et seq*. The GC held that the fact that the new product is introduced gradually does not necessarily mean that the old product exercises a competitive constraint on the new. The Commission was right therefore to treat the new product as occupying a separate relevant market from the old: on appeal Case C-457/10P *AstraZeneca v Commission*, not yet decided.

(iii) The SSNIP test

4.028 **Application of the SSNIP test in practice.** For a good example of the SSNIP test applied to establish the boundaries of a relevant downstream market see *Purple Parking Ltd v Heathrow Airport Ltd* [2011] EWHC 987 (Ch) (meet and greet airport parking in a separate market from short stay car park).

(iv) Limitations on the SSNIP test

4.029 **Circumstances where the SSNIP test cannot be applied.** See, eg the analysis of bidding data in Case M.4662 *Syniverse/BSG Wireless Business* (4 December 2007) (analysis of the participation of the data clearing houses in tenders and on the ranking data provided by customers was carried out on two datasets: one based on information received from the customers and the other one based on data received mainly from the parties) and Case M.4647 *AEE/Lentjes* (5 December 2007).

The 'cellophane fallacy'. In COMP/34579 *MasterCard MIF charges*, decn of **4.030** 19 December 2007 the Commission found that the SSNIP test was not a reliable indicator of what products should be included in the relevant market because there was a significant risk of the 'cellophane fallacy' applying in relation to charges imposed by acquirers on merchants in the MasterCard payment scheme: paras 286–287. The case is on appeal: Case T-111/08, not yet decided.

See also *Soda-Club*, WuW DE-R 2268, judgment of German Federal Supreme Court of 4 March 2008 in a case under Article 101 TFEU, holding that the SSNIP test there was only a guide and could not determine the market definition, in part because the prices charged by Soda-Club, a dominant company, could not be regarded as competitive market prices.

2. Product Market

(a) Demand-side substitution

Product characteristics and functional interchangeability. In Case T-446/05 **4.034** *Amann & Söhne GmbH v Commission*, judgment of 28 April 2010, [2010] 5 CMLR 789, the GC upheld the finding that thread used by the motor industry formed a separate market from other industrial thread. Undertakings in the automotive sector buy only thread which has specific intrinsic characteristics and which has been certified by those undertakings because of its special characteristics so that no demand substitutability existed: para 67.

There have been a number of cases recently where the Commission has considered the interchangeability of internet and non-internet retail distribution: in Case M.5996 *Thomas Cook/travel business of Co-operative Group/travel business of Midlands Co-operative Society* (6 January 2010) the Commission concluded that the competitive constraint of online distribution of holidays was not sufficiently strong to regard it as part of the same market as the distribution via bricks-and-mortar travel agencies: para 28; Case M.5838 *Bertelsmann/Planeta/Circulo* (5 July 2010), paras 32 and 33 (book retail); Case M.5721 *Otto/Primondo Assets* (16 February 2010) where the Commission found that home shopping on the internet and home shopping by catalogue were part of the same relevant market but that there was insufficient evidence to show that they were part of the same market as bricks-and-mortar shopping. The Commission did accept, however, that bricks-and-mortar shopping imposed some competitive constraint on home shopping.

In *Bookmakers' Afternoon Greyhound Services v Amalgamated Racing Ltd* [2009] EWCA Civ 750 the English Court of Appeal held that racecourses are not in competition with each other for the sale of rights to broadcast horse races to book-makers' premises. The Court took into account the fact that races held at British racecourses are deliberately scheduled by the British Horseracing Authority so as to take place at different times and not to coincide. Secondly, bookmakers have an incentive to show live coverage of as many British races as possible and to screen a succession of races throughout the day in order to maximise their betting turnover: paras 58 *et seq*. The case was therefore distinguishable from *UEFA Champions League* [2004] 4 CMLR 9.

4.035 **Switching data.** See the detailed analysis of switching in Case M.4731 *Google/DoubleClick* (11 March 2008) where the Commission identified three major steps that a customer would need to take before switching between ad serving providers and noted that perception of the switching process in terms of time and cost varied significantly among market players (para 138). The Commission found evidence that a large number of publishers and advertisers had switched from DoubleClick to other service providers (and vice versa) in the previous few years.

4.037 **Consumer preferences and perceptions.** The segmentation of spirits into markets for different spirit types has been confirmed by the Commission in a number of merger cases: see, eg Case M.5114 *Pernod Ricard/V&S Vin & Sprit* (17 July 2008) and the cases cited there. In that case the Commission also considered whether vodka should be further segmented according to price. The notifying party disputed this arguing that vodkas form a price continuum, meaning that there is a continuous distribution of prices with no clear break. They did acknowledge however that a limited number of brands sold at significantly higher prices may not form part of the price continuum. The Commission found that the econometric analysis available was inconclusive and left the question open.

See the description of 'conjoint analysis' in COMP/34579 *MasterCard MIF charges*, decn of 19 December 2007, para 292. Where a product has a range of attributes, conjoint analysis is used to determine which combinations of attributes the customer most values. The case is on appeal: Case T-111/08, not yet decided.

For a discussion of the merits of the consumer survey conducted by the Commission (among airline passengers and corporate customers), see Case T-342/07 *Ryanair Holdings plc v Commission*, judgment of 6 July 2010, [2011] 4 CMLR 245, paras 207 *et seq*.

Note also *Purple Parking Ltd v Heathrow Airport Ltd* [2011] EWHC 987 (Ch) where the High Court held that 'meet and greet' airport parking formed a separate relevant market from short stay parking because of the *perceived* convenience for customers, although in fact the journey time from the short stay car park to the terminal might be no longer than the journey from the meet and greet spot on the forecourt to the terminal: para 120.

As regards luxury goods see also Case T-427/08 *Confédération européenne des associations d'horlogers-réparateurs (CEAHR) v Commission*, judgment of 15 December 2010 where the GC noted that the essential function of a watch, namely to tell the time, is fully and accurately served by a watch costing around €25. Given that the price of watches sold by Swiss manufacturers was 60 to 160 times higher than the price of the cheapest watches, the GC found that the watches covered by the complaint were 'luxury/prestige watches': para 74. The GC went on to annul the rejection of the complaint because of the Commission's errors in analysing the markets for spare parts and for servicing of such watches.

See the interesting discussion of chocolate and candy purchasing habits in Case M.5644 *Kraft Foods/Cadbury* (6 January 2010), in particular the concept of the 'British heritage chocolate' which British consumers regard as 'extremely different' from continental chocolate, leading the Commission to conclude that there was low substitutability between the two: para 56.

Shock analysis or event evidence.   See, eg Case M.5141 *KLM/Martinair*   **4.040** (17 December 2008) where the Commission considered the effect on leisure travel of the introduction of a Dutch ticket tax at Schiphol airport: para 182.

Different absolute price levels.   In its decision of 27 February 2008 (COMP/   **4.042** 37792) fixing the periodic penalty payment for Microsoft's failure to offer non-patented interoperability information on reasonable terms, the Commission stressed that it was necessary to exclude from the assessment of the value of the technology the 'strategic value' stemming from Microsoft's market power in the client PC and work group server operating system markets: see paras 107 *et seq*. The decision is under appeal: Case T-167/08, not yet decided.

Critical loss analysis.   The Commission considered a critical loss analysis put for-   **4.044** ward by the parties in Case M.5141 *KLM/Martinair* (17 December 2008) and concluded that 'it appears more likely than not that any significant non transitory price increase on the part of the merged entity would be unprofitable': paras 296 *et seq*.

See also the analysis in Case M.4734 *INEOS/Kerling* (30 January 2008), paras 95 *et seq*. Having found that the results derived from econometric analysis were inconclusive, the Commission focused on other quantitative and qualitative evidence gathered during the market investigation to assess whether the estimated volumes needed to defeat a potential price increase by the merging parties could be provided by the Continental suppliers. The Commission therefore looked at the current level of imports, the role of importers, Continental suppliers' ability to expand their sales in the United Kingdom, transport costs and the future expansion of capacities: para 105. For an explanation of the Commission's methodology in conducting a critical loss analysis in this case see Amelio et al, 'Ineos/Kerling merger: an example of quantitative analysis in support of a clearance decision' (2008) 1 Competition Policy Newsletter 65.

(b) Supply-side substitution

4.052 **Use of supply-side substitution in practice.** The first step in considering supply substitution may be to examine the amount of spare capacity available to existing competitors. For example, in Case M.4525 *Kronospan/Constantia* (19 July 2007) (a case under the Merger Regulation) the Commission found that the main suppliers did not have significant spare capacity to increase supplies into the affected area and that expanding capacity would need considerable investment and a significant lead time (paras 60 and 61). The Commission also noted that capacity constraints are more likely to be important when goods are relatively homogeneous.

Supply-side substitutability was an important issue in Case M.4513 *Arjowiggins/M-Real Zanders' Reflect paper mill* (4 June 2008) concerning carbonless paper reels and sheets. The notifying party referred to the fact that the Relevant Market Notice specifically mentions the paper industry as an example of supply-side substitutability. The Commission noted that it is not simply a question of whether it is technically possible for suppliers to switch—marketing and distribution issues are also relevant. Supply-side substitutability is less likely in markets for heavily branded goods. The Commission adopted two techniques for analysing the market: 'correlation analysis' which measures the extent to which price movements of one product are associated with price movements of another product; and 'stationarity analysis' which uses sophisticated statistical tests to gauge whether the relative price of two products tends to revert to a constant value over time (that is to say, whether the relative price is 'stationary'); but ultimately the question was left open: paras 48 *et seq*.

See also the discussion in Case T-446/05 *Amann & Söhne GmbH v Commission*, judgment of 28 April 2010, [2010] 5 CMLR 789, para 88 (no supply-side substitutability between motor industry thread and other industrial thread); Case M.5599 *Amcor/Alcan* (15 December 2009) (flexible packaging for various end uses: paras 13 *et seq*).

4.057 **Supply-side substitution: shock analysis or event evidence.** In Case M.5046 *Friesland/Campina* (17 December 2008) the parties submitted evidence about the effect of a fire which had closed one of the parties' plants for the whole of 2005, leading to a significant reduction in production. However, the Commission concluded on the facts that the supply shock analysis was of limited informative value regarding the incentives of the merged entity to raise prices: para 799.

(c) Particular issues in determining the product market

(i) Connected markets

4.059 **Connected markets.** The GC carried out an interesting analysis of systems markets in Case T-427/08 *Confédération européenne des associations d'horlogers-réparateurs (CEAHR) v Commission*, judgment of 15 December 2010. The Commission had rejected a complaint from the CEAHR alleging anti-competitive conduct on the part of the manufacturers of Swiss watches because of their refusal to continue to supply spare parts to independent watch repairers. The Commission had concluded that the after-sales service market for luxury/prestige watches was an insignificant part of the general turnover achieved in the sale of luxury/prestige watches and that that 'luxury/prestige watches' were only a segment of the total watches market. The Commission had therefore decided that the market was very small and of limited economic importance. The GC noted that the spare parts market for primary products of a particular brand may not be a separate relevant market in two situations: first, if it is possible for a consumer to switch to spare parts manufactured by another producer; secondly, if it is possible for the consumer to switch to another primary product in order to avoid a price increase on the market for spare parts. As to the first issue, the Commission had failed to analyse whether the spare parts for one maker's watch were substitutable for the spare parts of another maker's watch: paras 89 and 90. As to the second issue, the Commission had not shown that consumers who already own luxury/prestige watches may reasonably switch to another primary product (ie buy another watch) in order to avoid a price increase for spare parts, so as to make that increase unprofitable. The factors raised by the Commission merely indicated a purely theoretical possibility of switching to another primary product and this is not a sufficient demonstration for the purposes of the definition of the relevant market. The GC also rejected the argument that this was a 'systems market' because, as the Commission had itself stated, the cost of servicing and repair is low over the lifetime of a luxury/prestige watch in comparison with the initial cost of the watch, with the result that it is unlikely that potential purchasers will calculate that cost over the life of the primary product.

Fn 167. For another example of a 'two sided market' see Case M.4523 *Travelport/ Worldspan* (21 August 2007) (global distribution systems for travel services provide a service to airlines, hotels and other travel services providers on one side and to travel agents on the other). See further new paragraph 4.022A, above.

Potential or hypothetical markets.   In COMP/38700 *Greek Lignite and Electricity*   **4.059A** *generation*, decn of 5 March 2008, [2009] 4 CMLR 495 the Commission considered whether PPC could be dominant in the market for the supply of lignite in Greece when no such market currently existed because PPC had the exclusive right to mine all available deposits of lignite to use in its own plants for generating electricity. The Commission referred to the statement of the CJ in Case C-418/01 *IMS Health* [2004] ECR I-5039, [2004] 4 CMLR 1543, [2004] All ER (EC) 813 to the effect that 'it is sufficient that a potential market or even a hypothetical market can be identified'. The Commission held that since the reason why there was no market for the sale of lignite was because PPC had already monopolised this activity and vertically integrated it, PPC could be held to be dominant in the market for the supply of lignite. The case is on appeal, Case T-169/08 *DEI v Commission*, not yet decided.

4.060   **Systems markets.**   See also Case T-427/08 *Confédération européenne des associa-tions d'horlogers-réparateurs (CEAHR) v Commission*, judgment of 15 December 2010, discussed in the update to paragraph 4.059, above.

In *Soda-Club* WuW DE-R 2268, judgment of 4 March 2008, the German Federal Supreme Court held that the supply of home water carbonation systems was dis-tinct from the market for refilling or replacing empty carbonators for such systems. Bottled sparkling water acted to constrain prices of the former systems, but once consumers had purchased a system, there was a distinct, secondary market for the carbonators.

Fn 178. See also COMP/39391 *Printers (EFIM complaint)*, decn of 20 May 2009, where the Commission rejected a complaint adopting similar reasoning to that relied on in *Pelikan/Kyocera* and *Info-Lab/Ricoh*. The case is on appeal: Case T-296/09, not yet decided.

4.061   **Market in licences or access to facilities.**   In Case M.5224 *EdF/British Energy* (22 December 2008) the Commission held that there is a separate product market akin to a real estate market for sites considered suitable for building new nuclear power stations: para 104. Clearance of the proposed merger was conditional on divestment of one of those sites.

Fn 182. In *Arriva Scotland West Limited v Glasgow Airport Ltd* [2011] CSOH 69 the Scottish Court of Session held that an allegation of abuse of a dominant position was arguable where Glasgow Airport had excluded Arriva's bus service from the airport's public transport zone following a tender exercise, but declined to grant interim relief. See also *Purple Parking Ltd v Heathrow Airport Ltd* [2011] EWHC 987 (Ch) where it was conceded for the purposes of the trial that Heathrow was dominant in the provision of access to Heathrow's facilities, including its roads and forecourts: para 73.

(ii) Branded goods

4.064   **Separate markets for branded and own label products.**   Note that this is a differ-ent question from the question whether the market for supplying branded prod-uct to retailers is different from the market for supplying own label product to retailers: see Case M.4842 *Danone/Numico* (31 October 2007), para 32 and the cases cited therein.

Fn 186. See also Case M.4533 *SCA/ P&G (European tissue business)* (5 September 2008) where the Commission held that the markets for the supply of consumer tissue products to retailers should be divided into (a) production and supply of manufacturer brands/branded products; and (b) production and supply of private labels/retailer brands and applied those distinctions separately to the three catego-ries of tissue products (toilet paper, kitchen towels, and handkerchiefs/facials). However, the Commission stressed that the competition at the retail level between the branded and unbranded products was crucial for the assessment of the case. Note that the Commission's market investigation established that 'toilet paper (as opposed to handkerchiefs/facials) is a "low emotion" commoditized product where brands do not play an important role': para 114.

(iii) In-house production

In-house production. In Case M.4731 *Google/DoubleClick* (11 March 2008) **4.065** the Commission found that the fact that major advertisers could and did opt to develop in-house technology for ad serving diminished the market position of DoubleClick substantially (para 178). The ability to develop in-house solutions imposed a constraint on the merged entity in two ways. First, publishers could develop an in-house solution for their own use in response to a price increase by third party ad serving tool providers. Secondly, in-house solutions could ultimately also be marketed and sold to third parties as well (that is to say customers could become competitors) as had in fact occurred in the relevant market. See also Case M.4781 *Norddeutsche Affinerie/Cumerio* (23 January 2008) where the Commission found that copper shapes were produced for selling on the merchant market and also for internal processing into downstream semi-finished copper products. In fact only 17 per cent of all copper shapes produced were sold on the merchant market, the rest were used in-house (para 130). The Commission found that the ability of users to increase production of copper shapes either for their own in-house use or for sale on the merchant market acted as a constraint on the merged entity: para 152.

In *Independent Media Support Ltd v OFCOM* [2008] CAT 13, the UK Competition Appeal Tribunal considered paragraph 98 of the Commission's Guidelines on Vertical Restraints which states that in assessing market share, in-house production should be left out of account.

(v) Procurement markets

Supply and procurement markets. In Case M.5224 *EdF/British Energy* **4.067** (22 December 2008) the Commission found that there was a market in the procurement of nuclear fuel: para 127.

Fn 199. The appeal against the *Sovion/HMG* merger clearance has been dismissed: Case T-151/05 *Nederlandse Vakbond Varkenshouders (NVV) v Commission* [2009] ECR II-1219, [2009] 5 CMLR 1613.

(vi) Technology and innovation markets

Technology markets. Fn 200. See also Case M.5675 *Syngenta/Monsanto sun-* **4.068** *flower seed business* (17 November 2010) (upstream market for the trading of sun-flower varieties constitutes a separate product market from the commercialisation of sunflower seed hybrids).

Fn 202. See now the Horizontal Cooperation Guidelines 2011, OJ 2011 C11/1: Vol II, App C22 which replace the 2001 Guidelines referred to. Technology markets are discussed in paras 116–122 of the Guidelines.

3. Geographic Market

(a) Overview

4.070   **Definition of the relevant product market.**   For a recent case which turned on the proper definition of the geographic market see Case T-151/05 *Nederlandse Vakbond Varkenshouders (NVV) v Commission* [2009] ECR II-1219, [2009] 5 CMLR 1613, concerning the merger of two Dutch pig slaughterhouses. An association of Dutch pig farmers challenged the clearance of the merger on the basis (among other arguments) that the Commission had erred in finding that German slaughterhouses competed with Dutch slaughterhouses for the business of Dutch pig farmers within a 150 km radius of the main cities of the pig breeding areas of the Netherlands. The GC upheld the Commission's decision, holding that 'the fundamental question for the purposes of defining the geographic market in the present case is therefore whether, if there were to be a small but sustainable reduction in the purchase price for pigs or sows in the areas concerned, the customers of the parties to the concentration and, in particular, the pig breeders, would switch to slaughterhouses located elsewhere' (para 122). The GC upheld the findings that (i) differences in the weight of German and Dutch pigs or in their type or breed did not preclude Dutch farmers using German slaughterhouses; (ii) fluctuations in the prices paid for pig meat in the two countries had a direct effect on the scale of exports; (iii) the effect of disease outbreaks leading to temporary bans on exports did not restrict the market to a national market because after such bans were lifted, exports quickly resumed their previous levels; and (iv) transport costs are not decisive inasmuch as their impact on the price of pigs for slaughter is marginal. As regards the use of 150 km radius in defining the geographic market, the decisive question was whether suppliers of pigs for slaughter would be willing to transport their animals over a distance of 150 km to competing slaughterhouses if there were to be a small but sustainable reduction in the purchase price for pigs, with the result that such a drop in prices would not be profitable for the body which emerged from the concentration. The fact that the majority of pigs for slaughter are usually transported over distances of less than 150 km did not therefore constitute, in itself, a decisive factor for defining the relevant market.

4.071   **Methodology.**   For an example, see Case M.4734 *INEOS/Kerling* (30 January 2008) where the geographic market definition for a certain kind of PVC was crucial for the assessment of the merger in particular with respect to the United Kingdom, as the position of the parties was substantially different depending on whether the market was national or wider than national. The Commission noted that certain customers indicated that concerns about flexibility and reliability of supply, short lead times and precise timing of deliveries made it unlikely that they would source product from outside the United Kingdom. To determine whether these concerns were justified, the Commission carried out an assessment of the sourcing and switching patterns of these customers and a quantitative and qualitative analysis to assess to what extent Continental suppliers would be in a position to defeat a hypothetical price increase in the United Kingdom (the SSNIP test). The analysis was supported by the qualitative evidence of the current level of imports, transport costs and reported planned capacity expansions compared with demand growth, and the assessment of barriers to expansion in the United Kingdom: see paras 83 *et seq*. The Commission concluded that the evidence showed that the market was wider than just the United Kingdom.

Geographic market definition in the context of the removal of barriers to **4.072** **trade.** In COMP/38700 *Greek Lignite and Electricity generation*, decn of 5 March 2008, [2009] 4 CMLR 495 the Commission noted that it had usually defined the geographic market for the wholesale supply of electricity as a national one. But in the case of Greece where only the part of the territory that was covered by the interconnector system had been opened up to competition so far as retail supply was concerned, the geographic market was held to be the territory of the interconnecter system: para 172. The case is on appeal: Case T-169/08 *DEI v Commission*, not yet decided.

(b) Demand-side substitution

Transport costs. Where transport costs are high relative to the value of the prod- **4.073** uct, the geographic market may be defined in terms of distance from the individual production plant: see, eg Case M.4525 *Kronospan/Constantia* (19 July 2007) (shipment data from suppliers and customers showed that the vast majority of shipments of raw particle board were within a 500 km radius of the plant regardless of national boundaries). This meant that national market shares were imperfect indicators of post-merger market power, as national boundaries did not necessarily reflect the competitive interaction between plants (paras 26 *et seq*). By contrast a significant amount of coated particle board was shipped more than 1000 km from the plant. See similarly Case T-151/05 *Nederlandse Vakbond Varkenshouders (NVV) v Commission* [2009] ECR II-1219, [2009] 5 CMLR 1613, where the territory within 150 km radius of the main pig breeding areas of the Netherlands was found to be the relevant geographic market, even if the radius covered territory across the border in Germany.

Pricing data. In Case M.4980 *ABF/GBI Business* (23 September 2008) the **4.074** Commission found that there was a striking difference between trends in the average price of compressed yeast in Portugal compared with trends in neighbouring Spain, in particular that a large price level drop which occurred in Portugal did not seem to have had any influence on the Spanish prices. This indicated that the dynamics of the market were different in these two Member States and that the competitive interplay between producers and demand was to a large degree independent: para 76.

4.075   **Differences in prices: further considerations.**   **Fn 224.** The appeals referred to were dismissed save for an adjustment to penalty: Case T-57/01, judgment of 17 December 2009; Case T-66/01, judgment of 25 June 2010.

4.076   **National preferences and cultural features.**   See also COMP/38113 *Prokent-Tomra* [2009] 4 CMLR 101, paras 47–55 where the Commission considered the geographic market for reverse vending machines for recycling empty containers. The Commission found that the existence and volume of demand in any country was very dependent on the existence of national legislation relating to waste management in general and deposit systems for used drink containers in particular. Further, the prevalence and volumes of particular drink containers in the individual countries, as they result from regulatory requirements, from the choices made by the beverage industry, or from retail sector or consumer preferences, played a decisive role. For these and other reasons the Commission concluded that the market was national in scope. Tomra's appeal was dismissed and this point was not discussed: Case T-155/06 *Tomra Systems v Commission*, judgment of 9 September 2010.

See also the discussion in Case T-151/05 *Nederlandse Vakbond Varkenshouders (NVV) v Commission* [2009] ECR II-1219, [2009] 5 CMLR 1613 of the weight and genetic differences between Dutch and German pigs; and the discussion of geographic market definition for the sale of books in Case M.5838 *Bertelsmann/Planeta/Circulo* (5 July 2010), para 28.

4.079   **Shock analysis or event evidence.**   In Case M.4734 *INEOS/Kerling* (30 January 2008) the Commission considered a 'natural experiment' in the form of an outage in one of the parties' United Kingdom plants. The Commission noted that this type of natural experiment, although it does not in itself provide sufficiently conclusive evidence with respect to the geographic market definition, provides for a picture of the flows of the product between regions during an unexpected event, namely the extent to which a shortage in supply is counterbalanced by local and external producers. This in turn can constitute an indication of the patterns of supply and demand within a national market, should production output in that market be restricted or the price for the product be increased on a longer term basis: para 140. The Commission concluded that the assessment of Ineos' outage in mid 2004 therefore suggested that, apart from Kerling, importers were in a position to react swiftly to any attempts by Ineos to reduce output so as to increase prices. This provided evidence that both Ineos and Kerling were constrained by importers, even in the event of an output shortage, which in turn suggested that the market was wider than the United Kingdom: para 149.

4. Temporal Market

Existence of temporal dimension.   For a case in which the temporal dimension of   **4.089**
market demand was expressly addressed see COMP/38113 *Prokent-Tomra* [2009]
4 CMLR 101, paras 56, 287, 343 and 344, concerning the market for reverse vending machines for recycling empty containers. The Commission noted that the volume of sales increased considerably during 'key years' which occurred when national
legislation mandating recycling of, or deposit systems for, used drinks containers
was introduced. In one Member State a key year also occurred on the introduction
of the euro when many customers chose to renew their equipment. Tomra's appeal
was dismissed and this point was not discussed: Case T-155/06 *Tomra Systems v
Commission*, judgment of 9 September 2010.

5. Market Definitions in Particular Sectors

Introduction.   In relation to the segmentation of the market in IT services see, eg   **4.091**
Case M.5301 *Cap Gemini/BAS* (13 October 2008) where the Commission referred
to a report produced by the Gartner Group, an independent industry analyst com-
pany which specialised in the IT industry: paras 9 and 10 and the other cases cited
therein. There have been other recent mergers in the IT sector in which the
Commission has had to consider the segmentation of the relevant markets: see, eg
Case M.5984 *Intel/McAfee* (26 January 2011) and Case M.5529 *Oracle Corporation/
Sun Microsystems* (21 January 2010).

Pharmaceuticals.   In Case M.5253 *Sanofi-Aventis/Zentiva* (4 February 2009) the   **4.092**
Commission noted that competition at the more detailed molecule level was particularly relevant in a case where the producer of an originator drug acquires an
important, or even the sole, producer of its generic equivalent on the market. The
role of the molecule level in the market analysis is important in those cases where
(i) doctors may, or are even required to, prescribe medicines using the international
non-proprietary name (INN) of the molecule rather than by brand name; (ii) reimbursement is based on the price of a generic version of the originator medicine; and
(iii) pharmacies may, or are required to, offer the patient the opportunity to substitute an originator medicine with a generic equivalent. The Commission also distinguished in this case between OTC and prescription-only medicines. In Case
M.5295 *Teva/Barr* (19 December 2008) the Commission considered a merger
between two companies which specialised in producing generic pharmaceuticals.
Due to the greater importance of competition between drugs based on the same
molecule in markets where generics were available—in particular for drugs aimed
at serious illnesses and procured by hospitals—the Commission analysed the
markets affected by the notified operation not only at the ATC3 level but also at

molecule level: para 18. The merger was approved conditional upon certain divestments. See more recently Case M.5661 *Abbott/Solvay Pharmaceuticals* (11 February 2010); Case M.5865 *Teva/Ratiopharm* (3 August 2010) (merger created largest generics manufacturer in the EEA; Commission noted that in older cases involving originator pharmaceutical companies, the third level, referred to as ATC3, which allows medicines to be grouped in most cases according to their therapeutic indications, has generally been taken as the starting point for market definition. However, in recent cases involving generic companies the Commission has tended to identify competition issues more often at the molecule level, at the ATC4 level, or on the basis of a group of molecules: para 12). See also the discussion of 'galenic forms' in, eg Case M.5778 *Novartis/Alcon* (9 August 2010), paras 18 *et seq*.

In Case T-321/05 *AstraZeneca v Commission*, judgment of 1 July 2010, [2010] 5 CMLR 1575, the GC analysed the markets for stomach ulcer treatments where a new product was gradually replacing or causing the re-positioning of an older product. The Court considered the impact of the prescribing habits of doctors on the development of the markets: see paras 98 *et seq*. The case is on appeal: Case C-457/10P *AstraZeneca v Commission*, not yet decided.

For market definition in the animal health sector see Case M.4691 *Schering-Plough/Organon Biosciences* (11 October 2007) where the Commission referred to three core areas, namely (i) biological (vaccines); (ii) pharmaceuticals; and (iii) medicinal feed additives, each containing hundreds of relevant markets; also Case M.5476 *Pfizer/Wyeth* (17 July 2009).

See now also the Horizontal Cooperation Guidelines 2011, OJ 2011 C11/1: Vol II, App C22, paras 119 *et seq* which discuss the analysis of the relevant market for the purposes of assessing R&D cooperation, particularly in the pharmaceutical industry. The Commission refers to 'R&D poles' which compete by aiming to develop substitutable products in a similar time frame. Credible competing poles to the goal being pursued by the R&D cooperation of the parties need to be identified and assessed. This is particularly relevant in the pharmaceutical industry where innovation is structured in such as way as to identify competing poles at an early stage. Five examples of different R&D arrangements are given and analysed, two of which concern pharmaceutical products.

Fn 269. The issue of market definition was not raised in the appeal Cases C-501/06P, etc, *GlaxoSmithKline Services Unlimited v Commission*, judgment of 6 October 2009.

Fn 271. See also Case M.5778 *Novartis/Alcon* (9 August 2010), para 12.

4.094 **Telecommunications: the Commission's Recommendation on Relevant Markets.** The 2003 Recommendation referred to in this paragraph has been replaced by the 2007 Recommendation, 2007 OJ L344/65. This Recommendation sets out the three cumulative criteria to be applied in determining whether a market is one in which *ex ante* regulation may be warranted, namely (a) the presence of high and non-transitory barriers to entry which may be of a structural, legal, or regulatory nature; (b) a market structure which does not tend towards effective competition within the relevant time horizon; and (c) the insufficiency of competition law alone adequately to address the market failure(s) concerned. The Annex to the Recommendation now lists only seven such markets identified by the Commission on the basis of those criteria. When considering whether SMP exists in markets not included in the Annex to the Recommendation, the Member States must apply those three criteria.

For the application of this Recommendation in the merger context see, eg Case M.5148 *Deutsche Telekom/OTE* (2 October 2008) and the cases cited therein.

Broadcasting and television.   In COMP/38698 *CISAC*, decn of 16 July 2008,   **4.096** [2009] 4 CMLR 577, the Commission identified a number of separate relevant product markets in a case concerning bilateral reciprocal licensing arrangements between collecting societies licensing music performance rights. The Commission noted that collective management of copyright covers different activities corresponding to many different relevant product markets: paras 48 *et seq*. The case is on appeal Cases T-398, 410, 411, 413–422, 425, 432, 434, 442, 451/08, not yet decided.

The Commission analysed the various markets in broadcasting and programme acquisition in Case M.5121 *News Corp/Premiere* (26 June 2008). However, many aspects of market definition, such as whether there were separate markets for feature films and other TV content did not need to be decided since the merger did not raise any competition concerns.

Transport routes.   The GC upheld the Commission's approach to analysing the   **4.097** relevant market by reference to airport or city pairs and the use of the 100 km or one hour driving time benchmark in defining the catchment areas of the airports in Case T-342/07 *Ryanair Holdings plc v Commission*, judgment of 6 July 2010, [2011] 4 CMLR 245, para 112.

In Case M.5403 *Lufthansa/British Midland* (14 May 2009) the Commission treated air and rail services between London and Brussels as operating in the same market: paras 63 and 64. In considering this concentration, the Commission adopted the 'point of origin/point of destination' approach to market definition and then considered in relation to each city pair which airports or other services were substitutable and whether indirect flights were substitutable for direct flights for long-haul pairs. See also Case M.5141 *KLM/Martinair* (17 December 2008), paras 122 *et seq*; Case M.5747 *Iberia/British Airways* (14 July 2010); Case M.5830 *Olympic Air/Aegean Airlines* (26 January 2011) (merger prohibited where it would have led to a quasi monopoly on routes where the airlines currently competed head to head: the case is on appeal: Case T-202/11 *Aeroporia Aigaiou Aeroporiki v Commission*, not yet decided, where one of the grounds is that the Commission erred in defining the market as time sensitive passengers only).

See now also COMP/39596 *BA/AA/IB*, decn of 14 July 2010 where the Commission considered point to point markets and the distinction between premium and non-premium markets in the context of an airline alliance.

The same principles regarding point to point markets and a distinction between time sensitive and non-time sensitive passengers were discussed in respect of cross-Channel rail routes: Case M.5655 *SNCF/LCR/Eurostar* (17 June 2010) and the earlier *Eurostar* case cited therein.

4.098 **Air transport: business and leisure passengers; cargo.** In Case T-342/07 *Ryanair Holdings plc v Commission*, judgment of 6 July 2010, [2011] 4 CMLR 245, the GC upheld the Commission's finding, based on survey evidence, that the distinction between time sensitive and non-time sensitive passengers was not relevant in the context of a proposed merger between two low cost airlines: para 107.

In Case M.5403 *Lufthansa/British Midland* (14 May 2009) the Commission confirmed that point of origin/point of destination analysis is not appropriate for air cargo markets (paras 18 *et seq*). As concerns intercontinental routes, the corresponding catchment areas broadly correspond to continents, at least for those continents where local infrastructure is adequate to allow for onward connections. For continents (eg Africa) where local infrastructure is less developed, the catchment area corresponds to the countries of destination. Market definition must also take account of the fact that cargo air transport is by nature unidirectional as the demand on each end of the route differs substantially. On air cargo markets see also Case M.5141 *KLM/Martinair* (17 December 2008), paras 28 *et seq* (which also considered the separate markets for the wholesale supply of seats to tour operators); Case M.5747 *Iberia/British Airways* (14 July 2010).

The distinction between business and leisure may extend to the market for the vessels themselves: see Case M.4956 *STX/Aker Yards* (5 May 2008) and the discussion of the distinction between ferries, cruise ships, and other commercial ships.

5

COMMON HORIZONTAL AGREEMENTS

1. Introduction

Other horizontal agreements: Commission Notice.   The 2001 Guidelines have   **5.004**
been replaced by the Guidelines on horizontal cooperation agreements issued in
2011: OJ 2011 C11/1: Vol II, App C22. They accompanied the two new block
exemption regulations for research and development agreements (Regulation
1217/2010, OJ 2010 L335/36: Vol II, App C7C) and for specialisation agreements
(Regulation 1218/2010, OJ L335/43: Vol II, App C7D).

2. Cartels and other Covert Conduct

(a) The Commission's approach to cartel activity

Increasing focus of law enforcement.   The Commission has established a settle-   **5.006**
ment procedure intended to enable it to handle cartel cases more quickly and efficiently. Regulation 773/2004 has been amended by Regulation 622/2008, OJ
2008 L171/3, [2008] 5 CMLR 1032 to incorporate this procedure as Article 10a
of Regulation 773/2004. The Commission has also issued a Notice on the Conduct
of Settlement Procedures in cartel cases, explaining how the procedure will operate:
see OJ 2008 C167/1, [2008] 5 CMLR 1055. The new settlement procedure introduced by Regulation 622/2008 is discussed in new paragraphs 13.113A–13.113D,
below.

In 2007 the Commission took eight decisions condemning cartels and imposed fines
totalling €3.3 billion; in 2008 it took seven decisions and imposed fines totalling
€2.3 billion; in 2009 it took six decisions and imposed fines totalling €1.5 billion
and in 2010 it took seven decisions and imposed fines totalling €2.8 billion.

(b) Anatomy of a classic cartel

How and why cartels form: *Choline Chloride*.   The appeal in the *Choline Chloride*   **5.008**
case mentioned in fn 18 has now been decided: Cases T-101&111/05 *BASF AG*

and UCB SA v Commission [2007] ECR II-4949, [2008] 4 CMLR 347. The GC quashed the Commission's finding that the global and European aspects of the cartel were a single continuous infringement (paras 208 *et seq*). The result of this was that the global cartel was time barred and the fine that had been imposed for the years covered only by the global cartel was quashed. Unfortunately for BASF, the reduction in fine it had been given because of its cooperation with the investigation of the global cartel was also quashed so that BASF's fine in fact increased as a result of its success on this ground of appeal: para 222.

5.009   *Choline Chloride*: **the global aspect of the cartel.   Fn 20.** The pending appeal mentioned has now been decided: Case C-511/06P *Archer Daniels Midland v Commission (citric acid)*, judgment of 9 July 2009 and related solely to the fine imposed.

5.011   *Choline Chloride*: **the Commission's findings.**   The appeal in the *Choline Chloride* case mentioned in fn 21 has now been decided: Cases T-101&111/05 *BASF AG and UCB SA v Commission* [2007] ECR II-4949, [2008] 4 CMLR 347. The GC quashed the Commission's finding that the global and European aspects of the cartel were a single continuous infringement.

(c) Ancillary restrictions supporting cartel activity

5.012   **Restrictions ancillary to the main anti-competitive restrictions.**   For a more recent example of information exchange and customer allocation in support of a price-fixing cartel see COMP/38638 *Butadiene Rubber and Emulsion Styrene Butadiene Rubber*, decn of 29 November 2006, [2009] 4 CMLR 421 (various appeals determined on other grounds in judgments delivered by the GC on 13 July 2011).

5.013   **Restrictions on advertising.**   Note that in COMP/39579 *Consumer detergents*, decn of 13 April 2010, OJ 2011 C193/14, the Commission treated restrictions on promotional activity as a form of price collusion.

Fn 30. The appeal in Case T-68/04 *SGL Carbon AG v Commission* has been decided: [2008] ECR II-2511, [2009] 4 CMLR 7 but related to fine only. A further appeal was dismissed: Case C-564/08P, judgment of 12 November 2009.

5.014   **Cartel 'consultancy'.**   The appeal by the trade association fined in *Organic Peroxides* for providing administrative and secretarial services to the cartel was dismissed by the GC: Case T-99/04 *AC-Treuhand AG v Commission* [2008] ECR II-1501, [2008] 5 CMLR 962. The GC noted that the Courts had given a broad meaning to the term 'agreement between undertakings' and that a contextual and teleological approach to interpreting Article 101 TFEU confirmed that the notions of a cartel and of an undertaking which is the perpetrator of an infringement are conceptually independent of any distinction based on the sector or the market on which the undertakings concerned are active. The principle of *nullum crimen, nulla* *poena sine lege* did not preclude the gradual clarification of legislative provisions through developing case law. Further, the GC held that it had been reasonably foreseeable that a consultancy firm would infringe Article 101 where it contributed actively and intentionally to a cartel between producers active on a market other than that on which the consultancy firm itself operates. On the facts, the GC upheld the Commission's finding of liability.

See also COMP/39181 *Candle Waxes*, decn of 1 October 2008, [2009] 5 CMLR 2441 where the Commission rejected, on the evidence, a claim by one company that it had only attended the legitimate, technical part of the meetings: paras 222 *et seq*. The decision is on appeal, Cases T-540, 541, 543, 544, 548, 550, 551, 558, 562/08, not yet decided.

3. Agreements on Prices and Trading Conditions

(a) Price-fixing

(i) *Generally*

Price-fixing prohibited.   For an example of a straightforward horizontal, price-fixing agreement see COMP/38432 *Professional Videotape* [2008] 5 CMLR 122 (price increases agreed and, when market circumstances would not allow further price increases, the parties agreed to maintain prices unchanged at the previously agreed level, or at least to prevent them 'from tumbling down uncontrollably' (para 127)). **5.015**

Fn 37. The appeals in *Industrial copper tubes* (all relating to fine only) were dismissed by the GC in three judgments given on 6 May 2009: Case T-127/04 *KME Europa Metal* [2009] ECR II-1167, [2009] 5 CMLR 1574 (on further appeal C-272/09P, not yet decided); Case T-122/04 *Outokumpu* [2009] ECR II-1135, [2009] 5 CMLR 1553; Case T-116/04 *Wieland-Werke AG* [2009] ECR II-1087, [2009] 5 CMLR 1517.

What constitutes price-fixing.   In Case C-8/08 *T-Mobile Netherlands BV v Raad van bestuur van de Nederlandse Mededingingsautoriteit*, judgment of 4 June 2009, the CJ confirmed that a concerted practice can have the object of price-fixing even if it does not relate to consumer end prices. Thus where the concerted practice concerned the payments made by mobile phone operators to phone dealers it could be an 'object' infringement even though there might not be a direct link between the practice and consumer prices. Article 101 TFEU is designed not only to protect the immediate interests of individual competitors or consumers but also to protect the structure of the market and thus competition as such: para 38. **5.016**

See also COMP/39188 *Bananas*, decn of 15 October 2008 where the Commission found that regular bilateral phone calls between importers of bananas took place in which they discussed price setting factors, that is factors relevant for setting of quotation prices for the upcoming week and/or discussed or disclosed their views about price trends and/or indications of quotation prices for the upcoming week for the Northern European region. Such conduct, which was monitored by subsequent disclosure of quoted prices, led to coordination of their quotation prices. Note that the Commission also held that even if the parties did not discuss their particular prices, discussions or disclosure of expectations as to the 'development' or 'evolution' of prices were liable to reveal to competitors their intentions concerning future pricing decisions for setting of quotation prices. Viewed in their context, the discussions and disclosures on either 'price trends' or specifically on quotation prices had the object of coordinating the setting of quotation prices by the parties: para 262. This led the Commission to find 'a concerted practice which concerned the fixing of prices': para 289. The decision is under appeal: Cases T-587&588/08, not yet decided.

Note that in COMP/39579 *Consumer detergents*, decn of 13 April 2010, OJ 2011 C193/14, the Commission treated restrictions on promotional activity as a form of price collusion.

Fn 41. The appeal in Case T-68/04 *SGL Carbon AG v Commission* has been decided: [2008] ECR II-2511, [2009] 4 CMLR 7 but related to fine only. A further appeal was dismissed: Case C-564/08P, judgment of 12 November 2009.

Fn 44. In Case T-384/06 *IBP Ltd v Commission*, judgment of 24 March 2011 the GC held that concerted action as to the percentage of an increase in packaging costs that would be passed on to customers rather than absorbed by the manufacturer was an infringement: para 67.

Fn 47. See also COMP/39510 *Ordre National des Pharmaciens en France (ONP)*, decn of 8 December 2010 (professional association prohibiting discounts of more than 10 per cent condemned).

5.017 **Price recommendations.** **Fn 64.** Reg 358/2003 has been replaced by Reg 267/2010 (OJ 2010 L83/1: Vol II, App E27A); see the updates to paragraphs 12.170 *et seq*, below.

5.018 **Price transparency.** See also the Commission's analysis in the Horizontal Cooperation Guidelines, OJ 2011 C11/1: Vol II, App C22, paras 63 and 94.

5.019 **Price agreements among distributors.** **Fn 69.** The appeal in the *French Beef* case was dismissed: Cases C-101&110/07P *Coop de France bétail et viande and FNSEA v Commission* [2008] ECR I-10193, [2009] 4 CMLR 743.

(iii) Resale and purchase prices

5.025 **Resale price maintenance for books.** Following on from the commitments given to settle the *Sammelrevers* case see now Case C-531/07 *Fachverband der Buch- und Medienwirtschaft v LIBRO Handelsgesellschaft* [2009] ECR I-3717. The Austrian court requested a preliminary ruling in the course of proceedings brought by an Austrian publishers trade association to enforce a minimum price set for retail books in Austria. That price was set pursuant to Austrian legislation allowing the association to fix minimum prices for books. The defendant was a book retailer which was importing books from Germany and selling them in Austria at the minimum retail price fixed for the book under the corresponding German law, that price being lower than the minimum price fixed in Austria. The CJ held that the legislation fell within Article 34 TFEU and was not justified under Article 36 TFEU (formerly Articles 28 and 30 EC). Referring to Article 167 TFEU (formerly Article 151 EC) the CJ noted that the protection of books as cultural objects can be considered as an overriding requirement in the public interest capable of justifying measures restricting the free movement of goods, on condition that those measures are appropriate for achieving the objective fixed and do not go beyond what is necessary to achieve it. However, the Court held that the objective of the protection of books as cultural objects can be achieved by measures less restrictive for the importer, for example by allowing the latter or the foreign publisher to fix a retail price for the Austrian market which takes the conditions of that market into account.

Note that the French Autorité de la Concurrence has recommended that the resale price maintenance arrangements in place for hard copy books should not be adapted to apply to digital books: ECN Brief 2/2010, p3.

Fn 92. Following the Council Resolution referred to in the footnote see also Council Resolution on the application of national fixed book-price systems, OJ 2001 C73/5.

Fixing of purchase prices. **Fn 96.** The appeals from the *Spanish Raw Tobacco* decision were decided in a series of judgments: Case T-24/05 *Alliance One, Standard Commercial Tobacco and Trans-Continental Leaf Tobacco v Commission*, judgment of 27 October 2010 (attribution of liability to one of the parent companies annulled; appeals otherwise dismissed); Case T-29/05 *Deltafina v Commission*, judgment of 8 September 2010 (appeal dismissed save for reduction in fine, on further appeal Case C-537/10P, not yet decided); Case T-33/05 *Cetarsa v Commission*, judgment of 3 February 2011 (reduction in fine, on further appeal C-181/11P, not yet decided); and Case T-37/05 *World Wide Tobacco España v Commission*, judgment of 8 March 2011 (reduction in fine for cooperation: on appeal Case C-240/11P, not yet decided); Case T-38/05 *Agroexpansión* and Case T-41/05 *Dimon* are not yet decided.   **5.027**

Fn 97. Appeals dismissed in Case T-25/06 *Alliance One International v Commission*, judgment of 9 September 2011; and Case T-12/06 *Deltafina v Commission*, judgment of 9 September 2011.

Fn 98. The appeal in the *French Beef* case was dismissed: Cases C-101&110/07P *Coop de France bétail et viande and FNSEA v Commission* [2008] ECR I-10193, [2009] 4 CMLR 743.

(iv) Application of Article 81(3)

5.028   **Relevance of state of the industry.**   A further appeal in the *French Beef* case was dismissed: Cases C-101&110/07P *Coop de France bétail et viande and FNSEA v Commission* [2008] ECR I-10193, [2009] 4 CMLR 743.

Fn 107. The appeal against the readoption of the decision condemning the steel beams cartel has been decided: Case T-405/06 *Arcelor Mittal v Commission* [2009] ECR II-771, [2010] 4 CMLR 787. The decision was annulled as against two of the addressees on the basis that the decision was adopted outside the limitation period (further appeals by the applicant and by the Commission dismissed: Cases C-201&216/09P *ArcelorMittal v Commission*, judgment of 29 March 2011).

(c) Professional services

5.039   **Professional services: other restrictions.**   The Portuguese Competition Authority found that the professional body for certified accountants had abused its dominant position by reserving a third of the obligatory training requirements to itself, and setting the criteria for the admission of other training bodies and the approval of their training courses. The case is on appeal to the Lisbon Commercial Court: *Association of Certified Accountants (OTOC)* ECN Brief 4/2010, p2.

5.040   **Professional services: current practice.**   The CJ has recently reiterated that in the absence of an agreement between undertakings, the competition rules do not apply to legislation adopted by a Member States prohibiting advertising: Case C-446/05 *Doulamis* [2008] ECR I-1377.

The recommendation of a fee scale by a professional association, although detailed and followed by the members, may not be a restriction by object when there would not in any event be appreciable price-related competition between those professionals. The Dutch Trade and Industry Appeals Tribunal thus upheld the quashing of a decision by the Dutch Competition Authority concerning the annual recommendations published jointly by the three Dutch associations of psychologists and psychotherapists concerning fees that were not covered by standard health insurance. The Authority had failed to consider whether the recommendations were likely to have an adverse impact on competition, in particular since the choice of psychologist was often made by the patient's general practitioner and based on the professional qualifications and experience of the psychologist, his or her availability and the urgency of treatment, and not on the level of fee; and even where patients approached a psychologist directly for treatment, the associations argued that fees were not relevant to the selection of specialist. This particular economic context meant that there was insufficient basis to condemn the recommendations as restrictions by object. *NMa v NIP, NVVP and LVE* (LJN: BF8820) judgment of 6 October 2008.

Fn 142. In the Hungarian Bar Association case, the Budapest Metropolitan District Court modified the GVH's decision, holding that the rules did not impose a complete ban on advertising and that some of the restrictions were proportionate to the need to preserve ethical standards in the profession (eg the prohibition of all internet advertising could not be justified but the prohibition on reference to names of clients was upheld): Case No. 2.K.30.863/2009, judgment of 29 October 2009.

(d) Banking and payment services

Credit cards and payment systems.   See also the analysis of the different kinds of credit and debit cards available and the definition of relevant product markets in the merger case Case M.5384 *BNP Paribas/Fortis* (3 December 2008).

5.045

Fn 162. For a discussion of the Dutch case *Interpay* see also COMP/34579 *MasterCard MIF charges*, decn of 19 December 2007, para 304. See also the judgments of the Austrian Courts in *Europay*, holding that a JV of Austrian commercial banks that offered payment card acquiring services to merchants infringed the domestic equivalents of Article 101 TFEU (in fixing the fees that the parent banks would charge competitors to the Europay system for processing transactions) and of Article 102 TFEU (by charging excessive fees both to competitors and by way of merchant service charges to small retailers): GZ 27 Kt 20, 24, 27/06, judgment of the Cartel Court of 22 December 2006; on appeal, 16 Ok 4/07, judgment of the Supreme Court of 12 September 2007.

Multilateral interchange fees.   The Commission adopted a prohibition decision under Article 101 in relation to the MasterCard MIF charges referred to in fn 164: COMP/34579 *MasterCard MIF charges*, decn of 19 December 2007. The Commission decided it was not necessary to reach a definite conclusion as to whether the MIF was a restriction by object since the effect of the fee clearly restricted competition: paras 401–407. The Commission held that the MIF restricted competition by inflating the base on which acquiring banks set charges for merchants. Prices set by acquiring banks would be lower in the absence of the rule. The MIF created an artificial cost base that was common for all acquirers and the merchant fee typically reflected the costs of the MIF: para 410. The Commission rejected an argument based on *Wouters* that banks could not operate a card payment system without MIFs. Turning to the application of Article 101(3), the Commission acknowledged, referring to the earlier *Visa MIF* decision, that in principle in a payment card system characterised by indirect network externalities, interchange fees can help optimise the utility of the network to its users. But both the existence and the level of the fee had to be justified by empirical evidence showing that the fee enhanced the output of the payment scheme. MasterCard had not provided any such analysis and hence the first condition of Article 101(3) was not shown to be fulfilled: paras 729–733. The Commission went on to find that the other conditions were also not fulfilled. MasterCard was allowed six months in

5.046

which to amend its rules and ordered to publicise the effect of the Commission's decision on its website in each country: para 766. No fine was imposed since the agreement had been notified under Regulation 17, but periodic penalty payments were imposed in the event that MasterCard failed to comply with the order to terminate the infringement: paras 773 *et seq*. The case is on appeal: Case T-111/08, not yet decided. MasterCard has temporarily withdrawn the MIF: see MEMO/08/397, 12 June 2008.

For a discussion of this case see Repa et al, 'Commission prohibits MasterCard's multilateral interchange fees for cross-border card payments in the EEA' (2008) 1 Competition Policy Newsletter 1.

The exemption granted in 2002 to Visa expired at the end of 2007. The Commission accepted commitments from Visa (i) to cap its yearly weighted average cross-border MIFs on certain transactions; (ii) to implement and improve its transparency measures in a number of ways; and (iii) to appoint a Monitoring Trustee to supervise the implementation of the commitments: COMP/39398 *Visa MIF*, decn of 8 December 2010.

See also the judgment of the Polish Court of Appeal in: *Visa—MasterCard*, Case No. XVII AmA 109/07, ECN Brief 3/2010, p2. The Court overturned the ruling of the Court for Competition and Consumer Protection (judgment of 12 November 2008) and held that the Competition Authority had correctly defined the relevant market and agreed with the EU approach set out in decisions on cross-border interchange fees for Visa and Mastercard payments. The Court examined the settlements between the payment card transaction participants and found that the prices for processing transactions had been determined by agreements made by the banks rather than free competition. The case was referred back to the CCCP for review.

5.047 **Sectoral inquiry and payment cards.** The Commission's analysis of this market was confirmed in its decision in COMP/37860 *Morgan Stanley/Visa International and Visa Europe*, decn of 3 October 2007 in which it imposed a fine on Visa for applying a rule which excluded competitors from the network to refuse membership to Morgan Stanley. The Commission found that barriers to entry made it unrealistic to expect Morgan Stanley to enter the European market to engage in inter-brand competition by expanding the card network it operates in the USA. But there was scope for it to contribute to intra-brand competition if it joined the Visa network as a card provider and merchant acquirer. The exclusion of Morgan Stanley therefore had appreciable restrictive effects on competition: para 201. The Commission considered that, nonetheless, the application of the Rule to Morgan Stanley would not fall under Article 101(1) if it was directly related to and necessary (proportionate and non-discriminatory) for the proper functioning of Visa's network. On the facts the Commission held that this was not the case, and the rule did not fulfil the conditions of Article 101(3) either. A fine of €10.2 million was imposed in relation to the application of the rule (which had been notified to the Commission under Regulation 17) during the period starting with the issue of the statement of objections (in which the Commission made it clear it was contemplating imposing a fine) and ending with the admission of Morgan Stanley to the network in 2006. The Commission's analysis was upheld on appeal: Case T-461/07 *Visa v Commission*, judgment of 14 April 2011. The GC held that the Commission had been correct to regard Morgan Stanley as a realistic potential market entrant and to reject Visa's contention that Morgan Stanley could have entered the market otherwise than by joining the Visa network. On appeal Visa did not contest the finding that the exclusion was not objectively justified.

See similarly, COMP/38606 *Groupement des Cartes Bancaires*, decn of 17 October 2007 (on appeal Case T-491/07 *CB v Commission*, not yet decided).

4. Output Restrictions

Limitation of production.   Where a professional body governing individual clinical laboratories takes steps to prevent the entry or expansion of laboratory groups in the market, this restricts production or investment: COMP/39510 *Ordre National des Pharmaciens en France (ONP)*, decn of 8 December 2010, para 667.   **5.049**

Domestic restructuring of a national industry: *Dutch Bricks*.   Restructuring arrangements must now be considered in the light of the CJ's judgment in Case C-209/07 *Beef Industry Development Society Ltd v Barry Brothers (Carrigmore) Meats Ltd* [2008] ECR I-8637, [2009] 4 CMLR 310, [2009] All ER (EC) 367 (mentioned in fn 177). There the CJ considered arrangements for the restructuring of the Irish beef and veal processing industry. Under the arrangements, total capacity would be reduced by 25 per cent by some processors leaving the market with each 'stayer' paying a levy in accordance with its share of the market. The Court held that this agreement had as its object the restriction of competition contrary to Article 101(1). The application of Article 101(3) was not raised in the request for a preliminary ruling. Following the CJ ruling, the Irish Supreme Court remitted the case back to the judge of first instance to determine whether the conditions of Article 101(3) were satisfied on the facts, referring expressly to *Synthetic Fibres* and *Dutch Bricks*: see *Competition Authority v Beef Industry Development Society Ltd* [2009] IESC 72. The case was settled by BIDS withdrawing its High Court action asserting the applicability of Article 101(3) and the Irish Competition Authority issuing a Guidance Notice to businesses considering entering into agreements to reduce capacity in specific industries in Ireland (N/11/001 issued on 16 June 2011 see ECN Brief 1/2011, p2).   **5.054**

Specialisation block exemption.   Regulation 2658/2000 has been replaced by Regulation 1218/2010 (OJ 2010 L335/43: Vol II, App C7D) which came into force on 1 January 2011. It also sets a 20 per cent market share threshold for the application of the exemption, see the updates to paragraphs 7.087 *et seq*, below.   **5.056**

5.057 **Joint production.** Regulation 2658/2000 has been replaced by Regulation 1218/2010 (OJ 2010 L335/43: Vol II, App C7D), see the updates to paragraphs 7.087 *et seq*, below.

5.058 **Production limitation under Article 81(3).** The 2001 Guidelines have been replaced by the Guidelines on horizontal cooperation agreements issued in 2011: OJ 2011 C11/1: Vol II, App C22: see paras 170 and 171 which are in more positive terms than para 101 in the earlier version.

5. Market-sharing and Customer Allocation

(a) Generally

5.059 **Market-sharing.** Another common mechanism by which markets and customers are allocated is by bid-rigging in relation to sales of products which are usually the subject of tenders by purchasers: for two recent examples see COMP/39406 *Marine Hoses*, decn of 28 January 2009 and COMP/39125 *Car glass*, decn of 12 November 2008. Both decisions are on appeal: *Marine Hoses*: Cases T-146, 147, 148, 154/09, not yet decided and *Car glass*: Cases T-56, 68, 72, 73/09, not yet decided.

Fn 185. The appeal referred to was dismissed save for an adjustment to the penalty: Case T-58/01, judgment of 17 December 2009 (see the update to paragraph 13.109A, below for a table setting out the *Solvay* and *ICI* appeals).

5.060 **Market-sharing between producers. Fn 189.** See also COMP/39129 *Power transformers*, decn of 7 October 2009 (agreement between European and Japanese producers not to sell into each other's markets); COMP/39401 *E.ON—GDF*, decn of 8 July 2009 (agreement by parties sharing a gas pipeline that they would not sell the transported gas into each other's home market).

5.062 **Market-sharing in product and geographic markets.** Substantial parts of the Commission's decision in *Needles* were overturned as regards Coats' involvement: Case T-36/05 *Coats Holdings Ltd v Commission* [2007] ECR II-110, [2008] 4 CMLR 45. The GC found that the mere fact that Coats had been informed about an anti-competitive agreement between two producers, Prym and Entaco, cannot give rise to liability for the infringement (para 105). Further, the GC found on the facts that Coats had not influenced the drafting of the anti-competitive Heads of Agreement between Prym and Entaco. The GC then considered the fact that the terms of the anti-competitive agreement between Prym and Entaco provided that its coming into effect would be triggered when Coats sold its business. The GC held that Coats' decision to proceed with the sale of its business was not capable by itself of proving that its purpose was to contribute to the objectives of the Prym/Entaco cartel. The fact that Prym and Entaco decided to make that event the date on which their cartel would come into force could not, at first sight, be attributed to Coats. However, in the circumstances of the case, the fact that Coats triggered the mechanism of the Prym/Entaco cartel could implicate Coats in that cartel, if that act was part of a common plan. The GC found that Coats' anti-competitive intentions were demonstrated by the fact that the Heads of Agreement were disclosed to it. In that regard, the Commission had rightly observed that suppliers do not generally inform their customers about the cartels of which they are members and this highly unusual step showed that, contrary to Coats' claim, it was not the 'victim' of a cartel. The very fact that Entaco and Prym discussed confidential issues (such as the creation of a cartel) showed, the GC found, that Coats' intentions must have been of an anti-competitive nature. By facilitating the entry into force of the Heads of Agreement between Prym and Entaco, Coats became liable until that agreement came to an end on 13 March 1997. The GC went on to overturn the Commission's finding of a trilateral arrangement arising from the several bilateral arrangements between Coats, Prym and Entaco. The Court examined the wording of the relevant clause, the structure and context of the clause, the intended objective and history of the clause. It found that Coats' alternative explanation of the clause was plausible and convincing and that there was no tripartite agreement established. Coats' fine was reduced to reflect the more limited nature of its involvement. Coats' appeal against this decision was dismissed: Case C-468/07P [2009] 4 CMLR 301. Prym's appeal to the GC against the same decision was also dismissed save for a small reduction in the fine: Case T-30/05 *Prym v Commission* [2007] ECR II-107* (further appeal dismissed: Case C-534/07, judgment of 3 September 2009, [2009] 5 CMLR 2377).

Market-sharing between purchasers.   **Fn 193.** The appeals from the *Spanish*   **5.063**
Raw Tobacco decision were decided in a series of judgments, see the update to paragraph 5.027, above.

Fn 194. Appeals dismissed in Case T-25/06 *Alliance One International v Commission*, judgment of 9 September 2011 and Case T-12/06 *Deltafina v Commission*, judgment of 9 September 2011.

Control over imports and exports.   See also COMP/39401 *E.ON—GdF collu-*   **5.065**
sion, decn of 8 July 2009 where the Commission imposed substantial fines on the joint owners of a pipeline importing Russian gas into Germany and France. The parties had agreed not to supply gas into each other's markets: see Press Release IP/09/1099 (8 July 2009).

Market-sharing and trade with third countries.   See also Case T-110/07 *Siemens*   **5.066**
v Commission, judgment of 3 March 2011, para 60 where the GC held that an understanding which seeks to respect the traditional privileged positions of parties to the cartel on the European and Japanese markets respectively, if established, would constitute, in itself, a cartel having effects on the common market, inasmuch as it suppresses the potential competition which Japanese producers would have

provided in the common market. That would be the case even if that the Commission did not succeed in showing that the European producers had, in addition, shared the European market among themselves.

(c) Bilateral market-sharing

5.074 **Generally.** **Fn 218.** Reg 2658/2000 has been replaced by Reg 1218/2010 (OJ 2010 L335/43: Vol II, App C7D) and Reg 2659/2000 has been replaced by Reg 1217/2010 (OJ 2010 L335/36: Vol II, App C7C).

(f) Customer allocation

5.083 **Customer allocation.** **Fn 240.** The appeal in the *Choline Chloride* case has now been decided: Cases T-101&111/05 *BASF AG and UCB SA v Commission* [2007] ECR II-4949, [2008] 4 CMLR 347. The GC quashed the Commission's finding that the global and European aspects of the cartel were a single continuous infringement (paras 208 *et seq*). The appeal in Case T-112/05 *Akzo Nobel* and a further appeal to the CJ have also now been decided: see Case C-97/08P *Akzo Nobel NV v Commission*, judgment of 10 September 2009.

6. Information Exchange

5.084 **Information agreements.** Chapter 6 of the new Horizontal Cooperation Guidelines discusses information agreements outside the context of a cartel: OJ 2011 C11/1: Vol II, App C22, paras 55 *et seq*. The Guidelines note the potential advantages of information exchange by solving problems of information asymmetries or allowing companies to improve efficiency by benchmarking against each other's best practice: para 57. However, it may also restrict competition by encouraging a collusive outcome or by foreclosing the market by excluding unaffiliated companies. The Guidelines describe the factors relevant to an assessment of whether an information exchange arrangement falls within Article 101(1):

- Market characteristics—the likelihood of information exchange resulting in a collusive outcome is increased where the market is transparent, concentrated, non-complex (ie there is a single priced homogeneous product rather than a range of differentiated products), stable (ie not subject to volatile demand or frequent new entry), and symmetric (ie where the undertakings concerned are homogeneous in terms of costs, demand, capacity etc). It is important to look not only at the characteristics of the market prior to the information exchange but at how the presence of exchange affects those characteristics.
- Characteristics of the information exchange—in particular whether the exchange covers strategic information such as prices, customer lists, quantities; whether it is aggregated or individualised, historic or recent, public or non-public.

The frequency of exchange and whether the companies involve cover all or most of the market are also important factors.

The Guidelines indicate how efficiency gains can arise for the purpose of applying Article 101(3) and how exchange can benefit consumers by helping them make more informed choices (paras 95 *et seq*). Several examples of information exchange arrangements are analysed.

Information exchange ancillary to a cartel. See also the discussion of **5.085** COMP/39188 *Bananas*, decn of 15 October 2008 in the update to paragraph 5.016, above. The Commission stated that the cartel in that case was distinguished from an information exchange of the kind discussed in *United Kingdom Agricultural Tractor Registration Exchange* because it concerned pre-pricing communications and not *ex post* exchanges of information about transactions already completed. The decision is under appeal: Cases T-587&588/08, not yet decided.

Fn 244. The appeals in *Industrial copper tubes* (all relating to fine only) were dismissed by the GC in three judgments given on 6 May 2009: Case T-127/04 *KM Europa Metal* [2009] ECR II-1167, [2009] 5 CMLR 1574 (on further appeal C-272/09P, not yet decided); Case T-122/04 *Outokumpu* [2009] ECR II-1135, [2009] 5 CMLR 1553; Case T-116/04 *Wieland-Werke AG* [2009] ECR II-1087, [2009] 5 CMLR 1517.

The United Kingdom Agricultural Tractor Registration Exchange. The principles **5.087** here were confirmed by the CJ in Case C-8/08 *T-Mobile Netherlands BV v Raad van bestuur van de Nederlandse Mededingingsautoriteit*, judgment of 4 June 2009: 'An exchange of information between competitors is tainted with an anti-competitive object if the exchange is capable of removing uncertainties concerning the intended conduct of the participating undertakings': para 43.

Wirtschaftsvereiningung Stahl. In Case T-53/03 *BPB plc v Commission* [2008] **5.088** ECR II-1333, [2008] 5 CMLR 1201 the GC emphasised the different effect of information exchange in different market structures. In a truly competitive market, an information exchange system is not likely to reduce or remove uncertainty about the foreseeable nature of competitors' conduct. However, on a highly concentrated oligopolistic market, the exchange of information does enable operators to know the market positions and strategies of their competitors and thus impairs competition appreciably: paras 107 *et seq*.

Artificial market transparency. In Case T-53/03 *BPB plc v Commission* [2008] **5.089** ECR II-1333, [2008] 5 CMLR 1201 the GC confirmed that the mere fact of receiving information concerning competitors, which an independent operator preserves as business secrets, is sufficient to demonstrate the existence of an anti-competitive intention. The fact that price information was known by customers before it was transmitted to the competitors and, therefore, could be collected on the market did not negate the existence of an anti-competitive agreement. It did not make the prices readily accessible. The fact that price lists were sent directly from one competitor to another allowed the competitors to become aware of that information more simply, rapidly, and directly than they would via the market. Further, that prior notification allowed them to create a climate of mutual certainty as to their future pricing policies: paras 235–236.

Fn 257. See also Horizontal Cooperation Guidelines OJ 2011 C11/1: Vol II, App C22, paras 62 and 63 where the Commission states that where only one undertaking discloses strategic information to its competitors this can amount to a concerted practice.

Fn 260. See also the example in para 109 of the Horizontal Cooperation Guidelines, above, where the Commission indicates that exchange by telephone of current prices among petrol stations would not be regarded as exchange of genuinely public information.

5.090 **Information on output and sales.**   Similarly, where a trade association publishes cost forecasts to its members, this is likely to affect their pricing decisions for the future and thus restrict competition. In separate decisions, the Danish Competition Council found that the two Danish Freight Transport Associations violated the domestic equivalent of Article 101 TFEU by issuing such forecasts to their members, along with cost calculation models that they can use to calculate their freight rates by applying their own costs according to a uniform programme: *Dansk Transport og Logistik (DTL)*, decn of 17 December 2008; *International Transport Danmark (ITD)*, decn of 25 February 2009 (taken also under Article 101). On appeal to the Competition Appeals Board, the DCC's decision in the *DTL* case was quashed in part on the grounds that the recommendations were of a general nature and did not involve the passing on of specific information about costs. However the CAB upheld the DCC's findings as regards DTL's infringements arising from the publication of the cost forecast for freight transport by road and the recommendation to transport companies to pass on a specific insurance cost to their customers: see judgment of 30 November 2009. On the same day the CAB issued its ruling in the appeal in the *ITD* case. The CAB upheld the DCC's decision that (i) a pre-fulfilled cost calculating program for freight transport by road; (ii) a version of the pre-fulfilled cost calculation programme above including index figures; (iii) a cost forecast for freight transport by road; and (iv) a specific rate for waiting hours were unlawful. However, it allowed the appeal as regards ITD's recommendation to transport companies to pass on oil-related costs to the members' customers.

A disclosure by one undertaking in a highly concentrated and oligopolistic market of the fact that it does not want a larger market share than the one it already holds is sufficient to inform competitors of an essential element of its strategy and therefore to restrict competition: see Case T-53/03 *BPB plc v Commission* [2008] ECR II-1333, [2008] 5 CMLR 1201, para 183.

Fn 269. In the *Bouygues Télécom* case, on reference back from the Cour de Cassation (now reported in translation at [2008] ECC 439), the Paris Court of Appeal rejected the appeals brought by the three French mobile network operators, Bouygues, Orange, and SFR. The court held that the information exchanged was confidential and, having regard to its detail and the frequency of exchange, was of considerable value to the commercial strategy of the individual companies since it enabled them to adapt to the evolution of the commercial policies of each other. Accordingly, the requisite anti-competitive effect was demonstrated: *Bouygues Télécom, SFR, Orange*, judgment of 11 March 2009, BOCCRF No. 7 of 17 July 2009. The appeal to the Cour de Cassation was dismissed: ECN Brief 3/2010, p2. The Court confirmed the Autorité's finding that, on an oligopolistic market, exchanges of strategic and sensitive information were likely to distort competition, as these pieces of information were effectively taken into account by the operators.

Other exchanges of information. The 2001 Guidelines have been replaced by the Guidelines on horizontal cooperation agreements issued in 2011: OJ 2011 C11/1: Vol II, App C22. Chapter 2 of the Guidelines provides a detailed analysis of the application of Article 101(1) and (3) to information exchange agreements of various kinds; see the update to paragraph 5.084, above. **5.091**

Information agreements under Article 81(3). The new Horizontal Cooperation Guidelines OJ 2011 C11/1: Vol II, App C22 set out the factors relevant to an analysis of when information exchange agreements will benefit from Article 101(3): paras 95 *et seq*. **5.096**

Regulation 358/2003 has been replaced by Regulation 267/2010 (OJ 2010 L83/1: Vol II, App E27A). The new block exemption covers only two of the categories of agreements previously exempted, namely collaboration between insurers in relation to joint compilations, tables and studies of risk and insurance pools.

7. Collective Trading Arrangements

(a) Boycotts and collective exclusive dealing

Collective refusal to deal. See also *Lottoblock*, WuW DE-R 2408, judgment of the German Federal Supreme Court of 14 August 2008 (resolution by Association of German Lottery Companies advising its members not to accept business generated by commercial brokers through certain channels of distribution, which threatened their regional monopolies, was a decision by an association of undertakings that infringed Article 101). **5.100**

(b) Collective selling of goods

5.106 **In general.** Chapter 6 of the new Horizontal Cooperation Guidelines (OJ 2011 C11/1: Vol II, App C22) analyses agreements on commercialisation which involve cooperation between competitors in the selling, distribution or promotion of their products. The Guidelines indicate the importance of assessing the impact of the arrangement on neighbouring markets as well as on the market to which the products directly covered by the arrangements belong. The Guidelines stress that price-fixing is a major concern arising from joint selling, even where the arrangement is non-exclusive: para 235. They also explain the factors relevant to an assessment of when such an agreement is likely to have restrictive effects on competition; describe when Article 101(3) is likely to apply; and give worked examples including the operation of a joint internet platform for selling gift fruit baskets.

5.110 **Joint ventures and specialisation agreements.** See now Chapter 6 of the new Horizontal Cooperation Guidelines (OJ 2011 C11/1: Vol II, App C22). The Guidelines explain where the Vertical Restraints block exemption (now Regulation 330/2010, OJ 2010 L102/1: Vol II, App C7A) does and does not apply to distribution agreements (para 226).

Fn 312. See now the Horizontal Cooperation Guidelines, para 237 and the examples analysed at paras 252 and 253.

Fn 313. See now Reg 330/2010, OJ 2010 L102/1: Vol II, App C7A, Art 2(4) to the same effect.

Fn 314. See the Horizontal Cooperation Guidelines, para 238.

Fn 315. See the Horizontal Cooperation Guidelines, para 240 setting the same 15 per cent market share threshold.

(c) Collective selling of intellectual property and media rights

5.111 **Joint selling of rights.** In COMP/38698 *CISAC*, decn of 16 July 2008, [2009] 4 CMLR 577, the Commission noted that individual management of rights is often not feasible: para 42. See also the Commission's market analysis in Case M.5533 *Bertelsmann/KRR/JV* (8 September 2009) (a case under the Merger Regulation).

5.112 **Collective selling of rights: music and films.** The Commission's increasingly interventionist approach to the licensing of music rights by collecting societies is demonstrated by COMP/38698 *CISAC*, decn of 16 July 2008, [2009] 4 CMLR 577. The Commission examined the provisions of the bilateral reciprocal licensing agreements between the EEA members of CISAC relating to the use of music in satellite, cable and internet transmission modes. Those agreements were based in part on the model clauses adopted by CISAC. Some of the clauses complained of had been deleted from those model clauses but were still found in the bilateral contracts. The Commission held that a membership clause whereby the collecting societies agreed that neither of them would, without the consent of the other, accept as member any member of the other society or any person having the nationality of one of the countries in which the other society operates infringed Article 101 TFEU. The clause restricted competition between collecting societies on the market for the provision of services to rights holders and, indirectly, may also affect competition between collecting societies on the market for the licensing of rights to commercial users: para 126. In line with the *Simulcasting* decision, the Commission held that the concerted practice among the societies whereby the territory licensed was limited to the domestic territory of the licensee society led to national monopolies for the multi-repertoire licensing of public performance rights and had the effect of segmenting the EEA into national markets (paras 204 *et seq*). The Commission was careful to make clear that it was only the coordination aspect of the grant of a limited territory that was condemned in the decision; 'in isolation, the granting of a licence limited to a certain territory, even to the domestic territory, is not automatically restrictive of competition' (para 201). The Commission also left open whether, as regards exploitation of performing rights in offline applications (bars, restaurants, discos, etc) the territorial delineation of licences along national borders might be justified on the basis that duplication of copyright usage monitoring structures in all territories would lack economic rationale. But that could not justify such limitations for the applications covered by the decision namely satellite, cable and internet transmission modes (para 184). The decision also contains an interesting analysis of the relevant product markets for the exploitation of rights for satellite, cable and internet transmission modes (paras 48 *et seq*). Note that the finding of infringement was addressed to the members and not to the collecting society itself. The decision is on appeal on the issue of whether the Commission was correct to find the existence of a concerted practice as regards the limitation of the licences to the domestic territory of the licensee: see Cases T-398, 410, 411, 413–422, 425, 432, 434, 442, 451/08, not yet decided. The GC rejected an application for interim measures to suspend parts of the Commission's order Case T-411/08R *Artijus Magyar v Commission* [2009] 4 CMLR 353. An appeal against that ruling was dismissed: Case C-32/09P(R) *Artijus Magyar v Commission*, order of 31 August 2010, [2010] 5 CMLR 1208.

Licensing use of rights on the internet. In COMP/38698 *CISAC*, decn of 16 July 2008, [2009] 4 CMLR 577, discussed above, the Commission applied the principles laid down in the *Simulcasting* decision. As regards the definition of the relevant product market, the Commission noted that technical and legal distinctions could point in favour of separate product markets for each of the satellite, cable and internet transmission modes. However, in view of the increasing convergence between television and internet services, this might change: para 57. The Commission relied on the particular characteristics of these applications as contrasted with offline applications (broadcast in bars, restaurants, discos, etc) in

5.113

finding that there was no need for local monitoring and enforcement and hence no economic rationale for territorial limitations: para 184. The case is on appeal Cases T-398, 410, 411, 413–422, 425, 432, 434, 442, 451/08, not yet decided.

In April 2007 the Commission issued a statement of objections alleging an agreement among Apple and the major record companies to the effect that consumers can only buy music from the iTunes' online store in their country of residence and are thereby restricted in the choice of where to buy music and at what price. The Commission later closed the case having ascertained that the organisation of the iTunes store in Europe is not determined by agreements between Apple and the major record companies. Apple nonetheless agreed to equalise prices for downloads of songs from its iTunes online store in Europe within six months. This put an end to the different treatment of UK consumers who previously paid higher prices for downloads: see COMP/39154 *Apple and iTunes* Press Release IP/08/22 (9 January 2008).

5.114   **Licensing of music rights: further steps.**   See the discussion of the Commission Recommendation 2005/737/EC in COMP/38698 *CISAC*, decn of 16 July 2008, [2009] 4 CMLR 577, paras 106–110. The case is on appeal Cases T-398, 410, 411, 413–422, 425, 432, 434, 442, 451/08, not yet decided.

The Commission has convened a 'roundtable' to discuss general principles to underpin the online distribution of music. The fourth meeting, in October 2009 led to a joint statement regarding access to repertoire: see Press Release IP/09/1548 (20 October 2009).

5.115   **Collective selling of rights: sporting events.**   In July 2007, the Commission adopted a White Paper on Sport (COM(2007)391 final) which was accompanied by a Staff Working Document 'The EU and Sport: Background and Context' (SEC(2007) 935). Annex I to that Staff Working Document entitled 'Sport and the EU Competition Rules' provides an overview of the principal case law on the application of Articles 101 and 102 TFEU to the sports sector, dealing both with the organisational aspects of sport (notably sporting rules) and with the revenue-generating aspects of sport (in particular the sale of sport media rights). The White Paper discusses product market definition, particularly the distinction between upstream markets where rights owners sell rights to media companies and downstream markets in which those media companies operate. It analyses the *UEFA Champions League*, *German Bundesliga* and *FA Premier League* decisions and lists the remedies that the Commission has used to redress the restrictive effects of collective selling such as limiting the duration of exclusive vertical contracts and imposing a 'no single buyer' obligation. See further new paragraphs 5.156A and 5.156B, below.

See also *Mediapro/Gol TV* ECN Brief 2/2011, p2 (Spanish Competition Authority imposed fine for abusive bundling of matches in the Spanish regular league and King's Cup).

Commission policy: sports content rights and broadcasting.   Fn 330. The appeal   **5.116**
in the *Infront* case has been decided: Case C-125/06P *Commission v Infront WM* [2008] ECR I-1451, [2008] 2 CMLR 785. The CJ upheld the GC's judgment that Infront, which was the holder, for the countries of Europe for the years 2002 and 2006, of the exclusive broadcasting rights in respect of the football World Cup finals organised by FIFA, was directly and individually concerned by the Commission's decision approving the designation by the United Kingdom of those events as listed events and so could challenge that decision.

Fn 332. The decision in the *Polish Football Association* case was upheld on further appeal by the Polish Supreme Court: case III SK 16/08, judgment of 7 January 2009.

Sponsoring of competing joint selling vehicle.   Where particular rights have   **5.116A**
been sold through a monopoly acquirer, an arrangement among sellers under which they grant exclusive rights to a competing joint venture will not fall within Article 101(1) where the exclusivity is necessary to enable the joint venture to compete with the incumbent. In *Bookmakers' Afternoon Greyhound Services v Amalgamated Racing Ltd* [2009] EWCA Civ 750 the English Court of Appeal upheld a decision that a joint venture to which a group of racecourses sold the exclusive right to broadcast horse races to licensed bookmakers' premises had neither the object nor the effect of restricting competition since it challenged the existing monopsony of an organisation owned by the bookmakers. Lloyd LJ stated: 'Given that the incumbent operator was dominated by the interests of the purchasers in the downstream market, given the high cost of entry, and given the very long period in which no other operator had shown any interest in entry to these markets, it seems to me that it was obviously necessary that the new entrant would have to be promoted by or in association with a number of racecourses, and that it would need to be protected, at the stage of its establishment, from competition from the incumbent, since otherwise it would never get off the ground': para 85. The Court of Appeal considered the Commission's decisions in *UEFA Champions League* and *FA Premier League* on the question of whether the racecourses could be regarded as being in competition with each other, given that the races were organised so as not to coincide with each other. The Court held that they were not in competition with each other. The Court upheld the first instance judge's decision ([2008] EWHC 1978 (Ch)) on the basis that the exclusivity was an ancillary restriction within the principles established in Case T-112/99 *Métropole Télévision (M6) v Commission* [2001] ECR II-2459 and Case C-309/99 *Wouters* [2002] ECR I-1577.

(d) Joint tendering

5.122 **'Cover' bidding.** Note that in Case T-210/08 *Verhuizingen Coppens v Commission*, judgment of 16 June 2011 the GC annulled the decision in COMP/38543 *International Removal Services*, decn of 11 March 2008 insofar as it applied to the applicant because the applicant had been involved only in a cover bidding agreement and not in the agreement relating to commissions condemned in that decision. Although the Court said that 'participation in the system of cover quotes may in itself constitute an infringement', the fine imposed indicated that the Commission had found Verhuizingen Coppens liable for the wider infringement but had not discharged the burden of proof in that regard.

In a series of appeals against an Office of Fair Trading decision fining 103 construction companies for cover bidding, the UK Competition Appeal Tribunal reduced the fines that had been imposed and, in some cases, overturned findings of liability on the grounds of lack of evidence. In the lead judgment, the Tribunal analysed the anti-competitive effect of such conduct: *Kier Group plc v Office of Fair Trading* [2011] CAT 3. At paras 78 onwards the Tribunal considered the seriousness of cover pricing as an infringement of the competition rules. See also *GF Tomlinson Group Ltd v Office of Fair Trading* [2011] CAT 7.

5.123 **Bidders' reciprocal sub-contracting arrangements.** The decision of the Hungarian Competition Office was upheld on appeal, by the Supreme Court of Hungary: Case Kfv.II.39162/2008, judgment of 17 June 2009.

(e) Collective buying of goods

5.124 **In general.** Chapter 5 of the new Horizontal Cooperation Guidelines (OJ 2011 C11/1: Vol II, App C22) focuses on agreements concerning the joint purchase of products, paras 194 *et seq*. The new Guidelines also indicate that the horizontal aspects of the arrangements should be considered first and if they do not give rise to competition concerns, a further assessment of the vertical aspects can be carried out under the Vertical Agreements block exemption and guidelines: para 195.

5.128 **Collective purchasing: economics-based approach.** The 2001 Guidelines have been replaced by the Guidelines on horizontal cooperation agreements issued in 2011: OJ 2011 C11/1: Vol II, App C22. Chapter 5 of the Guidelines provides a detailed analysis of the application of Article 101(1) and (3) to purchasing agreements.

Fn 356. See now para 205 of the new Horizontal Cooperation Guidelines.

Fn 357. See now paras 197 and 198, ibid.

Fn 358. See now para 212, ibid.

Fn 359. See now paras 200–216, ibid.

Fn 360. See now paras 217 *et seq* and the examples analysed, ibid.

8. Trade Associations, Cooperatives and Exhibitions

(a) Membership rules

The Commission's attitude to membership rules.   See also COMP/39416 *Ship*   **5.135**
Classification, decn of 14 October 2009 where the Commission accepted commitments to remove concerns about the decisions of the International Association of
Ships Classification Societies (IACS) relating to (i) the criteria and procedures ruling membership of IACS; and (ii) the elaboration and accessibility to non-IACS
classification societies of IACS' resolutions and technical background information
relating to these resolutions. The Commission considered the combined market
share of the IACS members and the significant competitive disadvantages faced by
classification societies who were not members of IACS. Concerns were expressed
that the membership rules were not sufficiently objective and determinate so as to
enable them to be applied uniformly and in a non-discriminatory manner and that
they were not in fact applied in an objective and non-discriminatory manner. The
commitments accepted included (i) changes to the membership rules to ensure that
they are objective, transparent, and non-discriminatory; (ii) the right of appeal
against membership decisions to an independent board; (iii) participation of non-
IACS members in IACS's technical work; (iv) access by non-members to IACS's
resolutions and technical background information via the IACS website; and (v) a
statement on the website that non-members are free to use IACS' technical material
without royalty or licence.

(b) Common standards

Agreements on technical standards.   The Horizontal Cooperation Guidelines   **5.139**
issued in 2011 (OJ 2011 C11/1: Vol II, App C22) substantially revised the chapter
on standardisation in the old Guidelines. The earlier Guidelines referred only to
agreements aimed at achieving environmental objectives such as the reduction of
pollution. The current Guidelines now cover all standardisations agreements,
defined as agreements which have as their object the definition of technical or quality requirements with which current or future products or services may comply: see
Chapter 7 of the Guidelines, paras 257 *et seq.* The Guidelines do not, however,
cover standards relating to the provision of professional services: para 258.

In *SEL-Imperial Ltd v British Standards Institution* [2010] EWHC 854 (Ch) the
English High Court considered (in the context of an application to strike out a
civil claim) an allegation that the interpretation by the BSI of which vehicle parts
were 'safety related' and which 'non-safety related' placed too many parts in the
former category. This had the effect of limiting the extent to which manufacturers
of replica parts could compete with the original manufacturer's spare parts. Referring
to para 33 of the 2001 Horizontal Cooperation Guidelines, Roth J held that a

multi-lateral agreement whereby the participants gave up their independent right to determine how 'safety-related' is interpreted and left that interpretation to the BSI could have the effect of restricting competition in the supply of replica parts, if the BSI took an overly restrictive view of which parts related to safety.

See also Piesiewicz and Schellingerhout, 'Intellectual property rights in standard setting from a competition law perspective' (2007) 3 Competition Policy Newsletter 36.

5.139A   **Disclosure of patents during the standard setting process:** *Rambus.* The Commission launched proceedings against Rambus alleging that it had failed to disclose patents and pending patent applications in the course of negotiations over the setting of standards for DRAM computer chips: COMP/38636 *RAMBUS*, decn of 9 December 2009. JEDEC, an industry-wide standard setting organisation in the USA, had developed a standard for DRAMs. DRAMs complying with that standard constituted the vast majority of DRAMs sold globally. Rambus asserted patents on all JEDEC-compliant DRAMs such that every manufacturer was forced either to pay Rambus royalties or litigate its patent rights. The Commission considered that Rambus may have engaged in intentional deceptive conduct in the context of the standard-setting process by not disclosing the existence of the patents and patent applications which it later claimed were relevant to the adopted standard. This led to an alleged abuse of its dominant position when Rambus claimed royalties at a level which, absent its allegedly intentional deceptive conduct, it would not have been able to charge. Rambus' conduct was a breach of 'the underlying duty of good faith in the context of standard-setting'. The Commission accepted commitments from Rambus offering a bundled worldwide licence for all of its relevant patents and setting maximum royalty rates for the different patents. Rambus also agreed not to charge royalties for the standards that were adopted during the time in which the Commission provisionally considered Rambus may have engaged in intentional deceptive conduct in the context of the standard-setting process, by not disclosing the existence of the patents and patent applications which it later claimed were relevant to the adopted standards. Following the decision making the commitments binding, the Commission issued a decision rejecting a complaint by Hynix relating to the same alleged abusive conduct: COMP/38636 *RAMBUS*, decn of 15 January 2010. That rejection decision is on appeal: Case T-149/10 *Hynix Conductor v Commission*, not yet decided.

5.140   **Agreements on standards outside Article 81(1).** The Horizontal Cooperation Guidelines 2011 (OJ 2011 C11/1: Vol II, App C22) state that standard setting can lead to anti-competitive effects in three situations: first where it leads the undertakings into collusive behaviour such as price fixing, secondly where competing technologies or companies are excluded from the market once the standard has been set, and thirdly where companies are discriminated against by not being given access to the results of the standard-setting process. The Guidelines outline the kinds of agreements that will not generally be caught by Article 101(1): see paras 277 *et seq.* These are agreements where:

- all competitors in the market can participate in the process leading up to the setting of the standard;
- the standard setting organisation has transparent procedures allowing stakeholders to be aware of standard setting work in good time and at each stage of the development of the market;
- the organisation's rules allow access to the standard on terms that are fair, reasonable and non-discriminatory (often referred to as 'FRAND' terms);
- there is a 'clear and balanced' IPR policy which requires participants who wish to have their IPR included in the standard to provide an irrevocable commitment in writing to offer to license their essential IPR to all third parties on FRAND terms;
- the policy should also require good faith disclosure by participants of any IPR under development that might be essential for use of the standard;
- the parties remain free to develop alternative standards or products that do not comply with the agreed standard.

Fn 388. See now para 258 of the Horizontal Cooperation Guidelines 2011 (OJ 2011 C11/1: Vol II, App C22) where the Commission indicates that such bodies are subject to the competition rules to the extent that they are undertakings or associations of undertakings.

See Case T-432/05 *EMC Development AB v Commission*, judgment of 12 May 2010, [2010] 5 CMLR 757 where the GC upheld the Commission's rejection of a complaint alleging that standards for cement set by a standards body recognised under Directive 98/34 contravened Articles 101 and 102. The GC held that the Commission had been correct to apply the criteria set out in paras 162 and 163 of the Guidelines on Horizontal Cooperation in order to assess (i) whether the procedure for adoption of the Standard had not been non-discriminatory, open, and transparent; and (ii) whether the Standard was binding. There was no evidence that the body had set the Standard to correspond to the products of Portland cement producers and exclude competing products or that the cement producers had had an undue influence over the decisions taken by the body.

Fn 390. The approach to market share indicated in para 296 of the 2011 Horizontal Cooperation Guidelines is somewhat more nuanced. The Commission notes that in many cases the market shares of the undertakings participating in the standard could be a proxy for estimating the likely market share of the standard. But high market shares will not necessarily lead to the conclusion that the standard is likely to give rise to restrictive effects on competition.

Use of standard forms, etc.   The Horizontal Cooperation Guidelines 2011 (OJ   **5.143**
2011 C11/1: Vol II, App C22) discuss the use of standard terms and conditions

between competitors and their consumers. Standard terms devised by a single company solely for use with its own suppliers or customers are not covered: see para 260. If a large part of the industry adopt these terms and choose not to deviate from them, there may be restrictive effects produced by the terms themselves or by restrictions on access to the terms by competing undertakings: paras 270–272, 275 and 276. The Guidelines go on to indicate that where participation in the establishment of the standard terms is unrestricted and where the terms are non-binding and accessible to all they are unlikely to give rise to anti-competitive effects: see paras 301 *et seq*. However, there may be instances where the standard terms include a definition of the product sold, thereby effectively limiting choice and innovation. This may arise for example where standard terms in insurance contracts limit the choice of key elements of cover. The extent of any restriction on competition resulting from such clauses will depend on the degree of market concentration. So far as the application of Article 101(3) is concerned, the Guidelines note that the use of standard terms can make it easier for customers to compare the conditions offered by competitors and may result in savings in transaction costs. The Guidelines give a number of worked examples of standard terms including standard insurance policy conditions: see paras 333, 334 and 335.

As regards the final sentence of paragraph in the main work, on 25 September 2007, the Commission published the Final Report of the sector inquiry into business insurance. The Final Report focuses in substance on two main issues. The first is competition in the wholesale subscription market, that is where an ad hoc syndication arrangement is set up by a broker or client to cover a given risk. The Report considers the use of 'Best Terms and Conditions' clauses whereby an insurer makes an offer to subscribe conditional on no other participant receiving better terms in respect of either a higher price or a more advantageous policy. The Commission notes that this may lead to an upward alignment of premiums and/or contract uncertainty. The second issue is broker conflicts of interest and the Commission has undertaken to look at these issues in the framework of the review of the Insurance Mediation Directive.

5.144 **Agreements on standards under Article 81(3).** The Horizontal Cooperation Guidelines issued in 2011 (OJ 2011 C11/1: Vol II, App C22) set out how the Commission approaches the application of Article 101(3) to standardisation agreements: see paras 308 *et seq*. For example, where standards facilitate technical interoperability and compatibility between products it can be assumed that the standard will benefit consumers.

Regulation 358/2003 has been replaced by Regulation 267/2010 (OJ 2010 L83/1: Vol II, App E27A). The new block exemption does not exempt agreements on technical specifications for security devices or rules to approve firms that carry out their installation and maintenance: see also the Commission's Communication (OJ 2010 C82/20: Vol II, App E27B), paras 25 *et seq*. Standard setting more generally is now covered by the Horizontal Cooperation Guidelines, as noted above, see in particular the example analysed at para 328 (group of insurance companies comes together to agree non-binding standards for the installation of certain security devices). Note that Article 8 of Regulation 267/2010 provided a transitional period of continued exemption until 30 September 2010 to agreements which complied with the earlier block exemption but not with the new Regulation.

Agreements protecting the environment.   The new Horizontal Cooperation **5.144** Guidelines (OJ 2011 C11/1: Vol II, App C22) do not contain specific provisions about standards for environmental objectives. Such agreements are now covered by the general provisions. The Commission has stated that this does not imply any downgrading of the assessment of environmental agreements: MEMO/10/676 (14 December 2010) para 12. See also the examples given at paras 329, 331, and 332 of the Guidelines.

(c) Joint marketing

Joint advertising.   The 2001 Guidelines have been replaced by the Horizontal **5.147** Cooperation Guidelines issued in 2011: OJ 2011 C11/1: Vol II, App C22. The new Guidelines also consider joint advertising in the chapter on joint commercialisation. The points made in the text remain pertinent: see paras 243 and 245 of the new Guidelines.

(d) Trade exhibitions and auctions

Application of Article 81(1).   Fn 426. See now *FBIAC v WEX* (2006/AR/2392), **5.153** [2008] ECC 9, judgment of the Brussels Court of Appeal of 15 June 2007, to the same effect as the judgment of 2005 cited in the footnote, which was a preliminary ruling on a reference from the Brussels Commercial Court. The subsequent decision of the Commercial Court determining the case was in turn appealed, giving rise to the 2007 judgment which is final.

Auctions.   Fn 433. The decision of the Dutch Competition Authority in *Dutch* **5.155** *shrimp producers and wholesalers agreement* was upheld by the Trade and Industry Appeals Tribunal: Cases AWB 06/599, etc, judgment of 19 January 2009, LJN: BD0436. However the Dutch Administrative High Court for Trade and Industry reduced the fine imposed on shrimp fishers for cartel activity because of a misunderstanding about the applicability of competition rules in the sector governed by European fishing regulation: ECN Brief 2/2011, p2.

9. Sporting Bodies and Competitions

Introduction.   For a case concerning the organisation of motorcycle racing events **5.156** see Case C-49/07 *Motosykletistiki Omospondia Ellados NPID (MOTOE) v Elliniko*

Dimosio [2008] ECR I-4863, [2008] 5 CMLR 790, [2009] All ER (EC) 150, esp para 22.

5.156A **Commission White Paper on Sport.**   In July 2007, the Commission adopted a White Paper on Sport (COM(2007)391 final) which was accompanied by a Staff Working Document 'The EU and Sport: Background and Context' (SEC(2007) 935). Annex I to that Staff Working Document entitled 'Sport and the EU Competition Rules' provides an overview of the principal case law on the application of Articles 101 and 102 TFEU to the sports sector, dealing with both the organisational aspects of sport, notably sporting rules and revenue-generating aspects of sport, in particular the sale of sport media rights. The Commission has now issued a Communication on Sport (COMM(2011) 12 Final: 18 January 2011) called *Developing the European Dimension in Sport*, discussed below.

5.156B **The White Paper: application of competition law to sporting rules.**   The White Paper confirms the importance of *Meca Medina* in establishing that there is no category of purely sporting rules excluded from the scope of competition law. Rather, it is necessary, once it has been established that the various elements in Article 101(1) are satisfied, to consider first, the overall context in which the rule was adopted or in which it has its effect; secondly, whether the restriction of competition arising from the rule is inherent in the pursuit of the objective of the rule; and thirdly, whether the rule is proportionate in the light of the objective pursued. It is also necessary to consider whether Article 101(3) applies or whether the rule can be objectively justified for the purposes of Article 102. The White Paper sets out an indicative list of rules that are more likely to comply with the competition rules, namely selection criteria for sport competitions, 'at home and away' rules, transfer periods, nationality clauses for national teams, rules prohibiting the multiple ownership of clubs, anti-doping rules, and the rules of the game. Sporting rules that are less likely to comply include rules prohibiting clubs or athletes from participating in competitions organised by a rival sporting body, rules regulating professions ancillary to sport such as football players' agents, and rules excluding legal challenges of decisions by sports associations before the ordinary courts. In addition, rules limiting the number of foreign players or requiring transfer payments for players whose contracts have expired may fall to be assessed under competition rules as well as under free movement provisions. The more recent Communication on Sport adopted by the Commission Sport (COMM(2011) 12 Final: 18 January 2011) *Developing the European Dimension in Sport* does not refer directly to *Meca Medina* but notes that exploitation of intellectual property rights in the area of sport, such as licensing of retransmission of sport events or merchandising, represents important sources of income for professional sports and that revenue derived from these sources is often partly redistributed to lower levels of the sports chain. Subject to full compliance with EU competition and free movement law, the Commission regards the effective protection of these sources of revenue as important in guaranteeing independent financing of sport activities in Europe.

The Communication goes on to cite the collective selling of media rights as a good example of financial solidarity and redistribution mechanisms within sports. Interestingly the Commission notes that collective selling of media rights *inherently* restricts competition but that it may bring about advantages which may outweigh the negative effects and therefore meet the criteria for the application of Article 101(3) TFEU if certain conditions are fulfilled. The Commission recommends sport associations to establish mechanisms for the collective selling of media rights to ensure adequate redistribution of revenues.

Meca-Medina: **the Court of Justice's analysis.**   Fn 454. In COMP/39471 *Certain*   **5.161**
joueur de tennis professionnel/Agence mondiale antidopage, decn of 13 October 2009 the Commission noted that the body against which complaint was directed by the tennis player did not organise sporting events itself and did not exploit rights arising from such events. Rather, its activities were limited to providing oversight and administration services to the sports tribunal which delivered rulings on disputes. The Commission considered that 'l'exercice de ces activités de jugement, ainsi que l'administration et le financement de ces activités par le CIAS, ne peuvent être considérés comme constituant une activité économique': para 23. Similarly the legislative activity of the anti-doping agency was unlikely to be an economic activity rendering that body an undertaking for the purposes of the competition rules. The Commission went on to apply the principles set out in *Meca-Medina* and rejected the complaint. The case is on appeal: Case T-508/09 *Cañas v Commission*, not yet decided.

Proportionality under Article 81 in the sporting context.   In *ADIPAV*,   **5.162**
Case 640/08, decn of 29 December 2008, the Spanish Competition Commission held that the provision in the technical regulations of the International Association of Patin Sailing Boats that wood is the only permitted material for manufacturing such boats was proportionate and legitimate for the objective of ensuring a neutral sporting competition; whereas the rule which limited the price of such boats was not so justified and infringed the Spanish domestic equivalent of Article 101 TFEU.

6

VERTICAL AGREEMENTS AFFECTING DISTRIBUTION OR SUPPLY

1. Introduction

Vertical restraints under Article 81. **Fn 2.** Some of the terms often used in the analysis of vertical restraints are explained in the 2010 Vertical Restraints Guidelines, OJ 2010 C130/1: Vol II, App C20 (discussed below), see, eg para 107(a) ('free-rider problem'); 107(c) ('certification free-rider issue'); 107(d) ('hold-up problem'); 107(f) ('vertical externality issue'). **6.002**

Appreciable effect: the Commission's presumption. **Fn 4.** See now para 8 of the 2010 Vertical Restraints Guidelines, OJ 2010 C130/1: Vol II, App C20 (discussed below) to the same effect. **6.003**

Situations where the presumption in the Notice does not apply. Paras 9–11 of the 2010 Vertical Restraints Guidelines cover *de minimis* in relation to vertical agreements which do not contain hard-core restrictions (in which case a 15 per cent market share threshold applies); vertical agreements which include hard-core restrictions (in which case Article 101(1) may apply even where market shares are below 15 per cent); and vertical agreements between small and medium enterprises which are regarded as 'rarely capable' of appreciably affecting competition. **6.004**

Legislative approach to vertical restraints. Regulation 2790/99 has been replaced by Regulation 330/2010 which came into force on 1 June 2010 and expires on 31 May 2022 (OJ 2010 L102/1: Vol II, App C7A). The new Regulation continues the 30 per cent market share ceiling approach of the earlier block exemption. It was accompanied by a new set of Guidelines on Vertical Restraints (OJ 2010 C130/1: Vol II, App C20). The motor vehicle block exemption, Regulation 1400/2002 has also been replaced in part by Regulation 461/2010 (OJ 2010 L129/52: Vol II, App C7B), also accompanied by new Guidelines (OJ 2010 C138/16: Vol II, App C21). Regulation 461/2010 distinguishes between agreements relating to the distribution of new motor vehicles and agreements relating to the aftersales markets of the supply of spare parts and the provision of repair and maintenance services. **6.006**

As regards the supply of new motor vehicles, the Commission has concluded that the provisions of the general Vertical Restraints block exemption are sufficient to deal with competition concerns. In respect of these agreements, the application of Regulation 1400/2002 is extended until 31 May 2013 as a transitional measure and thereafter the agreements will be covered by Regulation 330/2010. As regards agreements relating to the aftersales markets, they are exempt if they comply with Regulation 330/2010 and do not contain any of the three additional hard-core restrictions set out in Article 5 of Regulation 461/2010. Regulation 461/2010 expires on 31 May 2023.

6.007 **Economic analysis and market power.** **Fn 16.** A similar statement is made at para 6 of the 2010 Vertical Restraints Guidelines and see also paras 98 and 99 which refer to the self-restraining character of vertical agreements where both parties have an incentive to prevent the exercise of market power by the other. The negative and positive effects of vertical restraints generally are described in paras 100 *et seq* of the new Guidelines.

Fn 18. See now paras 100 *et seq* of the 2010 Vertical Restraints Guidelines.

Fn 19. The 2001 Guidelines have now been replaced by the Horizontal Cooperation Guidelines 2011, OJ 2011 C11/1: Vol II, App C22. The new Guidelines do not refer to the HHI though similar points are covered in para 97 and paras 111 *et seq*.

6.008 **The Guidelines.** New Guidelines on Vertical Restraints were published to accompany Regulation 330/2010 (OJ 2010 C130/1: Vol II, App C20) ('the 2010 Vertical Restraints Guidelines'). The 2010 Vertical Restraints Guidelines describe vertical agreements which generally fall outside Article 101 (including agency); clarify the application of the block exemption; describe how to define relevant markets and calculate market shares; and set out the Commission's general framework of analysis and its enforcement policy in relation to particular kinds of agreement. The 2010 Vertical Restraints Guidelines do not group agreements into the four categories set out in the previous Guidelines but they do cover single branding, exclusive distribution or customer allocation, selective distribution, franchising, and exclusive supply. They also cover two other kinds of vertical restraints not currently discussed in this Chapter, namely upfront access payments and category management agreements, see new paragraphs 6.085A and 6.085B, below.

6.008A **The Guidelines: negative and positive effects of vertical restraints.** The 2010 Vertical Restraints Guidelines set out a framework of analysis for vertical restraints generally in paras 96 *et seq*. Although the Commission regards vertical restraints as generally less harmful than horizontal restraints, the Guidelines set out negative effects that may arise, in particular anti-competitive foreclosure of other suppliers or other buyers, the softening of inter-brand competition or intra-brand competition, and the creation of obstacles to market integration. The Commission notes that restraints agreed for non-branded goods are in general less harmful than those for branded goods but that combinations of vertical restraints may in some cases be less harmful than restraints in isolation. The positive effects of vertical restraints are also outlined, in particular solving the 'free rider' problem, enabling entry into new markets and helping create a brand image by imposing uniformity and quality standards. Finally, in this general section of the Guidelines, the Commission sets out four steps for analysing vertical restraints: establishing the market shares of the parties; applying the 30 per cent threshold in Regulation 330/2010; and then individual assessment under Article 101(1) and Article 101(3) where the market share threshold is exceeded.

Relevant factors for individual assessment of agreements.   Where an agreement   **6.008B**
containing vertical restraints does not benefit from the block exemption in Regulation 330/2010, the parties will have to assess whether it falls within Article 101(1) and if so whether the conditions in Article 101(3) are fulfilled. The 2010 Vertical Restraints Guidelines set out the factors that the Commission considers are relevant at both stages. Where the parties' market shares exceed the 30 per cent threshold, the Commission will undertake a full analysis considering the nature of the agreement, the market position of the parties, their competitors and their customers, for example whether the customers exercise buyer power. Other factors include the maturity of the market, whether the products on the market are homogeneous or heterogeneous, and the cumulative effect of other similar agreements on the market. So far as the application of Article 101(3) is concerned, the Commission notes that when considering whether the restraints make it possible to distribute the goods more efficiently, undertakings invoking the benefit of Article 101(3) are not required to consider hypothetical or theoretical alternatives: para 125.

Structure of this Chapter.   Regulation 1400/2010 referred to in sub-para (iii) has   **6.009**
been replaced in part by Regulation 461/2010 (OJ 2010 L129/52: Vol II, App C7B).

2. Regulation 2790/99

In general.   Regulation 2790/99 has been replaced by Regulation 330/2010   **6.010**
which came into force on 1 June 2010 and expires on 31 May 2022 (OJ 2010 L102/1: Vol II, App C7A). The new Regulation was accompanied by a new set of Guidelines on Vertical Restraints (OJ 2010 C130/1: Vol II, App C20).

(a) Scope

'Vertical agreement'.   The term 'vertical agreement' is now defined in Article 1(a)   **6.011**
of Regulation 330/2010 and has the same meaning as under Regulation 2790/99. The definition is expanded upon in paras 24 *et seq* of the 2010 Vertical Restraints Guidelines. These make clear, amongst other things, that the block exemption

does not apply to agreements with final consumers who are not undertakings: para 25(b); that it does apply to goods sold and purchased for renting to third parties but not to rent and lease agreements: para 26.

6.012 **Competing undertakings.** The definition of 'competing undertakings' in Article 1(c) of Regulation 330/2010 differs from that in Article 2(4) of the earlier block exemption. The new definition distinguishes between actual and potential competitors. An actual competitor is one active 'on the same relevant market' and a potential competitor is one which it is realistic to suppose would enter that market in response to a small but permanent price rise. The reference to the 'relevant market' rather than the 'product market' presumably now encompasses the geographic market in the definition. So far as the application of the block exemption to non-reciprocal agreements between competing undertakings are concerned, the first exception relating to the buyer's annual turnover is not included in the new definition of non-reciprocal agreements in Article 2(4) of Regulation 330/2010. The other two exceptions for cases where the supplier operates on both the wholesale and retail level are carried forward in Article 2(4) of the new Regulation. Further clarification of the 'dual distribution' exceptions for goods and services is provided in the 2010 Vertical Restraints Guidelines, paras 27 and 28.

6.013 **Retailers' associations.** The provision as regards retailers' associations in the former block exemption is reproduced in identical terms in Article 2(2) of Regulation 330/2010. See also paras 29 and 30 of the 2010 Vertical Restraints Guidelines.

6.014 **Turnover calculations.** The provision as regards the calculation of turnover in the former block exemption is reproduced in identical terms in Article 10 of Regulation 330/2010. The same definition of 'connected undertakings' is also carried forward in Article 1(2) of the new block exemption.

6.015 **Other block exemptions.** Article 2(5) of Regulation 330/2010 provides that the Regulation does not apply to vertical agreements the subject-matter of which falls within the scope of any other block exemption regulations, unless otherwise provided for in such a regulation. However, the relationship between this block exemption and the new block exemption for motor vehicle distribution, Regulation 461/2010 (OJ 2010 L129/52: Vol II, App C7B) is more complex: see the update to paragraphs 6.006, above and 6.111, below.

As to vertical restraints in connection with agreements concerning specialisation or research and development, Regulation 2658/2000 has been replaced by Regulation 1218/2010 (OJ 2010 L335/43), and Regulation 2659/2000 has been replaced by Regulation 1217/2010 (OJ 2010 L335/36). See also the new Horizontal Cooperation Guidelines (OJ 2011 C11/1: Vol II, App C22) paras 195 and 196 which discuss the application of the Vertical Agreements block exemption to joint purchasing arrangements.

Intellectual property rights.   Article 2(3) of Regulation 330/2010 is in identical   **6.016**
terms to Article 2(3) of Regulation 2790/99. The relationship between vertical
agreements and IPR licensing is covered extensively in the 2010 Vertical Restraints
Guidelines, paras 31 *et seq*. The Commission there indicates the kinds of agreements which will not be covered by the block exemption, eg where a party provides
another party with a recipe and licenses the other party to produce a drink to that
recipe or where the contract confers the right to advertise oneself as being an official
sponsor of an event. The Guidelines also refer to sales of hard copies of software
where the buyer of the hard copy does not obtain a licence but rather the licence (in
the form of a 'shrink wrap' licence) is entered into between the supplier and the
ultimate consumer.

(b) Market share

Threshold.   One of the principal changes in the new block exemption, Regulation   **6.017**
330/2010 (OJ 2010 L102/1: Vol II, App C7A), is that the market share threshold
now applies to the buyer as well as the supplier of the goods or services. Article 3(1)
of Regulation 330/2010 provides that the exemption applies on condition that the
market share held by the seller does not exceed 30 per cent of the relevant market
on which it sells the contract goods or services and that the market share of the
buyer must also not exceed 30 per cent of the relevant market 'on which it purchases
the contract goods or services'. Article 3(2) makes provision for multi-party agreements, particularly where one party is both a supplier and a buyer under the agreement: see also para 90 of the 2010 Vertical Restraints Guidelines (OJ 2010 C130/1:
Vol II, App C20). A similar indication by the Commission that there is no presumption that agreements where the market share threshold are exceeded will fall
foul of Article 101 is given in para 96 of the 2010 Vertical Restraints Guidelines.

Relevant party.   Now that all parties to the agreement must meet the 30 per cent   **6.018**
threshold, there is no separate provision for exclusive supply agreements.

Calculation of market share.   Article 7 of Regulation 330/2010 largely repro-   **6.019**
duces Article 9 of the previous block exemption. Para 86 of the 2010 Vertical
Restraints Guidelines (OJ 2010 C130/1: Vol II, App C20) refers to the Notice on
Definition of Relevant Markets (OJ 1997 C372/5: Vol II, App C10). In the new
provisions, however, there is no distinction drawn between the use of volume data
for suppliers or buyers in the absence of market sales or purchase data. See also para
93 of the 2010 Vertical Restraints Guidelines.

The point about the relevant market being the market on which the buyer purchases
the good rather than the downstream market is now made in Article 3(1) itself.

For in-house production now see para 94 of the 2010 Vertical Restraints Guidelines;
for tripartite agreements now see para 90; for OEM suppliers see para 91; for dual
distribution see para 95.

6.020   **Relevant period.**   The provisions previously in Article 9(2) of Regulation 2790/99 are carried forward to Article 7(d)–(g) of Regulation 330/2010.

6.021   **Vertical agreement covering several products.**   Paras 68 and 69 of the previous Guidelines concerning portfolios of product are reproduced as paras 72 and 73 of the 2010 Vertical Restraints Guidelines (OJ 2010 C130/1:Vol II, App C20).

(c)   Terms and conditions

6.022   **Scheme of the block exemption.**   The scheme of the new block exemption is similar to that described here with Article 4 of Regulation 330/2010 (OJ 2010 L102/1: Vol II, App C7A) setting out the hard-core restrictions which preclude the application of the exemption at all and Article 5 listing the non-exempted restrictions. As to the severability of non-exempted restrictions, see paras 70 and 71 of the 2010 Vertical Restraints Guidelines (bringing forward paras 66 and 67 of the earlier Guidelines) which state that the 'rule of severability' applies to excluded restrictions so that the benefit of the block exemption is only lost in relation to that part of the vertical agreement which does not comply with the conditions set out in Article 5.

6.023   **Hard-core restrictions.**   The hard-core restrictions listed in Article 4 of Regulation 330/2010 (OJ 2010 L102/1: Vol II, App C7A) are almost identical to those set out in Article 4 of the earlier block exemption. Further clarification is provided by paras 47 *et seq* of the 2010 Vertical Restraints Guidelines, OJ 2010 C130/1: Vol II, App C20. Note that the 2010 Vertical Restraints Guidelines also consider exceptional cases where hard-core restrictions will fall outside the scope of Article 101(1) or may fulfil the conditions of Article 101(3): see paras 60–64 of the Guidelines and the update to paragraphs 6.054, below (exclusive distribution) and 6.106, below (selective distribution systems).

As regards the restriction of sales by members of a selective distribution system to unauthorised distributors, this is now only a hard-core restriction if it relates to unauthorised distributors within the territory reserved by the supplier to operate that system: see also para 57 of the 2010 Vertical Restraints Guidelines. As regards sales over the internet: see the update in paragraph 6.023A, below.

Fn 67. See now para 48 of the 2010 Vertical Restraints Guidelines regarding indirect imposition of RPM.

Fn 68. The term 'selective distribution system' is now defined in Article 1(e) of Regulation 330/2010. The definition is limited to arrangements where the distributors undertake not to supply to unauthorised distributors 'within the territory reserved by the supplier to operate that system'.

Fn 69. The point made in para 54 of the old guidelines is now made in para 57 of the 2010 Vertical Restraints Guidelines, which states that use by a distributor of its own website is not the same thing as opening a new outlet in a different location.

Fn 72. The point made in para 49 of the old guidelines concerning measures which indirectly restrict the buyer's sales to customers outside its territory is now made in para 50 of the 2010 Vertical Restraints Guidelines.

Fn 73. The point concerning health and safety as a possible justification for a hard-core restriction is now made in para 60 of the 2010 Vertical Restraints Guidelines. The point that an obligation to display the supplier's brand is not a hard-core restriction is now made in para 50.

Fn 74. For the use of the internet, see the update in paragraph 6.023A, below.

Fn 76. The ability to restrict a wholesaler from making either active or passive sales to end users is discussed in para 55 of the 2010 Vertical Restraints Guidelines.

Fn 77. The term 'component' is now defined in para 55 of the 2010 Vertical Restraints Guidelines.

'Active' and 'passive' sales: the internet.   The classification of a restriction as hard-   **6.023A**
core depends in part on whether the restriction relates to active or passive sales. The 2010 Vertical Restraints Guidelines (OJ 2010 C130/1: Vol II, App C20) define what is meant by these terms, taking into account the use of email and the internet: paras 51 *et seq*. Active selling thus includes sending unsolicited emails or specifically targeting advertisements at customers in the particular territory. However, in general, the use of a website to sell products is regarded as a form of passive selling (para 52), even if the website offers different language options. The Commission lists in detail the kinds of restrictions on internet sales that it will regard as restrictions on passive selling including the extent to which the supplier can insist on the proportion of overall sales made over the internet by the distributor. It also describes when an advertisement will be considered active rather than passive selling. Note also para 64 where the Commission states that though 'dual pricing' (ie charging a higher price for products intended to be resold online than for products intended to be resold offline) is generally a hard-core restriction, it may be justified under Article 101(3) where selling online leads to higher costs for the manufacturer than offline sales.

Non-exempted restrictions.   Article 5 of Regulation 330/2010 carries forward   **6.024**
the provisions of Article 5 of the earlier block exemption. Further clarification is set out in paras 65 *et seq* of the 2010 Vertical Restraints Guidelines (OJ 2010 C130/1: Vol II, App C20).

Fn 80. The point concerning indirect prolongation of non-compete obligations is now made in para 66 of the 2010 Vertical Restraints Guidelines.

Fn 82. The point concerning sales from the supplier's premises is now discussed in para 67 of the 2010 Vertical Restraints Guidelines.

Fn 83. 'Know-how' is now defined in Article 1(g) of Reg 330/2010. The new definition is somewhat wider than formerly in that in order to be 'substantial' it must be 'significant and useful' rather than having to include information which is 'indispensable'.

Fn 84. The point concerning suppliers sharing a distribution network is now made in paras 69 and 183 of the 2010 Vertical Restraints Guidelines.

(d) Withdrawal and disapplication

6.025 **Withdrawal by the Commission.** Regulation 330/2010 (OJ 2010 L102/1: Vol II, App C7A) contains no provision relating to the withdrawal of the block exemption because this power is conferred by Article 29(1) of Regulation 1/2003. The circumstances likely to trigger withdrawal are discussed in paras 74–78 of the 2010 Vertical Restraints Guidelines (OJ 2010 C130/1: Vol II, App C20) which make clear that withdrawal operates only *ex nunc* and cannot affect the status of the agreement until the date on which the withdrawal becomes effective. See also para 179 of the Guidelines as regards withdrawal of the block exemption where selective distribution agreements cover more than 50 per cent of a relevant market.

6.026 **Withdrawal by a national authority.** Similarly, this is now dealt with by Article 29(2) of Regulation 1/2003 rather than by a provision in the new block exemption itself, though see Recital (14) of Regulation 330/2010 and para 78 of the 2010 Vertical Restraints Guidelines (OJ 2010 C130/1: Vol II, App C20).

Where the effects result from a network of similar agreements, the national authority will need to consider whether withdrawal of the benefit of the block exemption as regards only one supplier would be discriminatory and thus itself distort competition. Thus the Hungarian Competition Authority decided not to withdraw the application of Regulation 2790/99 in respect of the beer-tie agreements of the supplier under investigation (Borsodi) when two other suppliers had equal shares of the market and it was the cumulative effect of all their agreements that restricted competition under the *Delimitis* test: see decision of 16 May 2008, Case No. Vj-28/20007/42.

6.027 **Disapplication by regulation.** The possible disapplication of the block exemption where a market is characterised by parallel networks of similar vertical restraints is dealt with in Article 6 of Regulation 330/2010. The obligation to allow a transitional period of six months which was stipulated by Article 8(2) of Regulation 2790/99 now applies by virtue of Article 1a of Regulation 19/65 (which article was inserted by Regulation 1215/1999 (OJ 1999 L148/1)): see paras 79–85 of the 2010 Vertical Restraints Guidelines.

3. Agency Agreements

6.029 **Commission Guidelines.** The Guidelines on Vertical Restraints referred to have been replaced by a new set of Guidelines on Vertical Restraints (OJ 2010

C130/1: Vol II, App C20) which accompanied the new block exemption, Regulation 330/2010 (OJ 2010 L102/1: Vol II, App C7A). The 2010 Vertical Restraints Guidelines define an agent rather than an agency agreement but the content of the definition is the same: para 12.

Financial or commercial risk. **Fn 105**. See similarly Case C-279/06 *CEPSA v* **6.030** *Tobar* [2008] ECR I-6681, para 40.

The analysis of the Court of First Instance in *DaimlerChrysler*. As regards the **6.031** criticism referred to in the penultimate sentence of the paragraph, the 2010 Vertical Restraints Guidelines (OJ 2010 C130/1: Vol II, App C20) state that the question of risk must be assessed 'with regard to the economic reality of the situation rather than the legal form' (para 17).

Types of risk. The 2010 Vertical Restraints Guidelines (OJ 2010 C130/1: Vol II, **6.032** App C20) describe three kinds of risk (para 14): contract specific risks such as the financing of stock; risks associated with market specific investments; and risks associated with other activities which the principal requires the agent to undertake on the same product market but which are not done on behalf of the principal but by the agent for its own risk. For the purposes of applying Article 101(1), the agreement will qualify as an agency agreement only where the agent does not bear any or any significant risk in relation to any of these three kinds of risk (para 15). The Guidelines go on to describe the characteristics of a relationship which will be considered an agency agreement: para 17.

Agent acting for more than one principal. The 2010 Vertical Restraints **6.033** Guidelines also state that it is not material whether the agent acts for one or several principals: para 13.

Cartels facilitated by agents. The same point is made in para 20 of the 2010 **6.034** Vertical Restraints Guidelines (OJ 2010 C130/1: Vol II, App C20).

Terms and conditions falling outside Article 81(1). Similar provision is made as **6.036** regards the terms which fall outside Article 101 in the case of a genuine agency agreement in para 18 of the 2010 Vertical Restraints Guidelines. See also para 49 of those Guidelines which states that where an agreement is not a true agency agreement, an obligation preventing or restricting the agent from sharing its commission with the customer would be a hard-core restrictions under Article 4(a) of Regulation 330/2010.

Other terms and conditions. The terms dealt with in para 19 of the old Guidelines **6.037** are dealt with in para 19 of the 2010 Vertical Restraints Guidelines. Post-termination non-compete provisions are covered by Article 5(a) of Regulation 330/2010 (OJ 2010 L102/1: Vol II, App C7A).

Application of Regulation 2790/99. This Regulation has been replaced by a new **6.038** block exemption: Regulation 330/2010 which came into force on 1 June 2010 and expires on 31 May 2022 (OJ 2010 L102/1: Vol II, App C7A). The definition of 'buyer' also includes an undertaking selling goods or services on behalf of another undertaking: Article 1(h) and the characterisation of a ban on sharing commission as a hard-core restriction still pertains: Article 4(a) of Regulation 330/2010 and para 49 of the 2010 Vertical Restraints Guidelines (OJ 2010 C130/1: Vol II, App C20).

4. Exclusive Distribution and Supply Agreements

(a) Generally

6.039 **Definitions.** The Guidelines on Vertical Restraints referred to have been replaced by a new set of Guidelines on Vertical Restraints (OJ 2010 C130/1: Vol II, App C20) which accompanied the new block exemption, Regulation 330/2010 (OJ 2010 L102/1: Vol II, App C7A). The 2010 Vertical Restraints Guidelines do not use the category 'limited distribution' to group these kinds of agreements. The definition of 'exclusive distribution' agreements is the same as under the old Guidelines (see para 151 of the 2010 Vertical Restraints Guidelines) but 'exclusive supply' is no longer defined in the block exemption and the definition in the new Guidelines does not refer to the appointment of only one purchaser in the Union but rather to one purchaser 'for a whole market': see paras 192 *et seq*. The definition of 'selective distribution agreements' is the same in the 2010 Vertical Restraints Guidelines as it was in the earlier Guidelines: para 174.

6.040 **Economic effects of exclusive distribution/supply agreements.** The 2010 Vertical Restraints Guidelines contain a similar analysis in paras 151 *et seq*. See more generally the Commission's views on the negative and positive effects of vertical agreements in paras 100 *et seq* of the Guidelines.

6.041 **Economic effects of exclusive customer allocation.** The 2010 Vertical Restraints Guidelines (OJ 2010 C130/1: Vol II, App C20) contain a similar analysis in paras 168 *et seq*.

6.042 **Combination with other vertical restraints.** The 2010 Vertical Restraints Guidelines analyse the effect of combining exclusive distribution with single branding at paras 161 and 162.

6.043 **Structure of this Section.** Regulation 2790/99 has been replaced by Regulation 330/2010 (OJ 2010 L102/1: Vol II, App C7A) but the points considered in this paragraph apply equally to the new block exemption.

(b) Application of Article 81(1)

6.044 **In general.** Fn 144. The Commission's framework for analysis of vertical restraints is set out in paras 96 *et seq* of the 2010 Vertical Restraints Guidelines (OJ 2010 C 130/1).

Inter-brand competition and market power. The new block exemption **6.045** Regulation 330/2010 sets the same 30 per cent market share threshold but applies it to both the supplier and the purchaser, see update to paragraph 6.017, above. As regards the supply of new products, or the expansion into new geographic markets, see now paras 107 and 61 of the 2010 Vertical Restraints Guidelines (OJ 2010 C130/1: Vol II, App C20). As regards multiple exclusive dealerships in an oligopolistic market see para 166 of those Guidelines.

Fn 145. See now para 153 of the 2010 Vertical Restraints Guidelines.

Fn 146. The same point is made in para 158 of the 2010 Vertical Restraints Guidelines.

Foreclosure issues. See now paras 155, 156, 161 of the 2010 Vertical Restraints **6.046** Guidelines to similar effect. As regards exclusive supply discussed in the final sentence, see now paras 192–202 of the new Guidelines (OJ 2010 C130/1: Vol II, App C20).

Fn 152. The equivalent provision as regards the length of non-compete obligation in Reg 330/2010 is Article 5(1).

Cumulative effect. See now paras 121 and 154 of the 2010 Vertical Restraints **6.047** Guidelines.

(i) The hard-core restrictions

Resale price maintenance. The 2010 Vertical Restraints Guidelines (OJ 2010 **6.050** C130/1: Vol II, App C20) deal in some detail with resale price maintenance: paras 223 *et seq*. The Commission confirms that an agreement involving RPM is presumed to restrict competition and is unlikely to fulfil the conditions in Article 101(3). However it is possible for undertakings 'to plead an efficiency defence' most notably where a manufacturer introduces a new product. In such a case RPM may be helpful during the introductory period to promote the product: para 225. The threshold at which the Commission considers that even hard-core restrictions may not have an appreciable effect has been increased from 10 to 15 per cent: paras 9 and 10.

In Case C-506/07 *Lubricantes y Carburantes Galaicos ('Lubricarga') v GALP Energía España*, Order of 3 September 2009 the CJ confirmed that a contract which fixes resale prices and which contains other hard-core clauses taking it outside Regulation 1984/83 can still fall outside Article 101(1) if it is *de minimis*.

Recommended resale prices. The 2010 Vertical Restraints Guidelines (OJ 2010 **6.051** C130/1: Vol II, App C20) consider recommended resale prices at paras 226 *et seq* and para 48.

Maximum retail prices. The 2010 Vertical Restraints Guidelines consider **6.052** maximum resale prices at paras 226 *et seq* and para 48. See also para 107(f) which considers the use of maximum price setting as way of avoiding the 'double margin-alisation problem'.

Fn 173. The appeal referred to in the footnote was found to be inadmissible: Case T-274/06 *Estaser El Mareny v Commission* [2007] ECR II-143*.

6.053   **Measures obstructing parallel imports.   Fn 175.** The discussion of export restrictions in the pharmaceutical market must be read in the light of the CJ's judgment in Cases C-501/06P, etc, *GlaxoSmithKline Services Unlimited v Commission*, judgment of 6 October 2009. The CJ did not regard the pharmaceuticals market as a special case and rejected the argument that an agreement limiting parallel trade only has the object of restricting competition if it disadvantages final consumers: para 62. The CJ held that the agreement setting different prices for product depending on whether it would be resold domestically or exported had as its object the restriction of competition so that there was no need to examine its effect on the market. But the CJ upheld the GC's decision that the Commission had failed properly to examine GSK's arguments for the application of Article 101(3) TFEU: para 104. See also Cases C-468/06, etc, *Sot Lelos kai Sia EE v GlaxoSmithKline* [2008] ECR I-7139, [2008] 5 CMLR 1382, [2009] All ER (EC) 1 (State regulation of prices does not mean that benefits of parallel trading for consumers are minimal).

Fn 177. The appeals in *Video Games, Nintendo Distribution* have now been decided: Case T-18/03 *CD-Contact Data v Commission* [2009] ECR II-1021 (fine reduced) (appeal dismissed Case C-260/09P *Activision Blizzard v Commission*, judgment of 10 February 2011); Case T-12/03 *Itochu* [2009] ECR II-883, [2009] 5 CMLR 1375 (appeal dismissed); Case T-13/03 *Nintendo* [2009] 5 CMLR 1421 (fine reduced); Case T-398/02 *Linea Gig* (removed from register 2 May 2005).

6.054   **'Active' and 'passive' sales and absolute territorial protection.**   The sentence ending with the marker for fn 184 should refer to the contract being limited to banning active sales not passive sales.

The distinction between active and passive sales is an important element in the new block exemption, Regulation 330/2010 (Article 4(b) and (c)) and the 2010 Vertical Restraints Guidelines (OJ 2010 C130/1: Vol II, App C20) (paras 51 *et seq*). The 2010 Guidelines analyse how these terms are to be applied to advertising on the worldwide web and to sales over the internet: see new paragraph 6.023A, above. The 2010 Guidelines also discuss certain 'exceptional cases' where a ban on both active and passive sales may be justified, namely where the distributor will be the first to sell a new brand or to enter a new market and has to commit substantial investment to generate a demand for the product. In such a case, the Commission considers that restrictions on passive sales may fall outside the scope of Article 101(1) for the first two years that the distributor sells the contract goods in the exclusive territory or to the exclusive customer group: see para 61 of the Guidelines.

Similarly, where a product is being tested in a limited territory or with a small customer group, or where introduction of the product is being staggered, restrictions on active selling may fall outside Article 101(1): para 62.

Unilateral conduct or unlawful infringement. This issue is now covered by the **6.055** 2010 Vertical Restraints Guidelines, para 25.

Financial disincentives for dealers who export. See also COMP/37811 *Algerian* **6.056** *gas imports* Press Release IP/07/1074 (11 July 2007) concerning a profit sharing mechanism under which the buyer/importer of gas from Algeria was obliged to share part of the profit with the supplier/producer if the gas was sold on by the importer to a customer outside the agreed territory or to a customer using the gas for a purpose other than the one agreed upon. A common understanding was reached between the Commission and Algeria that the conditions would be deleted.

Other indirect measures preventing parallel imports. Fn 207. In Cases **6.058** C-501/06P, etc, *GlaxoSmithKline Services Unlimited v Commission*, judgment of 6 October 2009 the CJ held that the agreement setting different prices for a product depending on whether it would be resold domestically or exported had as its object the restriction of competition so that there was no need to examine its effect on the market. See also Cases C-468/06, etc, *Sot Lelos kai Sia EE v GlaxoSmithKline* [2008] ECR I-7139, [2008] 5 CMLR 1382, [2009] All ER (EC) 1 (State regulation of prices does not mean that benefits of parallel trading for consumers are minimal).

Fn 211. The provision in Reg 2790/99 has been replaced by Article 4(b)(i) of Reg 330/2010 (OJ 2010 C130/1: Vol II, App C20).

Measures aimed at monitoring and identifying the source of parallel **6.061** **imports. Fn 217.** The appeals in *Video Games, Nintendo Distribution* have now been decided: Case T-18/03 *CD-Contact Data v Commission* [2009] ECR II-1021 (fine reduced) (appeal dismissed Case C-260/09P *Activision Blizzard v Commission*, judgment of 10 February 2011); Case T-12/03 *Itochu* [2009] ECR II-883, [2009] 5 CMLR 1375 (appeal dismissed); Case T-13/03 *Nintendo* [2009] 5 CMLR 1421 (fine reduced); Case T-398/02 *Linea Gig* (removed from register 2 May 2005). Nothing was stated in those appeals to detract from the points made in this paragraph.

(ii) Particular clauses

Distributor's obligation not to sell competing products. A non-compete obliga- **6.062** tion of more than five years will not benefit from exemption under Regulation 330/2010 (OJ 2010 C130/1: Vol II, App C20): see Article 5(1)(a).

Distributor's exclusive purchasing obligation. The 2010 Vertical Restraints **6.063** Guidelines (OJ 2010 C130/1: Vol II, App C20) deal with the point made here in similar terms: see para 162 (which, however, omits the earlier statement that such agreements were unlikely to merit exemption unless there were clear and substantial efficiencies).

6.065 **Restrictions as to persons to whom goods may be resold.** For a discussion of exclusive customer allocation clauses see paras 168 *et seq* of the 2010 Vertical Restraints Guidelines (OJ 2010 C130/1: Vol II, App C20).

(c) Application of Article 81(3) to individual agreements

6.081 **Application of Article 81(3) to exclusive distribution agreements.** The need to protect investments incurred in the launch of a new product was held by the Paris Court of Appeal not to be established as justification for restrictions in the agreement between Apple and Orange making the latter the exclusive network operator and wholesaler of the iPhone in France. Examining the investments relied on and the profits being made, the Court upheld the decision of the competition authority that the five-year exclusive contract was out of proportion to the investment risk. The judgment was on appeal from the authority's decision taking interim measures that prohibited Apple from refusing to distribute through other network operators: *Apple Sales International v Bouygues Télécom*, judgment of 4 February 2009, BOCCRF No. 4 of 8 April 2009; on appeal to the Cour de Cassation, not yet decided. The Court also held that the restrictions in the agreement took it outside the scope of Regulation 2790/99. In November 2009, Apple and Orange announced that they were abandoning their exclusivity arrangement.

6.082 **Application of Article 81(3) to exclusive customer allocation agreements.** For a discussion of exclusive customer allocation clauses see paras 168 *et seq* of the 2010 Vertical Restraints Guidelines (OJ 2010 C130/1: Vol II, App C20).

6.085A **Upfront access payments.** The 2010 Vertical Restraints Guidelines (OJ 2010 C130/1: Vol II, App C20) discuss agreements for upfront access payments, where a supplier pays a sum to a distributor at the start of a relevant period for eg access to shelf space (a 'slotting allowance', or for promotional campaigns: see paras 203–208. Where the parties to such an agreement do not have more than a 30 per cent share of their respective markets, the agreement will be covered by the block exemption in Regulation 330/2010, OJ 2010 C130/1: Vol II, App C20. Although such payments may result in foreclosure of other distributors or suppliers, they may contribute to the efficient allocation of shelf-space and prevent free riding by suppliers on the promotional effort of the distributor.

6.085B **Category management agreements.** The 2010 Vertical Restraints Guidelines (OJ 2010 C130/1: Vol II, App C20) discuss category management agreements where the distributor entrusts a supplier with the marketing of a category of products supplied by that supplier and its competitors: see paras 209–213. Where the parties to such an agreement do not have more than a 30 per cent share of their respective markets, the agreement will be covered by the block exemption in

Regulation 330/2010, OJ 2010 C130/1: Vol II, App C20. Although such agreements are not considered problematic in general, the Commission notes that they may facilitate collusion at both the suppliers' and the distributors' levels.

5. Selective Distribution Systems

(a) Generally

Preliminary. Selective distribution agreements are considered in paras 174 *et seq*   **6.086**
of 2010 Vertical Restraints Guidelines (OJ 2010 C130/1: Vol II, App C20).

Approach of this Section. Motor vehicle distribution and servicing agreements   **6.088**
are now governed by Regulation 461/2010, OJ 2010 L129/52: Vol II, App C7B
which continues the application of Regulation 1400/2002 to certain agreements:
see the updates to paragraphs 6.109, *et seq* below.

(b) Article 81(1)

Luxury and prestige products. As to when trade mark rights can be enforced in   **6.093**
respect of luxury goods sold by a licensee to a discount store outside the network see
Case C-59/08 *Copad SA v Christian Dior couture SA and SIL* [2009] ECR
I-3421where the CJ interpreted the reference in Article 8(2) of Directive 80/104 to
the 'quality' of goods as including 'the allure and prestigious image which bestows
on the goods an aura of luxury'.

Note also para 175 of the 2010 Vertical Restraints Guidelines (OJ 2010 C130/1:
Vol II, App C20) which indicate that one of the conditions which must be satisfied
before purely qualitative criteria fall outside Article 101(1) is that 'the nature of the
product in question must necessitate a selective distribution system . . . having regard
to the nature of the product concerned, to preserve its quality and ensure its proper
use'. Note also the points made in paras 184 and 185 of the new Guidelines.

Restrictions on sales over the internet. The classification of a restriction as   **6.095**
hard-core depends in part on whether the restriction relates to active or passive
sales. The 2010 Vertical Restraints Guidelines (OJ 2010 C130/1: Vol II, App C20)
define what restraints on sales over the internet and by email will be regarded as
hard-core restrictions on passive sales and what will be regarded as restraints on
active sales: paras 51 *et seq*. Active selling thus includes sending unsolicited emails
or specifically targeting advertisements at customers in the particular territory.
However, in general, the use of a website to sell products is regarded as a form of
passive selling (para 52), even if the website offers different language options. The
Commission lists in detail the kinds of restrictions on internet sales that it will
regard as restrictions on passive selling including the extent to which the supplier
can insist on the proportion of overall sales made over the internet by the distributor.

It also describes when an advertisement will be considered active rather than passive selling.

See also Case C-439/09 *Pierre Fabre Dermo-Cosmétique SAS v Competition Authority*, not yet decided (reference from Cour d'appel de Paris asking whether a general and absolute ban on selling contract goods to end users via the internet, imposed on authorised distributors in the context of a selective distribution network, constitutes a 'hard-core' restriction which is not covered by the block exemption provided for by Regulation 2790/1999 but which potentially benefits from Article 101(3)).

6.099 **Application of Regulation 2790/99.** The Regulation referred to in the text has been replaced by Regulation 330/2010 (OJ 2010 C130/1: Vol II, App C20) which brings forward the 30 per cent market share threshold but applies it to both the supplier and the purchaser, see the update to paragraph 6.017, above. See also paras 174 *et seq* of the 2010 Vertical Restraints Guidelines OJ 2010 C130/1: Vol II, App C20 and, as regards withdrawal of the block exemption see now para 75 of those Guidelines.

6.100 **Cumulative effect.** See now the discussion in para 179 of the 2010 Vertical Restraints Guidelines OJ 2010 C130/1: Vol II, App C20 where the Commission notes that as regards individual contributions, a supplier with a market share of less than 5 per cent is in general not considered to contribute significantly to a cumulative effect. See also the example analysed in para 188 of the Guidelines.

6.101 **Territorial and other restrictions on resale.** See also Case T-427/08 *CEAHR v Commission*, not yet decided (appeal against rejection of complaint alleging breach of Article 102 TFEU by watch manufacturer refusing to sell spare parts outside the distribution system).

Fn 380. See also *re the Léonidas Network* [2008] ECC 190 (Decn No 07-D-24) where the French Competition Council found that the distribution arrangements operated by the Belgian chocolate manufacturer infringed Article 101 TFEU and the equivalent provision in the French Commercial Code. The network comprised 13 resellers who were authorised to import products to sell in their own shops and also to sell to other authorised retailers who countersigned the reseller's contract with Léonidas. Each retailer could only buy supplies from the reseller who had introduced him to the network or from a subsequent replacement reseller but they could not buy from more than one specified supplier at any given time. Further, the retailers were required only to supply end-users. The Council held that these terms fell within Article 4(b) of Regulation 2790/1999 so that the block exemption did not apply. A fine of €120,000 was imposed.

(c) **Application of Article 81(3)**

6.106 **Hard-core restrictions.** As regards bans on cross supplies between appointed distributors, see the 2010 Vertical Restraints Guidelines, OJ 2010 C130/1: Vol II,

App C20, para 63 where the Commission indicates that if appointed wholesalers located in different territories are obliged to invest in promotional activities to support the sales of appointed retailers, restrictions on active sales by the wholesalers to appointed retailers in other wholesalers' territories may be permissible to overcome possible free riding and may, in an individual case, benefit from Article 101(3).

Combination with other restraints. Fn 408. See now paras 182 and 193 of the **6.107** 2010 Vertical Restraints Guidelines OJ 2010 C130/1: Vol II, App C20 which have replaced the earlier guidelines.

Fn 409. Similar provision is now made in Article 5(1) of the replacement block exemption Regulation 330/2010, OJ 2010 L102/1: Vol II, App C7A.

Fn 410. See now Article 1(d) of Reg 330/2010, to the same effect.

Fn 411. See now Article 5(1)(c), ibid and para 182 of the 2010 Vertical Restraints Guidelines.

(d) Motor vehicle distribution and servicing

Regulation 1400/2002. Regulation 1400/2010 has been replaced in part by **6.109** Regulation 461/2010, OJ 2010 L129/52: Vol II, App C7B which came into force on the same day as the new block exemption for vertical restraints, Regulation 330/2010, OJ 2010 L102/1: Vol II, App C7A. The relationship between the two block exemptions is more complex than that between their predecessor regulations: see the updates to the following paragraphs. Regulation 461/2010 was accompanied by Supplementary Guidelines, OJ 2010 C138/16: Vol II, App C21. These Guidelines deal not only with the specific provisions of Regulation 461/2010 but also provide clarification on the interpretation of Regulation 330/2010 as it now applies to motor vehicle agreements dealing with aftersales matters and as it will apply after 31 May 2013 to agreements for the distribution of new motor vehicles: paras 2 and 3. The Guidelines are expressed to be without prejudice to the applicability of the Guidelines on Vertical Restraints (OJ 2010 C130/1: Vol II, App C20): see para 2.

Aims of Regulation 1400/2002. The Commission carried out an in-depth evalu- **6.110** ation of the operation of Regulation 1400/2002 (SEC(2008) 1946: 28 May 2008) and issued a Communication on 22 July 2009 (COM(2009) 388). The Commission concluded that so far as distribution of new motor vehicles were concerned, the general vertical restraints block exemption was now adequate to meet any competition concerns raised: see Supplementary Guidelines, para 12. However, for agreements covering distribution of spare parts and/or the provision of repair and maintenance services, the new block exemption prohibits three hard-core restrictions which apply in addition to the provisions of Regulation 330/2010.

Regulation 1400/2002: summary. According to Regulation 461/2010 (OJ **6.111** 2010 L129/52: Vol II, App C7B) Regulation 1400/2002 will still apply to those provisions in an agreement relating to the conditions under which the parties may purchase, sell or resell new motor vehicles in the period between 1 June 2010 (when Regulation 461/2010 came into force) and 31 May 2013. Thereafter the general block exemption for vertical restraints, Regulation 330/2010 (OJ L102/1: Vol II, App C7A) will apply to agreements relating to new vehicles. Vertical agreements relating to the conditions under which spare parts are distributed or repair and maintenance services are provided are exempt as from 1 June 2010 provided that they meet the conditions in Regulation 330/2010 and do not contain the three hard-core restrictions set out in Article 5 of Regulation 461/2010. Thus agreements relating to after sales matters must not contain either the hardcore restrictions set out in Regulation 330/2010 or the three additional restrictions in Article 5 of Regulation 461/2010: see the Supplementary Guidelines which accompanied the new Regulation—OJ 2010 C138/16: Vol II, App C21, para 14. The former list of non-exempt conditions in Article 5 of Regulation 1400/2002 no longer, therefore applies to agreements dealing with aftersales matters (although *quaere* the final sentence of para 46 of the Guidelines). The Supplementary Guidelines indicate that where hard-core restrictions are included, not only will the agreement no longer benefit from the block exemption, but there is a rebuttable presumption that the criteria in Article 101(3) are not satisfied: see para 17. In summary: the discussion in the text of the provisions of Regulation 1400/2002 and the old Explanatory Brochure still apply to an analysis of agreements so far as the agreement concerns distribution of new vehicles: see Supplementary Guidelines, para 13. For agreements relating to spare parts and repair and maintenance service, the provisions of Regulation 461/2002 no longer apply—the relevant instruments are Regulation 330/2010, Regulation 461/2010 and the new Supplementary Guidelines. After 31 May 2013, the relevant instruments for agreements relating to the distribution of new motor vehicles will be Regulation 330/2010 and the new Supplementary Guidelines: see para 3 of those Guidelines.

6.112   **Selective and exclusive distribution.**   So far as agreements for distributing new motor vehicles are concerned, the principles discussed in the text continue to apply until 31 May 2013: see update to paragraph 6.111, above. Thereafter the general Vertical Restraints Agreements block exemption, Regulation 330/2010 applies. The Commission's Supplementary Guidance (OJ 2010 C138/16: Vol II, App C21) gives guidance as to how the general provisions regarding single branding and selective distribution will apply in the motor vehicle sector.

6.113   **Principles underlying Regulation 1400/2002.**   As far as distribution of new motor vehicles is concerned, the principles set out in the text apply until 31 May 2013; thereafter such agreements will be governed by the general principles in the Vertical Restraints block exemption Regulation 330/2010: see update to paragraph 6.111, above. Guidance as to the application of Regulation 330/2010 to motor vehicle distribution is set out in the Commission's Supplementary Guidance,

OJ 2010 C138/16: Vol II, App C21. The Guidance considers in particular single branding and selective distribution arrangements.

Underlying principles regarding exemption of repair and maintenance arrange- **6.114**
ments. Agreements relating to the repair and maintenance of motor vehicles are now covered by the general Vertical Restraints block exemption Regulation 330/2010 but must also not contain any of the three additional hard-core restrictions set out in Article 5 of Regulation 461/2010 (OJ 2010 L129/52: Vol II, App C7B): see Article 4 of that Regulation. See also the Commission's Supplementary Guidance, OJ 2010 C138/16: Vol II, App C21. Para 15 of the Guidance notes that the brand-specific nature of the markets for repair and maintenance services means that competition is less intense in those markets than in the market for new vehicles. Paragraphs 22–24 discuss the three additional hard-core restrictions in Article 5 of Regulation 461/2010.

Relationship with Regulation 2790/99 and Article 81(3). Regulation 2790/99 **6.115**
has been replaced by Regulation 330/2010, OJ 2010 L102/1: Vol II, App C7A and the relationship between that regulation and the block exemption of motor vehicle agreements under Regulation 461/2010 (OJ 2010 L129/52: Vol II, App C7B) is very different: see the update to paragraph 6.111, above.

Scope of application of Regulation 1400/2002. The text is still relevant as regards **6.116**
distribution agreements for new motor vehicles, until 31 May 2013. After that date, and as from 1 June 2010 in relation to agreements for spare parts and repair and maintenance services, the general provisions of the Vertical Restraints block exemption, Regulation 330/2010 will apply (subject to some additional conditions in respect of aftermarkets agreements): see Regulation 461/2010 discussed in the update to paragraph 6.111, above. The definitions of 'motor vehicle' and 'spare parts' are the same in the new Regulation as they were under Regulation 1400/2002: see Article 1(1)(g) and (h) of Regulation 461/2010.

Third parties. This paragraph must now be read subject to the substantial changes **6.117**
to the treatment of motor vehicle distribution arrangements brought about by Regulation 461/2010, OJ 2010 L129/52: Vol II, App C7B, discussed in the updates to the preceding paragraphs.

Types of vertical agreements covered by Regulation 1400/2002. So far as agree- **6.118**
ments for distributing new motor vehicles are concerned, Regulation 1400/2002 continues to apply until 31 May 2013: see update to paragraph 6.111, above. Thereafter the general Vertical Restraints Agreements block exemption, Regulation 330/2010 applies (OJ 2010 L102/1: Vol II, App C7A). As from 1 June 2010, Regulation 1400/2002 is no longer relevant to agreements for the distribution of spare parts or for the provision of repair and maintenance services; these are now governed by Regulation 330/2010, subject to the provision concerning three additional hard-core restrictions set out in Regulation 461/2010 Article 5.

6.119 **Agreements between competing undertakings.**   So far as agreements for distributing new motor vehicles are concerned, Regulation 1400/2002 continues to apply until 31 May 2013: see update to paragraph 6.111, above. Thereafter the general Vertical Restraints Agreements block exemption, Regulation 330/2010 applies. Regulation 1400/2002 is no longer relevant to agreements for the distribution of spare parts or for the provision of repair and maintenance services; these are now governed by Regulation 330/2010. Article 4 of Regulation 330/2010 provides that the block exemption does not apply to agreements between competing undertakings unless they are non-reciprocal arrangements and the buyer does not compete at the manufacturing level with the seller. Article 2 of that Regulation covers vertical agreements entered into by an association of undertakings.

6.120A **Single branding.**   The Supplementary Guidance (OJ 2010 C138/16: Vol II, App C21) issued by the Commission to accompany Regulation 461/2010 contains detailed guidance about single branding arrangements in the motor vehicle sector. This Guidance applies to arrangements for the distribution of new motor vehicles as from 31 May 2013 (when Regulation 1400/2002 ceases to apply) and to arrangements for spare parts and repair and maintenance as from 1 June 2010).

6.121 **Exclusive or selective distribution.**   So far as agreements for distributing new motor vehicles are concerned, Regulation 1400/2002 continues to apply until 31 May 2013: see update to paragraph 6.111, above. Thereafter the general Vertical Restraints Agreements block exemption, Regulation 330/2010 applies. Regulation 1400/2002 is no longer relevant to agreements for the distribution of spare parts or for the provision of repair and maintenance services; these are now governed by Regulation 330/2010, subject to the three additional hard-core restrictions set out in Regulation 461/2010, Article 5 (OJ 2010 L129/52: Vol II, App C7B). The Supplementary Guidance (OJ 2010 C138/16: Vol II, App C21) issued by the Commission to accompany Regulation 461/2010 contains detailed guidance about selective distribution arrangements.

6.122 **Market share thresholds.**   The market share thresholds discussed in the text apply to new motor vehicle distribution agreements until 31 May 2013. After that the market share thresholds in Regulation 330/2010 will apply. Those thresholds already apply for agreements relating to the distribution of spare parts and repair and maintenance services: see the update to paragraph 6.111, above. See also paras 26 and 46 of the Supplementary Guidance (OJ 2010 C138/16: Vol II, App C21) issued by the Commission to accompany Regulation 461/2010. They contain detailed guidance about selective distribution arrangements.

6.123 **Other conditions for the application of the exemption.**   The provisions described in the text now apply only to agreements for the distribution of new motor vehicles and will cease to apply on 31 May 2013: see updates to the previous paragraphs.

Fn 467. See also the judgment of the Higher Regional Court of Frankfurt, *Secondary Car Dealer*, 13 May 2008, WuW DE-R 2444 (one-year notice period economically justified).

Hard-core restrictions. As from 1 June 2010 the hard-core restrictions which will take an agreement relating to the distribution of spare parts or the provision of repair and maintenance services outside the exemption are those listed in Article 4 of Regulation 330/2010 *and* the three kinds of restrictions listed in Article 5 of Regulation 461/2010 (OJ 2010 L129/52: Vol II, App C7B). Guidance as to these additional restrictions is given in paras 22–24 of the Supplementary Guidance (OJ 2010 C138/16: Vol II, App C21) issued to accompany Regulation 461/2010. As regards agreements for the distribution of new motor vehicles, the hard-core restrictions set out in Regulation 1400/2002 apply until 31 May 2013. Thereafter only the hard-core restrictions in Article 4 of Regulation 330/2010 will apply: see Article 4 of Regulation 461/2010.   **6.124**

Hard-core restriction: price-fixing. See the update to paragraph 6.124, above. None of the three restrictions set out in Article 5 of Regulation 461/2010 relates to price-fixing. But see Article 4(a) of Regulation 330/2010.   **6.125**

Hard-core restrictions: territorial ban on sales. See the update to paragraph 6.124, above.   **6.126**

Other hard-core restrictions of general application. See the update to paragraph 6.124, above.   **6.127**

Active and passive sales. Guidance as to the meaning of active and passive sales is given in the 2010 Vertical Restraints Guidelines (OJ 2010 C130/1: Vol II, App C20): paras 50 *et seq.* So far as selling over the internet is concerned, see the update to paragraph 6.023A, above. In the Supplementary Guidance accompanying Regulation 461/2010 (OJ 2010 C138/16: Vol II, App C21) the Commission has stressed the importance of parallel trade: paras 47 *et seq.*   **6.128**

Hard-core restrictions concerning only the sale of new motor vehicles. The provisions described in the text will apply until 31 May 2013. Pursuant to Articles 2 and 3 of Regulation 461/2010 (OJ 2010 L129/52: Vol II, App C7B), Regulation 1400/2002 will then cease to apply to agreements for the sale of new motor vehicles and as from 1 June 2013, such agreements will fall within the ambit of the general Vertical Agreements Block Exemption, Regulation 330/2010. See the update to paragraph 6.111, above.   **6.129**

Hard-core restrictions concerning only the supply of repair and maintenance services and sales of spare parts. This paragraph has been superseded by Regulation 461/2010 (OJ 2010 L129/52: Vol II, App C7B). As from 1 June 2010, Regulation 1400/2002 ceased to apply to these kinds of agreements; they are now covered by Regulation 330/2010 though they are also subject to Article 5 of   **6.130**

Regulation 461/2010 which sets out three additional hard-core restrictions which will remove the benefit of the block exemption. Guidance as to these additional restrictions is given in paras 22–24 of the Supplementary Guidance (OJ 2010 C138/16: Vol II, App C21) issued by the Commission to accompany Regulation 461/2010.

6.131 **Hard-core restrictions concerning access to information.** The Supplementary Guidance emphasises the importance of access to technical information for independent operators in the paragraphs dealing with the assessment of selective distribution agreements outside the scope of the block exemption: paras 62 *et seq*.

The Commission opened proceedings against four car manufacturers alleging a breach of Article 101 TFEU in that the agreements between the manufacturer and its dealer network restricted the disclosure of information to independent repairers. The Commission accepted commitments under which (i) the manufacturers would ensure that all information provided to authorised repairers was also made available to independent repairers on a non-discriminatory basis; (ii) although manufacturers may withhold information relating to anti-theft or performance limiting functions of on-board electronics, they have to ensure that this does not prevent independent repairers from performing repairs not directly related to these functions; and (iii) the information made available to repairers must be unbundled and priced in a way which takes account of the extent to which they use it (eg by hourly charges for access to the website). All four manufacturers also agreed to accept arbitration or mediation mechanisms for disputes. The commitments expire at the same time as Regulation 1400/2002 expires: COMP/39140–39143 *Daimler Chrysler and others* Press Release IP/07/1332 (14 September 2007).

6.132 **Specific conditions: non-compete clauses.** The restrictions set out in Article 5 of Regulation 1400/2002 continue to apply in relation to agreements for the distribution of new motor vehicles until 31 May 2013. For agreements relating to spare parts and repair services, only the excluded restrictions in Article 5 of Regulation 330/2010 are now relevant.

6.134 **Specific conditions: leasing services and 'location clauses'.** See the update to paragraph 6.132, above.

Fn 503. On the definition of 'specified criteria' in the definition of selective distribution system in Article 1(1)(f) see Case C-158/11 *Auto 24 SARL v Jaguar Land Rover France*, not yet decided (request for preliminary ruling from the French Cour de Cassation).

6.135 **Withdrawal of the benefit of the block exemption.** The new Regulation 461/2010 does not contain provisions for withdrawal since this is now covered by Article 29 of Regulation 1/2003 (OJ 2003 L1/1: Vol II, App B3): see Recitals (21)–(23) of Regulation 461/2010.

Disapplication to parallel networks in a relevant market. This provision has **6.136** been brought forward in part in Article 6 of Regulation 461/2010. The 2010 Vertical Restraints Guidelines (OJ 2010 C130/1: Vol II, App C20) describe the circumstances in which this might occur: paras 79 *et seq*. According to para 84 of those Guidelines, a transitional period of six months (rather than one year) will need to be set.

6. Exclusive Purchasing, Single Branding and Tying

(a) Generally

Definitions. Fn 523. The definition is now set out in para 129 of the 2010 Vertical **6.139** Restraints Guidelines (OJ 2010 C130/1: Vol II, App C20). The Commission considers that a non-compete arrangement exists where an obligation or incentive scheme makes the buyer purchase more than 80 per cent of its requirements on a particular market from only one supplier.

Fn 524. Quantity forcing is also defined in para 129, ibid.

Fn 525. Tying is defined in para 214, ibid.

Economic effects of exclusive purchasing/single branding. These are now **6.140** discussed in the 2010 Vertical Restraints Guidelines, paras 130 *et seq*.

Economic effects of tying. These are now discussed in paras 214–222 of the 2010 **6.141** Vertical Restraints Guidelines.

(b) Application of Article 81(1)

Exclusive purchasing and single branding agreements: similar approach. The **6.144** Guidelines referred to in the text have been replaced by the 2010 Vertical Restraints Guidelines (OJ 2010 C130/1: Vol II, App C20). They cover single branding at paras 130 *et seq*.

Langnese-Iglo/Schöller. See also the example of a non-compete obligation **6.147** imposed by the market leader in a national market for an impulse consumer product at para 149 of the 2010 Vertical Restraints Guidelines.

Resale from supplier's premises. Fn 566. See Case C-260/07 *Pedro IV Servicios v* **6.152** *Total España* [2009] ECR I-2437, [2009] 5 CMLR 1291 where a long-term exclusive purchasing obligation on the lessor of a service station qualified for exemption under Reg 1984/83 but not under Reg 2790/99.

Fn 568. The appeal referred to in the footnote was found to be inadmissible: Case T-274/06 *Estaser El Mareny v Commission* [2007] ECR II-143*.

6.157 **Quantity forcing.** That quantity forcing can be achieved in various ways is illustrated by the arrangements between motor vehicle insurers and car dealers that were condemned by the Hungarian Competition Authority, under the domestic equivalent of Article 101, in a decision upheld by the Budapest Court of Appeal. The two major motor vehicle insurers in Hungary (who together accounted for about 80 per cent of the market) each had agreements with car dealers under which the rate of remuneration for repair work was significantly increased each year in return for the dealers selling a certain amount of policies for that insurer to customers purchasing cars. This provided an incentive to dealers to sell an even greater proportion of new policies on behalf of those insurers and thus operated to foreclose smaller, competing insurers (although they then had no choice but to offer the same, higher rates). The agreements between insurers and dealers were held to have the object of restricting competition: *Allianz Hungária, Generali-Providencia and ors*, 2.Kf.27.129/2009, judgment of the Budapest Court of Appeal of 23 September 2009.

6.159 **'English clause'.** See also the 2010 Vertical Restraints Guidelines (OJ 2010 C130/1: Vol II, App C20), para 129.

Fn 595. The decision in the *Polish Football Association* case was upheld on further appeal by the Polish Supreme Court: case III SK 16/08, judgment of 7 January 2009.

6.160 **Tying obligations.** See also the discussion in paras 214–222 of the 2010 Vertical Restraints Guidelines.

(c) **Application of Article 81(3)**

6.169 **Long-term industrial supply agreements.** See also the updates to paragraphs 12.066 and 12.080, below for more recent cases concerning long-term industrial supply.

6.170 **Hard-core restrictions.** Fn 622. The Guidelines referred to have been replaced by the 2010 Vertical Restraints Guidelines (OJ 2010 C130/1: Vol II, App C20), see particularly paras 47 *et seq* dealing with hard-core restrictions.

7. Franchising Agreements

(a) **Generally**

6.171 **Franchising.** The guidelines referred to in this section have been replaced by the 2010 Vertical Restraints Guidelines (OJ 2010 C130/1: Vol II, App C20), see particularly paras 189–191 which discuss the issues raised by franchising agreements.

(b) Application of Article 81(1)

(i) Clauses falling outside Article 81(1)

Protection of know-how and expertise.   See also *Pirtek (UK) Ltd v Joinplace*   **6.175**
Ltd [2010] EWHC 1641 (Ch), where the English High Court upheld a post-
termination restrictive covenant in a franchise agreement, following *Pronuptia* and
Charles Jourdan. Briggs J noted that the case law required a 'cautious, case-specific,
analysis' and based his assessment on the know-how and expertise in fact provided
to the franchisee rather than that said to be provided in the agreement itself. Having
concluded that the agreement did not fall within the domestic equivalent of
Article 101(1), the court went on to hold that it would have been justified under
the equivalent of Article 101(3). The agreement would not have benefited from
block exemption under Regulation 2790/1999 because it went beyond the limit
prescribed by Article 5(b) of that Regulation.

Protection of network reputation.   The 2010 Vertical Restraints Guidelines   **6.176**
para 190(b) states that a non-compete obligation falls outside Article 101(1) where
it is necessary to maintain the common identity and reputation of the franchised
network and the duration of the obligation is irrelevant, provided it does not exceed
the duration of the franchise agreement itself.

(c) Regulation 2790/99 and franchise agreements

Intellectual property rights.   Article 2(3) of Regulation 330/2010 is in identical   **6.183**
terms to Article 2(3) of Regulation 2790/99. The relationship between vertical
agreements and IPR licensing is covered extensively in the 2010 Vertical Restraints
Guidelines, paras 31 *et seq*. The Guidelines contain specific guidance for know-how
licences in franchise agreements, paras 43–45. In particular the Commission lists
IPR-related obligations which are generally considered necessary to protect the
franchisor's IPR rights and which are therefore covered by the block exemption if
they fall within Article 101(1).

Market share.   As to the calculation of market share in franchise agreements where   **6.184**
the franchisor does not himself supply goods, see now para 92 of the 2010 Vertical
Restraints Guidelines, OJ 2010 C130/1: Vol II, App C20.

Non-compete obligations.   In *Pirtek (UK) Ltd v Joinplace Ltd* [2010] EWHC   **6.186**
1641 (Ch) the English High Court held that a post-termination non-compete
clause fell outside the domestic equivalent of Article 101(1) but that it would not
have benefited from exemption under Regulation 2790/1999 because it went
beyond the limit prescribed by Article 5(b) because it was not limited to sales from
a particular premises.

Fn 679. Note that Reg 2659/2000 has been replaced by Reg 1217/2010 (OJ 2010 L335/36). Note that the new Reg adopts the definition of know-how in Reg 772/2004, ie that 'substantial' means 'significant and useful' rather than 'indispensable': see Art 1.1(k).

8. Subcontracting

6.189   **Generally.** **Fn 689.** The 2001 Guidelines have now been replaced by the Horizontal Cooperation Guidelines 2011, OJ 2011 C11/1: Vol II, App C22. See in particular paras 150–154.

6.190   **The Subcontracting Notice.** **Fns 690 and 692.** The 2001 Guidelines have been replaced by the Guidelines on horizontal cooperation agreements issued in 2011: OJ 2011 C11/1: Vol II, App C22: see paras 154 and 169.

6.193   **Application of Regulation 2790/99.** **Fn 700.** The 2001 Guidelines referred to have been replaced by the Horizontal Cooperation Guidelines issued in 2011: OJ 2011 C11/1: Vol II, App C22: see paras 154 and 169.

9. Waste Packaging Recycling Arrangements

6.196   **Generally.** In COMP/38113 *Prokent-Tomra* [2009] 4 CMLR 101 the Commission condemned a series of exclusivity arrangements and loyalty rebate schemes entered into by Tomra which was dominant in the supply of reverse vending machines for recycling empty containers in a number of EU and EEA Member States. The Commission noted that the volume of sales increased considerably during 'key years' which occurred when national legislation mandating recycling of, or deposit systems for, used drinks containers was introduced. Tomra's appeal was dismissed and this point was not discussed: Case T-155/06 *Tomra Systems v Commission*, judgment of 9 September 2010.

6.198   **Relationship between the system operator and the producers and distributors of packaged goods.** The appeal to the CJ in *DSD* was dismissed: Case C-385/07P *Der Grüne Punkt—Duales System Deutschland v Commission*, judgment of 16 July 2009, [2009] 5 CMLR 2215. The GC analysed the case under Article 102(a) TFEU, referring to settled case law according to which an undertaking abuses its dominant position where it charges fees which are disproportionate to the economic value of the service provided. The conduct objected to here, namely requiring payment of a fee for all packaging bearing the DGP logo and put into circulation in Germany, even where customers of the company show that they do not use the DGP system for some or all of that packaging, constituted an abuse of a dominant position within that case law. The CJ upheld this analysis, emphasising that the remedies imposed by the decision did not amount to an obligation to grant a licence to use the DGP logo. There was nothing in the decision which affects DSD's freedom of choice as to the grant of licences—the decision at issue merely obliges DSD not to claim payment from its contractual partners for take-back and recovery services which it has not provided. Note that the GC stated that the decision did not stop DSD levying an adequate fee for merely using the DGP mark even where it is shown that the packaging bearing the DGP logo has been taken back and recovered by another system. The green dot affixed to the packaging may have economic value as such, since it can inform the consumer that the packaging at issue may be brought to the DSD system: paras 193 and 194.

Fn 716. An appeal against the decision in *ARA and ARGEV, ARO* was dismissed: Case T-419/03 *Altstoff Recycling Austria AG v Commission*, judgment of 22 March 2011.

Arrangements with waste collectors. An appeal against the decision in *ARA and ARGEV, ARO* was dismissed: Case T-419/03 *Altstoff Recycling Austria AG v Commission*, judgment of 22 March 2011.   **6.199**

7

JOINT VENTURES AND SIMILAR COLLABORATIVE ARRANGEMENTS

1. Introduction

(a) Definitions

Functions of the joint venture.   **Fn 8.** The 2001 Guidelines have been replaced by   **7.003**
the Guidelines on horizontal cooperation agreements issued in 2011: OJ 2011
C11/1: Vol II, App C22.

Fn 10. The new Horizontal Cooperation Guidelines (OJ 2011 C11/1: Vol II,
App C22) also consider various categories of agreement.

Strategic alliances.   **Fn 30.** The 2001 Guidelines discussed in the text have been   **7.009**
replaced by the Horizontal Cooperation Guidelines issued in 2011: OJ 2011
C11/1: Vol II, App C22. Para 6 states that the Guidelines apply to most agreements
irrespective of the level of integration they entail, except for concentrations covered
by the Merger Regulation.

(b) Article 81 and the Merger Regulation

Duration and outcome of investigation.   **Fn 49.** Reg 2658/2000 has been   **7.015**
replaced by Reg 1218/2010 (OJ 2010 L335/43: Vol II, App C7D) and
Reg 2659/2000 has been replaced by Reg 1217/2010 (OJ 2010 L335/36: Vol II,
App C7C), but the point made in the text still applies.

2. Developing Treatment of JVs under EC Competition Law

Horizontal Cooperation Guidelines.   The 2001 Guidelines discussed in the text   **7.027**
have been replaced by the Horizontal Cooperation Guidelines issued in 2011: OJ
2011 C11/1: Vol II, App C22. The new Guidelines do cover information exchange
agreements (see Chapter 2 of the Guidelines). Para 6 states that the Guidelines
apply to most agreements irrespective of the level of integration they entail, except

for concentrations covered by the Merger Regulation. The Guidelines do not apply to the extent that sector specific rules apply as with agriculture, transport, or insurance: see para 18.

7.028   **Categories under the Guidelines.**   The same categories are covered in the 2011 Guidelines with the addition of information exchange. The chapter on standardisation agreements has been expanded such that the separate discussion of environmental agreements was no longer necessary.

7.029   **'Centre of gravity' test.**   **Fn 94.** See now paras 13 and 14 of the Horizontal Co-operation Guidelines 2011, OJ 2011 C11/1: Vol II, App C22.

7.030   **Block exemptions.**   The new Guidelines on horizontal cooperation agreements issued in 2011 (OJ 2011 C11/1: Vol II, App C22) accompanied two new block exemption regulations for research and development agreements (Regulation 1217/2010, OJ 2010 L335/36: Vol II, App C7C) and for specialisation agreements (Regulation 1218/2010, OJ L335/43: Vol II, App C7D). The points made in this paragraph remain valid.

3. The Application of Article 81(1) to Joint Ventures

(b) Formation of the JV

7.036   **Removal of actual or potential competitors.**   **Fn 104.** The 2001 Guidelines discussed have been replaced by the Horizontal Cooperation Guidelines issued in 2011: OJ 2011 C11/1: Vol II, App C22. See in particular paras 175 *et seq* on the relevance of commonality of costs to the assessment under Article 101(1) TFEU.

7.041   **Effect on competition: 'appreciability'.**   **Fn 112.** See now the Horizontal Co-operation Guidelines 2011, OJ 2011 C11/1: Vol II, App C22, paras 20 and 26 *et seq.*

7.042   **Appreciability and market share.**   **Fn 115.** See now the Horizontal Cooperation Guidelines 2011, OJ 2011 C11/1: Vol II, App C22, para 44.

Fn 116. See now the Horizontal Cooperation Guidelines 2011, OJ 2011 C11/1: Vol II, App C22, paras 45–47.

(c) Actual or potential competitors

7.044   **The emergence of a realistic economic analysis.**   The 2001 Guidelines discussed in the text have been replaced by the Horizontal Cooperation Guidelines issued in 2011: OJ 2011 C11/1: Vol II, App C22. The relevance of commonality of costs for production agreements is discussed in paras 175 *et seq.*

(g) Specific restrictions

Examples of ancillary restrictions.   The 2001 Guidelines discussed in the text   **7.055**
have been replaced by the Horizontal Cooperation Guidelines issued in 2011: OJ
2011 C11/1: Vol II, App C22. The new Guidelines also do not discuss expressly the
question of ancillary restrictions in a joint venture.

4. Application of Article 81(3)

(a) Introduction

Application of Article 81(3): the conditions.   The 2001 Guidelines discussed in   **7.057**
the text have been replaced by the Horizontal Cooperation Guidelines issued in
2011: OJ 2011 C11/1: Vol II, App C22. The point made in the text remains pertinent: see, eg paras 141 *et seq* (R&D agreements) or 183 *et seq* (production
agreements).

(b) Application of the Article 81(3) conditions

The first Article 81(3) condition: efficiencies or economic benefits.   Fn 186.   **7.058**
See now the Horizontal Cooperation Guidelines 2011, OJ 2011 C11/1: Vol II,
App C22. The new Guidelines do not contain a statement equivalent to that in
para 33 of the earlier version.

The second Article 81(3) condition: allowing consumers a fair share of the   **7.060**
benefit.   Fn 194. See now the Horizontal Cooperation Guidelines 2011, OJ 2011
C11/1: Vol II, App C22. The new Guidelines do not contain a statement equivalent
to that in para 35 of the earlier version.

Relationship between elimination of effective competition and dominant   **7.063**
position.   Fn 205. See now the Horizontal Cooperation Guidelines 2011, OJ
2011 C11/1: Vol II, App C22. The new Guidelines do not contain a statement
equivalent to that in para 36 of the earlier version.

5. R&D Agreements

(a) Generally

Introduction.   Regulation 2659/2000 has been replaced by Regulation 1217/2010   **7.067**
(OJ 2010 L335/36: Vol II, App C7C) which came into force on 1 January 2011.
This section should also be read together with the Commissions Guidelines on the
applicability of Article 101 TFEU to horizontal cooperation agreements (OJ 2011
C11/1: Vol II, App C22), particularly Chapter 3 of those Guidelines.

7.068   **R&D cooperation.   Fn 220.** Article 163 EC is now Article 179 TFEU. Article 179(1) refers to the achievement of a 'European research area in which researchers, scientific knowledge and technology circulate freely . . .'. Article 179(2) closely reflects the wording of Article 163(2) quoted here, though it refers also to the aim of permitting researchers to cooperate freely across borders as well as to enabling undertakings to exploit the internal market potential.

Fn 227. Reg 2659/2000 has been replaced by Reg 1217/2010 (OJ 2010 L335/36: Vol II, App C7C) which came into force on 1 January 2011.

7.069   **The Commission's approach.**   The Commission's approach is set out in Chapter 3 of the Horizontal Cooperation Guidelines (OJ 2011 C11/1: Vol II, App C22). The Chapter sets out how the Commission identifies the relevant market or markets affected by the agreement. This may comprise the market for an existing product (where the R&D is directed at slight improvements or variations of that product); a market for existing technology (where IPR are marketed separately from the products to which they relate); and markets in innovation and new product markets (where the R&D cooperation concerns the development of new products which may one day create completely new demand). The Commission refers to 'R&D poles' which compete by aiming to develop substitutable products in a similar time frame. Credible competing poles to that being pursued by the R&D cooperation of the parties need to be identified and assessed. This is particularly relevant in the pharmaceutical industry where innovation is structured in such as way as to identify competing poles at an early stage. The Guidelines also discuss how market share can be calculated (paras 123–126) and how the arrangement should be assessed under Article 101(1) and (3). Five examples of different arrangements are given and analysed.

(b) Application of Article 81 to R&D agreements

7.070   **Application of Article 81(1).   Fn 229.** See now Reg 1217/2010, OJ L335/36: Vol II, App C7C, Recital (6) and the Horizontal Cooperation Agreements Guidelines, OJ 2011 C11/1: Vol II, App C22, para 129.

7.072   **Access to results.**   For the payment of royalties as between the parties to the agreement see the Horizontal Cooperation Agreements Guidelines, OJ 2011 C11/1: Vol II, App C22 Article 3(2) and (3). Such payments are permissible provided they are not so high as effectively to impede access to the results.

Fn 237. See now the Horizontal Cooperation Agreements Guidelines, para 140 which makes a similar point and paras 141–146 which discuss the application of Article 101(3) to these agreements.

7.074   **Duration.   Fns 243, 245 and 247.** The 2001 Guidelines referred to have been replaced by the Horizontal Cooperation Guidelines issued in 2011: OJ 2011 C11/1: Vol II, App C22. See in particular paras 145 and 146.

(c) Regulation 2659/2000: the R&D block exemption

In general. Regulation 2659/2000 has been replaced by Regulation 1217/2010   **7.078**
(OJ 2010 L335/36: Vol II, App C7C) which came into force on 1 January 2011
and will expire on 31 December 2022. It has been adopted with appropriate amendments for the purpose of the EEA Agreement: see Decn 3/2011 (OJ 2011 L93/32).
Article 8 of Regulation 1217/2010 provides transitional exemption for agreements
which satisfied the conditions in Regulation 2659/2000 until 31 December 2012.
This section should also be read together with the Commission's Guidelines on the
applicability of Article 101 TFEU to horizontal cooperation agreements (OJ 2011
C11/1: Vol II, App C22), particularly Chapter 3 of those Guidelines. The scope of
the new Regulation has been widened in two ways; first to cover 'paid-for' research
where one party finances the R&D activities of the other and secondly to cover the
situation where only one party sells the contract products in the EU on the basis of
an exclusive licence by the other party.

The agreements covered. The definition of research and development agreements   **7.079**
is set out in Article 1.1 of Regulation 1217/2010. It includes the three categories
covered by the former Regulation and adds three further categories relating to (a)
paid-for R&D and joint exploitation of the results of that R&D; (b) the joint
exploitation of the results of paid-for R&D; and (c) paid for R&D excluding joint
exploitation of the results. 'Paid-for' R&D is defined as where R&D is carried out
by one party financed by a party which does not carry out any of the R&D activities
itself: Article 1.1(p) and (q).

Fn 252. Article 1.1(b) of Reg 1217/2010 is to the same effect.

Fn 253. Recital (6) of Reg 1217/2010 is to the same effect.

Definition of terms. The definition of 'research and development' in Article 1.1(c)   **7.080**
of Regulation 1217/2010 is the same as in Article 2(4) of Regulation 2659/2000
save for a reference to 'technologies' in addition to products or processes.

Fn 254. 'Know-how' is defined in Article 1.1(i), (j), (k), and (l) of Reg 1217/2010
generally in the same terms as under the old Reg. Note, however, that the requirement that the know-how must be 'substantial' now means that it must be 'significant
and useful' for the manufacture of the contract products rather than that it must
include information which is 'indispensable' for the manufacture as required by
Article 2(10) of Reg 2659/2000.

Fn 256. The definition of 'exploitation of the results' is set out in Article 1.1(g) of
Reg 1217/2010 in similar terms to former Article 2(8).

Fn 257. 'Contract product' is defined in Article 1.1(f) of Reg 1217/2010 in similar
terms.

Fn 258. The term 'contract process' has been replaced by the term 'contract technology' defined in similar terms in Article 1.1(e) of Reg 1217/2010.

7.081   **Meaning of 'joint' exploitation.**   'Joint exploitation' is defined in similar terms in Article 1.1(m) of Reg 1217/2010.

7.082   **Conditions for exemption.**   Article 3(2) of Regulation 1217/2010 (OJ 2010 L335/36: Vol II, App C7C) provides that R&D agreements must stipulate that all the parties have access to the final results of the R&D as soon as they become available for use in further R&D. However:

- research institutes, academic bodies or undertakings which supply R&D services on a commercial basis but which are not normally active in the exploitation of results may confine their use of the results of the R&D to further research; and
- where the parties limit their rights of exploitation in accordance with the Regulation, such as where they specialise in the context of exploitation, their access to the results may be limited accordingly.

Article 3(2) also provides that the parties may agree to compensate each other for access to the results provided that this is not 'so high as to effectively impede such access'. See also Recital (11) as to the justification for such payments.

Article 3(3) of Regulation 1217/2010 replacing Article 3(3) of Regulation 2659/2000 provides that in the case of R&D agreements up to the stage of industrial application the parties must have access to any pre-existing know-how of the other parties which is indispensable for the exploitation of the results. Again, the parties may agree to compensate each other provided the level of compensation does not impede such access.

As regards the scope of permissible joint exploitation, the wording of Article 3(4) of Regulation 1217/2010 differs from the earlier provision (Article 3(4) of Regulation 2659/2000) by providing that the resulting IPR or know-how which can by jointly exploited is only that which is 'indispensable'.

The requirement that all specialising undertakings must meet all orders for product is now set out in Article 3(5) of Regulation 1217/2010 though this is subject to an exception not only where the agreement provides for joint distribution but also where the agreement provides that only the party manufacturing the products may distribute them.

Fn 262. The sentence in Recital (14) of Reg 2659/2000 concerning parties with complementary skills is not included in the corresponding Recital (11) of the new Reg.

7.083   **Broad approach to exemption.**   Regulation 1217/2010 continues the economics-based approach of the earlier Regulation. Note also that Article 2(2) provides that the exemption applies to provisions relating to the assignment or licensing of IPR provided that those provisions are ancillary but directly related to and necessary for the implementation of the R&D agreement. This provision is different from the former Article 1(2) of Regulation 2569/2000. The point made in Recital (9) of the old Regulation is now made in Recital (7) of Regulation 1217/2010.

Market share limits and duration.   The market share limits and the duration of   **7.084**
the exemption are the same under Article 4 of Regulation 1217/2010 as they were under Regulation 2569/2000. For the definition of actual and potential competitors see now Article 1.1(r), (s), and (t) which differ from the earlier provisions in requiring that market entry must be likely within three years before an undertaking is regarded as a potential competitor (cf the new Horizontal Cooperation Guidelines, OJ 2011 C11/1: Vol II, App C22, para 10). The data to be used for calculating market share are described in Article 7 of Regulation 1217/2010 which also sets out similar safety margin extensions where market share rises.

Fn 271. See now the Horizontal Cooperation Guidelines, above, para 126.

Provisions which must not be included.   Article 5 of Regulation 1217/2010 sets   **7.085**
out a list of hard-core restrictions which preclude the application of the exemption. Note that the seven-year limitation previously imposed on active sales restrictions has been abolished where the parties allocate territories or customers between them in the context of joint exploitation of the R&D results. The following are hard-core restrictions:

- restrictions on carrying out R&D in unconnected fields or, after the completion of the agreement, in the field to which the agreement relates or in a connected field: Article 5(a);
- the limitation of output or sales except for (i) the setting of production or sales targets; (ii) provisions constituting specialisation in the context of exploitation; and (iii) restrictions on dealing in competing products or technologies during the period when the parties have agreed to exploit results jointly: Article 5(b);
- restrictions on fixing prices save that they may agree the prices charged to immediate customers when they undertake joint distribution or licensing: Article 5(c);
- restrictions on passive sales except where there is a requirement to license the results exclusively to another party: Article 5(d);
- restrictions on active sales except to customers who have been exclusively allocated to one of the parties by way of specialisation in the context of exploitation: Article 5(e);
- restrictions on meeting demand from customers who would market the contract product in other territories within the internal market or requirements to make it difficult for users or resellers to obtain the contract products from other resellers in the internal market: Article 5(f) and (g).

Excluded restrictions.   Two of the kinds of restrictions that were included in the   **7.085A**
hard-core list in Article 5 of Regulation 2569/2000 now appear in a list of excluded

restrictions in Article 6 of the new Regulation. These restrictions are not exempt but do not prevent the application of the exemption to the rest of the agreement:

- obligations not to challenge the validity of IPR, although a clause terminating the agreement in the event of such a challenge is permissible: Article 6(a);
- obligations not to grant licences to third parties, except where the agreement provides for exploitation of the results by at least one of the parties to the agreement and such exploitation 'takes place in the internal market vis-à-vis third parties': Article 6(b).

7.086 **Withdrawal of block exemption.** There is no specific provision in Regulation 1217/2010 dealing with withdrawal of the block exemption since this is now dealt with by Article 29(1) of Regulation 1/2003: see Recitals (19), (20), and (21) of Regulation 1217/2010. Recital (21) indicates the circumstances in which it may be appropriate to withdraw the exemption.

6. Specialisation/Production Agreements

(a) Generally

7.087 **Introduction.** Regulation 2658/2000 has been replaced by Regulation 1218/ 2010 (OJ 2010 L335/43: Vol II, App C7D) which came into force on 1 January 2011. This section should also be read together with the Commission's Guidelines on the applicability of Article 101 TFEU to horizontal cooperation agreements (OJ 2011 C11/1: Vol II, App C22), particularly Chapter 4 of those Guidelines.

7.089 **Joint production agreements.** The new Regulation 1218/2010, like its immediate predecessor, applies to all agreements for joint manufacture, not only those where the parties agree that all manufacture will be joint. The Horizontal Cooperation Agreements Guidelines issued in 2011 (OJ 2011 C11/1: Vol II, App C22) have replaced the Guidelines referred to in the text. They also treat specialisation and joint production as a single category: see Chapter 4 of the Guidelines.

7.090 **The Commission's approach.** Regulation 1218/2010 adopts an economics-based approach to exemption using a market share test.

(b) Assessment under Article 81

7.091 **Actual or potential competitors.** The 2001 Guidelines discussed in the text have been replaced by the Horizontal Cooperation Guidelines issued in 2011: OJ 2011 C11/1: Vol II, App C22. See in particular paras 163–166.

7.094 **Degree of commonality of costs.** The 2001 Guidelines discussed in the text have been replaced by the Horizontal Cooperation Guidelines issued in 2011: OJ 2011

C11/1: Vol II, App C22. See in particular paras 175 *et seq* on the relevance of commonality of costs to the assessment under Article 101(1).

(c) Regulation 2658/2000: the specialisation block exemption

In general. Regulation 2658/2000 has been replaced by Regulation 1218/2010 **7.097**
(OJ 2010 L335/43: Vol II, App C7D). It came into force on 1 January 2011 and
expires on 31 December 2022. Article 6 grants transitional exemption until
31 December 2012 for agreements already in force which do not meet the conditions of this Regulation but were exempt under its predecessor.

Scope. Regulation 1218/2010 covers specialisation agreements which are **7.098**
defined as comprising unilateral and reciprocal specialisation agreements and
joint production agreements broadly in the terms described in this paragraph: see
Article 1(a)–(d). However note that:

- The definitions of unilateral and reciprocal agreements refer to parties agreeing
  'fully or partly' to ceasing production, making clear that they will benefit from
  exemption even where, for example, one party closes one of its two plants and
  outsources the output of the closed plant. These two definitions also refer to the
  parties being active on the same product market but this is not a requirement for
  joint production agreements: see Recital (8) which also states that it is not necessary for the parties to be active on the same geographic market.
- The requirement for reciprocal supply continues for reciprocal specialisation
  agreements.

Ancillary restrictions. Article 2(2) of Regulation 1218/2010 is different from **7.099**
Article 1(2) of Regulation 2658/2000 in that it provides that the exemption applies
to ancillary provisions assigning or licensing IPR to one or more of the parties
but does not appear to treat these as an example of a broader range of exempted
ancillary restrictions.

Purchasing and marketing arrangements. Article 2(3) of Regulation 1218/2010 **7.100**
provides that a specialisation agreement is exempt whereby the parties accept an
exclusive purchase or exclusive supply agreement or where they do not independently sell the specialised products but jointly distribute them. 'Joint distribution' is
defined (Article 1.1.(q)) as including appointing a third party distributor on an
exclusive or non-exclusive basis provided that the third party is not a competing
undertaking, so the effect of former Article 3 of Regulation 2568/2000 appears to
be preserved.

Other obligations. Article 4 of Regulation 1218/2010 sets out the hard-core **7.101**
restrictions which will rule out exemption, namely fixing prices (except for prices
charged to immediate customers in the context of joint distribution); limiting output (except for agreeing the amount of product or setting sales targets for joint
distribution); and allocating markets or customers.

7.102   **Market share and turnover limits.**   The exemption under Regulation 1218/2010 applies provided that the combined market share of the parties does not exceed 20 per cent on any relevant market. The term 'parties' includes their connected undertakings: see Article 1.2. Note that where the specialisation products are intermediary products which one or more of the parties fully or partly use captively for the production of downstream products, the exemption is also conditional upon a 20 per cent market share threshold in that downstream market: see Article 1.1.(i). Recital (10) states that in such a case, looking at the parties' market position at the level of the intermediary product, would ignore the potential risk of foreclosing or increasing the price of inputs for competitors at the level of the downstream products.

Provisions about the calculation of market share and a safety margin where the threshold is exceeded are made in Article 5.

7.103   **Withdrawal of block exemption.**   There is no specific provision in Regulation 1218/2010 dealing with withdrawal of the block exemption since this is now dealt with by Article 29(1) of Regulation 1/2003: see Recitals (13), (14) and (15) of Regulation 1218/2010 (OJ 2010 L335/43: Vol II, App C7D). Recital (15) indicates the circumstances in which it may be appropriate to withdraw the exemption.

7. Joint Ventures in Practice

(c) TV and other media

7.119   *Telenor*: **specific restrictions.**   The Danish Competition Appeal Tribunal upheld a decision of the Competition Authority that the terms on which Viasat distributed its television channels was contrary to Article 101 TFEU. Viasat's terms of business stipulated that two of its popular tv channels must be inserted into the most advantageous programme package available to the commercial TV channels offered by the cable networks. Viasat also required that Viasat's TV channels were watched by at least 75 per cent of the subscribing households (ie the 'minimum penetration requirement'). These business terms were used in all distribution agreements between Viasat and the cable distributors' local cable networks, resulting in a TV market with a parallel network of vertical agreements. The CAT concluded that both Viasat's location requirements as well as Viasat's requirements of a minimum penetration level were restrictions of competition both by object and by effect: ECN 4/2010, p2.

(e) E-commerce platforms

7.131   **E-commerce platforms: subsequent practice.**   The Horizontal Cooperation Guidelines referred to in the text have been replaced by the Horizontal Cooperation Guidelines issued in 2011: OJ 2011 C11/1: Vol II, App C22.

(f) Airline alliances

Collaborative arrangements. In Case M.5403 *Lufthansa/British Midland* **7.133** (14 May 2009) the Commission considered the implications for assessing a merger of the two airlines of the fact that (a) Lufthansa was a member of the Star Alliance; and (b) the merging entities already operated a code-sharing arrangement. The Commission found that the issue of the treatment of the parties' alliance partners could be left open, as the proposed concentration did not raise serious doubts under the Merger Regulation, whether or not Lufthansa's alliance partners should be considered as competitors of Lufthansa (para 35) (see also on this point Case M.5141 *KLM/Martinair* (17 December 2008), para 23). The Commission held that pre-merger cooperation that was not contrary to Article 101 TFEU could form the relevant counterfactual for assessing the competitive effect of the merger. In such a case the proposed concentration could raise serious doubts only if (i) despite the code-share agreements, the operating carrier and the marketing carrier exert a significant constraint on each other as actual competitors (with respect to sales of seats on the operating carrier's flights); or (ii) if, in the presence of the code-share agreement, the marketing carrier were to be likely to enter the respective route as an operating carrier. In this case, the Commission found that there was no such significant constraint prior to the merger. See similarly, Case M.5889 *United Airlines/ Continental* (27 July 2010), paras 45 *et seq*.

See now also COMP/39596 *BA/AA/IB*, decn of 14 July 2010 where the parties entered into commitments to bring to an end proceedings under Article 101 in respect of an alliance under which they agreed to establish fares jointly, to regulate capacity, coordinate their respective schedules, and cooperate with respect to sales and marketing, share overall revenues and sell each other's products and services without regard to which party is operating the aircraft. The Commission identified a number of point to point markets, distinguishing in some instances between 'premium' and 'non-premium' sectors of those markets. The commitments given included: (i) making slots available to competitors at congested airports for a period of 10 years and allowing an applicant for slots to remain anonymous by using a monitoring trustee; (ii) offering fare combinability arrangements to competitors on particular routes; (iii) offering 'SPAs' (ie special pro-rate arrangements) for splitting the fare where a multi-segment flight combines the services of competing airlines; (iv) hosting competitors' services in their Frequent Flyer Programme; (v) reporting commitments enabling the Commission to review the take up of the commitments. The Commission rejected a request from Virgin Atlantic to adopt a 'fix it first' approach whereby the take-up of the commitments is a precondition to the implementation of the parties' cooperation on the routes on which slot commitments are offered given the interest that had been expressed by competing airlines during the investigation procedure. The Commission also accepted a clause in the slot commitment whereby any slots allotted to new services on the problematic routes would reduce the slot release obligation of the parties. See the impact of this alliance on the

Commission's assessment of the later concentration between Iberia and British Airways: M.5747 *Iberia/British Airways* (14 July 2010).

Fn 379. The exemption for the British Airways/Iberia/GB Airways alliance expired in September 2009 and was followed by the merger of Iberia and British Airways which was approved by the Commission: M.5747 *Iberia/British Airways* (14 July 2010).

Fn 380. The Commission market tested commitments in COMP/37984 *Sky Team* (making slots available to new competitors, sharing Frequent Flyer Programmes with new entrant, interlining, etc) but no final decision has been published: [2008] 4 CMLR 228.

8

MERGER CONTROL

1. Introduction

(a) Summary

Merger Regulation. The Commission has adopted a report on the operation of **8.001** the Merger Regulation as required by Article 1(4) of the Merger Regulation. The report concludes that overall, the jurisdictional and referral mechanisms have provided the appropriate legal framework for a flexible allocation and reallocation of cases by effectively distinguishing in most cases mergers that have an EU relevance from those which are primarily national. During the consultation, concerns were raised regarding cumbersome and lengthy referral procedures and it was suggested that efforts towards further convergence of national rules governing merger control and their relation to EU rules could reduce difficulties with regard to multiple filings: see Press Release IP/09/963 (18 June 2009) which contains a link to the Report.

(b) Commission guidance

Implementing Regulation and Notices **8.008**

(b) *Jurisdictional Notice.* The Consolidated Jurisdictional Notice has now been published: OJ 2008 C95/1.

(f) *Remedies Notice.* The revised Notice on Remedies has now been adopted: Notice on remedies acceptable under the EC Merger Regulation and under Commission Regulation (EC) No 802/2004, OJ 2008 C267/1: Vol II, App D15, see update to paragraph 8.162, below. The new Form RM was also incorporated into the Implementing Regulation as Annex IV by Commission Regulation 1033/2008, OJ 2008 L279/3: see Vol II, App D2.

(g) *Horizontal Merger Guidelines.* The proposed non-horizontal merger guidelines mentioned in sub-para (g) have now been adopted: OJ 2008 C265/6: Vol II, App D14.

(c) **Case law and statistics**

8.011 **Statistics.** Table (c) fn (i). The *Schneider Electric* case referred to in the footnote was partly overturned on appeal: see Case C-440/07P *Commission v Schneider Electric*, judgment of 16 July 2009 (Commission's liability confirmed in principle but appeal allowed in part on issue of causation of loss).

The tables can be updated as follows:

(a) **Total number of notifications and referrals by year**

Year	Notifications to Commission	Referrals from Member States to Commission		Referrals from Commission to Member States	
		Pre-notification (Art 4(5))	Post-notification (Art 22)	Pre-notification (Art 4(4))	Post-notification (Art 9)
2007	402	50	3	5	2
2008	347	22	2	9	4
2009	259	25	1	6	1
2010	274	24	3	7	7
Total	4,548	200	25	53	79

(b) **Different Phase I outcomes by year**

Year	Clearance decisions				No jurisdiction	Referred to Phase II decisions		Notifications withdrawn during Phase I	
	Unconditional		Conditional						
2007	368	(91%)	18	(4%)	–	15	(4%)	5	(1%)
2008	307	(89%)	19	(5%)	–	10	(3%)	10	(3%)
2009	225	(90%)	13	(5%)	–	5	(2%)	6	(3%)
2010	253	(92%)	14	(6%)	–	4	(1%)	4	(1%)
Total	3,950	(89%)	204	(4%)	52 (1%)	195	(4%)	100	(2%)

(c) **Different Phase II outcomes by year**

Year	Clearance decisions				Prohibition decisions		Notifications withdrawn during Phase II	
	Unconditional		Conditional					
2007	5	(42%)	4	(33%)	1	(8%)	2	(17%)
2008	9	(60%)	5	(33%)	–	–	1	(7%)
2009	0	–	3	(60%)	–	–	2	(40%)
2010	1	(33%)	2	(66%)	–	–	0	–
Total	47	(24%)	93	(48%)	20	(10%)	33	(18%)

2. Jurisdictional Scope of the Merger Regulation

(a) Overview of the 'one-stop shop' principle

In general.   The 'one-stop shop' principle has been considered in the context of   **8.012**
the retention by Ryanair of a minority shareholding in Aer Lingus following the
Commission's decision to prohibit a merger between the two companies. The
General Court upheld the Commission's decision that it did not have jurisdiction
to order the divestment of a holding that did not confer control and hence did not
amount to a concentration for the purposes of the Merger Regulation: Case
T-411/07 *Aer Lingus Group plc v Commission*, judgment of 6 July 2010, [2011]
4 CMLR 358. In earlier rejecting an application for interim (Case T-411/07R *Aer
Lingus Group plc v Commission* [2008] ECR II-411) the President of the GC noted
that where a merger had been prohibited by the Commission, the remaining minority shareholding was no longer linked to an acquisition of control, it ceases to be
part of a 'concentration' and lies outside the scope of the Regulation. The application of the 'one-stop shop principle', did not in principle, under those circumstances, prevent the application by NCAs or national courts of national legislation
which empowered them to take action against the remaining shareholding.
However, the UK Competition Appeal Tribunal later held that the duty of sincere
cooperation under Article 10 EC (now Article 4(3) TEU) did preclude the Office
of Fair Trading from investigating the minority shareholding pending Ryanair's
appeal to the GC from the prohibition decision and Aer Lingus' appeal from
the jurisdiction decision: *Ryanair Holdings v Office of Fair Trading* [2011] CAT 23,
para 106.

(b) Concentrations

(iii) Acquisitions

Definition of control.   **Fn 62.** The appeal in *Cementbouw* was dismissed: Case   **8.024**
C-202/06P *Cementbouw Handel & Industrie BV v Commission* [2007] ECR
I-12129, [2008] 4 CMLR 1324. The CJ confirmed that control of a company is
obtained by the power to block strategic decisions, including the appointment of
the company's management or board.

Object of control.   See also Case M.5721 *Otto/Primondo Assets* (16 February   **8.026**
2010) (assets acquired in the context of a home shopping business were the trade-
marks and the right to use the target's customer data and other assets. This constituted the acquisition of control for the purposes of Article 3(1)(b): para 10; Case
M.5727 *Microsoft/Yahoo! Search business* (18 February 2010) (assets acquired in the
context of an internet search and search advertising business comprised the transfer
of relevant technology, employees and a migration of customers, and target was
contractually required to exit the market).

(iv) Sole control

8.029   **Sole control through minority shareholding.**   Fn 76. See also Case M.4956 *STX/ Aker Yards* (5 May 2008). In Case M.5121 *News Corp/Premiere* (26 June 2008) the target company's most recent AGM had occurred after News Corp had acquired its interest in the company but before it was able to exercise the voting rights attached to the shares. The Commission considered that the unusually high attendance of shareholders was atypical and that the shareholders wanted 'to be able to influence the course of the company for one last time before News Corp would take control'. Attendance was likely to return to its earlier lower levels, giving News Corp *de facto* control: para 8. In Case M.5518 *Fiat/Chrysler* (24 July 2009) the Commission held that Fiat had obtained *de jure* control over Chrysler even though it held only a minority interest because it had extensive governance rights that no other share-holder enjoyed: para 7.

8.032   **Other factors leading to *de facto* control.**   See also Case M.5148 *Deutsche Telekom/ OTE* (2 October 2008) (DT to hold 25 per cent plus 12 shares; but the shareholder agreement gave DT rights to nominate the senior officers of the company who had a casting vote on decisions so DT acquired sole control). See also Case M.5545 *ArcelorMittal/Noble European Holding* (17 July 2009) where the Commission left open the question whether control was acquired in March 2008 when ArcelorMittal acquired 49.9 per cent of the shares and the right to nominate the majority of board members or in May 2009 when it acquired 100 per cent of the shares: para 7.

(v) Joint control

8.033   **Concept of joint control.**   In Case M.5533 *Bertelsmann/KRR/JV* (8 September 2009) the Commission considered a joint venture between a private equity com-pany (which would own 51 per cent of the joint venture) and one of the main music industry companies (which would own 49 per cent). The Commission examined the factors that gave each partner influence and concluded that in light of the terms of the proposed transaction and in view of the overall context of the planned opera-tion, the private equity partner would need to cooperate with Bertelsmann in order to determine the strategic behaviour of the proposed JV; and Bertelsmann could reasonably be expected to be in a position to block important strategic decisions in the proposed JV which were not in its interest. The Commission therefore con-cluded that the parties held joint control over the JV.

8.035   **Veto rights for minority shareholders.**   Rights which do not go beyond minority shareholder protection rights will not confer joint control: Case M.5996 *Thomas Cook/travel business of Co-operative Group/travel business of Midlands Co-operative Society* (6 January 2010).

8.036   **Focus on strategic business policy.**   Fn 88. An appeal against the GC's judgment in *Cementbouw* was dismissed: Case C-202/06P *Cementbouw Handel & Industrie BV v Commission* [2007] ECR I-12129, [2008] 4 CMLR 1324.

(vi) Changes in quality of control

Changes from joint to sole control. **Fn 100.** See also Case M.5141 *KLM/* **8.041**
Martinair (17 December 2008) (move from 50 per cent to 100 per cent holding
was a concentration). The Commission considered the question whether the effect
of the concentration should be assessed taking into account the pre-existing joint
control (which the parties argued meant that very little would change as a result of
the acquisition). The Commission stated that it is first necessary to analyse the
extent to which the parties have constrained each other pre-merger. This involves
considering the organisation and corporate governance of the target company as
well as the extent and nature of the competitive interaction between the parties
on the markets where their activities overlap. In this case, the Commission found,
the parties were, in principle, to be treated as competitors though the fact that
KLM already had control of Martinair pre-merger clearly reduced the likely anti-
competitive effects of the merger.

(vii) Interrelated transactions

Transactions involving different steps. The appeal against the GC's judgment in **8.044**
Cementbouw was dismissed: Case C-202/06P *Cementbouw Handel & Industrie BV
v Commission* [2007] ECR I-12129, [2008] 4 CMLR 1324.

Fn 113. See also Case M.5296 *Deutsche Bank/ABN AMRO Assets* (1 October
2008). In Case M.4980 *ABF/GBI Business* (23 September 2008) the Commission
found that the acquisition by ABF of GBI Holding's yeast operations in various
Member States as well as shares in other undertakings and assets in yet others
(including employees, customer contracts and intellectual property rights) constituted a single concentration. The Commission referred to the 'clear business
rationale' which was to gain sole control of what it called 'the GBI business'. In Case
M.5533 *Bertelsmann/KRR/JV* (8 September 2009) the proposed concentration
consisted of two transactions, one of which was *de facto* dependent on the other and
one of which was *de jure* dependent on the other. The Commission noted that
under the Jurisdictional Notice, even if several transactions are linked by condition
upon one another, they can only be treated as a single concentration if control is
acquired ultimately by the same undertakings. It held that the transactions did
result in a single concentration.

Break-up bids and other operations with on-sale arrangements. Fn 117. See, eg **8.046**
Case M.4844 *Fortis ABN Amro Assets* (3 October 2007), paras 6–8; Case M.4963
Rexel/Hagemeyer (22 February 2008), paras 5–9. In the case of the break-up of the
brewer Scottish & Newcastle which was shared between Carlsberg and Heineken,
the Commission cleared the Carlsberg acquisition of S&N assets (Case M.4952
Carlsberg/Scottish & Newcastle assets (7 March 2008)) and on the same day referred
the merger as regards the Irish beer markets back to the Irish competition authority
under Article 9(2) and cleared the remainder of the Heineken acquisition (Case
M.4999 *Heineken/Scottish & Newcastle* (3 April 2008)).

(viii) Specific operations that are not concentrations

8.049 **Temporary holdings by financial institutions.** This 'warehousing' exception (under Article 5 of Regulation 4064/89) was examined by the GC in Case T-279/04 *Éditions Odile Jacob SAS v Commission*, judgment of 13 September 2010. The applicant challenged the Commission's clearance, subject to divestment conditions, of the acquisition by Lagardère of the publishing assets of Vivendi Universal Publishing (M.2978 *Lagardère/Natexis/VUP*, OJ 2004 L125/54). Lagardère had arranged for a bank, through its subsidiary, to acquire the target assets from VUP on a temporary basis and to sell them back to Lagardère once the Commission had approved the VUP/Lagardère concentration. The GC held that the arrangement did not give Lagardère decisive influence, alone or jointly with the bank, over the activity associated with the target assets such as to affect the Commission's decision to approve the concentration (para 144). The holding of the target assets could not, therefore be deemed to be a concentration and so was not subject to control by the Commission. The GC rejected the applicant's assertion that the arrangement should be regarded as fraudulent. The GC went on to uphold the clearance of the merger but, in separate proceedings brought by the same applicant (Case T-452/04, judgment of 13 September 2010), annulled the Commission's approval of a purchaser of the assets to be divested on the grounds that the monitoring trustee on whose report the Commission had relied was not independent of the parties. The T-279/04 judgment is on appeal: Case 551/10P *Éditions Odile Jacob v Commission*, not yet decided.

(c) Full-function joint venture undertakings

(ii) Full functionality

8.054 **Key principles of full functionality.** Fn 143. See also Case M.5533 *Bertelsmann/ KRR/JV* (8 September 2009); Case M.5655 *SNCF/LCR/ Eurostar* (17 June 2010) (high speed cross-channel rail services).

(iii) Lasting basis

8.058 **Durability.** See also Case M.5727 *Microsoft/Yahoo! Search business* (18 February 2010): agreements comprising transfer of assets in a market characterised by rapid technological developments, (internet search and search advertising) amounted to control on a lasting basis.

Fn 154. An appeal against the *DaimlerChrysler/Deutsche Telekom/JV* decision was dismissed: Case T-48/04 *Qualcomm Wireless Business Solutions v Commission* [2009] ECR II-2029.

(d) Community dimension

(i) Turnover thresholds

8.060 **Worldwide and Community-wide turnover.** In Case C-202/06P *Cementbouw Handel & Industrie BV v Commission* [2007] ECR I-12129, [2008] 4 CMLR 1324 the CJ held that the competence of the Commission to make findings in relation to a concentration must be established, as regards the whole of the proceedings, at a fixed time. Having regard to the importance of the obligation of pre-notification, that time must necessarily be closely related to the notification of the concentration. It was accepted by the parties that the concentration had a EU dimension on the date when the two groups of transactions which comprised the concentration were concluded and on the date of the notification made at the Commission's request. The fact that during the course of the investigation the concentration may no longer have met the thresholds did not deprive the Commission of jurisdiction. The Court did not have to rule therefore on whether the relevant time for the purpose of determining the Commission's competence is the time at which the obligation to notify arose or the time at which the notification should have been made or even the time at which it was actually made: para 44.

(e) Pre-notification reallocation of jurisdiction

(ii) Article 4(5) referrals to Commission

Suitable case for Article 4(5) referral.   See, eg Case M.4942 *Nokia/Navteq* (2 July   **8.085**
2008) (proposed transaction could have been reviewed in 11 Member States); Case M.5597 *Towers Perrin/ Watson Wyatt* (3 December 2009) (four Member States); Case M. 5675 *Syngenta/Monsanto sunflower seed business* (17 November 2010) (two Member States); Case M.6007 *Nokia Siemens Networks/ Motorola Network Business* (15 December 2010) (nine Member States).

(f) Post-notification reallocation of jurisdiction

(i) Article 9 referrals from Commission to NCAs

Legal requirements under Article 9.   In Case M.5112 *Rewe/Plus Discount* (3 July   **8.091**
2008) the Commission considered a request by the Czech authorities for a reference back to them of the acquisition by the Rewe group of a chain of Czech discount stores engaged in the retail sale of daily consumer goods. The request was made under both Article 9(2)(a) and 9(2)(b). So far as the application of Article 9(2)(b) was concerned, the Commission concluded that there were strong indications that the criteria were fulfilled so far as the retail level of the relevant market was concerned but that they were not fulfilled as regards the procurement markets, that is the market for sales by producers to wholesalers and retailers. However, the Commission found that the criteria in Article 9(2)(a) were fulfilled in respect of both retail and procurement markets and exercised its discretion to refer the whole merger to the Czech authorities: an assessment of the procurement markets without the assessment of the retail markets was not appropriate.

In Case M.4999 *Heineken/Scottish & Newcastle* (3 April 2008) the Commission decided that the relevant markets for beer in Ireland presented the characteristics of a distinct market and the Irish aspect of the merger was referred back under

Article 9(2)(a). The rest of the merger (other than the Irish beer markets) was cleared under Article 6(1)(b) on the same day.

See also Case M.5557 *SNCF-P/CDPQ/ Keolis/EFFIA* (30 October 2009) where the Commission referred a merger in the passenger rail transport sector to the French authority noting that that authority had particular expertise in the subject matter of the case.

8.093 **Procedure.**   **Fn 253.** A number of appeals against refusals to refer cases back to the national authority are pending: Case T-202/11 *Italy v Commission*, not yet decided; Case T-224/10 *Association Belge des Consommateurs Tests-Achats v Commission*, not yet decided (appeal against rejection of referral and subsequent clearance of the merger); Case T-315/10 *Groupe Partouche v Commission*, not yet decided.

(g) National investigations on grounds other than competition

(i) Legitimate interests under Article 21(4)

8.104 **Other legitimate public interest grounds.**   **Fn 292.** The appeal in Case T-41/06 *Republic of Poland v Commission* was withdrawn, 10 April 2008.

Fn 293. The proceedings concerning the Article 21 decisions against Spain in Case M.4197 continued. The Commission brought an infringement action under Article 258 TFEU (formerly Article 226 EC): Case C-196/07 *Commission v Spain*, judgment of 6 March 2008, [2008] ECR I-41*, in which the CJ found that Spain had violated EU law by failing to comply with the Article 21 decisions. The CJ confirmed that, before adopting the contested measures, Spain should have communicated to the Commission the legitimate interests that those measures were intended to protect (namely, the guarantee of the supply of energy). The CJ also stated that, when a Member State disagrees with an Article 21 decision, it must challenge the legality of that decision before the EU Courts and cannot simply fail to comply with it. In the meantime, the original bid had been abandoned. The Endesa undertaking was then the subject of a subsequent public bid which was approved by the Commission on 5 July 2007: Case M.4685 *Acciona/Enel/Endesa* (2007 OJ C130/19). The Spanish authorities authorised the operation on 4 July 2007 but again subject to a number of conditions. By a decision of 5 December 2007, the Commission found that Spain had violated Article 21 ECMR, as well as the Treaty provisions on free movement of capital and goods and freedom of establishment. Spain's application for interim measures to suspend the implementation of the decision was rejected by the President of the GC: Case T-65/08R, Order of 30 April 2008, [2008] ECR II-69* and the substantive appeal (Case T-65/08) was later withdrawn. Note that the CJ has also held that, by attributing these powers to the Energy Regulator, Spain had infringed Articles 49 and 63 TFEU (formerly Articles 43 and 56 EC) (see Case C-207/07 *Spain v Commission*, judgment of 17 July 2008, [2008] ECR I-111*). For a description of the rather tangled procedural history of this matter see Busa and Zaera Cuadrado, 'Application of Article 21 of the Merger Regulation in the E.ON/Endesa case' (2008) 2 Competition Policy Newsletter 1.

3. Procedure

(a) In general

(i) Commission hierarchy for merger control proceedings

Case teams. The Commission has now published instructions for a case team allocation request: Vol II, App D18.   **8.107**

(iii) Obligation to notify

Timing of formal notification. The Commission has published a Merger Notification and Procedures Template to provide a starting point for the analysis of a particular transaction: Vol II, App D17.   **8.111**

(iv) Formalities

Form CO. The Form CO has been amended by Commission Regulation 1033/2008, OJ 2008 L279/3: see Vol II, App D2. Most of the amendments draw the parties' attention to the corresponding provisions of the EEA Agreement.   **8.117**

The Commission has issued a document called 'Best Practices for the Submission of Economic Evidence and Data Collection in Cases Concerning the Application of Articles 101 and 102 TFEU and in Merger Cases' (Vol II, App B21, and on the DG Competition website and linked to Press Release IP/10/02 (6 January 2010)). It describes the preferred content and presentation of economic and econometric data and best practice on responding to requests for quantitative data. The Best Practice describes the content and presentation of economic models stating, *inter alia*, that assumptions underlying the model should be carefully laid out and the sensitivity of its predictions to changes to the assumptions should be made explicit.

Business secrets. Note that the Implementing Regulation was amended in 2008 to provide that if the parties do not identify confidential information as required by Article 18(2) and (3), the Commission may assume that the documents or statements concerned do not contain confidential information: see Article 18(4) inserted by Commission Regulation 1033/2008, OJ 2008 L279/3: Vol II, App D2.   **8.120**

Need for full and accurate disclosure. The Commission has published guidance on the delivery of correspondence from the parties to the Commission, including the procedure for ensuring the security of documents: Vol II, App D16.   **8.121**

(v) Simplified procedure

8.124 **Short Form.** The Short Form has been amended by Commission Regulation 1033/2008, OJ 2008 L279/3: see Vol II, App D2. Most of the amendments draw the parties' attention to the corresponding provisions of the EEA Agreement.

(b) Initial Phase I investigation

(i) Phase I process

8.133 **Duration of Phase I investigation.** In Case T-151/05 *Nederlandse Vakbond Varkenshouders (NVV) v Commission* [2009] ECR II-1219, [2009] 5 CMLR 1613 the GC stated, in relation to a merger cleared at Phase I: 'in view of the need for speed and the very tight deadlines to which the Commission is subject in the procedure for the control of concentrations, the Commission cannot be required, in the absence of evidence indicating that information provided to it is inaccurate, to verify all the information it receives. Although the diligent and impartial examination which the Commission is obliged to carry out in the context of that procedure does not permit it to base itself on facts or information which cannot be regarded as accurate, the abovementioned need for speed presupposes that it cannot itself verify down to the last detail the authenticity and reliability of all the information it receives, since the procedure for the control of concentrations is based, of necessity and to a certain extent, on trust': para 184. The GC also referred to the fact that sanctions exist for the provision of inaccurate information and that clearance based on incorrect information can be revoked: para 185.

(ii) Possible outcomes at Phase I

8.137 **Deemed decisions.** The CJ has rejected an argument that the existence of this deeming provision means that a Commission clearance decision cannot be annulled on the basis of inadequate reasoning: see Case C-413/06P *Bertelsmann AG and Sony Corporation of America v Impala and Commission* [2008] ECR I-4951, para 175.

(c) In-depth Phase II investigation

(i) Phase II process

8.145 **Statement of objections.** In Case C-413/06P *Bertelsmann AG and Sony Corporation of America v Impala and Commission* [2008] ECR I-4951 the CJ, drawing an analogy with proceedings under Articles 101 and 102 TFEU, stressed that the statement of objections is a provisional account of the facts and is subject to amendment in the light of the observations submitted by the parties and of subsequent findings of fact: paras 63 *et seq*. The CJ held that the GC had erred in law in criticising inconsistencies between the facts as set out in the statement of objections and the findings set out in the decision. The GC can refer to the statement of objections to interpret a decision of the Commission, particularly as regards the examination of its factual basis. But the GC had gone beyond what was permissible by treating what it termed 'findings of fact made previously' in that statement as being more reliable and more conclusive than the findings set out in the contested decision itself: see paras 69 *et seq.*

Access to file.   Note that if the Commission was precluded from relying on docu-   **8.146**
ments because they had not been disclosed to the applicant, the GC cannot rely on them in its review of the Commission's decision: Case C-413/06P *Bertelsmann AG and Sony Corporation of America v Impala and Commission* [2008] ECR I-4951, para 102.

Reply to statement of objections.   The notifying parties cannot, as a rule, be criti-   **8.147**
cised for putting forward certain—potentially decisive—arguments, facts or evidence only in their arguments in reply to the statement of objections. It is only with that statement that the parties to the concentration know in detail what concerns the Commission has about the concentration and the arguments and evidence on which it relies in that regard: see Case C-413/06P *Bertelsmann AG and Sony Corporation of America v Impala and Commission* [2008] ECR I-4951, para 89. The CJ expressly disapproved para 414 of the GC's judgment referred to in fn 428, holding that the arguments set out in reply to the statement of objections cannot be subject to more demanding standards as to their probative value and their cogency than those applied to the arguments of competitors, customers and other third parties. Further, the GC had erred in finding that the absence of additional market investigation after communication of the statement of objections and the adoption by the Commission of the appellants' arguments in defence amounted to an unlawful delegation of the investigation to the parties to the concentration: paras 93 *et seq.*

(iii) Role of Member States

Advisory Committee.   For the problems that can arise when the Advisory   **8.155**
Committee objects to the Commission's proposed decision on a merger see Case T-145/06 *Omya AG v Commission* [2009] ECR II-145, [2009] 4 CMLR 827, paras 4 *et seq.*

(iv) Possible outcomes at Phase II

Decisions following a Phase II investigation.   As to adequacy of reasoning in the   **8.156**
decision, see Case C-413/06P *Bertelsmann AG and Sony Corporation of America v Impala and Commission* [2008] ECR I-4951. There the CJ confirmed that the extent of the Commission's reasoning had to take into account the need for speed and the short timescales set for the Commission under the Merger Regulation: paras 166–169 and 174–176. The GC had erred in holding that the Commission's decision was inadequately reasoned. The CJ rejected an argument that the deeming provision in Article 10(6) of the Merger Regulation meant that a Commission clearance decision could not be annulled for lack of reasoning: para 175.

8.160   **Dissolution of prohibited concentrations and other restorative measures.**   Following the prohibition of the acquisition by Ryanair of Aer Lingus (M.4439 decn of 27 June 2007) Ryanair bought a further 4.3 per cent of the share capital of Aer Lingus bringing its total shareholding to 29.4 per cent. Aer Lingus asked the Commission to open proceedings against Ryanair under Article 8(4) of the Merger Regulation and to adopt interim measures to prevent Ryanair from exercising its voting rights in Aer Lingus. The Commission rejected Aer Lingus's request on the grounds that it did not have power to intervene in a situation where Ryanair had not taken control of Aer Lingus. Aer Lingus appealed to the GC against this rejection (Case T-411/07). Ryanair had also appealed against the prohibition of the merger (Case T-342/07). Aer Lingus's request for interim measures pending the hearing of its appeal was rejected: Case T-411/07R *Aer Lingus v Commission* [2008] ECR II-411, [2008] 5 CMLR 538. The President held (a) interim measures could only ever extend until the disposal of the appeal in Case T-411/07, and could not extend until the disposal of Case T-342/07; (b) an order could not be issued suspending the effect of a negative administration decision by the Commission because the grant of suspension could not change the applicant's position (para 46); (c) the GC could not order the Commission to give directions under Article 8(4) and 8(5) because this would constitute an interference with the exercise of the Commission's powers; and (d) as regards the request that the GC issue orders against Ryanair directly, the President did not rule out the exercise of such a power against Ryanair as a third party to the instant appeal, provided that procedural safeguards were put in place (para 56). However, the GC held that Aer Lingus had failed to establish a *prima facie* case that Ryanair had 'implemented' a concentration within the meaning of Article 8(4) or 8(5) given that it was accepted that there had been no change of control by reason of the acquisition of the minority shareholding (paras 84 *et seq*).

The Commission's prohibition of the concentration was upheld by the GC: Case T-342/07 *Ryanair v Commission*, judgment of 6 July 2010, [2011] 4 CMLR 245. The Commission's decision that it did not have power to order Ryanair to dispose of its 29.4 per cent share in Aer Lingus was also upheld: Case T-411/07, judgment of 6 July 2010. In the latter judgment, the Court held that the condition for taking action under Article 8(4) of the Merger Regulation was not met, since the notified concentration had not been implemented: from the moment when the decision finding incompatibility with the common market was adopted, it was no longer possible for Ryanair, *de jure* or *de facto*, to exercise control over Aer Lingus or to exercise decisive influence on that undertaking (para 61). It would not be correct to treat the minority shareholding as a partial implementation of the prohibited merger (paras 65 and 84). Finally, the Court noted that since there was no concentration with a EU dimension, the Member States were free to apply their national competition law to Ryanair's shareholding in Aer Lingus in accordance with the rules in place to that effect (para 91). Following the GC's judgments the Office of

Fair Trading in the United Kingdom notified the parties that it intended to open an investigation into the minority holding under domestic merger legislation. Ryanair's challenge to the OFT's powers, arguing that the statutory time bar precludes such an investigation was rejected by the UK Competition Appeal Tribunal: *Ryanair Holdings v Office of Fair Trading* [2011] CAT 23.

(d) Commitments to enable clearance

(i) Commitments at Phase I or Phase II

In general.   The revised Notice on Remedies has now been adopted: Notice on   **8.162** remedies acceptable under the EC Merger Regulation and under Commission Regulation (EC) No 802/2004, OJ 2008 C267/1: see Vol II, App D15. The Notice sets out the general principles which will guide the Commission's assessment of proposed commitments at all stages of the process. It then covers particular kinds of commitments, primarily divestiture of a business to a suitable purchaser but also referring to removal of links with competitors and other remedies such as access commitments and amendments to long-term exclusive contracts. The Notice states that whatever the kind of commitment accepted, the Commission will require a review clause though the Commission makes clear that modification of the commitments will not heal retroactively any breach of the commitments which has been committed before the time of the modification. The Notice then sets out the procedure for the submission of commitments at Phase I or Phase II of the investigation and gives further guidance on implementation. The main changes from the earlier notice are (a) more stringent information requirements on the parties including the new 'Form RM'; (b) clarifying and tightening up the requirements for the sufficient scope of divestitures and for the suitability of purchasers, in particular explaining the application of 'up-front buyer' provisions and 'fix-it-first' solutions that can address possible uncertainties in finding a suitable purchaser; (c) providing that carve-outs from the divested business may be accepted in certain circumstances provided that they are finalised prior to the sale to a purchaser; and (d) as to non-divestiture remedies, the Notice underlines that such remedies are only acceptable where they are equivalent in their effects to a divestiture. Access commitments are only acceptable if there is a sufficient likelihood that they will actually be used by competitors in practice. The Notice further stresses that difficulties of monitoring and risks concerning effectiveness may lead to non-divestiture remedies being rejected.

Form RM.   The new Form RM referred to in fn 479 was also incorporated into the   **8.162A** Implementing Regulation as Annex IV by Commission Regulation 1033/2008, OJ 2008 L279/3: see Vol II, App D2. The form specifies the information and documents to be submitted by the undertakings concerned at the same time as offering commitments. The Form sets out in detail the information and documents required to be submitted when the commitments offered include the divestiture of a business.

8.163 **Phase I commitments.** For examples of commitments accepted at Phase I see Case M.5152 *Posten AB/Post Danmark A/S* (21 April 2009) (divestment of assets and customer contracts) and Case M.5406 *IPIC/MAN Ferrostaal* (13 March 2009) (divestment of shareholding in subsidiary).

Fn 484. The new Form RM referred to has now been incorporated into the Implementing Reg as Annex IV by Commission Reg 1033/2008, OJ 2008 L279/3: see Vol II, App D2.

8.164 **Phase II commitments.** **Fn 487.** Note that the Implementing Reg was amended in 2008 to provide that the undertakings must, at the same time as offering commitments, submit one original and 10 copies of the information and documents prescribed by the Form RM relating to remedies as set out in Annex IV to the Reg: see Article 20(1a) inserted by Commission Reg 1033/2008, OJ 2008 L279/3: see Vol II, App D2. Form RM has been incorporated as Annex IV of the Implementing Reg, see new paragraph 8.162A, above.

8.165 **Common principles.** **Fn 492.** The appeal to the CJ in relation to the Handel/ Cementbouw concentration was dismissed: Case C-202/06P *Cementbouw Handel & Industrie BV v Commission* [2007] ECR I-12129, [2008] 4 CMLR 1324. The CJ held that review by the Court of Justice of the EU of the exercise of the Commission's discretion as regards acceptance of commitments must take account of the discretionary margin implicit in the provisions of an economic nature. The GC had been right to hold that the Commission was not required to accept the first draft of the commitments offered since it considered that they were insufficient to resolve the competition problem it had identified: paras 53 *et seq*.

Fn 493. The new Form RM referred to has now been incorporated into the Implementing Reg as Annex IV by Commission Reg 1033/2008, OJ 2008 L279/3: see Vol II, App D2, see new paragraph 8.162A, above.

(ii) Scope of commitments

8.166 **Structural and behavioural commitments.** In Case M.5984 *Intel/McAfee* (26 January 2011) the Commission noted that although structural commitments are usually the preferred remedy, in the case of a conglomerate merger other remedies may be better suited to addressing concerns. Where the concern was that control of key technology and IP rights might lead to foreclosure of competitors whose products need to interoperate with the merged entity's technology, commitments to grant competitors access to the necessary information may eliminate the competition concerns. In such a case the commitments should foresee non-exclusive licences or the disclosure of information on a non-exclusive basis to all third parties which depend on the IP rights or information for their activities. Further the commitments must ensure that the terms and conditions under which the licenses are granted do not impede the effective implementation of such a licence remedy. The terms and conditions should be clear and transparent. This also applies to the pricing of the licence, or the commitment should take the form of royalty-free licences. The Commission will only accept such commitments if it can be concluded that they will be effective and that competitors are likely to use them: para 307. The commitments accepted included the appointment of a monitoring trustee (who the Commission said must be in a position to act as the Commission's 'eyes and ears' to ensure the compliance of the parties with the commitments) and a dispute settlement procedure.

In Case M.4842 *Danone/Numico* (31 October 2007) the commitments included the grant of a five-year exclusive licence of certain brands, followed by a five-year commitment not to reintroduce the divested brands in Belgium, the transfer of product formulations and recipes, and transfer of the contract with an existing supplier: paras 86 *et seq*. In Case M.4691 *Schering-Plough/Organon Biosciences* (11 October 2007) the divestiture was accompanied by technical assistance, at the option of the purchaser to help the purchaser to assume responsibility for the manufacture, sale and marketing of the divested businesses.

Note that in Case M.5529 *Oracle Corporation/Sun Microsystems* (21 January 2010), the Commission recorded that Oracle had published ten 'pledges' to customers of the competing database, MySQL, currently produced by the target setting out how it would manage and enhance that product post-merger. Although these did not constitute binding commitments, the Commission noted that 'it can be expected that all of the public pledges made by Oracle to reassure MySQL users, developers and storage engine vendors will be subject to close scrutiny from the open source community' (para 182 and paras 655 *et seq*). These factors led the Commission to conclude that it was unlikely that Oracle would downgrade or eliminate the competing product post-merger. This aspect of the decision has been challenged on appeal: Case T-292/10 *Monty Program v Commission*, not yet decided.

Fn 499. On the disposal of slots in aviation mergers see also Case M.5364 *Iberia/ Clickair/Vueling* (9 January 2009) (proposed acquisition by Spanish national carrier of two low cost Spanish airlines: Phase I clearance conditional on giving up slots at Spanish and other European airports).

Divestiture. In Case M.5153 *Arsenal/DSP* (9 January 2009) the Commission **8.167** accepted a commitment to divest in a case where it had found that the merged entity would have run the only two production plants of a particular chemical in the EEA and that imports of the product were very low.

The divestiture may also, of course, give rise to a concentration under the Merger Regulation and need to be cleared by the Commission: see, eg Case M.5220 *ENI/ Distrigaz* (15 October 2008) following Case M.4180 *Gaz de France/Suez* which required GDF and Suez to divest Suez's share in the capital of Distrigaz. Following a bid process, ENI was elected as proposed purchaser and was approved by the Commission as a suitable buyer in line with the previous procedure. See similarly Case M.5519 *E.ON/Electrabel Acquired Assets* (13 September 2009).

(iii) Implementation of commitments

8.170   **Role of trustees.**   The Implementing Regulation now provides that commitments offered at either Phase I or Phase II may include, at the expense of the undertakings concerned, the appointment of an independent trustee (or trustees) assisting the Commission in overseeing the parties' compliance with the commitments or having a mandate to implement the commitments. The trustee may be appointed by the parties, after the Commission has approved its identity, or by the Commission. The trustee carries out its tasks under the supervision of the Commission. The Commission may attach such trustee-related provisions of the commitments as conditions and obligations under Articles 6(2) or 8(2) of the Merger Regulation: see Article 20a inserted by Commission Regulation 1033/2008, OJ 2008 L279/3: see Vol II, App D2.

In Case T-452/04 *Éditions Odile Jacob SAS v Commission*, judgment of 13 September 2010, the GC annulled a Commission decision approving a purchaser of assets being divested as a condition of the clearance of a concentration (M.2978 *Lagardère/Natexis/VUP*, OJ 2004 L125/54). One of the conditions attached to the clearance was the appointment of a monitoring trustee to supervise the choice of purchaser. The GC held that the trustee chosen was not sufficiently independent and that since the Commission had substantially relied on his report in deciding to approve the purchaser, that approval must be annulled. Both the Commission and Lagardère have lodged appeals against this ruling: Cases C-554/10P and C-553/10P, not yet decided. A parallel appeal challenging the decision to clear the concentration was dismissed by the GC: Case T-279/04 *Éditions Odile Jacob SAS v Commission*, judgment of 13 September 2010 (on appeal: Case 551/10P *Éditions Odile Jacob v Commission*, not yet decided).

(e)   Commission's powers of investigation

(i) Means of obtaining information

8.172   **Information requests.**   In Case T-145/06 *Omya AG v Commission* [2009] ECR II-145, [2009] 4 CMLR 827 the GC interpreted the requirement in Article 11(1) that the information requested be 'necessary'. The Court held that the need for the information must be assessed by reference to the view that the Commission could reasonably have held, at the time the request in question was made, of the extent of the information necessary to examine the concentration. As to when it was necessary to ask the parties to correct information already communicated, the Court held that the Commission is entitled to request the correction of erroneous information if there is a risk that the errors identified could have a significant impact on its assessment of whether the concentration is compatible with the common market. These criteria were not to be applied strictly and the Court would have a limited role in reviewing the Commission's decisions in this regard. The Court rejected Omya's assertion that the Commission's request had been used as a pretext to suspend the time running under the Regulation in light of objections raised by the Advisory Committee to a proposed clearance of the merger.

The Commission has issued a document called 'Best Practices for the Submission of Economic Evidence and Data Collection in Cases Concerning the Application of Articles 101 and 102 TFEU and in Merger Cases' (Vol II, App B21, and on the DG Competition website and linked to Press Release IP/10/02 (6 January 2010)). It describes the preferred content and presentation of economic and econometric data and best practice on responding to requests for quantitative data. The Best Practice describes the content and presentation of economic models stating, *inter alia*, that assumptions underlying the model should be carefully laid out and the sensitivity of its predictions to changes to the assumptions should be made explicit. As regards responding to information requests, the Commission has indicated (i) problems of missing data should be flagged up and justified to the Commission well in advance of the submission deadline; (ii) submissions of data should be accompanied by a memo *inter alia* describing the data compilation process, identifying all relevant sources; describing any assumptions and estimations used to fill incomplete data; and reporting on consistency checking and all data cleaning operations; (iii) tests for accuracy of the data should always be undertaken and reported. The Commission also warns against ignoring a carefully drafted and limited data request by producing large amounts of data points, using non-obvious 'definitions' of common terms in construing requests, or making unilateral and undisclosed inferences about what DG Competition is effectively seeking. The Commission also states that it may send a 'draft' data request, inviting parties to propose any modifications that could alleviate the compliance burden while producing the necessary information.

(ii) Suspension of Phase I and Phase II timetables

Article 11 decisions.   The appeal in Case T-145/06 *Omya AG v Commission* was **8.175** dismissed: [2009] ECR II-145, [2009] 4 CMLR 827. The GC held that the information requested by the Commission and the request for correction of that information was not a misuse of power and had properly suspended the running of time under the Regulation.

(iii) Confidentiality and business secrets

Business secrets and other confidential information.   The Commission has pub- **8.177** lished 'Guidance on procedures of the Hearing Officers in proceedings relating to Articles 101 and 102 TFEU' (Vol II, App B22 and available on the DG Competition website and linked to Press Release IP/10/02 (6 January 2010)) which sets out the role of the Hearing Officer in resolving disputes over confidentiality in the context of an infringement investigation. It describes the '*AKZO* procedure' under which the Hearing Officer will review the disputed documents and arrive at a decision on disclosure.

(f) Commission's powers of sanction

(ii) Fines and penalty payments

8.181 **Fines for substantive infringement.** The Commission has imposed a fine of €20 million for failure to notify a concentration: Case M.4994 *Electrabel/Compagnie Nationale du Rhône* (10 June 2009). The acquisition was cleared by the Commission on 29 April 2008 but the Commission found that Electrabel had already acquired *de facto* control of CNR in December 2003. Although Electrabel at that time had acquired less than 50 per cent of the shares, the Commission found that the widespread dispersion of the remaining shareholding and other factors meant that Electrabel had acquired control. In setting the fine the Commission had regard to the fact that Electrabel should have known that the 2003 transaction triggered the obligation to notify but also to the fact that the transaction did not give rise to any competition concerns and Electrabel had subsequently voluntarily informed the Commission of the acquisition of control: see Press Release IP/09/895 (10 June 2009). The case is on appeal: Case T-332/09, not yet decided. Cf Case M.5545 *ArcelorMittal/Noble European Holding* (17 July 2009) where the Commission left open the question whether control was acquired in March 2008 when ArcelorMittal acquired 49.9 per cent of the shares and the right to nominate the majority of board members; or in May 2009 when it acquired 100 per cent of the shares: para 7.

4. Substantive Appraisal of Concentrations

(b) Market definition

(ii) Product market

8.189 **Other features specifically relevant to merger control.** See the discussion of the merits of the consumer survey conducted by the Commission among airline passengers and corporate customers in Case T-342/07 *Ryanair Holdings plc v Commission*, judgment of 6 July 2010, [2011] 4 CMLR 245, paras 207 *et seq*.

(c) SIEC test

(ii) Relationship with concept of dominance

8.196 **Dominance remains a relevant consideration.** In Case M.5529 *Oracle Corporation/Sun Microsystems* (21 January 2010) the Commission rejected the submission from Oracle that the theory of harm was unusual and unprecedented because it did not depend on showing either the creation of a dominant position or the acquisition of a close competitor. The Commission noted that concentrations involving the elimination of important competitive constraints that the merging parties had exerted upon each other, as well as a reduction of competitive pressure on the remaining competitors may, even in the absence of a likelihood of coordination between the members of the oligopoly, result in a significant impediment to effective competition. The closeness of competition between the merging parties was only one of the factors influencing whether significant non-coordinated effects are likely to result from a merger: para 163. In an in-depth investigation, the Commission must therefore examine the nature and degree of the competitive constraint exerted by the target before the proposed transaction, the extent to which such competitive constraint would be removed after the merger as well as the extent to which other actual or potential competitors would constrain the combined entity post-merger: para 167. In this instance it was also important to assess whether the acquiring company would have the incentive to downgrade or eliminate the competing product supplied by the target post-merger. The decision is on appeal: Case T-292/10 *Monty Program v Commission*, not yet decided.

In Case M.4513 *Arjowiggins/M-Real Zanders' Reflect paper mill* (4 June 2008) the Commission found that the merged entity would have more than 50 per cent of the market in carbonless paper. The merger was cleared following the acceptance of commitments.

(iii) Checks and balances

Prospect of judicial review.   **Fn 607.** The *Schneider Electric* case referred to at the end of the footnote was partly overturned on appeal: see Case C-440/07P *Commission v Schneider Electric*, judgment of 16 July 2009 (Commission's liability confirmed in principle but appeal allowed in part on issue of causation of loss).   **8.198**

(iv) General content of assessment

Impact on consumer welfare and the counterfactual.   Where the merging parties are already cooperating pursuant to an agreement exempted under Article 101(3), this will be taken into account when considering the counterfactual: M.5747 *Iberia/British Airways* (14 July 2010), para 63. Cf Case M.5889 *United Airlines/Continental* (27 July 2010) where the Commission stated that it cannot be required to accept as a counterfactual pre-merger cooperation that is contrary to Article 101 TFEU since it cannot reasonably be predicted that illegal cooperation would continue in the absence of the merger. The merger would change the contractual relation between the parties into a permanent structural link, removing the possibility that one of them would discontinue the cooperation and start competing again. When considering that merger, the Commission was also in the course of investigating the cooperation between the airlines under Article 101 TFEU (COMP/39595 *AC/CO/LH/UA*, not yet decided). However, the Commission concluded that the merger did not raise serious concerns, whichever counterfactual was used.   **8.200**

Horizontal and non-horizontal mergers and their economic effects.   For a helpful example of the application of the Horizontal Merger Guidelines and the Non-Horizontal Merger Guidelines see Case M.4731 *Google/DoubleClick* (11 March 2008). The Commission did not consider the parties to be actual competitors but analysed whether the removal of DoubleClick as a potential competitor could   **8.202**

impede competition: paras 222 *et seq*. Further, while DoubleClick might have grown into an effective competitive force in online ad intermediation services, there were likely to be sufficient other competitors left in the market to maintain competitive pressure after the merger: para 278. An analysis of the potential conglomerate effects of the merger did not reveal any competition concerns and the merger was cleared in Phase II, see update to paragraph 8.219, below.

Fn 626. The Commission has now published its Non-Horizontal Merger Guidelines, OJ 2008 C265/6: Vol II, App D14. These are discussed in new paragraphs 8.217A (vertical mergers) and 8.219A (conglomerate mergers), below.

(d) Unilateral effects

(i) In general

8.204 **Relevance of market shares and concentration levels.** In Case T-342/07 *Ryanair Holdings plc v Commission*, judgment of 6 July 2010, [2011] 4 CMLR 245, the GC noted that the Commission had described high market shares post-merger as 'useful first indications' of the effect of the merger on competition and had taken care to carry out an in-depth analysis of the conditions of competition by taking account of factors other than just market shares. The Court considered that this was consistent with the analytical approach which the Commission must adopt when assessing the anti-competitive effects of a concentration: para 44.

In Case M.4956 *STX/Aker Yards* (5 May 2008) the Commission considered the implications of possible State subsidies from South Korea to the merged entity. The Commission analysed the earlier ECSC case of Case T-156/98 *RJB Mining plc v Commission* [2001] ECR II-337 and held that it was not required to make a 'pre-assessment' of alleged subsidies within a merger control procedure by conducting a *quasi* State aid investigation to identify whether subsidies were granted by a non-Member State. In principle, the Commission accepted that it must take into account any subsidies as factors potentially increasing a merged entity's financial strength, insofar as evidence supports the existence or the likelihood of such subsidies. However, if there is no clear evidence of the existence of such subsidies provided by third countries, the Commission is not obliged to investigate further. Any alleged inadequacies of the international procedures, such as the WTO procedures, are not relevant in this respect: paras 75 *et seq*.

Where the acquisition involves assets acquired from an insolvency administration, the Commission will assess how much of the target's pre-administration turnover the acquirer is likely to achieve in order to assess the strength of the post-merger entity on the market: see, eg Case M.5721 *Otto/Primondo Assets* (16 February 2010).

Fn 634. See, eg Case M.4533 *SCA/ P&G (European tissue business)* (5 September 2008) where the merged entity would have an 80–90 per cent share in the supply of branded kitchen paper but would not have market power because of the strong competition from private label product at the retail level: 'high market shares did not reflect their real market power vis-à-vis retailers and, ultimately, end-consumers': para 126.

(ii) Relevant considerations

Potentially relevant factors. Note that the GC has said that the Horizontal **8.207** Merger Guidelines do not require an examination in every case of all the factors mentioned in the Guidelines, since the Commission enjoys a discretion enabling it to take account or not to take account of certain factors: Case T-282/06 *Sun Chemical Group v Commission* [2007] ECR II-2149, para 57.

In Case M.5141 *KLM/Martinair* (17 December 2008) the Commission found that an important element of the counterfactual was that Martinair's business was loss-making and the existing owner had no strategic interest in making the investment necessary to reverse this decline. It was likely that the competitive constraint exerted by Martinair on KLM would be eroded in the foreseeable future absent the merger: para 175. See also Case M.4647 *AEE/Lentjes* (5 December 2007) where the Commission noted that the past market position of Lentjes was likely to weaken because demand in the German market in which it had a strong reputation was likely to decline: para 101; Case M.5727 *Microsoft/Yahoo! Search business* (18 February 2010) (Yahoo's performance in the sector had declined markedly over the years: paras 147 and 159).

As to point (a) see Case M.5830 *Olympic Air/Aegean Airlines* (26 January 2011) (merger prohibited where it would have led to a quasi-monopoly on routes where the airlines currently competed head to head; the case is on appeal: Case T-202/11 *Aeroporia Aigaiou Aeroporiki v Commission*, not yet decided). Note that even where the merged entity will have high market shares, the merger may be cleared if there is sufficient competition in the market: Case M.5907 *Votorantim/Fischer* (4 May 2011) (many customers had multiple sources of supply and switching costs were low given the commodity-type nature of the product involved). Where one party exits some of the relevant markets shortly before the merger, the Commission may require an explanation in order to assess whether the counterfactual should include the possibility of that party resuming production: Case M.5865 *Teva/Ratiopharm* (3 August 2010), para 35.

As to point (e) (elimination of an important competitive force), the target company does not need to be either a recent entrant or an innovating firm in order to be characterised as an important competitive force: Case M.5529 *Oracle Corporation/ Sun Microsystems* (21 January 2010), para 163. In that case an important issue was whether Oracle would have an incentive to downgrade or eliminate the competing product currently being sold by the target company, given the Commission's finding that that product imposed a significant competitive constraint on Oracle pre-merger (para 616). The Commission accepted that any such behaviour would have a substantial negative impact on Oracle's reputation as a software vendor. The Commission also referred to public announcements or 'pledges' made by Oracle, in part in the form of binding obligations to third parties and in part to the software-using community more generally. The Commission concluded that 'If the leader of an open source project, who is at the centre of an open source ecosystem, damages its own reputation and loses the open source community's trust, there will be an increased risk of losing network effects due to fragmentation and reorientation of the community. The leader consequently risks losing control of a so far relatively unified community and damaging its open source project, as the ecosystem might reorient and move towards a different leader': para 655. There was therefore unlikely to be an incentive to downgrade the competing product. The Commission also considered the control that Oracle would acquire over IP rights that were an important licensed input for downstream rivals (para 895) and concluded that Oracle would not have either the ability or the incentive to foreclose its downstream competitors by downgrading the terms and availability of licences (para 938). The decision has been challenged on appeal: Case T-292/10 *Monty Program v Commission*, not yet decided, in particular in relation to the Commission's reliance on Oracle's public pledges. See also Case M.5675 *Syngenta/Monsanto sunflower seed business* (17 November 2010) (Syngenta would remove the competitive constraint Monsanto represented as a strong innovator in Spain thereby ensuring its leading position also in the long run).

As to mergers between close competitors, see the analysis of the Commission in Case M.4842 *Danone/Numico* (31 October 2007) as regards the Belgian market for baby meals: merged entity would have a market share of 75–80 per cent, far ahead of that of its closest rival and undertakings wishing to enter or expand would 'experience the utmost difficulties': paras 63 *et seq*. In Case M.4828 *Owens Corning/Saint Gobain Vetrotex* (26 October 2007) the Commission noted that the merger would create a market leader with significantly higher sales and capacity than any other competitors and that the parties were generally considered as the leading innovators in the industry, with high quality R&D departments capable of developing entirely new products to suit customer needs: para 71. The commitments accepted before the clearance of the merger included the divestment of a product R&D centre, including a team of 20 experienced engineers, chemists and technicians under the direction of the R&D leader and a fully equipped laboratory. Further, as to whether merging firms are close competitors see Case T-342/07 *Ryanair Holdings plc v Commission*, judgment of 6 July 2010, [2011] 4 CMLR 245, (GC held that differences in operating costs between two airlines did not prevent them being 'closest competitors': para 79). The judgment contains a detailed discussion of the Commission's and Ryanair's econometric analysis.

Fn 643. As to merger with a potential competitor see also Case M.5096 *RCA/MAV Cargo* (25 November 2008) where the Commission conditionally cleared a merger which led to the removal of the most likely new entrant in each of the parties' domestic rail freight markets. In Case M.4956 *STX/Aker Yards* (5 May 2008) the Commission, referring to para 60 of the Horizontal Merger Guidelines, found no plans or specific evidence indicating a likely and timely entry by STX in the relevant market in a significant way absent the merger. Other Far East shipbuilders were more advanced than STX in their steps towards entering into the cruise ship market. The Commission concluded that the merger would not have significant anti-competitive effects as a result of the elimination of STX as a potential competitor of the three current large builders of cruise ships.

Fn 645. In Case T-342/07 *Ryanair Holdings plc v Commission*, judgment of 6 July 2010, [2011] 4 CMLR 245, the GC discussed barriers to entry and the concept of 'timeliness' in para 74 of the Guidelines: see para 291 of the judgment. The GC also upheld the Commission's finding that Ryanair's reputation for aggressive price cutting in response to market entry constituted a barrier to entry: para 287.

Fn 647. See, eg Case M.5597 *Towers Perrin/Watson Wyatt* (3 December 2009) (barriers to entry into the market of actuarial and risk management software for life insurance included actuarial and regulatory know-how as well as development costs); Case M.5599 *Amcor/Alcan* (15 December 2009) (barriers to entry into packaging for pharmaceutical products included know-how, customer knowledge and credibility on the market, para 104).

Fn 653. As to pricing 'mavericks' see Case M.4919 *Statoil/ConocoPhillips (Jet)* (21 October 2008) where the Commission found that JET Sweden played a unique role in the Swedish market as a low price supplier in retail sales of motor fuels and that its removal from the market would have a greater effect than its market share would imply at first glance: paras 91 *et seq.* Similarly in Case M.4844 *Fortis/ABN Amro Assets* (3 October 2007) Fortis as a smaller competitor had the incentive to break into existing customer relations and compete on price and non-price parameters in order to increase its customer base. This incentive would disappear once it was acquired by the market leader. In Case M.4999 *Heineken/Scottish & Newcastle* (3 April 2008) the fact that S&N was regarded as a price maverick in the Irish beer market was relevant to the decision whether to refer the merger back to the Irish competition authorities under Article 9(2) of the Merger Reg: paras 41 *et seq.* In Case M.4523 *Travelport/Worldspan* (21 August 2007) the Commission rejected arguments that Worldspan acted as a price maverick since the market investigation did not establish that Worldspan's prices were lower than its competitors' before the merger and Worldspan's market share was declining: para 104. A similar submission was also rejected in Case M.4963 *Rexel/Hagemeyer* (22 February 2008), para 71. In Case M.5549 *EDF/Segebel* (12 November 2009) the Commission found that the proposed transaction would remove 'the most ambitious entrant' in the relevant market (para 83) but cleared the merger on accepting appropriate divestiture commitments. See also Case M.5650 *T-Mobile/Orange* (1 March 2010) where the Commission had concerns about the merged entity's incentives to terminate or downgrade an agreement on sharing facilities with a competitor which had played a key role in driving innovation and lowering prices for consumers: para 107. The Commission cleared the merger after commitments addressing this were accepted.

(e) Coordinated effects

(i) In general

8.210   **Opportunities for tacit collusion.**   This and the following paragraphs must now be read in the light of the CJ's judgment in Case C-413/06P *Bertelsmann AG and Sony Corporation of America v Impala and Commission* [2008] ECR I-4951. The CJ overturned the GC's judgment, finding that the GC had erred in a number of respects both procedural and substantive. The CJ set out the test that the Commission must apply in the case of an alleged creation or strengthening of a collective dominant position: see paras 119 *et seq*. The Court emphasised that in applying the criteria, it is necessary to avoid a mechanical approach involving the separate verification of each of those criteria taken in isolation, while taking no account of the overall economic mechanism of a hypothetical tacit coordination. See further the update to paragraph 10.053, below.

Where there was already an asymmetry between the market shares of the main suppliers, the merger may not change the market in a way which makes coordination more likely, stable or effective: Case M.5907 *Votorantim/Fischer* (4 May 2011).

(ii) Relevant considerations

8.211   **Characterising a market as oligopolistic.**   The test as set out by the CJ in the *IMPALA* judgment was applied by the Commission in granting conditional clearance at Phase II of the investigation into a merger in Case M.4980 *ABF/GBI Business* (23 September 2008) (paras 144 *et seq*). The Commission found as regards the Portuguese market: the three existing entities all had a strong presence in the market and faced virtually no threat of entry or expansion from competitors; the market was characterised by the high frequency of interaction between suppliers, indirectly via their distributors; demand for the product was relatively inelastic; there were high barriers to entry arising from the importance of having a local distribution network and a strong reputation for quality and reliability; the product was fairly homogeneous across suppliers and thus subject to similar supply or demand shocks; there was transparency of price, sales and capacity; and the technology used in the market was mature and not expected to change or improve. All these factors indicated that the market conditions were conducive to coordination. So far as mechanisms for policing the coordination were concerned, the Commission cited instances in the past where attempts by the *de facto* exclusive distributor of one supplier to expand its share of the market in an area had been disciplined by the supplier: 'This demonstrates how the system corrects itself when a distributor is trying to deviate from the paradigm imposed by the suppliers': para 219. The Commission went on to find that the other conditions set in *IMPALA* were also satisfied and that the merger, by creating a duopoly would increase the incentives for coordination. The merger was cleared on the basis of divestiture commitments.

By contrast in Case M.5114 *Pernod Ricard/V&S Vin & Sprit* (17 July 2008) the Commission found that the criteria for market coordination were not satisfied because prices were not transparent. Further, there were strong local producers present in most Member States who would be able to gain market shares in case of coordinated price increases from large, international players: paras 107 *et seq*. See also Case M.4942 *Nokia/Navteq* (2 July 2008) paras 395 *et seq*; and Case M.4854 *TomTom/Tele Atlas* (14 May 2008) paras 277 *et seq* (conditions for coordinated behaviour not met in vertical mergers); Case M.4781 *Norddeutsche Affinerie/Cumerio* (23 January 2008) paras 183 *et seq* (ability of actual and potential competitors to counteract any attempts of coordination reduced the ability and incentives for undertakings to try to coordinate their commercial behaviour); Case M.4523 *Travelport/Worldspan* (21 August 2007) paras 149 *et seq* (limited price transparency in the market for global distribution systems for travel services products). In Case M.5020 *Lesaffre/GBI UK* (11 July 2008) the merger would have created a duopoly in the relevant market aligning the merged entity with the existing market leader in terms of market shares, production capacity and geographic plant distribution. The merger was cleared subject to commitments which returned the position to the status quo.

Reaching terms of coordination.   The judgment of the GC in Case T-464/04   **8.212** *IMPALA v Commission* [2006] ECR II-2289, [2006] 5 CMLR 1049 was overturned by the CJ on appeal: see Case C-413/06P *Bertelsmann AG and Sony Corporation of America v Impala and Commission* [2008] ECR I-4951. The CJ approved the criteria for collective dominance as expressed by the GC in *Airtours* but held that the GC had been wrong to conclude that the discounts offered by the record companies (which the Commission had found meant that prices were not transparent in the market) would have been apparent to a 'hypothetical industry professional': para 131. See further the update to paragraph 10.053, below.

Case M.5549 *EDF/Segebel* (12 November 2009) considered the effect of State ownership on the existence of structural links that might lead to coordinated effects: paras 89 *et seq*. The Commission found that though both shareholdings would be managed by the same State agency, EDF was in fact able to set its business plans independently and in accordance with its own commercial interests so that this concern was not well founded.

Prospective analysis: *Impala*.   The judgment of the GC in *IMPALA* was over-   **8.214** turned by the CJ: see updates to paragraph 8.212, above and paragraph 10.053, below.

(f) Vertical and conglomerate effects

(i) Vertical effects

8.216 **Potential foreclosure effects.** In Case M.5121 *News Corp/Premiere* (26 June 2008) the Commission considered whether the vertical aspect of the merger would lead to 'input foreclosure', ie whether the upstream business of the merged entity would have the ability and incentive to stop supplying competitors in the downstream market and 'customer foreclosure', ie whether the downstream business would acquire all its requirements internally, thereby removing it as a potential outlet for competitors in the upstream market: paras 59 *et seq.* The Commission's concerns about the strengthening of Premiere's dominant position in the German pay-TV market were resolved by commitments which allowed the merger to be cleared.

In Case M.4854 *TomTom/Tele Atlas* (14 May 2008) and Case M.4942 *Nokia/ Navteq* (2 July 2008) the Commission considered whether a vertical merger may give the merged entity access to commercially sensitive information regarding the downstream activity of rivals. For instance, by becoming a supplier to its downstream competitors, the merged entity may obtain critical information allowing it to compete less aggressively or could put competitors at a disadvantage thereby making entry and expansion less attractive (para 360 of *Nokia/Navteq* and para 276 of *TomTom/Tele Atlas*). The Commission found that this was not a problem on the facts of the particular market. For a discussion of the Commission's approach to vertical mergers in *TomTom/TeleAtlas* and *Nokia/Navteq* see de Coninck, 'Economic analysis in vertical mergers' (2008) 3 Competition Policy Newsletter 48; and Esteva Mosso et al, 'Digital maps go vertical: TomTom/TeleAtlas and Nokia/NAVTEQ' (2008) 3 Competition Policy Newsletter 70. See similarly Case M.4731 *Google/ DoubleClick* (11 March 2008), para 257 (contractual restrictions on use of data collected on behalf of one customer to benefit other customers meant that there were no network effect benefits); Case M.5978 *GDF Suez/International Power* (26 January 2011) (acquirer's access to confidential information about the output of target's power generation plant enabled it to increase electricity prices and dissuade its competitor from expanding: para 78).

A particular kind of vertical effect can arise in two-sided markets: see, eg Case M.4523 *Travelport/Worldspan* (21 August 2007) where the Commission described a theory of harm arising from concentration in the market for global distribution systems for travel services. The Commission referred to potential 'vertical cross market effects' whereby the merged entity would have an incentive to offer favourable terms to attract more travel agents to join its network and recoup that investment (and generate margin) by extracting rents upstream from the travel service providers such as airlines, hotels and car rental companies: para 76.

In the Non-Horizontal Merger Guidelines, OJ 2008 C265/6: Vol II, App D14 the Commission notes that the integration of complementary activities within a single firm may produce significant efficiencies and be pro-competitive. Vertical integration may provide an increased incentive to seek to decrease prices and increase output because the integrated firm can capture a larger fraction of the benefits. This is often referred to as the 'internalisation of double mark-ups'. Similarly, other efforts to increase sales at one level (eg improve service or step up innovation) may provide a greater reward for an integrated firm that will take into account the benefits accruing at other levels. Integration may also decrease transaction costs and allow for a better coordination in terms of product design, the organisation of the production process, and the way in which the products are sold: paras 13 and 14.

Vertical mergers: the Non-Horizontal Merger Guidelines.   The Commission has   **8.217A**
now published its Non-Horizontal Merger Guidelines, OJ 2008 C265/6: Vol II, App D14. So far as vertical mergers are concerned, the Guidelines indicate that the Commission is unlikely to investigate a non-horizontal merger extensively where the market share post-merger of the new entity in each of the markets concerned is below 30 per cent and the post-merger HHI is below 2000 unless certain listed factors are present: para 26. The Guidelines discuss how the Commission will assess the likelihood of input foreclosure, that is, whether the upstream part of the entity is likely to restrict supplies or increase prices charged to undertakings in the downstream market which are now competing with the downstream arm of the merged entity. The Commission will examine first, whether the merged entity would have, post-merger, the ability to foreclose access to inputs; secondly, whether it would have the incentive to do so; and thirdly, whether a foreclosure strategy would have a significant detrimental effect on competition downstream. The Commission describes the kinds of circumstances in which input foreclosure is likely to be a problem.

The Commission notes that vertical mergers may generate efficiencies, in particular, a vertical merger allows the merged entity to internalise any pre-existing double mark-ups; it may further allow the parties better to coordinate the production and distribution process, and therefore to save on inventory costs and may align the incentives of the parties with regard to investments in new products, new production processes and in the marketing of products. So far as customer foreclosure is concerned, the Commission again describes the factors indicating whether the merged entity would have the ability and the incentive to engage in such conduct and whether this would have a significant detrimental effect on consumers in the downstream market: paras 58 *et seq.* Finally the Guidelines discuss the circumstances in which a vertical merger may lead to coordinated effects by making it easier for the firms in the upstream or downstream market to reach a common understanding on the terms of coordination.

In practice.   See also the Commission's analysis of possible vertical effects in a   **8.218**
merger between a manufacturer of sensors used in textile weaving and spinning machines and a manufacturer of those machines: Case M.4874 *Itema/Barco Vision* (4 August 2008). Both the upstream market (for the sensors) and the downstream

market (for the machines) were highly concentrated and competitors in the downstream market feared that they would no longer be able to buy sensors to incorporate into their machines. On analysis the Commission found that there was little risk of foreclosure and the merger was cleared. In Case M.4942 *Nokia/Navteq* (2 July 2008) the Commission considered a case of 'backward vertical integration' in the sense that a producer of a good (mobile phone handsets) acquired its main provider of an important input (navigable digital map databases). The Commission identified upstream, downstream, and intermediate markets (for navigation software) affected by the merger. Competitors in the downstream market expressed concerns that the merged entity might pursue a foreclosure strategy either by increasing prices, by providing degraded map sets, by delaying access to the latest maps or attributes or by reserving innovative features to Nokia. The Commission applied three criteria: (i) whether the merged entity would have the *ability* post-merger to foreclose access to inputs; (ii) whether it would have the *incentive* to do so; and (iii) whether a foreclosure strategy would have a significant detrimental effect in the intermediary downstream market for navigation software and in the downstream markets. As to the first, the Commission concluded that the merged entity would have a significant degree of market power on the upstream market for navigable digital map databases but that it was unclear whether they would have the ability to adopt a strategy of foreclosure. The Commission cleared the merger on the basis that the merged entity would have no incentive to foreclose. When the Nokia/Navteq merger was notified, the Commission was part way through investigating a very similar vertical merger in the same markets and the analysis and reasoning in *Nokia/Navteq* drew heavily on the earlier decision in Case M.4854 *TomTom/Tele Atlas* (14 May 2008).

See also Case M.5585 *Centrica/Venture Production* (21 August 2009) where the Commission considered the possible vertical effects in a merger in the gas and crude oil production markets.

Fn 683. An appeal against the *DaimlerChrysler/Deutsche Telekom/JV* decision was dismissed: Case T-48/04 *Qualcomm Wireless Business Solutions v Commission* [2009] ECR II-2029. See more recently Case M.5675 *Syngenta/Monsanto sunflower seed business* (17 November 2010).

(ii) Conglomerate effects

8.219 **Conglomerate effects.** In Case M.4731 *Google/DoubleClick* (11 March 2008), para 257 the Commission investigated non-horizontal theories of harm arising from the fact that intermediation and ad serving tools are products that publishers and advertisers can purchase together (though not necessarily). With the acquisition of DoubleClick, Google would therefore acquire the leading supplier of ad serving that publishers and advertisers can combine with intermediation services such as those offered by Google's ad network (AdSense). The Commission therefore analysed (i) foreclosure scenarios based on DoubleClick's market position in ad serving; (ii) foreclosure scenarios based on Google's market position in search advertising and online ad intermediation services; and (iii) foreclosure scenarios based on the combination of DoubleClick's and Google's databases on customer online behaviour. The Commission concluded (para 310) that the evidence reviewed did not support the view that the new entity would be able to foreclose competitors in intermediation markets through leveraging its leading position in ad serving. There were credible alternatives to which customers (publishers/advertisers/ad networks) could switch and network effects (ie the competitive advantages derived from having a large customer base) were not strong. Any strategy to attract publishers/advertisers to AdSense through input foreclosure or a variety of bundling/tweaking strategies was unlikely to be able to foreclose rivals in intermediation markets. For a helpful discussion of the issues in this rather complicated case see Brockhoff et al, 'Google/DoubleClick: The first test for the Commission's non-horizontal merger guidelines' (2008) 2 Competition Policy Newsletter 53.

In Case M.5984 *Intel/McAfee* (26 January 2011) the Commission considered various concerns arising from the merger of Intel, the dominant producer of central processing units (CPUs) and McAfee, a producer of endpoint computer security services. The Commission found that the merged entity would have both the ability and incentive to foreclose the market by downgrading interoperability and by technically bundling the products with the aim of leveraging Intel's dominance into the endpoint security markets, causing McFee's competitors to exit the market. These practices would have a significant effect on competition. Although it would also have the ability to engage in commercial bundling of its products, its incentives to do so would be limited. However, this possibility combined with the risk of foreclosure from the other practices reinforced the Commission's concerns. The Commission cleared the merger after accepting behavioural commitments to resolve these problems.

Conglomerate effects: Non-Horizontal Merger Guidelines. The Commission **8.219A** has now published its Non-Horizontal Merger Guidelines, OJ 2008 C265/6: Vol II, App D14. The Commission notes, as regards conglomerate mergers, that in practice its focus is on mergers between companies that are active in closely related markets (eg mergers involving suppliers of complementary products or of products which belong to a range of products that is generally purchased by the same set of customers for the same end use). The Guidelines indicate that the Commission is unlikely to investigate a non-horizontal merger extensively where the market share post-merger of the new entity in each of the markets concerned is below 30 per cent and the post-merger HHI is below 2000 unless certain listed factors are present: para 26. The main concern is that of foreclosure since the combination of products in related markets may confer on the merged entity the ability and incentive to leverage a strong market position from one market to another by means of tying or bundling or other exclusionary practices: paras 93 *et seq*. The Commission will therefore first examine whether the merged entity will have the ability to foreclose its rivals, secondly, whether it would have the economic incentive to do so and, thirdly, whether a foreclosure strategy would have a significant detrimental effect on competition, thus causing harm to consumers. Foreclosure in this context involves conditioning sales in a way that links the products in the separate markets together, usually by tying or bundling.

8.221 **Other conglomerate cases.** The Commission has now published its Non-Horizontal Merger Guidelines, OJ 2008 C265/6: Vol II, App D14 discussed in the preceding paragraphs.

Fn 702. The Commission also considered possible conglomerate effects in Case M.5114 *Pernod Ricard/V&S Vin & Sprit* (17 July 2008) but concluded that the merged entity would not be able to tie or bundle its brand portfolio: para 115.

(g) Other considerations relevant to substantive appraisal

(ii) Efficiencies

8.229 **Proving efficiency benefits.** See the evidence that the parties submitted in Case M.5141 *KLM/Martinair* (17 December 2008), paras 408 *et seq*. The Commission found that the underlying assumptions in the report were too strong to allow any inference on their ultimate quantification, and no clear-cut indication could be drawn from it. In Case M.4942 *Nokia/Navteq* (2 July 2008) the Commission considered whether pricing efficiencies would arise from the removal of double mark-ups in a vertical merger, referring to para 55 of the Non-Horizontal Merger Guidelines (paras 365 *et seq*).

(iii) Failing firm defence

8.230 **Failing firm defence.** See also Case M.5141 *KLM/Martinair* (17 December 2008) where the Commission found that Martinair's business was loss-making and the existing owner had no strategic interest in making the investment necessary to reverse this decline. It was therefore likely that the competitive constraint exerted by Martinair on KLM would be eroded in the foreseeable future absent the merger: para 175.

(h) Coordinative aspects of certain full-function joint ventures

(i) In general

8.232 **Spill-over effects.** In Case M.5332 *Ericsson/STM/JV* (25 November 2008) the Commission found that there were no likely coordinated effects because the market was characterised by differentiated products, long-term contracts, infrequent bidding and large volumes of individual tenders, asymmetry of players' market shares post joint venture, significant buyer power of customers and the importance of innovation in the market.

5. Judicial Review by the Community Courts

(a) Procedures

Expedited procedure.   The judgment of the GC in Case T-464/04 *IMPALA v*   **8.236**
Commission [2006] ECR II-2289, [2006] 5 CMLR 1049 was overturned by the CJ
on appeal: see Case C-413/06P *Bertelsmann AG and Sony Corporation of America v
Impala and Commission* [2008] ECR I-4951. The case was referred back to the GC
to consider the other grounds of appeal not dealt with. Costs were reserved.

(c) Persons entitled to appeal

(ii) Third parties

Competitors and customers.   Where a competitor has gone into liquidation and   **8.240**
hence is no longer active in the relevant market, it does not have standing to challenge the clearance of a merger: Case T-269/03 *Socratec v Commission*, judgment of
19 June 2009. The GC rejected the argument that Socratec's potential rights of
action for damages against either the parties to the concentration or the Commission
gave it standing.

Note that even if the Commission sends a copy of the approval decision to a complainant who has been involved in the investigation stage, the time for that
complainant to bring an appeal against the clearance decision still runs only from
the publication of the decision in the *Official Journal*: Case T-48/04 *Qualcomm
Wireless Business Solutions v Commission* [2009] ECR II-2029, para 58.

(d) Scope of judicial review

(i) Application of the law

Jurisdictional issues.   Fn 773. The appeal in *Cementbouw* was dismissed: Case   **8.246**
C-202/06P *Cementbouw Handel & Industrie BV v Commission* [2007] ECR
I-12129, [2008] 4 CMLR 1324.

Procedural issues.   As to adequacy of reasoning in the decision, see Case C-413/   **8.247**
06P *Bertelsmann AG and Sony Corporation of America v Impala and Commission*
[2008] ECR I-4951 where the CJ confirmed that the extent of the Commission's
reasoning had to take into account the need for speed and the short timescales set
for the Commission under the Merger Regulation: paras 166–169. The CJ rejected
an argument that the deeming provision in Article 10(6) of the Merger Regulation
meant that a Commission clearance decision could not be annulled for lack of
reasoning: para 175.

(iii) Economic issues

Effective but restrained review.   In Case C-413/06P *Bertelsmann AG and*   **8.252**
Sony Corporation of America v Impala and Commission [2008] ECR I-4951, the

CJ confirmed that while the GC must not substitute its own economic assessment for that of the Commission, that does not mean that the Court of Justice of the EU must refrain from reviewing the Commission's interpretation of information of an economic nature. Although the GC had carried out an in-depth examination of the evidence underlying the contested decision, it had acted in conformity with the requirements of the case law: paras 145–146.

In Case C-202/06P *Cementbouw Handel & Industrie BV v Commission* [2007] ECR I-12129, [2008] 4 CMLR 1324 the CJ referred to 'the discretionary margin implicit in the provisions of an economic nature which form part of the rules on concentrations' in the context of a challenge to the Commission's refusal to accept commitments offered by the parties to the concentration during a Phase II investigation: para 53.

(e) Standard of proof incumbent on Commission

8.255 **Borderline cases.** In Case C-413/06P *Bertelsmann AG and Sony Corporation of America v Impala and Commission* [2008] ECR I-4951 the CJ confirmed that there is no general presumption that a notified concentration is compatible with, or incompatible with, the common market. The burden of proof is the same whether the Commission is considering clearing or prohibiting the merger. Further, there is no particularly high standard of proof in mergers involving allegations of collective dominance: paras 46 *et seq*.

6. Application of Articles 81 and 82 in Field of Mergers and Acquisitions

Note that Articles 81 and 82 EC are now Articles 101 and 102 TFEU

(a) Background

8.259 **Article 82 and concentrations.** See the rather cautious approach in COMP/ 38113 *Prokent-Tomra*, decn of 29 March 2006, [2009] 4 CMLR 101, paras 86, 107 and 345 where the Commission referred to the dominant undertaking's exclusionary strategy as including acquisition of its competitors. The Commission stated that the acquisitions were described in order to illustrate Tomra's overall strategy and the means implemented to maintain its dominant position: 'This decision does not question the legality of these practices, which are outside its scope': para 107. Tomra's appeal was dismissed and this point was not discussed: Case T-155/06 *Tomra Systems v Commission*, judgment of 9 September 2010.

(c) Minority shareholdings and other structural links

8.273 **Links not conferring control.** On the question of when a minority shareholding confers control and the powers of the Commission under the Merger Regulation in respect of a minority shareholding that does not amount to a concentration see Case T-411/07 *Aer Lingus v Commission*, judgment of 6 July 2010, paras 67 *et seq.* The case is discussed in the update to paragraph 8.160, above.

7. National Merger Control and International Cooperation

(a) National merger control regimes within EEA

(ii) Summary of national regimes

Outline of national merger control rules in the EEA. The following entries should be substituted at the appropriate place in the table.   **8.279**

Jurisdiction	Jurisdictional criteria	Notification requirements
Bulgaria	(a) combined turnover in Bulgaria of BGN 25m (c. €12.8m); and (b) either (1) at least two parties each have turnover in Bulgaria of BGN 3m (c. €1.5m); *or* (2) target has turnover in Bulgaria of BGN 3m (c. €1.5m)	Mandatory prior notification to Commission for Protection of Competition
Cyprus	(a) at least two parties each have worldwide turnover of €3.4m; and (b) at least one party carries on business in Cyprus; and (c) combined turnover in Cyprus of €3.4m	Mandatory prior notification to Commission for the Protection of Competition
Czech Republic	(a) combined turnover in Czech Republic of CZK 1,500m (c. €59m); and (b) each of at least two parties has turnover in Czech Republic of CZK 250m (c. €9.9m); *or* (a) at least one party (which must be the target in the case of a share or asset acquisition) has turnover in Czech Republic of CZK 1,500m (c. €59m); and (b) at least one other party has worldwide turnover of CZK 1,500m (c. €59m)	Mandatory prior notification to Úřvad pro Ochranu Hospodářské Soutěže (Office for the Protection of Economic Competition)
Denmark	(a) combined turnover in Denmark of DKK 900m (c. €120.8m); and (b) at least two parties each have turnover in Denmark of DKK 100m (c. €13.4m); *or* (a) at least one party has turnover in Denmark of DKK 3.8 billion (c. €510m); and (b) at least one of the other parties has worldwide turnover of DKK 3.8 billion (c. €510m)	Mandatory prior notification to Koncurrencestyrelsen (Competition Authority)

Jurisdiction	Jurisdictional criteria	Notification requirements
France	(a) combined worldwide turnover of €150m; and (b) at least two parties each have turnover in France of €50m Special thresholds for concentrations in the retail trade sector or in the French Départements or Collectivités d'Outre-Mer	Mandatory prior notification to l'Autorité de la concurrence (Competition Authority)
Greece	Mandatory prior notification if: (a) combined turnover of €150m; and (b) each of at least two parties has turnover in Greece of €15m	Mandatory prior merger notification to Hellenic Competition Commission
Iceland	(a) combined turnover in Iceland of ISK 2,000m (c. €13m); and (b) at least two parties each have turnover in Iceland of ISK 200m (c. €1.3m); *or* (a) combined turnover in Iceland of ISK 1,000m (c. €6.5m); and (b) authority believes the merger can substantially reduce effective competition	Mandatory prior notification to Samkeppnisstofnun (Competition Authority)
Italy	(a) combined turnover in Italy of €472m; or (b) target has turnover in Italy of €47m (Thresholds are revised annually to take account of inflation; above figures were revised in May 2010)	Mandatory prior notification to the Autorità Garante della Concorrenza e del Mercato (Competition Authority)
Latvia	(a) combined turnover (in Latvia) of LVL 25m (c. €35m); or (b) combined market share in relevant market of 40% Exception: Merger notification may not be necessary if turnover of one of the parties does not exceed LVL 1.5 million (c. €2.1m)	Mandatory prior notification to Konkurences Padome (Competition Council)
Lithuania	(a) combined turnover in Lithuania exceeds LTL 30m (c. €8.7m); and (b) at least two parties each have turnover in Lithuania of LTL 5m (c. €1.4m)	Mandatory notification to Konkurencijos Taryba (Competition Council)
Malta	(a) combined turnover in Malta of €2,329,373.40; and (b) each of the undertakings concerned has turnover in Malta equivalent to at least 10% of parties' combined turnover	Mandatory prior notification to Director of the Office for Fair Competition
Slovakia	(a) combined worldwide turnover of €46m; and (b) at least two parties each have turnover in the Slovak Republic of €14m; *or* (a) at least one party has worldwide turnover of €46m; and (b) at least one other party has turnover in the Slovak Republic of €19m	Mandatory prior notification to Protimonopolného úrad (Antimonopoly Office)

Jurisdiction	Jurisdictional criteria	Notification requirements
Slovenia	(a) combined turnover in Slovenia of 35m; and (b) (i) target has turnover in Slovenia of €1m; or (ii) in cases of joint ventures of at least two parties, including affiliated companies, turnover in Slovenia of €1m NB: If thresholds are not met, but parties to the concentration, together with the affiliated companies, have more than 60 % market share in the Slovenian market, the undertakings concerned are obliged to inform the CPO of the concentration (but not submit a formal notification).	Mandatory prior notification to Urad RS za Varstvo Konkurence (Competition Protection Office)
Spain	(a) combined turnover in Spain of €240m; and (b) each of at least two parties has turnover in Spain of €60m; *or* combined market share in Spain of 30 per cent (Note that this market share threshold will not apply where target's turnover in Spain was under €10m in the last financial year provided that the parties' individual or combined market share is under 50 per cent)	Mandatory prior notification to Servicio de Comisión Nacional de Competencia
Sweden	(a) combined turnover in Sweden of SEK 1,000m (c. €104.8m); and (b) at least two parties each have turnover in Sweden of SEK 200m (c. €20.9m)	Mandatory prior notification to Konkurrensverket (Swedish Competition Authority). Voluntary notification may be submitted by the parties if only the first turnover threshold (SEK 1,000m) is met.
United Kingdom	(a) target has turnover in the UK of £70m (c. €81.6m); *or* (b) transaction results in or increases share of supply of goods or services of any description of 25 per cent or more in UK (or a substantial part of the UK)	Voluntary notification to Office of Fair Trading

9

INTELLECTUAL PROPERTY RIGHTS

1. Introduction

The move to a more economics-based analysis. **Fn 20.** The 2001 Guidelines **9.005**
referred to have been replaced by the Horizontal Cooperation Guidelines issued in
2011: OJ 2011 C11/1: Vol II, App C22.

2. Infringement Actions and the Free Movement Rules

(b) Patents

Pharmaceutical marketing authorisations. **Fn 100.** The appeal in *AstraZeneca* **9.028**
has been decided and is discussed in the update to para 10.154, below: Case
T-321/05 *AstraZeneca v Commission*, judgment of 1 July 2010, [2010] 5 CMLR
1575 (on appeal Case C-457/10P *AstraZeneca v Commission*, not yet decided).

(c) Trade marks

Specific subject-matter of the trade mark. In Case C-533/06 *O_2 Holdings v* **9.033**
Hutchison 3G UK Ltd [2008] ECR I-4231, [2008] 3 CMLR 397, the CJ considered the essential function of the trade mark when deciding whether the use in an
advertisement by one mobile phone network operator (H3G) of a sign very similar
to the registered trade mark of a competitor (O_2) was a breach of the latter's rights
when the sign was being used to emphasise that H3G's prices were lower than O_2's.
The Court considered the relationship between Article 5(1) of Directive 89/104
and Directive 84/450 concerning misleading and comparative advertising (1984
OJ L250/17 amended by Dir 2005/29 2005 OJ L149/22). O_2 accepted that the
comparison made in the advertisement was not misleading and further that the
advertisement did not suggest that there was any trade connection between the two
companies. The use of the O_2 sign did not therefore cause confusion or otherwise

jeopardise the essential function of O$_2$'s mark. The CJ held that the use made of the O$_2$ mark did constitute 'use' within the meaning of Article 5(1) and (2) of Directive 89/104. However, in order to reconcile Article 5 of Directive 89/104 with Article 3a(1) of Directive 84/450, these provisions must be interpreted as meaning that the trade mark owner is not entitled to prevent the use of its mark in a comparative advertisement which satisfies all the criteria of Directive 84/450, under which comparative advertising is permitted.

9.039   **Repackaging: recent case law.**   Following the judgment of the CJ on the second preliminary ruling reference (Case C-348/04 [2007] ECR I-3391, [2007] 2 CMLR 1445, [2008] All ER (EC) 411) the English Court of Appeal noted that both sides claimed to have won: *Boehringer Ingelheim v Swingward* [2008] EWCA Civ 83, [2008] All ER (EC) 411. Jacob LJ commented 'European trade mark law seems to have arrived at such a state of uncertainty that no one really knows what the rules are. . . . Big brand owners want bigger rights; small players, no change or less. The compromises which have emerged have very fuzzy lines'. The case concerned the practices of 're-boxing' (which generally involves re-affixing the original trade mark on the new information leaflet and box); 'de-branding' (using only the generic name of the drug on the box but not removing the brand name from the blister pack or the product itself); and 'co-branding' (where the packaging bears the trade mark of the drug but also the get up of the importer). Co-branding and de-branding were not in principle liable to damage a trade mark's reputation. The CJ in the second reference (Case C-348/04) specifically held that whether or not those activities caused damage was a question of fact for the national court. The evidence in relation to co-branding did not establish any damage to the trade marks. The Court of Appeal further considered that total de-branding, where all traces of the trade mark sued upon were removed, was clearly not an infringement, because there was simply no use of the trade mark in any shape or form. A trade mark owner had no right to insist that his trade mark stayed on the goods for the aftermarket and, because that was so, it was impossible to say that partial de-branding was damaging in itself. The manner or form of partial de-branding could hurt the image or prestige of a trade mark. That would depend on how it was done. The judge's conclusion of fact at first instance, that the specific de-branding complained of by M did not damage their trade marks, was not shown to be wrong. Further, the importer had complied with the fourth condition in *Bristol Myers Squibb* and their activities by way of re-boxing and re-labelling had not caused damage to the reputation of M's trade marks. However, the Court of Appeal deferred making a final decision to await the outcome of a further reference to the CJ in Case C-276/05 *Wellcome v Paranova* where the issue was whether the presentation of the new packaging was to be measured against the principle of minimum intervention or only against whether it was such as to damage the reputation of the trade mark and its proprietor. The CJ gave judgment in Case C-276/05 *Wellcome v Paranova* on 22 December 2008. The CJ held that Article 7(2) of Directive 89/104 is to be interpreted as meaning that, where it is established that repackaging of the pharmaceutical product is necessary for further marketing in the Member State of importation, the presentation of the packaging should be assessed only against the condition that it should not be such as to be liable to damage the reputation of the trade mark or that of its proprietor. Further, Article 7(2) of Directive 89/104 is to be interpreted as meaning that it is for the parallel importer to furnish to the proprietor of the trade mark the information which is necessary and sufficient to enable the latter to determine whether the repackaging of the product under that trade mark is necessary in order to market it in the Member State of importation. The English proceedings then settled before they were reinstated in the Court of Appeal.

See also recently Cases C400/09&C207/10 *Orifarm v Paranova Danmark*, judgment of 28 July 2011 (the trade mark proprietor cannot oppose the parallel import and further marketing of its pharmaceutical products in repackaged form on the sole ground that the new packaging indicates as the repackager not the undertaking which actually repackaged the product but the undertaking which holds the marketing authorisation for the product and on whose instructions the repackaging was carried out).

Marketing in a manner that may affect reputation.   In Case C-533/06 *O₂* **9.042**
Holdings v Hutchison 3G UK Ltd [2008] ECR I-4231, [2008] 3 CMLR 397, the CJ held that Article 5 of Directive 89/104 does not entitle the trade mark owner to prevent the use of its mark in a comparative advertisement which satisfies all the criteria of Directive 84/450 (1984 OJ L250/17 amended by Directive 2005/29, 2005 OJ L149/22) under which comparative advertising is permitted.

No international exhaustion: *Silhouette.*   The conflict between the CJ's judg- **9.044**
ments in *Silhouette* and *Sebago* and the EFTA Court's judgment in *Mag Instrument* has now been resolved in favour of a consistent interpretation of Article 7 of Directive 89/104 and a prohibition on international exhaustion within the EEA: Cases E-9&10/07 *L'Oréal Norge v Per Aarskog AS*, decn of the EFTA Court 8 July 2008. L'Oréal sought to prohibit the import into Norway of products bearing the 'Redken' mark which had been marketed by it in the USA but not within the EEA. Norwegian national law provided for international exhaustion so that L'Oréal's rights were exhausted by the marketing of the items in the USA. The EFTA Court held that the case law of the CJ had made clear that it was not open to EU Member States to introduce or maintain a principle of international exhaustion in the light of Article 7. The EFTA Court found that there were no compelling grounds for a divergent interpretation in the EEA. Article 7 therefore precludes the unilateral introduction or maintenance of international exhaustion of rights. The Court appears to have left open the question whether the result would be different if the EFTA State in question had entered into a treaty with a third country providing for exhaustion of rights: para 32.

9.045 **Consent: express or implied.** In Case C-59/08 *Copad SA v Christian Dior Couture SA and SIL* [2009] ECR I-3421 the CJ considered whether sales of marked goods by a licensee (SIL) to a discount store outside the selective distribution network (Copad) contrary to the terms of the licence with the trade mark owner (Dior) are an infringement of the trade mark or merely a breach of contract. The CJ interpreted Article 8(2) of Directive 89/104 which provides that the proprietor of a trade mark may invoke the rights conferred by that trade mark against a licensee who contravenes a provision in his licensing contract if that provision relates to certain matters including the quality of the goods. The CJ held that the list of matters in Article 8(2) was exhaustive and not illustrative; the mark owner could rely on its trade mark rights provided it was established that the breach of the licence terms damaged the allure and prestigious image which bestows on the goods an aura of luxury and hence damaged their quality. Further, Article 7(1) of the Directive meant that a licensee who puts goods bearing a trade mark on the market in disregard of a provision in a licence agreement does so *without* the consent of the proprietor of the trade mark where it is established that the provision in question is included in those listed in Article 8(2) of that Directive. In a case where a licensee puts luxury goods on the market in contravention of a provision in the licence agreement, but must nevertheless be considered to have done so *with* the consent of the proprietor of the trade mark, the proprietor of the trade mark can rely on such a provision to oppose a resale of those goods on the basis of Article 7(2) of the Directive only if it can be established that, taking into account the particular circumstances of the case, such resale damages the reputation of the trade mark. See also *Mastercigars Direct Ltd v Hunters & Frankau Ltd* [2007] EWCA Civ 176, [2007] RPC 24, paras 16–17 for a summary of the state of the law at that point.

9.046 **Exhaustion of rights: the burden of proof.** The burden of proving where goods were first put on the market for the purpose of determining whether rights conferred by a trade mark have been exhausted lies on the person asserting that rights have been exhausted: *Honda Motor Company v David Silver Spares Ltd* [2010] EWHC 1973 (Ch).

(d) Copyright and similar rights

9.052 **The specific subject-matter of the copyright.** In Case C-275/06 *Promusicae* [2008] ECR I-276, [2008] All ER (EC) 809 the CJ considered questions referred from a Spanish court arising in proceedings brought by Promusicae, a music publishers' trade association, against an internet service provider, seeking disclosure of the identities and physical addresses of persons who were using a file sharing internet site to download music in breach of the rights of Promusicae's members. The CJ held that neither Directive 2001/29 nor other relevant EU legislation requires Member States to oblige ISPs to disclose this information to support a civil action for breach of copyright. But the CJ added that EU law does require that, when transposing those directives, the Member States take care to rely on an interpretation of them which allows a fair balance to be struck between the various fundamental rights protected by the EU legal order. Further, when implementing the measures transposing those directives, the authorities and courts of the Member States must not only interpret their national law in a manner consistent with those directives but also make sure that they do not rely on an interpretation of them which would be in conflict with those fundamental rights or with the other general principles of EU law, such as the principle of proportionality.

(ii) Films and DVDs

The right to exhibit protected: *Coditel (No. 1)*.   See the discussion of *Coditel I* in   **9.061**
Cases C-403&429/08 *Football Association Premier League v QC Leisure/ Murphy v Media Protection Services*, Opinion of 3 February 2011, discussed below, in particular Advocate General's remarks about the historical nature of the decision.

Television broadcasts.   The interaction between free movement of services,   **9.064**
Directive 2001/29 and the competition rules is being considered by the CJ in Cases C-403&429/08 *Football Association Premier League v QC Leisure/ Murphy v Media Protection Services*, Opinion of 3 February 2011. The cases concerned references from the English High Court ([2008] EWHC 1411 (Ch)) arising out of attempts by the claimants in both cases to prevent the use in the United Kingdom of decoder cards that enabled encrypted satellite broadcasts intended for the Greek market to be viewed in the UK. The FAPL's exclusive rights to broadcast live matches are divided territorially and are granted on the basis of three-year terms. FAPL appoints only one broadcaster within any particular territory and restricts the circulation of authorised decoder cards outside the territory of each licensee. In order to protect this territorial exclusivity, each broadcaster undertakes in its licence agreement with the FAPL to encrypt its signal. The licensee transmits its encrypted signal via satellite to subscribers within its assigned territory. Subscribers with a satellite dish can decrypt and decompress the signal in a decoder, which requires a decoder card. The actions in the High Court were brought against companies who supply to pubs and bars the equipment and satellite decoder cards which make possible the reception of Greek satellite channels that carry live Premier League matches. Other actions involved licensees of pubs which had shown live Premier League matches broadcast on the channels of an Arabic broadcaster. The Advocate General rejected the suggestion that a decoder card lawfully sold in one Member State becomes an 'illicit device' for the purposes of Article 2(e) of Directive 98/84 if it is used in another Member State against the will of the undertaking broadcasting the protected service (paras 48 *et seq*). However, she advised that the recognition and enforcement of rights to satellite programmes on the basis of which the rights-holders can prohibit third parties not contractually linked to them from watching and showing those programmes in Member States other than those intended constituted a serious restriction on the freedom to use services from another Member State. That restriction was not justified by the need to safeguard the specific subject-matter of

these rights. The right to exploit commercially the transmission of football matches through the charge for the decoder cards was not undermined by the use of Greek decoder cards, as charges had been paid for those cards. Whilst those charges are not as high as the charges imposed in the United Kingdom, there is no specific right to charge different prices for a work in each Member State. Rather, it forms part of the logic of the internal market that price differences between different Member States should be offset by trade. The Advocate General distinguished *Coditel I* as a case in which the Court had recognised that a territorial restriction on the transmission of the German television broadcast into Belgium was necessary to protect the cinematic exhibition rights in Belgium as those rights would be impaired if television broadcast were not delayed: '[f]rom the perspective of the 1970s, [the Court] added that television showings were possible in purely practical terms only in the context of national monopolies' (para 196). In the instant case the partitioning of the internal market for live football transmissions was not intended to protect any other form of exploitation of the transmitted football match but rather to optimise exploitation of the same work within the different market segments. Further, *Coditel I* had involved the rebroadcast of the programme without the payment of a fee whereas here the user of the decoder did pay a fee, albeit at the Greek rather than the UK rates. Finally the Advocate General considered the application of Article 101 in the light of a question from the High Court seeking to ascertain whether it is sufficient that a licence agreement concerning the territorially limited transmission of a broadcast has an anti-competitive object or whether an actual impairment of competition must be shown. She advised that a contractual obligation linked to a broadcasting licence requiring the broadcaster to prevent its satellite decoder cards from being used outside the licensed territory has the same effect as agreements to prevent or restrict parallel exports. Such an obligation is intended to prevent any competition between broadcasters through a reciprocal compartmentalisation of licensed territories. Such licences with absolute territorial protection are incompatible with the internal market and there was no reason to treat such agreements any differently from agreements intended to prevent parallel trade. Citing her Opinion in Case C-169/08 *Presidente del Consiglio dei Ministri* [2009] ECR I-10821, points 134 *et seq*, she commented that her assessment of the freedom to provide services rules confirmed this conclusion 'since conflicting assessments of the fundamental freedoms and competition law are to be avoided in principle'. Hence she advised that the question be answered to the effect that where a programme content provider enters into a series of exclusive licences each for the territory of one or more Member States under which the broadcaster is licensed to broadcast the programme content only within that territory (including by satellite) and a contractual obligation is included in each licence requiring the broadcaster to prevent its satellite decoder cards which enable reception of the licensed programme content from being used outside the licensed territory, such licence agreements are liable to prevent, restrict or distort competition. They are therefore incompatible with Article 101(1) TFEU; it is not necessary to show that such effects have actually occurred.

3. Articles 81 and 82 and the Exercise of Intellectual Property Rights

Note that Articles 81 and 82 EC are now Articles 101 and 102 TFEU

Article 82 and infringement suits. The appeal in *AstraZeneca* has been decided: **9.072**
Case T-321/05 *AstraZeneca v Commission*, judgment of 1 July 2010, [2010]
5 CMLR 1575. The Court upheld the Commission's factual findings that
AstraZeneca defended various challenges to its SPCs in national courts by persisting in the misrepresentations that it had previously made to the various patent
offices in order to obtain those certificates and thus engaged in a 'persistent and
linear course of conduct': para 598. The case is on further appeal Case C-457/10P
AstraZeneca v Commission, not yet decided.

See Case T-119/09 *Protégé International v Commission*, not yet decided (appeal
against rejection of complaint alleging abuse of dominant position by Pernod
Ricard in filing legal proceedings against the applicant contesting the registration
of trade marks. It is alleged that the proceedings were aimed not at protecting
Pernod Ricard's intellectual property rights in its own marks ('Wild Turkey') but of
eliminating the applicant as a competitor of Pernod Ricard in the Irish whiskey
market). See also Case T-96/08 *Global Digital Disc v Commission*, not yet decided
(appeal against rejection of complaint alleging breach of Article 102 TFEU in
licensing practices in the CD-R field).

In the final Report on the sectoral inquiry into the pharmaceutical industry published on 8 July 2009, the Commission described the scale of infringement litigation
brought by originator pharmaceutical companies against both generic manufacturers and against competing originating companies. The Commission concluded
that in certain instances originator companies 'may consider litigation not so much
on its merits, but rather as a signal to deter generic entrants'. The Commission
examined the scale of applications for interim injunctions and noted that there is a
risk that settlements of litigation are concluded at the expense of consumers if they
limit generic entry and include a value transfer from an originator company to a
generic company. All stakeholders contributing to the inquiry emphasised the need
for a unified and specialised patent litigation system in Europe.

'Patent ambush' in standard setting. The Commission brought proceedings   **9.072A**
against Rambus alleging that it had failed to disclose patents and pending patent
applications in the course of negotiations over the setting of standards for DRAM
computer chips and as a result was able to charge royalties at a level which it would
not otherwise have been able to charge: COMP/38636 *RAMBUS*, decn of 9
December 2009, discussed in the update to paragraph 5.139A, above.

Article 82 and refusal to licence. **Fn 235.** Note also that the German Federal   **9.073**
Supreme Court has held that a patent user cannot resist an infringement action by

alleging the right to a compulsory licence (and thus that a refusal to license is an abuse of a dominant position) unless it has made an unconditional, binding offer to the patent-holder and, if that was not accepted, paid the offered licence fees into an escrow account: *Orange-Book Standard*, judgment of 6 May 2009, WuW/E DE-R2613. However, this decision is based on the jurisprudence concerning the good faith provision of the German Civil Code (Article 242); in the absence of a ruling from the CJ, it is unclear to what extent national law can restrict the application of EU competition law in this way.

9.074 **Acquisition of technology by dominant undertaking.** **Fn 238.** AstraZeneca's appeal against the findings of abuse in this respect was dismissed by the GC: see Case T-321/05 *AstraZeneca v Commission*, judgment of 1 July 2010, [2010] 5 CMLR 1575 discussed in the update to paragraph 10.154, below. The case is on appeal Case C-457/10P *AstraZeneca v Commission*, not yet decided.

5. The Block Exemption for Technology Transfer Agreements

(g) Relationship between Regulation 772/2004 and other block exemptions

9.169 **Generally.** The other block exemptions referred to in this paragraph have all been replaced:

- for specialisation agreements Regulation 2658/2000 has been replaced by Regulation 1218/2010 (OJ L335/43: Vol II, App C7D);
- for research and development agreements Regulation 2659/2000 has been replaced by Regulation 1217/2010 (OJ 2010 L335/36: Vol II, App C7C); and
- for vertical agreements Regulation 2790/1999 has been replaced by Regulation 330/2010 (OJ 2010 L102/1: Vol II, App C7A).

9.170 **Specialisation and research and development agreements.** **Fn 484.** See now Reg 1218/2010 (OJ 2010 L335/43: Vol II, App C7D), Article 2(1) together with the definitions in Article 1.1(a) and (d).

Fn 486. See also Article 2(2) of Reg 1218/2010 and Article 2(2) of Reg 1217/2010 as regards the similar provision regarding licences in a research and development agreement.

6. Licences of other Intellectual Property Rights

(a) Trade marks

9.172 **Trade mark licences generally.** As to when a breach by a licensee of a provision in the licence allows the mark owner to invoke his trade mark rights see Case C-59/08

Copad SA v Christian Dior couture SA and SIL [2009] ECR I-3421, discussed in the update to paragraph 9.045, above.

Royalties for the use of the mark.   The appeal to the CJ in *DSD* was dismissed: **9.178**
Case C-385/07P *Der Grüne Punkt—Duales System Deutschland v Commission*, judgment of 16 July 2009, [2009] 5 CMLR 2215. The GC analysed the case under Article 102(a) TFEU, referring to settled case law, according to which an undertaking abuses its dominant position where it charges for its services fees which are disproportionate to the economic value of the service provided. The conduct objected to here, namely requiring payment of a fee for all packaging bearing the DGP logo and put into circulation in Germany, even where customers of the company show that they do not use the DGP system for some or all of that packaging, constituted an abuse of a dominant position within that case law. The CJ upheld this analysis, emphasising that the remedies imposed by the decision did not amount to an obligation to grant a licence to use the DGP logo. There was nothing in the decision which affects DSD's freedom of choice as to the grant of licences—the decision at issue merely obliges DSD not to claim payment from its contractual partners for take-back and recovery services which it has not provided. Note, however, that the GC stated that the decision did not stop DSD levying an adequate fee for merely using the DGP mark even where it is shown that the packaging bearing the DGP logo has been taken back and recovered by another system. The green dot affixed to the packaging may have economic value as such, since it can inform the consumer that the packaging at issue may be brought to the DSD system: paras 193 and 194.

(b) Copyright

Copyright licences generally.   Fn 513. But note *Harry Potter*, WuW DE-R 2018,   **9.179**
judgment of the Frankfurt am Main Higher Regional Court of 17 April 2007, holding that two merchandising agreements entered into regarding *Harry Potter and the Sorcerer's Stone* (one for products related to the book and the other for products related to the film) that limited the rights granted to the German-speaking States (ie Austria, Germany and Switzerland) and to certain means of supply (eg internet sales were excluded) did not infringe Article 101 TFEU. The experience of a licensee may relate only to certain markets, and the copyright holder could have decided to grant no licences and to decide itself which markets to enter.

10

ARTICLE 82

1. Introduction

Note that Article 82 EC is now Article 102 TFEU

(a) Generally

Link between dominant position and abuse. On the basis of European jurispru- **10.004**
dence, the Paris Court of Appeal annulled the decision of the French competition
authority finding that GlaxoSmithKline (GSK) had abused its dominant position
on the market for injectable acyclovir by predatory pricing on the market for sodic
cefuroxime. GSK was not dominant on the latter market and although its prices for
sodic cefuroxime were below average variable cost, the two markets were not sufficiently closely connected for conduct on the latter market to constitute an abuse of
GSK's position on the former market. The Court noted that competitors on the
non-dominated market were not potential competitors of GSK on the dominated
market so that the pricing could not have the alleged effect of a 'message' to deter
their entry into the dominated market: *Laboratoire GlaxoSmithKline (France) v
Competition Council*, judgment of 14 March 2007, BOCCRF No. 7 of 15 September
2008; appeal dismissed by the Cour de Cassation, Case No. E08-14.503, judgment
No. 259 of 17 March 2009.

DG Comp Discussion Paper. In February 2009 the Commission formally **10.005**
adopted its Guidance on the Commission's enforcement priorities in applying
Article 82 to abusive exclusionary conduct by dominant undertakings: OJ 2009
C45/7: Vol II, App C19. The Guidance is not intended to be a statement of the law
but aims to provide greater clarity and predictability as regards the general framework of analysis that the Commission will employ when determining whether to
pursue cases (para 2). It applies only to exclusionary conduct and only to conduct
of a single dominant firm, not to cases of collective dominance (para 4). The
Guidance sets out the Commission's approach to assessing market power
(paras 9–18); a general description of what is termed 'anti-competitive foreclosure' and the factors that are relevant in assessing whether such foreclosure is likely
(paras 19–22); a description of price-based exclusionary conduct including the

cost benchmarks that the Commission is likely to use (paras 23–27) and how the Commission will assess claims by dominant undertakings that the conduct is objectively justified (paras 28–31). There then follows a section dealing with specific abuses, exclusive dealing (including rebates); tying and bundling; predation and refusal to supply; and margin squeeze. The Commission issued a Question and Answer Memo responding to frequently asked questions: MEMO/08/761 (3 December 2008). As to the adoption by the Commission of a more economics-based analysis of infringements see the discussion of COMP/37990 *Intel*, decn of 13 May 2009 in the update to paragraph 10.096, below.

As to the status of this Guidance, see *Purple Parking Ltd v Heathrow Airport Ltd* [2011] EWHC 987 (Ch), para 95.

3. Dominant Position

(b) The market position of the undertaking itself

10.021 **Market share as an indicator of dominance.** In the Commission's Guidance on the enforcement of Article 82, OJ 2009 C45/7: Vol II, App C19, the Commission states that market shares 'provide a useful first indication' of the market structure and the relative importance of the different undertakings on the market. However, market shares will be interpreted in the light of the dynamics of the market and the extent to which products are differentiated: para 13.

10.022 **General caution about market shares.** In Case M.4513 *Arjowiggins/M-Real Zanders' Reflect paper mill* (4 June 2008) the Commission recognised that 'Theoretically, a market where four competitors that are not capacity-constrained supply a more or less homogenous product can generate competitive outcomes, even if one firm has a 50% initial market share': para 363. However, the Commission's market analysis of customers' switching patterns did not allay the competition concerns arising from the merged entity's market share.

As regards 'bidding markets' see COMP/38113 *Prokent-Tomra*, decn of 29 March 2006, [2009] 4 CMLR 101, para 90 (market in reverse vending machines not a bidding market). Tomra's appeal was dismissed and this point was not discussed: Case T-155/06 *Tomra Systems v Commission*, judgment of 9 September 2010.

See also Case M.4533 *SCA/ P&G (European tissue business)* (5 September 2008) where the merged entity would have an 80–90 per cent share in the supply of branded kitchen paper but would not have market power because of the strong competition from private label product at the retail level: 'high market shares did not reflect their real market power vis-à-vis retailers and, ultimately, end-consumers': para 126.

Fn 66. See also Case M.4956 *STX/Aker Yards* (5 May 2008) where the Commission examined market shares in the cruise ship building market over a four-year period because market shares computed over a shorter period would not be a good proxy of market power, given the limited number of orders and deliveries: para 40; Case M.4647 *AEE/Lentjes* (5 December 2007) where the Commission looked at the market position over a five-year period, supplementing this information with a detailed analysis of those tenders and projects in which both AEE and Lentjes had taken part as bidders. The Commission asked competitors and customers to furnish additional details of individual tenders, in particular those in which both parties had participated to see whether the two companies had been close competitors such that the planned merger would eliminate a significant competitive factor: paras 57 *et seq*; Case M.4662 *Syniverse/BSG Wireless Business* (4 December 2007); Case M.5669 *Cisco/Tandberg* (29 March 2010), para 46 (the fact that end users tend to look for interoperability with the installed base when launching a request for tenders meant that the fact that that sales were typically organised through a bidding process was not in itself sufficient to alleviate competition concerns (in a merger context). Rather, an analysis of tender data was necessary to determine whether the merging parties were close competitors); Case M.5983 *Tyco Electronics/ADC Telecommunications* (7 December 2010) (the parties' major customers usually launched tenders every 1–2 years. This implied that even relatively high market shares did not give a clear indication of merged entity's market power: para 29. The Commission also noted there was spare capacity among existing competitors); Case M.6007 *Nokia Siemens Networks/Motorola Network Business* (15 December 2010), para 35.

Market share levels: *Hoffmann-La Roche*. Fn 71. See more recently Case T-66/01 **10.024** *ICI v Commission*, judgment of 25 June 2010, para 258.

Market shares in other cases. In Case T-321/05 *AstraZeneca v Commission*, judg- **10.025** ment of 1 July 2010, [2010] 5 CMLR 1575, the GC held that AstraZeneca's possession of a particularly high market share and, in any event, a share which was much higher than those of its competitors, was an entirely relevant indicator of its market power. The fact that this market power may have been the result of successful innovation in the pharmaceutical sector did not detract from its relevance: para 252. The case is on appeal: Case C-457/10P *AstraZeneca v Commission*, not yet decided.

Relative market shares. In COMP/38113 *Prokent-Tomra*, decn of 29 March **10.027** 2006, [2009] 4 CMLR 101 the Commission relied on the high market shares of Tomra and on the fact that in the relevant national markets Tomra's market share was a multiple of the market shares of its competitors: see paras 84 and 85. Tomra's appeal was dismissed and this point was not discussed: Case T-155/06 *Tomra Systems v Commission*, judgment of 9 September 2010.

Stability of market shares. Fn 87. The appeal in *Der Grüne Punkt* was dismissed: **10.028** Case C-385/07P *Der Grüne Punkt—Duales System Deutschland v Commission*, judgment of 16 July 2009, [2009] 5 CMLR 2215 and did not concern the finding of dominance.

10.029 **Market shares indicating dominance.** In the Commission's Guidance on the enforcement of Article 82, OJ 2009 C45/7: Vol II, App C19, the Commission states that dominance is not likely if the undertaking's market share is below 40 per cent: para 14. In COMP/37990 *Intel*, decn of 13 May 2009 the Commission found that Intel had held very high market shares in excess of or around 80 per cent in an overall x86 CPU market and in excess of around 70 per cent in any of the sub-markets examined throughout the six-year observation period. The Commission noted that such large market shares are in themselves a clear indication of the existence of a dominant position but went on to say that this insight was subject to further verification in any given case by reference to contextual factors such as barriers to entry and expansion and buyer power: para 852.

10.030 **Overall size and strength.** In Case T-321/05 *AstraZeneca v Commission*, judgment of 1 July 2010, [2010] 5 CMLR 1575 the GC noted that AstraZeneca's superiority in terms of financial resources was derived almost exclusively from its pharmaceutical business, on which it also focused almost all its resources, whereas its competitors had more limited resources which were not devoted exclusively to their pharma business. The GC held that the superiority of AstraZeneca's R&D effort was also relevant for assessing the position of that undertaking relative to its competitors on the market. The Court concluded that although these facts were not sufficient in themselves to warrant the conclusion that AstraZeneca was in a dominant position, they constituted a series of relevant indicia which permitted the inference that AstraZeneca had resources superior to those of its competitors such as to reinforce its market position in relation to them: para 286. The case is on appeal: Case C-457/10P *AstraZeneca v Commission*, not yet decided.

Fn 96. The appeal referred to in the footnote was dismissed by the CJ: Case C-202/07P *France Télécom v Commission*, judgment of 2 April 2009. The CJ judgment did not consider issues concerning dominance.

10.031 **Anti-competitive conduct as evidence of dominance.** **Fn 102.** As regards the firm's own attitude to its market position see COMP/38113 *Prokent-Tomra*, decn of 29 March 2006, [2009] 4 CMLR 101 where the Commission relied (*inter alia*) on internal documents showing that Tomra believed that it held a dominant position: para 91. Tomra's appeal was dismissed and this point was not discussed: Case T-155/06 *Tomra Systems v Commission*, judgment of 9 September 2010.

(c) **Barriers to entry and expansion**

10.032 **Barriers to entry: generally.** See also the comments on barriers to entry and expansion in the Commission's Guidance on the enforcement of Article 82, OJ 2009 C45/7: paras 16 and 17.

10.034 **Scale economies.** See, eg the Commission's analysis in COMP/37990 *Intel*, decn of 13 May 2009, para 866. The Commission also discussed the link between high fixed costs and barriers to entry: paras 875 *et seq*.

Ownership of intellectual property. See also the discussion in Case T-321/05   **10.036**
AstraZeneca v Commission, judgment of 1 July 2010, [2010] 5 CMLR 1575 of the
strength of the patent protection owned by AstraZeneca over its new drug and its
vigorous enforcement of its rights: paras 270 *et seq*. The Court firmly rejected the
assertion that taking into account intellectual property rights and their exercise,
even if not abusive, in order to establish the existence of a dominant position was
liable to reduce the incentive to create innovative products. Separately, the Court
upheld the Commission's reliance on AstraZeneca's 'first mover status' as relevant
to the finding of dominance: para 283. The case is on appeal: Case C-457/10P
AstraZeneca v Commission, not yet decided.

In COMP/37990 *Intel*, decn of 13 May 2009 the Commission noted that Intel's
main competitor AMD manufactured its x86 CPUs on the basis of a cross licence
agreement with Intel. That agreement followed on from a number of patent
infringement cases brought by Intel against AMD and a global settlement between
the two companies in 1995. The Commission commented that 'the extensive litigation history highlights the significant intellectual property-related barriers that any
new entrant to the x86 CPU market would have to overcome': para 858.

For an analogous situation see *Neurendale Ltd t/a Panda Waste Services v Dublin City
Council* [2009] IEHC 588 (local authorities providing refuse collection services
were dominant not only because of their own provision of services but because they
could, by regulation, control who else was able to provide services: 'The undertakings involved are unlike private dominant undertakings in that not only do they
have a significant share of the market, but more importantly, they have the power
to regulate it: to decide entry or no entry, to decide conditions of entry, and if
allowed, to decide operative conditions. It is that regulation, independently of any
given market share which they might enjoy, which gives them the power to act
independently and therefore makes them dominant in their respective markets':
para 133).

Advertising. In COMP/37990 *Intel*, decn of 13 May 2009 the Commission   **10.038**
noted Intel's substantial spend on marketing and concluded that its 'brand equity
resulting from its investment in product differentiation and its installed base have
given it "must-stock" status at the OEM level, in other words, it is an unavoidable
trading partner for OEMs': para 870.

On an analogous point, an incumbent's reputation for aggressive price cutting
in response to market entry can constitute a barrier to entry: Case T-342/07
Ryanair Holdings plc v Commission, judgment of 6 July 2010, [2011] 4 CMLR 245,
para 287.

(d) Countervailing market power

Countervailing power of buyers. See the discussion in Case T-321/05 *Astra*   **10.041**
Zeneca v Commission, judgment of 1 July 2010, [2010] 5 CMLR 1575 of the

relative bargaining power of a pharmaceutical company supplying a new product and the national health services. The Court noted that national authorities which set reimbursement levels or prices of medicines are encouraged, on account of their public interest mission, to ensure the inclusion in their health systems of products which contribute significantly to the improvement of public health: para 256. The Court upheld the Commission's finding that AstraZeneca was able to behave independently *vis-à-vis* the health systems to a significant extent: para 268. The case is on appeal: Case C-457/10P *AstraZeneca v Commission*, not yet decided.

See also the interesting analysis of countervailing buyer power in COMP/38113 *Prokent-Tomra*, 29 decn of March 2006, [2009] 4 CMLR 101. Tomra argued that the customers for its reverse vending machines were the large supermarket retail chains who were difficult negotiating partners. But the Commission found that in some markets the customers' market shares were more fragmented and even in concentrated markets the customers' market shares did not equal Tomra's. Further the existence of buyer power requires that there are either credible alternative suppliers to which the customers could turn, or that customers are able to sponsor new entrants. In the absence of established competitors with significant and stable market shares, there was no credible threat of even the largest customers moving from Tomra. Procurement of reverse vending equipment is not part of the core activities of retail groups so they were unlikely to act in a strategic manner in order to subsidise and actively build up competing suppliers. There was therefore no countervailing buyer power: paras 88 and 89. Tomra's appeal was dismissed and this point was not discussed: Case T-155/06 *Tomra Systems v Commission*, judgment of 9 September 2010.

In Case M.4662 *Syniverse/BSG Wireless Business* (4 December 2007) the Commission found that the consolidation of customers as well as a more sophisticated bidding process may give customers countervailing power. In particular, they may have a strong bargaining position by virtue of their relative financial size and the scale of their operations which they may use to influence the buying process and to sponsor new entry. Customers were also able to design sophisticated procurement processes in order to derive the best possible price and service level agreements (para 99). In Case M.4523 *Travelport/Worldspan* (21 August 2007) the Commission identified various factors in the market which were changing the bargaining interaction between GDS providers and customers on both sides of the two-sided market, resulting in increased bargaining strength of those customers relative to GDS providers. These elements (effective bargaining power of one set of customers, and ongoing or possible development of additional bargaining tools) were enough to counter the potentially detrimental effect of the reduction from four to three GDS providers (para 110).

See also the comments on countervailing buyer power in the Commission's Guidance on the enforcement of Article 82, OJ 2009 C45/7: Vol II, App C19, para 18.

The scale of countervailing buyer power was considered by the Competition Appeal Tribunal in *National Grid v The Gas and Electricity Markets Authority* [2009] CAT 10, in particular the economic effect of substantial sunk costs on the part of the allegedly dominant firm. The Tribunal's decision was upheld by the Court of Appeal: *National Grid plc v Gas and Electricity Markets Authority* [2010] EWCA Civ 114.

Fn 127. As regards the *Hutchison 3G* case there mentioned, OFCOM held that there was insufficient buyer power to counteract Hutchison's dominance: this was upheld on appeal by the Competition Appeal Tribunal and then by the Court of Appeal: *Hutchison 3G UK Ltd v OFCOM* [2009] EWCA Civ 683.

(e) Appraisal of market power in more complex cases

The relevant market and the market in which the abuse took place. **Fn 137.** The **10.047** appeal in *AstraZeneca* has been decided but this point was not discussed: Case T-321/05 *AstraZeneca v Commission*, judgment of 1 July 2010, [2010] 5 CMLR 1575 (on appeal Case C-457/10P *AstraZeneca v Commission*, not yet decided).

(f) Collective or joint dominance

(i) Generally

Abuse by one or more undertakings. In COMP/39388&39389 *E.ON German* **10.048** *electricity markets*, decn of 26 November 2008, the Commission indicated (in a decision accepting commitments) that for Article 102 to be infringed it is not necessary for all the undertakings which are considered to be collectively dominant also to be involved in the alleged abusive conduct. Thus although a collective dominant position might be held by two or three electricity companies in the German wholesale market, only E.ON was suspected of the abusive conduct: para 27.

(ii) Legal links between jointly dominant undertakings

Relationship between collective dominance and anti-competitive agreements. **10.050** In *Neurendale Ltd t/a Panda Waste Services v Dublin City Council* [2009] IEHC 588 the Irish High Court considered an allegation of collective dominance against a number of local authorities who issued regulations purporting to exclude private companies from offering competing refuse collection services. Collaboration of the councils as to the content of these regulations could not be condemned since this was specifically provided for by the relevant national legislation. However, the fact that such collusion is provided for by statute will not prevent a finding of collective dominance. The fact that there was no competition between the respondents could also not be criticised since they were local authorities who exercise their power within defined geographic bounds. However, McKechnie J continued 'such a situation, where there is collaborative action and no competition between the undertakings, supports a finding of collective dominance. They act in concert on many issues and viewed from the outside do constitute, in many respects, a collective entity: certainly *vis-à-vis* their competitors and consumers on this market'. He therefore found that the local authorities were collectively dominant in the greater Dublin area, as well as being dominant individually within each of their respective geographical areas.

(iii) Links arising from market structure

10.053 **Market structures and coordinated policy.** This and the following paragraphs must now be read in the light of the CJ's judgment in Case C-413/06P *Bertelsmann AG and Sony Corporation of America v Impala and Commission* [2008] ECR I-4951. The CJ overturned the GC's decision finding that the GC had erred in a number of respects, both procedural and substantive. The CJ set out the test that the Commission must apply in the case of an alleged creation or strengthening of a collective dominant position: see paras 119 *et seq.* In an important passage the CJ described the conditions in which collective dominance will arise as the relationship of interdependence existing between the parties to a tight oligopoly within which, on a market with the appropriate characteristics, in particular in terms of market concentration, transparency and product homogeneity, those parties are in a position to anticipate one another's behaviour and are therefore strongly encouraged to align their conduct on the market in such a way as to maximise their joint profits by increasing prices, reducing output, the choice or quality of goods and services, diminishing innovation, or otherwise influencing parameters of competition. In such a context, each operator is aware that highly competitive action on its part would provoke a reaction on the part of the others, so that it would derive no benefit from its initiative: para 121. The Court went on to elaborate on the conditions under which such a situation is likely to arise:

> 'Such tacit coordination is more likely to emerge if competitors can easily arrive at a common perception as to how the coordination should work, and, in particular, of the parameters that lend themselves to being a focal point of the proposed coordination. . . . Moreover, having regard to the temptation which may exist for each participant in a tacit coordination to depart from it in order to increase its short-term profit, it is necessary to determine whether such coordination is sustainable. In that regard, the coordinating undertakings must be able to monitor to a sufficient degree whether the terms of the coordination are being adhered to. There must therefore be sufficient market transparency for each undertaking concerned to be aware, sufficiently precisely and quickly, of the way in which the market conduct of each of the other participants in the coordination is evolving. Furthermore, discipline requires that there be some form of credible deterrent mechanism that can come into play if deviation is detected. In addition, the reactions of outsiders, such as current or future competitors, and also the reactions of customers, should not be such as to jeopardise the results expected from the coordination' (para 123).

The Court emphasised that in applying the criteria, it is necessary to avoid a mechanical approach involving the separate verification of each of those criteria taken in isolation, while taking no account of the overall economic mechanism of a hypothetical tacit coordination: para 125. Following the annulment of the Commission's decision, the case was re-notified to the Commission who reassessed the concentration under the current market circumstances and approved it. This decision is now under appeal: Case T-229/08 *Impala v Commission*, not yet decided.

Collective dominance in oligopolistic markets.   In COMP/39388&39389 *E.* **10.054**
ON German electricity markets, decn of 26 November 2008 the Commission accepted commitments in relation to E.ON's conduct on the electricity wholesale market in Germany. The Commission considered that at least two companies were collectively dominant: they were linked by a network of agreements on production and wholesale supply; the product was homogenous and 'not evolving'; the price was transparent; decisions on capacity were transparent; the market was growing at a modest rate; and new entry was severely restricted. A common policy on pricing and production was possible because they could detect and counter any deviation and react immediately by doing the same: paras 19–22.

See also the Bundeskartellamt's 'Final Report on the Fuel Sector Inquiry' (26 May 2011) finding that an oligopolistic market structure enables the large oil companies to set prices more or less uniformly at their petrol stations.

Three conditions for establishing collective dominance.   The test as set out by **10.055**
the CJ in the *IMPALA* judgment was applied by the Commission when granting conditional clearance at Phase II of the investigation into a merger in Case M.4980 *ABF/GBI Business* (23 September 2008) (paras 144 *et seq*). The Commission found various features of the Portuguese market for compressed yeast indicated that the conditions were conducive to coordination. So far as mechanisms for policing the coordination were concerned, the Commission cited instances in the past where attempts by the *de facto* exclusive distributor of one supplier to expand its share of the market in an area had been disciplined by the supplier: 'This demonstrates how the system corrects itself when a distributor is trying to deviate from the paradigm imposed by the suppliers': para 219. The Commission went on to find that the other conditions set in *IMPALA* were also satisfied and that the merger, by creating a duopoly, would increase the incentives for coordination. By contrast, in the French market the Commission found that there was no evidence of a coordinated effect for the same product. The merger was cleared on the basis of divestiture commitments. See also the other merger cases referred to in the update to paragraph 8.211, above.

IMPALA: **retaliatory measures.**   The GC's judgment in *IMPALA* was overturned **10.057**
on appeal by the CJ: see update to paragraph 10.053, above. The CJ did not deal specifically with the issue of retaliatory measures.

4. Abuse of a Dominant Position

(a) Introduction

10.058 **In general.**   In *National Grid plc v Gas and Electricity Markets Authority* [2010] EWCA Civ 114 the English Court of Appeal held, citing this paragraph, that there was no need for a finding of abuse to be based on a benchmark. Although benchmarks were often used in pricing cases, '[t]here is, however, no rule requiring the use of a benchmark in every case, let alone a benchmark that will tell one precisely where the line between lawful and unlawful conduct is to be drawn' (para 54). The Court of Appeal also held that the use of counterfactuals as a tool of appraisal is plainly permissible and of potential value. What is appropriate by way of counterfactual, however, is a matter of judgment for the decision-maker and there is no rule of law that the counterfactual has to take a particular form. The purpose of the counterfactual is simply to cast light on the effect of the conduct in issue. It is for the decision-maker to determine whether a counterfactual is sufficiently realistic to be useful, and to decide how much weight to place on it: 'This is an area of appreciation, not of legal rules'.

Fn 174. The appeal in *AstraZeneca* was in large part dismissed: Case T-321/05 *AstraZeneca v Commission*, judgment of 1 July 2010, [2010] 5 CMLR 1575. The GC held that by submitting data with its application, without disclosing that the data were computed on the basis of an interpretation of the relevant legislation which AstraZeneca knew was not the generally accepted interpretation, AstraZeneca had abused its dominant position. The GC noted that that 'such conduct, characterised by a manifest lack of transparency, is contrary to the special responsibility of an undertaking in a dominant position not to impair by its conduct genuine undistorted competition in the common market': para 493. However, the GC disagreed with the Commission on one point, holding that the abuse only started when the documents containing the misleading statements were sent to the relevant patent offices by AstraZeneca's patent attorney, not when AstraZeneca sent the misleading information to those attorneys: paras 370–372. The case is on further appeal Case C-457/10P *AstraZeneca v Commission*, not yet decided.

10.059 **Governing principles.**   The concept of abuse covers not only practices which may cause damage to consumers directly but also practices which are detrimental to them through their impact on competition: Case C-52/09 *Konkurrensverket v TeliaSonera Sverige AB*, judgment of 17 February 2011, para 24.

10.060 **Abuse as an objective concept.**   See also Case T-301/04 *Clearstream Banking v Commission*, judgment of 9 September 2009. The GC emphasised that the concept of abuse is an objective one so that it was not necessary to rule on whether the Commission was right in finding that Clearstream's intention was to exclude EB from the provision of their services and, therefore, to hinder competition in the provision of cross-border secondary clearing and settlement services: para 143.

The proper interpretation of the CJ's definition in *Hoffmann-La Roche*, in particular the reference to 'recourse to methods different from those which condition normal competition' was discussed by the English Court of Appeal in *National Grid plc v Gas and Electricity Markets Authority* [2010] EWCA Civ 114. The Court held that there was no legal requirement to establish first what normal competition entailed in respect of a particular product before going on to consider the effect of the allegedly abusive conduct: para 36. Thus the Competition Appeal Tribunal (in *National Grid v The Gas and Electricity Markets Authority* [2009] CAT 10, paras 88 *et seq.*) had been 'entitled not to isolate the question of normal competition as a separate issue but to ask itself whether the foreclosing effect of the agreements was too severe and to look at matters in the round in deciding whether the conduct was abusive': para 40.

The 'special responsibility' of dominant firms.   This paragraph was cited by the Court of Appeal in *National Grid plc v Gas and Electricity Markets Authority* [2010] EWCA Civ 114, discussed above: see para 39.   **10.061**

Abusive intent.   See also COMP/38113 *Prokent-Tomra*, decn of 29 March 2006, [2009] 4 CMLR 101 where the Commission cited some colourful extracts from Tomra's internal documents evidencing an exclusionary intent: paras 98–105. Tomra's appeal against the decision was dismissed: Case T-155/06 *Tomra Systems v Commission*, judgment of 9 September 2010, see paras 33 *et seq.* The GC held that the Commission had been right to examine the applicants' internal documents to see whether they show that the exclusion of competition was intended or alternatively suggest another explanation for the practices. In this instance, Tomra's internal correspondence allowed the Commission to place their practices in context and to substantiate its own assessment of those practices. The GC however affirmed that an abuse is an objective concept: para 38. The case is on appeal: Case C-459/10P, *Tomra Systems*, not yet decided.   **10.062**

Advantage from abuse for dominant undertaking.   In *SEL-Imperial Ltd v British Standards Institution* [2010] EWHC 854 (Ch) the English High Court considered (in the context of an application to strike out a civil claim) whether conduct could be an abuse even if the dominant undertaking derived no competitive advantage from it. The court examined in particular the comment of the GC in Case T-155/04 *SELEX Sistemi Integrati v Commission* [2006] ECR II-4797, para 108 that it was not apparent that Eurocontrol 'could have derived any competitive advantage' from the conduct alleged to be abusive. Roth J held that although this comment supported the BSI's contention that competitive advantage was an element in the concept of abuse, the position was insufficiently clear on this point, and thus the allegation of abuse should not be struck out.   **10.062A**

10.063   **Objective justification.**   In Case T-321/05 *AstraZeneca v Commission*, judgment of 1 July 2010, [2010] 5 CMLR 1575, AstraZeneca sought to argue objective justification before the Court when it had not raised such arguments during the Commission's administrative process. The GC noted that although the Commission is required to take into account a possible objective justification for conduct which might otherwise be abusive, it is still necessary for the undertaking concerned to raise that objective ground of justification during the administrative procedure and put forward arguments and evidence in support thereof: para 686. The case is on appeal: Case C-457/10P *AstraZeneca v Commission*, not yet decided.

In *Purple Parking Ltd v Heathrow Airport Ltd* [2011] EWHC 987 (Ch) the Court agreed with the criticism by Advocate General Jacobs of the two-stage analysis of abuse and objective justification but nonetheless applied it: para 180. The Court rejected arguments based on traffic congestion, airport security, safety, and environmental considerations put forward to justify excluding competing undertakings from providing 'meet and greet' valet parking services at the airport terminals.

10.064   **Comparison of objective justification with criteria in Article 81(3).**   In the Commission's Guidance on the enforcement of Article 82, OJ 2009 C45/7: Vol II, App C19, the Commission has stated that a dominant undertaking can show that its conduct is objectively justified either by showing that it is 'objectively necessary' or by demonstrating that the conduct produces substantial efficiencies which outweigh any anti-competitive effect on consumers: paras 28–31. Objective necessity for the purposes of Article 102 can arise only from factors external to the dominant undertaking, for example health and safety reasons related to the nature of the product. In order to demonstrate efficiencies the dominant undertaking must show that (i) efficiencies have been or are likely to result from the conduct; (ii) the conduct is indispensable to the realisation of those efficiencies; and (iii) the efficiencies outweigh any likely negative effects on competition and consumer welfare in the affected markets.

See also the approach of the Irish High Court in *Neurendale Ltd t/a Panda Waste Services v Dublin City Council* [2009] IEHC 588, para 140.

Fn 192a. See also Case T-321/05 *AstraZeneca v Commission*, judgment of 1 July 2010, [2010] 5 CMLR 1575, para 686. The case is on appeal: Case C-457/10P *AstraZeneca v Commission*, not yet decided.

10.065   **Exclusionary and exploitative abuses.**   In the Commission's Guidance on the enforcement of Article 82, OJ 2009 C45/7: Vol II, App C19, the Commission sets out the criteria relevant for its assessment of whether there is anti-competitive foreclosure in a market: paras 19–22. The factors include the strength of the dominant position; whether there are economies of scale or scope and network effects which entrench the dominant firm's position; whether there is a specific competitor which is particularly innovative or has the reputation of systematically cutting prices; whether the conduct has been applied to selected customers; what percentage of total sales in the market are affected by the conduct; whether there is evidence of actual foreclosure if the conduct has been in place for a sufficient period of time; whether there is evidence from internal documents of exclusionary intent. However, there may be conduct which the Commission regards as raising obstacles to competition and creating no efficiencies, in which case it is not necessary to carry out a detailed assessment before concluding that there is likely to be consumer harm: para 22.

Efficiency and abuse.   Note that the Commission has issued a document called   **10.067**
'Best Practices for the Submission of Economic Evidence and Data Collection in Cases Concerning the Application of Articles 101 and 102 TFEU and in Merger Cases' (Vol II, App B21, and on the DG Competition website and linked to Press Release IP/10/02 (6 January 2010)). It describes the preferred content and presentation of economic and econometric data and best practice on responding to requests for quantitative data.

Fn 197. The appeal by Deutsche Telekom was dismissed both by the GC and the CJ: Case T-271/03 *Deutsche Telekom v Commission* [2008] ECR II-477; and Case C-280/08P *Deutsche Telekom v Commission*, judgment of 14 October 2010, [2010] 5 CMLR 1485. The GC defined the margin squeeze abuse as occurring '[i]f the applicant's retail prices are lower than its wholesale charges, or if the spread between the applicant's wholesale and retail charges is insufficient to enable an equally efficient operator to cover its product-specific costs of supplying retail access services, a potential competitor who is just as efficient as the applicant would not be able to enter the retail access services market without suffering losses': para 237. The CJ upheld this definition (see para 255 of its judgment).

Abuses considered in this Section.   In *Purple Parking Ltd v Heathrow Airport Ltd*   **10.068**
[2011] EWHC 987 (Ch) the High Court rejected the submission that because the alleged abuse could be described as an 'essential facilities' type abuse, the claimants were precluded from arguing that it was any other kind of abuse. The court held that such pigeon-holing of conduct was inconsistent with the case law: para 105. Note that the CJ arrived at a similar conclusion in Case C-52/09 *Konkurrensverket v TeliaSonera Sverige AB*, judgment of 17 February 2011. TeliaSonera argued that they should remain free to fix their terms of trade, unless those terms are so disadvantageous that they may be regarded, in the light of the relevant criteria set out in *Bronner,* as entailing a refusal to supply. The Court rejected this, holding that the conditions to be met in order to establish that a refusal to supply is abusive do not apply to conduct which consists in supplying services or selling goods on conditions which are disadvantageous or on which there might be no purchaser. Such conduct may, in itself, constitute an independent form of abuse distinct from that of refusal to supply.

(b) Own market abuses: exclusionary pricing practices

(i) Predatory pricing

10.070 **Predatory pricing.** In the Commission's Guidance on the enforcement of Article 82, OJ 2009 C45/7 the Commission states that it will normally only intervene where the conduct has already been, or is capable of, hampering competition from competitors who are as efficient as the dominant undertaking. The Commission's focus will therefore be on economic data relating to the costs of the dominant undertaking itself: paras 23–27. However, the Commission recognises that sometimes a less efficient competitor may also exert a competitive constraint which should be taken into account: para 24. See also paras 63 *et seq* of the Guidance.

10.071 **The Court of Justice's approach.** As to the last sentence of this paragraph, note that in Case C-202/07P *France Télécom v Commission*, judgment of 2 April 2009, para 109, the CJ said that prices below AVC 'must be considered prima facie abusive' but (at para 111) referred to the possibility of economic justification of such pricing.

10.075 **Other measures of cost.** The costs benchmarks that the Commission is likely to use are average avoidable cost (AAC) and long run incremental cost: see the Commission's Guidance on the enforcement of Article 82, OJ 2009 C45/7, paras 26, 27, 64, and 65.

See Case C-209/10 *Post Danmark v Konkurrencerådet*, not yet decided (reference from Danish court asking whether the grant by a dominant postal undertaking with a universal service obligation of selective price reductions to a level lower than the postal undertaking's average overall costs, but higher than the provider's average incremental costs, can constitute an exclusionary abuse if it is established that the prices are not set at that level for the purpose of eliminating a competitor).

As to the last sentence of this paragraph, the judgment of the Paris Court of Appeal in *Régie départmentale des passages d'eau de la Vendée* was annulled by the Cour de Cassation. The Cour de Cassation remitted the case for further consideration of what costs truly had to be incurred to fulfil the operator's public service obligation and thus whether any of the costs of the express ferry at issue should properly be regarded as common costs to be left out of account in a predatory pricing analysis: Cass. Com., 17 June 2008, BOCCRF No. 4 of 8 April 2009, [2009] ECC 63. In its second judgment, the Paris Court of Appeal confirmed the conclusion of the prior ruling, with additional reasoning that expressly drew on the approach of the Commission decision in *Deutsche Post* and emphasised the difference in the economic aspects of operating a mandated public service as compared to a private competitive service: judgment of 9 June 2009, BOCCRF No. 8 of 3 August 2009.

Potential for recoupment of losses: *Tetra Pak II*. The CJ has confirmed that **10.076** 'demonstrating that it is possible to recoup losses is not a necessary precondition for a finding of predatory pricing': Case C-202/07P *France Télécom v Commission*, judgment of 2 April 2009: lack of recoupment does not prevent damage to customers through the reduction in choice that results from the elimination of a competitor: paras 110–112. The CJ noted that the possibility of recoupment may nonetheless be relevant in excluding economic justifications for pricing below AVC or in establishing a plan to eliminate a competitor under the second limb of the *AKZO* rule.

In the Commission's Guidance on the enforcement of Article 82, OJ 2009 C45/7, the Commission indicates that it is unlikely that consumers are harmed by predatory conduct unless the dominant undertaking is likely to benefit from its sacrifice. This does not mean that the dominant undertaking must be likely to be able to increase its prices; it is sufficient if, for instance, the conduct would be likely to prevent or delay a decline in prices that would otherwise have occurred: paras 70 and 71.

Possible justifications for below-cost pricing. The further appeal in the *Wanadoo* **10.078** *Interactive* case was dismissed by the CJ: Case C-202/07P *France Télécom v Commission*, judgment of 2 April 2009. The CJ rejected the appellant's claim that the GC failed to state adequate reasons for rejecting arguments based on a right to align its prices on those of its competitors.

The Commission has indicated that it is unlikely that predatory conduct will create efficiencies though it will consider claims that low pricing enables the dominant firm to achieve economies of scale or efficiencies relating to expanding the market: see the Commission's Guidance on the enforcement of Article 82, OJ 2009 C45/7, para 74.

Proof of 'intention'. The CJ dismissed the further appeal in the *Wanadoo* **10.079** *Interactive* case: Case C-202/07P *France Télécom v Commission*, judgment of 2 April 2009. The CJ rejected arguments concerning the 'plan of predation': see paras 89 *et seq*. In the Commission's Guidance on the enforcement of Article 82, OJ 2009 C45/7 the Commission refers to 'direct evidence' of predatory strategy in documents from the dominant undertaking: see para 66.

(ii) Price discrimination or targeting

Selective price cutting: the Courts' approach. Fn 245. The appeal referred to in **10.082** the footnote was dismissed by the GC, Case T-276/04 *Compagnie maritime belge SA v Commission* [2008] ECR II-1277.

Price discrimination: differential tariffs. In *PKP Cargo v Office of Competition*, **10.084** judgment of 9 May 2011, the Polish Court of Competition and Consumer Protection upheld a fine of PLN60 million imposed on a dominant freight carriage provider for failing to make attractive discount terms available to competitors using its services.

10.086 **Price discrimination on grounds of nationality.** As regards the penultimate sentence of this paragraph the CJ in Cases C-501/06P, etc, *GlaxoSmithKline Services Unlimited v Commission*, judgment of 6 October 2009 overturned the GC's analysis insofar as it held that it was necessary to prove that an agreement entails disadvantages for final consumers as a prerequisite for a finding of anti-competitive object. The judgment did not discuss Article 102.

10.089 **Identifying equivalent transactions.** The terms on which facilities are made available to an undertaking's own ancillary business can form the basis of a comparison for the terms offered to independent undertakings seeking to operate a competing business: *Purple Parking Ltd v Heathrow Airport Ltd* [2011] EWHC 987 (Ch), paras 134 *et seq*.

10.090 **Objective justification for differential pricing.** By contrast, heavy expenditure on advertising to promote special prices, above cost, that are designed to match those of a new entrant on the market but are offered to customers generally, is not in itself an abuse. The Spanish Supreme Court thus annulled the decision of the Spanish competition authority which had held the massive expenditure by the incumbent fixed line telephone operator on advertising to promote its new special tariffs for national and international calls at the time that another company was about to enter the market offering cheap calls with a dialling prefix constituted an abuse: *Telefónica de España SA v Retevisión SA*, Case 9174/2003, judgment of 20 June 2006. Applying the Spanish domestic equivalent of Article 102, the Court held that the question of abuse depended more on objective considerations, and that intent to hinder a new entrant was not in itself unlawful. Furthermore, the new entrant in this case also had significant financial resources so that the incumbent's level of advertising expenditure did not constitute a barrier to entry.

In Case C-52/07 *Kanal 5 Ltd and TV 4 AB v Föreningen Svenska Tonsättares Internationella Musikbyrå (STIM) upa* [2008] ECR I-9275, [2009] 5 CMLR 2175 the CJ considered whether the practice of a collecting society of calculating royalties on different bases as between public service and commercial broadcasters amounted to applying dissimilar conditions to equivalent transactions. In a preliminary ruling under Article 267 TFEU (formerly Article 234 EC), the CJ held that this could be an abuse if it placed the commercial broadcasters at a competitive disadvantage, unless such a practice could be objectively justified. This was for the national court to determine.

(iii) Fidelity rebates and similar practices

10.091 **Fidelity rebates and similar practices.** The principles set out in this paragraph were reiterated by the GC in Case T-155/06 *Tomra Systems v Commission*, judgment of 9 September 2010. The Court upheld the Commission's decision condemning an exclusionary strategy involving exclusivity agreements, individualised quantity commitments and individualised retroactive rebate schemes: COMP/38113 *Prokent/Tomra*, decn of 29 March 2006. Tomra challenged the decision, *inter alia*, on the basis that the Commission had regarded such practices as *per se* infringements of Article 102. The GC confirmed that in order to determine whether the arrangements breached Article 102, it is necessary to ascertain whether, following an assessment of all the circumstances and of the context in which those agreements operate, those practices are intended to restrict or foreclose competition on the relevant market or are capable of doing so. The Court held that the Commission had examined the context and not just the content of the arrangements. It was not necessary for the Commission to prove that the proportion of the market covered by the agreements was so large that the remaining contestable section was insufficient to enable viable market entry: 'the foreclosure by a dominant undertaking of a substantial part of the market cannot be justified by showing that the contestable part of the market is still sufficient to accommodate a limited number of competitors. First, the customers on the foreclosed part of the market should have the opportunity to benefit from whatever degree of competition is possible on the market and competitors should be able to compete on the merits for the entire market and not just for a part of it. Second, it is not the role of the dominant undertaking to dictate how many viable competitors will be allowed to compete for the remaining contestable portion of demand': para 241. Further it was not necessary to show that competitors would have to offer negative prices to customers in order to compete for their remaining business: para 258. In the decision the Commission had explored at some length the likely foreclosing effect of the agreements. The GC rejected the challenges to these findings on the basis that they were not necessary for the finding of infringement and had not been relied on by the Commission otherwise than to 'complete its analysis'. The GC further stated that even if the Commission had made a manifest error of assessment in holding that those agreements actually eliminated competition, the legality of the contested decision would not be affected (para 290). Finally the Court found that the non-binding nature of the arrangements did not preclude their illegality: para 300. The case is on appeal: Case C-459/10P, *Tomra Systems*, not yet decided.

In COMP/37990 *Intel*, decn of 13 May 2009 the Commission fined Intel €1.6 billion for exclusionary practices. The Commission found that Intel engaged in two specific forms of illegal practice. First, Intel gave wholly or partially hidden rebates to computer manufacturers on condition that they bought all, or almost all, their x86 CPUs from Intel. Intel also made direct payments to a major retailer on condition it stock only computers with Intel x86 CPUs. Secondly, Intel made direct payments to computer manufacturers to halt or delay the launch of specific products containing competitors' x86 CPUs and to limit the sales channels available to these products. The Guidance on enforcement priorities did not apply in *Intel* but the Commission noted that the decision was in line with the orientations of that guidance: para 916. The Commission also rejected the suggestion that it was necessary to show actual foreclosure and said that the Guidance made no difference in this respect either: paras 919 and 925. The case is on appeal: Case T-286/09, not yet decided.

As to the willing acceptance by the customer of the rebate scheme, the Commission has noted that it may be in the individual interest of the customer to enter into the exclusive purchasing obligation; but this does not mean that the obligation is beneficial for customers overall or for final consumers: see the Commission's Guidance on the enforcement of Article 82, OJ 2009 C45/7, para 34. See also paras 37 *et seq* of the Guidance regarding the cases which the Commission will treat as an enforcement priority: the anti-competitive foreclosure is likely to be higher where competitors are not able to satisfy the entire demand of each individual customer and the dominant undertaking can use the 'non contestable' portion of the demand as leverage to decrease the price to be paid for the 'contestable' portion: para 39.

See also the rather unusual arrangement that was condemned as abusive by the Competition Appeal Tribunal in *National Grid v The Gas and Electricity Markets Authority* [2009] CAT 10. The Tribunal's decision was upheld by the Court of Appeal: *National Grid plc v Gas and Electricity Markets Authority* [2010] EWCA Civ 114.

10.092 **Turnover related discounts: annual sales targets.** **Fn 286.** See also Case T-66/01 *ICI v Commission*, judgment of 25 June 2010, para 328. The appeal from the *Prokent/Tomra* decision was dismissed by the GC: see Case T-155/06 *Tomra Systems v Commission*, judgment of 9 September 2010 discussed in the update to paragraph 10.091, above.

10.093 **Stepped discount arrangements.** See also COMP/38113 *Prokent-Tomra*, decn of 29 March 2006, [2009] 4 CMLR 101 (upheld on appeal Case T-155/06 *Tomra Systems v Commission*, judgment of 9 September 2010) discussed in the update to paragraph 10.091, above.

On the question of objective justification for the discount scheme see the Commission's Guidance on the enforcement of Article 82, OJ 2009 C45/7, para 46 which refers to transaction-related cost advantages and cases where relationship-specific investment is needed by the dominant undertaking.

10.094 **Discounts dependent on the dominant firm's discretion.** Similarly in *Prokent-Tomra*, discussed in the update to paragraph 10.091, above, the Commission held that the lack of transparency in a discount scheme was liable to strengthen its loyalty-building character: para 324. The decision was upheld on appeal: see Case T-155/06 *Tomra Systems v Commission*, judgment of 9 September 2010 discussed in the update to paragraph 10.091, above.

Across-product rebates. In the Commission's Guidance on the enforcement of   **10.095**
Article 82, OJ 2009 C45/7, the Commission treats multi-product rebates as a form
of tying or bundling: paras 59 *et seq.*

Fn 308. On US antitrust law see also *Cascade Health Solutions v PeaceHealth*, 515
F.3d 883 (9th Cir, 2008): 'discount attribution' test applied instead of approach in
LePage to determine whether bundled rebate excludes an 'as efficient' competitor.

Turnover related discounts: summary. See now the approach of the Commission   **10.096**
in COMP/37990 *Intel*, decn of 13 May 2009. The Commission firmly rejected
Intel's argument that it was necessary to establish actual foreclosure in order to find
an infringement. Further, although the Commission asserted that the exclusivity
rebates granted by the dominant firm were in themselves enough to establish an
infringement, it went on to demonstrate that the rebates were capable of causing or
likely to cause anti-competitive foreclosure likely to result in consumer harm: para
925. It did this by conducting an 'as efficient competitor analysis': paras 1003 *et seq.*
This analysis examines whether Intel itself, in view of its own costs and the effect of
the rebate, would be able to enter the market at a more limited scale without incurring losses. It thereby establishes at what price a competitor which is 'as efficient' as
Intel would have to offer x86 CPUs in order to compensate an OEM for the loss of
any Intel rebate. The Commission concluded that if Intel's rebate scheme means
that in order to compensate an Intel trading partner for the loss of the Intel rebate,
an as efficient competitor has to offer its products below a viable measure of
Intel's cost, then it means that the rebate was capable of reducing access to Intel
trading partners which could offer products from the as efficient competitor, or
in other words capable of foreclosing a hypothetical as efficient competitor: paras
1154–1574.

The approach of the *Michelin II* and *British Airways* judgments has been applied by
the Danish courts and competition authority. In *Schneider Electric Danmark A/S v
Competition Council*, U.2008.851/1H, the Supreme Court (judgment of 7 January
2008) upheld the finding of the Danish Competition Council that the advance
order and delivery rebate system applied for the supply of electrical socket outlets
infringed the domestic equivalent of Article 102 TFEU. The Court rejected the
argument that since the marginal price of each unit supplied was not below the total
cost of production of that unit, the price could be matched by an equally efficient
competitor so that the scheme had no exclusionary effect; the Court held that
the advance order rebates created loyalty effects equivalent to progressive yearly
bonuses. See also *Viasat Broadcasting UK Ltd v Competition Council*, Ø´LR B-3926-
06, judgment of the High Court of Eastern Denmark, reversing the holding of
the lower court that the television advertising market had special characteristics
so as to displace the finding that progressive annual rebates had a loyalty-inducing
effect and thus forced competitors of the dominant commercial channel to
charge lower rates. The High Court's judgment was later upheld by the Danish

Supreme Court: ECN Brief 2/2011, p2. In *Post Danmark* (decn of the Danish Competition Council of 24 June 2009) the Council found the loyalty rebate scheme for direct, bulk mail delivery operated by the Danish postal operator with a share of over 90 per cent of this market violated Article 102 and its domestic equivalent even if the reduced price could be charged by an 'as efficient' competitor: the scheme involved retroactive, stepped rebates and was likely to have loyalty inducing and anti-competitive effects in a market where Post Danmark enjoyed substantial economies of scale and scope and even less efficient competitors would have a constraining effect on the dominant undertaking.

Fn 310. The description of the Swedish Market Court case in the first sentence should read: 'Swedish Market Court upheld a decision of the Swedish NCA that SAS had abused its dominant position on the market for domestic scheduled air transportation services by applying on domestic routes its international frequent flyer programme. . . .'.

Further, by decision No. 324/2008 of 9 January 2009, the Swedish NCA held that the previous ruling and injunction applied to the situation as at the time of the Market Court's judgment and therefore would not apply to potential operation of the programme in current conditions on domestic routes exposed to competition. Since the NCA does not give negative clearance, it was then for SAS to decide whether conditions were sufficiently altered for it to reintroduce the scheme without committing an abuse.

(c) Own market abuses: exclusionary non-price conduct

10.097 **Discrimination on grounds of nationality.** See also COMP/39388&39389 *E. ON German electricity markets*, decn of 26 November 2008 where the Commission accepted commitments in respect of alleged discrimination by E.ON in favour of acquiring domestic supplies of energy for balancing and against importing supplies: para 54.

In COMP/39351 *Swedish Interconnectors*, decn of 14 April 2010 the Commission's concerns were that SvK (which was dominant in the market for electricity transmission in Sweden) may have abused its dominant position by curtailing capacity on the Swedish interconnectors when it anticipated internal congestion within the Swedish transmission system by treating requests for transmission for the purpose of consumption within Sweden differently from requests for transmission. The concerns were met by commitments made binding on SvK.

10.098 **Long-term exclusive dealing.** In COMP/38113 *Prokent-Tomra*, decn of 29 March 2006, [2009] 4 CMLR 101 the Commission condemned as abusive a wide range of exclusivity arrangements entered into by Tomra which was found to be dominant in the market for the supply of reverse vending machines for recycling empty containers: paras 281 *et seq*. The Commission found that because there was a peak in demand in the years when national legislation mandating recycling or the introduction of empty container deposit schemes was introduced, even a short-term exclusive agreement could have a significant foreclosure effect if it covered a 'key year': para 287, paras 303 *et seq*, and para 343. The decision was upheld on appeal see Case T-155/06 *Tomra Systems v Commission*, judgment of 9 September 2010 discussed in the update to paragraph 10.091, above.

See also the Commission's Guidance on the enforcement of Article 82, OJ 2009 C45/7, paras 33–36 as regards the factors that the Commission will consider when deciding whether to intervene.

Fn 321. The Commission's decision in *De Beers* was reinstated when the CJ set aside the judgment of the GC in Case T-170/06 and dismissed Alrosa's challenge to the decision: Case C-441/07P *Commission v Alrosa*, judgment of 29 June 2010, [2010] 5 CMLR 643.

De facto **exclusive dealing: the 'ice cream wars'.**   Van den Bergh's share of the **10.100** market for impulse ice cream in Ireland was over 75 per cent not 40 per cent as stated in the text.

Abusive enforcement of exclusivity provisions.   Fn 332. The appeal referred to in **10.101** the footnote was dismissed by the GC, Case T-276/04 *Compagnie maritime belge SA v Commission* [2008] ECR II-1277.

Litigation as an exclusionary abuse.   The appeal in *AstraZeneca* has been decided: **10.103** Case T-321/05 *AstraZeneca v Commission*, judgment of 1 July 2010, [2010] 5 CMLR 1575. The Court upheld the Commission's factual findings that AstraZeneca defended various challenges to its SPCs in national courts by persisting in the misrepresentations that it had previously made to the various patent offices in order to obtain those certificates and thus engaged in a 'persistent and linear course of conduct': para 598. The case is on further appeal Case C-457/10P *AstraZeneca v Commission*, not yet decided.

(d) Own market abuses: exploitative pricing

Unfairly high prices.   To propose, in the course of negotiations, prices which are **10.105** excessive is not of itself abusive conduct: *Humber Oil Terminals v Associated British Ports* [2011] EWHC 352 (Ch), para 20.

The Commission's approach: *Port of Helsingborg*.   The Commission's approach **10.106** to assessing the reasonableness of prices for the transfer of technology can be seen in its decision in *Microsoft* of 27 February 2008 (COMP/37792). This decision fixed the periodic penalty payment imposed on Microsoft for setting too high a price for the non-patented information it made available in one of the packages it offered competitors in purported compliance with the obligations under the 2004 decision. In assessing whether the remuneration charged by Microsoft was unreasonable, the Commission referred to the 'WSPP Pricing Principles' ('WSPP' stands for Work Group Server Protocol Program) that had been devised by Microsoft in negotiation with the Commission during 2005 and 2006. The WSPP Pricing Principles were based on the Commission's assertion that the upshot of the 2004 Decision was that in order for it to be reasonable, 'any remuneration charged by Microsoft for access to or use of the Interoperability Information should be justified by showing that it allows competitors to viably compete with Microsoft's work group server operating system and that it represents a fair compensation for the value of the technology that is transferred by Microsoft to recipients of the Interoperability Information beyond the mere ability to interoperate, namely excluding the "strategic value" stemming from Microsoft's market power in the client PC and work group server operating system markets': para 107. The WSPP Pricing Principles thus stated that the assessment of what reflects such value conferred upon a licensee to the exclusion of strategic value should in particular take into account three factors. The first was whether the protocols described in the specifications were Microsoft's own creations (as opposed to Microsoft's implementation of a publicly available standard). If Microsoft simply uses protocols that it takes from the public domain, then the only information that it is providing pursuant to the Decision is to indicate which of the protocols available in the public domain it is actually using. The Commission considered that Microsoft should not be entitled to charge any price for that information. The second factor was whether these creations by Microsoft constitute innovation. If the protocol technology currently used by Microsoft, although different from protocol technology available in the public domain, is not novel then Microsoft should not be entitled to charge for it. The third factor was to carry out a market valuation of technologies deemed comparable, excluding the strategic value that stems from the dominance of any such technologies. The Commission found that most of the information being made available in the non-patent package was not innovative and that comparable protocol technology was provided royalty-free by other undertakings. The Commission therefore found that Microsoft had charged an unreasonable fee for this information. This decision is under appeal: Case T-167/08, not yet decided.

Fn 352. The appeal in Case T-306/05 *Scippacercola and Terezakis v Commission* was dismissed, [2008] ECR II-4*, [2008] 4 CMLR 1418. The GC upheld the Commission's rejection of the complaint on the ground of lack of EU interest and did not address the issue of excessive pricing. Further appeal dismissed Case C-159/08P, Order of 25 March 2009.

10.107 **Benchmark comparator.** See, eg *Europay*, 16 Ok 4/07, judgment of 12 September 2007, where the Austrian Supreme Court upheld a finding of infringement of the domestic equivalent of Article 102 TFEU by a joint venture of Austrian commercial banks that offered card transaction processing systems to merchants, for the excessive charges that it was agreed would be made by the JV parent banks to competing systems. The charge was found to be excessive both on the basis of a comparison with the much lower price charged by the parent banks to Europay and by reference to the actual costs (€0.06 per transaction, for which the charge levied was €0.36–0.40). (The agreement was also found to violate the Austrian equivalent of Article 101 TFEU).

In *Iberdrola Generación*, Case 166/07, judgment of 2 July 2009, the Spanish National High Court upheld the competition tribunal's finding of infringement of the Spanish equivalent of Article 102 in the prices charged over relatively short periods when there were so-called 'technical restrictions' that prevent supply in a particular area being met from the electricity pool and enabled supplies to be required from the generator in the area at above the 'pool' price. This could give rise to a situation of temporary monopoly since there were often no other generators in the area. The Court compared the impugned prices with those charged by Iberdrola in preceding periods and also the difference between variable cost and prices charged in the daily market pool, a measure whereby Iberdrola's prices were found to be some 40 per cent higher.

Fn 361. See, eg *Canarias de Explosivos*, Case 626/07, decn of 12 February 2008, where the Spanish competition authority found the sole distributor in the Canary Islands of explosives for demolitions committed an abuse contrary to the domestic equivalent of Article 102 by charging prices that were about eight times higher than those charged in mainland Spain where the market was more competitive; transport costs could not account for this difference.

Benchmark price.   When the imposition of prices which incorporate a very high **10.108** margin over costs has an exclusionary effect on the market, that may lead to the conclusion that the prices are abusive. In its first decision to find excessive pricing, the French competition authority found that France Télécom was abusing its dominant position on the fixed telephony and internet markets in the French overseas departments (DOM), which it previously monopolised, by making its competitors' entry into these markets more difficult and costly. In particular, its annual profit margin on rental of lines on the undersea connection between la Réunion and the mainland was 493 per cent in 2002 and rose to 1794 per cent in 2004. Charging such prices made it impossible for competing operators to develop in the retail market on la Réunion. Thus excessive pricing operated as an exclusionary abuse (along with other forms of exclusionary conduct): Decision No. 09-D-24 of 28 July 2009.

In *SEA SpA and AdR SpA* the Italian Competition Authority found that the operators of Rome and Milan airports had abused their respective dominant positions by charging excessive prices on the markets for access to infrastructure for the provision of refuelling services, catering services and rent of operational areas for cargo operators (relevant product markets) where tariffs were above average costs plus capital remuneration. However, the ICA held that there was insufficient evidence of abuse relying on the findings of a regulatory body which had examined the prices charged and concluded that they were aligned with costs. The Tribunale Amministrativo partially overturned the ICA's decision as being insufficiently reasoned because it was based on the regulatory authority's conclusions rather than the ICA's own assessment. But on further appeal, the Consiglio di Stato considered that the ICA had conducted an autonomous assessment on the existence of the anti-competitive conduct. The fact that the ICA had relied on the outcome of the regulatory proceedings to conclude that the prices for the provision of a specific service were not excessive, appeared to the judge a reasonable approach, due to the difficulty of verifying the relationship between prices and costs: ECN Brief 4/2010, p2.

Fn 369. Cf the Austrian case, *Europay*, discussed in the update to paragraph 10.107, above.

10.109   **Economic value.**   In Case C-52/07 *Kanal 5 Ltd and TV 4 AB v Föreningen Svenska Tonsättares Internationella Musikbyrå (STIM) upa* [2008] ECR I-9275, [2009] 5 CMLR 2175 the CJ held that no abuse was committed where a copyright association set a royalty for the performing rights of its repertoire calculated as a percentage of the revenue earned by the broadcaster from television broadcasts directed at the general public and/or subscription sales. The percentage varied according to the amount of music broadcast by the TV station. The Court noted that the royalties must be analysed with respect to the value of that use in trade. Insofar as such royalties are calculated on the basis of the revenue of the television broadcasting societies, they are, in principle, reasonable in relation to the economic value of the service provided by STIM: para 37. The CJ held that there was no abuse unless another method was available which enabled the use of those works to be identified more precisely with the audience, without a disproportionate increase in the costs incurred in the management of contracts and the supervision of the use of the copyright works.

(e) Related market abuses: exclusionary pricing

(i) Margin squeezing

10.112   **Price or margin squeezing.**   There have been several important cases on margin squeeze recently: the appeals to the GC and the CJ from the Commission's decision in *Deutsche Telekom* referred to in the text: Case T-271/03 *Deutsche Telekom v Commission* [2008] ECR II-477 and Case C-280/08P *Deutsche Telekom v Commission*, judgment of 14 October 2010, [2010] 5 CMLR 1485; the Commission's decision in COMP/38784 *Wanadoo España/Telefónica*, decn of 4 July 2007 and, in the English Court of Appeal *Albion Water Ltd v Water Services Regulation Authority (Dŵr Cymru/Shotton Paper)* [2008] EWCA Civ 536 on appeal from the Competition Appeal Tribunal. These cases are discussed in the following paragraph updates.

In Case C-52/09 *Konkurrensverket v TeliaSonera Sverige AB*, judgment of 17 February 2011, the CJ (on a reference from the Stockholm court) reiterated the principles established in *Deutsche Telekom* (discussed below) and *France Télécom* and held further that although in general the analysis should focus on the costs incurred by the dominant undertaking itself and on its strategy, the costs and prices of competitors may also be relevant. For example where the cost structure of the dominant undertaking is not precisely identifiable for objective reasons, or where the service supplied to competitors consists in the mere use of an infrastructure the production cost of which has already been written off, access to such an infrastructure no longer represents a cost for the dominant undertaking which is economically comparable to the cost which its competitors have to incur to have access to it. Similarly the particular market conditions of competition may dictate it, where, for example, the level of the dominant undertaking's costs is specifically attributable to the competitively advantageous situation in which its dominant position places it. The Court also considered the relationship between margin squeeze and refusal to grant access to essential facilities in the *Bronner* line of cases. TeliaSonera argued that they should remain free to fix their terms of trade, unless those terms are so disadvantageous that they may be regarded, in the light of the relevant criteria set out in *Bronner*, as entailing a refusal to supply. The Court rejected this, holding that the conditions to be met in order to establish that a refusal to supply is abusive do not apply to conduct which consists in supplying services or selling goods on conditions which are disadvantageous or on which there might be no purchaser. Such conduct may, in itself, constitute an independent form of abuse distinct from that of refusal to supply. In answer to a question from the referring court as to whether an anti-competitive effect had to be established, the Court held that the practice must have an anti-competitive effect on the market, but the effect does not necessarily have to be concrete. It is sufficient to demonstrate that there is an anti-competitive effect which may potentially exclude competitors who are at least as efficient as the dominant undertaking. Whilst it was therefore not necessary to show that the dominant undertaking's purpose of driving competitors from the relevant market had been achieved, the conduct was not exclusionary where the penetration of those competitors in the market concerned is not made any more difficult by that practice. It was for the national court to decide whether this was so. The Court also held: (i) although it was not necessary for the input product to be indispensable for would-be competitors, if it was not, this may make it less likely that competitors were excluded by the margin squeeze; (ii) it was not necessary to show that the dominant firm was also dominant in the downstream retail market; (iii) it is irrelevant whether the competitor is a new or existing customer; and (iv) it is irrelevant that the market concerned is growing rapidly or that it involves new technology requiring high levels of investment.

By contrast the US Supreme Court (by a 5-4 majority) has robustly rejected the concept of price squeezing as an independent form of abuse under the

US antitrust laws: *Pacific Bell Telephone Co v Linkline Communications Inc* 129 S. Ct. 1109 (2009).

10.113   **The Commission's practice.**   The appeal by Deutsche Telekom was dismissed both by the GC and the CJ: Case T-271/03 *Deutsche Telekom* v *Commission* [2008] ECR II-477; and Case C-280/08P *Deutsche Telekom v Commission*, judgment of 14 October 2010, [2010] 5 CMLR 1485. The Court of Justice rejected arguments based on the involvement of the German telecoms regulator in the setting of DT's retail prices. The appeal proceeded in the CJ on the premiss that the wholesale price for local loop access was fixed by the regulator without leaving DT scope for changing those prices. The CJ held that this did not preclude a finding of margin squeeze since there was still scope for DT to adjust its retail prices to avoid the squeeze (para 85). Further, since the existence of the abuse arose from the unfairness of the spread rather than the precise levels of the wholesale or retail prices, the level of the wholesale price (and in particular whether it had been set too high by the regulator) was irrelevant to the question of abuse (paras 167–168). So far as the level of retail prices were concerned, although DT was encouraged by the intervention of the national regulator to maintain the *retail* prices that led to the margin squeeze, this did not absolve DT of responsibility for the abuse (paras 82 *et seq*). In any event the regulator's decisions were not binding on the Commission (para 90). The CJ upheld the GC's decision that it was not necessary to show that the retail price was excessive and abusive in itself (para 183); the essence of the abuse is the spread between the prices. Indeed, the fact that DT would have to increase its retail prices for end-user access services in order to avoid squeezing its competitors was not relevant (para 181). The CJ held that the GC had correctly rejected the Commission's assertion that the very existence of a margin squeeze constituted an abuse without the need to demonstrate an anti-competitive effect (para 250). It was not necessary to show that equally efficient competitors had actually be driven from the market but it was necessary to show that market penetration was made more difficult (para 254). The CJ held that the GC had been correct in finding that the Commission had established that DT's pricing practices had given rise to actual exclusionary effects on 'as efficient' competitors (para 259). The Courts upheld the Commission's decision to base the finding of abuse on the costs and charges of the dominant undertaking and not to examine the costs and prices of its actual or potential competitors (paras 196–204 of CJ's judgment). In response to various other challenges to the way the Commission had calculated the margin, the GC held that this was a matter of complex economic assessment as to which the Commission had a margin of appreciation: para 185. All DT's pleas on the detail of what revenues should or should not have been included in the calculations were rejected by both Courts.

In COMP/38784 *Wanadoo España/Telefónica*, decn of 4 July 2007 the Commission imposed a fine for a margin squeeze in the Spanish broadband internet access markets. The Commission found that the incumbent, Telefónica, was the only Spanish telecommunications operator with a nationwide fixed telephone network and that it controlled the entire ADSL value chain in Spain. Alternative network operators wishing to provide retail broadband services had no other option but to contract wholesale broadband access products, all of which are built on Telefónica's local access network. From September 2001 to December 2006, the margin between Telefónica's retail prices and the price for wholesale access at regional level, on the one hand, and the margin between the retail prices and the price for wholesale access at national level, on the other hand, was insufficient to cover the costs that an operator as efficient as Telefónica would have to incur to provide retail broadband access. The methodology applied was to assess whether Telefónica's downstream arm would operate profitably on the basis of the upstream charges levied by Telefónica's upstream arm. Two profitability methods were used: the so-called period-by-period method (which assessed Telefónica's profitability every year), and the discounted cash flows method (which allowed below-cost pricing in the initial phase of an expanding market but required Telefónica to be profitable over 2001–2006) proposed by Telefónica itself. Both methods led to the same conclusion. The Commission rejected Telefónica's argument that the case should be analysed as an 'essential facilities' refusal to supply case so that the criteria laid down in *Oscar Bronner* applied. A substantial fine was imposed. The case is on appeal Cases T-336&398/07 *Telefónica and Telefónica de España v Commission*, not yet decided.

Note that in the Commission's Guidance on the enforcement of Article 82, OJ 2009 C45/7, the Commission treats margin squeeze as a form of refusal to supply: paras 75 *et seq*.

Domestic cases on margin squeezing: *Genzyme*. Fn 393. The case of *Albion Water Ltd v Water Services Regulation Authority (Dŵr Cymru/Shotton Paper)* went to the Court of Appeal: see the update to paragraph 10.114A, below. See also the decision on the practices of France Télécom in French overseas departments (DOM), Decision No. 09-D-24 of 28 July 2009, discussed in the update to paragraph 10.108, above, where the French Competition Authority found a margin squeeze in the pricing of broadband internet connections in la Réunion in addition to a distinct abuse of excessive pricing.   **10.114**

Domestic cases on margin squeezing: *Albion Water*. The English Court of Appeal delivered an important judgment on margin squeeze in *Albion Water Ltd v Water Services Regulation Authority (Dŵr Cymru/Shotton Paper)* [2008] EWCA Civ 536 on appeal from the decision of the Competition Appeal Tribunal [2006] CAT 23, [2007] CompAR 22 (referred to in fn 393 of the main work). The *Albion Water* judgment contains a helpful analysis of the EU and domestic case law and drew the following conclusions as to the present state of the law: paras 87 *et seq*. First, there are some features which are common to the various formulations of the test for margin squeeze in the authorities. These are the existence of two markets (upstream and downstream); a vertically integrated undertaking which is dominant on the upstream market and active (whether or not also dominant) on the   **10.114A**

downstream market; the need for access to an input from the upstream market in order to operate on the downstream market; and the setting of upstream and downstream prices by the dominant undertaking that leave an insufficient margin for an equally efficient competitor to operate profitably in the downstream market. As to the last feature, the Court of Appeal held that the earlier controversy over whether the test should refer to an 'equally efficient competitor' (in which case the analysis focuses on the costs of the dominant undertaking's own downstream operation) or a 'reasonably efficient competitor' (which focuses on the costs of an actual or potential competitor in the downstream market) was settled by the GC in *Deutsche Telekom* in favour of the former test. The Court of Appeal rejected the arguments of the dominant water supplier Dŵr Cymru Cyfyngedig for an additional requirement, namely that the competitor must either be engaged in a 'transformative activity' (that is adding value to the product or service offered downstream by the dominant undertaking) or must displace part of the service offered by the dominant thereby enabling the dominant undertaking to avoid some of its costs. The Court referred to the fact that in *Deutsche Telekom* the Commission had found that as regards the period 1998–2001 there was a negative spread between the wholesale and retail prices (that is, the retail prices were lower than the wholesale prices) and had used that negative spread as a direct measure of the margin squeeze without any need to consider the downstream costs. This approach had been approved by the GC, indicating that the avoidance of downstream costs is not a necessary feature of margin squeeze: para 101 of *Albion Water*. The Court of Appeal acknowledged that it is possible for the dominant undertaking to put forward an objective justification for the squeeze and that arguments over displacement of the dominant undertaking's activity and avoided costs are relevant and important considerations when considering that: para 106. Note that the Competition Appeal Tribunal had rejected reliance by the water regulator on an approach known as the Efficient Component Pricing Rule to calculate what access price would have been appropriate, [2006] CAT 23, [2007] CompAR 22, para 875. The appellant was not given permission to appeal against that aspect of the Tribunal's reasoning: see *Albion Water*, para 40.

See also *PT Group/ZON Group*, ECN Brief 1/2010, p2 (Portuguese Competition Authority imposed substantial fine for margin squeeze in the retail broadband access market. PT Group was the sole provider of wholesale broadband access and had over 70 per cent of the retail market. By raising wholesale prices and reducing retail prices PT Group prevented an as efficient competitor from competing profitably. Over the period of the margin squeeze competitors saw their market share shrink from 36 per cent to 19 per cent whilst PT Group experienced a 193 per cent growth rate in customers. The companies were fined over €53 million).

10.115   *Genzyme*: **remedies.**   Following the finding of margin squeeze in *Albion Water*, discussed above, the Tribunal issued a separate judgment dealing with remedies: [2009] CAT 12. For various procedural and practical reasons the Tribunal held that it was not appropriate to set a minimum retail margin in that case and the relief granted was limited to a declaration that the abuse had taken place and an order that Dŵr Cymru bring the infringement to an end and refrain from any conduct having the same or equivalent effect.

(f) Related market abuses: exclusionary non-price practices

(i) Tying and bundling

Introduction. The Commission has stated that, as regards its own enforcement priorities, it will normally take action where an undertaking is dominant in the tying market and (i) the tying and tied products are distinct products; and (ii) the tying practice is likely to lead to anti-competitive foreclosure. The risk of such fore-closure is greater where the tying or bundling strategy is a lasting one, for example in technical tying which is costly to reverse: see the Commission's Guidance on the enforcement of Article 82, OJ 2009 C45/7: Vol II, App C19, paras 47 *et seq.* **10.119**

'Pure', 'technical' and 'mixed' bundling. Fn 414. As regards US jurisprudence see also *Cascade Health Solutions v PeaceHealth*, 515 F.3d 883 (9th Cir, 2008) for discussion as to when bundled discounts have an anti-competitive effect. **10.120**

Consumables tied with machinery. See also *Soda-Club*, WUW DE-R 2268, judgment of the German Federal Supreme Court of 4 March 2008 in relation to the terms offered to customers by the dominant supplier of home water carbonation systems that enabled consumers to make their own soda water. The restriction imposed in the rental agreement for the gas carbonation bottles that prevented consumers from obtaining gas refills from anyone other than a Soda-Club licensed dealer was found to be an abuse. **10.121**

Microsoft: **technical bundling.** The Commission launched further investigations into Microsoft's conduct: COMP/39294 which concerned allegations that Microsoft had illegally refused to disclose interoperability information across a broad range of products, including information related to its Office suite. In COMP/39530 the Commission accepted commitments from Microsoft in relation to alleged abuses in the tying of its web browser Internet Explorer to its dominant PC operating system: COMP/39530 *Microsoft (Tying)*, decn of 16 December 2009. The Commission stated that although according to the case law, it could assume that the tying of a specific product and a dominant product has, by its nature, a foreclosure effect, the Commission had in this case examined such effects more closely. In considering existing barriers to entry, the Commission noted that while downloading a competing browser from the internet is in itself a technically inexpensive way of distributing web browsers, it considered that, for that distribution mode to be successful, vendors of competing browsers must first overcome users' inertia and persuade them not to limit themselves to the pre-installed Internet Explorer. Downloading a new web browser thus requires an active decision from the user who must be aware of the existence of that alternative product. The commitments (the effect of which readers may have noticed) included distributing **10.122** a choice screen software update to users who have Internet Explorer set as their default web browser giving users an opportunity to install a competing web browser. Note that the Commission has rejected a complaint against Microsoft alleging anti-competitive behaviour on the market for the provision of Enterprise Resource Planning or Enterprise Application Software and that rejection is on appeal: COMP/39784 *Omnis/Microsoft*, decn of 1 December 2010 (on appeal Case T-74/11 *Omnis Group v Commission*, not yet decided).

(ii) Refusal to supply

10.125   **Conceptual and policy difficulties relating to refusal to supply.**   Interestingly, the Commission has stated that it 'starts from the position' that even a dominant firm should have the right to choose its trading partners and dispose freely of its property: see the Commission's Guidance on the enforcement priorities in applying Article 82, OJ 2009 C45/7: Vol II, App C19, para 75. The Commission also notes that (i) it is not necessary for the refused product to have been already traded provided that there is a demand from potential purchasers; and (ii) there can be a 'constructive refusal' to supply where there is undue delay or other impediments to supply (para 79).

An abuse whereby an airport operator provided meet and greet parking services from the terminal forecourt but excluded competing operators from the forecourt and imposed a charge on the service they provided from the car park, was treated as discriminatory behaviour which operated to the detriment of consumers: *Purple Parking Ltd v Heathrow Airport Ltd* [2011] EWHC 987 (Ch). The Court rejected the suggestion that the case had to be analysed as an 'essential facilities' case.

Fn 431. In *Intecare Direct Ltd v Pfizer Ltd* [2010] EWHC 600 (Ch), [2010] ECC 28, the English High Court, when it refused to grant an injunction, held that the condition set by the allegedly dominant pharmaceutical company for supplying a scarce drug, namely that the purchaser demonstrate that the drug was intended for UK patients, was not applied in a discriminatory manner and so did not give rise to a distortion of competition.

10.127   **Discontinuing supply of services.**   See also *Europe Direct AB and ors v VPC AB*, Case No. T-32799-05, judgment of the Stockholm District Court of 20 November 2008, awarding damages for breach of the Swedish equivalent of Article 102 TFEU against the operator of the central share security depository for ceasing to supply share registers in electronic form to the claimants whose businesses involved mailings to shareholders, although VPC was not itself a competitor of the claimants; on appeal to the Svea Court of Appeal, not yet decided.

10.128   **The limited scope of 'objective justification' as regards an existing customer.**   The Court of Justice's decision in the reference from the Athens Court of Appeal has now been delivered: Cases C-468/06, etc, *Sot Lelos kai Sia EE v GlaxoSmithKline* [2008] ECR I-7139, [2008] 5 CMLR 1382, [2009] All ER (EC) 1. The CJ rejected

GlaxoSmithKline's argument that the pressure brought to bear on price levels by parallel trading brought only minimal benefits to consumers, since lower prices benefit patients who have to pay a proportion of the price of medicines: para 56. Referring to earlier case law condemning agreements aimed at partitioning national markets or at restricting parallel imports, the CJ held that 'there can be no escape' from the prohibition in Article 102 for a dominant undertaking trying to avoid all parallel exports. However, the Court also noted that it was the disparities in the degree of regulation in the different Member States which created the opportunities for parallel imports by setting prices at different levels. The competition rules should not be interpreted in such a way that in order to defend its own commercial interests, the only choice left for a dominant pharmaceuticals company is not to place its medicines on the market at all in low price Member States: para 68. The CJ therefore concluded that it would be a reasonable and proportionate measure in relation to the threat that parallel exports represent to its legitimate commercial interests for a dominant undertaking to refuse to supply a wholesaler with orders which are 'out of the ordinary' ('présentent un caractère anormal'). Thus, although a dominant pharmaceutical company cannot cease to honour the ordinary orders of an existing customer for the sole reason that the customer is exporting some of those quantities, it could refuse to supply 'significant quantities of products that are essentially destined for parallel export'. It was for the referring court to decide whether the orders at issue in the national proceedings were ordinary or not, in the light of the size of those orders in relation to the requirements of the market in the relevant Member State and the previous business relations between the dominant undertaking and the wholesalers concerned.

In *VIP Communications v OFCOM* [2009] CAT 28, the United Kingdom Competition Appeal Tribunal struck out an appeal against a rejection of a complaint which had alleged that a mobile phone operator's cessation of supply of SIM cards for use in GSM-Gateways was contrary to Article 102. The Tribunal held that since the use proposed to be made of the SIM cards by the appellant was illegal under domestic law, the phone operator's conduct could not be abusive. This was the case even if, as the appellant alleged, the provision making that use unlawful was contrary to the European telecoms directives. Cf *SIM-Card*, WuW DE-R 2427, judgment of the Oberlandesgericht Düsseldorf of 13 March 2008 where the Court rejected arguments in a similar case that the use of SIM cards in GSM-Gateways would jeopardise the position of the plaintiff under German telecommunications law and that it could cause a technical deterioration of network connectivity.

Refusal to license intellectual property rights. Fn 455. The appeal in *Der* **10.129** *Grüne Punkt* was dismissed: Case C-385/07P *Der Grüne Punkt—Duales System Deutschland v Commission*, judgment of 16 July 2009, [2009] 5 CMLR 2215. The GC analysed the case under Article 102(a) TFEU, referring to settled case law according to which an undertaking abuses its dominant position where it charges for its services fees which are disproportionate to the economic value of the service provided. The conduct objected to here, namely requiring payment of a fee for all packaging bearing the DGP logo and put into circulation in Germany, even where customers of the company show that they do not use the DGP system for some or all of that packaging, constituted an abuse of a dominant position within that case law. The CJ upheld this analysis, emphasising that the remedies imposed by the decision did not amount to an obligation to grant a licence to use the DGP logo. There was nothing in the decision which affected DSD's freedom of choice as the grant of licences—the decision at issue merely obliges DSD not to claim payment from its contractual partners for take-back and recovery services which it has not provided. Note that the GC stated that the decision did not stop DSD levying an adequate fee for merely using the DGP mark even where it is shown that the packaging bearing the DGP logo has been taken back and recovered by another system. The green dot affixed to the packaging may have economic value as such, since it can inform the consumer that the packaging may be brought to the DSD system: paras 193 and 194.

Fn 458. The appeal in *AstraZeneca* has been decided and the findings of abuse in relation to the information submitted by AstraZeneca when applying for patent protection extensions were upheld: Case T-321/05 *AstraZeneca v Commission*, judgment of 1 July 2010, [2010] 5 CMLR 1575. However, the GC disagreed with the Commission on one point, holding that the abuse only started when the documents containing the misleading statements were sent to the relevant patent offices by AstraZeneca's patent attorney, not when AstraZeneca sent the misleading information to those attorneys: paras 370–372. The case is on further appeal Case C-457/10P *AstraZeneca v Commission*, not yet decided.

10.134 **Copyright associations.**   In a dispute between a collecting society, STIM, and two commercial television broadcasters, the Swedish Market Court referred questions as to whether it was an abuse for STIM to charge royalties calculated as a percentage of the revenue earned by the broadcaster from television broadcasts directed at the general public and/or subscription sales. The percentage varied according to the amount of music broadcast by the TV station. The CJ held that there was no abuse unless another method was available which enabled the use of those works to be identified more precisely with the audience, without a disproportionate increase in the costs incurred in the management of contracts and the supervision of the use of the copyright works. The CJ left it to the national court to decide whether calculating royalties on different bases as between public service and commercial broadcasters amounted to applying dissimilar conditions to equivalent transactions, or whether such a practice was objectively justified: see Case C-52/07 *Kanal 5 Ltd and TV 4 AB v Föreningen Svenska Tonsättares Internationella Musikbyrå (STIM) upa* [2008] ECR I-9275, [2009] 5 CMLR 2175.

10.135 **Refusal of access to 'essential facilities'.**   Note that the Commission has said that cases will take priority as regards enforcement if (i) the refusal relates to a product or service which is objectively necessary to be able to compete effectively on a downstream market; (ii) the refusal is likely to lead to elimination of effective competition on the downstream market; and (iii) the refusal is likely to lead to consumer harm: see the Commission's Guidance on the enforcement of Article 82, OJ 2009 C45/7: Vol II, App C19, paras 81 *et seq*. These criteria apply to both cessation of existing supply and refusal of *de novo* supply: para 84.

In *Purple Parking Ltd v Heathrow Airport Ltd* [2011] EWHC 987 (Ch) the High Court considered the requirements for an abuse relating to access to essential facilities although ultimately found the existence of an abuse based on discrimination. The Court acknowledged that the law recognised the principles of freedom to contract with those one chooses and also the rights of the property owner to do as he pleases with his property. But the judge doubted whether the essential facilities cases required that competition be eliminated before an abuse was established. Note also that the court held that much less weight fell to be given to the rights of the airport operator as the creator of the facility because the meet and greet parking service which the claimants wanted to provide was ancillary to the purpose for which the airport forecourts had been developed. This was not, therefore, a case where the creator of the facility was being asked to 'share the real fruits of ownership with a competitor': para 174.

The criterion of 'necessity': application. Fn 497. In the case of *MLP v NMPP*, **10.138** the Cour de Cassation, judgment of 20 February 2007, rejected an appeal against the second judgment of the Paris Court of Appeal regarding the interim measures decision: BOCCRF No. 4 of 7 June 2007. NMPP then presented commitments to the French Competition Authority which were accepted, thereby concluding the proceedings.

Dominant undertakings' presence in downstream market. In *SE Vilnius Inter-* **10.140** *national Airport*, ECN Brief 3/2010, p2, the Lithuanian Supreme Administrative Court upheld a finding that the airport abused its dominant position in the market of management and organisation services on the territory of Vilnius International Airport by refusing to provide access to its infrastructure to UAB Naftelf. The Court held that the infrastructure was an essential facility to enable UAB Naftelf to enter the downstream market for the supply of fuel to aircraft at the airport, in competition with the Airport which itself operated as a supplier of fuel.

Essential facilities and cross-border discrimination. The Commission's decision **10.141** in *Clearstream* was upheld as regards both the refusal to supply and the discriminatory pricing infringements: Case T-301/04 *Clearstream Banking v Commission*, judgment of 9 September 2009. The GC emphasised that the concept of abuse is an objective one so that it was not necessary to rule on whether the Commission was right in finding that Clearstream's intention was to exclude EB from the provision of their services and, therefore, to hinder competition in the provision of cross-border secondary clearing and settlement services: para 143.

10.143 **Essential facilities in the energy sector.** See COMP/39315 *ENI*, decn of 29 September 2010; and COMP/39317 *E.ON gas foreclosure*, decn of 4 May 2010 both discussed in the update to paragraph 12.081, below.

(g) Other forms of abuse

10.146 **Unfair trading conditions.** In *CNIM v Electricité de France* [2008] ECC 208 the French Cour de Cassation (Commercial Chamber) held that a clause limiting the electricity supplier's liability for damage caused by unexpected power cuts was not an abuse even though the supplier had a legal monopoly of supply.

10.150 **Unfair trading conditions: IP licences.** Fn 535. The appeal in *Der Grüne Punkt* was dismissed: Case C-385/07P *Der Grüne Punkt—Duales System Deutschland v Commission*, judgment of 16 July 2009, [2009] 5 CMLR 2215: see update to paragraph 10.129, above.

10.151 **Limiting production, markets or technical development.** In COMP/39388&39389 *E.ON German electricity markets*, decn of 26 November 2008 the Commission accepted commitments in a case where E.ON was suspected of having limited its own production of electricity in order to raise prices in the wholesale market.

Other examples of practices that limit the access of entrants to new markets or of access generally by competitors are found in national decisions. Hence, the requirement by the Hungarian State Railway of bank guarantees from private rail companies as a condition of securing network use agreements at the time of liberalisation of the rail network was held to be part of a strategy to hinder access to the market by new entrants and thus among the practices condemned under both Article 102 TFEU and its domestic Hungarian equivalent: *Magyar Államvasutak ('MÁV')*, case 2.Kf.27.165/2008/14, judgment of the Budapest Court of Appeal of 18 February 2009; on appeal to the Supreme Court. In Italy, the Council of State upheld the Authority's decision condemning, under the Italian equivalent of Article 102, the inadequate information provided by the dominant operator of dry docks in Naples harbour regarding the times when its docks would be available to third party ship refitters. As a result of this lack of transparency, the operator, which itself had full information as to when the docks would be available, obtained a competitive advantage for its own refitting services and secured the overwhelming majority of refitting work: *O.N.I.—Cantieri del Mediterraneo*, Case No. 7589, judgment of 3 April 2009.

In Spain, the monopoly supplier and distributor of electricity in Majorca was held to have infringed Article 102 by using the information that a new client was requesting connection to the network to make an immediate offer to carry out the related installation works, and thus obtain a competitive advantage over independent electrical installers: *ASINEM-ENDESA*, Case 606/05, decn of the Spanish Court for the Defence of Competition of 14 December 2006.

Abusive alteration of the structure of the market. Where local authorities   **10.152**
adopted regulations which purported to exclude private undertakings from competing with them in the supply of refuse collection services, this was an abusive
alteration of the structure of the market by foreclosing competition and strengthening the market position of the local authorities themselves: *Neurendale Ltd t/a Panda
Waste Services v Dublin City Council* [2009] IEHC 588, para 140.

Misconduct in acquisition of property rights: *AstraZeneca*. The penultimate   **10.153**
sentence of this paragraph should read 'Moreover, it was not necessary to establish
that the misleading representations were relied on by patent agents, patent offices
and courts.' AstraZeneca's appeal was dismissed by the GC: Case T-321/05
AstraZeneca v Commission, judgment of 1 July 2010, [2010] 5 CMLR 1575. The
Court held first that the submission by a dominant undertaking to the patent offices
of objectively misleading representations which led those offices to grant it extended
patent protection to which it was not entitled constituted an abuse. The question
whether those representations were objectively misleading must be assessed in the
light of the specific circumstances and context of each individual case: para 361.
Having examined the facts in detail, the GC upheld the Commission's findings of
infringement, stating that there was no need to demonstrate bad faith or positively
fraudulent intent on AstraZeneca's part. It was sufficient to note that such conduct,
characterised by a manifest lack of transparency, was contrary to the special responsibility of an undertaking in a dominant position not to impair by its conduct genuine undistorted competition in the common market: para 493. However, the GC
disagreed with the Commission on one point, holding that the abuse only started
when the documents containing the misleading statements were sent to the relevant
patent offices by AstraZeneca's patent attorney, not when AstraZeneca sent the
misleading information to those attorneys: paras 370–372. The case is on appeal:
Case C-457/10P *AstraZeneca v Commission*, not yet decided.

See also COMP/38636 *RAMBUS*, decn of 9 December 2009, discussed in the
new paragraph 5.139A, above, where the Commission accepted commitments to
bring to an end proceedings against Rambus alleging that it had failed to disclose
patents and pending patent applications in the course of negotiations over the setting of standards for DRAM computer chips and as a result was able to charge
royalties at a level which it would not otherwise have been able to charge.

Impeding parallel imports and launch of competing products: *AstraZeneca*. The   **10.154**
GC also upheld most of the Commission's findings so far as this second abuse was
concerned: Case T-321/05 *AstraZeneca v Commission*, judgment of 1 July 2010,
[2010] 5 CMLR 1575, paras 619 *et seq*. The Court said that a dominant undertaking cannot use regulatory procedures in such a way as to prevent or make more
difficult the entry of competitors on the market, in the absence of grounds relating
to the defence of the legitimate interests of an undertaking engaged in competition
on the merits or in the absence of objective justification: para 672. However, in

relation to the deregistration of products in Denmark, the GC held that the Commission had failed to prove that the Danish or Norwegian authorities would revoke the parallel import licences of AstraZeneca's competitors when AstraZeneca deregistered its capsules. To that extent the appeal was allowed: paras 852 and 859. The GC's judgment is on appeal: Case C-457/10P *AstraZeneca v Commission*, not yet decided.

See also the conclusions of the Commission's final report on the pharmaceutical sector published on 8 July 2009. The Commission examined the practices of the pharmaceutical companies in relation to a sample of 219 different molecules. They found that entry of generic products following the expiry of patent protection was delayed by several months and that this resulted in a substantial loss of savings by health authorities. The conduct examined included patent strategies such as filing numerous patent applications for the same medicine (forming so-called 'patent clusters' or 'patent thickets'). These strategies tended to extend the breadth and duration of their patent protection. The Commission found that the number of patent litigation cases between originator and generic companies increased by a factor of four between 2000 and 2007. In total, 698 cases of patent litigation between originator companies and generic companies were reported in relation to the medicines investigated. There were 255 applications for interim injunctions by patent originator companies. Further, patent companies regularly opposed the grant of patents to generic producers and intervened in the market authorisation process by which generic companies sought licences for their products. The inquiry also examined similar trends in litigation between originating companies. The Commission stressed the need to intensify competition scrutiny both at European level and by national authorities, The Report refers to cases at the national level such as *Napp* (discussed in para 10.110); *Arrow Génériques*, judgment of the Cour de Cassation of 13 January 2009, Pourvoi No. P 08-12.510 (interim measures granted by the French competition authority to a generic company whose products were systematically criticised by a competing originator company's sales staff even after marketing authorisation) and *Glaxo-PRINCIPI ATTIVI* (Case A363), decn of Autorità Garante della Concorrenza e del Mercato of 8 February 2006, No. 15175 (refusal of an originator company to grant a licence for the production of an active ingredient, needed by producers of generic medicines to access national markets where the originator did not have any exclusive rights, infringed Article 102).

11

THE COMPETITION RULES AND THE ACTS OF MEMBER STATES

2. State Compulsion

Compliance with State measures. The stringency of the test was confirmed **11.004** recently by the Court of Justice in Case C-280/08P *Deutsche Telekom v Commission*, judgment of 14 October 2010, [2010] 5 CMLR 1485. The Court reiterated that it is only if anti-competitive conduct is required of undertakings by national legislation or if that legislation itself eliminates any possibility of competitive activity that Articles 101 and 102 will not apply. The fact that national law merely encourages or make it easier to engage in autonomous anti-competitive conduct is not enough. In that case even though the retail prices charged by DT had been investigated and approved by the German regulator, the price could still constitute a margin squeeze contrary to Article 102. The German regulator's decisions were not binding on the Commission and a dominant undertaking was still responsible for its own actions even if the regulator might itself have been open to separate infringement proceedings: paras 80 *et seq*.

For an interesting analogous situation see Case C-431/07P *Bouygues SA v Commission* [2009] ECR I-2665. The CJ upheld the finding of the GC that the apparent advantage granted by the State when it waived part of the fees to be paid by telecoms licensees did not constitute a State aid because the waiver was necessary to avoid unequal treatment of those licensees which would be contrary to the EU telecoms regulatory scheme then in force. The waiver brought their fees in line with the fees that Bouygues had agreed to pay in a later auction of the same licences. Since the GC had been right to hold that the principle of non-discrimination required the French authorities to align the fees due with those charged to Bouygues, there was no State aid.

A different approach was adopted by the Italian Competition Authority assessing whether the operators of Rome and Milan airports were charging excessive prices for access to centralised infrastructure. The ICA held that there was insufficient evidence of abuse relying on the findings of a regulatory body which had examined the prices charged and concluded that they were aligned with costs. The Tribunale Amministrativo partially overturned the ICA's decision as being insufficiently reasoned because it was based on the regulatory authority's conclusions rather than the ICA's own assessment. But on appeal, the Consiglio di Stato considered that the ICA had conducted an autonomous assessment on the existence of the anti-competitive conduct. The fact that the ICA had relied on the outcome of the regulatory proceedings to conclude that the prices for the provision of a specific service were not excessive, appeared to the judge a reasonable approach, due to the difficulty of verifying the relationship between prices and costs: *SEA SpA and AdR SpA* ECN Brief 4/2010, p2.

Fn 7. The appeal in the *French Beef* case was dismissed: Cases C-101&110/07P *Coop de France bétail et viande and FNSEA v Commission* [2008] ECR I-10193, [2009] 4 CMLR 743.

11.006   **Scope for residual competition.**   Fn 15. The appeal in *GlaxoSmithKline* has been decided: Cases C-501/06P, etc, *GlaxoSmithKline Services Unlimited v Commission*, judgment of 6 October 2009. The judgment did not consider the point raised here.

11.008   **Liability of undertakings when State compulsion is lifted.**   In *VIP Communications v OFCOM* [2009] CAT 28, the United Kingdom Competition Appeal Tribunal applied the principles in *CIF* in striking out an appeal against a rejection of a complaint which had alleged that a mobile phone operator's cessation of supply of SIM cards for use in GSM-Gateways was contrary to Article 102 TFEU. The Tribunal held that since the use proposed to be made of the SIM cards by the appellant was illegal under domestic law, the phone operator's conduct could not be abusive. This was the case even if, as the appellant alleged, the provision making that use unlawful was contrary to the European telecoms directives and the national telecoms regulator was under a duty to disapply the domestic provision. Unless or until a decision was taken to disapply the domestic provision, the phone operator was shielded from sanction for any alleged abuse. Cf *SIM-Card*, WuW DE-R 2427, judgment of the Oberlandesgericht Düsseldorf of 13 March 2008 where the Court rejected arguments in a similar case that the use of SIM cards in GSM-Gateways would jeopardise the position of the plaintiff under German telecommunications law and that it could cause a technical deterioration of network connectivity.

3. The Application and Enforcement of the Prohibition in Article 86(1)

Note that Article 86 EC is now Article 106 TFEU

11.011   **Undertakings granted special or exclusive rights.**   In COMP/38700 *Greek Lignite and Electricity generation*, decn of 5 March 2008, [2009] 4 CMLR 495 the

Commission held that it did not matter that the special or exclusive rights challenged had been granted to the electricity generating company before liberalisation of the electricity market and therefore at a time when competition was not possible. It was the maintenance of the rights (in that case the exclusive access to the cheapest form of fuel for power generation) that distorted competition once liberalisation had occurred: para 236. The case is on appeal, Case T-169/08 *DEI v Commission*, not yet decided.

See also Case C-437/09 *AG2R Prevoyance v Beaudout*, judgment of 3 March 2011, para 66 (a decision by the public authorities to make compulsory affiliation to a scheme for supplementary reimbursement of healthcare costs for all of the traditional bakery sector necessarily implies a grant to that body of an exclusive right to receive and manage the contributions paid by the employers and employees in that sector under that scheme for the purposes of Article 106).

Application in conjunction with Treaty provisions.   Fn 51. See also *Special rights* **11.015**
granted to La Banque Postale, Caisses d'Epargne and Crédit Mutuel for the distribution of the livret A and livret bleu, decn of 10 May 2007, C(2007) 2110 final, where the Commission found that the rights granted contravened Article 106 in conjunction with Article 49 TFEU (formerly Articles 86 and 43 EC). Appeals lodged against this decision (Cases T-279&289/07) were withdrawn.

Link between the measure and the breach by the undertaking.   The 'is led' for- **11.016**
mulation was used by the CJ in Case C-49/07 *Motosykletistiki Omospondia Ellados NPID (MOTOE) v Elliniko Dimosio* [2008] ECR I-4863, [2008] 5 CMLR 790, [2009] All ER (EC) 150, para 49. The CJ held that 'it is not necessary that any abuse should actually occur' and that 'in any event' Articles 102 and 106(1) 'are infringed where a measure imputable to a Member State, and in particular a measure by which a Member State confers special or exclusive rights within the meaning of Article 86(1) EC, gives rise to a risk of an abuse of a dominant position'.

Inability to satisfy demand.   In COMP/39562 *Slovakian postal legislation relat-* **11.017**
ing to hybrid mail services, decn of 7 October 2008, [2009] 4 CMLR 663 the Commission found that before the Slovakian legislation was amended to reserve a monopoly in hybrid postal services to the State-run undertaking, competitors had offered additional services such as track-and-trace which the State-run undertaking did not offer. Citing *Höfner and Elser* the Commission found that Slovakia was in breach of Article 106(1) TFEU in conjunction with Article 102 TFEU: by reserving the delivery of hybrid mail to Slovenská Pošta's, the Slovak Republic had limited the services available to users: paras 150 *et seq*. The decision is on appeal Case T-556/08 *Slovenská pošta v Commission*, not yet decided.

In Case C-437/09 *AG2R Prevoyance v Beaudout*, judgment of 3 March 2011 the CJ distinguished between a complaint that the body providing insurance services was unable to satisfy demand and a complaint that because affiliation was compulsory, a member was unable to obtain better cover offered by other providers.

11.018　**Extension of dominance into neighbouring markets.**　**Fn 58.** See also COMP/ 39562 *Slovakian postal legislation relating to hybrid mail services*, decn of 7 October 2008, [2009] 4 CMLR 663 (extension of postal services monopoly to hybrid electronic mail services), para 116. The decision is on appeal Case T-556/08 *Slovenská pošta v Commission*, not yet decided.

11.019　**Creation of conflict of interest.**　In Case C-49/07 *Motosykletistiki Omospondia Ellados NPID (MOTOE) v Elliniko Dimosio* [2008] ECR I-4863, [2008] 5 CMLR 790, [2009] All ER (EC) 150 the CJ held that Article 106(1) TFEU in conjunction with Article 102 was infringed by a national rule which confers on a legal person which organises motorcycling events and enters into sponsorship, advertising, and insurance contracts, the power to authorise such competitions, without that power being made subject to restrictions, obligations, and review. The situation of unequal conditions of competition created by the power could lead the legal person entrusted with conferring authorisations to distort competition by favouring events which it organises or those in whose organisation it participates: paras 48 *et seq*.

11.020　**Fee tariffs.**　See also the rejection of a complaint alleging breach by France of Article 106 in relation to the national telecoms regulator ARCEP's failure to prevent alleged abuses by France Télécom: COMP/39653 *Vivendi, Iliad/France Télécom*, decn of 2 July 2010 (on appeal Case T-568/10 *Vivendi v Commission*, not yet decided).

11.020A　**Creating an inequality of opportunity.**　In Case C-462/99 *Connect Austria* [2003] ECR I-5197, [2005] 5 CMLR 302 the CJ stated that a system of undistorted competition can be guaranteed only if equality of opportunity is secured as between the various economic operators. Hence if inequality of opportunity between economic operators, and therefore distorted competition, results from a State measure, such a measure constitutes an infringement of Article 106(1) TFEU in conjunction with Article 102 TFEU (see paras 83 and 84). The Commission applied this principle in COMP/38700 *Greek Lignite and Electricity generation*, decn of 5 March 2008, [2009] 4 CMLR 495 where Greece had granted the former monopoly generator of electricity quasi-monopolistic rights to explore for and exploit lignite which is the cheapest source of fuel for electricity generation. Greece had thereby created inequality of opportunity between economic operators in the wholesale electricity market and distorted competition in favour of the public undertaking, reinforcing its dominance in that market. The case is on appeal: Case T-169/08 *DEI v Commission*, not yet decided.

11.023　**Commission's discretion as to enforcement.**　**Fn 77.** See also Case T-60/05 *Union française de l'express (UFEX) v Commission* [2007] ECR II-3397, [2008] 5 CMLR 580, paras 189 *et seq*.

11.028　**Postal services.**　**Fn 91.** See also COMP/39562 *Slovakian postal legislation relating to hybrid mail services*, decn of 7 October 2008, [2009] 4 CMLR 663 (extension of postal services monopoly to hybrid electronic mail services). The decision is on appeal: Case T-556/08 *Slovenská pošta v Commission*, not yet decided.

4. Unenforceability of National Measures: Article 10

Note that the substance of Article 10 EC is now incorporated into Article 4 TEU

Development of the *INNO* principle: *Van Eycke v ASPA*.   For a post-Lisbon **11.030** case applying these principles see Case C-437/09 *AG2R Prevoyance v Beaudout*, judgment of 3 March 2011 where the CJ held there was no breach of Article 101 TFEU in conjunction with Article 4(3) TEU where public authorities enforced a collective labour agreement to make affiliation to a health insurance scheme compulsory.

Narrow application of Articles 81, 3(1)(g) and 10.   Note that Article 3(1)(g) EC **11.033** was repealed by the Lisbon Treaty and replaced in substance by Articles 3–6 TFEU. In Case C-446/05 *Doulamis* [2008] ECR I-1377 the CJ held that these Articles do not preclude a national law which prohibits dentists from advertising their services; see also Case C-386/07 *Hospital Consulting v Esaote SpA*, Order of 5 May 2008 (Treaty provisions do not preclude a national law which prohibits derogation from minimum fees approved by ministerial decree, on the basis of a draft drawn up by a professional body of lawyers and which also prohibits the court, when assessing costs, from derogating from those minimum fees); Case C-393/08 *Sbarigia v Azienda USL RM/A,* judgment of 1 July 2010 (CJ held in a reference from an Italian court that legislation which obliged a pharmacist to close her shop during the summer months could not affect trade between Member States so that the question as to the application of Articles 101, 102 and 106 was inadmissible); Case C-338/09 *Yellow Cab Verkehrsbetriebs v Landeshauptmann von Wien,* judgment of 22 December 2010 (national legislation in question did not fall within the two categories of legislation which can contravene the competition rules read in conjunction with Article 4(3) TEU).

See also *Hemat v The Medical Council* [2010] IESC 24 (advertising rules promulgated by Medical Council); *Neurendale Ltd t/a Panda Waste Services v Dublin City Council* [2009] IEHC 588 (Irish High Court held that a regulation by which local authorities purported to exclude private undertakings from offering competing refuse collection services was economic rather than administrative in nature and constituted an agreement or at least a concerted practice between them).

On national legislation which may have an anti-competitive effect, see the interaction of competition rules and the application of Article 34 TFEU in Case C-531/07 *Fachverband der Buch- und Medienwirtschaft v LIBRO Handelsgesellschaft* [2009] ECR I-3717.

Direct applicability of Article 10.   Note that the substance of what was Article 10 **11.034** EC is now found in Article 4 TEU. In *Online lotteries*, WuW DE-R 2034, judgment of 8 May 2007, the German Federal Supreme Court upheld a decision of the German competition authority prohibiting as a violation of what was then Article 10 EC, in conjunction with what is now Article 101 TFEU, an agreement between the German regional states (Länder) that they would restrict the operation of licensed lottery companies to the territory of the state granting the licence. This was found to have a particularly restrictive effect in the light of the development of online sales. But the Court quashed the authority's imposition of a mandatory requirement on the companies to offer internet sales beyond the State boundaries. A distinct agreement between the lottery companies themselves to the same effect was also prohibited as a clear violation of Article 101.

5. State Monopolies of a Commercial Character: Article 31

Note that Article 31 EC is now Article 27 TFEU

11.040 **Monopolies for import and export.**   Fn 134. The proceedings against Malta were closed after Malta adopted legislative measures to create a framework for a new licensing procedure to allow companies other than the former State monopoly to apply for a licence to import: Press Release IP/07/1952 (18 December 2007).

6. Derogations under Articles 86(2) and 296

Note that Article 86(2) EC is now Article 106(2) TFEU and Article 296 EC is now Article 346 TFEU

(a) Article 86(2): services of general interest

11.048 **Article 86(2) and State aids.**   See also Case T-442/03 *SIC v Commission* [2008] ECR II-1161 where the GC considered the alleged grant of State aid to a public service television broadcaster.

11.049 **The task entrusted.**   Fn 159. The Supreme Court of Ireland allowed the appeal: see update to paragraph 11.053, below.

11.050 **Services of general economic interest.**   Member States have a wide discretion to define what they regard as SGEIs and the definition of such services by a Member State can be questioned by the Commission only in the event of manifest error: Case T-289/03 *BUPA v Commission* [2008] ECR II-81, para 166 (a State aid case). The GC went on to hold that a private medical insurance scheme adopted by Ireland did have an SGEI mission. The GC held that to be an SGEI, the service in question does not need to be a universal service in the strict sense of responding to a need common to the whole population or being supplied throughout a territory. The fact that the SGEI obligations in question have only a limited territorial or material application or that the services concerned are enjoyed by only a relatively limited group of users does not necessarily call in question the universal nature of an SGEI mission. Thus the GC found that a private medical insurance scheme was an SGEI even though the complainant argued that the insurance represented only optional, indeed 'luxury', financial services. Further, the compulsory nature of the SGEI mission does not preclude a certain latitude being left to the operator on the market, including in relation to the content and pricing of the services which it proposes to provide. The compulsory nature of the service and, accordingly, the existence of an SGEI mission are established if the service provider is obliged to contract, on consistent conditions, without being able to reject the other contracting party. That element makes it possible to distinguish a service forming part of an SGEI mission from any other service provided on the market.

As regards public service television broadcasting see Case T-442/03 *SIC v Commission* [2008] ECR II-1161 (a State aid case) where the GC upheld the power of the Member States to designate as a service of general economic interest, the service provided by a public broadcasting undertaking even though the undertaking broadcasts a wide range of programmes and was able to carry on commercial activities, such as the sale of advertising space. The GC held that the Commission must satisfy itself that there is in place a mechanism for the State to monitor compliance by the undertaking of its public service remit: para 213. On the facts, the GC found that the Commission had failed to ensure that it had reliable information available to determine what public services were actually supplied and what costs were actually incurred in supplying them. In the absence of such information, the GC held, the Commission was unable to proceed to a meaningful verification of whether the funding under challenge was proportionate to the public service costs and was unable to make a valid finding that there had been no overcompensation of the public service costs. The Commission's decision was therefore annulled.

The Commission has published a Communication on Services of general interest, including social services of general interest, COM(2007) 725 adopted on 20 November 2007. The Communication refers to the Protocol to be annexed by the Treaty of Lisbon to the TEU and the TFEU as part of an attempt to establish a 'transparent and reliable' EU framework which respects the principles of subsidiarity and proportionality. For the Protocol now see OJ 2007 C306/158.

Fn 166. The appeal by Deutsche Telekom was dismissed both by the GC and the CJ: Case T-271/03 *Deutsche Telekom v Commission* [2008] ECR II-477; and Case C-280/08P *Deutsche Telekom v Commission*, judgment of 14 October 2010, [2010] 5 CMLR 1485.

Fn 169. The appeal in Case T-490/04 was removed from the register. Note that the correct citation for the article referred to is (2005) 1 EC Competition Policy Newsletter 31.

Fn 174. See now COMP/38698 *CISAC*, decn of 16 July 2008, [2009] 4 CMLR 577 where the Commission noted that in the *GVL* case the German legislation had not conferred the management of copyright or related rights on specific undertakings.

The Commission left open whether Article 106(2) TFEU could apply to collecting societies in a Member State where legislation describes the function and the status of the collecting society in a way which allows the assumption that the collecting society is entrusted with the operation of services of general economic interest: para 257. The decision is on appeal: Cases T-398, 410, 411, 413–422, 425, 432, 434, 442, 451/08, not yet decided.

Fn 175. Note that the Commission has accepted that the provision of banking services to sections of the population who have difficulty accessing basic banking services can be a service of general economic interest: see *Special rights granted to La Banque Postale, Caisses d'Epargne and Crédit Mutuel for the distribution of the livret A and livret bleu*, decn of 10 May 2007, C(2007) 2110 final, where the Commission found that the rights granted contravened Article 106 in conjunction with Article 49 TFEU (formerly Articles 86 and 43 EC). Appeals against this decision (Cases T-279&289/07) were withdrawn.

11.052   **Obstructing the performance of the tasks.**   In COMP/39562 *Slovakian postal legislation relating to hybrid mail services*, decn of 7 October 2008, [2009] 4 CMLR 663 the Commission stated that even though there is a presumption of *prima facie* justification under Article 106(2) TFEU for services covered by the reserved area as defined in the Postal Directive (cf Point 8.3 of the Postal Notice), that did not apply in this case because the hybrid service had at first been liberalised by Slovakia and the functioning of the public service had not been endangered: para 165. The subsequent extension of the monopoly to cover the service therefore needed specific justification. The Commission agreed with using the net avoided cost methodology to calculate the costs of providing the universal service, but did not accept the evidence as to those costs put forward by Slovakia. In particular, the Commission held that it is not permissible under the Postal Directive to finance services other than the universal postal services by maintaining or extending those reserved areas. The cost of providing other services, such as financial services, cannot be included in the cost of the universal service. The Commission therefore found that Slovakia was in breach of Article 106(1) in conjunction with Article 102. The decision is on appeal Case T-556/08 *Slovenská pošta v Commission*, not yet decided.

11.053   The *Dutch Sectoral Pension Funds* cases.   The principles set out here were applied in Case C-437/09 *AG2R Prevoyance v Beaudout*, judgment of 3 March 2011.

Fn 186. The Supreme Court allowed the appeal in *BUPA Ireland Ltd v Health Insurance Authority* [2008] IESC 42, holding that the 'risk equalisation scheme' was *ultra vires* the Irish statute. The Supreme Court therefore did not address the Article 106(2) argument and BUPA's damages claim against the State for violation of Article 106 is continuing in the High Court. The State argues that there was nonetheless objective justification for the anti-competitive nature of the scheme so that it did not violate competition law; and further that BUPA caused its own loss by leaving the market before its appeal was determined.

12

SECTORAL REGIMES

2. Transport

(a) Introduction

Implementation of Articles 81 and 82 in the transport sector. Regulation **12.006**
1017/68 has been replaced by Regulation 169/2009 (OJ 2009 L61/1) which codifies the amendments previously made to the earlier Regulation. See further the
updates to subsequent paragraphs.

(b) Rail, road and inland waterway transport

(i) Application of Community competition rules

Introduction. Regulation 1017/68 has been replaced by Regulation 169/2009 **12.009**
(OJ 2009 L61/1) which codifies the amendments previously made to the earlier
Regulation.

Scope of Regulation 1017/68. The much amended Regulation 1017/68 has **12.010**
been replaced by a codifying measure, Regulation 169/2009 (OJ 2009 L61/1).
Article 1 of the new Regulation repeats Article 1 of Regulation 1017/68, listing the
kinds of agreements decisions or concerted practices covered. It also states that the
Regulation applies to the abuse of a dominant position in the transport market.

Exception for technical agreements. Article 2 of Regulation 169/2009 repeats **12.011**
Article 3 of the old Regulation, as amended. The word 'sole' does not appear before
'object or effect' in the new Article 2 or in preamble para (7).

Exemption for groups of small- and medium-sized undertakings. The equiva- **12.012**
lent provision in Regulation 169/2009 is Article 3.

Article 82. See also *Magyar Államvasutak ('MÁV')*, case 2.Kf.27.165/2008/14, **12.014**
judgment of the Budapest Court of Appeal of 18 February 2009, discussed in
the update to paragraph 10.151, above. The Court upheld the decision of the
Hungarian Competition Authority condemning various acts engaged in by the
Hungarian State Railway company to hinder access by new entrants at the time of

rail liberalisation in Hungary (including the conclusion of long-term exclusive agreements with major shippers of bulk products). The case is on appeal to the Supreme Court.

(c) Maritime transport

(i) Scope of application of the competition rules

12.019   **Repeal of Regulation 4056/86.**   The Commission has issued guidelines concerning the application of Article 101 TFEU to liner shipping services, cabotage and tramp services, see Guidelines on the application of Article 81 of the EC Treaty to maritime transport services, OJ 2008 C245/2, [2008] 5 CMLR 1037: Vol II, App E7C. The Guidelines cover the definition of relevant product and geographic markets, indicating that containerised liner shipping services are likely to constitute a separate relevant market from other forms of transport, because only an insufficient proportion of the goods carried by container can easily be switched to other modes of transport, such as air transport services. See Bermig and Ritter, 'The new Guidelines on the application of Article 81 of the EC Treaty to the maritime sector' (2008) 3 Competition Policy Newsletter 25.

12.020   **Agreements outside Article 81(1).**   See now the Commission's Guidelines on the application of Article 81 of the EC Treaty to maritime transport services, OJ 2008 C245/2, [2008] 5 CMLR 1037: Vol II, App E7C. These describe the kinds of agreements among liner shipping carriers and tramp shipping operators that generally do not come within Article 101 TFEU. These include technical agreements (such as agreements aimed at implementing technical improvements or achieving technical cooperation or relating to the implementation of environmental standards, but excluding agreements relating to price or capacity); certain kinds of information exchange agreements and pool agreements in tramp shipping where the participants are not actual or potential competitors. Conversely pool agreements between competitors limited to joint selling have as a rule the object and effect of coordinating the pricing policy of these competitors and will fall within Article 101(1). Tramp shipping pools which do not involve joint selling but nevertheless entail some degree of coordination on the parameters of competition (eg joint scheduling or joint purchasing) will be subject to Article 101(1) if the parties to the agreement have some degree of market power.

See also COMP/39416 *Ship Classification*, decn of 14 October 2009 discussed in the update to paragraph 5.135, above.

(ii) Block exemption for liner conferences

12.022   **Transitional period of application.**   See now the Guidelines on the application of Article 81 of the EC Treaty to maritime transport services, OJ 2008 C245/2: Vol II, App E7C discussed in the updates to paragraphs 12.019 and 12.020, above.

(iii) Block exemption for consortia

Generally. The Commission has replaced Regulation 479/92 with a consolidated **12.029** enabling regulation: Regulation 246/2009 on the application of Article 81(3) of the Treaty to certain categories of agreements, decisions and concerted practices between liner shipping companies (consortia), OJ 2009 L79/1: Vol II, App E7A.

Regulation 823/2000. The Commission has also adopted a new block exemp- **12.030** tion for liner consortia: Regulation 906/2009, OJ 2009 L256/31: Vol II, App E7B. The Regulation entered into force on 26 April 2010 when Regulation 823/2000 expired. The Regulation applies only to consortia insofar as they provide international liner shipping services from or to one or more European Union ports. But the new Regulation extends to all liner shipping cargo services, whether containerised or not. The definition of a consortium has been revised slightly so that it is now:

> '[A]n agreement or a set of interrelated agreements between two or more vessel-operating carriers which provide international liner shipping services exclusively for the carriage of cargo relating to one or more trades, the object of which is to bring about cooperation in the joint operation of a maritime transport service, and which improves the service that would be offered individually by each of its members in the absence of the consortium, in order to rationalise their operations by means of technical, operational and/or commercial arrangements.'

The list of exempted activities has been revised in order to reflect current market practices and hard-core restrictions such as price-fixing and market- or customer-sharing will still deprive the agreement of the benefit of the exemption. The market share threshold has been reduced from 35 per cent to 30 per cent and the method of its calculation has been clarified. The permissible restrictions on a member withdrawing from the consortium have also been revised.

(d) Air transport

(i) Scope of application of the competition rules

Developments following the '*Open Skies*' judgment. See also Gremminger, **12.038** 'New EU–US cooperation agreement in air transport' (2007) 2 Competition Policy Newsletter 27.

(ii) The sectoral rules applicable to the air transport sector

Scope of Regulation 3976/87. Regulation 3976/87 and the regulations amend- **12.041** ing it have been repealed and replaced by a consolidating instrument: Regulation 487/2009 on the application of Article 81(3) of the Treaty to certain categories of agreements and concerted practices in the air transport sector, OJ 2009 L148/1: Vol II, App E9A. The kinds of block exemption regulations that the Commission may adopt remain as set out in the text.

(iii) Particular issues

12.048 **Computer reservation systems.** Note that in a merger case, Case M.4523 *Travelport/Worldspan* (21 August 2007) the Commission defined global distribution systems as a separate relevant product market.

12.049 **CRS code of conduct.** Regulation 2299/89 has been repealed and replaced by Regulation 80/2009, OJ 2009 L35/47 as from 29 March 2009. The new Regulation prohibits the imposition of unfair and/or unjustified conditions by the system vendor on participating carriers. It also provides that transport providers must not discriminate against competing CRSs by refusing to provide data. Information on bus services for air transport products or rail transport products which are incorporated alongside air transport products should be included in the principal display. The Commission has also published an explanatory note with regard to the definition of 'parent carrier' in the Regulation: OJ 2009 C53/4.

12.050 **Groundhandling services.** In COMP/38469 *Athens International Airport*, decn of 2 May 2005, the Commission rejected a number of complaints about charges for ground services provided at Athens airport. The decision was primarily based on lack of EU interest although the Commission did carry out a comparison of the charges with those at other airports. The Commission also indicated that the carrying out of passenger security checks was not an economic activity covered by Article 102 TFEU (para 49) and that it was likely that car parking services did not form a relevant product market but competed with other means of travelling to the airport (paras 120 *et seq*). On appeal, the GC upheld the Commission's decision that there was no EU interest: Case T-306/05 *Scippacercola and Terezakis v Commission* [2008] ECR II-4*, [2008] 4 CMLR 1418, see paras 145 *et seq* (further appeal dismissed Case C-159/08P, Order of 25 March 2009).

3. Energy

(b) Electricity

(i) Generally

12.059 **Market structure generally.** In COMP/39351 *Swedish Interconnectors*, decn of 14 April 2010, the Commission defined the electricity transmission market including the transmission grid at the voltage level of 220–400 kV and the interconnectors connected to this voltage level, in line with previous decisional practice cited there: para 19. See also Case M.5549 *EDF/Segebel* (12 November 2009) where the Commission also included instruments for trading electricity in the relevant market but did not segment the market according to the source of the electricity (decn on appeal Case T-224/10 *Association Belge des Consommateurs Tests-Achats v Commission*, not yet decided).

(ii) Liberalisation

The Electricity Directive. Directive 2003/54 is being repealed and replaced by **12.061**
Directive 2009/72 concerning common rules for the internal market in electricity,
OJ 2009 L211/55. This new directive is part of the 'Third Energy Package', intended
to improve the functioning of the European Union's internal market for gas and
electricity. The Directive establishes common rules for the generation, transmission, distribution, and supply of electricity, together with consumer protection
provisions. It lays down rules on the organisation and functioning of the electricity
sector, open access to the market, calls for tender, granting of authorisations and
system operation. The Directive requires Member States to ensure that electricity
companies are operated so as to achieve a competitive, secure and environmentally
sustainable market in electricity. It also requires Member States to ensure universal
service (ie the right to be supplied with electricity of a specified quality at reasonable, easily and clearly comparable, transparent and non-discriminatory prices).
Final customers must be protected, especially vulnerable customers and those in
remote areas. From 3 March 2012, Member States must ensure the separation
('unbundling') of transmission systems and transmission system operators. The
Directive had to be implemented by 3 March 2011, on which date all its requirements are to be applied other than Article 11. That Article, which relates to certification of transmission systems owned or operated by persons in third countries,
will apply from 3 March 2013.

(iii) Long-term arrangements and exclusivity

Length of exclusivity. The Commission opened proceedings under Article 102 **12.066**
TFEU against EDF (the French electricity supplier) because of concerns over a
contract concluded between EDF and Exeltium, a consortium of large industrial
electricity consumers in France. Under the arrangement, EDF would supply
significant volumes of electricity to the consortium on a very long term basis, subject to restrictions on resale. The Commission closed its file after substantial amendments were made to address these concerns: (i) securing an effective opt-out for
the members of the consortium wishing to contract with other suppliers; (ii) removing various contractual resale restrictions; and (iii) other resale restrictions being
lifted by amendments to certain provisions of the legal and regulatory framework by the French authorities: COMP/39386 *EDF/Exeltium*, MEMO/08/533
(31 July 2008).

See also COMP/39386 *Long term contracts—France*, decn of 17 March 2010 where
the Commission accepted commitments from EDF to allay concerns arising from
the long term exclusive supply contracts it had entered into with large industrial
customers. The contracts also contained clauses preventing the customers from
reselling the electricity. Under the commitments, EDF undertook (i) to return a
significant volume of its electricity supply to the market each year to enable those
volumes to be made available to its competitors; (ii) to limit the duration of new

contracts to five years (or to include a free opt out from the contract every five years); (iii) to offer the option of non-exclusive supply to all customers; and (iv) to drop the resale restrictions imposed on customers and inform customers with a contract that any clause restricting resale will be deemed null and void. The commitments last for 10 years or until EDF's market share drops below a set threshold.

12.066A **Market definition in electricity supply.** So far as the geographic market is concerned, the Commission noted in COMP/38700 *Greek Lignite and Electricity generation*, decn of 5 March 2008, [2009] 4 CMLR 495 that the market for wholesale electricity (generation and imports of electricity for further resale) is national or smaller in scope. A further distinction may be made between 'the inter-connected system', ie mainland Greece and the interconnected islands, and 'the non-interconnected system'. Given that there is no competition possible at the wholesale level in 'the non-interconnected system', the decision addressed only the 'interconnected system'. Thus the geographical scope of the electricity whole-sale market concerned was the territory of the 'interconnected system'. The case is on appeal: Case T-169/08 *DEI v Commission*, not yet decided.

See also COMP/39388&39389 *E.ON German electricity markets*, decn of 26 November 2008 where the Commission distinguished between the wholesale electricity market in which electricity is bought for further resale and the market for balancing power needed to maintain the appropriate tension level in the grid. Because of certain technical differences and differences in demand the Commission also distinguished between secondary balancing reserves on the one hand and tertiary balancing reserves on the other. The relevant product market was therefore limited to the market for secondary balancing reserves: para 46.

The Commission has identified three distinct markets for the retail supply of elec-tricity to final customers: (i) the supply of electricity to large industrial and commercial customers; (ii) the supply of electricity to small industrial and com-mercial customers; and (iii) the supply of electricity to residential customers: see COMP/39386 *Long term contracts—France*, decn of 17 March 2010 and the cases cited there. In that case, the Commission also distinguished between those custom-ers who had exercised their 'eligibility' under French law, ie who had opted not to pay a regulated price but to pay according to unregulated tariffs. The Commission excluded from the relevant market the supply of electricity to make good network losses, and the self-supply by electricity generators ('auto-consumption'). The retail markets are generally separate from the electricity transmission market, the geo-graphic scope of which is regarded as each transmission operator's network: COMP/39351 *Swedish Interconnectors*, decn of 14 April 2010.

12.067 **Exclusivity and Article 82.** In a combined decision, the Commission accepted commitments in investigations under Article 102 TFEU into the electricity wholesale market and the electricity balancing market in Germany: COMP/39388&39389 *E.ON German electricity markets*, decn of 26 November 2008.

The Commission came to the provisional conclusion that E.ON and two other electricity companies held a collective dominant position on the wholesale market (that is generation and import of electricity for resale) and that the suspected practices of E.ON of withholding capacity and deterring investment in generation raised Article 102 concerns. Further the Commission considered that E.ON might be dominant on the market for secondary reserves and was suspected of favouring its affiliated companies as well as preventing power producers from other Member States from selling balancing energy into the balancing markets, in possible breach of Article 102.

Other abuses in relation to electricity production. In COMP/38700 *Greek* **12.067A**
Lignite and Electricity generation, decn of 5 March 2008, [2009] 4 CMLR 495 the Commission held that Greece was in breach of Article 106(1) TFEU by maintaining in place rights which gave the former monopoly electricity generating company exclusive access to lignite deposits; lignite being the cheapest available source of fuel for electricity generation. The case is on appeal: Case T-169/08 *DEI v Commission*, not yet decided.

National or European markets. Fn 193. The Commission has followed its previ- **12.069**
ous practice in Case M.3440 *ENI/EDP/GdP* in defining relevant markets in the electricity sector: see COMP/39388&39389 *E.ON German electricity markets*, decn of 26 November 2008.

(v) Imports and exports

National monopolies investigated under Article 31. Note that Article 31 EC is **12.071**
now Article 27 TFEU.

Cumulative effect to establish import/export ban. The Commission has also **12.072**
brought proceedings where a dominant electricity transmission undertaking (SvK) treated transmission services for domestic supply differently from transmission services intended to export electricity through an interconnector: COMP/39351 *Swedish Interconnectors*, decn of 14 April 2010. The Commission alleged that demand for domestic transmission services was satisfied where transmission capacity was available, whereas in a significant number of hours and to a significant extent demand for transmission services to or over interconnectors was refused despite transmission capacity being available. The Commission accepted commitments to subdivide the Swedish transmission system into two or more bidding zones after which SvK would manage congestion in the Swedish transmission system without limiting trading capacity on interconnectors.

(c) **Gas**

(i) Generally

Market structure. In Case M.5585 *Centrica/Venture Production* (21 August **12.073**
2009) the Commission considered the definition of relevant product markets

at each stage of the production and supply of gas from exploration to retail supply. The Commission indicated that exploration, ie the finding of new hydrocarbon reserves, constitutes a separate product market and that there is no distinction between the exploration for oil on the one hand and exploration for natural gas on the other. However, it is appropriate to define separate product markets for the upstream production of crude oil and another relevant market for the upstream production of natural gas.

See also the discussion of market definition in COMP/39317 *E.ON gas foreclosure*, decn of 4 May 2010 where the Commission distinguished between the market for gas transport from that of gas supply or sale; between interruptible and firm capacity and between transport of high calorific and low calorific gas; in COMP/39316 *Gaz de France (GDF Suez)*, decn of 8 July 2009 the Commission discussed, as regards gas supply, dividing the market between the wholesale supply of gas to shippers, such as local distribution companies, and retail supply to final customers and, further, into supply via the transmission network and supply via the distribution network, on the one hand, and supply by type of customer—household, professional, or industrial—on the other. In the case of supply via distribution networks, the Commission found that a distinction could be drawn between non-household customers and household customers as the two categories have somewhat different consumer habits and needs. So far as gas infrastructure is concerned, the Commission in its preliminary assessment defined a market in gas import capacity, including import capacity via gas pipelines and via LNG terminals and distinguished between firm capacity and interruptible (including conditional) capacity and between H gas, with a high calorific value, and B gas, with a low calorific value, both in the gas import capacity market and in the gas supply markets. The geographic market for the supply of gas was defined as the balancing zone of the transport network in France and as regards the market for gas import capacity, the Commission concluded that the capacities of all the gas import infrastructures in each balancing zone of the transport network in France, including interconnection capacity between the balancing zones of the GRTgaz network, could be considered as belonging to a single relevant geographic market; Case M.5549 *EDF/Segebel* (12 November 2009), paras 167 *et seq*.

(ii) Liberalisation

12.075 **The Gas Directive.**   Directive 2003/55 is being repealed and replaced by Directive 2009/73 concerning common rules for the internal market in natural gas, OJ 2009 L211/94. This new Directive is part of the 'Third Energy Package', intended to improve the functioning of the European Union's internal market for gas and electricity. The Directive establishes common rules for the transmission, distribution, supply and storage of natural gas. It lays down rules on the organisation and functioning of the natural gas sector, access to the market, the criteria and procedures applicable to the granting of authorisations for transmission, distribution, supply and storage of natural gas, and systems operation. The Directive also applies to biogas and to gas from biomass and other types of gas able to be injected into, and transported through, the natural gas system. Member States are required to ensure that natural gas companies are operated so as to achieve a competitive, secure and environmentally sustainable market in natural gas. Final customers must be protected, especially vulnerable customers and those in remote areas. Member States must ensure that all customers connected to the gas network are entitled to have their gas provided by a supplier from any Member State. Member States must also ensure the separation ('unbundling') of transmission systems and transmission system operators. The Directive is to be implemented by 3 March 2011, on which date all its requirements are to be applied other than Article 11. That Article, which relates to certification of transmission systems owned or operated by persons in third countries, will apply from 3 March 2013.

In Case C-347/06 *ASM Brescia v Comune de Rodengo* [2008] ECR I-5641, [2008] 3 CMLR 1024 the CJ held, in an Article 267 TFEU reference, that Article 23(1) of Directive 2003/55 concerns the supply of natural gas not its distribution and therefore does not oblige Member States to bring to an end distribution contracts previously granted without a competitive tendering procedure. The Directive does not require existing concessions for the distribution of gas to be called into question and indeed the CJ stated that the principle of legal certainty requires the early termination of such a concession to be coupled with a transitional period which enables the contracting parties to untie their contractual relations in a satisfactory manner.

(iii) Application of competition rules

Territorial restrictions.   The Commission has negotiated the removal of territo-   **12.079**
rial restrictions in gas supply contracts concluded by the Algerian gas producer Sonatrach. Algeria agreed to delete territorial restrictions and also not to include profit sharing mechanisms whereby the buyer/importer was obliged to share part of the profit with the supplier/producer if the gas was sold on by the importer to a customer outside the agreed territory or to a customer using the gas for a purpose other than the one agreed upon. These mechanisms had been used as an alternative to territorial restrictions: COMP/37811 *Algerian gas imports* Press Release IP/07/1074 (11 July 2007).

See also COMP/39401 *E.ON—GDF*, decn of 8 July 2009 where the Commission imposed fines of €533 million each on E.ON and Gaz de France for a market-sharing agreement entered into in respect of Russian gas transported by them through the MEGAL pipeline under which each of them agreed that they would not supply the transported gas into the other's home market.

Long-term contracts and developing markets.   In COMP/39316 *Gaz de France*   **12.080**
(GDF Suez), decn of 8 July 2009 the Commission accepted commitments to

overcome competition concerns raised by GDF's reservations for itself of a substantial part of total firm import capacity in each of the balancing zones of the gas transmission network over a very long period of time. This meant that third party shippers did not have access to this capacity under conditions that would allow them to exert effective competition on the downstream gas supply markets in these zones. The Commission analysed this as amounting to a refusal by GDF Suez to supply an essential input. The refusal to supply also took the form of a strategic limitation of investment in additional import capacity. The commitments bound GDF Suez to release capacity onto the market and to limit its future reservations of capacity.

Fn 224. The Commission accepted commitments from Distrigas as mentioned in the footnote: COMP/37966 *Distrigas*, decn of 11 October 2007. The Commission calculated the proportion of the relevant market tied to Distrigas by its existing contracts and decided that the contracts concluded by Distrigas significantly foreclosed the relevant market in a way that could constitute an abuse of its dominant position. Distrigas gave commitments whereby, first, on average a minimum of 70 per cent of the gas volumes supplied by Distrigas to industrial users and electricity producers in Belgium will return to the market each year. Secondly, contracts with industrial users and electricity producers would not be for longer than five years. Thirdly, Distrigas undertook not to conclude any gas supply agreements with resellers with a duration of over two years.

12.081   **Third party access.**   In COMP/39402 *RWE (gas foreclosure)*, decn of 18 March 2009, [2009] 5 CMLR 1667 the Commission has accepted a commitment from RWE to divest its entire high pressure West German gas transmission network to allay Commission concerns about access to the network. The Commission had suspected a possible refusal to supply gas transmission services to other companies and a margin squeeze aimed at lowering the margins of RWE's downstream competitors in gas supply.

In COMP/39315 *ENI*, decn of 29 September 2010, the Commission accepted commitments to bring to an end proceedings under Article 102 alleging ENI managed and operated its natural gas transmission pipelines with the aim of limiting third party access to available and new capacity. The allegations included refusing to grant competitors access to capacity available on the transport network (capacity hoarding), granting access in an impractical manner (capacity degradation), and strategically limiting investment (strategic underinvestment) in ENI's international transmission pipelines. The commitments required divestment of shareholdings in companies related to international gas transmission pipelines since this would remove the inherent conflict of interest ENI faced operating both as a transmission system operator and as a company active on the Italian wholesale market. The Commission stated that only a structural remedy was effective: 'Decisions both with respect to day-to-day management of gas transmission systems and to invest in transport capacity should be taken not only independently by the TSO [transmission systems operator], but also having regard to the commercial interests (i.e. profit maximising) of the TSO alone and not of any particular gas supplier. Only by this means is it possible to remove the link between the decisions on the TSO level and the interests of downstream profitability': para 91. See similarly COMP/39317 *E.ON gas foreclosure*, decn of 4 May 2010 where the Commission described E.ON's gas transmission system as an essential supply facility. The Commission was concerned that E.ON had made long term bookings for almost all the capacity in its own pipe line system, thereby excluding competitors from being able to transport their gas through its network. The Commission regarded these bookings as a refusal to supply an essential input. The Commission accepted commitments by E.ON to release capacity in the short and long term.

(d) Energy and the environment

Competition rules. The Horizontal Cooperation Guidelines referred to in the text have been replaced by the Horizontal Cooperation Guidelines issued in 2011: OJ 2011 C11/1: Vol II, App C22. The new Guidelines do not contain specific provisions about standards for environmental objectives. Such agreements are now covered by the general Guidelines. The Commission has stated that this does not imply any downgrading of the assessment of environmental agreements: MEMO/10/676 (14 December 2010) para 12. See also the examples given at paras 329, 331 and 332 of the Guidelines.   **12.086**

4. Electronic Communications

(a) Regulatory framework

Overview of regulatory framework. At the end of November 2009 a new pack-   **12.089** age of measures amending certain aspects of the regulatory framework was adopted. The new package comprised three measures (i) Directive 2009/140/EC, OJ 2009 L337/37, known as the Better Regulation Directive which amends the Framework Directive, the Authorisation Directive and the Access Directive; (ii) Directive 2009/136/EC, OJ 2009 L337/11, known as the Citizens' Rights Directive which amends the Universal Services Directive and the e-Privacy Directive; (iii) Regulation 2009/1211, OJ 2009 L337/1 which establishes a new European Telecoms Authority 'BEREC' (Body of European Regulators for Electronic Communications) to replace the European Regulators Group. The Framework Directive was also amended by Regulation 544/2009 OJ 2009 L167/12 which primarily deals with roaming.

Among the main reforms introduced by these measures were:

- an enhancement of the Commission's powers in relation to remedies proposed by national communications authorities to deal with significant market power (see the new paragraph 12.104A, below);

- various measures to benefit consumers, for example setting minimum time limits for number portability; requiring more information to be provided about the services acquired, in particular minimum service quality levels; and enhancing protection against personal data breaches and spam: see the amendments to the Universal Services Directive made by the Citizen's Rights Directive;
- rules to strengthen the political independence of national regulators: see the new Article 3(3a) of the Framework Directive inserted by Article 1(3) of the Better Regulation Directive;
- introduction of functional separation as a new regulatory remedy available to all national regulators: see the new Articles 13a and 13b of the Access Directive inserted by Article 2(10) of the Better Regulation Directive;
- a new chapter in the Framework Directive covering security and integrity of networks and services.

The Member States were obliged to implement the new provisions by 26 May 2011. The provisions which proved most controversial were the safeguards to be put in place to restrict the rights of Member States to impose limits on an individual's access to the internet. A new Article 1(3a) inserted into the Framework Directive provides that any measures taken by Member States regarding end-users' access to the internet shall respect the individual's human rights under the ECHR.

12.090 **Scope of the regulatory framework.**   In Case C-262/06 *Deutsche Telekom v Bundesrepublik Deutschland* [2007] ECR I-10057, [2008] 4 CMLR 240, the CJ held, on an Article 267 TFEU reference, that the transitional provisions in Article 27 of the Framework Directive maintained in force temporarily all obligations that had been imposed on a dominant provider under the previous regulatory framework.

(i) The Framework Directive

12.092 **Harmonisation.**   Fn 257. Many of these provisions have been amended by the package of reforms adopted at the end of 2009, particularly by the Better Regulation Directive, see update to paragraph 12.089, above. The Commission has published a consolidated version of the Framework Directive on the Information Society section of its website.

12.093 **Obligations on NRAs.**   Note that the amendments to Article 3 of the Framework Directive inserted by Article 1(3) of the Better Regulation Directive (Directive 2009/140/EC, OJ 2009 L337/37), expand on the need for the NCA to be independent and properly resourced.

Fn 263. For the relationship between the NRA's dispute resolution function and its analysis of SMP in a relevant market see *Hutchison 3G UK Ltd v OFCOM* [2009] EWCA Civ 683.

Fn 264. The wording of Article 4 of the Framework Directive was amended by Article 4(4) of the Better Regulation Directive and an additional provision added requiring Member States to collect information about appeals and decisions granting interim relief.

Technology neutrality.   Article 8 of the Framework Directive has been amended   **12.094**
by Article 1(8) of the Better Regulation Directive.

Ex ante **conditions on operators with SMP.**   Article 7 of the Framework Directive   **12.098**
has been replaced by a new version inserted by Article 1(6) of the Better Regulation
Directive. Article 16 of the Framework Directive has also been substantially
amended by Article 1(18) of the Better Regulation Directive, in particular imposing an obligation on NRAs to carry out an analysis of each relevant market every
three years (though this period may be extended where the NRA has notified a
reasoned proposed extension to the Commission and the Commission has not
objected) or two years after a revised Recommendation on Relevant Markets in
respect of a market not previously notified to the Commission.

SMP requires a 'prospective' analysis.   Fn 289. As regards the *Hutchison 3G* case   **12.100**
there mentioned, OFCOM held that there was insufficient buyer power to counteract Hutchison's dominance: this was upheld on appeal by the Competition
Appeal Tribunal and then by the Court of Appeal: *Hutchison 3G UK Ltd v OFCOM*
[2009] EWCA Civ 683.

The Recommendation on Relevant Markets.   The 2003 Recommendation   **12.101**
referred to in this paragraph has been replaced by the 2007 Recommendation, OJ
2007 L344/65. This Recommendation sets out the three cumulative criteria to be
applied in determining whether a market is one where *ex ante* regulation may be
warranted, namely (a) the presence of high and non-transitory barriers to entry
which may be of a structural, legal or regulatory nature; (b) a market structure
which does not tend towards effective competition within the relevant time horizon; and (c) the insufficiency of competition law alone adequately to address the
market failure(s) concerned. The Annex to the Recommendation now lists only
seven markets identified by the Commission on the basis of those criteria. When
considering whether SMP exists in markets not included in the Annex to the
Recommendation, the Member States must apply those three criteria. For the
application of this Recommendation in the merger context see, eg Case M.5148
Deutsche Telekom/OTE (2 October 2008) and the cases cited therein. For the application of the new Recommendation in two recent notifications by the Polish NRA
see Szarka, 'Rolling back regulation in the telecoms sector: a practical example'
(2008) 3 Competition Policy Newsletter 21. The article describes two notifications
under Article 7 of the Framework Directive where the Polish NRA had proposed *ex
ante* regulation for two markets which were listed in the 2003 Recommendation
but not in the new one. Applying the three criteria test the Commission issued
serious doubts letters in both cases and the proposed measures were withdrawn.
See also the Commission's approach to the finding of sub-national markets by
OFCOM in the United Kingdom: Bringer and Schumm, 'Revolution or evolution

in telecoms? Sub-national markets in sector-specific regulation when competition develops unevenly' (2008) 2 Competition Policy Newsletter 23.

12.103   **SMP Conditions.**   Note the new Article 13a inserted into the Access Directive by Article 2(10) of the Better Regulation Directive. This provides that where an NRA concludes that other SMP obligations have failed to achieve effective competition it may, as an exceptional measure, impose an obligation on vertically integrated undertakings to place their activities relating to the wholesale provision of relevant access products in an independent operated business entity. Where an undertaking designated with SMP intends voluntarily to transfer its local access network assets to a separate legal or business entity, it must provide details of its proposals to the NRA in advance to enable the NRA to assess the effect of the proposed transaction on existing regulatory obligations: see the new Article 13b of the Access Directive.

Fn 314. The Commission has issued a Recommendation on the Regulatory Treatment of Fixed and Mobile Termination Rates in the EU, OJ 2009 L124/67 giving guidance to NRAs on how to calculate costs incurred by an efficient operator for the purpose of imposing price controls and cost-accounting obligations for mobile call termination rates.

12.104   **The Commission's review of SMP designations.**   A letter sent by the Commission pursuant to Article 7(3) of the Framework Directive (stating that it does not have serious doubts about the proposed measure) is not a reviewable act for the purposes of appeal to the GC under Article 263 TFEU (formerly Article 230 EC): see Case T-109/06 *Vodafone España v Commission* [2007] ECR II-5151, [2008] 4 CMLR 1378. The GC's order contains an interesting discussion of the consultation procedure under Article 7.

12.104A   **The Commission's review of remedies imposed by NRAs.**   The Better Regulation Directive introduced Article 7a into the Framework Directive, strengthening the scope of the Commission's review of the NRAs' decisions beyond the designation of undertakings with SMP. Under Article 7(3) of the Framework Directive before the new reforms, the Commission's powers as regards proposed measures imposing SMP conditions were limited to providing comments within one month of being notified of the measure by the NRA. Article 7a now provides that where the Commission considers that a measure proposed by an NRA imposing SMP conditions would create a barrier to the single market or raises serious doubts about its compatibility with EU law, the Commission has one month to notify the NRA of its concerns. The draft measure must not then be adopted for three months. During that three month period, the Commission, BEREC and the NRA must cooperate closely to identify the most appropriate and effective measure taking due account of the view of market participants and the need to ensure the development of consistent regulatory practice. After the first six weeks of the three month period, BEREC is required to issue a reasoned opinion on the Commission's objections.

If BEREC shares the Commission's concerns, the NRA may decide within the three-month period to amend the draft measure or to maintain the draft. Where BEREC does not share the Commission's concerns, or where the NRA decides, despite BEREC's opinion, to maintain its draft measure, the Commission may, within one month after the three month period has expired, issue a recommendation requiring the NRA to amend or withdraw the draft measure, setting out specific proposals to that end. If the NRA still decides not to amend or withdraw the draft measure, it may then adopt it and notify the Commission and BEREC of the adopted final measure. Thus the reform stopped short of conferring a power of veto on the Commission as regards remedies. A revised text of Article 19 of the Framework Directive (amended by Article 1(21) of the Better Regulation Directive) empowers the Commission to adopt recommendations or decisions if divergences in implementation by the NRAs of their regulatory tasks risk creating a barrier to the internal market.

(ii) The Access Directive

Access and interconnection. The Access Directive has been substantially amended **12.105** by the Better Regulation Directive (Directive 2009/140/EC, OJ 2009 L337/37) including amendments to the definition of 'access' in Article 2(a) of the Access Directive: see Article 2(1) of the Better Regulation Directive. The Commission has published an informal consolidated text of the amended Access Directive on the Information Society pages of its website.

(iii) The Authorisation Directive

The general authorisation regime. The Authorisation Directive has been sub- **12.110** stantially amended by Article 3 of the Better Regulation Directive (Directive 2009/140/EC, OJ 2009 L337/37). The Commission has published an informal consolidated text of the amended Access Directive on the Information Society pages of its website.

Special provisions for radio frequencies and numbers. See also Case C-380/05 **12.112** *Centro Europa 7 v Ministero delle Comunicazioni* [2008] ECR I-349, [2008] 2 CMLR 512 where the Italian Court requested a preliminary ruling in the context of an action for compensation brought by Centro Europa 7. The applicant had been awarded a licence to broadcast but had not been allocated any radio frequency to enable it to start up its service. The CJ concluded that Article 56 TFEU (formerly Article 49 EC) in conjunction with the directives of the common regulatory framework precluded, in television broadcasting matters, national legislation which makes it impossible for an operator holding rights to broadcast in the absence of broadcasting radio frequencies granted on the basis of objective, transparent, non-discriminatory and proportionate criteria. It was for the national court to decide whether compensation was payable by reason of the breach.

(iv) The Universal Service Directive

12.113 **Overview.** The Universal Service Directive has been substantially amended by the Citizen's Rights Directive (Directive 2009/136/EC, OJ 2009 L337/11). The Commission has published an informal consolidated text of the amended Universal Services Directive on the Information Society pages of its website.

(vi) Overview of the current position on radio spectrum policy.

12.117 **Radio spectrum policy.** Article 9 of the Framework Directive has been replaced and substantially expanded by Article 1(10) of the Better Regulation Directive. Further:

- Article 8a was inserted into the Framework Directive by Article 1(9) of the Better Regulation Directive, requiring Member States to cooperate with each other and with the Commission in the strategic planning, coordination and harmonisation of the radio spectrum;
- Article 9a was inserted by Article 1(11) of the Better Regulation Directive allowing Member States to establish a mechanism for the review of certain existing restrictions placed on the holders of spectrum rights;
- Article 9b was inserted also by Article 1(11) requiring Member States to confer a right on undertakings to transfer or lease the right to use radio frequencies in specified bands other than frequencies used for broadcasting.

(vii) Forthcoming changes

12.120 **Reform.** The new package of regulatory measures has now been adopted, see preceding updates. Further, the new Recommendation on relevant markets referred to in this paragraph has been adopted: OJ 2007 L344/65.

(b) Application of competition law

(ii) Relationship of competition rules and sector-specific regulation

12.125 **The role of competition rules in a regulated sector.** The Framework Directive and the Specific Directives have all been substantially amended by the two Directives adopted in late 2009: see the update to paragraph 12.089, above and the subsequent updates in that section.

(iv) Joint ventures and mergers

12.145 **Joint venture decisions under Article 81.** The Horizontal Cooperation Guidelines referred to in the text have been replaced by the Horizontal Cooperation Guidelines issued in 2011: OJ 2011 C11/1: Vol II, App C22.

12.146 **Mergers and full-function joint ventures.** The Commission cleared the acquisition of the UK subsidiary of Tiscali SpA by the Carphone Warehouse Group: see Case M.5532 *Carphone Warehouse/Tiscali UK* (30 June 2009). The parties' activities overlap horizontally in retail and wholesale internet access provision, as well as in retail fixed line telephony services. The Commission analysed in particular the domestic sector of broadband services but found that the merged entity would continue to face competition from a number of strong players, especially BT, as well as from a number of strong alternative operators, including those based on the cable platform. Competition from other technologies, such as mobile telecommunications, was also growing: see Press Release IP/09/1054 (30 June 2009).

(v) Application of Article 82

Types of abuse.   Use of information held by the former dominant incumbent for targeted marketing to customers of newer entrants to the market can also amount to abuse: see *Fastweb SpA v Telecom Italia SpA*, decn of Milan Court of Appeal of 16 May 2006, Giur. It. 2007, 4, 919. An interim injunction was granted to stop Telecom Italia using information from number portability requests to engage in aggressive 'win-back' strategies directed at its former customers. Since Telecom Italia subsequently discontinued the practice the case did not proceed to final judgment but a claim by Fastweb for resulting damages is pending in the Italian courts.

12.151

Similarly, in its decision on the practices of France Télécom in French overseas departments (DOM), the French Competition Authority found as an aspect of the infringement the use by France Télécom of the information which it held as administrator of the local loops to direct its marketing efforts at customers who had migrated to other providers, while also denigrating the services of those competitors: Decision No. 09-D-24 of 28 July 2009.

Restricting activities of competitors.   See also COMP/39525 *Telekomunikacja Polska*, decn of 22 June 2011 where the Commission imposed a fine of €127 million for abusive practices preventing access to wholesale broadband by competitors in the downstream broadband markets (appeal Case T-533/08 withdrawn).

12.152

Predatory behaviour.   The elements of predatory pricing were considered by the CJ in Case C-202/07P *France Télécom v Commission*, judgment of 2 April 2009. First, the CJ held that the GC's judgment under appeal had set out sufficiently clearly why the circumstances of the present case, in particular the relationship between the level of prices applied by Wanadoo and the average variable costs and average total costs borne by Wanadoo, were analogous to those in *Tetra Pak v Commission*. Many of Wanadoo's arguments concerning the calculation of costs were rejected as inadmissible or unfounded. However, the CJ did expressly uphold the GC's conclusion that 'demonstrating that it is possible to recoup losses is not a necessary precondition for a finding of predatory pricing': para 113.

12.157

Bundling.   The Polish Supreme Court upheld a fine imposed on Telekomunikacja Polska SA for making it a condition for the conclusion of an agreement on broadband Internet access that the user also have a fixed line telephone service from TP: ECN Brief 3/2010, p2.

12.160

12.162 **Imposing excessive prices.** See also the decision of the French Competition Authority regarding the practices of France Télécom in French overseas departments (DOM) (Decision No. 09-D-24 of 28 July 2009) discussed in the update to paragraph 10.108, above. As well as charging excessive prices for line rental to competitors, France Télécom refused to provide adequate security on the lines, making it impossible for them to offer services of equivalent quality.

12.164 *Deutsche Telekom.* The appeal by Deutsche Telekom was dismissed both by the GC and the CJ: Case T-271/03 *Deutsche Telekom v Commission* [2008] ECR II-477, para 314; and Case C-280/08P *Deutsche Telekom v Commission*, judgment of 14 October 2010, [2010] 5 CMLR 1485. The Court of Justice rejected arguments based on the involvement of the German telecoms regulator in the setting of DT's retail prices. The appeal proceeded in the CJ on the premiss that the wholesale price for local loop access was fixed by the regulator without leaving DT scope for changing those prices. The CJ held that this did not preclude a finding of margin squeeze since there was still scope for DT to adjust its retail prices to avoid the squeeze (para 85). Further, since the existence of the abuse arose from the unfairness of the spread rather than the precise levels of the wholesale or retail prices, the level of the wholesale price (and in particular whether it had been set too high by the regulator) was irrelevant to the question of abuse (paras 167–168). So far as the level of retail prices were concerned, although DT was encouraged by the intervention of the national regulator to maintain the *retail* prices that led to the margin squeeze, this did not absolve DT of responsibility for the abuse (paras 82 *et seq*). In any event the regulator's decisions were not binding on the Commission (para 90). The CJ upheld the GC's decision that it was not necessary to show that the retail price was excessive and abusive in itself (para 183); the essence of the abuse is the spread between the prices. Indeed, the fact that DT would have to increase its retail prices for end-user access services in order to avoid squeezing its competitors was not relevant: para 181. The CJ held that the GC had correctly rejected the Commission's assertion that the very existence of a margin squeeze constituted an abuse without the need to demonstrate an anti-competitive effect (para 250). It was not necessary to show that equally efficient competitors had actually be driven from the market but it was necessary to show that market penetration was made more difficult (para 254). The CJ held that the GC had been correct in finding that the Commission had established that DT's pricing practices had given rise to actual exclusionary effects on 'as efficient' competitors (para 259). In response to various challenges to the way the Commission had calculated the margin, the GC held that this was a matter of complex economic assessment as to which the Commission had a margin of appreciation: para 185. All DT's pleas on the detail of what revenues should or should not have been included in the calculations were rejected by both Courts.

Fn 537. In *ETNA v France Télécom and SFR*, the case was referred back to the Paris Court of Appeal which followed the position set out by the Cour de Cassation and upheld the decision of the Competition Authority: judgment of 2 April 2008,

BOCCRF No. 7 of 15 September 2008. However this judgment was annulled by the Cour de Cassation for procedural reasons (judgment of 3 March 2009) so the case has been referred back to the Court of Appeal for a second time (not yet decided).

International roaming charges. The proceedings against T-Mobile and Vodafone in Germany and against O$_2$ and Vodafone in the UK were dropped following the adoption of Regulation 717/2007: Press Release IP/07/1113 (18 July 2007). The validity of the Roaming Regulation was challenged by four mobile network operators in proceedings in the High Court in England and a reference was made to the CJ under Article 267 TFEU (formerly Article 234 EC): Case C-58/08, not yet decided. The action challenged the legal base for the Regulation (Article 114 TFEU, formerly Article 95 EC) and alleged that the Regulation was invalid on the grounds that the imposition of a price ceiling in respect of retail roaming charges infringes the principle of proportionality and/or subsidiarity. Meanwhile the Roaming Regulation has been amended by Regulation 544/2009 OJ 2009 L167/12, *inter alia*, extending the Regulation to cover SMS and data roaming charges. **12.165**

(vi) Application of Article 86

Discriminatory licensing by Member States. The disputes arising out of the Spanish operator Telefónica's refusal (i) to conclude a roaming agreement with the Gibraltar operator for mobile phone services; and (ii) to recognise the international dialling code for Gibraltar were resolved by negotiation between the UK, Spain and Gibraltar. The challenge to the Commission's rejection of the Gibtel complaint was withdrawn: Cases T-433/03, etc, *Gibtelcom v Commission*, Order of 26 June 2008, [2009] 4 CMLR 344. **12.168**

5. Insurance

Generally. The Commission investigated various markets for insurance in Case M.5075 *Vienna Insurance Group/Erste Bank* (17 June 2008) where the merger was cleared after the parties offered commitments. In September 2007, the Commission published the Final Report of the sector inquiry into business insurance. The Final Report focuses in substance on two main issues. The first is competition in the wholesale subscription market, that is where an ad hoc syndication arrangement is set up by a broker or client to cover a given risk. The Report considers the use of 'Best Terms and Conditions' clauses whereby an insurer makes an offer to subscribe conditional on no other participant receiving better terms in respect either of a higher price or a more advantageous policy. The Commission notes that this may lead to an upward alignment of premiums and/or contract uncertainty. The second issue is broker conflicts of interest and the Commission has undertaken to look at these issues in the framework of the review of the Insurance Mediation Directive. **12.169**

See also *Asefa, Mapfre Empresa, Caser* ECN Brief 1/2010, p2 (Spanish competition authority imposed substantial fines on insurers and reinsurers who had agreed minimum prices for insurance premia for latent building defects).

12.170 **Insurance block exemption.** Regulation 358/2003 has been replaced by Regulation 267/2010 (OJ 2010 L83/1: Vol II, App E27A). It was accompanied by a Communication from the Commission on the application of Article 101(3) to certain agreements in the insurance sector: OJ 2010 C82/20, Vol II, App E27B. The new block exemption came into force on 1 April 2010 and will expire on 31 March 2017. The new Regulation continues the exemption for only two of the four kinds of agreements exempted under Regulation 358/2003: (i) joint compilations, tables and studies; and (ii) common coverage of certain types of risks (pools). The other two categories, agreements relating to technical specifications for security devices and standard policy conditions have not been renewed in Regulation 267/2010. Agreements relating to those two matters are discussed in the Commission's Horizontal Cooperation Guidelines (OJ 2011 C11/1), Chapter 7. Regulation 237/2010 was adopted under Regulation 1534/91 and Preamble (3) notes that the Commission still considers that it does not have sufficient experience of handling agreements relating to settlement of claims and registers of, and information on, aggravated risks and these matters are still not covered by the exemption. Note that Recital (8) of Regulation 267/2010 states that there is no presumption that agreements falling outside the Regulation are either caught by Article 101(1) or that they fail to satisfy the conditions in Article 101(3).

12.172 **Joint calculation, tables and studies of risk.** Collaboration between insurers in relation to information is now covered by Articles 2, 3 and 4 of Regulation 267/2010 (OJ 2010 L83/1: Vol II, App E27A). See also Recitals (9)–(12) of the Regulation and paras 7–10 of the Commission's Communication (OJ 2010 C82/20: Vol II, App E27B). Agreements (which term includes, for the purposes of the Regulation, concerted practices and decisions of associations) which were previously exempted continue to benefit from exemption. Some minor changes are introduced in the new Regulation; the term 'joint calculation' has been changed to 'joint compilations' (which may also include some calculations); the exemption is expressed to apply only where the exchange of information is 'necessary' for the purposes specified in Article 2(a); and access to data is now also required, subject to certain conditions, for consumer organisations except where non-disclosure is objectively justified on grounds of public security: Article 3(2)(e).

12.173 **Standard policy conditions and models.** The new block exemption Regulation 267/2010 (OJ 2010 L83/1: Vol II, App E27A) does not exempt these agreements since the Commission's review of the functioning of the earlier exemption revealed that it was no longer necessary to include such agreements in a sector specific regulation (see Recital (3) of Regulation 267/2010). See also paras 21 *et seq* of the Commission's Communication (OJ 2010 C82/20: Vol II, App E27B).

Agreements relating to standard terms are covered by the Horizontal Cooperation Guidelines (OJ 2011 C/11/1: Vol II, App C22), particularly paras 300–307 and the example analysed at para 335 (national association for the insurance sector distributes non-binding standard policy conditions for house insurance contracts). Note that Article 8 of Regulation 267/2010 provided a transitional period of continued exemption until 30 September 2010 to agreements which complied with the earlier block exemption but not with the new Regulation.

Common coverage of certain types of risk: insurance pools. The exemption provided by Regulation 358/2003 for insurance pools has been continued in the new exemption Regulation 267/2010 (OJ 2010 L83/1: Vol II, App E27A) but with some important modifications. First, the turnover considered when applying the market share thresholds has been expanded to cover gross premium income earned outside as well as inside the pool. Secondly, the definition of 'new risks' has been expanded: Article 1(6): see the Commission's Communication (OJ 2010 C82/20: Vol II, App E27B), paras 11 *et seq*. The Communication confirms that ad hoc co-insurance or co-reinsurance agreements on the subscription market remain outside the scope of the block exemption. **12.174**

Exemption for pool covering new risks. See now Article 6(1) of Regulation 267/2010 (OJ 2010 L83/1: Vol II, App E27A) and the wider definition of 'new risks' in Article 1(6). **12.175**

Exemption for pools covering risks that are not new. See now Article 6(2) of Regulation 267/2010 (OJ 2010 L83/1: Vol II, App E27A) and the wider ambit of the turnover that is taken into account in assessing market share. **12.176**

Individual application of Article 81(3) to insurance pools. Note the Commission's comment in its Communication (OJ 2010 C82/20: Vol II, App E27B), para 16 that many insurers have been 'incorrectly using the pool exemption in the BER as a "blanket" exception, without carrying out the required careful legal assessment of a pool's compliance with the conditions of the BER'. The Communication provides guidance as to how self-assessment should be carried out. **12.177**

Security devices. The new block exemption Regulation 267/2010 (OJ 2010 L83/1: Vol II, App E27A) does not exempt these agreements; see also the Commission's Communication (OJ 2010 C82/20: Vol II, App E27B), paras 25 *et seq*. Standard setting more generally is now covered by the Horizontal Cooperation Guidelines (OJ 2011 C/11/1: Vol II, App C22), Chapter 7 (paras 257 *et seq*), and the example analysed at para 328 (group of insurance companies comes together to agree non-binding standards for the installation of certain security devices). Note that Article 8 of Regulation 267/2010 provided a transitional period of continued exemption until 30 September 2010 to agreements which complied with the earlier block exemption but not with the new Regulation. **12.178**

12.179 **Insurance intermediaries.**   Note that where the insurance broker is acting for the insured but the agreement at issue concerns arrangements between the insurer and the broker regarding the level of broker's commission, that will not be a vertical agreement since the relationship between insurer and broker in that regard is not that of seller and purchaser: cf *Allianz Hungária, Generali Providencia*, 2. Kf.27.129/2009, judgment of the Budapest Court of Appeal of 23 September 2009 (re the Hungarian domestic vertical restraints block exemption).

A 'captive' insurance company, that is an insurance company wholly owned by a non-insurance company the purpose of which is to provide reinsurance cover exclusively for the risks of the undertaking to which it belongs, is itself an undertaking for the purpose of State aid rules: Cases E-4/10 etc, *Reassur Aktiengesellschaft v EFTA Surveillance Authority*, judgment of 10 May 2011.

See also Case C-32/11 *Allianz Hungária Biztosító v Gazdasági Versenyhivatal*, not yet decided (request for a preliminary ruling as to whether bilateral agreements between an insurance company and individual car repairers, or between an insurance company and a car repairers' association, under which the hourly repair charge paid by the insurance company to the repairer for the repair of vehicles insured by the insurance company depends, among other things, on the number and scale of insurance policies taken out with the insurance company by the repairer, as the insurance broker for the insurance company in question, are object infringements contravening Article 101(1) TFEU).

6. Postal Services

(b) Liberalisation

12.183 **The Postal Directive.**   The Postal Directive was amended substantially by Directive 2008/6, OJ 2008 L52/3. This took the final step of abolishing the grant of a monopoly for any part of the postal service, at the same time imposing an obligation on Member States to ensure the provision of a universal service at all points in their territory at affordable prices for at least five working days a week. Under Article 4 of the revised Directive 97/67, Member States may designate one or more undertakings as universal service providers. But instead of allowing Member States to reserve part of the service, the Directive now sets out various means by which the Member State may finance provision of the universal service. Where a Member State determines that the universal service obligations entail a net cost and 'represent an unfair financial burden' it may introduce a mechanism to compensate the provider either from public funds or by sharing the net costs between providers of services and/or users (Article 7(3)). Where the costs are to be shared among providers or users, the Member State may establish a compensation fund to which those providers or users contribute and which is administered by an independent body (Article 7(4)). For services which fall outside the scope of the universal service, Member States may introduce general authorisation to the extent necessary to guarantee compliance with the 'essential requirements' defined as non-economic issues such as the confidentiality of correspondence. But such authorisations must not be limited in number (Article 9(2)). The amendments introduced by Directive 2008/6 also laid down tariff principles for the universal service, namely that it must be affordable and cost-oriented, transparent and non-discriminatory. It also provides ancillary provisions for the financial accounts of universal service providers, for postal users' complaints procedures and, in Annex I, provides guidance on calculating the net cost, if any, of universal service. The dismantling of any remaining postal monopolies must be implemented by most Member States by 31 December 2010 though 11 Member States have a further two years in which to implement the Directive.

In Case C-162/06 *International Mail Spain SL v Administración del Estado* [2007] ECR I-9911, [2008] 4 CMLR 18 the CJ held in an Article 267 TFEU reference that Article 7(2) of Directive 97/67 allows Member States to reserve cross-border mail to the universal provider only insofar as they establish either that, in the absence of such a reservation, that universal service could not be achieved, or that such a reservation is necessary to enable that service to be carried out under economically acceptable conditions: 'mere expediency' was not enough. The CJ agreed with the Commission's submissions that it would be contrary to the objective of Directive 2002/39, which is to pursue the gradual and controlled opening of postal services to competition, to interpret the fourth subparagraph of Article 7(1) of Directive 97/67, as amended, as increasing the scope of discretion afforded to Member States: para 46.

Reservation of services.   Article 7 of the Postal Directive was unsuccessfully relied   **12.184** on by Slovakia to rebut an allegation of breach of Article 106 TFEU in conjunction with Article 102: COMP/39562 *Slovakian postal legislation relating to hybrid mail services*, decn of 7 October 2008, [2009] 4 CMLR 663. The Commission found that Slovakia had amended its legislation to extend the monopoly of the State-owned postal service to cover 'hybrid' mail services, that is services where data are sent electronically by the client to the service provider who then prints out and delivers the individual items to the client's customers. The Commission stated that even though there is a presumption of *prima facie* justification under Article 86(2) for services covered by the reserved area as defined in the Postal Directive (cf Point 8.3 of the Postal Notice), that did not apply here because the hybrid service had at first been liberalised by Slovakia and the functioning of the public service had not been endangered: para 165. The extension of the monopoly to cover the service needed specific justification. The Commission agreed with using the net avoided cost methodology to calculate the costs of providing the universal service but did not accept the evidence as to those costs put forward by Slovakia. In particular, the Commission held that it is not permissible under the Postal Directive to finance services other than the universal postal services by maintaining or extending those reserved areas. Thus the cost of providing other services, such as financial services, cannot be included in the cost of the universal service. The decision is on appeal Case T-556/08 *Slovenská pošta v Commission*, not yet decided.

(c) Application of competition rules

12.188 **Jurisprudence of the Community Courts and the Commission.** In COMP/ 39562 *Slovakian postal legislation relating to hybrid mail services*, decn of 7 October 2008, [2009] 4 CMLR 663 the Commission considered whether hybrid mail services form a separate relevant product market from traditional postal services for the purposes of applying Article 106(1) in conjunction with Article 102 TFEU. The Commission found that they fulfil different business and service needs. While a part of these services is similar in that both of them ultimately concern the delivery of an item to the addressee, from the point of view of customers they are perceived as two alternative, different means of effecting the transmission of content. Further, the two services were subject to different regulatory constraints. The regulatory environment of a service is a distinguishing factor for the purposes of market definition. In Slovakia, prior to the adoption of the State measure being challenged, traditional postal services were reserved while hybrid mail services, including the delivery of hybrid mail items, were not (on this aspect see update to paragraph 12.184, above). It follows that the two categories of services were subject to different market dynamics: paras 92 *et seq.* The decision is on appeal, Case T-556/08 *Slovenská pošta v Commission*, not yet decided.

12.191 **Article 82 and cross-subsidy issues.** See Case C-209/10 *Post Danmark v Konkurrencerådet*, not yet decided (reference from Danish court asking whether selective price reductions by a dominant postal undertaking with a universal service obligation to a level lower than the postal undertaking's average overall costs, but higher than the provider's average incremental costs, can constitute an exclusionary abuse, if it is established that the prices are not set at that level for the purpose of eliminating a competitor).

12.193 **Article 82 and consumer loyalty issues.** Similarly, in Denmark, Post Danmark was held to have abused its dominant position in the market for distribution of unaddressed items and weeklies by selectively charging lower prices to some customers of its main competitor and using progressive loyalty rebates awarded against a target agreed with the customer, which rebates did not reflect underlying cost savings: *Post Danmark v Competition Council*, Ø'LR (13 Afd) B 2656/05, judgment of the High Court of Eastern Denmark of 21 December 2007. The case is on appeal to the Supreme Court (Case No. 2/2008) which decided on 28 October 2009 to make a reference to the European Court of Justice. See also *Post Danmark*, decision of the Danish Competition Council of 24 June 2009 discussed in the update to paragraph 10.096, above.

7. Agriculture

Note that Article 33 EC is now Article 39 TFEU

(a) The objectives of Article 33 of the EC Treaty

Relationship between Article 36 and competition law objectives. The *Milk* **12.195** *Marque* case was discussed by the CJ in Case C-505/07 *Compañía Española de Comercialización de Aceite SA*, judgment of 1 October 2009, [2010] 4 CMLR 11 where the Court held (in a reference for preliminary ruling by a Spanish Court) that national competition authorities can apply national competition law to an agreement which is likely to affect the market in olive oil at EU level provided that they refrain from taking any measure which might undermine or create exceptions to the common organisation of the market in olive oil and from taking decisions which conflict with those of the Commission or which create the risk of such conflict.

The agricultural sector. In December 2008 the Commission published a **12.196** Communication on Food Prices in Europe (COM(2008) 821 final (9.12.2008)) in response to the substantial increases in food commodity prices during 2007/08. The Communication lists a number of anti-competitive practices which might give rise to concerns including buying alliances and single branding obligations.

The Dutch Administrative High Court for Trade and Industry reduced the fine imposed on shrimp fishers for cartel activity because of a misunderstanding about the applicability of competition rules in the sector governed by European fishing regulation: ECN Brief 2/2011, p2.

(b) Application of competition rules

The first Article 2(1) exception: national market organisations. Fn 641. The **12.202** appeal in the *French Beef* case was dismissed: Cases C-101&110/07P *Coop de France bétail et viande and FNSEA v Commission* [2008] ECR I-10193, [2009] 4 CMLR 743.

The second Article 2(1) exception: necessary under Article 33. Fn 644. The **12.023** appeal in the *French Beef* case was dismissed: Cases C-101&110/07P *Coop de France bétail et viande and FNSEA v Commission* [2008] ECR I-10193, [2009] 4CMLR 743.

13

ENFORCEMENT AND PROCEDURE

1. Introduction

The Commission's role in enforcing Article 81 and 82.   The Commission has   **13.002**
issued a document called 'Best Practices on the conduct of proceedings concerning
Articles 101 and 102 TFEU' (Vol II, App B20, available on the DG Competition
website and linked to Press Release IP/10/02 (6 January 2010)). It describes each
stage of the Commission's procedure starting with the investigation stage and
covering commitments, complaints and adoption and publication of decisions.

2. The Former Enforcement Regime under Regulation 17

Comfort and discomfort letters.   For a case where the Commission reversed the   **13.011**
stance taken in a comfort letter because of developments in the market, in particular the development of the internet, see COMP/38698 *CISAC*, decn of 16 July
2008, [2009] 4 CMLR 577, paras 120–122. The case is on appeal Cases T-398,
410, 411, 413–422, 425, 432, 434, 442, 451/08, not yet decided.

3. The European Competition Network and the Allocation of Cases

Case allocation under Regulation 1/2003.   In its report to the European   **13.017**
Parliament and Council on the functioning of Regulation 1/2003 (COM/2009/
0206 final 29 April 2009), the Commission noted that work sharing has been
'unproblematic' and that discussions on case allocation have come up in very few
cases and have been resolved swiftly.

The European Competition Network.   A special issue of the ECN Brief pub-   **13.018**
lished in December 2010 provides information and contact details for each NCA
in the Union.

13.021 **Challenging decisions as to case allocation.** But see Case T-201/11 *Si.mobil v Commission*, not yet decided (appeal from the rejection of a complaint alleging that the Commission should have intervened where an NCA was unduly drawing out proceedings and where the Commission was the 'best placed' authority to adjudicate on the issues).

4. The Commission's Powers of Investigation

(a) Fundamental rights and the Commission's powers of investigation

13.026 **General principles of EC law.** See also Case T-69/04 *Schunk GmbH v Commission* [2008] ECR II-2567, [2009] 4 CMLR 2 where the GC considered the case law of the Court of Human Rights on Article 7 ECHR in relation to an assertion that the wide discretion given to the Commission when imposing a fine infringed the principle of legal certainty: paras 28–50.

13.028 **Relevant rights.** In Case T-99/04 *AC-Treuhand AG v Commission* [2008] ECR II-1501, [2008] 5 CMLR 962 the GC considered the principle of *nullum crimen, nulla poena sine lege* which is a general principle of Union law by analogy with Article 7 of the ECHR. This principle is described as requiring 'that any Community legislation, in particular where it imposes or permits the imposition of penalties, must be clear and precise so that the persons concerned may know without ambiguity what rights and obligations flow from it and may take steps accordingly': para 139. Although the principle allows the rules governing criminal liability to be gradually clarified through interpretation by the courts, it may preclude the retroactive application of a new interpretation of a rule establishing an offence. That is particularly true if the result of that interpretation was not reasonably foreseeable at the time when the offence was committed, especially in the light of the interpretation attributed to the provision in the case law at the material time. The GC held that the principle had not been infringed when the Commission imposed a fine on a trade association which had facilitated the operation of a cartel by providing administrative and secretarial support.

Fn 82. For an example of a breach of the principles of sound administration and equal treatment see Case T-410/03 *Hoechst GmbH v Commission* [2008] ECR II-881, [2008] 5 CMLR 839, paras 134–138 (Commission had assured Chisso that it would be given 'fair warning' if another undertaking looked like overtaking it in the application for leniency but had decided that it would not inform Hoechst that Chisso had applied for leniency).

13.029 **Right to a fair trial.** A ground of appeal alleging an irregularity in the composition of the GC involves a matter of public policy which must be raised by the Court of its own motion and can be raised at any time in the proceedings: Cases C-341&342/06P *Chronopost and La Poste v UFEX* [2008] ECR I-4777, [2008]

3 CMLR 568. That case concerned an appeal against the judgment of the GC, that GC judgment having been delivered following the reference back of the case by the CJ which had overturned an earlier GC judgment in the same appeal. The duties of the Judge-Rapporteur in the Chamber which delivered the judgment under appeal were entrusted to the member who had been both President and Judge-Rapporteur in the Chamber which had delivered the earlier judgment successfully appealed against. The CJ held, referring to jurisprudence of the Court of Human Rights, that this was not a breach of the right to a fair trial: para 60.

Where the Commission is itself the 'victim' of a cartel (in this case because it reimbursed the costs of removal services for officials where a bid rigging cartel had operated) the Commission is not obliged on grounds of bias to decline jurisdiction in favour of the relevant NCA: Case T-199/08 *Ziegler SA v Commission*, judgment of 16 June 2011, paras 99 *et seq*.

'Criminal charge'.   **Fn 95.** As to the case law of the ECtHR see also *Menarini*   **13.030**
Diagnostics v Italy No. 43509/08, judgment of 27 September 2011.

(b) Power to obtain information

Information from undertakings.   The Commission has issued a document called   **13.032**
'Best Practices for the Submission of Economic Evidence and Data Collection in Cases Concerning the Application of Articles 101 and 102 TFEU and in Merger Cases' (Vol II, App B21, and on the DG Competition website and linked to Press Release IP/10/02 (6 January 2010)). It describes the preferred content and presentation of economic and econometric data and best practice on responding to requests for quantitative data. As regards the latter, the Commission has indicated (i) problems of missing data should be flagged up with the Commission well in advance of the submission deadline and justified; (ii) submissions of data should be accompanied by a memo *inter alia* describing the data compilation process, identifying all relevant sources; describing any assumptions and estimations used to fill incomplete data; and reporting on consistency checking and all data cleaning operations; (iii) tests for accuracy of the data should always be undertaken and reported. The Commission also warns against ignoring a carefully drafted and limited data request by producing large amounts of data points, using non-obvious 'definitions' of common terms in construing requests, or making unilateral and undisclosed inferences about what DG Competition is effectively seeking. The Commission also states that it may send a 'draft' data request, inviting parties to propose any modifications that could alleviate the compliance burden while producing the necessary information.

As to the language in which the request is made see 'Best Practices on the conduct of proceedings concerning Articles 101 and 102 TFEU' (Vol II, App B20, available on the DG Competition website and linked to Press Release IP/10/02 (6 January 2010)), para 26 (initial request will be sent in English and include information about the addressee's rights to obtain a translation into the language of the addressee's location, as well as his/her right to reply in that language). On information requests more generally, see the Best Practices, paras 30 *et seq.*

Fn 108. In Case T-99/04 *AC-Treuhand AG v Commission* [2008] ECR II-1501, [2008] 5 CMLR 962 the GC considered the scope of the Commission's obligation to inform the undertaking concerned of the subject-matter and purpose of the investigation under way. The GC held that there had been a breach of the rights of the defence where the information request to an industry association had not made clear that the association itself, and not just its members, was considered a potential wrongdoer. But no detriment had arisen for the association from this breach, so the ground of appeal was rejected. *Quaere* whether this is correct having regard to the CJ's judgment in Cases C-322/07P, etc, *Papierfabrik August Koehler AG and Bolloré SA v Commission*, judgment of 3 September 2009, [2009] 5 CMLR 2301 discussed in the update to paragraph 13.084, below.

13.033   **Addressees of requests for information.**   See Case T-171/10 *Slovak Telekom v Commission*, not yet decided (challenge to information request on the grounds that Commission has no jurisdiction to request information relating to a period before the Slovak Republic joined the EU).

13.037   **Statements.**   On the exercise of this power to take statements see 'Best Practices on the conduct of proceedings concerning Articles 101 and 102 TFEU' (Vol II, App B20, available on the DG Competition website and linked to Press Release IP/10/02 (6 January 2010)), paras 42 *et seq.* The Commission has stated there that although it is within the discretion of DG Competition to decide when to conduct an interview, a request by a party to have its statement recorded as an interview will in principle be accepted, subject to the needs and requirements of the proper conduct of the investigation.

13.039   **Investigations into sectors of the economy and types of agreements.**   **Fn 145.** See, eg the Commission carried out 'dawn raids' at the outset of its inquiry into the pharmaceutical sector: Press Release IP/08/49 (16 January 2008).

(c) **Powers of inspection**

13.043   **Inspection of undertakings pursuant to decision.**   The Commission may address an inspection decision to a professional body without explaining in detail why it considers that the body is an undertaking for the purposes of Article 20 of Regulation 1/2003: Case T-23/09 *CNOP and CCG v Commission*, Order of 26 October 2010 (challenge by professional association of pharmacists to inspection decision dismissed).

13.048   **Powers that can be exercised during an inspection.**   As regards the sealing of premises see Case T-141/08 *E. ON Energie v Commission*, judgment of 15 December 2010 where the GC upheld a fine of €38 million imposed for breach of a seal placed overnight by Commission officials to secure a room containing documents which they were in the course of inspecting. The Court held that the Commission had been justified in finding that, at the very least, the seal had been broken negligently. The Commission had rejected various other reasons for the seal being voided including the fact that a cleaning woman may have wiped the seal with a particular brand of cleaning fluid or the possibility that frequent opening and closing of doors close by might have caused vibrations resulting in the failure of the seal (see COMP/39326 *E.ON (breach of seal)*, decn of 30 January 2008, [2009] 4 CMLR 371). The case is on further appeal: Case C-89/11P, not yet decided. See similarly COMP/39796 *Suez Environnement—breach of seal*, decn of 24 May 2011, where the Commission imposed a fine of €8 million for breach of a seal.

Penalties in respect of inspections. **Fn 213.** See now Case T-141/08 *E.ON* **13.050**
Energie v Commission, judgment of 15 December 2010 where the GC upheld a fine of €38 million imposed for breach of a seal placed overnight by Commission officials to secure a room containing documents which they were in the course of inspecting. The case is on further appeal: Case C-89/11P, not yet decided. See similarly COMP/39796 *Suez Environnement—breach of seal*, decn of 24 May 2011, where the Commission imposed a fine of €8 million for breach of a seal.

Consequences of breach. In Case T-452/05 *Belgian Sewing Thread v Commission*, **13.054**
judgment of 28 April 2010, [2010] 5 CMLR 889, the GC discussed the relevant case law when rejecting a claim for damages arising out of the Commission's disclosure of confidential price lists, on the grounds that the applicant had not established a causal link between the disclosure and the alleged loss: paras 163 *et seq.*

(d) Privilege

Lawyer/client privilege: *Akzo.* The Court of Justice rejected the appeal in *Akzo* **13.056**
and upheld the reasoning of the GC on all issues: Case C-550/07P *Akzo Nobel Chemicals v Commission*, judgment of 14 September 2010, [2010] 5 CMLR 1143. The Court held that the appellants had an interest in bringing the appeal even though they did not contest the Commission's assertion that it had not relied on the disputed documents in its decision and had not passed them to national authorities.

Subsequent case law of the Community Courts. As to the practical application **13.059**
of the case law by the Commission see 'Best Practices on the conduct of proceedings concerning Articles 101 and 102 TFEU' (Vol II, App B20, available on the DG Competition website and linked to Press Release IP/10/02 (6 January 2010)), paras 47 *et seq.*

5. Complaints

Legitimate interests: the practice. **Fn 282.** The appeals against the decision in **13.065**
Nintendo have now been decided: Case T-18/03 *CD-Contact Data v Commission*

[2009] ECR II-1021 (fine reduced) (appeal dismissed Case C-260/09P *Activision Blizzard v Commission*, judgment of 10 February 2011); Case T-12/03 *Itochu* [2009] 5 CMLR 1375 (appeal dismissed); Case T-13/03 *Nintendo* [2009] 5 CMLR 1421 (fine reduced); Case T-398/02 *Linea Gig* (removed from register 2 May 2005). No issue arose in the appeals concerning the point made in this paragraph.

13.067 **Extent of the Commission's duty to consider a complaint.** The principles described in this paragraph were applied in Case T-306/05 *Scippacercola and Terezakis v Commission* [2008] ECR II-4*, [2008] 4 CMLR 1418, paras 91 *et seq* (further appeal dismissed Case C-159/08P, Order of 25 March 2009). The GC also held that the decision rejecting a complaint must be based on the Commission's consideration of all relevant matters of law and of fact which exist at the time the decision is adopted not at the time the complaint was made: para 149. See also, eg Case T-432/05 *EMC Development AB v Commission*, judgment of 12 May 2010, [2010] 5 CMLR 757, paras 54–60 where the duties imposed on the Commission, the rights of the complainant and the role of the GC on reviewing the rejection of a complaint are set out.

Following the CJ's judgment in Case C-119/97P *Ufex v Commission* [1999] ECR I-1341, [2000] 4 CMLR 268, the GC annulled the decision dismissing the complaint (Case T-77/95 *UFEX and others v Commission* [2000] ECR II-2167). The Commission re-examined the complaint but rejected it again. On appeal from that decision, the GC upheld the Commission's rejection on the ground of lack of Union interest: see Case T-60/05 *Union française de l'express (UFEX) v Commission* [2007] ECR II-3397, [2008] 5 CMLR 580.

Fn 309. The Commission has stated that it will endeavour to inform complainants of the action that it proposes to take on a complaint within four months from the receipt of the complaint: see 'Best Practices on the conduct of proceedings concerning Articles 101 and 102 TFEU' (Vol II, App B20, available on the DG Competition website and linked to Press Release IP/10/02 (6 January 2010)), para 15.

13.071 **Decision upon a complaint.** For an example of continuing confusion giving rise to uncertainty as to the date on which the period for appealing had commenced see Case T-200/09 *Abertis Infraestructuras v Commission*, Order of 18 May 2010. The GC noted that where a party becomes aware of a decision which affects it but which has not been published or notified to it, that party is bound to ask the Commission for fuller details of the reasoning of that decision within a reasonable time. Thus where a complainant was informed that the Commission had rejected its complaint, but waited six months before requesting a copy of the full decision, its appeal against that rejection was out of time.

See the discussion of the appeals arising from the Commission's rejection of a complaint by Athinaïki Techniki concerning alleged State aid: Case C-362/09P *Athinaïki Techniki v Commission*, judgment of 16 December 2010, discussed in the update to paragraph 13.220, below.

The Commission has described the procedure followed when rejecting a complaint in 'Best Practices on the conduct of proceedings concerning Articles 101 and 102 TFEU' (Vol II, App B20, available on the DG Competition website and linked to Press Release IP/10/02 (6 January 2010)), paras 119 *et seq.*

Lack of Community interest. In Case T-60/05 *Union française de l'express (UFEX)* **13.072** *v Commission* [2007] ECR II-3397, [2008] 5 CMLR 580 the GC interpreted paras 93 and 95 of the earlier CJ judgment in Case C-119/97P *Ufex v Commission* in holding that the Commission was obliged to consider the seriousness and duration of an alleged infringement, even where the Commission found that the conduct complained of had terminated some time earlier and had no continuing anti-competitive effects. However, the GC confirmed that it is possible for the Commission to take account of the seriousness and duration of the alleged infringement in assessing the EU interest in pursuing the complaint without determining the existence and precise characteristics of the alleged infringement: see paras 70 *et seq.* The GC also held (a) that the Commission was entitled to assess the existence of a EU interest at the date of its decision re-examining the complaint (following the various appeals) rather than as at the time of the original complaint: para 122; and (b) that the difficulty of being able to establish an infringement to the requisite legal standard in order to adopt a decision is a matter which may be taken into account in the context of the assessment of the EU interest.

The criteria listed in (a) and (c) of para 13.072 were particularly relevant in the Commission's decision to reject a complaint about charges imposed by Athens International Airport for various groundhandling services: COMP/38469 *Athens International Airport*, decn of 2 May 2005. The decision was upheld on appeal: Case T-306/05 *Scippacercola and Terezakis v Commission* [2008] ECR II-4*, [2008] 4 CMLR 1418 (further appeal dismissed Case C-159/08P, Order of 25 March 2009).

Where the Commission's decision that the complaint does not merit investigation is in fact based on conclusions about the significance of the market which are vitiated by manifest errors of assessment, the decision rejecting the complaint will be annulled: Case T-427/08 *Confédération européenne des associations d'horlogers-réparateurs (CEAHR) v Commission*, judgment of 15 December 2010, paras 172 *et seq.*

Note that the question whether there is a serious impediment to intra-Union trade (which is a criterion that the Commission may apply when deciding whether there is a EU interest in investigating a particular complaint) is different from a question whether the conduct affects trade between Member States: see Case C-425/07P *AEPI v Commission* [2009] ECR I-3205, [2009] 5 CMLR 1337, paras 49 *et seq* (on appeal from Case T-229/05 referred to in fn 338).

The Commission may reject a complaint relying both on Article 13 of Regulation 1/2003 and on Article 7 of Regulation 773/2004 (see paragraph 14.017, below) and lack of EU interest: COMP/39707 *Si.mobil/Mobitel*, decn of 24 January 2011. The decision is on appeal: Case T-201/11 *Si.Mobil v Commission*, not yet decided.

13.073 **Complainant's rights after initiation of procedure.** Conversely, even if the complaint is withdrawn, the Commission may still proceed to an infringement decision and impose a fine: see, eg COMP/37860 *Morgan Stanley/Visa International and Visa Europe*, decn of 3 October 2007 (appeal on other grounds dismissed: Case T-461/07 *Visa v Commission*, judgment of 14 April 2011).

The complainant's right to a non-confidential copy of the statement of objections does not apply where the new settlement procedure introduced by Regulation 622/2008 applies. In such a case the Commission must inform the complainant of the nature and subject-matter of the procedure: see amended version of Article 6.1 of Regulation 773/2004 substituted by Regulation 622/2008, OJ 2008 L171/3, [2008] 5 CMLR 1032 Article 1.2. The new settlement procedure is discussed in new paragraphs 13.113A–13.113D, below. Note that the complainant does not have access to settlement submissions: Notice on the Conduct of Settlement Procedures in cartel cases: OJ 2008 C167/1: Vol II, App B17, para 34.

6. Formal Procedure Prior to an Adverse Decision

(a) The nature of Commission proceedings

13.075 **An 'administrative' procedure.** In COMP/37990 *Intel*, decn of 13 May 2009 the Commission responded to serious allegations of malfeasance and bias levelled by Intel at the case team. The Commission stated that it was under no obligation to take minutes of meetings it held with industry participants: para 40.

Fn 364. The citation for Cases T-125&253/03 *Akzo Nobel Chemcials v Commission* should read [2007] ECR II-3523, para 86. The appeal against that judgment was dismissed: Case C-550/07P *Akzo Nobel Chemicals v Commission*, judgment of 14 September 2010, [2010] 5 CMLR 1143. The Court again stressed the importance of the rights of the defence (para 92) but held that these were not infringed by the failure to extend legal privilege to communications with in-house lawyers.

13.076 **Presumption of innocence and burden of proof.** See also Case T-36/05 *Coats Holdings Ltd v Commission* [2007] ECR II-110, [2008] 4 CMLR 45 where the GC stated that any doubt in the mind of the Court must operate to the advantage of the addressee of the decision finding an infringement: 'Given the nature of the infringements in question and the nature and severity of the ensuing penalties, the principle of the presumption of innocence applies in particular to the procedures relating to infringements of the competition rules applicable to undertakings that may result in the imposition of fines or periodic penalty payments': para 70. Coats' appeal against this decision was dismissed: Case C-468/07P [2009] 4 CMLR 301.

However, in Case T-53/03 *BPB plc v Commission* [2008] ECR II-1333, [2008] 5 CMLR 1201 the GC discussed the burden of proof on the Commission and expressly rejected the appellant's assertion that the Commission must adduce proof 'beyond reasonable doubt' of the existence of the infringement in cases where it imposes heavy fines: paras 61 *et seq*.

It is contrary to the presumption of innocence for the Commission to allege in the decision that an undertaking was party to a cartel at a time subject to the limitation period where there is no finding of infringement in the operative part of the decision and where, therefore, the undertaking could not challenge the allegation on appeal: Case T-474/04 *Pergan Hilfsstoffe für industrielle Prozesse GmbH v Commission* [2007] ECR II-4225, [2008] 4 CMLR 148, para 76.

The standard of proof is the same in the case of a vertical arrangement as in respect of a horizontal arrangements: Case C-260/09P *Activision Blizzard v Commission*, judgment of 10 February 2011, para 71.

For a case under Article 102 where the burden of proof and Article 6(2) ECHR was discussed see Case T-321/05 *AstraZeneca v Commission*, judgment of 1 July 2010, [2010] 5 CMLR 1575, para 476. The case is on appeal: Case C-457/10P *AstraZeneca v Commission*, not yet decided.

See also the discussion of the shifting burden of proof in Case T-110/07 *Siemens v Commission*, judgment of 3 March 2011, paras 43 *et seq*. The GC, referring to Article 6(2) ECHR and the fundamental principles of European Union law, held that the Court cannot conclude that the Commission has established the infringement at issue to the requisite legal standard if it still entertains any doubts on that point, in particular in proceedings for annulment of a decision imposing a fine. The Court went on to consider where the burden lies as regards proof of the end date of the undertaking's involvement in a cartel: paras 171 *et seq*. The Commission asserted that once it has shown that the undertaking participated in the cartel, that participation is presumed to continue until the undertaking proves that it ceased participating. The GC rejected this, holding that the end date of participation is an essential element of the infringement so that the burden of proving it lies with the Commission. However, once the Commission has established participation to a particular date, it is up to the undertaking then to adduce evidence capable of undermining the Commission's findings. The case is on further appeal: Case C-239/11P, not yet decided.

In *Bookmakers' Afternoon Greyhound Services v Amalgamated Racing Ltd* [2009] EWCA Civ 750 the English Court of Appeal was considering a case where the agreement in question was *prima facie* contrary to Article 101(1) but a party sought to persuade the court that the restriction on competition was justified in the particular circumstances of the case. Where this happens, the Court said, the legal burden of proving an infringement of Article 101(1) remains with the party who so asserts but the evidential burden of demonstrating that the apparent restriction on competition is justified falls upon the undertaking advancing such assertion: para 393 (citing *The Racecourse Association v Office of Fair Trading* [2005] CAT 29 at paras 132–133).

Fn 366. See also Case C-413/08 *Lafarge v Commission*, judgment of 17 June 2010, [2010] 5 CMLR 586, para 30 where the CJ said that where the burden of proof rests on one party, the evidence on which that party relies may be of such a kind as to require the other party to provide an explanation or justification, failing which it is permissible to conclude that the rules on the burden of proof have been satisfied.

13.078   **Delay.**   The principles established in Case C-105/04P *Nederlandse Federatieve Vereniging voor de Groothandel op Elektrotechnisch Gebied ('FEG') v Commission* [2006] ECR I-8725, [2006] 5 CMLR 1223 were applied in Case T-60/05 *Union française de l'express (UFEX) v Commission* [2007] ECR II-3397, [2008] 5 CMLR 580. The GC reiterated that it is a general principle of EU law that the administrative procedure be completed within a reasonable time but found that no prejudice to the rights of the defence had been demonstrated: see para 55. As to the effect of delay on the penalty imposed see update to paragraph 13.180, below.

Fn 376. See also Case T-58/01 *Solvay v Commission*, judgment of 17 December 2009, para 120 (on further appeal, Case C-110/10P, not yet decided).

Fn 377. See also the approach of the Dutch courts in *AUV v NMa, Aesculaap v NMa*, judgments of the Trade and Industry Appeals Tribunal of 3 July 2008 (Cases AWB 06/526, etc, LJN: BD6629 & 6635) (although two years for the administrative proceedings by the Dutch Competition Authority was not in itself unreasonable, the fines were reduced by 20 per cent because the process had been lengthened by periods of unjustified delay by the Authority).

13.079   **Effect of unreasonable delay.**   In Case T-60/05 *Union française de l'express (UFEX) v Commission* [2007] ECR II-3397, [2008] 5 CMLR 580 the Post Office, whose conduct was the subject of a complaint that the Commission had repeatedly rejected, argued that it would not be possible for it to defend itself properly if the Commission now commenced an investigation. The GC held that since it was impossible to know what allegations would be made by the Commission if it decided to pursue the complaint, it was also impossible to know whether the Post Office would be prejudiced: para 57. The GC also rejected the Post Office's argument that to be under continuous investigation is seriously damaging to it, 'in the sense of its departments being deployed for unproductive ends, incurring fruitless expenses and its competitors gaining access to a large amount of commercial information'.

13.080   **The right to be heard.**   Article 11(1) of Regulation 773/2004 has been substituted by Regulation 622/2008, OJ 2008 L171/3, [2008] 5 CMLR 1032 Article 1.5.

That Regulation introduces the new cartel settlement procedure into Regulation 773/2004: see Vol II, App B4. The new wording of Article 11(1) is identical save that it refers to parties to whom the Commission addresses a statement of objections rather than to parties to whom the Commission has addressed a statement of objections. It is not clear what difference in substance the amendment is intended to make.

Hearing by 'an independent and impartial tribunal'. The principle established in *Enso Española* was reiterated in Case T-54/03 *Lafarge v Commission* [2008] ECR II-120*. The point was not considered in the further appeal which was dismissed: Case C-413/08 *Lafarge v Commission*, judgment of 17 June 2010, [2010] 5 CMLR 586. **13.081**

(b) Initiation of procedure and the statement of objections

Initiation of proceedings. In Case T-99/04 *AC-Treuhand AG v Commission* [2008] ECR II-1501, [2008] 5 CMLR 962 the GC referred to the two 'distinct and successive' stages of the Commission's investigation of an infringement, the preliminary investigation stage and the *inter partes* stage. The issue of the statement of objections marks the move from the first to the second and it is only in the second stage that the rights of the defence are fully engaged. However, there are some rights of the defence relevant to the preliminary stage also: paras 47 *et seq*. **13.082**

As to the possible dates which trigger the initiation of proceedings, Article 2(1) of Regulation 773/2004 has been amended so that a request that the parties express their interest in engaging in settlement discussions is added to the other dates listed: see Regulation 622/2008, OJ 2008 L171/3, [2008] 5 CMLR 1032, Article 1.1. The new settlement procedure introduced by Regulation 622/2008 is discussed in new paragraphs 13.113A–13.113D, below.

Informal and 'state of play' meetings. During the investigative phase, DG Competition may hold informal meetings with the parties, complainants, or third parties: see 'Best Practices on the conduct of proceedings concerning Articles 101 and 102 TFEU' (Vol II, App B20, available on the DG Competition website and linked to Press Release IP/10/02 (6 January 2010)), para 38. As regards the parties being investigated, state of play meetings may be held at different stages of the investigation: ibid, paras 54 *et seq*. In some, more exceptional, cases the Commission will hold 'triangular' meetings if, for example, two or more opposing views have been put forward as to key data or evidence. It is also normal practice to offer executive officers of the parties an opportunity to discuss the case with the Director-General of DG Competition or when appropriate, with the Commissioner responsible for Competition, if the parties so request: ibid para 64. **13.082A**

Closure of the investigation. If the Commission decides at any point not to proceed with the investigation, it will usually publish an announcement to that effect on its website: Best Practices (cited above), para 70. **13.082B**

13.083   **The statement of objections: its purpose and status.**   In Case C-413/06P
Bertelsmann AG and Sony Corporation of America v Impala and Commission [2008]
ECR I-4951 the CJ laid down some important principles regarding the relationship between the facts as set out in the statement of objections and the facts as set
out ultimately in the decision. Although this was in the context of a statement of
objections issued under the Merger Regulation, there is nothing to suggest that it
does not also apply to proceedings under Regulation 1/2003. The CJ stressed that
the statement of objections is a provisional account of the facts and is subject to
amendments in the light of the observations submitted to it by the parties and subsequent findings of fact: paras 63 *et seq*. The CJ held that the GC had erred in law
in criticising inconsistencies between the facts as set out in the Commission's statement of objections and the findings in the decision. The CJ held that the GC can
refer to the statement of objections in order to interpret a decision of the Commission,
particularly as regards the examination of its factual basis. But the GC had gone
beyond what was permissible by treating what it termed 'findings of fact made
previously' in that statement as being more reliable and more conclusive than the
findings set out in the contested decision itself: see paras 69 *et seq*.

Article 10(1) of Regulation 773/2004 was amended so that it now does not require
the Commission to inform the persons concerned of the objections raised against
them in writing. However, the statement of objections, once issued must be sent in
writing to each party against whom objections are raised. The purpose of the amendment is to allow for early disclosure of the Commission's concerns and a response to
that disclosure by the parties prior to the issue of the statement of objections as part
of the settlement procedure now incorporated into Regulation 773/2004: see
Regulation 622/2008, OJ 2008 L171/3, [2008] 5 CMLR 1032 Article 1.3 and
Recital (2). The new settlement procedure introduced by Regulation 622/2008 is
discussed in new paragraphs 13.113A–13.113D, below.

See also the description in 'Best Practices on the conduct of proceedings concerning
Articles 101 and 102 TFEU' (Vol II, App B20, available on the DG Competition
website and linked to Press Release IP/10/02 (6 January 2010)), paras 76 *et seq*.

Fn 410. On appeal from the GC's decision in Case T-351/03, the CJ confirmed
that the statement of objections is essential to the application of the principle of
respect for the rights of the defence: para 163. The CJ, however, overturned the
GC's judgment in part on the basis that there was no adequate causal link between
the manifest and serious breach of the rights of the defence and the loss for which
compensation had been awarded by the GC: Case C-440/07P *Commission v
Schneider Electric*, judgment of 16 July 2009.

13.084   **Contents of the statement of objections.**   The statement of objections must also
make clear whether it is alleged that the undertaking was the leader of a cartel if the
Commission intends to increase the amount of the fine to be imposed on this

ground: Case T-410/03 *Hoechst GmbH v Commission* [2008] ECR II-881, [2008] 5 CMLR 839, paras 423 *et seq*.

The CJ has held that it is important that the statement of objections indicates in what capacity allegations are being made against a recipient: see Cases C-322/07P, etc, *Papierfabrik August Koehler AG and Bolloré SA v Commission*, judgment of 3 September 2009, [2009] 5 CMLR 2301. Bolloré had been found liable in the Commission's decision both as the parent company of Copiograph and because of its own independent involvement in the *Carbonless paper* cartel. The GC had found that the statement of objections had not made the latter allegations clear but declined to annul the decision on the grounds that Bolloré had had an opportunity to exercise its rights of defence as regards the former allegation. The CJ held that the GC had erred in law in failing to draw any legal conclusion from its finding that Bolloré's rights of defence had not been observed and annulled the whole of the contested decision so far as it concerned Bolloré.

As regards what must be included if the Commission intends to impose a fine: see Cases C-101&110/07P *Coop de France bétail et viande and FNSEA v Commission* [2008] ECR I-10193, [2009] 4 CMLR 743, paras 47 *et seq*: it is not appropriate for the Commission to give an indication of the level of fine proposed since this anticipates the Commission's decision. But the Commission must indicate expressly that it will consider whether it is appropriate to impose fines on the undertakings concerned and must set out the principal elements of fact and of law that may give rise to a fine, such as the gravity and the duration of the alleged infringement and the fact that it has been committed 'intentionally or negligently'.

Where the Commission sets out the facts in the statement of objections on which its theory is based and it is clear from the addressee's response that it understood the significance of those facts, the statement is adequate even if the Commission did not expressly state the inferences it drew from those facts: Case T-133/07 *Mitsubishi Electric v Commission*, judgment of 12 July 2011, para 68.

Where the statement of objections follows the adoption of the settlement procedure now incorporated into Regulation 773/2004 by Regulation 622/2008, OJ 2008 L171/3, [2008] 5 CMLR 1032, it will reflect the infringement admitted by the parties.

Fn 416. ADM's appeal has now been decided: Case C-511/06P *Archer Daniels Midland v Commission*, judgment of 9 July 2009. The CJ held that it was not necessary for the statement of objections to spell out the details of why the Commission intended to classify ADM as the leader of the cartel for the purposes of the fine. But the Commission was nonetheless required, at the very least, to state those facts in the statement of objections. The GC had held that it was sufficient that the facts on which the Commission later relied in the decision were contained in documents that had been annexed to the statement of objections even though they had not been referred to in the body of the statement of objections. The CJ held that in the circumstances of the case, this was not sufficient to enable ADM to dispute those facts and therefore to exercise its rights of defence effectively: para 94.

Fn 423. This point was confirmed by the CJ in Case C-511/06P *Archer Daniels Midland v Commission*, judgment of 9 July 2009, para 69.

Fn 425. Following the judgment in *ARBED*, the Commission retook the decision condemning the steel beams cartel: an appeal against that decision by ARBED was dismissed but the decision was annulled as against two of the addressees on the basis that the decision was adopted outside the limitation period: Case T-405/06 *Arcelor Mittal v Commission* [2009] ECR II-771, [2010] 4 CMLR 787 (appeals by the applicant and by the Commission dismissed: Cases C-201&216/09P *ArcelorMittal v Commission*, judgment of 29 March 2011).

13.086 **Reply to the statement of objections.** The Commission is not under any obligation to allow an addressee to comment on the reasoning it intends to rely on to refute arguments put forward by the addressee in response to the statement of objections: Case T-18/05 *IMI plc v Commission*, judgment of 19 May 2010, para 111.

Fn 438. The Commission's 'Best Practices on the conduct of proceedings concerning Articles 101 and 102 TFEU' (Vol II, App B20, available on the DG Competition website and linked to Press Release IP/10/02 (6 January 2010)), para 87 indicates that a period of two months will usually be given in complex cases. Disputes about the period allowed can be resolved by the Hearing Officer: see 'Guidance on procedures of the Hearing Officers in proceedings relating to Articles 101 and 102 TFEU' (Vol II, App B22 and available linked to the same Press Release) para 26.

Fn 440. See also Case T-73/04 *Le Carbone-Lorraine v Commission* [2008] ECR II-2661, [2010] 5 CMLR 81 where the GC held that it was open to the applicant to raise on appeal a factor in mitigation of the fine even though this had not been raised in its reply to the statement of objections: para 194. A further appeal was dismissed: Case C-554/08P, judgment of 12 November 2009.

As to the effect of factual admissions in the reply to the statement of objections referred to in fn 440, see now Case T-69/04 *Schunk GmbH v Commission* [2008] ECR II-2567, [2009] 4 CMLR 2. Some of the points raised by Schunk in relation to the fine included various challenges to the findings of infringement. The Commission argued that these were inadmissible because Schunk had made admissions in its response to the statement of objections and should not be allowed to challenge them for the first time before the Court. The GC agreed, holding that it is on the basis of the replies to the statement of objections that the Commission has to adopt its position regarding the future course of the administrative procedure: paras 79 *et seq*.

As to disclosure of one alleged cartel member's reply to the statement of objections to the other undertakings being investigated see Case T-53/03 *BPB plc v Commission* [2008] ECR II-1333, [2008] 5 CMLR 1201, para 41.

See also Case C-407/08P *Knauf Gips KG v Commission*, judgment of 1 July 2010, [2010] 5 CMLR 708. The GC in dismissing an appeal against the Commission's attribution of the group's infringement to the applicant company, had relied, amongst other things, on the fact that during the administrative procedure the applicant company had presented itself as the sole interlocutor with the Commission on behalf of the group and had not raised the issue of whether liability for the infringement could be attributed to it. The CJ held that the GC had erred in finding that this conduct precluded the applicant from disputing its liability on appeal; there is no requirement under the EU law that the addressee must challenge the various matters of fact or law during the administrative procedure, or otherwise be barred from doing so on appeal: para 89. The CJ said 'Although an undertaking's express or implicit acknowledgement of matters of fact or of law during the administrative procedure before the Commission may constitute additional evidence when determining whether an action is well founded, it cannot restrict the actual exercise of a natural or legal person's right to bring proceedings before the General Court under the fourth paragraph of Article 263 TFEU': para 90.

Supplementary statement of objections and 'letters of fact'. Where after the   **13.087A**
statement of objections has been issued, new evidence is identified which the Commission intends to rely upon, the Commission will issue a supplementary statement or a letter of facts to give the undertakings an opportunity to present their observations on these new aspects. The procedural rights which are triggered by the sending of the initial statement apply *mutatis mutandis* where a supplementary statement is issued, including the right of the parties to request an oral hearing: 'Best Practices on the conduct of proceedings concerning Articles 101 and 102 TFEU' (Vol II, App B20, available on the DG Competition website and linked to Press Release IP/10/02 (6 January 2010)), paras 95–98.

(c) **Access to the file**

Access to the file. In cases where the cartel settlement procedure in Article 10a of   **13.088**
Regulation 773/2004 is adopted, the Commission will, on request, disclose a limited number of documents on the file to the parties involved in settlement discussions. Those parties will then confirm to the Commission in their settlement submissions that they will only require access to the file if the statement of objections does not reflect the content of their settlement submissions: see Article 15(1a) inserted by Regulation 622/2008, OJ 2008 L171/3, [2008] 5 CMLR 1032 Article 1.7. The new settlement procedure introduced by Regulation 622/2008 is discussed in new paragraphs 13.113A–13.113D, below.

Fn 448. See also Case T-53/03 *BPB plc v Commission* [2008] ECR II-1333, [2008] 5 CMLR 1201, para 31.

13.091 **Exculpatory and incriminating documents.** The principles set out in this paragraph and derived from *Aalborg Portland v Commission* were applied in Case T-410/03 *Hoechst GmbH v Commission* [2008] ECR II-881, [2008] 5 CMLR 839, paras 145–148 and in many other cases, see recently, eg Case 113/07 *Toshiba Corp v Commission*, judgment of 12 July 2011, paras 40 *et seq*; Case T-58/01 *Solvay v Commission*, judgment of 17 December 2009, paras 223 *et seq* (on further appeal, Case C-110/10P, not yet decided). In that case the Commission had lost various files and was not therefore able to give access to the documents on them. The GC concluded however, that the material on the file was unlikely to have been relevant to the issues in the case so that its loss did not result in the annulment of the decision: para 263.

In Case T-53/03 *BPB plc v Commission* [2008] ECR II-1333, [2008] 5 CMLR 1201 the GC reiterated that 'A document can be regarded as a document that incriminates an applicant only where it is used by the Commission to support a finding of an infringement in which that party is alleged to have participated': para 32. The GC went on to apply the principles laid down in *Aalborg Portland* as to when non-disclosure of an incriminating document affects the validity of the decision: paras 43–45.

In Case C-407/08P *Knauf Gips KG v Commission*, judgment of 1 July 2010, [2010] 5 CMLR 708 the CJ held that the fact that the Commission had listed an undisclosed document in the preambles to the challenged decision was not enough to establish that the Commission's decision would have been different if the Commission had not relied on that document: para 14. The Court went on to hold that other, exculpatory, documents which had also not been disclosed could not have affected the outcome of the case: para 27.

Fn 463. See also Case T-379/06 *Kaimer v Commission*, judgment of 24 March 2011, para 32.

13.093 **The documents to which access is granted.** The replies to the statement of objections lodged by other addressees of a decision do not form part of the Commission's file: the Commission is not obliged to disclose the reply of its own initiative unless it intends to rely on something in that response as against the addressee: Case T-195/06 *Solvay Solexis v Commission (hydrogen peroxide and perborate)*, judgment of 16 June 2011, paras 165 *et seq*.

Fn 480. See also Case T-410/03 *Hoechst GmbH v Commission* [2008] ECR II-881, [2008] 5 CMLR 839, para 147: 'it should be emphasised that it is not solely for the Commission, . . . to determine the documents which are of use to the defence of the undertakings concerned. However, the Commission may exclude from the administrative procedure the evidence which has no relation to the allegations of fact and of law in the statement of objections and which therefore has no relevance to the investigation. An applicant cannot properly put forward as a ground of annulment the fact that irrelevant documents were not communicated to it'.

Internal Commission documents. In Case T-410/03 *Hoechst GmbH v Commission* [2008] ECR II-881, [2008] 5 CMLR 839, the GC confirmed that the Commission's internal documents can be made available only if the exceptional circumstances of the case so require 'on the basis of serious indicia which it is for the party concerned to supply': para 165. The Court found that there were no serious indicia in this case, but for the sake of completeness the Court called for the internal records of phone conversations which Hoechst had been asking for and ascertained—without disclosing them to the parties—that they were not relevant to the case. The Court returned the records to the Commission and ordered that they be removed from the file: para 170.   **13.094**

Business secrets and other confidential information. The Commission cannot make a general reference to confidentiality to justify a total refusal to disclose documents in its file. The right of undertakings to protect their business secrets must be balanced against the safeguarding of the right of an undertaking being investigated to have access to the whole of the file: Case T-410/03 *Hoechst GmbH v Commission* [2008] ECR II-881, [2008] 5 CMLR 839, para 153. In that case where Hoechst had expressly requested sight of a particular letter sent by another alleged cartel member, the Commission had provided it with almost all the 101 pages blanked out. The GC held that this was tantamount to not providing the letter at all and that the Commission ought to have drawn up a non-confidential version of the documents in issue or, if that proved difficult, to have prepared a list of the documents concerned and a sufficiently precise non-confidential summary of their content: para 154. The GC adopted measures of organisation which gave Hoechst access to a better non-confidential version of the document so that they could make submissions as to how it might have affected their case.   **13.095**

For a procedure whereby information may be disclosed to a confidentiality ring, see the update to paragraph 13.099, below.

Other confidential documents. As regards information provided to the Commission on condition of anonymity see Case T-53/03 *BPB plc v Commission* [2008] ECR II-1333, [2008] 5 CMLR 1201, paras 31–38.   **13.096**

Obligation to identify confidential information when submitted. As to the role of the Hearing Officer in resolving disputes over confidentiality, see 'Guidance on procedures of the Hearing Officers in proceedings relating to Articles 101 and 102 TFEU' (Vol II, App B22 and available on the DG Competition website and linked to Press Release IP/10/02 (6 January 2010)), paras 19 *et seq* which includes a description of the '*AKZO* procedure' under which the Hearing Officer will review the disputed documents and arrive at a decision on disclosure.   **13.098**

13.099 **Procedure for granting access to the file.** In addition to the practical information set out in the Notice on Access to the File, see 'Best Practices on the conduct of proceedings concerning Articles 101 and 102 TFEU' (Vol II, App B20, available on the DG Competition website and linked to Press Release IP/10/02 (6 January 2010)), paras 83 *et seq*. The Commission outlines two additional procedures aimed at alleviating the burden on the parties to redact their submissions in relation to confidential information. In a case where the file is very voluminous, the Commission may accept the use of a 'negotiated disclosure procedure'. Under this procedure, the party being granted access to file agrees bilaterally with interested third parties to receive the entirety of their information on the file including confidential information (instead of only being given access to the redacted version of their submissions). The party being granted access to file limits access to the information to a confidentiality ring to be decided on a case-by-case basis. The second procedure is the grant of access through a so called 'data room' procedure organised by DG Competition. Under this procedure, part of the file, also including confidential information, is gathered in a room, the data room, at the Commission's premises. Access is thereafter given to this room, to a restricted group of persons, normally the external counsel or the economic advisers of the party, under the supervision of a Commission official. The external counsel may record information contained in the data room but may not disclose any confidential information to their client. Given that both these procedures involve a waiver of rights on both sides, they can normally be adopted only with the consent of both parties. However if parties unduly refuse to waive their right to access to the file or their right to confidentiality to the extent it would be necessary to implement the data room procedure, this waiver can be replaced by a decision pursuant to Articles 8 or 9 of the Hearing Officer's Mandate.

13.100 **Provision of documents from the file to third parties.** As regards the application of Regulation 1049/2001 in competition cases see Case C-506/08P *Sweden v Commission*, judgment of 21 July 2011 (on appeal from Case T-403/05 *MyTravel Group v Commission* [2008] ECR II-2027, [2008] 3 CMLR 1517). Following the annulment of the Commission's decision in Case T-342/99 *Airtours v Commission*, the Commission established a working group of officials of DG Comp to consider whether it was appropriate to bring an appeal against that judgment and to assess the implications of that judgment on procedures for merger control. The report of the working group was presented to the Commissioner for Competition. In 2003 Airtours, now renamed MyTravel, brought an action for damages arising from the Commission's handling of the concentration. In 2005, MyTravel requested documents under Regulation 1049/2001 namely the working group report, the working papers and other internal documents. The Commission granted access to a limited number of the documents but refused to supply others relying on three exceptions: the protection of the decision-making process; the protection of inspections, investigations and audit; and the protection of court proceedings and legal advice. The GC upheld the Commission's rejection of the request in relation to all but one of the documents requested but the CJ overturned much of that ruling, holding that the GC had erred in its application of the exceptions. The Court stressed that since the exceptions relied on derogate from the principle of the widest possible public access to documents, they must be interpreted and applied strictly. If an institution refuses access to a document, it must, in principle, explain how disclosure of that document could specifically and effectively undermine the interest protected by the exception and show that the risk of that undermining must be reasonably foreseeable and not purely hypothetical. As regards the exception aimed at protecting the decision-making process in Article 4(3) of the Regulation, the Court noted the distinction made in the two paragraphs of the Article between documents relating to a matter where the decision has not yet been taken and documents relating to a matter where the decision has already been adopted. In the *Mytravel* case, the decision was not only adopted at the time that Mytravel requested the documents, but the appeal against the prohibition of the merger had been determined and the time for a further appeal had expired. The Court considered each of the documents requested in turn:

- As regards the working group's report, the Court held that the GC's ruling that the exception in Article 4(3) applied had not been supported by detailed evidence, based on the actual content of the report, explaining why disclosure would seriously undermine the Commission's decision-making process. The GC should have required the Commission to indicate the specific reasons why there was still a risk of the decision-making process being seriously undermined even though the administrative procedure had closed.
- As regards the report of the Hearing Officer, the note from DG Competition to the Advisory Committee and the file note concerning a site visit to First Choice, the Court agreed with the applicant that these documents constituted opinions for internal use as part of deliberations and preliminary consultations within the Commission, and so fell within the scope of Article 4(3). But the Court held that the GC had erred in failing to verify whether the Commission had specific reasons why the exception applied, even though the administrative procedure to which those documents related had been closed.
- As regards the working group's papers which enabled the report to be produced and comprised preparatory assessments or provisional conclusions for internal use, the Court again held that there was insufficient consideration of specific reasons why disclosure would undermine the decision-making process.
- As regards the notes to the other services and the notes in reply from services other than the legal service, the Court endorsed the opinion of Advocate General Kokott that the GC's reasoning was not adequate to justify the application of the exception in Article 4(3).
- As regards the advice from the Commission's legal service, the Court considered the application of the second indent of Article 4(2) which protects court

proceedings and legal advice unless there is an overriding public interest in disclosure. The Court roundly rejected concerns that disclosure of legal advice, which might contradict the stance ultimately taken by the Commission, might be damaging: 'it is … precisely openness in this regard that contributes to conferring greater legitimacy on the institutions in the eyes of European citizens and increasing their confidence in them by allowing divergences between various points of view to be openly debated. It is in fact rather a lack of information and debate which is capable of giving rise to doubts in the minds of citizens, not only as regards the lawfulness of an isolated act, but also as regards the legitimacy of the decision-making process as a whole' (para 113).

The Court therefore allowed the appeal against the Commission's reliance on those grounds for refusing disclosure and referred the matter back to the GC for the lower court to consider the application of other exceptions also relied on by the Commission.

See also Case 28/08P *Bavarian Lager Co v Commission*, judgment of 29 June 2010 where the CJ held that where a request based on Regulation 1049/2001 seeks to obtain access to documents including personal data, the provisions of Regulation 45/2001 concerning the protection of personal data become applicable in their entirety. The Commission had been correct therefore to rely on the exception for the protection of private material in Article 4(1)(b) of Regulation 1049/2001 in refusing to include the names of people attending a meeting when disclosing a minute of that meeting, when the people concerned had not given their consent to the disclosure.

Fn 531. A similar ruling was handed down in Case T-237/05 *Éditions Odile Jacob SAS v Commission*, judgment of 9 June 2010 where the GC annulled most of a Commission decision refusing the applicant access to the document relating to the decision to clear a concentration under the Merger Regulation. The applicant had brought two appeals challenging that clearance decision. The GC again stressed that the Commission must examine each document individually to assess whether the exceptions to the obligation to disclose apply. However, the GC held that the Commission was entitled to withhold an opinion provided by the Commission's legal service. See also Case T-111/07 *Agrofert Holding v Commission*, judgment of 7 July 2010 where the GC held that it does not have power to order the Commission to disclose the documents to the applicant but the Court annulled the refusal to disclose (including the refusal to disclose legal advice) on the basis that it was not clear that the Commission had weighed the need for reliance on the exemptions against the public interest in disclosure in respect of each document.

The Commission has indicated that normally public disclosure of documents and written and recorded statements received in the context of the cartel settlement procedure would undermine the public interest within the meaning of Article 4 of Reg 1049/2001: see Notice on the Conduct of Settlement Procedures in cartel cases, OJ 2008 C167/1: Vol II, App B17, para 40. For the settlement procedure generally see new paragraphs 13.113A–13.113D, below.

See also Case C-360/09 *Pfleiderer v Bundeskartellamt*, judgment of 14 June 2011, discussed in the update to paragraph 13.198, below.

(d) The hearing and subsequently

Hearings. Article 12 of Regulation 773/2004 has been substituted by Regulation 622/2008, OJ 2008 L171/3, [2008] 5 CMLR 1032, Article 1.6. That Regulation introduces the new cartel settlement procedure into Regulation 773/2004. The new wording of Article 12 provides that when making settlement submissions, the parties should confirm that they will only require an oral hearing if the statement of objections does not reflect the content of their settlement submissions. For the settlement procedure generally see new paragraphs 13.113A–13.113D, below. **13.101**

Hearing Officer. The Commission has recently published Guidance on the role of the Hearing Officer: 'Guidance on procedures of the Hearing Officers in proceedings relating to Articles 101 and 102 TFEU' (Vol II, App B22 and available on the DG Competition website and linked to Press Release IP/10/02 (6 January 2010)) covering all their responsibilities, particularly regarding the conduct of the oral hearing. **13.102**

The Hearing Officer may also be called upon by parties involved in the cartel settlement procedure: see Notice on the Conduct of Settlement Procedures in cartel cases, OJ 2008 C167/1: Vol II, App B17, para 18. For the settlement procedure generally see new paragraphs 13.113A–13.113D, below.

Fn 545. As to the Hearing Officer's reports see Guidance referred to above, paras 61 *et seq.*

Conduct of the hearing. See now also the Guidance referred to in the preceding update. As to the language in which the hearing is conducted, participants may request to be heard in an EU official language other than the language of proceedings. In such a case, interpretation into the language of the proceedings from this language, if it is another official EU language, will be provided as long as sufficient advance notice of such a language requirement is given to the Hearing Officer. **13.103**

The fact that a hearing in a Dutch case is conducted in English is not a breach of the rights of the defence unless the parties can show that they were prejudiced by this: Case T-151/05 *Nederlandse Vakbond Varkenshouders (NVV) v Commission* [2009] ECR II-1219, [2009] 5 CMLR 1613, para 211. Note also, as to the language in which the hearing can be conducted, 'Best Practices on the conduct of proceedings concerning Articles 101 and 102 TFEU' (Vol II, App B20, available on the DG Competition website and linked to Press Release IP/10/02 (6 January 2010)), para 29.

Fn 556. See also Cases T-122/07, etc, *Siemens AG Österreich v Commission*, judgment of 3 March 2011, para 234.

13.104 **Third party participation in the hearing.** The admission of interested parties other than complainants to the proceedings is the responsibility of the Hearing Officer: see 'Guidance on procedures of the Hearing Officers in proceedings relating to Articles 101 and 102 TFEU' (Vol II, App B22 and available on the DG Competition website and linked to Press Release IP/10/02 (6 January 2010)), paras 32 *et seq*. Potential interested third parties are encouraged to submit formal applications at the time the statement of objections is issued. The relevant factors where an association applies to be admitted are set out in the Guidance.

13.108 **Adoption and authentication of the decision.** The fact that a Commission spokesman was reported as having said, the day before a decision was adopted, that the Commission was going to adopt it did not breach the principle of collegiality because the statement was not binding on the Commissioners: Case T-58/01 *Solvay v Commission*, judgment of 17 December 2009, paras 132 *et seq*. The case is on further appeal, Case C-110/10P, not yet decided.

Note that after adopting the decision in COMP/38543 *International Removal Services*, decn of 11 March 2008, the Commission adopted a decision revising the turnover figures on which the fines had been calculated: decn of 24 July 2009.

13.109 **Rules of Procedure on adoption of decisions.** In Case T-110/07 *Siemens v Commission*, judgment of 3 March 2011, the GC considered a case where, before the adoption of the contested decision, essential components of the draft decision submitted to the College of Commissioners for definitive approval were leaked by someone in the Commission's service to a press agency and published. However, there were no grounds for supposing that if the information at issue had not been disclosed, the College of Commissioners would have altered the proposed amount of the fine or the content of the draft decision. In particular, there was no evidence indicating that the College of Commissioners as a whole or certain Commissioners felt bound or took the view that they could not depart from those aspects of the draft decision which were leaked to the press. The leak did not therefore affect the validity of the decision: para 402. The case is on appeal on other grounds: Case C-239/11P, not yet decided.

The legality of the Rules can be challenged by an applicant seeking the annulment of a decision but the measure challenged must be applicable directly or indirectly, to the issue with which the action is concerned and there must be a direct legal connection between the contested individual decision and the general measure in question: Case T-58/01 *Solvay v Commission*, judgment of 17 December 2009, para 148. The case is on further appeal, Case C-110/10P, not yet decided.

Note that in Case T-192/07 *Comité de défense de la viticulture charentaise v Commission*, not yet decided, the applicant has challenged a decision rejecting a complaint on the grounds, *inter alia* of lack of competence of the Commission member who was the signatory to the contested measure, when he signed it 'on behalf of the Commission'.

Readoption of decision following annulment.   Where a decision is annulled by   **13.109A**
the GC on procedural grounds, the Commission may readopt the decision and reimpose the fines originally imposed. The procedure which it must follow in this situation has been considered in recent appeals against such readopted decisions. The GC rejected arguments challenging the ability of the Commission to readopt annulled decisions. In Case T-57/01 *Solvay v Commission*, judgment of 17 December 2009, the GC held that (i) the earlier appeals had suspended the running of the limitation period under Regulation 2988/74 so that the Commission was not time barred from readopting the decisions (para 99); (ii) the time taken by the earlier appeals must be left out of account when considering whether the Commission was in breach of the principle that it must take decisions within a reasonable time (para 124); and (iii) the Commission was not required to conduct a fresh oral hearing before readopting the decision (para 184) or to consult the Advisory Committee (para 202). See also Case T-66/01 *ICI v Commission*, judgment of 25 June 2010, paras 149 *et seq*. In that case (T-66/01) the GC held (para 209) that a challenge based on alleged lack of access to the file was *res judicata* as a similar challenge had been in the Court's judgment in the appeal against the decision which had been annulled on other grounds in Case T-37/91. The *Solvay* and *ICI* decisions and appeals are as set out in the following table:

Original decision	Appeal to GC	Appeal to CJ	Readopted Decision	Appeal to GC	Further appeal to CJ
91/297/EEC *Soda ash— Solvay ICI* OJ 1991 L152/1 Art 101 market-sharing arrangements confining sales to home markets UK/ Western Europe	ICI appeal T-36/91 *ICI v Comn* [1995] ECR II-1847 Annulled decn for breach of right of access to the file Solvay appeal T-30/91 *Solvay v Comn* [1995] ECR II-1775 Annulled for breach of right of access to the file				

Original decision	Appeal to GC	Appeal to CJ	Readopted Decision	Appeal to GC	Further appeal to CJ
91/298/EEC *Soda ash— Solvay, CFK* OJ 1991 L152/16 Art 101 market-sharing arrangements in Germany	Solvay appeal T-31/91 *Solvay v Comn* [not published] Annulled for improper authentication CFK did not appeal	Commission appeal Cases C-287 &288/95P *Comn v Solvay* [2000] ECR I-2391 Appeal dismissed	Decn 2003/5/EC COMP/33133-B *Soda Ash—Solvay, CFK* OJ 2003 L10/1	T-58/01 *Solvay v Comn*, judgment of 17 December 2009 Fine reduced	C-110/10P *Solvay v Comn* not yet decided
91/299/EEC *Soda Ash— Solvay* OJ 1991 L152/21 Art 102 long term supply and exclusivity contracts	Solvay appeal T-32/91 *Solvay v Comn* [1995] ECR II-1825 Annulled for improper authentication	Commission appeal Cases C-287&288/95P *Comn v Solvay* [2000] ECR I-2391 Appeal dismissed	Decn 2003/6/EC COMP 33.133-C *Soda ash-Solvay* OJ 2003 L10/10	T-57/01 *Solvay v Comn*, judgment of 17 December 2009 Fine reduced	C-109/10P *Solvay v Comn* not yet decided
91/300/EEC *Soda ash- ICI* OJ 1991 L152/40 Art 102 rebate and exclusivity abuse	ICI appeal T-37/91 *ICI v Comn* [1995] ECR II-1901 Annulled for improper authentication	Commission appeal Case C-286/95P *Comn v ICI* [2000] ECR I-2341 Appeal dismissed	Decn 2003/7/EC *Soda Ash—ICI* OJ 2003 L10/33	T-66/01 *ICI v Comn*, judgment of 25 June 2010 Fine reduced	

13.110 **Relationship between the decision and the statement of objections.** Fn 592. See also Case T-461/07 *Visa v Commission*, judgment of 14 April 2011, para 57.

13.112 **Publication of decisions.** In Case T-474/04 *Pergan Hilfsstoffe für industrielle Prozesse GmbH v Commission* [2007] ECR II-4225, [2008] 4 CMLR 148 the applicant challenged the fact that the Commission had stated in the published decision that the applicant had been involved in the organic peroxides cartel at an early stage but that there had been insufficient evidence of their involvement in the cartel at a time not barred by the limitation period. The Court analysed the reference in Article 21 of Regulation 17 (now Article 30 of Regulation 1/2003) to the need to protect 'business secrets' and found that the obligation to redact in fact extended not only to business secrets but to other kinds of confidential information covered by Article 339 TFEU (formerly Article 287 EC) (see para 64 of the judgment). The applicant had not been an addressee of the decision and so any challenge to the allegation of involvement in the cartel would have been inadmissible before the GC. The Court held that in these circumstances the allegation was contrary to the presumption of innocence and infringed the protection of professional secrecy. The Hearing Officer's decision to allow the Commission to include the allegation was annulled.

The procedure for publishing decisions is now described by the Commission in 'Best Practices on the conduct of proceedings concerning Articles 101 and 102 TFEU' (Vol II, App B20, available on the DG Competition website and linked to Press Release IP/10/02 (6 January 2010)), paras 130 *et seq*.

7. Commitments and Settlement

Cartel settlement.   The Commission has established a settlement procedure intended to enable it to handle cartel cases more quickly and efficiently. Regulation 773/2004 has been amended by Regulation 622/2008, OJ 2008 L171/3, [2008] 5 CMLR 1032 Article 1.4 to incorporate this procedure as Article 10a of Regulation 773/2004: see Vol II, App B4. The Commission has also issued a Notice on the Conduct of Settlement Procedures in cartel cases, explaining how the procedure will operate: see OJ 2008 C167/1: Vol II, App B17. See Tierno Centella, 'The new settlement procedure in selected cartel cases' (2008) 3 Competition Policy Newsletter 30. The settlement procedure was adopted first in COMP/38511 *DRAMS*, decn of 19 May 2010, where the Commission imposed fines of over €331 million on 10 producers of memory chips used in computers. A further settlement procedure decision was adopted in COMP/39579 *Consumer detergents*, decn of 13 April 2010, OJ 2011 C193/14 where those participants who did not achieve complete immunity under the Leniency Notice had their fines reduced by 10 per cent. There have been no appeals against these decisions, cf COMP/39258 *Airfreight*, decn of 9 November 2010 against which 13 appeals have been lodged.   **13.113A**

Commencement of the settlement procedure.   After proceedings have been initiated, the Commission may set a time limit for the parties to indicate in writing whether they are prepared to discuss settlement (Article 10a(1)). The Notice sets out the factors that the Commission will take into account in deciding whether a case is suitable for the settlement procedure (Notice, para 5). Those then taking part in the settlement discussions may be informed by the Commission of the objections it envisages raising against them and the evidence relied on. They may also request non-confidential versions of documents on the file so far as relevant to enable the party to ascertain its position *vis-à-vis* the cartel and the range of potential fines. The parties to the proceedings may not disclose to any third party in any jurisdiction the contents of the discussions or of the documents to which they have had access.   **13.113B**

Cartel settlement: settlement submissions and the statement of objections.   When progress made during the settlement discussions leads the Commission to conclude that procedural efficiencies are likely to be achieved, the Commission will set a deadline for final settlement submissions. In the submissions the parties make a formal request to settle by (i) acknowledging in clear and unequivocal terms the parties' liability for the infringement; (ii) indicating the   **13.113C**

maximum amount of the fine which the parties would accept; (iii) confirming that they have been sufficiently informed of the Commission's objections and have been given sufficient opportunity to make known their views; (iv) confirming that they do not want access to the file or an oral hearing provided that the settlement submissions are reflected in the statement of objections; and (v) agreeing to receive the statement of objections and the decision in one of the Union languages (Notice, para 20). The Commission will then issue a statement of objections which reflects the settlement submissions and the parties' reply is limited to confirming that this is the case.

13.113D   **Cartel settlement: other procedural aspects.**   Once the parties have confirmed that the statement of objections reflects the settlement submissions, the Commission proceeds immediately to the adoption of the final decision (Notice, para 28). If the statement of objections does not reflect the settlement submissions, the acknowledgements made by the parties are deemed to be withdrawn and cannot be used in evidence against any of the parties (Notice, para 27). Similarly, if the final decision is not going to endorse the settlement, a new statement of objections will be issued and the full rights of the defence will be granted (Notice, para 29). If the Commission decides to reward a party for settlement, the fine will be reduced by 10 per cent and this reduction will be added to the leniency reduction where the Leniency Notice also applies (Notice, paras 32 and 33). Article 17 of Regulation 773/2004 has been amended to include time limits for various stages in the settlement process: Regulation 622/2008, Article 1.8. The Notice sets out how settlement submissions will be protected from disclosure: see paras 35–40. The settlement procedure entered into force on 1 July 2008 (Regulation 622/2008, Article 2).

See also *Crest Nicholson v Office of Fair Trading* [2009] EWHC 1875 (Admin) where the application of a 'Fast Track Offer' procedure established by the Office of Fair Trading for a particular investigation into collusion in the construction industry was successfully challenged on the basis that it had not been applied fairly to the applicant.

13.114   **Article 9 of Regulation 1/2003.   Fn 607.** The judgment of the GC in Case T-170/06 was set aside by the CJ which held that the GC had erred in its analysis of the principle of proportionality as it applies to the Commission's consideration of commitments proposed by the parties: see Case C-441/07P *Commission v Alrosa*, judgment of 29 June 2010, [2010] 5 CMLR 643 discussed in the update to paragraph 13.116, below.

13.115   **Procedure.** The judgment of the GC in Case T-170/06 was set aside by the CJ which held that the GC had erred in finding that Alrosa's right to be heard had been infringed: see Case C-441/07P *Commission v Alrosa*, judgment of 29 June 2010, [2010] 5 CMLR 643 discussed in the update to paragraph 13.116, below.

See also 'Best Practices on the conduct of proceedings concerning Articles 101 and 102 TFEU' (Vol II, App B20, available on the DG Competition website and linked to Press Release IP/10/02 (6 January 2010)), paras 104 *et seq*, describing in particular the 'market test notice' issued by the Commission prior to deciding whether to accept the commitments.

Effects of a commitment decision. The judgment of the GC in the *De Beers* **13.116** case was overturned by the Court of Justice: Case C-441/07P *Commission v Alrosa*, judgment of 29 June 2010, [2010] 5 CMLR 643. The CJ held that the GC was wrong to hold that a decision which would be disproportionate if adopted under Article 7(1) of Regulation 1/2003 must be disproportionate if adopted as a binding commitment under Article 9(1). Although the principle of proportionality does apply to the Commission's role in considering commitments, there was no reason why the potential remedy under Article 7 should serve as a reference point for the commitments which the Commission was entitled to accept under Article 9. Undertakings which offer commitments 'consciously accept that the concessions they make may go beyond what the Commission could itself impose on them in a decision adopted under Article 7 of the regulation after a thorough examination. On the other hand, the closure of the infringement proceedings brought against those undertakings allows them to avoid a finding of an infringement of competition law and a possible fine' (para 48). Further, the CJ held that the Commission was not required itself to seek out less onerous or more moderate solutions than the commitments offered to it and that its only obligation in relation to the proportionality of the commitments was to ascertain whether the commitments were sufficient to address the concerns it had identified. The GC had erred by examining other less onerous solutions for the purpose of applying the principle of proportionality, including possible adjustments of the joint commitments. This went beyond the GC's proper function because it put forward its own assessment of complex economic circumstances and thus substituted its own assessment for that of the Commission, thereby encroaching on the discretion enjoyed by the Commission instead of reviewing the lawfulness of the Commission's assessment: para 67. The CJ also rejected the assertion that Alrosa's rights to be heard had been infringed. The GC had been wrong to treat Alrosa as 'a person concerned' in the Article 102 proceedings for the purposes of Article 27(2) of Regulation 1/2003 and had also erred in holding that the Commission was required to give reasons for rejecting the joint commitments and to suggest to Alrosa that it offer new joint commitments with De Beers: para 95. In addition to setting aside the GC's judgment, the CJ dismissed Alrosa's appeal against the Commission's decision.

9. Declarations of Infringement and Orders to Terminate

Declaratory decisions. A national competition authority does not have power **13.124** to declare that Article 102 has **not** been infringed; at most it can decide that there are no grounds for action on its part in respect of an alleged abuse: see Case C-375/09 *Tele 2 Polska*, judgment of 3 May 2011, para 29 '... the Commission alone is empowered to make a finding that there has been no breach of Article 102 TFEU, even if that article is applied in a procedure undertaken by a national competition authority'.

Fn 656. See also COMP/37860 *Morgan Stanley/Visa International and Visa Europe*, decn of 3 October 2007 where the infringing conduct (the exclusion of Morgan Stanley from the Visa payment card network) had ceased in 2006 and Morgan Stanley had withdrawn its complaint in accordance with its settlement agreement with Visa. The Commission held that it still had a legitimate interest in adopting a decision because (i) Visa continued to deny that their behaviour was contrary to Article 101(1); (ii) it was important for the proper functioning of the single market for payments that anti-competitive practices committed by market players were not tolerated; and (iii) the Commission wished to impose a fine (appeal on other grounds dismissed: Case T-461/07 *Visa v Commission*, judgment of 14 April 2011). The appeals from *Thread* were decided in judgments delivered on 28 April 2010: this point was not considered.

13.126 **Orders to terminate.** **Fn 668.** The judgment of the GC in *Alrosa* was overturned by the Court of Justice: Case C-441/07P *Commission v Alrosa*, judgment of 29 June 2010, [2010] 5 CMLR 643. The CJ went on to dismiss Alrosa's challenge to the commitments holding that Alrosa had not succeeded in showing that the individual commitments offered by De Beers and made binding by the Commission manifestly went beyond what was necessary to address the concerns identified by the Commission in its preliminary assessment: para 120.

13.127 **'Like effect' orders.** In Case T-410/03 *Hoechst GmbH v Commission* [2008] ECR II-881, [2008] 5 CMLR 839, Hoechst complained that it was wrong for the Commission to include an order prohibiting future similar conduct because Hoechst had left the sorbates market several years earlier. The GC rejected this argument, holding that the prohibition 'is by nature preventive and does not depend on the situation of the undertakings concerned at the time of adoption of the Decision': para 200. The GC does not appear thereby to be saying that the order would apply to similar conduct in a market other than the sorbates market.

The Commission may impose such an order even if the undertaking is no longer active on the market: Cases T-456&457/05 *Gütermann AG and Zwicky v Commission*, judgment of 28 April 2010, [2010] 5 CMLR 930, para 66.

13.128 **Power to order positive action.** In COMP/34579 *MasterCard MIF charges*, decn of 19 December 2007, where the Commission found that the imposition of a particular fee was unlawful, the Commission noted that the cost reduction made possible by the removal of the fee should be passed on to the customer and this was only likely to happen if the customer was aware that lower prices were now possible. The

Commission therefore ordered MasterCard to publicise the Commission's decision on the front page of each of its country-specific websites: para 766. The case is on appeal: Case T-111/08, not yet decided.

A further appeal in *Der Grüne Punkt* was dismissed: Case C-385/07P *Der Grüne Punkt—Duales System Deutschland v Commission*, judgment of 16 July 2009, [2009] 5 CMLR 2215.

10. Fines for Substantive Infringements

(b) Intentional or negligent infringement

Generally. Fn 716. The appeal against the *Thread* decision was largely dismissed; **13.137** this point was not considered: Case T-446/05 *Amann & Söhne GmbH v Commission*, judgment of 28 April 2010, [2010] 5 CMLR 789. Two of the appeals against the *Raw Tobacco (Italy)* decision have been dismissed: Case T-25/06 *Alliance One International v Commission*, judgment of 9 September 2011; and Case T-12/06 *Deltafina v Commission*, judgment of 9 September 2011.

'Intentionally'. Fn 717. The appeal referred to has now been decided: Case **13.138** T-85/06 *General Química v Commission*, judgment of 18 December 2008 (appeal on other grounds dismissed: Case C-90/09P *General Química v Commission*, judgment of 20 January 2011).

Knowledge of Treaty not prerequisite to intention. Fn 726. The appeal in **13.139** *AstraZeneca* has been decided and the findings of abuse based on the internal documents relating to the information submitted by AstraZeneca when applying for patent protection extensions were upheld: Case T-321/05 *AstraZeneca v Commission*, judgment of 1 July 2010, [2010] 5 CMLR 1575 (on appeal Case C-457/10P *AstraZeneca v Commission*, not yet decided).

(c) The calculation of the fine

Generally. In Case T-69/04 *Schunk GmbH v Commission* [2008] ECR II-2567, **13.144** [2009] 4 CMLR 2 the Commission submitted that the amount of the fine imposed should be increased because the applicant had attempted to challenge facts which it had admitted during the investigation. The GC rejected this submission holding that the amount of a fine can be determined only on the basis of the gravity and duration of the infringement. The fact that the Commission had had to prepare for the appeal on the basis that the applicant might be allowed to withdraw its previous admissions did not justify an increase of that fine. The expenses incurred by the Commission as a result of the proceedings before the Court must only be taken into account when applying the provisions of the Rules of Procedure relating to costs: para 262.

13.145 **Discretion of the Commission.** In Case T-69/04 *Schunk GmbH v Commission* [2008] ECR II-2567, [2009] 4 CMLR 2 the GC rejected a submission that the discretion conferred on the Commission was so wide that the power to fine infringed the principle of legal certainty. The GC considered the jurisprudence of the Court of Human Rights on Article 7 ECHR and concluded that the fact that a law confers a discretion is not in itself inconsistent with the requirement of foreseeability, provided that the scope of the discretion and the manner of its exercise are indicated with sufficient clarity, having regard to the legitimate aim in question, to give the individual adequate protection against arbitrary interference. The Court held that the Commission's power to fine did not breach the principle: paras 28–50. See similarly, Case C-266/06P *Degussa v Commission*, judgment of 22 May 2008; Case T-11/05 *Wieland-Werke AG v Commission*, judgment of 19 May 2010, paras 66 *et seq.*

As to the level of detail which the Commission must set out in the decision as regards the computation of the fine, the GC has emphasised that too much detail may be counterproductive: 'it is important to ensure that fines are not easily foreseeable by economic operators. If the Commission were required to indicate in its decision the figures relating to the method of calculating the amount of fines, the deterrent effect of those fines would be undermined. If the amount of the fine were the result of a calculation which followed a simple arithmetical formula, undertakings would be able to predict the possible penalty and to compare it with the profit that they would derive from the infringement of the competition rules': see Case T-53/03 *BPB plc v Commission* [2008] ECR II-1333, [2008] 5 CMLR 1201, para 336. See also the discussion of Cases T-204&212/08 *Team Relocations v Commission*, judgment of 16 June 2011 in the update to paragraph 13.150, below, regarding the effect of the changes made in the 2006 Guidelines on Fines.

A general argument that the total fine imposed on the applicant was disproportionate because it was more than five times the total value of the EEA market in the relevant product was rejected by the GC in Case T-410/03 *Hoechst GmbH v Commission* [2008] ECR II-881, [2008] 5 CMLR 839, para 342.

The Commission has a discretion as regards the uplift imposed for duration and the reduction for cooperation so that the GC will only interfere where there has been a manifest error; Case T-18/05 *IMI plc v Commission*, judgment of 19 May 2010, paras 120 *et seq*. See also Case T-21/05 *Chalkor v Commission*, judgment of 19 May 2010, [2010] 5 CMLR 1295, paras 60 *et seq* where the GC considered the interaction between the binding nature of the Guidelines on Fines and the Commission's discretion when setting the fine.

Fn 755. The same point was made by the GC in Case T-68/04 *SGL Carbon AG v Commission* [2008] ECR II-2511, [2009] 4 CMLR 7, paras 43–44. A further appeal was dismissed: Case C-564/08P, judgment of 12 November 2009.

Retroactive application of revised Guidelines. The retroactive application of the **13.147** new fining Guidelines has now been confirmed several times: see, eg Case C-510/ 06P *Archer Daniels Midland v Commission (sodium gluconate)* [2009] ECR I-1843, [2009] 4 CMLR 889, para 59.

(d) Basic amount

The basic amount: the 2006 Guidelines on Fines. See the comparison of various **13.148** points in the 1998 and the 2006 Guidelines in Cases T-204&212/08 *Team Relocations v Commission*, judgment of 16 June 2011.

In Case C-510/06P *Archer Daniels Midland v Commission (sodium gluconate)* [2009] ECR I-1843, [2009] 4 CMLR 889 (a case under the 1998 Guidelines) the CJ held that it is permissible to take into account both the undertaking's overall turnover as an indication, however approximate and imperfect, of the size of the undertaking and its economic strength, and that part of the turnover which derives from the goods which are the subject of the infringement and which therefore is capable of giving an indication of the scale of the infringement. The Court stated that it is important not to confer on one or other of those figures an importance which is disproportionate. The Court said that there is no general principle that the penalty must be proportionate to the undertaking's turnover from sales of the product in respect of which the infringement was committed: para 75.

Value of sales. The sales to be included are those in the relevant market not only **13.149** those affected by the infringing conduct: Case T-211/08 *Putters International v Commission*, judgment of 16 June 2011, para 59. Note the GC's comment that this is clearer from the German version of para 13 of the Guidelines ('Umsatz auf den vom Verstoß betroffenen Märkten'): Cases T-204&212/08 *Team Relocations v Commission*, judgment of 16 June 2011, para 62. See also the discussion in Case T-375/06 *Viega v Commission*, judgment of 24 March 2011, paras 82 *et seq* (on appeal Case C-276/11P, not yet decided).

In Case T-127/04 *KM Europa Metal v Commission* [2009] ECR II-1167, [2009] 4 CMLR 1574 the GC rejected an argument that because a large element of the relevant product, namely industrial copper tubes, was determined by the price of copper and that commodity price was determined on the London Metal Exchange by the buyers of the tubes, the Commission should have deducted the cost of the copper from the parties' turnover before arriving at the starting point for the fine: paras 89 *et seq*. The GC also rejected an argument that profits rather than turnover should be used to calculate the basic amount of the fine. The GC stated that it is undeniable that, as a factor for assessing the seriousness of the infringement, the turnover of an undertaking in a market is necessarily vague and imperfect. It does not distinguish between sectors with a high added value and those with a low added value, or between undertakings which are profitable and those which are less so.

However, despite its approximate nature, turnover is an adequate criterion for assessing the size and economic power of the undertakings concerned: para 93. On further appeal: Case C-272/09P, not yet decided. See similarly Case T-25/05 *KME Germany v Commission*, judgment of 19 May 2010, para 101; Case T-20/05 *Outokumpu Oyj v Commission (copper plumbing tubes)*, judgment of 19 May 2010, [2010] 5 CMLR 1276, para 77. This principle was distinguished by the UK Competition Appeal Tribunal in *Hays Specialist Recruitment Ltd v Office of Fair Trading* [2011] CAT 8, para 56 where the CAT held that where the turnover included in the statutory accounts of a recruitment agency includes the wages of temporary workers placed by them because the wages are paid by the client to them and then passed on to the worker, the fine calculation should be based on the net fees excluding these wages.

In Case T-452/05 *Belgian Sewing Thread v Commission*, judgment of 28 April 2010, [2010] 5 CMLR 889, the GC held that the Commission is free to take into account the turnover figure of its choice, provided that this does not appear unreasonable by reference to the circumstances of the case: para 77.

The Commission has applied point 18 of the 2006 Guidelines on Fines. This provides a calculation method for assessing the value of sales for cartels that are geographically wider than the EEA: COMP/39180 *Aluminium Fluoride*, decn of 25 June 2008 (on appeal: Case T-406/08 *ICF v Commission*, not yet decided) and COMP/39406 *Marine Hoses*, decn of 28 January 2009, para 432 (on appeal: Cases T-146, 147, 148, 154/09, not yet decided). See also COMP/39129 *Power transformers*, decn of 7 October 2009 where the Commission did not use turnover figures for the EEA only because, since the parties were being punished for a market-sharing cartel in accordance with which the Japanese members had refrained from selling into the EEA 'the Japanese parties' fine would be zero and they would be rewarded for having complied with the cartel arrangement not to compete on this market': para 232. The Commission therefore applied point 18 of the 2006 Guidelines on Fines and applied the parties' worldwide market shares to the value of the total EEA market for power transformers to arrive at a value for EEA sales turnover to which a seriousness percentage of 16 per cent was applied. The decision is on appeal Cases T-517/09 *Alstom*, T-519/09 *Toshiba*, T-521/09 *Areva T&D*, not yet decided.

Note that in COMP/39125 *Car glass*, decn of 12 November 2008 the Commission took the unusual step of limiting, for part of the period covered by the fine, the value of sales to those sales to car manufacturers in respect of which the Commission had direct evidence of collusion. This applied both to a 'roll out phase' trial period at the start of the collusion when the Commission thought the carglass suppliers rigged the bids only within selected large accounts and to the end phase of the cartel when collusion broke down. Nonetheless, the fine imposed on St Gobain was the largest ever imposed on a single company for cartel activity. The decision is on appeal: Cases T-56, 68, 72, 73/09, not yet decided. The GC has indicated that the

Commission's 'nuance' in *Car Glass* did not affect the general principle that the value taken is of all sales in the relevant market, not just those which the Commission has proved were affected by the anti-competitive conduct: Cases T-204&212/08 *Team Relocations v Commission*, judgment of 16 June 2011, para 67.

Value of sales: relevant year for turnover.   The question of which year's turnover **13.149A** should be used to calculate the basic amount was considered by the GC in two appeals from the *Industrial Bags* decision which had condemned a cartel which lasted from January 1982 to June 2002: Case T-26/06 *Trioplast Wittenheim v Commission* and Case T-40/06 *Trioplast Industrier v Commission*, both judgments delivered on 13 September 2010. In T-26/06 an appeal by the company which had been directly involved in the infringement was dismissed. In that case the GC upheld the Commission's use of the year 1996 as the reference year for assessment of the basic amount. As Trioplast Wittenheim reduced its activities significantly after 1997, its market share in 1996 better reflected its position in the relevant market throughout the infringement period than its position in 2001 which was the last complete year of the infringement. However, as regards Trioplast Industrier which was held liable as a parent company for Trioplast Wittenheim's infringement, the GC held that 1996 was not the appropriate year because Trioplast Industrier was not yet present at that time on the relevant market. Because the subsidiary's market share had decreased considerably by the time Trioplast Industrier became its parent, that year was not indicative of the scope of the infringement that should be attributed to the new parent company which acquired Trioplast Wittenheim in 1999. Cf Case T-133/07 *Mitsubishi Electric v Commission*, judgment of 12 July 2011, para 276; and Case T-113/07 *Toshiba Corp v Commission*, judgment of 12 July 2011, para 292 where the GC annulled the fine imposed on the applicants because the Commission could not adequately justify using a different year's turnover for calculating the fines imposed on the Japanese producers from the reference year used for the Europeans. Although the Commission's reason for choosing the different year was legitimate (because the year chosen was the last year in which Mitsubishi and Toshiba had independent turnover before entering a joint venture) there would have been other ways of reflecting this.

See also COMP/39129 *Power transformers*, decn of 7 October 2009 where the Commission took the value of sales in an earlier year than the last year of the infringement because in the last year of the infringement the Japanese cartel members had transferred the relevant business into a joint venture which distorted the figures: para 228.

The Commission is entitled to base the fine on turnover in the last year of the infringement even if mergers during the course of the infringement mean that the undertaking's turnover in that year is greater than it was during earlier phases of the cartel: Cases T-122/07, etc, *Siemens AG Österreich v Commission*, judgment of 3 March 2011, para 124.

13.150 **Appropriate proportion of the value of sales.** In Cases T-204&212/08 *Team Relocations v Commission*, judgment of 16 June 2011 the GC stressed that in deciding the appropriate percentage, the relative gravity of the participation of each addressee in a single continuous infringement must be examined to ensure that the principle of equal treatment and non-discrimination is respected. However, the General Court's practice is to assess individual circumstances not in the context of the assessment of the gravity of the infringement, that is, when the basic amount of the fine is set, but in the context of the adjustment to the basic amount to reflect mitigating or aggravating circumstances. The GC stressed that the 2006 Guidelines had brought about 'a fundamental change' in the calculation of fines (para 89). First the abandonment of the three-fold classification of infringements in the 1998 Guidelines (very serious, serious and minor) to the application of a percentage between 0 and 30 per cent enables finer distinctions to be made according to the gravity of the infringements. Secondly the move away from flat rates makes it easier to take into account the extent of the individual participation of each undertaking in the infringement when the gravity of that infringement is assessed. It also makes it possible to take into account any reduction in the gravity of a single infringement over time. Thirdly, the Commission had confirmed at the hearing that its decisional practice is no longer necessarily to apply a single percentage to all the participants in such an infringement but rather to apply different percentages to different categories of participant in the cartels at issue according to the relative gravity of their participation in the infringement. However, the GC held that the new methodology does not impose such an approach on the Commission and upheld the Commission's decision to apply the same percentage (17 per cent) to all addressees, on the basis that the applicant's individual circumstances could be adequately considered at the mitigation/aggravation stage. Note also that the GC stated that the move from the three-fold classification of fines to a more finely-tuned percentage increased the Commission's obligation to set out the reasons for the choice of a particular percentage in its decision. Although the Commission's reasoning in the contested decision was not very detailed, it was adequate given that the 17 per cent chosen was very close to the lower end of the scale laid down for the most serious restrictions and hence highly favourable to the applicant (para 100). See similarly, Cases T-208&209/08 *Gosselin Group v Commission*, judgment of 16 June 2011, para 132.

In Case T-452/05 *Belgian Sewing Thread v Commission*, judgment of 28 April 2010, [2010] 5 CMLR 889, the GC discussed the factors relevant to the gravity of the infringement in the context of applying the 1998 Guidelines. The Court held that the overall size of the (small) relevant market was a less important factor in assessing the proportionality of the fine than the fact that this was a price-fixing horizontal cartel but that it had been taken into account by the Commission in setting the starting amount: para 66.

Basic amount: the 1998 and 2006 Guidelines on Fines compared.   See the dis-   **13.152**
cussion of Cases T-204&212/08 *Team Relocations v Commission*, judgment of
16 June 2011 in the update to paragraph 13.150, above.

Fn 784. This point was considered in Case T-452/05 *Belgian Sewing Thread v
Commission*, judgment of 28 April 2010, [2010] 5 CMLR 889, para 66.

Fn 786. For a case where there was a considerable disparity in the size of the undertakings fined, see Case T-68/04 *SGL Carbon AG v Commission* [2008] ECR II-2511,
[2009] 4 CMLR 7. A further appeal was dismissed: Case C-564/08P, judgment of
12 November 2009. Where two undertakings' turnover in the relevant market was
similar, the Commission is not bound to differentiate between the basic amount of
fine because one undertaking is, overall, smaller than the other. It is turnover in the
relevant market which constitutes an objective criterion, giving a proper measure of
the harm which the offending conduct represents for normal competition, and it is
therefore a good indicator of the capacity of each undertaking to cause damage:
Case T-448/05 *Oxley Threads v Commission*, judgment of 28 April 2010, [2010] 5
CMLR 864, para 68 (a case under the 1998 Guidelines).

Hard-core cartels.   In Case T-53/03 *BPB plc v Commission* [2008] ECR II-1333,   **13.153**
[2008] 5 CMLR 1201 (a case under the 1998 Guidelines) the GC held that the
Commission was entitled to refer to the actual impact on the market of a cartel
having an anti-competitive object even though the Commission did not quantify
that impact or provide any assessment in figures in this respect. The actual impact
of a cartel on the market was sufficiently demonstrated if the Commission provides
specific and credible evidence indicating with reasonable probability that the cartel
had an impact on the market.

Where the Commission imposes a percentage at or near 30 per cent for a hard-core
cartel it must give reasons for its choice of percentage over and above the fact that
the cartel is a very serious infringement: Cases T-204&212/08 *Team Relocations v
Commission*, judgment of 16 June 2011, para 100.

Basic amount: seriousness of the infringements.   Fn 796. See also Case T-127/04   **13.154**
KM Europa Metal v Commission [2009] ECR II-1167, [2009] 4 CMLR 1574 where
the GC confirmed that the actual impact of a cartel on the market is sufficiently
demonstrated if the Commission can provide specific and credible evidence indicating with reasonable probability that the cartel had an impact on the market: para
68. On further appeal: Case C-272/09P, not yet decided. Note that under the 1998
Guidelines (para 1.A) the assessment of the gravity of the infringement could take
into account its actual impact on the market 'where this can be measured'. The
importance of that qualification was noted in Case C-511/06P *Archer Daniels
Midland v Commission (citric acid)*, judgment of 9 July 2009, para 125. In Case
C-534/07P *Prym and Prym Consumer v Commission*, judgment of 3 September

2009, [2009] 5 CMLR 2377 the CJ held that the GC had been right to reduce the fine imposed on Prym on the basis that the Commission had not given adequate reasons for concluding that the cartel had had an actual impact on the market. The CJ held that the Commission did not have to demonstrate actual impact in order to classify the infringement as 'very serious' under the 1998 Guidelines. But if the Commission wished to increase the fine beyond the minimum then applicable to a very serious infringement, on the grounds that the cartel had an actual impact on the market, it could not simply assume that the cartel had had such an effect because it had been implemented: 'it cannot just put forward a mere presumption but . . . must provide specific, credible and adequate evidence with which to assess what actual influence the infringement may have had on competition in that market': para 82. The 2006 Guidelines do not include the 'where this can be measured' phrase.

Fn 793. The appeal referred to has now been decided: Case T-450/05 *Automobiles Peugeot SA and Peugeot Nederland NV* [2009] ECR II-2533. The GC reduced the fine imposed because, in finding that the restrictions had led to a reduction in exports, the Commission had not taken into account the possible effect of relative changes in price on the level of exports.

Fn 792. An appeal against the fine was dismissed: see Case T-155/06 *Tomra Systems v Commission*, judgment of 9 September 2010.

13.155   **Duration of infringement.**   Note the comment of the GC in Case T-211/08 *Putters International v Commission*, judgment of 16 June 2011, para 75 that the use in the 2006 Guidelines on Fines of a multiplier rather than a percentage uplift to reflect duration is likely to result in the 10 per cent cap becoming the rule rather than the exception and that this may make it more difficult to distinguish between participants in accordance with their relative culpability. This problem is inherent in the new methodology introduced by the 2006 Guidelines and may require the Court to exercise its full jurisdiction to amend fines more freely in appropriate cases.

Where there is no direct evidence to show that a cartel continued during a particular period, the Commission may rely on evidence sufficiently close in time to enable one to conclude that the cartel continued uninterrupted during that period: See Case T-18/05 *IMI v Commission*, judgment of 19 May 2010, para 89; Case T-40/06 *Trioplast Industrier v Commission*, judgment of 13 September 2010, para 39.

In Cases T-204&212/08 *Team Relocations v Commission*, judgment of 16 June 2011 the GC, whilst noting the fundamental change in methodology as regards the treatment of duration between the 1998 and the 2006 Guidelines, did not interfere with the Commission's application of the new multiplier: para 110.

13.156   **Legal considerations affecting duration.**   In COMP/38113 *Prokent-Tomra*, decn of 29 March 2006, [2009] 4 CMLR 101 (a case under Article 82) the Commission treated the duration of the infringement as five years even though it was not claimed that all the abusive components identified in the decision existed throughout the entire period in question in each of the national markets investigated. The single fine imposed dealt globally with all of the infringements established, which together covered the entire period in question. The fact that the infringement did not always cover the entire period in each of the national markets considered, and that within each national market the intensity of the infringement may have varied over time, was taken into account in establishing the basic amount of the fine (€16 million): para 418. Tomra's appeal was dismissed and this point was not discussed: Case T-155/06 *Tomra Systems v Commission*, judgment of 9 September 2010.

Fn 801. The GC has stressed many times that the burden of proving duration lies on the Commission since this is an element of the infringement itself: see, eg Case T-42/07 *Dow Chemical v Commission*, judgment of 13 July 2011, para 89 and the cases cited there (decision annulled in respect of part of the period alleged).

Fn 805. In Case T-461/07 *Visa v Commission*, judgment of 14 April 2011 (on appeal from COMP/37860 *Morgan Stanley/Visa International and Visa Europe*, decn of 3 October 2007) the GC held that immunity from fines for notified conduct terminated when Regulation 1/2003 came into force so that Commission would have been entitled to impose a fine from that date: para 211. In fact the Commission had imposed a fine only in relation to conduct from a later date, the date in August 2004 when the SO had been served.

The 'entry fee'.   The application of the additional amount referred to in para 25 **13.157** of the 2006 Guidelines was approved by the GC in Cases T-204&212/08 *Team Relocations v Commission*, judgment of 16 June 2011, paras 116–118.

(e) Aggravating and mitigating circumstances and deterrence

Generally.   In Case T-127/04 *KM Europa Metal v Commission* [2009] ECR **13.158** II-1167, [2009] 4 CMLR 1574 the GC confirmed that the mere fact that the Commission has in its previous decisions granted a certain rate of reduction for specific conduct does not imply that it is required to grant the same proportionate reduction when assessing similar conduct in a subsequent administrative procedure: para 140. On further appeal: Case C-272/09P, not yet decided.

Repeat infringements.   In Case T-122/04 *Outokumpu Oyj v Commission (indus-* **13.160** *trial tubes)* [2009] 5 CMLR 1553 the GC held that the Commission was right to treat a decision taken under the ECSC Treaty as a previous infringement for this purpose and to do so even though no fine had been imposed in the previous case because of the unusual circumstances surrounding the earlier infringement: paras 55 *et seq.* See similarly, Case T-20/05 *Outokumpu Oyj v Commission (copper plumbing tubes)*, judgment of 19 May 2010, [2010] 5 CMLR 1276, para 63 (an infringement under Article 65 ECSC can justify an increase in the fine for the subsequent infringement of Article 101; the GC upheld an increase of 50 per cent on this ground).

Provided that the statement of objections makes clear that the Commission intends to increase the fine for recidivism, the Commission does not have to refer expressly to the previous infringements on which it relies: Case T-343/08 *Arkema France v Commission (sodium chlorate)*, judgment of 17 May 2011, para 61.

The Commission is entitled to increase the fine for recidivism as against a subsidiary within one group with reference to a past infringement by a different subsidiary within the same group, even where the parent company was not held liable for the earlier fine: COMP/39396 *Calcium carbide and magnesium based reagents*, decn of 22 July 2009, [2010] 5 CMLR 1368, para 311. But it must be clear that the undertaking on which the fine is being imposed is in fact part of the same economic entity which was previously found to have infringed: Cases T-144/07, etc, *ThyssenKrupp Liften Ascenseurs v Commission*, judgment of 13 July 2011 (increase in fine removed where the parent company had not been held liable for the earlier fines and it was not clear that the subsidiaries fined for the earlier cartel were the same as the subsidiaries being fined for the elevators cartel); and see similarly Case T-39/07 *ENI v Commission*, judgment of 13 July 2011; and Case T-59/07 *Polimeri Europa v Commission*, judgment of 13 July 2011 (both appeals from COMP/38638 *Butadiene Rubber and Emulsion Styrene Butadiene Rubber*, decn of 29 November 2006, [2009] 4 CMLR 421. The GC reduced the fines because the Commission had not proven that those companies had repeated an earlier infringement, given the complex changes in the control and structure of the companies concerned.

Fn 813. The same point was made in Cases T-101&111/05 *BASF AG and UCB SA v Commission* [2007] ECR II-4949, [2008] 4 CMLR 347, para 67. See also Case T-53/03 *BPB plc v Commission* [2008] ECR II-1333, [2008] 5 CMLR 1201, para 384 (a case under the 1998 Guidelines); Case T-343/08 *Arkema France v Commission (sodium chlorate)*, judgment of 17 May 2011, para 68 (Court held that three earlier decisions, taken in 1984, 1986 and 1994 were all before the current cartel activity started and were evidence of Arkema France's tendency to infringe the competition rules: an uplift of 90 per cent upheld).

In Case C-413/08 *Lafarge v Commission*, judgment of 17 June 2010, [2010] 5 CMLR 586 the CJ confirmed that there is no maximum period of time beyond which a past infringement cannot be taken into account but held that the principle of proportionality requires that the time elapsed between the infringement in question and a previous breach of the competition rules must be taken into account in assessing the undertaking's tendency to infringe those rules. The GC and CJ may therefore be called upon to scrutinise whether the Commission has complied with that principle when it increased the fine for this reason: see paras 66 *et seq*. In that case the CJ also upheld the GC's finding that the Commission may rely on an earlier infringement decision even if that decision is still subject to review by the courts. If the fine imposed in the earlier decision is later annulled, the Commission would have to comply with that judgment by amending, as appropriate, the later decision insofar as it includes an increase of the fine for repeated infringement: see paras 81 *et seq.*

Fn 814. The same point was made in *BASF and UCB*, above, para 64 where the GC said that it is sufficient if the previous infringement was under the same provision of the EC Treaty. See also Case T-410/03 *Hoechst GmbH v Commission* [2008] ECR II-881, [2008] 5 CMLR 839, para 474. An infringement of Article 102 is not of a similar nature as an infringement of Article 101, so the fine for the former cannot be increased on the basis of a previous infringement of the latter kind: Case T-66/01 *ICI v Commission*, judgment of 25 June 2010, para 380.

Effect of conduct on the market. In Case T-25/05 *KME Germany v Commission*, **13.160A**
judgment of 19 May 2010 the GC rejected the submission that if the Commission relied on the actual impact of the cartel in determining the amount of the fine, it was under a duty scientifically to demonstrate the existence of a tangible economic effect on the market and a link of cause and effect between that effect and the infringement: para 85. The Court held that actual impact of a cartel is sufficiently demonstrated if the Commission provides 'specific and credible evidence indicating with reasonable probability that the cartel had an impact on the market'. The Commission had rightly relied on the implementation of an information exchange system in relation to sales volumes and price levels, the existence of documents showing price increases during certain periods of the cartel and indicating that the cartel had enabled the undertakings concerned to achieve their price targets, the significant market share held by all the participants, and the fact that the respective market shares of those participants had remained relatively stable throughout the period of the infringement at issue. This evidence entitled the Commission to infer that the infringement had an actual impact on the market. The case is on appeal Case C-389/10P, not yet decided.

Refusal to cooperate with Commission investigation. In COMP/38432 **13.161**
Professional Videotape, decn of 20 November 2007, [2008] 5 CMLR 122, Sony's fine was increased by 30 per cent because of conduct during the Commission's visit (refusal to answer questions and shredding of documents). The Commission held that it was irrelevant whether the conduct had any effect on the investigation (para 221) or that the time limit for taking separate action under Article 23 of Regulation 1/2003 had expired (para 224).

The fact that the Commission is empowered to impose a fine for provision of misleading information does not prevent that conduct being treated as an aggravating factor in assessing the fine for the substantive infringement: Case T-384/06 *IBP Ltd v Commission*, judgment of 24 March 2011, para 109 (GC held that Commission had not proved that the information provided was misleading).

Fn 818. The appeals from the *Nintendo* decision have now been decided: Case T-13/03 *Nintendo* [2009] 5 CMLR 1421 (the GC upheld the Commission's imposition of a 25 per cent increase in the fine because Nintendo had continued with the infringement after the Commission investigation had started: para 144); Case T-18/03 *CD-Contact Data v Commission* [2009] ECR II-1021 (fine reduced) (appeal dismissed Case C-260/09P *Activision Blizzard v Commission*, judgment of 10 February 2011); Case T-12/03 *Itochu* [2009] 5 CMLR 1375 (appeal dismissed); Case T-398/02 *Linea Gig* (removed from register 2 May 2005). No issue arose in the appeals concerning the uplift imposed on John Menzies for inaccurate answers.

13.162   **'Ring leaders' of infringements and retaliatory measures.**   In Case T-13/03 *Nintendo and Nintendo Europe v Commission* [2009] 5 CMLR 1421 which concerned a vertical agreement, the GC held that in order to classify an undertaking as a 'leader', it is not necessary to prove that, in the absence of the role played by that undertaking, the infringement committed would have been less serious. The GC also rejected Nintendo's argument that a role of leader or instigator of the infringement can be found only in restrictive horizontal agreements. The fact that, in the case of vertical agreements, the role of leader or instigator generally merges with that of the manufacturer (rather than the distributors) does not preclude an increase of the fine on this ground: para 131.

In Case T-410/03 *Hoechst GmbH v Commission* [2008] ECR II-881, [2008] 5 CMLR 839 the GC held that the elements relied on by the Commission to establish that Hoechst had been the ring leader were not sufficiently drawn together in the statement of objections to make clear to Hoechst that this aggravating factor was alleged against it. Hoechst was thus not placed in a position to adopt an effective defence and the fine was reduced to strip out that element: paras 423 *et seq*. See also the update to paragraph 13.084, above.

See two appeals from the *Gas Insulated Switchgear* cartel decision: Case T-110/07 *Siemens v Commission*, judgment of 3 March 2011 paras 337 *et seq* (on further appeal: Case C-239/11P, not yet decided); and Cases T117&121/07 *Areva v Commission*, judgment of 3 March 2011 paras 277 *et seq*. In the former the GC upheld the increase imposed by the Commission because of Siemens' role as the 'secretary' to the cartel but in the latter an identical fine was reduced because Areva had been secretary for a much shorter time than Siemens. A failure to distinguish the amount of the fine to reflect the different periods for which the undertakings had filled the leadership role infringed the principles of equal treatment and proportionality. The case is on appeal Cases C-247&253/11P, not yet decided.

Fn 819. The uplift of 50 per cent of Deltafina's fine in *Raw Tobacco (Spain)* was overturned on appeal: Case T-29/05 *Deltafina v Commission*, judgment of 8 September 2010. The GC found (para 335) that there was no evidence to prove that Deltafina assumed responsibility for activities usually associated with acting the part of leader of a cartel, such as chairing meetings or centralising and distributing certain data. Similarly, although Deltafina had acted as mediator in disputes between the processors, its interventions in that capacity were few and limited to the first two years of the processors' cartel. Moreover, they were not accompanied by any real threat or disciplinary measure. The GC also increased the reduction granted to Deltafina to reflect its cooperation with the Commission's investigation since the Commission had limited the reduction because of Deltafina's supposed leadership role. The case is on appeal Case C-537/10P, not yet decided. The other appeals against *Raw Tobacco (Spain)* have also now been decided: Case T-24/05 *Alliance One, Standard Commercial Tobacco and Trans-Continental Leaf Tobacco v Commission,* judgment of 27 October 2010 (decn annulled as against one parent company; remainder of appeal dismissed); Case T-33/05 *Cetarsa v Commission,* judgment of 3 February 2011 (reduction in fine, on further appeal C-181/11P, not yet decided); Case T-37/05 *World Wide Tobacco España v Commission,* judgment of 8 March 2011 (reduction in fine for cooperation: on appeal Case C-240/11P, not yet decided); Cases T-38/05 *Agroexpansión* and Case T-41/05 *Dimon* are not yet decided.

The appeal in Case T-492/04 *Jungbunzlauer v Commission* was withdrawn on 10 July 2008.

Mitigating circumstances.   It is open to an applicant to raise on appeal a factor in
13.163
mitigation of the fine even though this has not been raised in its reply to the statement of objections: Case T-73/04 *Le Carbone-Lorraine v Commission* [2008] ECR II-2661, [2010] 5 CMLR 81, para 194. A further appeal was dismissed: Case C-554/08P, judgment of 12 November 2009.

In Cases T-208&209/08 *Gosselin Group v Commission,* judgment of 16 June 2011 the GC considered the relationship between the assessment of the seriousness of an individual participant's infringement when determining the basic amount of the fine and the assessment of mitigation based on that participant's limited involvement in the infringing conduct: para 183. If the Commission applies the same initial seriousness percentage to all the participants in a single continuous infringement at the first stage, it must then distinguish between them according to their relative culpability when considering mitigation at the later stage of the calculation: para 186.

The Commission is not bound always to take account separately of each of the attenuating circumstances listed in the Guidelines and it is not obliged to grant an additional reduction on such grounds automatically. The earlier case law concerning the Commission's discretion in this regard is not superseded by the Guidelines: Case T-25/05 *KME Germany v Commission,* judgment of 19 May 2010, paras 125 and 126. The case is on appeal Case C-389/10P, not yet decided.

Prompt termination of infringement.   Conversely, a substantial increase in the
13.164
fine may be imposed if the infringement continues despite the start of the

Commission's investigation: Case T-13/03 *Nintendo v Commission* [2009] 5 CMLR 1421, para 144.

In recent cartel appeals the GC has robustly confirmed that a reduction in fine is not appropriate in a cartel case: see, eg Case T-127/04 *KM Europa Metal v Commission* [2009] ECR II-1167, [2009] 4 CMLR 1574, para 121: '. . . termination constituted an appropriate and normal reaction to the Commission's intervention, and cannot be assimilated to the merits flowing from an independent initiative on the part of the applicants. Similarly, that termination merely constituted a return to lawful conduct and did not contribute to making the Commission's investigations more effective'. On further appeal: Case C-272/09P, not yet decided. Similarly, in Case T-53/03 *BPB plc v Commission* [2008] ECR II-1333, [2008] 5 CMLR 1201, paras 437–438, the GC held that the Commission was entitled to abandon the 'generous practice' of reducing the fine for prompt termination in cases of flagrant infringement. Thus the appropriateness of any such reduction depends on whether the applicant could reasonably doubt the illegality of its conduct. This approach has been confirmed by the CJ: see, eg Case C-510/06P *Archer Daniels Midland v Commission (sodium gluconate)* [2009] ECR I-1843, [2009] 4 CMLR 889 (a case under the 1998 Guidelines), para 149; and Case C-511/06P *Archer Daniels Midland v Commission (citric acid)*, judgment of 9 July 2009, para 105.

Fn 831. A further appeal in the *French Beef* case was dismissed: Cases C-101&110/07P *Coop de France bétail et viande and FNSEA v Commission* [2008] ECR I-10193, [2009] 4 CMLR 743.

13.165 **Negligent commission of infringement.**   As regards whether the existence of a compliance programme is a mitigating factor see Cases T-101&111/05 *BASF AG and UCB SA v Commission* [2007] ECR II-4949, [2008] 4 CMLR 347 (fine imposed under 1996 Guidelines), para 52: 'even though the measures to ensure compliance with competition law are important, they cannot affect the reality of the infringement committed'.

13.166 **Limited involvement and non-implementation.**   In Case T-18/03 *CD-Contact Data v Commission* [2009] ECR II-1021, the GC granted a 50 per cent reduction to one infringer on the basis that it had played 'an exclusively passive role' in the agreement and should have been treated in the same way as another undertaking who had been granted that level of reduction: para 199 (appeal dismissed Case C-260/09P *Activision Blizzard v Commission*, judgment of 10 February 2011).

13.167 **Cooperation with Commission investigation.**   See, eg *Industrial copper tubes*, OJ 2004 L125/50 where one cartel member gave the Commission a memorandum showing that the cartel had operated for much longer than the Commission had previously thought. This resulted in a substantial uplift of the fine on account of its duration; an uplift which could not be mitigated under the Leniency Notice 1996 because a 50 per cent reduction was the maximum that that cartel member could earn. The Commission dealt with this by granting a *de facto* immunity under the 1998 Guidelines (ie outside the Leniency Notice) as regards the additional duration of the cartel. See also in the appeal to the GC; Case T-127/04 *KM Europa Metal v Commission* [2009] ECR II-1167, [2009] 4 CMLR 1574, para 127 (on further appeal: Case C-272/09P, not yet decided). A similar point arose in respect of Zeon in COMP/38628 *Nitrile Butadiene Rubber*, decn of 23 January 2008. Since Zeon was the first to have disclosed that the cartel operated from October 2000 to May 2002, this period was not taken into consideration when considering the multiplier for duration in the calculation of the fine for Zeon.

In Case T-452/05 *Belgian Sewing Thread v Commission*, judgment of 28 April 2010, [2010] 5 CMLR 889, the GC increased the reduction for cooperation granted to the applicant because the differential granted by the Commission as between the applicant and other addressees did not adequately reflect the much greater assistance that the applicant gave: paras 150 *et seq*.

See now also the settlement procedure for cartels: Regulation 773/2004 Article 10a as inserted by Regulation 622/2008, OJ 2008 L171/3, [2008] 5 CMLR 1032 Article 1.4 and the Commission's Notice on the Conduct of Settlement Procedures in cartel cases: OJ 2008 C167/1: Vol II, App B17. For the settlement procedure generally see new paragraphs 13.113A–13.113D, above.

Fn 848. The GC has noted that unlike the 1996 Leniency Notice, the subsequent versions do not provide for any reduction of fines for undertakings which do not substantially contest the facts in the statement of objections. But an undertaking which expressly states that it is not contesting the allegations of fact may be regarded as having facilitated the Commission's task of finding infringements of the EU competition rules and bringing them to an end such that the Commission may grant a reduction to reflect this: Case T-151/07 *Kone Oyj v Commission*, judgment of 13 July 2011, paras 204 *et seq*.

Fn 849. See Case T-37/05 *World Wide Tobacco España v Commission*, judgment of 8 March 2011 (Commission erred in refusing to reduce the fine to take account of admission of facts: on appeal Case C-240/11P, not yet decided).

Encouragement by public authorities. In Case T-271/03 *Deutsche Telekom AG v* **13.168** *Commission* [2008] ECR II-477, [2008] 5 CMLR 631 the GC upheld a 10 per cent reduction in the fine for margin squeeze to reflect the fact that DT's retail and wholesale charges were subject to sector-specific regulation at the national level and the fact that the national telecoms regulator had, on several occasions during the period covered by the contested decision, considered the question of the existence of a margin squeeze resulting from the applicant's tariff practices and found that there was no abuse: para 312. This was further upheld on appeal to the CJ: Case C-280/08P *Deutsche Telekom v Commission*, judgment of 14 October 2010, [2010] 5 CMLR 1485, para 286.

A further appeal in the *French Beef* case was dismissed: Cases C-101&110/07P *Coop de France bétail et viande and FNSEA v Commission* [2008] ECR I-10193, [2009] 4 CMLR 743.

Where employees of a public authority encourage anti-competitive practices which are to the disadvantage of the authority itself, this is not a mitigating factor: Cases T-204&212/08 *Team Relocations v Commission*, judgment of 16 June 2011, paras 131 *et seq* (Commission officials requesting cover quotes from removal firms for relocations paid for by Commission).

In *National Grid plc v Gas and Electricity Markets Authority* [2009] CAT 14, the UK Competition Appeal Tribunal reduced the fine imposed for abusive conduct because of the involvement of senior officials of the regulator in the evolution of a contract which the regulator then condemned as having an abusive foreclosing effect on the market. On appeal, the Court of Appeal held that the regulator's involvement provided mitigation of considerable weight and further substantially reduced the fine: [2010] EWCA Civ 114.

13.169 **Uncertainty as to the law.** In *AstraZeneca*, the GC upheld the Commission's categorisation of the abuses as serious even though they were regarded as novel: Case T-321/05 *AstraZeneca v Commission*, judgment of 1 July 2010, [2010] 5 CMLR 1575, para 903 (on appeal Case C-457/10P *AstraZeneca v Commission*, not yet decided).

In Case T-461/07 *Visa v Commission*, judgment of 14 April 2011 the GC rejected a claim that the fine should be reduced on this ground because the Commission had limited the fine to conduct in the period following the issue of the SO: para 252.

Fn 862. The correct citation for the *CEWAL* decision is OJ 1993 L34/20, [1995] 5 CMLR 198.

Fn 867. The appeal by Deutsche Telekom was dismissed as was a further appeal to the CJ: Case T-271/03 *Deutsche Telekom v Commission* [2008] ECR II-477; and Case C-280/08P *Deutsche Telekom v Commission*, judgment of 14 October 2010, [2010] 5 CMLR 1485, see update to paragraph 13.168, above.

13.170 **No penalty or nominal fine.** In Case T-271/03 *Deutsche Telekom AG v Commission* [2008] ECR II-477, [2008] 5 CMLR 631 the GC set out the three criteria as applied by the Commission in *Deutsche Post—interception of cross border mail*, OJ 2001 L331/40, [2002] 4 CMLR 598, namely (1) the undertaking concerned had behaved in accordance with the case law of the German courts; (2) there was no EU case law relating specifically to the cross-border letter mail services concerned; and (3) the undertaking concerned had taken steps to avoid practical difficulties and facilitate the detection of future interference with free competition, should it occur. The GC held that none of the criteria applied to Deutsche Telekom's margin squeeze abuse. The GC's approach was upheld on further appeal: Case C-280/08P *Deutsche Telekom v Commission*, judgment of 14 October 2010, [2010] 5 CMLR 1485, paras 294–299.

The GC has stated that the decision whether to impose only a symbolic fine is within the discretion of the Commission: Case T-192/06 *Caffaro v Commission*, judgment of 16 June 2011, para 39.

The appeal by AC Treuhand fined in the *Organic Peroxides* decision for providing administrative and secretarial services to the cartel was dismissed by the GC: Case T-99/04 *AC-Treuhand AG v Commission* [2008] ECR II-1501, [2008] 5 CMLR 962.

Fn 871. The appeal in *Clearstream* was dismissed: Case T-301/04 *Clearstream Banking v Commission*, judgment of 9 September 2009.

Other aggravating and mitigating circumstances.   In COMP/39188 *Bananas*,   **13.171** decn of 15 October 2008 a reduction of 60 per cent in the fines of all the parties to the cartel was granted to reflect the fact that during the relevant period the banana sector was subject to a very specific regulatory regime: para 467. The decision is under appeal: Cases T-587&588/08, not yet decided.

Fn 874. Two of the appeals against the *Raw Tobacco (Italy)* decision have been dismissed: Case T-25/06 *Alliance One International v Commission*, judgment of 9 September 2011; and Case T-12/06 *Deltafina v Commission*, judgment of 9 September 2011.

Pressure from others.   **Fn 879.** This principle was applied in Case T-192/06   **13.172** *Caffaro v Commission*, judgment of 16 June 2011, where the GC reiterated that the case of a participant in a horizontal cartel is different from that of a distributor in a vertical arrangement: paras 42 *et seq*. The GC rejected the applicant's comparison of its case with that of *Spanish Raw Tobacco*. See also Case T-21/05 *Chalkor v Commission*, judgment of 19 May 2010, para 72 (on appeal Case C-386/10P, not yet decided).

Compensation paid to third parties.   The appeals against the *Nintendo* decision   **13.173** have now been decided: Case T-18/03 *CD-Contact Data v Commission* [2009] ECR II-1021 (fine reduced) (appeal dismissed Case C-260/09P *Activision Blizzard v Commission*, judgment of 10 February 2011); Case T-12/03 *Itochu* [2009] 5 CMLR 1375 (appeal dismissed); Case T-13/03 *Nintendo* [2009] 5 CMLR 1421 (fine reduced); Case T-398/02 *Linea Gig* (removed from register 2 May 2005). In Case T-13/03 *Nintendo*, the GC rejected the appellant's claim that a greater reduction should have been granted on this ground, holding that there had been no assurance from the Commission that the reduction in fine would exactly match the amount of compensation paid: see paras 202 *et seq*.

Fn 882. ADM's appeal referred to in fn 882 has now been decided: Case C-511/06P *Archer Daniels Midland v Commission (citric acid)*, judgment of 9 July 2009. The question of compensation to third parties was not considered in the appeal.

13.174   **Dismissal of staff responsible for the infringement.**   See also Case T-53/03 *BPB plc v Commission* [2008] ECR II-1333, [2008] 5 CMLR 1201, paras 423–424; Cases T-101&111/05 *BASF AG and UCB SA v Commission* [2007] ECR II-4949, [2008] 4 CMLR 347 (fine imposed under 1996 Guidelines), para 129 (dismissal not regarded as an attenuating circumstance).

Fn 885. See also Cases T-141/07, etc, *General Technic-Otis v Commission*, judgment of 13 July 2011, para 247.

13.176   **Other factors.**   The fact that an undertaking had recently been ordered to pay other fines, for partially simultaneous infringements, cannot justify a reduction of the fine: Case T-206/06 *Total and Elf Aquitaine v Commission (methacrylates)*, judgment of 7 June 2011.

13.177   **Specific increase for deterrence.**   A substantial increase for deterrence can be imposed in relation to vertical infringements as well as traditional horizontal cartels: Case T-13/03 *Nintendo v Commission* [2009] 5 CMLR 1421. The GC confirmed in that case that the Commission is not required to evaluate how likely the undertaking is to reoffend in the future before imposing an increase for deterrence: 'the pursuit of deterrent effect does not concern solely the undertakings specifically targeted by the decision imposing fines. It is also necessary to prompt undertakings of similar sizes and resources to refrain from participating in similar infringements of the competition rules': para 73.

In Cases T-101&111/05 *BASF AG and UCB SA v Commission* [2007] ECR II-4949, [2008] 4 CMLR 347 (fine imposed under 1996 Guidelines) the GC upheld a 100 per cent increase in the fine for deterrence based on the size of BASF. The GC confirmed that there is no need for the Commission to assess the likelihood of reoffending: para 47. See similarly Case T-410/03 *Hoechst GmbH v Commission* [2008] ECR II-881, [2008] 5 CMLR 839 (fine doubled to ensure deterrence: para 379).

Where a parent company and its subsidiary no longer form a single undertaking at the date of the decision imposing the fine, the Commission cannot rely on the turnover of the former parent company in the year preceding the adoption of that decision in order to determine the deterrence aspect applicable to two companies which formed a single undertaking at the material time but which have since been separated. That turnover does not reflect the effective economic capacity of that undertaking to cause damage to other operators at the time of the infringement: Case T-386/06 *Pegler v Commission*, judgment of 24 March 2011, para 133.

The uplift for deterrence need not be left to the final stage of the fine calculation. But where on the date that the fine was imposed, the applicant was no longer part of a larger group of companies, the Commission was not justified in taking into account the global turnover of the larger group when determining the uplift for deterrence—the objective of deterrence can be legitimately attained only by reference to the situation of the undertaking on the day when it is imposed: Case T-217/06 *Arkema France v Commission (methacrylates)*, judgment of 7 June 2011 (uplift reduced from 200 per cent to 25 per cent).

Fn 899. See also Case T-37/05 *World Wide Tobacco España v Commission*, judgment of 8 March 2011 (on appeal Case C-240/11P, not yet decided).

Benefit from the infringement. **Fn 911.** See also Case T-192/06 *Caffaro v Commission*, judgment of 16 June 2011, para 60 applying this principle; Case T-66/01 *ICI v Commission*, judgment of 25 June 2010, para 443. **13.178**

Ability to pay and performance of the sector. In COMP/38543 *International Removal Services*, decn of 11 March 2008, the Commission exceptionally took into account the inability to pay and particular circumstances of Interdean and reduced its fine by 70 per cent: paras 633 *et seq*. The case is under appeal: Cases T-208/08, etc, not yet decided. **13.179**

See the discussion of this factor in COMP/39396 *Calcium carbide and magnesium based reagents*, decn of 22 July 2009, [2010] 5 CMLR 1368, paras 362 *et seq* where the Commission rejected submissions based on 'the general economic crisis' but exceptionally granted a reduction of 20 per cent to one company on the basis that, although it had not shown that its economic viability was jeopardised by the proposed fine, it was a small independent company operating in a low margin industry with a focused product portfolio. The case is on appeal Cases T-410/09 *Alamet*, T-384/09 *SKW Stahl-Metallurgie Holding*, T-391/09 *Evonik Degussa and AlzChem Hart*, T-392/09 *1.garantovaná*, T-395/09 *Arques Industries*, T-400/09 *ECKA Granulate and non ferrum Metallpulver*, T-406/09 *Donau Chemie*, T-399/09 *HSE*, T-352/09 *Nováčke chemické závody*, not yet decided. Contrast the comments of the Competition Commissioner in the Press Release announcing COMP/38344 *Prestressing Steel*, decn of 30 June 2010, that 'the Commission will have no sympathy for cartelists; recidivists will be fined more and inability-to-pay claims will be accepted only when it is clear the fine would send a company into bankruptcy, which is rare even in the current difficult times': IP/10/1297 (6 October 2010) with the Press Release announcing COMP/39092 *Bathroom fittings and fixtures*, decn of 23 June 2010 'as the objective of anti-cartel enforcement is not to precipitate the fall of companies in financial difficulties, the Commission reduced the fines on five companies to a level they could afford': IP/10/790 (23 June 2010).

In Cases T-204&212/08 *Team Relocations v Commission*, judgment of 16 June 2011, the GC stated that there are three cumulative conditions for the grant of a reduction in fine on the basis of 'specific social and economic context' within the meaning of para 35 of the 2006 Guidelines on Fines: namely the submission of a request during the administrative procedure; the existence of a specific social and economic context; and the inability to pay of the undertaking, the undertaking having to provide objective evidence showing that the imposition of the fine would irretrievably jeopardise its economic viability and cause its assets to lose all their value: para 171. In Cases T-456&457/05 *Gütermann AG and Zwicky v Commission,* judgment of 28 April 2010, [2010] 5 CMLR 930, the GC reiterated that the Commission is under no obligation to take financial hardship into account, para 262.

See also Case T-25/05 *KME Germany v Commission,* judgment of 19 May 2010, paras 166 *et seq* (on appeal Case C-389/10P, not yet decided).

Fn 919. See also Case T-452/05 *Belgian Sewing Thread v Commission,* judgment of 28 April 2010, [2010] 5 CMLR 889, paras 95 and 96.

13.180 **Reduction of fine for delay.**   Unreasonable delay in the progress of the administrative proceedings before the Commission did not result in the decision being annulled or render a reduction in the fine where the applicants could not show that their rights of defence had been prejudiced (para 303). However, the GC considered that the reduction that the Commission had granted in the fine of €100,000 was inadequate and did not reflect the levels of the fines imposed and was not sufficient to provide redress for the unreasonable delay. The GC substituted a reduction of 5 per cent: see Cases T-235/07 *Bavaria v Commission,* judgment of 16 June 2011, para 343; and T-240/07 *Heineken Nederland v Commission,* judgment of 16 June 2011, para 434 (both on appeal from COMP/37766 *Dutch Beer,* decn of 18 April 2007).

In Case T-410/03 *Hoechst GmbH v Commission* [2008] ECR II-881, [2008] 5 CMLR 839 the GC held that while unreasonable delay might justify annulling the decision as a whole, it cannot be relied on when only the fine is challenged by the applicant because the limitation period for imposing the fine is set by regulation: para 220.

Fn 923. This principle was applied in Case T-276/04 *Compagnie maritime belge SA v Commission* [2008] ECR II-1277 where the GC held that Reg 2988/74 establishes a complete system of rules covering in detail the periods within which the Commission was entitled, without undermining the fundamental requirement of legal certainty, to impose fines and that there is therefore no room for consideration of a more general duty to exercise its power to impose fines within a reasonable period.

Fn 924. A claim for a reduction based on delay was rejected in Case T-461/07 *Visa v Commission,* judgment of 14 April 2011, paras 231 *et seq* where the GC confirmed that the case law under Reg 2988/74 was applicable to Article 25 of Reg 1/2003.

Maximum fine and consequential adjustment.   In Case T-68/04 *SGL Carbon AG*   **13.181**
v Commission [2008] ECR II-2511, [2009] 4 CMLR 7, the appellant complained
that by finding four separate infringements and adopting four separate decisions
imposing fines in relation to cartel activity involving graphite products, the
Commission had circumvented the 10 per cent ceiling. The GC rejected this and
upheld the fine: paras 131 *et seq*. A further appeal was dismissed: Case C-564/08P,
judgment of 12 November 2009. See similarly Case T-446/05 *Amann & Söhne GmbH
v Commission*, judgment of 28 April 2010, [2010] 5 CMLR 789, paras 149 *et seq*.

As regards the turnover to which the 10 per cent maximum is applied, where several
companies are held jointly and severally liable for a fine on the ground that they form
an undertaking for the purposes of Article 101, the cap on the fine is calculated on
the basis of the total turnover of all the companies constituting the single economic
entity acting as an undertaking. Only the total turnover of the component companies can constitute an indication of the size and economic power of the undertaking
in question: see Case T-112/05 *Akzo Nobel NV v Commission* [2007] ECR II-5049,
[2008] 4 CMLR 321, para 90 (further appeal dismissed Case C-97/08P, judgment
of 10 September 2009 not dealing with this point). Thus the 10 per cent maximum
is applied to the turnover of the parent company on whom the fine has been imposed,
not the subsidiary which was involved in the infringing conduct: Case T-12/03
Itochu Corp v Commission [2009] 5 CMLR 1375, para 157.

See the treatment of 1.garantovaná in COMP/39396 *Calcium carbide and magnesium based reagents*, decn of 22 July 2009, [2010] 5 CMLR 1368, para 334
(shareholders decision to sell off assets in the relevant year led to a 90 per cent reduction in turnover so that a previous year's turnover was used to calculate the 10 per
cent cap).

For the application of the 10 per cent maximum in the case of a trade association
see: Cases T-217&245/03 *FNCBV and Others v Commission* [2006] ECR II-4987,
paras 317 *et seq*, upheld on appeal Cases C-101&110/07P *Coop de France bétail et
viande and FNSEA v Commission* [2008] ECR I-10193, [2009] 4 CMLR 743. See
further update to paragraph 13.204, below.

Fn 928. See also Cases T-456&457/05 *Gütermann AG and Zwicky v Commission*,
judgment of 28 April 2010, [2010] 5 CMLR 930, paras 78 *et seq* where the GC
held that the Commission had erred in taking the turnover of the undertaking to
whom the infringer had sold the relevant business as the basis for the 10 per cent
cap. The Court, following *Britannia Alloys*, substituted the turnover in the last full
year of business.

(f) The Leniency Notice: cartel cases

The Leniency Notice 2006.   For a useful description of the aims of the leniency   **13.182**
regime see Case T-12/06 *Deltafina v Commission*, judgment of 9 September 2011,
paras 103 *et seq* (a case in which the 2002 Notice was applied).

The leniency regime applies only to horizontal cartels and not to vertical agreements even if the vertical infringement is regarded as very serious: Case T-13/03 *Nintendo v Commission* [2009] 5 CMLR 1421, para 157 (a case under the 1996 Notice).

See Case T-381/06 *FRA.BO SpA v Commission*, judgment of 24 March 2011 where the GC held that the 1996 Leniency Notice, rather than the 2002 Notice, applied to the cooperation provided by the applicant in respect of the period from March 2001 to April 2004 because the first leniency application in respect of the cartel was made before the 2002 Notice came into force. The Court noted that the 1996 Notice did not provide for a particular reward for cooperation relating to the gravity and duration of a cartel. The concept of 'partial immunity' was introduced by the 2002 Leniency Notice. However, the 1998 Fining Guidelines applied and these did allow the Commission to apply the 'partial immunity rule' by treating the undertaking's cooperation as an attenuating circumstance. The GC held that the Commission had adequately rewarded the applicant in the way it applied the 1998 Guidelines, albeit that the reduction had been applied at an earlier stage in the fine calculation than it would, if it had been applied under the Leniency Notice.

In addition to the Leniency Notice arrangements the Commission operates a procedure for settlement of cartel cases: see new paragraphs 13.113A–13.113D, above. Adoption of this procedure may lead to a reduction in the fine of 10 per cent, in addition to any reduction resulting from leniency.

Fn 933. For a case where this transitional provision was applied see Case T-410/03 *Hoechst GmbH v Commission* [2008] ECR II-881, [2008] 5 CMLR 839, paras 507–511.

13.186 **Additional conditions.** The scope of the duty of cooperation was discussed in Case T-12/06 *Deltafina v Commission*, judgment of 9 September 2011, paras 123 *et seq*. Deltafina had been the first undertaking to disclose to the Commission the existence of the cartel in Italian raw tobacco. It was therefore granted conditional immunity from fines (under the 2002 Notice). However, it then disclosed to its competitors, voluntarily and without informing the Commission, that it had applied for leniency, before the Commission had had an opportunity to investigate the cartel. The GC upheld the Commission's finding that Deltafina had not demonstrated a genuine spirit of cooperation and was not therefore entitled to full immunity.

13.188 **Securing a marker for immunity.** In Case T-410/03 *Hoechst GmbH v Commission* [2008] ECR II-881, [2008] 5 CMLR 839 the GC held that there had been a breach of the principle of sound administration where the Commission had assured Chisso that it would be given 'fair warning' if another undertaking looked like overtaking it in the application for leniency but had decided not to tell Hoechst that Chisso was already providing information: paras 134–138. A 10 per cent reduction in the fine was applied by the GC: para 582.

Level of reduction.   In *Industrial copper tubes*, OJ 2004 L125/50 one cartel mem- **13.193** ber gave the Commission a memorandum showing that the cartel had operated for much longer than the Commission had previously thought. This resulted in a substantial uplift of the fine on account of its duration; an uplift which could not be mitigated under the Leniency Notice 1996 because a 50 per cent reduction was the maximum that that cartel member could earn. The Commission dealt with this by granting a *de facto* immunity under the 1998 Guidelines (ie outside the Leniency Notice) as regards the additional duration of the cartel: see also in the appeal to the GC; Case T-127/04 *KM Europa Metal v Commission* [2009] ECR II-1167, [2009] 4 CMLR 1574, para 127 (on further appeal: Case C-272/09P, not yet decided).

Multiple leniency applications in different Member States.   Fn 974. If a Member **13.196** State only introduces a leniency programme later, an application should be made to the NCA as soon as the national programme takes effect. Hence the Austrian Supreme Court held that an earlier leniency application to the Commission could not be accepted as an application for leniency under national competition law, although there had been no leniency programme in Austria at that time: *Elevator Cartel (I)*, 16 Ok 5/08, judgment of 18 October 2008.

Oral applications for leniency.   See similarly the possibility of making settlement **13.197** submissions orally under the new cartel settlement procedure: Notice on the Conduct of Settlement Procedures in Cartel Cases, OJ 2008 C167/1: Vol II, App B17, para 38. For the settlement procedure generally see new paragraphs 13.113A–13.113D, above.

Note, however that the application for leniency will be treated as having been made when the oral statement is provided and not when the applicant contacts the Commission to make that statement: Case T-186/06 *Solvay SA v Commission (Hydrogen peroxide and perborate)*, judgment of 16 June 2011: 'It is precisely because the oral disclosure of information is as a rule a slower means of cooperation than the disclosure of information in writing that the undertaking in question must, by deciding to disclose information orally, take account of the risk that another undertaking may disclose to the Commission, in writing and before it, decisive evidence of the cartel's existence': para 374.

Fn 981. ADM's appeal referred to in fn 882 has now been decided: Case C-511/06P *Archer Daniels Midland v Commission (citric acid)*, judgment of 9 July 2009. The application of the Leniency Notice was not considered in the appeal.

Protection of corporate statements from disclosure.   In Case C-360/09 *Pfleiderer* **13.198** *v Bundeskartellamt*, judgment of 14 June 2011 the CJ delivered a preliminary ruling in the context of a claim for damages for breach of Article 101 in the national court. The applicant sought disclosure of documents provided to the NCA by an applicant for leniency. The CJ held that it is for the national court to weigh the respective interests in favour of disclosure of the information and in favour of the protection of information provided voluntarily by the applicant for leniency. However, the applicable national rules must be not less favourable than those governing similar domestic claims and must not operate in such a way as to make it practically impossible or excessively difficult to obtain such compensation for loss arising from the infringement. A slightly different point has arisen in proceedings in the English High Court in the context of a claim for damages following on from the Commission's cartel findings in *Gas Insulated Switchgear*: see *National Grid Electricity Transmission v ABB Ltd* [2011] EWHC 1717 (Ch). The claimants sought disclosure from the defendants of documents including the confidential version of the decision and of their replies to the statement of objections, parts of which include information provided by leniency applicants. The judge adjourned the application to allow the Commission an opportunity to make written submissions pursuant to Article 15(3) of Regulation 1/2003 as to the parties' duties of confidentiality to the Commission and the application of the *Pfleiderer* judgment to this situation.

See by analogy the decision of the US District Court of the Eastern District of New York (27 August 2010) in *Re payment card interchange fee and merchant discount*. The Court overturned an earlier decision ordering disclosure of the transcript of an oral hearing before the Commission and the Commission's statement of objections on the grounds that the order was contrary to the law of international comity. The judge held the Commission's interests would be significantly undermined if its confidentiality rules were disregarded by American courts in cases like this: ECN Brief 4/2010, p2.

Note that the Commission's White Paper on Damages Actions for Breach of the EC Antitrust Rules COM(2008) 165 (2 April 2008) also envisages that corporate statements will be exempt from disclosure in national courts.

13.199 **Review by the Community Courts.**   The GC has held that the Commission has a wide discretion in deciding the reduction to be granted and the Court will only interfere if there has been a manifest error: Case T-381/06 *FRA.BO SpA v Commission*, judgment of 24 March 2011, para 96; Case T-141/07, etc, *General Technic-Otis v Commission*, judgment of 13 July 2011, para 263.

The Commission also has a wide discretion in assessing whether or not the evidence provided by an undertaking brings added value within the meaning of Point 22 of the Leniency Notice and whether a reduction should be granted to that undertaking under that notice. That assessment is subject to a limited judicial supervision: see Case T-110/07 *Siemens v Commission*, judgment of 3 March 2011, para 376 and the cases cited therein. The case is on further appeal: Case C-239/11P, not yet decided.

(g) **Periodic penalty payments**

13.201 **Periodic penalty payments.**   Note that in COMP/34579 *MasterCard MIF charges*, decn of 19 December 2007, the Commission imposed a periodic penalty payment at the same time as it held that there was an infringement, in view of the risk that MasterCard would not comply with the six-month time limit for terminating the infringement: see paras 773 *et seq*. The case is on appeal: Case T-111/08, not yet decided.

Periodic penalty payments: *Microsoft*.   On 27 February 2008 the Commission **13.202** took a further decision in COMP/37792, following on from the findings of non-compliance in November 2005. The February 2008 decision concerned the finding that Microsoft had charged an unreasonable fee for the information that it had made available as at 15 December 2005. The decision was limited to examining the fees charged by Microsoft in only one of the packages that it made available, namely the remuneration schemes for *non-patented* Interoperability Information. The decision did not assess whether the remuneration rates requested by Microsoft for patent licences prior to 22 October 2007 were reasonable and did not establish non-compliance in this respect: see para 297. In the earlier decision dealing with the first element of non-compliance (decision of 12 July 2006) the Commission had left open the possibility of imposing a periodic penalty for the second failure to cover the period covered by its 12 July 2006 decision. But in fact the February 2008 decision fixed the fine for the second failure only for the period after the period covered by the 12 July 2006 decision until Microsoft was regarded as having complied with both requirements; namely from 21 June 2006 to 22 October 2007. The amount set was €899 million: see paras 281 *et seq*. This decision is under appeal: Case T-167/08, not yet decided. Various parties have been granted permission to intervene in the appeal: see Case T-167/08R order of 20 November 2008, [2009] 4 CMLR 775.

(h) Ancillary matters of law and practice

Allocation of fines between infringing parties.   In Case T-68/04 *SGL Carbon AG* **13.203** *v Commission* [2008] ECR II-2511, [2009] 4 CMLR 7 the GC rejected an appeal against a fine in respect of a cartel where there had been a substantial disparity in the size of the undertakings involved. The Commission had grouped the undertakings concerned into three categories on the basis of the EEA-wide turnover of each of them in relation to the goods concerned. The Commission then grouped the undertakings into bands, each band representing a 10 per cent increment of market share. The GC rejected the argument that the undertakings should have been differentiated by grouping into 5 per cent bands. The GC held that a division of the undertakings in three categories, namely large, medium and small operators, was not an unreasonable way of taking account of their relative importance on the market in order to set the starting amount, as long as it did not lead to a grossly inaccurate representation of the market concerned (para 70). A further appeal was dismissed: Case C-564/08P, judgment of 12 November 2009. See similarly *Nintendo Video games distribution*, OJ 2003 L255/33 where the undertakings concerned were divided into three groups according to the relative importance of each undertaking with regard to Nintendo, as distributor of the relevant products in the EEA. This decision was approved by the GC: see, eg Case T-12/03 *Itochu Corp v Commission* [2009] 5 CMLR 1375, paras 73–84; and Case T-18/03 *CD-Contact Data v Commission* [2009] ECR II-1021, para 109. The GC held that even if the effect of the division into groups is that certain undertakings are allocated the same basic amount even though they differ in size, the difference in treatment is objectively justified by the greater importance attached to the nature of the infringement than to the size of the undertakings in the assessment of the gravity of the infringement. There was no breach of the principle of equal treatment. However, in Case T-13/03 *Nintendo v Commission* [2009] 5 CMLR 1421 the GC reduced the fine imposed on Nintendo on the basis that the Commission had granted a larger reduction for cooperation to John Menzies and the degree of cooperation of the two undertakings was the same: paras 169 *et seq*.

In Case T-127/04 *KM Europa Metal v Commission* [2009] ECR II-1167, [2009] 4 CMLR 1574 the GC confirmed that even without proof of actual impact of the infringement on the market, the Commission is entitled to carry out differentiated treatment of the cartel participants by reference to the shares held in the market concerned; market share constitutes an objective factor which gives a fair measure of the responsibility of each of them as regards the potential harm to competition: paras 61 and 62. On further appeal: Case C-272/09P, not yet decided; Case T-25/05 *KME Germany v Commission*, judgment of 19 May 2010, [2010] 5 CMLR 1329 (Commission is entitled to distinguish among the infringers on the basis of their market shares, without proof of actual impact of the infringement at issue on the market: para 79. The case is on appeal Case C-389/10P, not yet decided).

Fn 1025. See Case T-452/05 *Belgian Sewing Thread v Commission*, judgment of 28 April 2010, [2010] 5 CMLR 889, para 77 which refers to 'every difference' in a similar context.

Fn 1029. The appeals from *Thread* were decided in judgments delivered on 28 April 2010.

13.203A **Relevance of previous fining decisions.** The GC has generally rejected claims of discrimination based on comparison with fines imposed in other Commission decisions. In Case T-155/06 *Tomra Systems v Commission*, judgment of 9 September 2010 the GC held that the Commission's practice in earlier decisions cannot in itself serve as a legal framework for fines in competition matters: the Commission 'cannot be compelled to set fines which display perfect coherence with those imposed in other cases': para 314.

13.204 **Trade associations.** The question whether the 10 per cent maximum for fines should be calculated on the basis of the turnover of the members of the association was considered by the GC in Cases T-217&245/03 *FNCBV and others v Commission* [2006] ECR II-4987, paras 317 *et seq*. The GC held that the earlier case law, particularly Case C-298/98P *Finnboard v Commission* [2000] ECR I-10157, did not restrict the ability of the Commission to consider the turnover of the members to those cases where the association had power, under its rules, to bind its members. The 10 per cent maximum could be based on the turnover of the members in particular where an infringement by an association involves its members' activities and where the anti-competitive practices at issue are engaged in by the association directly for the benefit of its members and in cooperation with them. This was upheld on appeal Cases C-101&110/07P *Coop de France bétail et viande and FNSEA v Commission* [2008] ECR I-10193, [2009] 4 CMLR 743, paras 93 *et seq*. Further the CJ upheld the GC's finding that the principle of *ne bis in idem* was not infringed by the Commission imposing penalties on three associations and on a fourth association of which the first three were members: para 130 of CJ judgment.

In COMP/39510 *Ordre National des Pharmaciens en France (ONP)*, decn of 8 December 2010 the Commission considered for the first time the operation of the new provision in Article 23(4) of Regulation 1/2003 and para 37 of the 2006 Guidelines on Fines enabling members of a professional body to be required to contribute to the fine imposed on that body: paras 749 *et seq*. The Commission imposed a fine of €5 million. The case is on appeal Case T-90/11 *ONP and others v Commission*, not yet decided.

Fn 1032. Following the CJ's judgment in Cases C-395&396/96P, the Commission retook the decision and reimposed fines on the members of the liner conference. An appeal against that decision was dismissed: Case T-276/04 *Compagnie maritime belge SA v Commission* [2008] ECR II-1277.

Fines on parents and subsidiaries.   After a brief period of uncertainty generated **13.205** by paras 28 and 29 of the CJ's judgment in Case C-286/98P *Stora Kopparbergs v Commission* [2000] ECR I-9925, the CJ confirmed the operation of a rebuttable presumption of decisive influence arising from 100 per cent ownership: Case C-97/08P *Akzo Nobel NV v Commission*, judgment of 10 September 2009, [2009] 5 CMLR 2633 para 61. The presumption has been applied many times in recent cases: see, eg Case T-175/05 *Akzo Nobel (monochloroacetic acid)*, judgment of 30 September 2009. During the period when it was unclear whether the 100 per cent ownership presumption applied, the Commission relied, from an abundance of caution, on additional factors before attributing liability. The GC held in Case T-24/05 *Alliance One v Commission, Standard Commercial Tobacco and Trans-Continental Leaf Tobacco v Commission*, judgment of 27 October 2010 that where the Commission had chosen to adopt a higher standard of proof than is in fact required by the jurisprudence, it must do so consistently as regards all addressees of the decision. The GC held that the evidence in relation to one parent was not sufficient to establish decisive influence. The case is on further appeal and cross appeal: Cases C-628/10P and C-14/11P, not yet decided.

In Case C-90/09P *General Química v Commission*, judgment of 20 January 2011 the CJ stressed that where the presumption reaffirmed in *Akzo Nobel* applies, the GC must still examine fully the evidence put forward to rebut the presumption and set out in clear and unequivocal terms why it rejects that evidence. The GC's judgment in that case was vitiated for lack of reasoning on this point. However the CJ considered the evidence itself and upheld the Commission's attribution of liability and hence dismissed the appeal against the decision. The CJ also confirmed that 'what counts is not whether the parent company encouraged its subsidiary to commit an infringement of the EU competition rules, or whether it was directly involved in the infringement committed by its subsidiary, but the fact that those two companies constitute a single economic unit and thus a single undertaking for the purposes of Article [101 TFEU]': para 102.

Note that in Case T-69/04 *Schunk GmbH v Commission* [2008] ECR II-2567, [2009] 4 CMLR 2, Schunk also argued that the fact that the subsidiary was a holding company meant that it operated independently from the parent but the GC held that this was not established.

A fine may be imposed on the ultimate parent which indirectly owns the entity which was involved in the infringement: see, eg COMP/38432 *Professional Videotape* [2008] 5 CMLR 122, para 169 and the cases cited therein; and Case C-90/09P *General Química v Commission*, judgment of 20 January 2011, para 90.

The liability of the parent company does not exonerate the subsidiary from liability for its own participation in the cartel: Cases T-122/07, etc, *Siemens AG Österreich v Commission*, judgment of 3 March 2011, para 196.

The presumption of decisive influence does not conflict with the presumption of innocence applied by analogy with Article 6 ECHR: eg Cases T-141/07, etc, *General Technic-Otis v Commission*, judgment of 13 July 2011, para 73. The GC also noted that the fact that the parent has deployed formal written policies for compliance with competition law does not rebut the presumption of influence but rather tends instead to support the proposition that the subsidiaries are not managed independently: para 85. See also Case T-299/08 *Elf Aquitaine v Commission (Sodium chlorate)*, judgment of 17 May 2011 (GC rejected submissions to the effect that the presumption arising from 100 per cent ownership has become, in practice, impossible to rebut and hence is contrary to the presumption of innocence: para 122); Case T-25/06 *Alliance One International v Commission*, judgment of 9 September 2011, paras 198–200.

Note that the Commission must make clear in the statement of objections if it intends to find a company liable both for its own conduct and for that of its subsidiary: see Cases C-322/07P, etc, *Papierfabrik August Koehler AG and Bolloré SA v Commission*, judgment of 3 September 2009, [2009] 5 CMLR 2301. Bolloré had been found liable in the Commission's decision both as the parent company of Copiograph and because of its own independent involvement in the *Carbonless paper* cartel. The GC held that the statement of objections had not made the latter allegations clear but declined to annul the decision on the grounds that Bolloré had had an opportunity to exercise its rights of defence as regards the former allegation. The CJ held that the GC had erred in law in failing to draw any legal conclusion from its finding that Bolloré's rights of defence had not been observed and annulled the whole of the contested decision so far as it concerned Bolloré.

In order to be held liable for an infringement, the parent entity must itself be an undertaking for the purposes of competition law: Cases T-208&209/08 *Gosselin Group v Commission*, judgment of 16 June 2011, para 42. Moreover, its control of the subsidiary entity which is an undertaking is not enough to establish that the parent is an undertaking unless it is shown that the parent involved itself in the business of the subsidiary: para 47.

Rebutting the presumption arising from 100 per cent ownership. In Case **13.205A** T-185/06 *L'Air Liquide v Commission*, judgment of 16 June 2011 the GC annulled the decision *vis-à-vis* a parent company because the Commission had not explained why it had rejected the evidence put forward to rebut the presumption arising from 100 per cent ownership. See also Case T-196/06 *Edison v Commission*, judgment of 16 June 2011 (liability of parent annulled for lack of reasoning for rejecting evidence put forward by applicant to rebut the presumption).

The fact that the parent regards its holding of the shares in the subsidiary as purely a financial investment and operates a policy whereby it delegates as much as possible to its subsidiaries is not enough to rebut the presumption of decisive influence: Case T-376/06 *Legris Industries v Commission*, judgment of 24 March 2011, para 53; and also Case T-38/07 *Shell Petroleum v Commission*, judgment of 13 July 2011, para 70: 'a holding company that coordinates, *inter alia*, financial investments within the group is in a position to regroup shareholdings in various companies and has the function of ensuring that they are run as one, including by means of such budgetary control'. Contrast, however, with Cases T-208&209/08 *Gosselin Group v Commission*, judgment of 16 June 2011, para 42 where the Court went on to hold that, even if the parent Portielje had been an undertaking (which the Court found it was not), the evidence that it had put forward had succeeded in rebutting the presumption of decisive influence that arose from its ownership of Gosselin.

In Cases T-141/07, etc, *General Technic-Otis v Commission*, judgment of 13 July 2011, the GC also noted that the fact that the parent has deployed formal written policies for compliance with competition law does not rebut the presumption of influence but rather tends instead to support the proposition that the subsidiaries are not managed independently: para 85.

The presumption of decisive influence arises where the parent owns 97 per cent of the shares in the subsidiary: Case T-299/08 *Elf Aquitaine v Commission (Sodium chlorate)*, judgment of 17 May 2011.

The entrustment of day-to-day business to the local management of a wholly-owned subsidiary is a common practice and is not therefore capable of proving that subsidiaries have real independence: Case T-25/06 *Alliance One International v Commission*, judgment of 9 September 2011, para 130.

13.205B **Fines on parents and subsidiaries where no presumption applies.**   In COMP/39188 *Bananas*, decn of 15 October 2008 the Commission held Del Monte jointly and severally liable with Weichert for the latter's infringement. Weichert was a partnership between Del Monte and the Weichert family. The Commission analysed the partnership and distribution agreements between them and concluded that Del Monte exercised decisive influence: paras 382 *et seq*. The decision is under appeal: Cases T-587&588/08, not yet decided.

See also Case C-407/08P *Knauf Gips KG v Commission*, judgment of 1 July 2010, [2010] 5 CMLR 708 where the shares in the various companies were held by members of the same family. The Court upheld the GC's reliance on the fact that when participating in the unlawful exchange of information, data relating to the whole corporate group was provided to other cartel members. However, the GC had also relied on the fact that during the administrative procedure the applicant company had presented itself as the sole interlocutor with the Commission on behalf of the group and had not raised the issue of whether liability for the infringement could be attributed to it. The CJ held that the GC had erred in finding that this conduct precluded the applicant from disputing its liability on appeal; there is no requirement under EU law that the addressee must challenge the various matters of fact or law during the administrative procedure, or otherwise be barred from doing so on appeal: para 89. The CJ therefore set aside the judgment of the GC but went on to dismiss the appeal against the Commission's attribution of liability.

A minority interest may enable a parent company actually to exercise a decisive influence if it is allied to rights greater than those normally granted to minority shareholders and if 'consistent legal or economic indicia' show that a decisive influence was in fact exercised over the subsidiary's market conduct: Case T-132/07 *Fuji v Commission*, judgment of 12 July 2011, paras 182 *et seq*. In that case the GC upheld an attribution of liability to a partner in a joint venture after considering the terms of the joint venture agreement, the role of senior management of the parents in the business of the JV, and the overlap of senior executives.

13.205C **Effect on parent's liability of annulment of infringing company's liability.**   Case T-382/06 *Tomkins plc v Commission*, judgment of 24 March 2011 considered the effect on the parent company of a successful appeal by the subsidiary. Tomkins had been held jointly and severally liable for the fine imposed on its subsidiary Pegler Ltd for its participation in the copper fittings cartel. The Commission had found that Pegler participated in the cartel between 31 December 1988 and 22 March 2001. Both the applicant and Pegler had brought proceedings to annul the Commission's decision in respect of duration but Pegler asserted that it was not liable for any infringement prior to 29 October 1993 whereas the applicant only contested Pegler's participation prior to 7 February 1989. In Pegler's appeal (Case T-386/06) the GC annulled the decision in respect of participation before 1993. The GC held that, given that Tomkins had brought an appeal and had challenged the duration of the infringement, it would not be *ultra petita* to give Tomkins the benefit of the whole reduction in duration achieved by Pegler. By contrast, Pegler's success in challenging the uplift imposed by the Commission for deterrence could not be applied by the Court to Tomkins' benefit because Tomkins had withdrawn an initial ground challenging this in its application. However, the GC made clear that Tomkins' liability could not in fact exceed that of Pegler so the Commission was bound, under Article 266 TFEU to 'draw the appropriate conclusions' from the *Pegler* judgment when enforcing the fine against Tomkins. The Commission has lodged an appeal against this decision: on appeal Case C-286/11P, not yet decided.

In COMP/38638 *Butadiene Rubber and Emulsion Styrene Butadiene Rubber*, decn of 29 November 2006, [2009] 4 CMLR 421 the Commission imposed a fine on Kaučuk which had participated in the cartel through its agent Tavorex. The Commission held that it was clear that Tavorex participated on behalf of Kaučuk because Kaučuk was kept informed of developments and the final responsibility for price policy was with Kaučuk: paras 415 *et seq*. The decision was therefore addressed to Kaučuk and to Kaučuk's parent Unipetrol, but not to Tavorex because Tavorex had gone into voluntary liquidation: para 423. Trade-Stomil was also an addressee of the decision as a direct participant in cartel meetings. However, there was not enough evidence to show that Trade-Stomil had been acting as agent for Dwory so no liability was imposed on Dwory: para 440. The decision was later annulled for lack of proof as against Trade-Stomil: Case T-53/07 *Trade-Stomil v Commission*, judgment of 13 July 2011. In further appeals by Kaučuk and Unipetrol the GC found that there was insufficient evidence of Tavorex's participation in the cartel: Case T-44/07 *Kaučuk v Commission*, judgment of 13 July 2011; and Case T-45/07 *Unipetrol v Commission*, judgment of 13 July 2011. The GC did not discuss the attribution of liability issue.

Note the point raised in Case T-42/11 *Universal v Commission*, not yet decided. Universal was held jointly and severally liable to pay the fine imposed on Deltafina in *Raw Tobacco, Italy*. Universal withdrew its appeal (T-34/06) against that decision but Deltafina continued with its appeal (T-12/06, judgment of 9 September 2011). The Commission wrote to Universal asking for payment of the fine before the *Deltafina* appeal was resolved. Universal has appealed against the decision to make that demand, alleging that in the event that Deltafina is wholly or partially successful the Commission will be obliged to reduce or eliminate the amount for which Universal is held jointly and severally liable.

Allocation of fines among different parents. In Cases T-122/07, etc, *Siemens* **13.205D** *AG Österreich v Commission*, judgment of 3 March 2011 the GC considered the principles to be applied where more than one parent is jointly and severally liable for the participation of a particular cartel member: see paras 152 *et seq*. The Court rejected the Commission's contention that it had a discretion as to how to allocate the joint and several liability among the various parents: each company must be able to discern from the decision how much it is liable to pay and to that end, the Commission must specify the periods during which the companies concerned were jointly liable for the unlawful conduct and, where necessary, the degree of liability of those companies for that conduct. This must be based on the Commission's findings regarding the periods of joint responsibility of the various companies belonging to the undertaking. Insofar as possible, those amounts must reflect the weighting of the individual shares of the joint liability of those companies (para 154)—although this does not have to be in direct proportion to the duration of their respective involvement: para 181. The task of sharing out the joint and several liability among the parents was exclusively for the Commission to perform and could not be left, as the Commission had suggested to the national courts. If the decision does not specify the respective shares of the parents, then the assumption is that they bear an equal share. This means that if the Commission proceeds against one of them for the whole amount, that parent may, on the basis of the Commission's decision, make a claim for recovery against each of the other joint and several debtors in respect of its share. Therefore, in the absence of any finding in the decision that, within the overall undertaking, certain companies are more responsible than others for the participation of that undertaking in the cartel during a given period, it must be assumed that they are all equally liable and, consequently, that the shares of the fine imposed on them jointly and severally are equal. No company can be held jointly and severally liable to pay more that the fine imposed on the infringing entity.

Where a company which is directly involved in an infringement has belonged to a series of successive parent companies during the period of infringement, the Commission may impose fines on the parents which add up to more than the fine imposed on the subsidiary. However, the amount recovered from one parent may be contingent on the amount recovered from the other parents and where successive parents have never formed part of the same undertaking, the actual amount paid by either parent must not exceed the share of its joint and several liability. That share corresponds to that parent's appropriate portion of the total amount which the successive parents are together held liable to pay. The Commission must therefore specify what that appropriate portion is and where it had failed to do so, the Commission annulled the decision to that extent: see Case T-26/06 *Trioplast Wittenheim* and Case T-40/06 *Trioplast Industrier v Commission*, both judgments delivered on 13 September 2010.

13.206 **Liability of successor undertaking.** The principles set out in this paragraph were applied by the GC in Cases T-117&121/07 *Areva v Commission*, judgment of 3 March 2011 (on appeal Cases C-247&253/11P, not yet decided); Case T-25/06

Alliance One International v Commission, judgment of 9 September 2011, paras 216 *et seq*. See also COMP/38432 *Professional Videotape*, decn of 20 November 2007, [2008] 5 CMLR 122, paras 158, 183; COMP/38638 *Butadiene Rubber and Emulsion Styrene Butadiene Rubber*, decn of 29 November 2006, [2009] 4 CMLR 421, paras 337 and 338. In the latter case the Dow Chemical Company in the US was held jointly and severally liable for the conduct of three Dow subsidiaries which had been involved in the cartel at different times. The parent's liability was therefore of a longer duration than any of the subsidiaries' looked at individually.

A clause in a contract transferring ownership of a company whereby the buyer assumes liability for any as yet unknown cartel activity previous engaged in by the company is not binding on the Commission which may still impose a fine on the seller of the company: see, eg COMP/39396 *Calcium carbide and magnesium based reagents*, decn of 22 July 2009, [2010] 5 CMLR 1368, para 238. For an example of a contractual warranty included in the sale of a business providing for indemnification for penalties and costs incurred in responding to investigations of pre-sale anti-competitive conduct see *B.S.A. International S.A v Irvine* [2010] CSOH 12.

The English High Court declined to make a reference to the CJ where the claimant brought proceedings for a declaration that the claimant was not liable as a successor undertaking: *Conex Banninger Ltd v Commission* [2010] EWHC 1978 (Ch).

Note that the Commission intervened in an appeal before the Slovakian Supreme Court to make submissions on the importance of successor companies being held liable for the fines of its predecessor. The Commission indicated in its written observations that any reduction of the fine imposed on the successor company solely on the ground that the infringement was committed by its predecessor can be contrary to the concept of economic continuity under EU law: *Železničná spoločnosť Cargo Slovakia*, ruling of 27 October 2010, ECN Brief 5/2010, p2.

Fn 1046. See also Case T-194/06 *SNIA v Commission*, judgment of 16 June 2011 applying this principle where the appellant had absorbed the business of the parent of the infringing company and so was held liable because of that parent's decisive influence: para 60.

Double jeopardy.   The principle of *ne bis in idem* was not infringed by the **13.207** Commission imposing penalties on three associations and on a fourth association of which the first three were members: Cases T-217&245/03 *FNCBV and others v Commission* [2006] ECR II-4987, para 344; upheld on appeal Cases C-101&110/07P *Coop de France bétail et viande and FNSEA v Commission* [2008] ECR I-10193, [2009] 4 CMLR 743, para 130.

On the relevance of fines imposed in the USA see also Case T-410/03 *Hoechst GmbH v Commission* [2008] ECR II-881, [2008] 5 CMLR 839, paras 599 *et seq*.

A different point on *non bis in idem* was considered by the GC in Case T-11/05 *Wieland-Werke AG v Commission*, judgment of 19 May 2010. The GC held that the principle was not infringed where the Commission imposed separate fines for cartel activity in separate but related markets: para 95.

13.208 **Limitation period for imposition of fines.** For the proper interpretation of the requirement in Article 25(3) that in order to interrupt the limitation period the Commission's action must be notified to an undertaking 'which has participated in the infringement', see Case T-405/06 *Arcelor Mittal v Commission* [2009] ECR II-771, [2010] 4 CMLR 787where the Commission's decision was annulled as against two of the addressees. Appeals by the applicant and by the Commission were dismissed: Cases C-201&216/09P *ArcelorMittal v Commission*, judgment of 29 March 2011. That judgment led to the repeal of a decision against two addressees in COMP/38589 *Heat Stabilisers*, decn of 11 November 2009: see Press Release IP/11/820 (4 July 2011).

For the application of the limitation period in a case where the GC and CJ upheld the Commission's finding of infringement but annulled some of the fines on procedural grounds see Case T-276/04 *Compagnie maritime belge SA v Commission* [2008] ECR II-1277. First the GC held that such a decision should not be treated as a decision finding an infringement since the fact of infringement was definitively established by the Commission in the parts of the earlier decision that were not annulled. The GC then held that both the five-year limit under Article 25(1)(b) and the ten-year limit under Article 25(5) had been complied with, having regard to the various interruptions and suspensions arising from the earlier investigation and the appeals from the earlier decision. The GC further applied the principle in Case T-213/00 *CMA CGM and others v Commission (FETTCSA)* [2003] ECR II-913, [2003] 5 CMLR 268 that Regulation 2988/74 establishes a complete system of rules covering in detail the periods within which the Commission was entitled to impose fines and that there is therefore no more general duty to exercise its power to impose fines within a reasonable period.

See also Case T-110/07 *Siemens v Commission*, judgment of 3 March 2011, paras 241 *et seq*. In that case the Commission had found that Siemens had participated in the gas insulated switchgear cartel for the periods from 15 April 1988 to 1 September 1999 and from 26 March 2002 to 11 May 2004. The cartel had continued uninterrupted in Siemens absence and the GC upheld the Commission's finding, for the purposes of applying the limitation period in Regulation 1/2003 that the cartel was a single continuous infringement. This meant that the earlier period of Siemens' participation was not time barred because the two phases of the infringement in which it is alleged to have participated were part of the same single and continuous infringement. The case is on further appeal: Case C-239/11P, not yet decided.

Where a decision is annulled by the GC on procedural grounds, the appeal proceedings are treated as interrupting the running of time for the purposes of

Article 25 so that the Commission may readopt the infringement decision more than five years after the cessation of the infringement: Case T-58/01 *Solvay v Commission*, judgment of 17 December 2009, para 87. The case is on further appeal, Case C-110/10P, not yet decided. The same point was made in Case T-66/01 *ICI v Commission*, judgment of 25 June 2010, para 77.

Fn 1053. The fact that the limitation period for imposing a fine in respect of obstruction of an investigation may have expired does not prevent the Commission from treating the conduct as an aggravating factor when imposing a fine for the substantive infringement: COMP/38432 *Professional Videotape*, decn of 20 November 2007, [2008] 5 CMLR 122, para 224.

Payment of the fine. In Case T-68/04 *SGL Carbon AG v Commission* [2008] **13.209** ECR II-2511, [2009] 4 CMLR 7 the GC rejected an appeal against the rate of default interest set for non-payment of the fine, holding that the Commission is entitled to adopt a point of reference higher than the applicable market rate offered to the average borrower, to an extent necessary to discourage dilatory behaviour. Interest rates of 5.5 per cent and 3.5 per cent could not be regarded as disproportionate. A further appeal was dismissed: Case C-564/08P, judgment of 12 November 2009.

Note that where two parties are held jointly and severally liable to pay the fine (for example the company which participated in the infringement and its parent) the payment of the fine by one extinguishes the liability of the other: see, eg Case T-386/06 *Pegler v Commission*, judgment of 24 March 2011, para 106.

The costs of providing a bank guarantee pending an appeal are generally not recoverable if the appeal succeeds: Case T-113/04 *Atlantic Container Line AB v Commission* [2007] ECR II-171*, [2008] 4 CMLR 1357.

The CJ has hinted strongly that fines are not tax deductible: Case C-429/07 *Inspecteur van de Belastingdienst v X BV*, judgment of 11 June 2009, para 39: 'The effectiveness of the Commission's decision by which it imposed a fine on a company might be significantly reduced if the company concerned, or at least a company linked to that company, were allowed to deduct fully or in part the amount of that fine from the amount of its taxable profits, since such a possibility would have the effect of offsetting the burden of that fine with a reduction of the tax burden'. On receipt of the CJ's ruling, the Dutch Court of Appeal which had referred the question ruled (on 11 March 2010) that the fines imposed were not tax deductible: ECN Brief 2/2010, p2.

See also Case T-574/10 *Quimitécnica.com and de Mello v Commission*, not yet decided (appeal against a requirement that bank guarantee must be an AA rated bank at a time when no bank in Portugal was granted that rating).

11. Review by the Court of First Instance

13.212 **The Court of First Instance.**   The Court of First Instance has been renamed the General Court following the coming into effect of the Lisbon Treaty. Article 229 EC is now Article 261 TFEU and Article 230 EC is now Article 263 TFEU.

(a) Review under Articles 229 and 230

(i) The scope of review

13.215 **Increase in fines.**   In Case T-25/05 *KME Germany v Commission*, judgment of 19 May 2010, the applicant complained that the Commission's repeated requests before the Court for an increase in the fine was 'part of a "vexatious strategy" aimed at preventing them from fully exercising their right of independent judicial review'. The GC rejected all the grounds for an increase without commenting on this allegation.

As to the power to increase fines when admissions are withdrawn on appeal, see now Case T-69/04 *Schunk GmbH v Commission* [2008] ECR II-2567, [2009] 4 CMLR 2. The GC held that the amount of a fine can be determined only on the basis of the gravity and duration of the infringement. The fact that the Commission had had to prepare for the appeal on the basis that the applicant might be allowed to withdraw its previous admissions did not justify an increase of that fine. In other words, the expenses incurred by the Commission as a result of the proceedings before the Court are not a criterion for determining the amount of the fine and must only be taken into account when applying the provisions of the Rules of Procedure relating to costs: para 262.

13.216 **Adjustment of fines in cases of unequal treatment.**   The *Hoek Loos* approach was referred to in Case T-68/04 *SGL Carbon AG v Commission* [2008] ECR II-2511, [2009] 4 CMLR 7, though the GC did not find that there had been an error in the calculation of another undertaking's fine: paras 136–137. A further appeal was dismissed: Case C-564/08P, judgment of 12 November 2009.

Fn 1087. See also Case T-410/03 *Hoechst GmbH v Commission* [2008] ECR II-881, [2008] 5 CMLR 839, para 371.

Fn 1088. In the appeals from the *Copper Plumbing Tubes* decision, the GC reduced the fines for some appellants on equal treatment grounds and rejected the submission that the fines on other addressees who had also brought appeals should be increased instead: see Case T-21/05 *Chalkor v Commission*, judgment of 19 May 2010, [2010] 5 CMLR 1295, para 105 (on appeal Case C-386/10P, not yet decided); and Case T-25/05 *KME Germany v Commission*, judgment of 19 May 2010, paras 188 *et seq* (the Commission asked for an increase in the applicants' fines if the GC held in other appeals that the Commission had failed to give other addressees of the decn sufficient credit for their lesser involvement in the cartel; however the GC reduced the fines of the other addresses rather than increasing the fines of the more egregious infringers) (on appeal Case C-389/10P *KME Germany v Commission*, not yet decided.)

Non-reviewable 'acts' of the Commission.   Note that the Court should examine   **13.220**
the substance of the alleged act, not just the form in which the Commission has communicated to the applicant: in Case C-521/06P *Athinaïki Teckniki v Commission* [2008] ECR I-5829, [2008] 3 CMLR 979 the CJ held that a letter in which the Commission informed the complainant that it was closing the file because on the basis of information available there were no grounds to justify an investigation, was in fact a statement by the Commission that the review initiated had not enabled it to establish the existence of State aid within the meaning of Article 107 TFEU. It had thereby implicitly refused to initiate the formal investigation procedure pro-vided for in Article 108(2) TFEU. The informal nature of the decision and the fact that it left it open for the complainant to provide more information did not change its nature and it was a reviewable act. The CJ therefore referred the matter back to the GC. The Commission then purported to withdraw the letter and reopen its examination of the complaint, leading the GC to dismiss the appeal asserting that since the contested act (ie the letter) had been withdrawn the appeal was devoid of purpose (Case T-94/05 *Athinaïki Techniki v Commission*, order of 29 June 2009). In a sharply worded judgment, the CJ annulled the GC's Order: Case C-362/09P *Athinaïki Techniki v Commission*, judgment of 16 December 2010. The Court stated that if the Commission were entitled to withdraw its act in those circum-stances, it could perpetuate a state of inaction during the preliminary examination stage and avoid any judicial review. If that were the position, it would be sufficient for the Commission to decide to take no further action on a complaint lodged by an interested party and then, after that party brought an action, to reopen the pre-liminary examination stage and repeat those operations as many times as are neces-sary in order to avoid any judicial review of its actions. The Court annulled the order and referred the matter back again to the GC.

The *IBM* judgment was considered by the English High Court in *Conex Banninger Ltd v Commission* [2010] EWHC 1978 (Ch) where the claimant sought a declara-tion that it was not liable to pay fines imposed by the Commission on other undertakings that had gone into receivership. The claim followed the Commission's decision to issue a request for information against Conex. Conex did not appeal against that decision but asked the Court to refer questions to the CJ regarding its liability. The Court considered that the CJ would be likely to hold that the Commission's preparatory acts in this regard were not justiciable and that the national courts were not required 'to fill the gap left' in respect of the Commission's preparatory acts.

Fn 1106. Similarly the GC does not have jurisdiction to hear a challenge to a decision of a national competition authority on the applicability of the competition rules: Case T-386/09 *Grúas Abril Asistencia v Commission*, Order of 24 August 2010 (on appeal Case C-521/10P, not yet decided).

13.221   **Standing to bring appeal.**   Where one applicant challenging the rejection of a complaint undoubtedly has standing, there is no need to examine the standing of the other applicant: see Case T-306/05 *Scippacercola and Terezakis v Commission* [2008] ECR II-4*, [2008] 4 CMLR 1418, paras 71 and 72 (appeal dismissed Case C-159/08P, Order of 25 March 2009); Case C-313/90 *CIRFS and others v Commission* [1993] ECR I-1125, para 31; Case T-282/06 *Sun Chemical Group v Commission* [2007] ECR II-2149, para 50. But where two appeals are joined, one appellant in each appeal must have standing to bring an appeal: see, eg Cases T-273&297/06 *ISD Polska v Commission* [2009] ECR II-2185.

The rights conferred on Member States to bring proceedings before the Court are not conferred on regional authorities within the State: Case C-461/07P(I) *Provincia di Ascoli Piceno and Comune di Monte Urano v Sun Sang Kong Yuen Shoes Factory* [2008] ECR I-11*, [2008] 2 CMLR 425.

As regards the last sentence of this paragraph, see Case C-506/08P *Sweden v MyTravel and Commission*, judgment of 21 July 2011 where Sweden brought an appeal against the GC's judgment in Case T-403/05 *MyTravel Group v Commission* [2008] ECR II-2027, [2008] 3 CMLR 1517 (access to documents under Regulation 1049/2001).

See also Case T-335/08 *BNP Paribas v Commission*, judgment of 1 July 2010 (in the State aid context).

Fn 1109. The judgment of the GC in *Alrosa* was overturned by the Court of Justice: Case C-441/07P *Commission v Alrosa*, judgment of 29 June 2010, [2010] 5 CMLR 643. The CJ held that the GC had been wrong to regard Alrosa as anything more than an interested third party for the purposes of the scope of its procedural rights. However, this does not appear to have affected Alrosa's standing to bring the appeal as the CJ, having set aside the GC's judgment, went on to dismiss Alrosa's challenge to the commitments decision.

(ii)   The grounds of annulment

13.223   **Procedural irregularities.**   **Fn 1117.** Following the judgment in *ARBED* the Commission retook the decision condemning the steel beams cartel: an appeal against that by ARBED was dismissed but the decision was annulled as against two of the addressees on the basis that the decision was adopted outside the limitation period: Case T-405/06 *ArcelorMittal v Commission* [2009] ECR II-771, [2010] 4 CMLR 787 (appeals by the applicant and by the Commission dismissed: Cases C-201&216/09P *ArcelorMittal v Commission*, judgment of 29 March 2011).

Inadequacy of reasoning.   For a recent exposition of the test of adequacy of rea-   **13.225**
sons see Case T-151/05 *Nederlandse Vakbond Varkenshouders (NVV) v Commission*
[2009] ECR II-1219, [2009] 5 CMLR 1613, paras 191 *et seq* in the context of a
merger Phase I clearance.

Where the Commission uses some data from a particular source, it is not required
to explain in the decision why it has rejected other data from that source unless the
parties have put forward arguments specifically based on the rejected data: Case
T-321/05 *AstraZeneca v Commission*, judgment of 1 July 2010, [2010] 5 CMLR
1575, para 81 (on appeal Case C-457/10P *AstraZeneca v Commission*, not yet
decided).

Fn 1142. The appeal in *SELEX Sistemi* was dismissed: Case C-113/07P *SELEX
Sistemi Integrati SpA v Commission*, judgment of 26 March 2009.

Lack of adequate proof.   As regards evidence from anonymous informants, in   **13.226**
Case T-53/03 *BPB plc v Commission* [2008] ECR II-1333, [2008] 5 CMLR 1201
the GC considered whether the right of access to the file included access to information provided by an anonymous informant. In that case, the GC noted that although
the Commission accepted that the information was a factor in triggering the investigations, the information was ultimately not referred to in the contested decision
and the Commission's objections were proved by other evidence. In any event,
where information was supplied on a purely voluntary basis, accompanied by a
request for confidentiality in order to protect the informant's anonymity, the
Commission if it accepts such information is bound to comply with such a condition. The GC held that proceedings initiated on the basis of information from an
undisclosed source are lawful, provided that this does not affect the ability of the
person concerned to make known his views on the truth or implication of the facts,
on the documents communicated or on the conclusions drawn by the Commission
from them.

The standard of proof is the same in the case of a vertical arrangement as in respect
of a horizontal arrangements: Case C-260/09P *Activision Blizzard v Commission*,
judgment of 10 February 2011, para 71.

The Commission is entitled to rely on information provided by third parties as well
as on that gleaned from its own investigation: Case T-321/05 *AstraZeneca v
Commission*, judgment of 1 July 2010, [2010] 5 CMLR 1575, para 80 (on appeal
Case C-457/10P *AstraZeneca v Commission*, not yet decided).

See also Case C-413/08 *Lafarge v Commission*, judgment of 17 June 2010, [2010]
5 CMLR 586, para 30.

Where the decision contained a number of contradictions as to the precise timing
of the alleged unlawful meeting and there was some doubt as to whether the applicant had participated in that meeting, the GC held that that doubt must operate to

the benefit of the applicant and annulled the decision *vis-à-vis* the applicant for lack of proof: Case T-53/07 *Trade-Stomil v Commission*, judgment of 13 July 2011; and Case T-44/07 *Kaučuk v Commission*, judgment of 13 July 2011, both appeals from the *Butadiene Rubber and Emulsion Styrene Butadiene Rubber* decision.

13.227 **Scope of review by the Court of First Instance.** In the appeal, the CJ upheld the GC's approach to reviewing the Commission's analysis: Cases C-501/06P, etc, *GlaxoSmithKline Services Unlimited v Commission*, judgment of 6 October 2009. The GC has also referred to the 'complex economic assessment' involved in defining the relevant market: Case T-446/05 *Amann & Söhne GmbH v Commission*, judgment of 28 April 2010, [2010] 5 CMLR 789, para 54. In that case the GC also considered the implications of this more limited form of review for Article 7 ECHR in holding that the breadth of the Commission's discretion in finding infringements was not too broad: para 131.

As regards issues of complex economic analysis, the GC has recently stressed that although the courts recognise that the Commission has a margin of assessment in economic or technical matters, that does not mean that the GC must decline to review the Commission's interpretation of economic or technical data. In order to take due account of the parties' arguments, the Courts must not only establish whether the evidence put forward is factually accurate, reliable and consistent but must also determine whether that evidence contains all the relevant data that must be taken into consideration in appraising a complex situation and whether it is capable of substantiating the conclusions drawn from it: see, eg Case T-321/05 *AstraZeneca v Commission*, judgment of 1 July 2010, [2010] 5 CMLR 1575, para 33 (on appeal Case C-457/10P *AstraZeneca v Commission*, not yet decided).

Fn 1172. See also Case T-427/08 *Confédération européenne des associations d'horlogers-réparateurs (CEAHR) v Commission*, judgment of 15 December 2010, paras 157 *et seq*.

Fn 1173. The judgment of the GC in *Alrosa* was overturned by the Court of Justice: Case C-441/07P *Commission v Alrosa*, judgment of 29 June 2010, [2010] 5 CMLR 643. The Court held that the GC had erred in substituting its own assessment of a complex economic matter for that of the Commission, 'thereby encroaching on the discretion enjoyed by the Commission instead of reviewing the lawfulness of its assessment' (para 67). The Court approved the passage in the Opinion of Advocate General Kokott where she said (para 84) 'it is not sufficient, in order to assume a manifest error of assessment, for the [GC] merely to take a different opinion to the Commission. If the factual and evidential position reasonably allows different assessments, there can be no legal objection if the Commission adopts one of them, even if it is not the one which the Court considers to be preferable. A manifest error of assessment exists only where the conclusions drawn by the Commission are no longer justifiable in the light of the factual and evidential position, that is to say if no reasonable basis can be discerned'. In addition to setting aside the GC's judgment, the CJ dismissed Alrosa's appeal against the Commission's decision.

Fn 1176. In Case T-461/07 *Visa v Commission*, judgment of 14 April 2011 the GC appears to have regarded the Commission's assessment of conduct under Article 101(1) as involving a complex economic assessment where there was no question of the application of Article 101(3): para 70.

Error of substantive law. For an unusual case where the GC exceptionally **13.228** upheld the Commission's decision despite finding that it had erred in failing to define the relevant market see Case T-199/08 *Ziegler SA v Commission*, judgment of 16 June 2011.

Fn 1180. The judgment of the GC in *Alrosa* was overturned by the Court of Justice: Case C-441/07P *Commission v Alrosa*, judgment of 29 June 2010, [2010] 5 CMLR 643. The CJ held that there had been no breach of the principle of proportionality.

Misuse of powers. In Case T-145/06 *Omya AG v Commission* [2009] ECR **13.230** II-145, [2009] 4 CMLR 827 Omya asserted that the Commission's request for the correction of certain information previously supplied was simply a pretext to suspend the time running under the Merger Regulation. The Advisory Committee had objected to the Commission's proposed clearance of the merger and Omya had refused an extension of time prior to the request being made. The GC stated (para 99) that a decision may amount to a misuse of powers only if it appears, on the basis of objective, relevant and consistent factors, to have been taken for a purpose other than the purpose for which the relevant powers were conferred. Where more than one aim is pursued, even if the grounds of a decision include, in addition to proper grounds, an improper one, that would not make the decision invalid for misuse of powers, since it does not nullify the main aim.

(iii) Procedural aspects

Time limits for bringing actions. As to the uncertainty referred to in the last **13.232** sentence of fn 1196, see Case T-48/04 *Qualcomm Wireless Business Solutions v Commission* [2009] ECR II-2029 where the GC held that time starts to run only once the decision is published in the *Official Journal* even if the Commission had sent a copy of the merger approval decision to the appellant before that: para 56. See similarly Cases T-273&297/06 *ISD Polska v Commission* [2009] ECR II-2185: although publication of the decision in that case (concerning State aid) was not a precondition for the decision to come into effect, it was consistent practice for Commission decisions closing a State aid investigation to be published in the *Official Journal*. Therefore, the applicants could legitimately expect the decision to be published and time started to run only from that publication (para 57). See similarly, Case T-354/05 *TF1 v Commission* [2009] ECR II-4719, para 34.

As regards what constitutes publication in the *Official Journal* see Case T-388/02 *Kronoply and Kronotex v Commission*, judgment of 10 December 2008 where the GC held that publication of a notification of a decision in the C series of the *Official Journal* with a hyperlink to the full text of the decision on the Commission's website is sufficient publication of the decision to start time running for an appeal. See also Case T-274/06 *Estaser El Mareny v Commission* [2007] ECR II-143* (publication of a decision on the DG Competition website may not of itself start the time for lodging an appeal; but where a notification is published in the *Official Journal* that the decision can be found on the website, the time for appealing runs from that notification).

See also Case T-2/09 *Internationale Fruchtimport Gesellschaft Weichert v Commission*, Order of 30 November 2009 for the correct way to calculate the time limit. The Court also emphasised the need for circumstances to be 'quite exceptional, in the sense of being unforeseeable or amounting to force majeure' before a derogation will be made. See similarly, Case C-112/09P *SGAE v Commission*, Order of 14 January 2010.

See also Case T-45/08 *Transportes Evaristo Molina SA v Commission*, Order of 14 November 2008 where the GC held that the application was brought out of time (further appeal dismissed: Case C-36/09P *Transportes Evaristo Molina SA v Commission*, Order of 11 November 2010).

13.234 **Whether decisions can be supported by new material.**   If the Commission was precluded from relying on documents because they had not been disclosed to the applicant, the GC cannot rely on them in its review of the Commission's decision: Case C-413/06P *Bertelsmann AG and Sony Corporation of America v Impala and Commission* [2008] ECR I-4951, para 102.

13.238 **Powers of partial annulment.**   In Case T-276/04 *Compagnie maritime belge SA v Commission* [2008] ECR II-1277 the GC held that those parts of a Commission decision which are not annulled on appeal 'definitively form part of the Community legal structure and produce all their legal effects'. In that case the annulment of a fine for purely procedural reasons did not in any way affect the legality of the finding of infringement. The Commission was entitled to rely on the parts of the decision that were not annulled for the purpose of adopting a later decision imposing a fine on the applicant for the abuses established in that earlier decision.

13.240 **Consequences of total annulment.**   The Commission's obligation to take measures to comply with the GC's judgment includes, where a fine imposed is annulled or reduced, repaying that fine or that part of it. That obligation applies not only to the principal amount of the fine overpaid but also to default interest on that amount: Case T-48/00 *Corus UK v Commission* [2004] ECR II-2325, para 223; and Case T-53/03 *BPB plc v Commission* [2008] ECR II-1333, [2008]

5 CMLR 1201, para 487. There is no need, therefore, for the GC to order this on disposing of the appeal.

As regards the Commission's obligations to comply with the GC's judgments under Article 266 TFEU (formerly Article 233 EC) see Case T-382/06 *Tomkins plc v Commission*, judgment of 24 March 2011 (where subsidiary's fine is reduced on appeal, the Commission cannot enforce a larger amount against a parent held jointly and severally liable only because of its relationship with that subsidiary. The Commission has lodged an appeal against this ruling: Case C-286/11P, not yet decided).

Fn 1232. On the ability of the Commission to pick up the investigation when a decision is annulled because the investigation was incomplete see Case T-301/01 *Alitalia v Commission* [2008] ECR II-1753, paras 97 *et seq*. The GC confirmed that where the obligation under Article 266 TFEU (formerly Article 233 EC) to comply with the Court's judgment calls for the adoption of a number of administrative measures, the institution is allowed a reasonable period within which to comply with a judgment annulling one of its decisions. The question whether or not the period was reasonable depends on the nature of the measures to be taken and the attendant circumstances (para 155).

Powers of the Court of First Instance following annulment of decision. The **13.241** judgment of the GC in *Schneider Electric* was appealed to the CJ: Case C-440/07P *Commission v Schneider Electric*, judgment of 16 July 2009. The CJ upheld the GC's finding that the Commission's decision to prohibit the merger based on an objection that had not been raised in the statement of objections was a sufficiently grave and manifest breach of the rights of the defence to trigger the Commission's liability to pay damages. But the CJ held on the facts that there was no sufficient causal link between that breach and the loss that Schneider Electric had incurred as a result of the reduction in the transfer price of Legrand conceded in consideration for the deferral of completion of the sale. The CJ therefore ordered that the compensation payable to Schneider Electric was limited to the costs they incurred as a result of the reopened investigation of the merger following the annulment of the original decision. The Court subsequently quantified Schneider Electric's damages at €50,000: Order of 9 June 2010.

A claim for damages against the Commission in a State aid case was dismissed by the GC on the grounds that there was insufficient causal link between the invalidity of the decision annulled and the loss alleged. The GC did not consider whether the defects in the decision were sufficiently serious to give rise to a cause of action: Case T-344/04 *Bouychou v Commission*, judgment of 17 July 2007, [2007] ECR II-91*. See also Cases T-362&363/05 *Nuova Agricast v Commission*, judgment of 2 December 2008 (Commission's errors not sufficiently serious to give rise to liability: appeal dismissed Case C-67/09P *Nuova Agricast v Commission*, judgment of

14 October 2010). See also the dismissal by the GC of a damages claim for alleged loss arising out of the Commission's rejection of a complaint: Case T-186/05 *SELEX Sistemi Integrati SpA v Commission*, Order of 29 August 2007 (appeal dismissed Case C-481/07P, judgment of 16 July 2009).

The GC does not have power to issue directions or assume the role of the institution challenged: see Case T-111/07 *Agrofert Holding v Commission*, judgment of 7 July 2010, para 40 and the cases cited there.

Fn 1238. See also Case T-145/06 *Omya AG v Commission* [2009] ECR II-145, [2009] 4 CMLR 827, para 23.

13.242 **Costs and other orders.** Where the CJ annuls the decision of the GC but then goes on itself to dismiss the challenge to the decision rather than referring the matter back to the GC, it may order each party to bear its own costs relating to the appeal and the applicant to pay all the costs at first instance: see, eg Case C-407/08P *Knauf Gips KG v Commission*, judgment of 1 July 2010, [2010] 5 CMLR 708.

For an example of a costs order where the applicant won the battle but lost the war, see Case C-113/07P *SELEX Sistemi Integrati SpA v Commission*, judgment of 26 March 2009 where the CJ found significant legal errors in the GC's reasoning but upheld the overall result (the rejection of the applicant's complaint by the Commission). The applicant was ordered to pay the Commission's costs but only half of Eurocontrol's costs.

The GC does not have power under Article 340 TFEU (formerly Article 288 EC) to order the Commission to compensate a successful appellant for the costs of providing a bank guarantee in lieu of paying the fine pending appeal, because there is an insufficient causal link between the expense and the Commission's error: Case T-113/04 *Atlantic Container Line AB v Commission* [2007] ECR II-171*, [2008] 4 CMLR 1357. The applicants' claim that the Commission's failure to pay for the bank guarantee was a breach of its obligation under Article 266 TFEU (formerly Article 233 EC) to take all necessary steps to comply with the judgment annulling the decision was also rejected. The GC held that given that the Commission would have had to pay interest on any fine paid pending the appeal, there was no loss suffered by the applicant for which the Commission should make recompense. The GC noted that Article 266 TFEU requires the administration to make good further damage which may be caused by the unlawful act annulled only if the conditions laid down in the second para of Article 340 TFEU are satisfied and they were not satisfied in this case.

In Case T-423/07 *Ryanair v Commission*, judgment of 19 May 2011 where Ryanair had brought an action based on the Commission's failure to act, the GC did not have to determine the appeal because the Commission had adopted a position by the time the matter came before the Court. However, the GC held that as Ryanair could not be criticised for having brought that action in order to protect its rights, the GC reflected that in the order made as to costs.

Fn 1249. In the appeal Cases C-501/06P, etc, *GlaxoSmithKline Services Unlimited v Commission*, judgment of 6 October 2009, the CJ overturned part of the GC's analysis though it ultimately upheld the outcome of the case. All parties were ordered to bear their own costs.

(b) Action under Article 232 in respect of failure to act

Conditions for successful application.   In Case T-423/07 *Ryanair v Commission*, judgment of 19 May 2011 the GC found that the complaint lodged by Ryanair had not made clear that it encompassed an allegation of abuse of dominance (as well as of State aid) such that the Commission could not be criticised for failure to act on the complaint.   **13.244**

(c) Interim relief from the Court

Generally.   Fn 1273. Where the main action is manifestly inadmissible, the claim for interim measures can be rejected on that ground: Case T-457/08R *Intel Corp v Commission*, Order of 27 January 2009.   **13.246**

Interim relief to suspend fine.   In Case T-113/04 *Atlantic Container Line v Commission* [2007] ECR II-171, [2008] 4 CMLR 1357 the GC confirmed that because an undertaking has the option of paying the fine pending its appeal, there is an insufficient causal link between the annulled decision and the bank guarantee charges incurred to found a claim in damages. In Case T-398/02R *Linea Gig v Commission* [2003] ECR II-1139 the GC rejected a request for interim measures to suspend the fine even though Linea was in liquidation and the GC found that the company had shown to the requisite legal standard that its situation made it objectively impossible for it to obtain the guarantee from a bank. The GC balanced this point against the fact that suspension of the fine would prevent the Commission from bringing any action before the national court to recover the fine and to protect, as well as its own interests, the European Union's financial interests. If the appeal was later dismissed, the applicant's assets might then no longer be adequate to pay the fine, in whole or in part. It was therefore necessary to maintain the enforceability of the decision in order not to preclude any measures which the Commission considers it necessary to take for the purposes of recovering the fine. An appeal against this rejection was dismissed: Case C-233/03 [2003] ECR I-7911. Contrast this with the decision of the GC in Case T-11/06R *Romana Tabacchi SpA v Commission* [2006] ECR II-2491 where the President of the GC found that the applicant (which had been fined €2.5 million for the Italian Raw Tobacco cartel) had established that it was impossible for it to acquire a bank guarantee and further found that the balance of interest lay in favour of ordering the applicant to provide   **13.248**

a bank guarantee of €400,000, pay €200,000 to the Commission and pay the rest of the fine (with interest) in instalments.

Applicants for interim relief must include evidence of the impossibility of obtaining a bank guarantee in their initial application and cannot add evidence on that point after the application has been lodged: Case T-30/10R *Reagens SpA v Commission*, Order of 12 May 2010, [2010] 5 CMLR 237.

> **Fn 1279.** For rare cases in which the President of the GC found that it was impossible for the applicant to provide a bank guarantee and held that the balance of interest lay in favour of granting interim measures see Case T-392/09R *1. garantovaná a.s. v Commission*, Order of 2 March 2011. The obligation to provide the guarantee was suspended until certain long term loans owned by the undertaking matured; Case T-393/10R *Westfälische Drahtindustrie v Commission*, Order of 13 April 2010.

> For a case where the President of the GC was somewhat sceptical of the efforts made by the applicant to secure a bank guarantee see Case T-410/09R *Almamet GmbH Handel mit Spänen und Pulvern aus Metall v Commission*, order of 7 May 2010, [2010] 5 CMLR 219.

13.249 Suspension of Commission order. A negative administration order by the Commission rejecting a request for interim measures cannot be suspended by the GC because such a suspension could not affect the applicant's position: Case T-411/07R *Aer Lingus v Commission* [2008] ECR II-411, [2008] 5 CMLR 53, para 47.

> **Fn 1285.** But see Case T-411/08R *Artisjus Magyar v Commission* [2009] 4 CMLR 353 where the GC rejected an application for interim measures to suspend parts of the Commission's order in the *CISAC* case. An appeal against the order was dismissed: Case C-32/09P(R) *Artisjus Magyar v Commission*, order of 31 August 2010, [2010] 5 CMLR 1208.

13.250 Interim measures at complainant's behest. Note however the comments of the President of the GC in Case T-411/07R *Aer Lingus v Commission* [2008] ECR II-411, [2008] 5 CMLR 53 that a request that the GC direct the Commission to take action under Article 8(4) or 8(5) of the Merger Regulation would constitute an interference with the exercise of the Commission's powers, incompatible with the distribution of powers between the various European Union institutions. The President did not, however, rule out the grant of interim measures as against a third party to the appeal provided that procedural safeguards were put in place: para 56.

13.253 Restricted review by the Court of Justice. The principles set out in this paragraph were reiterated and applied in Case C-413/08 *Lafarge v Commission*, judgment of 17 June 2010, [2010] 5 CMLR 586.

12. Appeals to the Court of Justice

Exercise of the jurisdiction. In Case C-413/06P *Bertelsmann AG and Sony* **13.254**
Corporation of America v Impala and Commission [2008] ECR I-4951 the CJ held
that the extent of the obligation to state reasons is a question of law reviewable by
the Court on appeal. Such a review must consider the facts on which the GC based
itself in reaching its conclusion as to the adequacy or inadequacy of the statement
of reasons: para 30. The CJ overturned the GC's decision which had itself annulled
the decision of the Commission approving a merger.

14

THE ENFORCEMENT OF THE COMPETITION RULES IN THE MEMBER STATES

1. Introduction

Relationship between Community and domestic competition law. Note that **14.007** an NCA does not have power to declare that Article 102 has **not** been infringed; at most it can decide that there are no grounds for action on its part in respect of an alleged abuse: see Case C-375/09 *Tele 2 Polska*, judgment of 3 May 2011, para 29 '. . . the Commission alone is empowered to make a finding that there has been no breach of Article 102 TFEU, even if that article is applied in a procedure undertaken by a national competition authority'. The Court of Justice stated further that Article 5 of Regulation 1/2003 overrides any national rule which precludes an NCA from bringing proceedings to an end with a finding that there are no grounds for action on its part.

2. Enforcement by National Competition Authorities

(a) The National Competition Authorities

Regulation 1/2003 and the Joint Statement. The Commission reported to the **14.011** European Parliament and Council on the functioning of Regulation 1/2003 at the end of April 2009 (COM/2009/0206 final). The Commission noted that after five years 'the challenge of boosting enforcement of the EC competition rules, while ensuring their consistent and coherent application, has been largely achieved' and that work sharing has been unproblematic.

Members of the European Competition Network. For an interesting discus- **14.014** sion of the effect of Article 35 of Regulation 1/2003 see Case C-439/08 *VEBIC*, judgment of 7 December 2010 discussed in the update to paragraph 14.070A, below.

(b) Avoidance of multiple proceedings

14.015 **Effect of initiation of Commission proceedings on jurisdiction of NCAs.**　See Case C-17/10 *Toshiba Corp v Czech Competition Authority*, not yet decided (reference from Czech court asking whether the initiation of proceedings and taking of a decision by the Commission automatically relieves the NCA of competence to deal with the matter, including under domestic law containing provisions parallel to Article 101).

14.017 **Effect of initiation of proceedings by one NCA on the jurisdiction of other NCAs.**　The Commission relied on Article 13 of Regulation 1/2003 in rejecting a complaint of abusive conduct which was already being actively dealt with by the Slovenian competition authority: COMP/39707 *Si.mobil/Mobitel*, decn of 24 January 2011. The decision is on appeal alleging that the shortcomings of the Slovenian authority's procedures oblige the Commission to take over handling the complaint: Case T-201/11 *Si.Mobil v Commission*, not yet decided.

(c) Cooperation within the Network

14.020 **Generally.**　The NCAs' obligations under Articles 11 and 12 of Regulation 1/2003 do not preclude the disclosure to potential damages claimants of information provided to the NCA by a leniency applicant in domestic proceedings. It is, however, for the courts of the Member States, on the basis of their national law, to determine the conditions under which such access should be permitted or refused by weighing the interests protected by EU law: Case C-360/09 *Pfleiderer v Bundeskartellamt*, judgment of 14 June 2011, see the discussion in the update to paragraph 14.028, below.

14.021 **Investigations on behalf of another NCA: Article 22(1).**　This procedure has been operated on a number of occasions: see, eg French Conseil de la Concurrence request to the Office of Fair Trading in the UK to carry out inspections at the UK head offices of three oil companies later found to have colluded in a tender for refuelling Air France aircraft in La Réunion. The Paris Court of Appeal upheld the decision, rejecting challenges to the legality of the process and to the admissibility of the documents found during the inspections: *Chevron Products Company* ECN Brief 1/2010, p2; see also *Envases Hortofruticolas* ECN Brief 3/2010, p2 (Spanish Comision Nacional de la Competencia requested the Italian authority to carry out inspections of the leading makers and sellers of plastic containers for fruit and vegetable packaging).

The Austrian Supreme Court has held that on receipt of a request under Article 22(1) from another NCA, the Austrian NCA is entitled to determine whether the facts could give rise to an infringement of EU competition law so as to justify the request, but that it is irrelevant whether the Austrian NCA would have jurisdiction to take proceedings regarding the alleged infringement: *Deutsches Amtshilfeersuchen*, 16 Ok 7/09, judgment of 15 July 2009.

(ii) Exchange of information and leniency programmes

Exchange of information and leniency programmes. The NCAs' obligations   **14.028**
under Articles 11 and 12 of Regulation 1/2003 do not preclude the disclosure to
potential damages claimants of information provided to the NCA by an applicant
under a domestic leniency regime. It is, however, for the courts of the Member
States, on the basis of their national law, to determine the conditions under which
such access must be permitted or refused by weighing the interests protected by EU
law. The applicable national rules must be not less favourable than those governing
similar domestic damages claims and they must not operate in such a way as to
make it practically impossible or excessively difficult to obtain such compensation:
Case C-360/09 *Pfleiderer v Bundeskartellamt*, judgment of 14 June 2011. A slightly
different point has arisen in proceedings in the English High Court in the context
of a claim for damages following on from the EU Commission's cartel findings in
Gas Insulated Switchgear: see *National Grid Electricity Transmission v ABB Ltd*
[2011] EWHC 1717 (Ch). The claimants sought disclosure from the defendants of
documents including the confidential version of the EU Commission's decision
and of their replies to the statement of objections, parts of which include information provided to the Commission by applicants under the EU leniency regime. The
judge adjourned the application to allow the Commission an opportunity to make
written submissions pursuant to Article 15(3) of Regulation 1/2003 as to the
parties' duties of confidentiality to the Commission and the application of the
Pfleiderer judgment to this situation.

Information exchange under Article 12. Settlement submissions made under   **14.030**
the new cartel settlement procedure will only be transmitted pursuant to Article 12
provided that the conditions set out in the Network Notice are met: see Notice on
the Conduct of Settlement Procedures in cartel cases, OJ 2008 C167/1: Vol II,
App B17, para 37. For the settlement procedure generally see new paragraphs 13.113A–13.113D, above.

The legal effect of the Network Notice limitations. In Case C-360/09 *Pfleiderer*   **14.031**
v Bundeskartellamt, judgment of 14 June 2011 the CJ noted that the Network
Notice and the Leniency Notice are not binding on the Member States and that
even if the guidelines set out by the Commission may have some effect on the practice of the national competition authorities, it is, in the absence of binding regulation under EU law, for Member States to establish and apply national rules on
access to leniency documents.

Disclosure of leniency programme information to national courts. Similar   **14.032**
protection is conferred on settlement submissions under the new cartel settlement
procedure referred to above.

Note also *In re Rubber Chemicals Antitrust Litigation*, 486 F Supp 2d (ND Ca,
2007), where the US Court refused to order discovery of a defendant's leniency
statements to the Commission, holding that the EU is entitled to comity as a

sovereign entity and relying on the strong objection communicated by DG Competition to such discovery as undermining its leniency programme.

(d) Enforcement of Community competition rules in the United Kingdom

14.033A **The 'cartel offence'.** Section 188 of the Enterprise Act 2002 provides for a criminal offence which is committed where an individual dishonestly agrees to arrangements of specified kinds. As to the meaning of 'dishonestly' in this context see *R v George, Burns, Burnett, Crawley* [2010] EWCA Crim 1148 concerning the prosecution of British Airways employees for alleged price-fixing arrangements with Virgin Atlantic Airways regarding fuel surcharges for passenger air transport. The Court of Appeal held that it was sufficient to show that the defendants were dishonest and it was not necessary to show mutual dishonesty on the part of both the BA and the VAA employees. The Court stated that the interpretation of the statutory offence was not assisted by reference to the case law on the common law offence of conspiracy (as to the application of that common law offence to cartel agreements see *Norris v Government of the United States of America* [2008] UKHL 16; and *R v GG* [2008] UKHL 17). The prosecution of the BA employees came to a premature end on 10 May 2010 with the withdrawal of the prosecution and acquittal of the defendants on discovery of a substantial amount of undisclosed electronic correspondence.

Note also *IB v The Queen* [2009] EWCA Crim 2575 (a statutory offence criminalising cartel activity did not form part of 'national competition law' for the purposes of Article 3 of Regulation 1/2003; the NCA did not have the exclusive power to prosecute the offence).

(ii) Jurisdiction of sectoral regulators to apply Articles 81 and 82

14.038 **Concurrent powers of sectoral regulators.** Note in the table that the Northern Ireland Authority for Energy Regulation has become the Northern Ireland Authority for Utility Regulation whose remit covers gas, electricity and water.

14.040 **Case allocation in the United Kingdom.** In *R (oao Cityhook Ltd) v Office of Fair Trading* [2009] EWHC 57 (Admin) the High Court considered the application of the Concurrency Regulations in a case where a complainant was challenging the decision by the Office of Fair Trading not to investigate a complaint because the complaint was not an administrative priority. The Court held that the OFT ought to have considered whether to refer the case to OFCOM under the Regulations. The Court did not quash the OFT's decision but directed that proper consideration be given to the possible transfer of the case to OFCOM.

3. Enforcement by National Courts: Jurisdiction

14.042 **Jurisdiction of national courts.** See Case C-17/10 *Toshiba Corp v Czech Competition Authority*, not yet decided (reference from Czech court asking whether

Article 101 and Regulation 1/2003 must be applied (in proceedings brought after 1 May 2004) to the whole period of operation of a cartel, which commenced in the Czech Republic before that State's entry to the European Union (that is, before 1 May 2004) and continued and ended after the Czech Republic's entry to the European Union).

(ii) Limitations on personal jurisdiction over defendants

The Brussels I Regulation and the Lugano Convention. The final text of a new Lugano Convention was published at OJ 2007 L339/3. On 18 May 2009, the EU ratified the 2007 Lugano Convention with effect for all Member States except Denmark. The 2007 Lugano Convention was ratified by Norway on 1 July 2009 and by Denmark on 24 September 2009, and entered into force as between the EU Member States and Norway on 1 January 2010. Switzerland ratified the 2007 Lugano Convention on 20 October 2010, with effect from 1 January 2011. The 2007 Lugano Convention was ratified by the Republic of Iceland on 25 February 2011 and entered into force as between the EU and Iceland on 1 May 2011. The 1988 Lugano Convention will only remain relevant for proceedings commenced before the applicable date of its entry into force in the relevant State of origin. **14.046**

In *Cooper Tire & Rubber Company Europe v Dow Deutschland Inc* [2010] EWCA Civ 864 the English Court of Appeal lifted a stay that had been granted under Article 21 of the Lugano Convention. Teare J had granted a stay of proceedings under Article 21 of the Lugano Convention in respect of one defendant domiciled in Switzerland. This was on the basis of a difference between the Lugano Convention and the Brussels I Regulation in respect of determining the Court first seised of proceedings: so far as concerns English law, the Lugano Convention looks to the date of *service* of proceedings, whereas the Brussels I Regulation looks to the date of *issue* of proceedings. On appeal, the Court of Appeal, referring to *The Trademark Licensing Company Ltd v Leofelis SA* [2009] EWHC 3285 (Ch) held that the Lugano Convention had no application when the rival proceedings were *both* in the courts of Member States. Such a case was governed by the Brussels I Regulation regardless of the domicile of the defendant so the stay was lifted.

Co-defendants. The application of Articles 6(1) and 28 of the Brussels I Regulation and of Article 21 of the Lugano Convention has been considered at various stages of litigation between tyre manufacturers and rubber producers concerning alleged losses arising from the cartel condemned by the Commission in the *Butadiene Rubber and Emulsion Styrene Butadiene Rubber* decision. The history of the proceedings in Milan and London is set out in the judgment of the English Court of Appeal in *Cooper Tire & Rubber Company Europe v Dow Deutschland Inc* [2010] EWCA Civ 864. One issue considered in that judgment was whether a cause of action for loss could be maintained against the UK subsidiaries of addressees of the decision, even if those subsidiaries were not alleged to have **14.050**

been involved in, or known about, the cartel activity of other entities within the addressee undertaking. The High Court had held ([2009] EWHC 2609 (Comm), Teare J) that they could, following the judgment of Aikens J in *Provimi*. The judge therefore held that the claim against the UK subsidiaries was properly brought and that those defendants could act as 'anchor defendants' for the purposes of Article 6(1) of the Brussels I Regulation to establish the English court's jurisdiction against other non-domiciled defendants. On appeal, the Court of Appeal held that the pleaded case, properly construed, did encompass both the possibility that the anchor defendants were parties to or aware of the anti-competitive conduct of their parent company and the other addressees and the possibility that they were not. The issue decided in *Provimi* did not therefore need to be considered. The Court of Appeal nonetheless stated that the liability of a subsidiary for losses arising from anti-competitive conduct elsewhere within the undertaking of which it was unaware was unclear and that a reference to the CJ would be necessary. The Court of Appeal went on to uphold Teare J's decision to refuse a stay under Article 28 on the grounds that there was no particular 'centre of gravity' for a claim arising from a European-wide cartel and the fact that the pre-emptive Italian proceedings had started first did not 'operate as a sort of trump card or even as a primary factor'. A second issue arising was that at first instance Teare J had granted a stay of proceedings under Article 21 of the Lugano Convention in respect of one defendant domiciled in Switzerland. In the appeal, the Court of Appeal, referring to *The Trademark Licensing Company Ltd v Leofelis SA* [2009] EWHC 3285 (Ch) held that the Lugano Convention had no application when the rival proceedings were both in the courts of Member States. Such a case was governed by the Brussels I Regulation regardless of the domicile of the defendant so the stay was lifted. Note that in an earlier decision, Teare J had refused an application to adjourn the consideration of the jurisdiction of the English court until the Italian courts had finally determined the Italian proceedings: [2009] EWHC 1529 (Comm).

14.051   **Declining jurisdiction.** In *Cooper Tire & Rubber Company Europe v Dow Deutschland Inc* [2010] EWCA Civ 864 the Court of Appeal considered, *inter alia*, whether the fact that the Italian appeal against the dismissal of the pre-emptive action brought by the rubber companies, though likely to succeed, would not be heard until January 2014 was a relevant factor in determining whether to grant a stay under Article 28. The Court rejected the suggestion that this would impliedly criticise the Italian court system, stating '[t]he fact that it may take different periods of time for similar proceedings to come to a conclusion in different jurisdictions, for whatever reasons, is not a criticism; it is merely a fact of life to which a judge cannot be expected to close his eyes' (para 55). The case was the appeal against the decision of Teare J to refuse a stay of proceedings *Cooper Tire & Rubber Europe v Shell Chemicals* [2009] EWHC 1529 (Comm).

4. Convergence, Cooperation and Consistency in the Application of the Competition Rules

(a) Parallel application of Community and national competition law

Duties to apply Articles 81 and 82.   Note that an NCA does not have power to declare that Article 102 has **not** been infringed; at most it can decide that there are no grounds for action on its part in respect of an alleged abuse: see Case C-375/09 *Tele 2 Polska*, judgment of 3 May 2011.   **14.056**

A statutory offence criminalising cartel activity does not form part of 'national competition law' for the purposes of Article 3 of Regulation 1/2003; the NCA did not have the exclusive power to prosecute the offence: *IB v The Queen* [2009] EWCA Crim 2575.

Raising competition law of the court's own motion.   The distinction is brought out by two contrasting Belgian judgments. See *Bima NV v Sodrepe NV*, Case 2002/AR/2580, judgment of 10 October 2008: on a claim under an agreement that expressly sought to share customers and exchange pricing information, the Brussels Court of Appeal of its own motion held that the agreement was void as a hard-core violation of Article 101 and the domestic Belgian equivalent. Cf *Brouwerij Haacht v BM*, Case C.08.0029.N, judgment of 15 May 2009: the Belgian Supreme Court held that where a party had relied only on a block exemption, the court was not required of its own motion, insofar as the agreement did not come within the block exemption, to consider the individual applicability of the conditions of Article 101(3) where this had not been raised by the parties to the dispute.   **14.058**

(b) The convergence rule

The convergence rule and Article 82.   In its report to the European Parliament and Council on the functioning of Regulation 1/2003 (COM/2009/0206 final 29 April 2009) the Commission describes provisions of this type that apply in a number of Member States: para 26. They include national provisions which regulate the abuse of economic dependence, 'superior bargaining power' or 'significant influence'; legal provisions concerning resale below cost or at loss; national laws that foresee different standards for assessing dominance; and stricter national provisions governing the conduct of dominant undertakings.   **14.061**

Convergence and the English doctrine of restraint of trade.   In *Jones v Ricoh UK Ltd* [2010] EWHC 1743 (Ch) the English High Court struck down a clause restricting competition and stated that once EU competition law applies and either strikes down or permits the restriction involved, the court is not permitted to reach   **14.063**

a different result as regards the application of a restriction to trade between EU Member States under the domestic law of restraint of trade.

Note that where only the domestic equivalent of Article 101 is applied and not Article 101 itself, the common law doctrine is still relevant: *Pirtek (UK) Ltd v Joinplace Ltd* [2010] EWHC 1641 (Ch).

(c) Cooperation between the Commission and the national authorities

(i) Mutual assistance

14.069 **The Commission's opinion on questions concerning the application of competition rules.**   A request was made under Article 15 by the Lithuanian Supreme Administrative Court in *UAB Schneidersöhne Baltija/UAB Libra Vitalis* concerning exchanges of confidential information. The Court however subsequently held that there was no effect on trade between Member States so that Article 101 was not infringed but upheld the finding of infringement of the domestic competition rules: ECN Brief 1/2010, p2.

14.070 **Submission of observations to the national court.**   The Commission's power to intervene in national court proceedings under Article 15(3) is subject to the sole condition that the coherent application of Articles 101 and102 TFEU so requires. That condition may be fulfilled even if the proceedings concerned do not pertain to issues relating to the application of those articles. Thus, the CJ held in Case C-429/07 *Inspecteur van de Belastingdienst v X BV*, judgment of 11 June 2009 that the Commission could intervene in proceedings in the German courts concerning whether fines imposed for cartel infringements were deductible from tax.

See, eg *National Grid Electricity Transmission v ABB Ltd* [2011] EWHC 1717 (Ch) where the English High Court was considering a claim for damages following on from the Commission's cartel findings in *Gas Insulated Switchgear.* The claimants sought disclosure from the defendants of documents including the confidential version of the decision and of their replies to the statement of objections, parts of which include information provided by leniency applicants. The judge adjourned the application to allow the Commission an opportunity to make written submissions pursuant to Article 15(3) of Regulation 1/2003 as to the parties' duties of confidentiality to the Commission.

The Commission intervened in an appeal before the Slovakian Supreme Court to make submissions on the importance of successor companies being held liable for the fines of their predecessor: *Zeleznicna spolocnost Cargo Slovakia*, ruling of 27 October 2010, ECN Brief 5/2010, p2.

Fn 198. The *Garage Gremeau* judgment is now reported at [2008] ECC 25.

14.070A **Ability of NCA to defend its decisions before national courts.**   In Case C-439/08 *VEBIC*, judgment of 7 December 2010 the CJ considered questions sent by a

Brussels court hearing an appeal by VEBIC against an infringement decision adopted by the Belgian Competition Council. According to court rules, the Competition Council was not entitled to appear as a party to the proceedings or to lodge written observations. The Court held neither Article 2 nor Article 15(3) of Regulation 1/2003 conferred a right on an NCA to be a party to such proceedings. However Article 35(1) requires the Member State to designate competition authorities in a way which ensures that the provisions of the Regulation are effectively complied with. If the NCA is not allowed to defend its decision there was a risk that the appeal court would be 'wholly "captive"' to the arguments of the appellant. Thus the NCA's obligation to ensure that Articles 101 and 102 are applied effectively require it to be entitled to participate as a party in the proceedings. Further, if the NCA consistently failed to exercise this right, the Member State remained competent to designate other bodies to perform this role.

Assistance to the Commission from the national court. Fn 200. The Commission **14.071** has noted that this provision 'has not functioned optimally': Report to the European Parliament and Council on the functioning of Regulation 1/2003 (COM/2009/ 0206 final 29 April 2009).

(ii) Effect of national authority's action on the Commission

Effect of national decision on the Commission. In COMP/39388&39389 *E.* **14.072** *ON German electricity markets*, decn of 26 November 2008, para 23, the Commission referred to German decisional practice in OLG Düsseldorf, VI-2 KART 7/04 (V), *Stadtwerke Eschwege*, 6 June 2007 upheld by the Bundesgerichtshof on 11 November 2008, KVR 60/07—*E.ON/Stadtwerke Eschwege* when leaving open whether the collective dominant position in the German wholesale electricity market involved two or three undertakings.

(iii) Effect of commencement of Commission investigation

Effect on proceedings in national courts. In *National Grid Electricity Transmission* **14.074** *plc v ABB Ltd* [2009] EWHC 1326 (Ch) the English High Court considered at what point in the preliminary stages of a follow-on action for damages arising from a cartel, the proceedings should be stayed pending an appeal from the Commission's decision to the GC. The Chancellor noted that since a number of the defendants had made leniency applications during the Commission's investigation, the court was entitled to take into account the likelihood that the appeal to the GC might not result in the cartel decision being annulled in its entirety. The Court ordered that the action should not be fixed for hearing until three months have elapsed from the end of the Luxembourg appeal process but that in the meantime pleadings should be served by the parties and the parties should meet to consider and if possible agree on the scope of disclosure of documents to be made pending the conclusion of the appeals.

(d) Duty to ensure consistency with decisions of European Commission

14.075 **The importance of consistent decision-making.** The scope of the duty under Article 10 EC (now Article 4(3) TEU) was considered by the UK Competition Appeal Tribunal in a merger context: see *Ryanair Holdings v Office of Fair Trading* [2011] CAT 23. The CAT held that the risk of inconsistent decisions meant that the OFT was required to delay investigating Ryanair's retained minority shareholding in Aer Lingus pending the parties' respective appeals to the GC.

14.078 **Subsequent infringement decisions.** The principles in *Masterfoods* were applied by the GC in Case T-271/03 *Deutsche Telekom AG v Commission* [2008] ECR II-477, [2008] 5 CMLR 631 where the Court considered the relevance of price regulation in the telecoms sector on an allegation of margin squeezing by a dominant undertaking. The GC rejected the argument that because the regulator approved the charges set by the applicant, that meant that they could not be contrary to Article 102 TFEU. The regulator was not a competition authority of the Member State and in any event, even if the regulator had decided that the charges were not contrary to Article 102, that finding did not bind the Commission: paras 113–124. The GC's ruling was upheld on appeal: Case C-280/08P *Deutsche Telekom v Commission*, judgment of 14 October 2010, [2010] 5 CMLR 1485 where the Court noted that even if the competition authority had itself been in breach of its obligations under the Treaty, that did not affect the scope which the appellant had to adjust its retail prices for end-user access services and avoid the squeeze: paras 77–96.

14.080 **Commission decisions in similar or related cases.** In its judgment on *Visa— MasterCard*, Case No. XVII AmA 109/07, judgment of 12 November 2008, the Polish Court for Competition and Consumer Protection held that the Polish NCA had not infringed Article 16(2) by adopting a market definition different from that applied by the Commission in its decision in *Visa International* (see paragraph 5.046 of the main work) since the Commission's decision concerned cross-border interchange fees whereas the Polish decision concerned only domestic fees and analysis of the national market. On appeal, however the Polish Court of Appeal overturned the judgment of the Court of Competition and Consumer Protection holding that the relevant market had been correctly defined and agreeing with the EU approach set out in decisions on cross-border interchange fees for Visa and Mastercard payments. The Court examined the settlements between the payment card transaction participants and found that the prices for processing transactions had been determined by agreements made by the banks rather than free competition. The case was referred back to the CCCP for review: ECN Brief 3/2010, p2.

14.081 **Non-applicability decisions.** Note that an NCA does not have power to declare that Article 102 has **not** been infringed: see Case C-375/09 *Tele 2 Polska*, judgment of 3 May 2011.

Decisions of NCAs. Note that an NCA does not have power to declare that **14.087** Article 102 has **not** been infringed; at most it can decide that there are no grounds for action on its part in respect of an alleged abuse: see Case C-375/09 *Tele 2 Polska*, judgment of 3 May 2011, para 29 '… the Commission alone is empowered to make a finding that there has been no breach of Article 102 TFEU, even if that article is applied in a procedure undertaken by a national competition authority'. The Court of Justice stated further that Article 5 of Regulation 1/2003 overrides any national rule which precludes an NCA from bringing proceedings to an end with a finding that there are no grounds for action on its part.

(e) Relationship between national courts and the Community courts

Article 234 references. Article 234 EC is now Article 267 TFEU. As to the obli- **14.090** gation on a national administrative body to reopen a final decision which a later ruling of the CJ (in another case) indicates was based on a misinterpretation of EU law see Case C-453/00 *Kühne & Heitz* [2004] ECR I-837, [2006] 2 CMLR 17; and Case C-2/06 *Kempter v Haupzollamt Hamburg-Jonas* [2008] ECR I-411, [2008] 2 CMLR 586.

Fn 266. Note that *inter partes* procedure is not a necessary condition: Case C-210/06 *Cartesio Okato* [2008] ECR I-9641, [2009] All ER (EC) 296, paras 55–59.

The approach of English courts to making a reference. See also the position **14.094** which arose in the reference from the English High Court regarding satellite broadcast decoder cards. The High Court referred questions to the CJ in the case of *Football Association Premier League Ltd and Ors v QC Leisure* [2008] EWHC 1411 (Ch). After the questions were referred (becoming Cases C-403&429/08, not yet decided) the judge allowed other parties to join the English proceedings for the purpose of being able to make representations to the CJ in the course of the reference: *FAPL v QC Leisure* [2008] EWHC 2897 (Ch). However, the President of the Court of Justice rejected their subsequent applications to submit observations on the referred questions before the Court on the grounds that they did not have a sufficient interest in the outcome of the proceedings. Those parties therefore subsequently brought their own separate action in the English High Court and the same judge referred similar questions in that new case to the CJ, inviting the Court of Justice to consider whether this reference should proceed with the Cases C-403&429/08 having regard to the similar legal and factual issues which they raise: *Union of European Football Associations (UEFA) v Euroview Sport Limited* [2010] EWHC 1066 (Ch).

See also *Conex Banninger Ltd v Commission* [2010] EWHC 1978 (Ch) (reference refused).

5. Enforcement by National Courts: Remedies

14.095 **Introduction.**   As to the obligations on a national court to provide effective judicial protection see *Conex Banninger Ltd v Commission* [2010] EWHC 1978 (Ch) which discusses, *inter alia* Case C-432/05 *Unibet (London) Ltd v Justitiekanslern* [2007] ECR I-2271. In *Unibet* Swedish law did not provide for a free-standing application for a declaration that a provision of national law is incompatible with a higher ranking rule, such as a rule of EU law. Unibet was placing advertising in the Swedish media for its internet betting service. The Swedish authorities took action against the advertisers on the basis that the advertisements contravened the Swedish law on lotteries, but no action was taken against Unibet. Unibet accordingly started an action in Sweden for a declaration that it had the right under EU law to promote its betting service and that it was not prevented from doing so by the relevant provision of Swedish domestic law (the Law on Lotteries) together with other relief including damages. The action for a declaration was dismissed on the above basis, leaving the action for damages in place. The CJ stated that it was not necessary for the national court to create specific new remedies if the existing remedies gave Unibet the opportunity to challenge the EU law measure in question. It concluded that Swedish national law provided such opportunities, including the opportunity in the action for damages to challenge the validity of the relevant Community measure. However the CJ held that the fact that Unibet could have challenged the law if it had decided to act in breach of the law and then challenge its validity in defending any proceedings taken against it was not sufficient judicial protection. In *Conex* the High Court rejected the suggestion that the effect of *Unibet* is that European Union law now requires national courts to provide a means of challenging a preparatory act of the Commission that the CJ would not consider a reviewable act for the purposes of Article 263 TFEU.

(a) Declarations of invalidity

14.098 **Generally.**   A claim that a contract contravenes the competition rules would defeat a defence of issue estoppel as the legal claim relied on represents a social policy in the interests of the public generally: *South Somerset District Council v Tonstate (Yeovil Leisure) Ltd* [2009] EWHC 3308 (Ch).

Fn 300. The appeal in *English, Welsh & Scottish Railway v E.ON UK plc* was withdrawn.

(ii) Severance

14.101A **Effect on resulting agreements.**   The question of whether, and in what circumstances, Article 101(2) will apply to an agreement entered into separately but in consequence of the agreement or arrangement that infringes Article 101(1) has been little explored, despite its obvious significance. An unlawful horizontal agreement between competitors will often be implemented by a series of vertical agreements. As with other parts of the agreement to which Article 101(1) applies, it seems that the invalidity of resulting but distinct contracts is probably a matter of national law: Case 319/82 *Soc de Vente de Ciments et Betons v Kerpen & Kerpen* [1983] ECR 4173, [1985] 1 CMLR 511, paras 11–12. If, for example, competing suppliers of a product X entered into a cartel to raise prices, in consequence of which each supplier sold X at inflated prices, it seems clear that the individual contracts of sale would not be void under Article 101(2). Independent purchasers would have a remedy in damages but could not have the purchase declared void, or indeed fail to have acquired good title to the X that they had bought. In *Courage Ltd v Crehan* [1999] UKCLR 110, the English Court of Appeal articulated a test of whether the 'contract can be considered to be so closely connected with the breach of Article [101] that it should be regarded as springing from or founded on the agreement rendered illegal by Article [101]' (at para 60). On that basis, the Court there held that individual contracts for the supply of beer to tenants of a pub subject to an unlawful beer tie were not void. See also *BAGS v AMRAC* [2009] EWCA Civ 750, at paras 124–127, where the English Court of Appeal expressly reserved its position on the application of this test to the facts. The Swedish Supreme Court adopted a similar approach in applying domestic competition law in *Boliden Mineral AB v Birka Värme Stockholm AB*, Case NJA 2004 s. 804, judgment of 23 December 2004. In 1997, the arrangement between two trade associations whereby they promulgated a standard form agreement for the supply of electricity, incorporating a price adjustment clause, was found to violate competition law and they were ordered to cease their cooperation. The claimant argued that the price adjustment clause in its contract for the purchase of electricity which had been entered into on that standard form was accordingly void. The Supreme Court held that, in general, for such a 'follow-on' agreement to be void it must in itself constitute a restriction of competition; but that depending on the circumstances there may be such a close connection between that agreement and the original infringing agreement that the public interest in protecting competition might lead to the follow-on agreement also being declared void. In that case, the price adjustment clause in the claimant's contract could not in itself be considered incompatible with competition law and it was therefore valid and enforceable.

Severance under English law: a summary. In *Pirtek (UK) Ltd v Joinplace Ltd* **14.106** [2010] EWHC 1641 (Ch) the geographic scope of a post-termination non-compete clause in a franchise agreement was cut down: para 63.

(b) Action for damages

The Ashurst Report and the Green Paper. The Commission adopted a White **14.109** Paper on Damages Actions for Breach of the EC Antitrust Rules COM(2008) 165 (2 April 2008). This was followed by a Study produced by the economics consultancy firm Oxera Consulting Ltd working with a multi-jurisdictional team of lawyers and published in December 2009 called *Quantifying antitrust damages: toward non-binding guidance for courts.* In June 2011 the Commission issued for public consultation a draft Guidance Paper on quantifying harm for damages based on breaches of Article 101 or 102 TFEU. The purpose of the Guidance is said to be 'to place at the disposal of courts and parties . . . economic and practical insights that may be of use when national rules and practices are applied': para 6 of the Draft Guidance. The Guidance describes various possible approaches to the assessment of loss including the choice of counterfactual, or non-infringement scenario, comparator-based methods, simulation models and cost-based analysis and methods for quantifying an overcharge. The main focus of the guidance is on the harm caused by cartels and by exclusionary practices. The Commission has also carried out a public consultation exercise on the issue of collective redress: *Towards a Coherent European Approach to Collective Redress* (SEC(2011)173 final) was issued in February 2011: see the update to paragraph 14.113, below.

14.112   **Qualifying interest.**   As to the last sentence of this paragraph, the German Federal Supreme Court upheld the decision that Cartel Damage Claims ('CDC') could pursue the cement cartel damages claims as assignee: *Cartel Damage Claims v Dyckerhoff AG*, Case KZR42/08, judgment of 7 April 2009. See Bundesgerichtshof Press Release No. 80/2009 of 17 April 2009. Subsequently, CDC commenced a follow-on claim in Germany on behalf of 32 customers against six producers arising from the Commission's decision in the hydrogen peroxides cartel.

14.113   **Indirect purchasers.**   In October 2010 a Joint Information Notice was issued by the EU Commissioners for Justice, Competition and Consumer Policy (SEC (2010) 1192, 5 October 2010) *Towards a Coherent European Approach to Collective Redress: Next Steps.* Subsequently, on 4 February 2011, a public Consultation Document *Towards a Coherent European Approach to Collective Redress* was issued (SEC(2011)173 final). The Consultation Paper notes that existing mechanisms for collective redress to compensate a group of victims harmed by illegal business practices vary widely throughout the EU. The purpose of the consultation was therefore to identify common legal principles on collective redress and examine how such common principles could fit into the EU legal system and into the legal orders of the 27 EU Member States Views were therefore sought on issues such as what role associations representing victims' interests should have in the context of litigation on multiple claims, in particular, in a cross-border context; the role of alternative dispute resolution mechanisms and safeguards against abusive litigation.

14.114   **Co-contractor's right to claim damages.**   An analogous point was raised in *Safeway Stores v Twigger* [2010] EWCA Civ 1472 where the English Court of Appeal held that an undertaking that had been fined for cartel activity by the NCA could not seek reimbursement from the directors and employees who had attended the cartel meetings. At first instance the High Court held that infringement of the competition rules was sufficiently illegal or unlawful to engage the maxim and this was not challenged on appeal where the main issue was whether the individuals' conduct was sufficiently separate from that of the corporation. The Court of Appeal held that the claim was barred by the rule *ex turpi causa non oritur actio* because the liability is personal to the claimants and that they are not entitled to pass it on to their employees.

Who can be sued: the *Provimi* case.   The decision in *Provimi* was discussed by   **14.117**
the Court of Appeal in *Cooper Tire & Rubber Company Europe v Dow Deutschland Inc* [2010] EWCA Civ 864. One issue considered in that judgment was whether a cause of action for loss could be maintained against the UK subsidiaries of addressees of the decision, even if those subsidiaries were not alleged to have been involved in or known about the cartel activity of other entities within the addressee undertaking. The High Court had held ([2009] EWHC 2609 (Comm), Teare J) that they could, following the judgment of Aikens J in *Provimi*. He therefore held that the claim against the UK subsidiaries was not liable to be struck out. On appeal, the Court held that the pleaded case, properly construed, did encompass both the possibility that the anchor defendants were parties to or aware of the anti-competitive conduct of their parent company and the other addressees, and the possibility that they were not. The issue decided in *Provimi* did not therefore arise in the appeal. The Court of Appeal nonetheless stated that the liability of a subsidiary for losses arising from anti-competitive conduct elsewhere within the undertaking of which it was unaware was unclear and that a reference to the CJ would be necessary: 'Although one can see that a parent company should be liable for what its subsidiary has done on the basis that a parent company is presumed to be able to exercise (and actually exercise) decisive influence over a subsidiary, it is by no means obvious even in an Article 81 context that a subsidiary should be liable for what its parent does, let alone for what another subsidiary does. Nor does the *Provimi* point sit comfortably with the apparent practice of the Commission, when it exercises its power to fine, to single out those who are primarily responsible or their parent companies rather than to impose a fine on all the entities of the relevant undertaking.' (para 45).

Note, however, that in 'follow-on' damages claims where statutory jurisdiction depends on a pre-existing decision finding an infringement, only addressees of the decision named in the operative part of the EU Commission's decision may be sued: *Emerson Electric v Morgan Crucible Company* [2011] CAT 4.

Fault.   The Commission's White Paper on damages actions (COM(2008) 165   **14.118**
(2 April 2008)) suggested that the full application of a fault requirement whereby it must be shown that the infringer acted intentionally or negligently cannot be reconciled with the principle of effectiveness. However, there may be room for some defence of 'excusable error' in novel or complex situations where the infringer has taken every reasonable precaution but is still found to have infringed. However, this topic is not included in the public consultations launched so far by the Commission.

14.120   **Extent of damages recoverable.**   In the White Paper on damages actions, the Commission stresses that national rules must not make it excessively difficult for victims to calculate the extent of the harm suffered and commits to producing non-binding guidance for courts on the calculation of damages.

14.121   **Damages cases.**   The Hungarian Competition Act, by an amendment that came into force on 1 June 2009, provides that on a claim for damages resulting from a supply-side price cartel, there is a presumption that the prices charged by the participants in the cartel were increased by 10 per cent by reason of the infringement. The declared aim of the amendment is to assist victims of the cartel in recovering compensation but the claimants will still have to prove their loss, for example that they did not pass on any part of the increase to their customers. They can contend that in fact prices were raised by more than the presumed 10 per cent and equally a defendant can seek to rebut the statutory presumption.

See also the developments at the European level attempting to address these problems discussed in the update to paragraphs 14.112 and 14.113, above.

Fn 385. In *Conduit Europe v Telefónica*, an appeal to the Madrid Provincial Court of Appeal was dismissed: judgment of 25 May 2006.

Fn 386. Cf the judgment of the Italian Corte di Cassazione, 3rd section, No. 2305 of 2 February 2007, quashing the decision of the Naples Court of Appeal that awarded damages to a consumer in a follow-on claim after the decision condemning the exchange of information among motor insurers: see fn 261 to paragraph 5.089 of the main work. It was held that the lower court should not have assumed that the increase in the premiums during the period of the infringement was caused by the infringement: causation had to be established on the evidence. Similarly, see judgment of the Corte di Cassazione, No. 3640, of 13 February 2009.

14.121A   **Access to evidence.**   In the White Paper the Commission noted that in many Member States the current systems of civil procedure offer no effective means for the victim to overcome the information asymmetry that is typical of antitrust cases. However, this topic is not included in the public consultations launched so far by the Commission.

14.122   **Exemplary damages.**   In *Devenish Nutrition v Sanofi-Aventis* [2007] EWHC 2394 (Ch) the English High Court held that EU rules precluded the award of exemplary damages in a follow-on action for damages against participants in the vitamins cartels condemned by the European Commission (OJ 2003 L6/1). First the principle of *non bis in idem* applied where the defendants have already been fined (or had fines imposed and then reduced or commuted under the Leniency Notice) by the Commission: para 52. Secondly, to award exemplary damages would 'run counter' to the decision already adopted by the Commission and therefore contravene Article 16 of Regulation 1/2003. This was because if the national court were to award exemplary damages that could only be because the national court had concluded that the fines imposed by the Commission (including those fines that had been reduced or commuted) were insufficient to punish and deter: para 54. The point was not challenged on appeal: [2008] EWCA Civ 1086. The scope of the ruling in *Devenish* was discussed by the UK Competition Appeal Tribunal in *Albion Water Ltd v Dŵr Cymru* [2010] CAT 30 where the Tribunal held that the principle did not apply where there had been no fine imposed in either EU or domestic infringement proceedings.

Restitution and prevention of unjust enrichment. In *Devenish Nutrition v* **14.123**
Sanofi-Aventis [2008] EWCA Civ 1086, the English Court of Appeal held that EU law neither required nor precluded the availability of a restitutionary remedy but that under English law no such remedy was available on the facts of the case (follow-on claim for damages resulting from the vitamins cartels). Restitutionary remedies were only available in tortious claims where compensatory damages were an inadequate remedy. The judge at first instance had held that damages could not be regarded as an inadequate remedy if the difficulty facing the claimant was only one of evidential proof ([2007] EWHC 2394 (Ch), para 93). Arden LJ held that this went too far: it is at least arguable that the court should order an account of profits where the evidential difficulties were not the claimant's responsibility: para 105 of her judgment. However, in the instant case the claimants were not alleging that it was exceptionally difficult or impossible for them to prove their claim: para 106.

Fn 390. The *Consumers' Association v JJB Sports* case referred to in this footnote settled before judgment.

'Passing-on' defence. The Commission's White Paper on damages actions refers **14.124**
to the 'thorny issue' of passing on of overcharges. The Commission states that as regards the passing-on defence, purchasers of an overcharged product or service who had actually passed on that overcharge to their customers should not be entitled to compensation for that overcharge, though they may be entitled to loss of profits if that passing on has led to a reduction in sales. As a corollary of this, the customer to whom the overcharge has been passed should be able to claim compensation for the resulting harm. Recognising that these customers may be reluctant to bring actions, the Commission suggests that they be able to aggregate their claims via collective actions and that there should be a presumption operating in their favour that the overcharge has been passed on in its entirety to their level. That presumption can be rebutted by the infringer, for example by showing that he has already paid compensation for that same overcharge to someone higher up in the distribution chain.

Note how this topic is treated in the Commission's Draft Guidance Paper on quantifying harm in actions for damages based on breaches of Articles 101 or 102 TFEU, issued for consultation in June 2011: paras 142 *et seq*. The Draft Guidance notes that the pass on of overcharges by direct customers to final customers, 'normally entails a volume effect' that is, fewer products are bought due to the rise in prices.

The price increase through pass on and the reduction in sales are thus connected. The Draft Guidance considers methods for assessing the likelihood of passing-on having taken place in a particular downstream market (for example the extent to which the direct purchaser's competitors were buying their input from sources outside the cartel) and for quantifying the harm caused by the volume effect.

14.125 **Examples of passing-on in the Member States.** In *Cement Cartel II*, Case 2 U 10/03 Kart., judgment of the Berlin Higher Regional Court (Kammergericht) of 1 October 2009, the court indicated that direct and indirect purchasers should constitute 'joint and several creditors' under German civil law, whereby each can sue the cartel participant directly for the damage it sustained. However, if only the direct purchaser sues it can recover for the full overcharge and then becomes liable to sub-purchasers to 'distribute' the damages to the extent that the overcharge was passed on. The claim there concerned only German competition law (as in force before the 7th Amendment referred to in the main text) but under the principle of equivalence the same reasoning would apply to a claim for violation of EU law. In that case, only the direct purchaser sued and the court awarded about a third of the damages claimed, illustrating the scrutiny applied to calculation of damages.

(c) Injunctive relief

14.131 **Conditions for relief.** In a claim alleging abusive predatory pricing, injunctive relief was refused where the claimant failed to show that its loss would not be capable of being compensated by an award of damages: *Goode Concrete v Cement Roadstone Holdings* [2011] IEHC 15.

14.132 **The balance of convenience.** In *Arriva Scotland West Limited v Glasgow Airport Ltd* [2011] CSOH 69 the Scottish Court of Session held that it would require a clear-cut case of abuse of dominant position to justify an interim interdict without detailed consideration of evidence. A case which depended on an extension of the existing case law to establish abuse, was not a strong *prima facie* case. Interim relief was declined on the balance of convenience.

Where an injunction was sought to require supplies of a scarce pharmaceutical product, the fact that shortages for UK patients might arise if the allegedly dominant supplier then felt obliged to supply all those who requested supplies was regarded as something that could not be compensated in damages: *Intecare Direct Ltd v Pfizer Ltd* [2010] EWHC 600 (Ch), [2010] ECC 28.

14.133 **Mandatory relief.** In *Software Cellular Network Ltd v T-Mobile (UK) Limited* [2007] EWHC 1790 (Ch) the High Court granted an interim injunction to the applicant who alleged that T-Mobile's refusal to route calls from its subscribers to the applicant's phone numbers was a breach of Article 102 TFEU. The judge noted that the injunction sought was a mandatory order rather than a prohibitory order but held that the balance of convenience favoured the grant of the injunction pending trial.

See however the discussion of awarding interim relief in a predatory pricing case: *Goode Concrete v Cement Roadstone Holdings* [2011] IEHC 15, para 32.

(d) Reliance on Articles 81 and 82 as a defence

Articles 81 and 82 as a defence to infringement of intellectual property rights. Fn 440. See also *Oracle America, Inc (Formerly Sun Microsystems, Inc) v M-Tech Data Limited* [2010] EWCA Civ 997 (defence to trade mark infringement proceedings).   **14.138**

The nexus between infringement and abuse under Article 82: the Community Courts' approach. See also Case T-119/09 *Protégé International v Commission*, not yet decided (appeal against rejection of complaint alleging abuse of dominant position by Pernod Ricard in filing legal proceedings against the applicant contesting the registration of trade marks. It is alleged that the proceedings were aimed not at protecting Pernod Ricard's intellectual property rights in its own marks ('Wild Turkey') but of eliminating the applicant as a competitor of Pernod Ricard in the Irish whiskey market). See also Case T-96/08 *Global Digital Disc v Commission*, not yet decided (appeal against rejection of complaint alleging breach of Article 102 TFEU in licensing practices in the CD-R field).   **14.140**

Fn 451. The appeal in *AstraZeneca* has been decided and the findings of abuse in relation to the information submitted by AstraZeneca when applying for patent protection extensions were upheld: Case T-321/05 *AstraZeneca v Commission*, judgment of 1 July 2010, [2010] 5 CMLR 1575 (on appeal Case C-457/10P *AstraZeneca v Commission*, not yet decided).

6. Practice and Procedure in the UK

Follow-on damages claims. For further examples of follow-on actions brought in the High Court see *Cooper Tire & Rubber Europe v Shell Chemicals* [2009] EWHC 1529 (Comm) (stay of proceedings to determine the Court's jurisdiction in the light of proceedings pending in Italy refused); *National Grid Electricity Transmission plc v ABB Ltd* [2009] EWHC 1326 (Ch).   **14.145**

Note that the Commission's White Paper on damages actions proposes that a final decision by any national competition authority and a final judgment by a national court reviewing such a decision should be accepted in every Member State as irrebuttable proof of the infringement in subsequent civil damages claims.

It may sometimes be difficult to identify precisely what findings of infringement are contained in the regulator's decision: see, eg *Enron Coal Services Ltd v English Welsh and Scottish Railway* [2009] EWCA Civ 647 where the English Court of Appeal said 'The purpose of s.47A is to obviate the necessity for a trial of the question of infringement only where the regulator has in fact ruled on that very issue. We were not referred to any procedure for seeking clarification of any points of uncertainty from the decision-maker. The Tribunal ought therefore, . . . to be astute to recognise and reject cases where there is no clearly identifiable finding of infringement and where they are in effect being asked to make their own judgment on that issue': para 31. The claim for damages was ultimately dismissed by the Tribunal: [2009] CAT 36 and the Tribunal's judgment was upheld by the Court of Appeal: *Enron Coal Services v English, Welsh and Scottish Railways* [2011] EWCA Civ 2.

In 'follow-on' damages claims where statutory jurisdiction depends on a pre-existing decision finding an infringement, only addressees of the decision named in the operative part of the EU Commission's decision may be sued: *Emerson Electric v Morgan Crucible Company* [2011] CAT 4.

14.146   **Other private actions: binding OFT determination.**   Note that section 58 applies to proceedings in follow-on actions before the Competition Appeal Tribunal as well as in proceedings in the High Court: *Enron Coal Services v English, Welsh and Scottish Railways* [2011] EWCA Civ 2.

14.149   **Limitation period.**   **Fn 485.** Where an appeal to the GC against a cartel decision is limited to issues relating to the fine imposed and does not challenge the finding of infringement, the limitation period is not suspended by the appeal and the follow-on action must be brought within two years of the expiry of the right to appeal: *BCL Old Company Ltd v BASF* [2009] EWCA Civ 434.

Fn 487. There has been a series of cases clarifying the operation of the two-year time limit under section 47A of the Competition Act 1998 within which to bring a damages claim following on from an infringement decision of the EU Commission. Where an appeal to the General Court against the Commission's decision challenges the fine only and does not contest liability, the appeal does not prevent the two-year period from running as against that infringer: *BCL Old Co Limited v BASF SE* [2009] EWCA Civ 434. Where an appeal to the GC on liability is lodged by one addressee of the decision, that does not prevent the two-year period running against other addressees who have not appealed: *Deutsche Bahn AG v Morgan Crucible* [2011] CAT 16 (departing from the Tribunal's earlier ruling to the contrary in *Emerson Electric Co v Morgan Crucible plc* [2007] CAT 28). Once the two-year limit has expired, the CAT does not have a discretion to extend time to bring a claim for damages: *BCL Old Co v BASF AG* [2010] EWCA Civ 1258 (on appeal to the UK Supreme Court).

14.151   **Pleading.**   **Fn 490.** See also *SEL-Imperial Ltd v British Standards Institution* [2010] EWHC 854 (Ch), para 17.

Strike out.   See also the comments of the court in *Humber Oil Terminals v   14.152
Associated British Ports* [2011] EWHC 352 (Ch), para 34: 'The fact that expert
evidence will be required to establish the allegation, so far from being a reason not
to particularise it, is a powerful indication of the opposite'.

Burden of proof.   Fn 497. The correct citation for the *Attheraces* decision is [2006]   14.153
ECC 24 and not [2006] ECC 12, [2006] EuLR 76.

Admissible evidence.   See the comments of Morgan J in *Bookmakers' Afternoon   14.157
Greyhound Services v Amalgamated Racing Ltd* [2008] EWHC 1978 (Ch), paras
287 and 288 that the expert witnesses did not confine themselves to matters of
microeconomics on which they could give admissible opinion evidence for the
assistance of the court but also summarised their understanding of the legal principles which fell to be applied and then offered their conclusions as to the result of
applying those legal principles to this case. Although the parties did not distinguish
between parts of their statements which were truly admissible expert evidence on
matters of microeconomics and those parts which went beyond the proper bounds
of expert evidence, the learned judge considered it important to do so. See also
Chester City Council v Arriva Buses [2007] EWHC 1373 (Ch) where the judge,
when assessing rival evidence relating to the definition of the relevant product market, compared the approach of an expert economics consultant witness with that of
a witness without economics qualifications but with long experience in the relevant
industry.

As regards economic evidence, see also Niels, Jenkins & Kavanagh, *Economics for
Competition Lawyers* (2011) for an analysis of the relevant economics principles,
aimed specifically at competition lawyers.

Disclosure of documents as between parties.   For pre-action disclosure between   14.158
potential parties to a claim for breach of Articles 101 and 102 TFEU see *Hutchison
3G UK Ltd v O2 (UK) Ltd* [2008] EWHC 55 (Comm) where Steel J held that under
the relevant Civil Procedure Rules, the applicants 'have to show that it is more
probable than not that the documents are within the scope of standard disclosure
in regard to the issues that are likely to arise': para 44.

See also *British Sky Broadcasting v Virgin Media Communications* [2008] EWCA
Civ 612. The applicant was involved in proceedings in the High Court, in the
Competition Appeal Tribunal and in an investigation by OFCOM. A confidentiality ring was established in the High Court proceedings, limiting disclosure of
commercially sensitive documents to external legal advisers. The question was
whether the defendant should be able to use the same legal advisers (who were part
of the ring) in the proceedings before the CAT and in the OFCOM investigation.
The CA held that they could, indicating that it was hard to conceive of circumstances where disclosure in one set of proceedings would preclude lawyers from
acting in other proceedings between the same parties.

See also *National Grid Electricity Transmission v ABB Ltd* [2011] EWHC 1717 (Ch) discussed in the update to paragraph 14.028, above.

14.160A **Stay of proceedings pending appeals in Luxembourg.** In *National Grid Electricity Transmission plc v ABB Ltd* [2009] EWHC 1326 (Ch) the English High Court considered at what point in the preliminary stages of a follow-on action for damages arising from a cartel the proceedings should be stayed pending an appeal from the Commission's decision to the GC. The Chancellor noted that since a number of the defendants had made leniency applications during the Commission's investigation, the appeal to the GC might not result in the cartel decision being annulled in its entirety. The Court ordered that the action should not be fixed for hearing until three months has elapsed from the end of the Luxembourg appeal process but that in the meantime pleadings should be served by the parties and the parties should meet to consider and if possible agree on the scope of disclosure of documents to be made pending the conclusion of the appeals.

14.160B **Class actions in cartel damages claims.** In *Emerald Supplies v British Airways* [2009] EWHC 741 (Ch) the Chancellor considered an application to strike out part of an action according to which the claimants purported to be claiming 'on their own behalf and on behalf of all other direct or indirect purchasers of air freight services the prices for which were inflated by the agreements or concerted practices' alleged. Applying CPR Rule 19.6, the Chancellor noted that there were two conditions to be satisfied before a representative action could properly be brought. The first pre-condition is that there should be more than one person who satisfies the remaining pre-condition. The second is that those persons have the relevant interest at the time the claim is begun. There is no limit to the number of persons in the class to be represented and the mere fact that the relevant class is both numerous and geographically widely spread is not of itself an objection to a representative action. Nevertheless the more extensive the class the more clearly should the second precondition be satisfied. The Court held that the class referred to in the pleadings was inconsistent with the rule because it was impossible to say of any given person that he was a member of the class *at the time the claim form was issued.* The defect was not that the class consisted of a fluctuating body of persons but that the criteria for inclusion in the class could not be satisfied at the time the action is brought because they depend on the action succeeding. The Chancellor's judgment was upheld on appeal: *Emerald Supplies v British Airways* [2010] EWCA Civ 1284.

See also developments on the EU front in the Consultation Document *Towards a Coherent European Approach to Collective Redress* was issued (SEC(2011)173 final) discussed in the update to paragraph 14.112, above.

14.161 **Summary judgment.** Summary judgment was refused in *Football Association Premier League Limited v QC Leisure* [2008] EWHC 44 (Ch) (Article 101 TFEU defence was the legitimate subject for a trial). The judge also refused an alternative application that the trial of the Article 101 defence be stayed until the other issues in the case were resolved.

For a case where English High Court granted summary judgment to a defendant, striking down a clause found to be contrary to Article 101 see *Jones v Ricoh UK Ltd* [2010] EWHC 1743 (Ch).

Fn 532. See also the comments of Roth J in *SEL-Imperial Ltd v British Standards Institution* [2010] EWHC 854 (Ch), para 16.

7. Arbitration Proceedings

Separability of the arbitration agreement. The decision of the Court of Appeal **14.164** in *Fiona Trust Corporation v Primalov* was upheld by the House of Lords: [2007] UKHL 40. Lord Hoffmann emphasised the importance of adopting a construction of an arbitration agreement consistent with what could be assumed to be the commercial rationale behind the parties' decision to enter into such an agreement. This meant that one should start from the assumption that the parties, as rational businessmen, are likely to have intended any dispute arising out of the relationship into which they have entered or purported to enter to be decided by the same tribunal. The clause should be construed in accordance with this presumption unless the language makes it clear that certain questions were intended to be excluded from the arbitrator's jurisdiction. The effect of section 7 of the Arbitration Act 1996 was that the arbitration agreement must be treated as separate from the main agreement and that the former can be invalidated only on a ground which relates to the arbitration agreement and is not merely a consequence of the invalidity of the main agreement. Where, therefore, the appellants argued that they were entitled to rescind the charterparties, including the arbitration agreements, because the charter parties were induced by bribery, this did not undermine the application of the arbitration agreement.

8. Table of National Enforcement Regimes

The Table of National Enforcement Regimes has not been updated for the Second **14.171** Supplement. The Reader is referred to the Commission's ECN Briefs available on the website. In particular the special issue published in December 2010 provides information and contact details for each NCA in the Union. Subsequent legislative developments are noted in the Briefs and will provide more up-to-date information than this Supplement can attempt.

15

STATE AIDS

1. Introduction

Generally. **Fn 1.** As to the application of the State aid rules to the sectors previ- **15.001**
ously covered by the ECSC Treaty see Case T-25/04 *González y Díez v Commission*,
judgment of 12 September 2007. The GC held that the Commission had been correct to apply Article 108(2) TFEU and the Procedural Regulation in its decision
adopted after the ECSC Treaty expired relating to an aid granted before that
expiry. But the Commission erred in deciding that a State aid put into effect without its prior approval would be subject to the provisions of Regulation 1407/2002
which was adopted after the aid was put into effect. (Note that this conclusion may
need to be reconsidered in the light of Case C-334/07P *Commission v Freistaat
Sachsen* [2008] ECR I-9465). However, since the relevant provisions of Reg
1407/2002 were identical to earlier provisions which were in force at the relevant
time, the GC in *González y Díez* found that the error did not affect the validity of
the decision.

As regards textbooks on State aids see now Bacon (ed), *European Community Law
of State Aid* (2009); Vesterdorf and Nielsen, *State Aid Law of the European Union*
(2008).

Recent legislative developments. Since the 6th edition a number of significant **15.003**
legislative instruments have been adopted:

- measures responding to the banking and financial crisis: see new paragraphs
  15.003A–15.003C, below;
- the General Block Exemption Regulation: Regulation 800/2008, OJ 2008
  L214/3: Vol II, App G16, see update to paragraph 15.067, below;
- new EU guidelines on State aid for environmental protection, OJ 2008 C82/1:
  Vol II, App G22A replacing the 2001 Guidelines (fn 18 refers), see update to
  paragraph 15.060, below;
- a new Notice on the application of Articles [107 and 108] to State aid in the form
  of guarantees, OJ 2008 C155/10: Vol II, App G26A, see update to paragraph
  15.038, below;

- a Notice Towards an effective implementation of Commission decisions ordering Member States to recover unlawful and incompatible State aid, OJ 2007
  C272/4: Vol II, App G8A, see update to paragraph 15.102, below.
- a new Notice on the enforcement of State aid law by national courts, OJ 2009
  C85/1: Vol II, App G8B, see update to paragraph 15.111, below;
- a 'Simplification Package' comprising a Notice on a simplified procedure for
  treatment of certain types of State aid, OJ 2009 C136/3: Vol II, App G8C and a
  Code of Best Practice: Vol II, App G8D: see new paragraph 15.075A, below;
- amendments to Regulation 794/2004 in Regulation 271/2008, OJ 2008 L82/1
  and Regulation 1147/2008, OJ 2008 L313/1, see update to paragraph 15.069,
  below.

15.003A **The global financial and economic crisis.** Since the second half of 2008, State aid
rules and procedures have had to accommodate the measures taken by Member
States to respond to the banking crisis which followed on from the collapse of
Lehmann Bros bank. There have been two strands to this response so far as concerns
State aid. The first strand is a series of Communications from the Commission dealing specifically with measures taken to rescue and support banking institutions.
The second strand concerns aid measures which could be described as part of the
'stimulus' package adopted by Member States to mitigate the effects of the severe
recession which followed the global crisis. The Commission published an Overview
of national measures adopted as a response to the financial/economic crisis,
MEMO/09/380 (9 September 2009) which contains links to the relevant
documents.

15.003B **Banking aid measures.** In October 2008 the Commission issued a Communication 'The application of State aid rules to measures taken in relation to financial
institutions in the context of the current global financial crisis', OJ 2008 C270/8:
Vol II, App G26B. This provides guidance on the criteria relevant for the compatibility with the State aid provisions of general schemes to safeguard the stability of
the financial system as well as the stabilisation of individual financial institutions of
systemic relevance. While noting that assistance to undertakings in difficulty was
usually assessed under Article 107(3)(c) TFEU, the Commission indicated that in
the light of the level of seriousness that the current crisis in the financial markets
had reached and of its possible impact on the overall economy of Member States,
Article 107(3)(b) is available in limited circumstances as a legal basis for aid measures. The Communication then went on to explain how the rules would be applied
to particular measures. On 5 December 2008 a further Communication giving
more detail about banking recapitalisation was adopted (OJ 2009 C10/2: Vol II,
App G26C), and in January 2009 further guidance was given on the treatment of
impaired assets in the EU banking sector (OJ 2009 C72/1). A Communication
explaining how the Commission will examine aid for the restructuring of banks was
published in August 2009 (OJ 2009 C195/10). It sets out a model restructuring

plan and applies to aids notified to the Commission on or before 31 December 2010. In December 2010 the Commission issued a further Communication (OJ 2010 C329/7) setting out the parameters for the temporary acceptability of crisis-related assistance to banks as from 1 January 2011 (referred to by the Commission as the 'Exit Communication'). More recently the Commission has published a Staff Working Paper (published 1 June 2011) on the application of State aid rules to government guarantee schemes covering bank debt to be issued after 30 June 2011. The Paper states that the ultimate goal must be the return to the normal State aid regime for the rescue and restructuring of banks, based on Article 107(3)(c), which should re-apply as of 1 January 2012, 'market conditions permitting'.

The Commission also adopted a large number of individual decisions approving particular aid schemes and aids to individual institutions: see MEMO/11/516 (18 July 2011) listing the decisions taken as at 14 July 2011 both as regards financial institutions and decisions relating to the real economy under the Temporary Framework.

'Recovery Plan' aids.   On 26 November 2008, the Commission adopted 'A **15.003C** European Economic Recovery Plan' (COM(2008) 800). This prompted the adoption of a Commission Communication 'Temporary Community framework for State aid measures to support access to finance in the current financial and economic crisis' which applies from 17 December 2008 (published OJ 2009 C16/1: Vol II, App G22B). The Communication noted that 'while State aid is no miracle cure to the current difficulties', well targeted public support for companies could help to unblock lending to companies and to encourage continued investment in a low-carbon future. The Communication described a number of measures that a Member State could take without falling within the State aid provisions, for example payment deadlines for social security and similar charges, or even taxes could be extended. The Communication referred to the existing State aid legislative measures which could be relied on by Member States. It goes on to state that the Commission will consider aids of various kinds as being compatible with the common market on the basis of Article 107(3)(b) TFEU. The kinds of aids covered are (a) limited aids above the existing *de minimis* threshold; (b) aids in the form of guarantees; (c) aid in the form of subsidised interest rates; (d) aid for the production of green products; and (e) risk capital measures. The Recovery Plan Communication also adapts the Communication relating to short-term export credit insurance (OJ 1997 C281/4: Vol II, App G24). Some amendments to the detail of this Communication were made in February 2009 and a consolidated version of the Recovery Plan Communication was published in OJ 2009 C83/1. At the end of 2010 the Commission issued a further Communication (OJ 2011 C6/5) prolonging the State aid crisis framework until the end of 2011 but subject to some stricter conditions designed to facilitate a gradual return to normal State aid rules limiting the impact of their prolonged application on competition: see Press Release IP/10/1636 (1 December 2010). The conditions for aid were tightened particularly for larger companies (rather than SMEs).

15.004 European Economic Area. For a recent judgment of the EFTA Court concerning the application of the State aid provisions in the EEA Agreement see Case E-5/07 *Private Barnehagers Landsforbund v EFTA Surveillance Authority*, decn of the EFTA Court 8 February 2008, [2008] 2 CMLR 818 (municipal kindergartens not undertakings for the purpose of the State aid provisions).

2. The Concept of an Aid

(a) Generally

15.010 An advantage. In Case T-25/07 *Iride SpA v Commission* [2009] ECR II-245 the GC rejected an argument that a payment did not confer an advantage because it only compensated the recipient for stranded costs arising from the liberalisation of the electricity market and so did no more than restore normal market conditions as compared with rival undertakings which did not have to bear the stranded costs. The GC held that the alteration of the legislative framework in the electricity sector which occurred as a result of Directive liberalisation was part of normal market conditions and that, when the recipients of the aid made the investments that gave rise to the stranded costs in question, it was taking the normal risks related to possible legislative amendments.

In Case C-431/07P *Bouygues SA v Commission* [2009] ECR I-2665 the CJ upheld the finding of the GC that the apparent advantage granted by France when it waived part of the fees to be paid by telecoms licensees did not constitute a State aid because the waiver was necessary to avoid unequal treatment of those licensees under the EU telecoms regulatory scheme then in force. The waiver brought their fees into line with the fees that Bouygues had agreed to pay in a later auction of the same licences. Since the GC had been right to hold that the principle of non-discrimination required the French authorities to align the fees due with those charged to Bouygues, there was no State aid. See also Case T-53/08 *Italy v Commission* and Case T-62/08 *ThyssenKrupp Acciai Speciali Terni v Commission*, both judgments of 1 July 2010 where the GC rejected a submission that the extension of a preferential electricity tariff was justified as compensation for the earlier nationalisation of some of the recipients' assets.

See also Tosics and Gaál, 'Public procurement and State aid control—the issue of economic advantage' where the authors note that the Commission has received State aid notifications in which Member States ask the Commission to confirm in advance that the complex public procurement transactions that they are planning would not lead to a State aid. The article clarifies the Commission's practice in that regard: (2007) 3 Competition Policy Newsletter 17.

Fn 42. As regards the principle established in the Case C-237/04 *Enirisorse v Sotacarbo,* the GC in Cases T-254/00, etc, *Hotel Cipriani v Commission* [2008] ECR II-3269 rejected the argument that social security exemptions granted to undertakings in Venice and Chioggia were justified as compensation for the additional costs connected with the specific structural problems resulting from the fact that the towns are situated in a lagoon. There was no direct connection between the additional costs actually incurred and the amount of the aid received by the various operators. Appeals against the GC's judgment were dismissed: Cases C-71/09P, etc, *Comitato 'Venezia vuole vivere' v Commission*, judgment of 9 June 2011.

Compensation for public service obligations. As to the margin of discretion **15.011** conferred on the Member State in designating an activity as being a service of general economic interest see Cases T-309/04, etc, *TV2/Danmark v Commission* [2008] ECR II-2935 (public service broadcasting channel funded partly by licence fee and partly by advertising was such a service).

The *Altmark* criteria. In Cases T-309/04, etc, *TV2/Danmark v Commission* **15.012** [2008] ECR II-2935 the Commission had found that the licence fee arrangements for TV2 failed to meet the second and fourth *Altmark* criteria. The Commission found that the fee had resulted in a build-up of capital reserves and hence overcompensated TV2 for the public service broadcasting function. The Commission rejected the Danish Government's contention that these reserves were necessary to protect TV2 from fluctuations in advertising revenue by which it was also partly funded. The GC annulled the decision for lack of reasoning. The Court held that the Commission had failed to examine the Danish Government's contentions seriously. The fact that TV2 did not have to draw on its reserves did not support the inference that those reserves had to be regarded as disproportionate to the funding needs of providing the public service. It is in the very nature of a reserve which is built up to deal with an uncertainty that it does not necessarily have to be used.

See also Case T-8/06 *FAB Fernsehen aus Berlin GmbH v Commission*, judgment of 6 October 2009 (first criterion of *Almark* not met).

See also Case T-266/02 *Deutsche Post v Commission* [2008] ECR II-1233 where the GC annulled the prohibition of a State aid because the Commission had failed to check or determine whether the transfer payment alleged to constitute the aid in fact exceeded the applicant's net additional costs associated with the provision of a service of general economic interest for which, in accordance with the conditions laid down in the *Altmark* judgment, it had the right to claim compensation. An appeal by the Commission was dismissed Case C-399/08P *Commission v Deutsche Post*, judgment of 2 September 2010.

Note that the criteria can be applied when assessing the validity of a Commission decision which predates the *Altmark* judgment since the CJ did not place any temporal limitation on the scope of its findings in that case: Case T-388/03 *Deutsche Post et DHL International v Commission* [2009] ECR II-199 (on appeal Case C-148/09P, not yet decided).

See also Case C-206/06 *Essent Netwerk Noord v Aluminium Delfzijl* [2008] ECR I-5497, [2008] 3 CMLR 895 (it is for the national court to decide whether and to what extent a levy paid over to an electricity generating company to compensate it for investment in 'non-market-compatible costs' prior to market liberalisation should be regarded as compensating for the discharge of public service functions for the purposes of the *Altmark* criteria).

As regards the public service obligation, the GC has confirmed that this concept has the same meaning here as the service of general economic interest for the purposes of Article 106(2) and that Member States have a wide discretion to define what they regard as SGEIs. The definition of such services by a Member State can be questioned by the Commission only in the event of manifest error: Case T-289/03 *BUPA v Commission* [2008] ECR II-81, para 166. The GC went on to hold that a private medical insurance scheme adopted by Ireland did have an SGEI mission and that the other *Altmark* criteria were also satisfied.

See also Case C-140/09 *Fallimento Traghetti del Mediterraneo v Presidenza del Consiglio dei Ministri*, judgment of 10 June 2010 (preliminary reference concerning subsidies allegedly paid 'on account' of public service obligations entered into many years later were an advantage capable of constituting a State aid).

15.013 **The 'market economy investor' principle.** In Case T-455/05 *Componenta v Commission*, judgment of 18 December 2008 the GC annulled a Commission decision which had held that a transaction by which the Finnish town of Karkkila bought out the applicant's half share in a property company amounted to a State aid because the price exceeded the value of the interest. The GC rejected the applicant's challenge to the way the Commission had valued the shares in the company but found that the Commission had not sufficiently explained how it had valued the land holdings of the company.

As to the application of this principle when the aid is granted by a State body allegedly exercising its a legislative or regulatory function see Case T-196/04 *Ryanair v Commission* [2008] ECR II-3643 on appeal from the *Ryanair/Charleroi* decision cited in fn 53. There the GC considered an arrangement under which the Walloon Region of Belgium which owns the Charleroi airport infrastructure agreed to grant Ryanair, first, a reduction in landing charges at the airport and, secondly, an indemnity in the event of losses which Ryanair might suffer following any change in the airport charges or opening hours of Charleroi airport. The GC concluded that the Commission had been wrong to treat the Walloon Region and the airport operating company BSCA as separate entities; they were in fact a single undertaking.

The GC then considered whether the private investor principle could be applied to this single entity, given that the measures in question were said by the Commission to have been adopted by the Walloon Region in its legislative, regulatory role. The Court noted that for the purposes of determining whether a measure of State aid constitutes an 'advantage', a distinction must be drawn between the obligations which the State assumes when exercising an economic activity and its obligations as a public authority. It is necessary, when the State acts as an undertaking to analyse its conduct by reference to the private investor principle. But application of that principle is excluded where the State acts as a public authority. In the latter case, the conduct of the State can never be compared to that of an operator or private investor in a market economy. However, the GC disagreed with the Commission's characterisation of the relevant activities as part of the public function and held that they were economic activities. The Commission's refusal to apply the private investor principle to the measures adopted by the Walloon Region was, the GC held, vitiated by an error in law.

For evaluation by a national court, see, eg *Svensson v Stockholm Municipality*, Case No. 4514-07, judgment of the Stockholm Administrative Court of Appeal of 25 May 2007, annulling the decision of the Municipality to approve a proposed investment by municipal housing companies for the purpose of extending the connection to broadband networks. Examining the commercial aims and financial calculations underlying the investment, the court held that it was unlikely that a private investor would have made an investment under those conditions. An application for permission to appeal to the Swedish Supreme Administrative Court is pending.

As to the last sentence regarding the private creditor comparator, see Case T-36/99 *Lenzing AG v Commission* [2004] ECR 3597, [2006] 1 CMLR 1213 (appeal dismissed: Case C-525/04P *Spain v Lenzing* [2007] ECR I-9947, [2008] 1 CMLR 1068) (debt-rescheduling agreements and the non-enforcement of debts following the breach of those agreements). These cases were considered in Case T-11/07 *Frucona Košice v Commission*, judgment of 7 December 2010 where the Slovak tax authorities had remitted a liability to tax in the course of bankruptcy proceedings. The GC upheld the Commission's findings that bankruptcy proceedings had been more advantageous to the company than a creditor arrangement and that the Slovak Republic had not acted like a private creditor in a market economy in that regard. See also Case T-1/08 *Buczek Automotive v Commission*, judgment of 17 May 2011 (GC upheld the finding of the Commission that the fact that the Polish authorities had not made the recipient of an unrecovered loan bankrupt was capable of constituting an 'advantage' even though the State had taken vigorous but ineffective measures to recover the money. The GC went on to annul the decision because the Commission has not proved that a private creditor would have chosen to push the company into liquidation rather than trying to recover the money); Cases T-267&279/08 *Région Nord-Pas-de-Calais v Commission*, judgment of 12 May 2011 (aid can be the difference between the interest that would have been paid if the interest had been charged at the rate that would have prevailed under normal market conditions and the interest in fact due: para 112); Cases T-415/05, etc, *Greece v Commission*, judgment of 13 September 2010 (classification of low rents as State aid annulled on the basis that the Commission had not examined the relationship between the rents paid by Olympic Airlines and those available in normal competitive conditions on the market and so had not established the anti-competitive nature of the rents).

For a discussion of the application of this principle by the Commission in a case concerning the roll out of a high speed broadband fibre access network in Amsterdam see Gaál, Papadias and Riedl, 'Citynet Amsterdam: an application of the market economy investor principle in the electronic communications sector' (2008) 1 Competition Policy Newsletter 82.

Fn 51. Where the State lends capital to a bank in return for remuneration, the question raised by the application of this principle is not whether the State could have obtained a better return on its special fund by investing it differently, but whether, by investing that special fund in the bank under the agreed conditions, the State conferred an advantage on the bank which the latter could not have obtained in any other way: Case T-163/05 *Bundesverband deutscher Banken v Commission*, judgment of 3 March 2010, para 58 (appeal against decn adopted after the earlier decn was annulled by the GC in Case T-228/99: appeal dismissed, upholding Commission's finding that the investment did not constitute an aid because no advantage was granted beyond what would have been available from a private investor).

Fn 53. Following the GC's annulment of the decision in Case T-296/97 *Alitalia v Commission* cited in the footnote, the Commission retook the decision, explaining in more detail why it considered that the minimum rate of return that had been used in the *Iberia* case was also appropriate for applying the private investor test to the Italian Government's investment in Alitalia. Alitalia's appeal against this decision was dismissed: Case T-301/01 *Alitalia v Commission* [2008] ECR II-1753. After noting that the Commission's assessment of whether an investment satisfies the private investor test is a complex economic matter so that judicial review of such a measure was limited, the GC held that there were no manifest errors in the Commission's application of the test.

15.014   **Absence of private investor comparator.**   The *Chronopost* saga has continued. The CJ overturned the GC's judgment in Case T-613/97 on the basis both that the GC had been wrong to say that the Commission decision was inadequately reasoned and because the GC had erred in finding that there had been a State aid: Cases C-341&342/06P *Chronopost and La Poste v UFEX* [2008] ECR I-4777, [2008] 3 CMLR 568. The GC had held that the transfer of a client base by La Poste to Chronopost had taken place without any payment of consideration by Chronopost for this valuable intangible asset. The CJ held that the GC had ignored the legal and economic context of the transaction and had also failed to establish that the transfer had distorted or threatened to distort competition. The Court decided not to remit the matter a second time to the GC but went on to determine the matter itself, setting aside the GC's judgment and then dismissing the appeal against the Commission's decision to reject the complaint.

'By a Member State or through State resources'.   In Case T-233/04 *Netherlands*   **15.017**
v Commission (emission trading scheme) [2008] ECR II-591 the GC considered an emissions trading scheme for nitrogen oxides. The GC held that although the Dutch Government did not directly grant emission allowances to the undertakings concerned, it authorised the undertakings subject to a binding emissions standard to trade between themselves the emission allowances which indirectly result from that standard, up to the limit of the ceiling applicable to each of them. Having examined the system, the Court concluded that the State had forgone State resources. The GC however annulled the decision on the grounds that the aid was not selective. The judgment is on appeal: Case C-279/08P, not yet decided.

Bodies caught.   Fn 81. See also Cases T-267&279/08 *Région Nord-Pas-de-Calais*   **15.018**
v Commission, judgment of 12 May 2011, para 110.

State resources.   The distinction between *PreussenElecktra* and *France v Ladbroke*   **15.019**
Racing and Commission was considered in Case T-25/07 *Iride SpA v Commission* [2009] ECR II-245 which concerned sums collected from electricity consumers and deposited in an account opened within the Equalisation Fund, before finally being transferred to a private undertaking. The Equalisation Fund was a public body appointed by the Italian State to arrange for the electricity distributors to receive compensation for stranded costs. The GC held that the sums were properly characterised as State resources, not only because they were under constant State control, but also because they were State property. See also Case T-136/05 *EARL Salvat père & fils v Commission* [2007] ECR II-4063 (aid was not entirely funded by contributions levied but included State funds). See similarly, Case C-206/06 *Essent Netwerk Noord v Aluminium Delfzijl* [2008] ECR I-5497, [2008] 3 CMLR 895 (the company designated to collect the levy and transfer it to the beneficiary was not entitled to use the proceeds from the charge for purposes other than those provided for by the national law and was strictly monitored in carrying out its task: hence the case fell on the *Pearle* side of the line and was distinguished from *PreussenElecktra*).

In Cases T-309/04, etc, *TV2/Danmark v Commission* [2008] ECR II-2935 the GC held that a television licence fee was 'State resources' because the amount is determined by the Danish authorities; the obligation to pay the licence fee does not arise from a contractual relationship between TV2 and the person liable to pay, but simply from the ownership of a television or radio receiver; where necessary, the licence fee is collected in accordance with the rules on the collection of personal taxes; and, lastly, it is the Danish authorities who determine TV2's share of the income from licence fees (para 158). However the GC held that the Commission had failed adequately to explain why it also treated the advertising revenue which partly funded TV2 as State resources.

15.020   **No transfer of resources required.**   See also Case C-431/07P *Bouygues SA v Commission* [2009] ECR I-2665 (waiver of fees for telecoms licence not an aid because it was required in order to avoid unequal treatment between licensees); Cases T-415/05, etc, *Greece v Commission*, judgment of 13 September 2010 (continued forbearance on the part of the Greek State regarding unpaid tax and social security contributions amounted to an aid).

15.021   **Imputability of the measure to the State.**   The principles established in *Staurdust Marine* were applied in Case T-442/03 *SIC v Commission* [2008] ECR II-1161 where the GC held that the applicant SIC had not succeeded in showing that the payment facility granted to the public service broadcaster which was late paying its network fee was imputable to the Portuguese Government: paras 93 *et seq*.

In *Skyways v Kristianstad Airport*, Case No. Ö 916-08, judgment of 7 May 2007 the Court of Appeal of Skåne and Blekinge upheld the grant of interim relief prohibiting the provision of various forms of financial assistance that the defendant airport had agreed to give to a competitor airline. The airport was 51 per cent owned by the Kristianstad municipality and 49 per cent by other public authorities and the Swedish courts considered that this probably constituted State aid. The proceedings were subsequently settled so no final judgment was given. But cf Case N791/2006 *Business case Norrköpping*, decn of 10 July 2007, where the European Commission held that assistance given by Norrköpping airport was not attributable to the State as the municipality held only a 50 per cent interest in the airport operating company and the balance was held by private investors.

Fn 97. A claim for damages against the Commission by Stardust Marine was dismissed by the GC on the grounds that there was insufficient causal link between the invalidity of the decision annulled and the loss alleged. The GC did not consider whether the defects in the decision were sufficiently serious to give rise to a cause of action: Case T-344/04 *Bouychou v Commission*, judgment of 17 July 2007, [2007] ECR II-91*.

15.023   **Favouring certain undertakings.**   An advantage granted directly to certain natural or legal persons who are not necessarily undertakings may constitute an indirect advantage, hence State aid, for other natural or legal persons who are undertakings: see Case C-156/98 *Germany v Commission* [2000] ECR I-6857, paras 22–35; Case C-382/99 *Netherlands v Commission* [2002] ECR I-5163, paras 38 and 60–66; Case T-445/05 *Associazione italiana del risparmio gestito v Commission* [2009] ECR II-289, paras 127 and 135 (tax reductions for investors in a certain kind of investment vehicle was an indirect benefit to those vehicles and was a selective benefit since it did not apply to the whole financial sector); similarly see Case T-424/05

Italy v Commission, judgment of 4 March 2009 'les mesures sélectives en faveur des petites et moyennes entreprises n'échappent pas non plus à la qualification d'aide d'État'; para 147.

In Case T-233/04 *Netherlands v Commission (emission trading scheme)* [2008] ECR II-591 the GC annulled a decision relating to the trading of emission credits on the grounds that it was not selective. All large industrial facilities were subject to the emission ceiling laid down by the measure in question and could benefit from the advantage offered by the tradability of emission allowances for which it provided. The criterion for application of the measure in question was therefore an objective one, without any geographic or sectoral connotation. To the extent that the measure was aimed at the undertakings which are the biggest polluters, that objective criterion was consistent with the goal of the measure, that is the protection of the environment, and with the internal logic of the system: para 88. The judgment is on appeal: Case C-279/08, not yet decided.

See also Case T-177/07 *Mediaset v Commission*, judgment of 15 June 2010: scheme providing a subsidy to each consumer who acquired a decoder when purchasing or renting equipment for the reception of digital terrestrial TV signals enabled cable operators and digital terrestrial broadcasters to benefit, as compared with satellite broadcasters and so was a selective advantage. Mediaset was thus an indirect beneficiary of the aid paid to the consumer (appeal dismissed: Case C-403/10P *Mediaset v Commission*, judgment of 28 July 2011).

Difference in treatment not always favouring certain undertakings. Fn 116. An **15.024** appeal against the GC's judgment in Case T-475/04 was dismissed: Case C-431/07P *Bouygues SA v Commission* [2009] ECR I-2665.

The effect on trade between Member States. In Case C-494/06P *Commission v* **15.026** *Italy and WAM* [2009] ECR I-3639 the CJ upheld the GC's judgment in Cases T-304&316/04 (referred to in fn 135). The CJ noted that the GC had correctly stated that the Commission was not obliged to carry out an economic analysis of the actual situation on the relevant market or to examine the patterns of the trade in question between Member States or to show the real effect of the aid at issue. In this case the aid was not directly connected to the activity of the beneficiary on that market, but was intended to finance expenditure for a third country market penetration programme. In those circumstances where it involved aid, the grant equivalent of which was of relatively low value, the effect of the aid on trade and on intra-Union competition was less immediate and less discernible. The GC had been right therefore to conclude that this required a greater effort to state reasons on the part of the Commission.

cf Cases T-254/00, etc, *Hotel Cipriani v Commission* [2008] ECR II-3269 where the GC stated that a relatively small amount of aid may affect such trade where there is strong competition in the sector in which the beneficiary undertakings operate. Thus, where a sector has a large number of small companies, aid potentially available to all or a very large number of undertakings in that sector can, even if individual amounts are small, have an effect on trade between Member States. The Commission's decision had already excluded aids which were *de minimis* and the GC upheld the finding that an aid may affect trade and distort competition even if the beneficiary undertakings which are in competition with producers in other Member States engage in their activities exclusively at local level. Where a Member State grants aid to an undertaking, domestic production may for that reason be maintained or increased with the result that undertakings established in other Member States have less chance of exporting their products to the market in that Member State: para 248. Appeals against the GC's judgment were dismissed: Cases C-71/09P, etc, *Comitato 'Venezia vuole vivere' v Commission*, judgment of 9 June 2011.

See also Cases T-81/07, etc, *Jan Rudolf Maas v Commission* [2009] ECR II-2411. The GC confirmed that when State aid strengthens the position of an undertaking compared with other undertakings competing in intra-EU trade, that trade must be regarded as affected by the aid (para 76). See also Case T-189/03 *ASM Brescia SpA v Commission* [2009] ECR II-1831, paras 66 *et seq* (there is no threshold or percentage below which trade between Member States can be said not to be affected and the fact that the companies eligible under a sectoral aid scheme did not operate outside their national territory did not preclude an effect on trade).

It is not necessary that the beneficiary undertaking itself be involved in intra-EU trade. Furthermore, the strengthening of an undertaking which, until then, was not involved in intra-EU trade may place that undertaking in a position which enables it to penetrate the market of another Member State: Case C-222/04 *Ministero dell'Economia e delle Finanze v Cassa di Risparmio di Firenze SpA* [2006] ECR I-289, [2008] 1 CMLR 705, para 143. See similarly, Case T-211/05 *Italy v Commission*, judgment of 4 September 2009, para 153; Case T-369/06 *Holland Malt BV v Commission*, judgment of 9 September 2009 (fact that the beneficiary of the aid sold its product 'almost exclusively' to third countries did not prevent the subsidy being an aid; appeal dismissed: Case C-464/09P *Holland Malt v Commission*, judgment of 2 December 2010).

15.027   *De minimis*: **the case law.**   See also Cases T-227/01, etc, *Diputación Foral de Álava and Comunidad autónoma del País Vasco—Gobierno Vasco v Commission*, judgment of 9 September 2009, para 148: the fact that the tax advantages constituting the aid were temporary and that their influence was 'small and not decisive' did not prevent them from falling within Article 107 since there is no requirement in case law that the distortion of competition, or the threat of such distortion, and the effect on intra-EU trade, must be significant or substantial.

15.028   *De minimis*: **The Commission's approach and the adoption of block exemptions.**   See now the temporary measure that the Commission has adopted for cash grants of no more than €500,000 for companies that got into difficulties after 1 July 2008 because of the financial crisis: Commission Communication 'Temporary Community framework for State aid measures to support access to finance in the current financial and economic crisis' (consolidated version published OJ 2009 C83/1), para 4.2.2.

Calculating the amount of the advantage.   Fn 152. This Notice has been replaced **15.029** by the Commission's Communication on the revision of the method for setting the reference and discount rates, OJ 2008 C14/2: Vol II, App G29.

(b) Particular applications

Examples of State aids.   An aid which is intended to relieve an undertaking of the **15.030** expenses which it would normally have had to bear in its day-to-day management or its usual activities in principle distorts competition: Cases T-81/07, etc, *Jan Rudolf Maas v Commission* [2009] ECR II-2411, para 75 (aid intended to meet contractual commitments and cover the costs of a social plan by the recipient which was in liquidation).

Fn 158. The 2000 Notice referred to has been replaced by a new Commission Notice on the application of Articles 107 and 108 TFEU] to State aid in the form of guarantees, OJ 2008 C155/10: Vol II, App G26A.

Fn 161. See also Case T-332/06 *Alcoa Trasformazioni v Commission*, judgment of 25 March 2009 on alleged Italian aid in the form of lower electricity tariffs.

Fn 169. As regards TV licence fees see Case T-354/05 *TF1 v Commission*, judgment of 11 March 2009 where the GC upheld the Commission's conclusion that the French system satisfied the *Altmark* criteria and so did not constitute State aid. See also Cases T-309/04, etc, *TV2/Danmark v Commission*, judgment of 22 October 2008 (decision that the licence fee had overly compensated the public service broadcaster for its services was annulled). On the funding of public service broadcasting see Tosics, Van de Ven and Riedl, 'Funding of public service broadcasting and State aid rules—two recent cases in Belgium and Ireland' (2008) 3 Competition Policy Newsletter 81.

Tax measures.   A tax advantage granted directly to natural or legal persons who **15.031** are not necessarily undertakings may constitute an indirect advantage, and hence a State aid, for other natural or legal persons who are undertakings: Case T-445/05 *Associazione italiana del risparmio gestito v Commission* [2009] ECR II-289, para 127 (tax reduction for investors in a certain kind of investment vehicle was an indirect benefit to those vehicles).

Taxes do not fall within the scope of the provisions concerning State aid unless they constitute the method of financing an aid measure so that they form an integral part of that measure: Case C-206/06 *Essent Netwerk Noord v Aluminium Delfzijl* [2008]

ECR I-5497, [2008] 3 CMLR 895, para 89. For a tax to be regarded as forming an integral part of an aid measure, it must be hypothecated to the aid measure under the relevant national rules, in the sense that the revenue from the tax is necessarily allocated for the financing of the aid and has a direct impact on the amount of that aid, *ibid*, para 90.

In Case T-442/03 *SIC v Commission* [2008] ECR II-1161 the GC annulled a Commission decision which had held that legislative measures by which the Portuguese public broadcaster was (a) exempted from the payment of registration charges and fees relating to its transformation into a public limited company; and (b) benefited from an unlimited exemption from payment to all authorities of any charges and fees in respect of any act of inscription, registration or annotation did not amount to State aid. In order to be able to find that the exemption from notarial charges was justified by the nature and the general logic of the system of which it was a part, it was not sufficient to find, as the Commission did, that the recourse to legislation for the purpose of transforming public undertakings into public limited companies meant that the chargeable event for the notarial charges did not occur. The question which the Commission ought to have examined was whether it was compatible with the logic of the Portuguese legal system for the transformation of public undertakings into public limited companies to occur by legislation, or whether the recourse to legislation for such operations constituted a derogation which, in view of the consequences which resulted from that (namely rendering a notarial deed unnecessary so that no charges were incurred), was intended to confer an advantage on public undertakings in relation to other undertakings.

As to the selectivity of tax measures see Cases T-211&T-215/04 *Gibraltar v Commission* [2008] ECR II-3745 (Commission had not demonstrated that tax measures in Gibraltar constituted derogations from the common or 'normal' tax regime). The case is on appeal: Cases C-106&107/09, not yet decided.

Fn 176. See also Case C-222/04 *Ministero dell'Economia e delle Finanze v Cassa di Risparmio di Firenze SpA* [2006] ECR I-289, [2008] 1 CMLR 705, para 132.

Fn 177. See also Cases T-227/01, etc, *Diputación Foral de Álava and Comunidad autónoma del País Vasco—Gobierno Vasco v Commission*, judgment of 9 September 2009, para 126 (tax credits constituted an aid). The GC's ruling in relation to the exemptions from, and tax credits relating to, corporation tax granted by the Territorios Históricos of Álava, Vizcaya and Guipúzcoa in Spain was upheld by the CJ: Cases C-471/09P, etc, *Territorio Histórico de Vizcaya - Diputación Foral de Vizcaya v Commission*, judgment of 28 July 2011. See also Cases C-465/09P, etc, *Territorio Histórico de Vizcaya—Diputación Foral de Vizcaya v Commission*, judgment of 9 June 2011; upholding the GC's judgment in Cases T-30/01, etc, *Territorio Histórico de Vizcaya—Diputación Foral de Vizcaya v Commission* [2009] ECR II-2919.

Fn 181. These principles were applied in Case T-335/08 *BNP Paribas v Commission*, judgment of 1 July 2010.

Tax measures: objective justification. The GC's judgment in *British Aggregates* **15.033** was overturned by the CJ on appeal: Case C-487/06P *British Aggregates Association v Commission* [2008] ECR I-10505. The CJ held that the objective pursued by State measures is not sufficient to exclude those measures outright from classification as 'aid' for the purposes of Article 107 TFEU. Article 107(1) does not distinguish between the causes or the objectives of State aid, but defines them in relation to their effects. The unavoidable conclusion was that the GC erred in holding that Member States are free, in balancing the various interests involved, to set their priorities as regards the protection of the environment and, as a result, to determine which goods or services they decide to subject to an environmental levy. The CJ confirmed that protection of the environment constitutes one of the essential objectives of the European Union. However, that cannot justify the exclusion of selective measures, even specific ones such as environmental levies, from the scope of Article 107(1). Account may in any event usefully be taken of the environmental objectives when the compatibility of the State aid measure with the common market is being assessed pursuant to Article 107(3). The CJ held that the GC had erred in a number of other respects, including by applying only a limited standard of review to the Commission's decision. The CJ referred the case back to the GC for further consideration. The GC then annulled the Commission's decision to approve the aid without opening the full investigation procedure under Article 108(2). The GC noted that the scheme led to crude aggregates extracted in Northern Ireland by producers having entered into environmental agreements being taxed at 20 per cent of the normal level whereas identical products imported from Ireland were taxed at the full rate. Aggregates producers established in Ireland could not, under the United Kingdom legislation, enter into an environmental agreement and were not otherwise eligible to benefit from the exemption scheme by showing, for example, that their activities in fact complied with analogous environmental standards: Case T-359/04 *British Aggregates Association v Commission*, judgment of 9 September 2010.

See also Case T-442/03 *SIC v Commission* [2008] ECR II-1161, discussed in the update to paragraph 15.031, above.

The principles in this paragraph were applied in Case T-211/05 *Italy v Commission*, judgment of 4 September 2009 where the GC held that a tax exemption conferred on newly listed companies in Italy was selective and was inconsistent with the nature and overall scheme of the Italian tax system.

Selectivity of regional taxation measures. The principles laid down in the *Azores* **15.034** judgment were applied by the GC in relation to a tax measure adopted by the Government of Gibraltar: Cases T-211&T-215/04 *Gibraltar v Commission* [2008] ECR II-3745. The CFI examined whether the tax reform satisfies the three conditions set out in para 67 of the *Azores* judgment namely (i) whether the tax reform has been devised by a regional or local authority which has, from a constitutional point of view, a political and administrative status separate from that of the central Government of the United Kingdom; (ii) whether the tax reform has been devised without the central Government of the United Kingdom being able to intervene directly as regards its content; and (iii) whether the financial consequences for Gibraltar of introducing the tax reform are offset by aid or subsidies from other regions or from the central Government of the United Kingdom. The Court rejected the argument that there was a fourth condition, namely the condition that the infra-State body must occupy a fundamental role in the definition of the political and economic environment in which the undertakings present on the territory within its competence operate. Nor was there a condition relating to the tax measure at issue being circumscribed by harmonisation criteria which are imposed by European Union law on tax measures adopted by the Member State to which the infra-State body in question belongs. The GC concluded that the reference framework corresponds exclusively to the geographical limits of the territory of Gibraltar, without there being any need to examine the applicants' arguments relating to Gibraltar not forming part of the United Kingdom and to Gibraltar and the United Kingdom lacking a common tax system. This meant that no comparison can be made between the tax regime applicable to companies established in Gibraltar and that applicable to companies established in the United Kingdom for the purpose of establishing a selective advantage favouring the former. As regards selectivity within the Gibraltar framework, the GC held that the Commission had not demonstrated this to the requisite legal standard and the Commission's decision was therefore annulled. The case is on appeal: Cases C-106&107/09, not yet decided.

See also Cases C-428/06, etc, *UGT Rioja v Juntas Generales de Territorio Histórico de Vizcaya* [2008] ECR I-6747, [2008] 3 CMLR 1397 in relation to the regional introduction of lower tax rates and possible tax deductions that were not available in the rest of Spain. The CJ confirmed that the only conditions which must be satisfied in order for the territory falling within the competence of an infra-State body to be the relevant framework for assessing whether the tax advantage is selective are the conditions of institutional autonomy, procedural autonomy and economic and financial autonomy as set out in para 67 of the *Azores* judgment. The CJ, noting that the institutional system of Spain 'is particularly complex', found that the infra-State bodies had institutional autonomy but that it was for the national court to determine whether they also had procedural and economic and financial autonomy. The CJ stated that an infra-State body cannot be said to lack autonomy solely on the ground that the acts that it adopts are subject to judicial review in the national courts.

15.035 **Privatisation and the sale of public assets.**   For the application of the principles discussed here in three recent Commission decisions see von Buttlar et al, 'State aid issues in the privatisation of public undertakings—some recent decisions' (2008) 2 Competition Policy Newsletter 77.

Sales of land and buildings. The sale of public land at a price lower than the mar- **15.036** ket value might constitute State aid. In the context of domestic proceedings, it is for the national court to determine whether national law laying down calculation methods for determining the value of agricultural and forestry land offered for sale by public authorities in the context of a privatisation plan is an aid, taking into account the methods provided for the updating of the prices where prices for such land are rising sharply, so that the price actually paid by the purchaser reflects, insofar as is possible, the market value of that land: Case C-239/09 *Seydaland Vereinigte Agrarbetriebe v BVVG Bodenverwertungs-und-verwaltungs*, judgment of 16 December 2010.

Fn 205. The GC's judgment in Case T-366/00 *Scott* was annulled by the CJ: Case C-290/07P *Commission v Scott*, judgment of 2 September 2010. The Court held that the GC had exceeded its review jurisdiction insofar as it held that, by giving preference to the costs-based method, the Commission had acted in breach of its duty to exercise due diligence, but without demonstrating that the information thus overlooked could have led to a different assessment of the aid value. The GC had also failed to identify any manifest error of assessment on the part of the Commission in the choice of method and its application as regards a valuation exercise that constituted a complex economic assessment. The CJ remitted the case back to the GC.

State guarantees. The 2000 Notice referred to has been replaced by a new **15.038** Commission Notice on the application of Articles [107 and 108 TFEU] to State aid in the form of guarantees, OJ 2008 C 155/10 (corr. OJ 2008 C244/32): Vol II, App G26A. The Notice defines when a guarantee can be regarded as an advantage granted 'through State resources': the benefit of a State guarantee is that the risk associated with the guarantee is carried by the State. Where the State forgoes all or part of the premium which would normally be payable for taking on that risk, there is both a benefit for the undertaking and a drain on the resources of the State. Thus, even if it turns out that no payments are ever made by the State under a guarantee, there may nevertheless be State aid under Article 107(1) TFEU. The Notice clarifies that the market investor principle applies to determining whether a market premium is being charged for the guarantee and that this involves an assessment of the risk involved in guaranteeing the loan. Factors to be taken into account when assessing this risk include the amount and duration of the transaction; the security given by the borrower and other experience affecting the recovery rate evaluation; the probability of default of the borrower due to its financial position, its sector of activity and prospects; as well as other economic conditions. This analysis should allow the borrower to be classified by means of a risk rating, for example by an internationally recognised rating agency or, where available, by the internal rating used by the bank providing the underlying loan. However, the new Notice contains specific provisions for SMEs. If the borrower is an SME, the Commission can accept a simpler evaluation of whether or not a loan guarantee involves aid. In that case, and provided all the other conditions laid down in the Notice are met, a State guarantee would be deemed as not constituting aid if a minimum annual premium, as set out in a table in the Notice, is charged on the amount effectively guaranteed by the State, based on the rating of the borrower. The Commission has published a useful summary of the provisions of the Notice, highlighting where it differs from the earlier notice: MEMO/08/313 (20 May 2008). On the calculation of the aid element in guarantee schemes and the Commission's approval of notified methods for that calculation see also Tuchhardt, Tar and Galand, 'Approved guarantee methods for regional aid or de-minimis aid—the German and the Hungarian example' (2008) 3 Competition Policy Newsletter 41.

In Case T-442/03 *SIC v Commission* [2008] ECR II-1161 the GC stated that in considering whether a State guarantee constituted a State aid, it was important not to confuse the question whether the State granted, expressly or implicitly, a guarantee with that of how the market reacted to the fact that the issuer of a bond was not just another private operator, but a wholly State-owned undertaking. The fact that the market agreed to subscribe to the 1994 bond issue—allegedly because the market considered that the State would guarantee *de facto* its repayment—does not mean that there was State aid, since it is not disputed that the State did not give its guarantee, either expressly or implicitly. Only objective findings leading to the conclusion that the State legally had to repay that issue in the event of default by the public undertaking would permit a finding of the existence of a State guarantee: see paras 121 *et seq*.

See also Case T-452/08 *DHL Aviation v Commission*, judgment of 7 October 2010 (comfort letter from the State providing an unlimited warranty held to be an incompatible aid); Cases T-443&455/08 *Freistaat Sachsen and Land Sachsen-Anhalt v Commission*, judgment of 24 March 2011 (unlimited guarantee granted by Germany to cover DHL's operational risks when it moved its European operation to Leipzig-Halle airport held an incompatible State aid as it was not something that a market investor would have granted).

3. Aids that are Compatible with the Common Market

15.039   **Article 87(2).**   Following the closure of US airspace immediately after the terrorist attacks of 11 September 2001, the Commission issued a Communication (COM(2001) 574 final of 10 October 2001) stating that Article 107(2)(b) TFEU enabled certain problems facing the airlines because of those events to be dealt with. Having regard to the exceptional nature of the occurrences in question, the provisions of that article could authorise compensation for, first, the costs caused by the closure of American airspace for four days and, secondly, the extra cost of insurance.

In Case T-268/06 *Olympiaki Aeroporia Ypiresies v Commission* [2008] ECR II-1091 the GC considered the application of the criteria set out in the Communication to aid granted by the Greek Government in respect of particular flights between Greece and the USA and Canada. The GC held that in order to qualify for approval under Article 107(2)(b) there must be a direct link between the damage caused by the exceptional occurrence and the State aid and as precise an assessment as possible must be made of the damage suffered. But the requirement of a direct connection between the exceptional occurrence and the damage caused does not presuppose that they occur at the same time. On the contrary, there may be such a connection even where the loss arises shortly after the exceptional occurrence. The GC disagreed with the Commission over the characterisation of some of the flights in contention so that the decision was annulled in part. Cf Case T-70/07 *Cantieri Navali Termoli v Commission*, judgment of 12 November 2008, [2008] ECR II-250*, where the GC rejected an argument that the attacks of 11 September 2001 affected the relevant sector of the shipbuilding industry.

4. Aids that may be Compatible with the Common Market

(a) Generally

The exercise of the Commission's discretion. In Case T-162/06 *Kronoply v Commission* [2009] ECR II-1167 the GC upheld a decision by the Commission that 'the two fundamental elements of incentive and necessity' required for the aid to fall within Article 107(2) or (3) TFEU were not present. The GC held that those two conditions governing the compatibility of aid each have their own specific meaning, so that the lack of incentive and the lack of necessity must each be regarded as autonomous reasons for finding that the aid was incompatible: para 60.   **15.042**

The CJ has stressed that the method by which aid is financed may render the entire aid scheme which it is intended to finance incompatible with the common market. Therefore, the aid cannot be considered separately from the effects of its method of financing and the Commission must take into account the method of financing the aid in a case where that method forms an integral part of the measure: see Case C-333/07 *Société Régie Networks v Direction de contrôle fiscal Rhône-Alpes Bourgogne* [2008] ECR I-10807, para 89 and the cases cited there.

Operating aid. See, eg Case T-211/05 *Italy v Commission*, judgment of 4 September 2009 where the GC held that a tax advantage available to newly listed companies in Italy was an operating aid and incompatible with the common market. Similarly, in Cases T-30/01, etc, *Territorio Histórico de Álava—Diputación Foral de Álava v Commission*, judgment of 9 September 2009 the GC upheld the Commission's finding that corporate tax exemptions constituted operating aid: para 227 (upheld by the CJ: Cases C-465/09P, etc, *Territorio Histórico de Vizcaya—Diputación Foral de Vizcaya v Commission*, judgment of 9 June 2011).   **15.043**

(b) Article 87(3)(a)

15.051 **Other aspects of entitlement to regional aid.** See also the Communication from the Commission concerning the criteria for an in-depth assessment of regional aid to large investment projects, OJ 2009 C223/3: Vol II, App G22E.

15.052 **Block exemption for regional aid.** Regulation 1628/2006 was repealed by the General Block Exemption Regulation; Regulation 800/2008, OJ 2008 L214/3: Vol II, App G16 (the GBER), see update to paragraph 15.067, below.

(c) Article 87(3)(b)

15.053 **Article 87(3)(b): aid for important projects or to remedy a serious disturbance.** The Commission has stated that in the light of the seriousness of the financial crisis which enveloped the global economy in the second half of 2008, certain State aids can be justified under Article 107(3)(b) TFEU: see Commission Communication 'Temporary Community framework for State aid measures to support access to finance in the current financial and economic crisis' (consolidated version published OJ 2009 C83/1).

(d) Article 87(3)(c)

15.059 **Guidelines and rules on sectoral aid.** The Commission has also issued guidelines on the application of State aid rules in relation to rapid deployment of broadband networks (17 September 2009) available on the Commission's website.

Fn 302. The 2001 Cinema Communication has been extended until such time as new rules on State aid to cinematographic and other audiovisual works come into effect, or, at the latest, until 31 December 2012: see Communication, OJ 2009 C31/1.

Fn 303. A Revised Draft Communication from the Commission on the application of State aid rules to public service broadcasting has been consulted upon: see Press Release IP/09/564 (8 April 2009).

Fn 307. The Framework on State aid to shipbuilding has been further extended until 31 December 2011: see OJ 2008 C173/3.

15.060 **Guidelines on horizontal aid.** Fn 315. The 2001 Guidelines for environmental protection have been replaced by new EU guidelines on State aid for environmental protection, OJ 2008 C82/1: Vol II, App G22A. The Guidelines identify a series of measures for which State aid may, under specific conditions, be compatible with Article 107(3)(c) TFEU. The main changes from the 2001 Guidelines are (i) a number of new kinds of aid are covered, eg aid for early adaptation to standards, aid for environmental studies and aid for waste management; (ii) permissible aid intensities have increased; and (iii) the Guidelines distinguish between a standard assessment and a detailed assessment. A detailed assessment method applies to large aid amounts to individual enterprises and involves greater scrutiny of individual cases which have the greatest potential to distort competition and trade. For comment on the new Guidelines see Winterstein and Tranholm Schwarz, 'Helping to combat climate change: new State aid guidelines for environmental protection' (2008) 2 Competition Policy Newsletter 12. See also the modifications made to the form for notifying environmental protection aids following the adoption of this Notice: Reg 1147/2008, OJ 2008 L313/1.

Fn 315. An appeal against the GC's judgment in Case T-176/01 was dismissed: Case C-49/05P *Ferriere Nord v Commission*, judgment of 8 May 2008, [2008] ECR I-68*.

Fn 319. The 2000 Notice referred to has been replaced by a new Commission Notice on the application of Articles [107 and 108 TFEU] to State aid in the form of guarantees, OJ 2008 C155/10: Vol II, App G26A, see further the update to paragraph 15.038, above.

Aid for rescuing and restructuring firms in difficulty.   The validity of the Rescue   **15.061**
Guidelines has been extended until 9 October 2012: OJ 2009 C156/3.

(e) Article 87(3)(d)

Aid to promote culture and heritage conservation.   Following the annulment of   **15.064**
the decision by the GC in Case T-49/93, the Commission adopted a new decision approving the aid. This decision was also annulled by the GC (Case T-155/98 [2002] ECR II-1179) on the grounds that the Commission had committed a manifest error of assessment as regards the definition of the relevant market. The Commission adopted a third decision approving the aid in 2004. This decision was annulled by the GC in 2008: Case T-348/04 *SIDE v Commission* [2008] ECR II-625. In the most recent judgment the GC held that the Commission had erred in law by applying Article 107(3)(d) TFEU to the period before 1 November 1993 instead of applying the substantive rules in force during the period in question. (Note that this conclusion may need to be reconsidered in the light of Case C-334/07P *Commission v Freistaat Sachsen* [2008] ECR I-9465.) The Commission argued in the alternative before the GC that the derogation relating to cultural objectives in Article 107(3)(d) was previously covered by subparagraph (c) of that provision and has simply been more clearly identified by the addition of subparagraph (3)(d). But the GC held that since the decision relied only on Article 107(3) (d) as its legal base, the Court did not need to consider this alternative argument: para 69. The GC went on to hold that the Commission had committed a manifest error of assessment in the way it calculated the costs of processing small orders of books and had therefore overestimated the costs of processing small orders which were actually incurred by CELF and were supposed to be strictly and proportionately offset by the contested aid.

(f) Aid authorised by the Council

15.065 **Authorisation by the Council: Article 87(3)(e).** See the discussion in Case T-584/08 *Cantiere Navale De Polic v Commission*, judgment of 3 February 2011 as to the temporal application of a Regulation made under this power. With regard to aid which has been notified but not paid, the rules, principles and criteria for assessing the compatibility of State aid which are in force at the date on which the Commission takes its decision may generally be regarded as those best adapted to the conditions of competition. That is because the aid in question would not create real advantages or disadvantages in the common market until, at the earliest, the date on which the Commission decides whether or not to authorise it. On the other hand, in the case of aid which has been paid unlawfully without prior notification, the applicable substantive rules are those in force at the time when the aid was paid, where the advantages and disadvantages created by such aid arose during the period in which the aid in question was paid. The Commission had therefore been correct to decline to apply a Regulation adopted under Article 107(3)(e) (providing a temporary defensive mechanism to assist shipyards which had suffered serious harm caused by the unfair competition from shipyards in Korea) since the planned aid had been notified but not paid and the Commission's decision on the compatibility of the aid was taken after the date of expiry of the regulation. The case is on appeal Case C-167/11P, not yet decided. See similarly Case T-3/09 *Italy v Commission*, judgment of 3 February 2011.

15.067 **Block exemptions pursuant to Regulation 994/98: SMEs, training and employment aids.** The three block exemptions referred to in this paragraph, Regulation 68/2001 (training), Regulation 70/2001 (SMEs), and Regulation 2204/2002 (employment) all expired on 30 June 2008 and have been replaced by the General Block Exemption Regulation; Regulation 800/2008, OJ 2008 L214/3: Vol II, App G16 (the GBER). The GBER was adopted on 7 July 2008 and takes effect as from 29 August 2008 but it applies to individual aid granted before its entry into force, if the aid fulfils all the conditions laid down in the Regulation (Article 44). The GBER also repealed Regulation 1628/2006 (regional aid). As well as substantially increasing the aid intensities and notification ceilings of measures covered by the earlier exemptions, the GBER covers additional aid measures. The categories of aid to which the GBER applies are (a) regional aid; (b) SME investment and employment aid; (c) aid for the creation of enterprises by female entrepreneurs; (d) aid for environmental protection; (e) aid for consultancy in favour of SMEs and SME participation in fairs; (f) aid in the form of risk capital; (g) aid for research, development and innovation; (h) training aid; and (i) aid for disadvantaged or disabled workers. To qualify for exemption the aid must be 'transparent' as defined in Article 5 of the Regulation and must have an 'incentive effect' as defined by Article 8. Article 6 sets the individual notification thresholds for various kinds of aid. Chapter II of the GBER then sets out the criteria for exempting 26 different kinds of aid. The Member State granting the aid is required by the GBER to publish on the internet the full text of any exempted aid measure (Article 9). The text must set out the conditions laid down in national law which ensure that the relevant provisions of the GBER are complied with and must remain accessible on the internet as long as the aid measure concerned is in force. The GBER remains in force until 31 December 2013. Article 44 of the GBER sets out transitional provisions for agreements fulfilling the conditions set in the previous regulations. For general comment see Nyssens, 'The General Block Exemption Regulation (GBER): bigger, simpler and more economic' (2008) 3 EC Competition Policy Newsletter 12. Since the adoption of the GBER, the Commission has issued guidance on criteria for the compatibility analysis of training aid (OJ 2009 C188/1: Vol II, App G22C) and of aid for disadvantaged and disabled workers (OJ 2009 C188/6: Vol II, App G22D).

The State aid general block exemption was adopted by the EEA: OJ 2008 L339/111; EEA Supp No. 79, 18.12.2008, p. 20 Annex 15 State Aid.

Note that the rules that apply to the consideration of an aid which has been notified by a Member State are the rules in force at the date the Commission takes its decision, not as at the date of notification, provided the parties are given an opportunity to comment on the application of any new rules: Case C-334/07P *Commission v Freistaat Sachsen* [2008] ECR I-9465, para 49.

(g) Article 86(2)

Individual exemptions for service of general economic interest: Article 86(2). Article 86(2) EC is now Article 106(2) TFEU. In Case T-442/03 *SIC v Commission* [2008] ECR II-1161, the GC held that the application of the derogation in Article 86(2) depended on the fulfilment of three conditions: first, the service in question must be a service of general economic interest and clearly defined as such by the Member State; secondly, the undertaking in question must have been explicitly entrusted by the Member State with the provision of that service; thirdly, the application of the competition rules of the Treaty—in this case, the ban on State aid—must obstruct the performance of the particular tasks assigned to the undertaking and the exemption from such rules must not affect the development of trade to an extent that would be contrary to the interests of the European Union. There was **no** requirement to the effect that the Member State must have followed a competitive or any tendering procedure for the award of the service. The GC went on to uphold the power of the Member States to designate the service provided by a public broadcasting undertaking as a service of general economic interest, even though the undertaking broadcast a wide range of programmes and was able to carry on commercial activities, such as the sale of advertising space. The GC further held that the Commission must satisfy itself that there is in place a mechanism for the State to monitor compliance by the undertaking with its public service remit: para 213. On the facts, the GC found that the Commission had failed to place itself in a position in which it had sufficiently reliable information available to

15.068

it to determine what public services were actually supplied and what costs were actually incurred in supplying them. In the absence of such information, the GC held, the Commission was unable to proceed to a meaningful verification of whether the funding under challenge was proportionate to the public service costs and was unable to make a valid finding that there had been no overcompensation of the public service costs. The Commission's decision was therefore annulled.

As to the margin of discretion conferred on the Member State in designating an activity as being a service of general economic interest see Cases T-309/04, etc, *TV 2/Danmark v Commission* [2008] ECR II-2935 (public service broadcasting channel funded partly by licence fee and partly by advertising was such a service).

Fn 369. The Commission has published a Staff Working Document answering frequently asked questions about Decision 2005/842. See also the Communication on services of general interest adopted on 20 November 2007 (COM (2007) 725).

Fn 371. For further litigation regarding the aid to the Tirrenia Group see Cases T-265/04, etc, *Tirrenia di Navigazione v Commission*, judgment of 4 March 2009 (subsequent Commission decision annulled for inadequate reasoning as regards whether the aid was an existing or a new aid).

5. Supervision under Article 88

Note that Article 88 EC is now Article 108 TFEU

15.069 **Procedures under Article 88 and Regulation 659/1999.** **Fn 372.** Reg 794/2004 has been amended: see update to paragraph 15.074, below.

(a) Review of existing aids

15.070 **Concept of an existing aid.** In Cases T-265/04, etc, *Tirrenia di Navigazione v Commission*, judgment of 4 March 2009 a Commission decision was annulled for inadequate reasoning as regards whether the aid was an existing or a new aid.

Fn 379. Once a general scheme of aid has been approved, the individual implementing measures do not need to be notified to the Commission, unless the Commission has issued certain reservations to that effect in the approval decision: Case T-20/03 *Kahla/Thüringen Porzellan v Commission* [2008] ECR II-2305, para 92 (GC upheld Commission's finding that the disputed aid was not in fact granted pursuant to a previously approved scheme and hence was properly analysed as new aid; further appeal dismissed: Case C-537/08P *Kahla Thüringen Porzellan v Commission*, judgment of 16 December 2010).

Fn 382. In Cases T-30/01, etc, *Territorio Histórico de Álava—Diputación Foral de Álava v Commission*, judgment of 9 September 2009 the GC held that the

Commission had never explicitly made a decision declaring that the schemes at issue did not constitute State aid schemes when they were put into effect so that the aids were not existing aids within Article 1(b)(v). It was not possible to construe the Commission's silence as a tacit decision that the scheme was not an aid. Further, the GC held that the concept of 'evolution of the common market' can be understood as a change in the economic and legal framework of the sector concerned by the measure in question, for example as a result of the liberalisation of a market initially closed to competition. That concept does not cover the situation where the Commission alters its appraisal on the basis only of a more rigorous application of the Treaty rules on State aid. The mere finding that there has been an evolution of State aid policy is not in itself sufficient to constitute an 'evolution of the common market' within the meaning of Article (1)(b)(v) of Reg 659/1999, provided that the objective concept of State aid, as defined by Article 107, is not itself altered. The GC's judgment was upheld by the CJ: Cases C-465/09P, etc, *Territorio Histórico de Vizcaya—Diputación Foral de Vizcayav Commission*, judgment of 9 June 2011.

Review of existing aids.   For the position of a complainant where the Commission   **15.071**
refuses to investigate an alleged existing aid see Case T-152/06 *NDSHT v Commission* [2009] ECR II-1517.

Existing aids no longer compatible with the common market.   On the nature of   **15.073**
a recommendation which is accepted by the Member State see Case T-354/05 *TF1 v Commission*, judgment of 11 March 2009 where the GC held that it was an act capable of legal challenge.

(b) Notification of new aids

Pre-notification of new aids.   Regulation 794/2004 has been amended by the   **15.074**
following instruments:

- Regulation 271/2008, OJ 2008 L82/1 making use of certain web electronic applications compulsory for notification of aids and making amendments to the time limits for such notifications; adjusting the interest rate to be used for recovering State aid granted in breach of Article 108(3) TFEU and amending the Annexes which set out how the aid is to be notified;
- Regulation 1147/2008, OJ 2008 L313/1 amending the form for notification of environmental aids, following the adoption by the Commission of new guidelines on State aid for environmental protection; and
- Regulation 257/2009, OJ 2009 L81/15.

Fn 399. The extension of existing tax advantages enjoyed by municipal and special undertakings to a new class of beneficiaries which have different statutory characteristics constitutes an alteration that is severable from the initial scheme so that the aid granted to the new companies is a new aid and not an existing aid: Case T-189/03 *ASM Brescia SpA v Commission* [2009] ECR II-1831, para 106. Similarly, see Case T-332/06 *Alcoa Trasformazioni v Commission*, judgment of 25 March 2009 (extension of preferential electricity tariff to cover subsequent years was a new aid not an existing aid: para 132). Further, the GC held in that case that an earlier decision finding that the tariff as applied between 1996 and 2005 did not constitute aid did not create a legitimate expectation that an extension of the tariff from 2005 to 2010 would be approved: para 108.

15.075   **The tailpiece to Article 87(3)(c): not contrary to the common interest.** These principles were applied in Case C-464/09P *Holland Malt v Commission*, judgment of 2 December 2010.

15.075A   **Simplified procedure.**   As part of the reform of State aid regulation, the Commission has issued a Notice setting out a simplified procedure under which the Commission intends to examine within an accelerated timeframe certain types of State support measures which only require the Commission to verify that the measure is in accordance with existing rules and practices without exercising any discretionary powers: see Notice on a simplified procedure for treatment of certain types of State aid, OJ 2009 C136/3 (corr. OJ 2009 C157/20): Vol II, App G8C. The categories of measures to which the procedure in principle applies are (i) aid measures falling within the 'standard assessment' sections of existing frameworks or guidelines; (ii) measures corresponding to well-established Commission decision-making practice; and (iii) prolongation or extension of existing schemes. Member States wishing to take advantage of the procedure should provide the Commission with a draft notification form which may include a request to omit certain information. Within a specified timescale, the Commission will inform the Member State whether the simplified procedure is appropriate. The Member State must notify the aid within two months of being informed that the simplified procedure applies. There is no separate form for simplified notification; the ordinary form should be used. If the Commission is satisfied that the notified measure fulfils the criteria for the simplified procedure it will issue a short-form decision after the consultation process is complete. The second plank of the 'simplification package' is the publication of a Code of Best Practice: Vol II, App G8D. The Best Practice Code details how State aids procedures should be carried out in practice, in particular as regards regular pre-notification contact and the response by Member States to requests for information. It will apply to all cases which are not covered by the General Block Exemption Regulation and are not subject to the Notice on the Simplified Procedure. The Code also covers improvements to the procedure for dealing with complaints, including indicative deadlines and better information for complainants.

15.076   **Aids covered by a block exemption.**   The block exemptions for aids for training and to SMEs and the block exemption for employment aids have been replaced by the General Block Exemption Regulation; Regulation 800/2008, OJ 2008 L214/3: Vol II, App G16, see update to paragraph 15.067, above.

Time limit for review of new aid.   Article 4(1) of the Procedural Regulation,   **15.078**
which provides that the Commission must examine a notification 'as soon as it is
received', imposes merely an obligation of particular diligence on the Commission.
It is therefore not a rule of application *ratione temporis* of the criteria for assessment
of the compatibility of notified proposed aid with the common market. The rules
that apply to the consideration of the notification are therefore the rules in force at
the date the Commission takes its decision, not as at the date of notification, provided the parties are given an opportunity to comment on the application of any
new rules: Case C-334/07P *Commission v Freistaat Sachsen* [2008] ECR I-9465,
para 49.

Preliminary examination of a notification.   In Case E-5/07 *Private Barnehagers*   **15.080**
Landsforbund v EFTA Surveillance Authority, decn of the EFTA Court 8 February
2008, [2008] 2 CMLR 818, the Court described the notion of 'doubts' which
trigger proceedings under the equivalent provisions in the EEA as being an objective notion: 'whether or not doubts exist with regard to the facts, points of law or
economic or social assessments requires investigation of both the content of the
contested aid scheme and the circumstances under which it was adopted or operated'. It follows from this that judicial review by the Court of the existence of
'doubts' under Article 4(4) in Part II of Protocol 3 SCA will go beyond simple consideration of whether or not there has been a manifest error of assessment by ESA
in not initiating a formal investigation procedure.

(c) The formal investigation procedure under Article 88(2)

The operation of the formal investigation procedure.   Fn 440. The GC's judg-   **15.083**
ment in Case T-366/00 *Scott* was overturned by the CJ: Case C-290/07P *Commission
v Scott*, judgment of 2 September 2010. The CJ held, *inter alia*, that the GC had
erred in holding that the Commission had acted in breach of its duty to exercise due
diligence by failing to request either Scott or the French authorities to produce the
valuations of the land at issue to which they referred merely in order to call in question the valuation used by the Commission: para 98. The case has been referred
back to the GC.

Fn 446. The 18-month period is indicative only and a period of 22 months may, in
the circumstances of the case, be acceptable: Case C-49/05P *Ferriere Nord v
Commission*, judgment of 8 May 2008, [2008] ECR I-68*, para 51.

Final decision under Article 88(2).   As to whether the Commission must calcu-   **15.085**
late the amount of the aid when it adopts a decision that the aid is compatible with
the common market: see Cases T-443&455/08 *Freistaat Sachsen and Land Sachsen-
Anhalt v Commission*, judgment of 24 March 2011.

Final decision under Article 88(2).   In Case C-334/07P *Commission v Freistaat*   **15.086**
Sachsen [2008] ECR I-9465, Regulation 70/2001 came into force between the date

when the planned aid scheme was notified to the Commission and the date on which the Commission took its decision under Article 108(2) TFEU. The Commission applied the new rules to the aid, holding that in order to be considered compatible with the common market, that aid must come within the scope of Regulation 70/2001 and not exceed the intensity thresholds laid down therein. The GC annulled this decision on the basis that the contested decision infringed the principle of non-retroactivity (Case T-357/02). The CJ overturned the GC's judgment finding that there was no retrospectivity here. The notification by a Member State of aid or a proposed aid scheme does not give rise to a definitively-established legal situation which requires the Commission to rule on their compatibility with the common market by applying the rules in force at the date on which that notification took place. On the contrary, it is for the Commission to apply the rules in force at the time when it gives its decision, the only rules on the basis of which the lawfulness of the decision it takes in that regard falls to be assessed: para 59.

15.086 **Conditional positive decisions.** In Case T-25/07 *Iride SpA v Commission* [2009] ECR II-245 the GC applied the principle of *TWD Textilewerke Deggndorf* to a case where the unrecovered aid was not an individual aid granted to the undertaking but aid granted pursuant to an earlier sectoral scheme that had been held to be illegal and hence where there was no Commission order directing that the particular sum be recovered by the Member State from that undertaking. The principle applied where the unlawful aid received earlier was part of a tax exemptions scheme, the exact benefit of which for the recipient undertakings could not, because of the lack of cooperation from the Italian authorities, be determined and specified in the tax exemptions decision. Any other approach would be tantamount to rewarding Member States which, after granting unlawful aid, go on to disregard their duty to cooperate in good faith.

The burden lies with the potential recipient of the new aid to provide the Commission with evidence capable of showing that the new aid and the earlier unlawful aid that has not been repaid do not have a cumulative effect: C-480/09P *AceaElectrabel Produzione v Commission*, judgment of 16 December 2010, para 100.

In Case T-301/01 *Alitalia v Commission* [2008] ECR II-1753 the GC held that Alitalia had locus to challenge the conditions imposed by the Commission for clearing the State aid but the challenge was rejected on the facts.

7. Unlawful Aid and Misuse of Aid

15.092 **Unnotified aid not automatically incompatible with the common market.** As to the point discussed in the last sentence of this paragraph and in fn 483, see now the CJ's judgments in Case C-199/06 *CELF v SIDE* [2008] ECR I-469, [2008] 2 CMLR 561; and Case C-384/07 *Wienstrom v Bundesminister für Wirtschaft und Arbeit* [2008] ECR I-10393, discussed in the update to paragraph 15.109, below.

Request for information and information injunction. Fn 492. Even if the **15.094**
Commission is entitled to take a decision on the basis of information available to
it, Article 13(1) of the Procedural Reg does not allow the Commission to impose on
a particular undertaking an obligation to repay, even jointly and severally, a fixed
part of the amount of the aid declared to be incompatible, where it cannot be established on the facts that the undertaking benefited from the transfer of State resources:
Case T-196/02 *MTU Friedrichshafen v Commission* [2007] ECR II-2889 (upheld
on appeal Case C-520/07P, judgment of 17 September 2009).

The GC's judgment in *Scott* was annulled on appeal: Case C-290/07P *Commission
v Scott*, judgment of 2 September 2010 (see update for paragraph 15.083, above).

Interrelationship between Article 88(3) and national courts. See also the guid- **15.097**
ance given to national courts about enforcing recovery of illegal aid in the Commission notice on the enforcement of State aid law by national courts, OJ 2009
C85/1: Vol II, App G8B, discussed in the update to paragraph 15.111, below.

Recovery decision. Where the incompatible aid comprised a comfort letter from **15.098**
the State providing an unlimited warranty, the value to be recovered was the fee the
recipient would have had to pay to obtain such a warranty for the period between
the grant and withdrawal of the letter: Case T-452/08 *DHL Aviation v Commission*,
judgment of 7 October 2010, para 39. The fact that the warranty might have been
treated as null and void under Article 108(3) by the German court if the recipient
had tried to enforce it did not affect this: 'the objective of the obligation to recover
unlawful aid would be seriously compromised if the applicants' argument were to
be accepted, for that would make it possible for Member States whose domestic law
treats measures granting unlawful aid as null and void to grant undertakings the
benefit of such aid, while precluding its recovery should the Commission find the
aid to be incompatible and order it to be recovered': para 47.

Fn 508. For further proceedings regarding the recovery of the aid to Olympic
Airways see Case C-369/07 *Commission v Greece (Olympic Airways)*, judgment of
7 July 2009.

Recovery where recipient's assets have been sold. See also Cases T-415/05, etc, **15.099**
Greece v Commission, judgment of 13 September 2010 where the GC considered
aid granted to Olympic Airways both before and after all its flying activities had
been transferred to a new entity, Olympic Airlines, in a manner which made recovery of the aid from the old entity impossible. The GC held that in respect of unlawful aid granted to Olympic Airways after the transfer of the assets, the new company
Olympic Airlines could not be regarded as the effective recipient of that aid. But aid
paid to Olympic Airways before the transfer of assets could be recovered from
the new entity since there was financial continuity between the two companies.
Note further that the GC found that the Commission had erred in classifying some
of the measures as aid and annulled some parts of the decision and held that the two

companies were not liable to repay the sums which had been wrongly classified as anti-competitive State aid.

The Commission need not show that a corporate restructuring carried out by a recipient of aid was undertaken with the objective of circumventing the recovery of the aid; it is sufficient to show that there is a risk that that will be the result: Case C-480/09P *AceaElectrabel Produzione v Commission*, judgment of 16 December 2010, para 59.

See also Cases T-273&297/06 *ISD Polska v Commission*, judgment of 1 July 2009.

15.100 **Interest and tax.** Where the Commission sets a rate of interest for the recovery of a particular aid, that is a decision which can be challenged by any company which is required to reimburse aid increased at that rate of interest: Cases T-273&297/06 *ISD Polska v Commission*, judgment of 1 July 2009, para 73.

As to the imposition of compound interest, however, see Case T-369/00 *Département du Loiret v Commission* [2007] ECR II-851 where the GC found that the imposition of compound interest was the first manifestation of a new and important policy of the Commission, which the Commission had wholly failed to explain. The Commission ought, first, to have indicated that it had decided to capitalise the interest and, secondly, to have justified its approach. That obligation to state reasons was all the greater since, in the light of the time which had elapsed between the grant of the aid and the contested decision, namely 13 years, the imposition of compound interest had had significant financial consequences on the amount of the aid to be recovered. The GC indicated that the use of a compound rate would only be justified where the beneficiary still retains such an advantage at the date the aid is recovered. On appeal, the CJ upheld the GC's ruling on the interest rate but held that the inadequacy of reasoning as regards interest payable did not entitle the GC to annul the Commission's decision as to the incompatibility of the aid: Case C-295/07P *Commission v Département du Loiret* [2008] ECR I-9363.

15.102 **The duty of a Member State to seek repayment.** The Commission has issued a Notice 'Towards an effective implementation of Commission decisions ordering Member States to recover unlawful and incompatible State aid', OJ 2007 C272/4: Vol II, App G8A, to explain the Commission's policy towards the implementation of recovery decisions. The Notice describes the Member States' obligation to recover unlawful and incompatible State aid and the exceptions to that obligation, stressing the duty of loyal cooperation and the importance of informing the Commission of unforeseen or unforeseeable difficulties which arise in executing the recovery decision within the required time limit. It describes how to identify the undertaking from whom aid must be recovered and how to calculate the amount to be recovered. In the final section of the Notice, the Commission sets out the steps that can be taken against a Member State which fails to fulfil these obligations.

Note that Article 260 TFEU which replaces Article 228 EC removes one of the steps that the Commission had to take before seeking a penalty for non-compliance by a Member State with a judgment of the Court of Justice. Under Article 228 EC, the Commission had to issue a reasoned opinion specifying the points on which the Member State had failed to comply and set a deadline for the Member State to comply. Only if the Member State failed to comply with that deadline could the Commission bring an action before the Court seeking a penalty. Under Article 260 TFEU, the Commission may, if it considers the Member State has not complied with the judgment, bring a case before the Court of Justice seeking a penalty, provided that it has given the State the opportunity to submit observations.

On recovery of State aid by a Member State see Case C-369/07 *Commission v Greece (Olympic Airways)*, judgment of 7 July 2009. That case related to a decision by the Commission in December 2002 that certain aids granted by Greece to Olympic Airways were incompatible with the common market. The Commission subsequently brought infringement proceedings in which the CJ found that Greece had failed to recover the aid (Case C-415/03 *Commission v Greece* [2005] ECR I-3875). The Commission then brought a further action against Greece alleging that it had failed to comply with the judgment in Case C-415/03 and seeking daily penalties for non-compliance. The CJ held that the question whether Greece had failed to comply had to be assessed as at the expiry of the time allowed for compliance in a reasoned opinion issued by the Commission after the judgment in Case C-415/03 (para 50). When it came to assessing the penalties to be imposed, Greece argued that the amount of the aid had effectively been set off against damages that had been awarded to Olympic Airways by a Greek court in an unconnected action brought by the airline against the Greek Government. The CJ held that in principle, so long as it is provided for under the national legal system as a mechanism for extinguishing debts, a set-off operation can constitute an appropriate means by which State aid may be recovered (para 68). The CJ further held that it was for the Greek Government to prove that the set off had in fact taken place. After examining the relevant documentation provided by Greece, the CJ found that some, but not all, of the incompatible aid had been duly recovered. As to the amount of the penalty to be imposed, the CJ held that it had power to impose both a lump sum penalty for non-compliance and a daily penalty payable until full compliance took place (para 143). The CJ held penalties imposed for non-compliance therefore related only to the parts of the aid that had not been recovered. The CJ imposed a lump sum penalty of €2 million and a daily penalty of €16,000.

The task of the Member State when implementing a recovery decision adopted by the Commission was clarified in Cases C-71/09P, etc, *Comitato 'Venezia vuole vivere' v Commission*, judgment of 9 June 2011. The Court held that the Commission was required to set out in the decision all the criteria needed for the Member State to implement the decision and could not properly supplement the decision by setting out such details in accompanying letters. The GC had been wrong to hold otherwise. However, the Court went on to hold that the decision had in fact contained all the necessary information to enable the Member State to implement the decision and that the letters had contained only information to assist the Member State in that implementation.

The annulment by a national court of a national measure implementing a Commission decision ordering recovery of unlawful aid impedes the immediate and effective implementation of that decision and is irreconcilable with the Member State's obligations: Case C-305/09 *Commission v Italy*, judgment of 5 May 2011. As regards the power of the national court to grant interim relief suspending the operation of measures aimed at recovering the aid see Case C-304/09 *Commission v Italy*, judgment of 22 December 2010, paras 45 *et seq*.

Fn 519. For subsequent proceedings in respect of the aid to Olympic Airways see Cases T-415/05, etc, *Greece v Commission*, judgment of 13 September 2010 (classification of some elements as aid annulled and successor undertaking only liable to repay some of the aid).

15.103 **Defences open to the Member State: absolute impossibility.** Where the recipient of the aid has gone into liquidation before the Commission adopts its decision requiring the recovery of the aid, restoration of the previous situation and removal of the distortion of competition resulting from aid unlawfully paid may, in principle, be achieved by registration as one of the liabilities of the undertaking in liquidation of an obligation relating to repayment of the aid concerned, except insofar as that aid has benefited another undertaking: see Cases T-81/07, etc, *Jan Rudolf Maas v Commission* [2009] ECR II-2411, paras 192 *et seq* and the cases there cited.

See also Case C-331/09 *Commission v Poland*, judgment of 14 April 2011 (insolvency arising after the date on which the Commission's decision fell to be implemented does not excuse non-recovery) and Case C-507/08 *Commission v The Slovak Republic*, judgment of 22 December 2010 (national measure alleged to be unenforceable because of national court regarding earlier debt write off which constituted the aid as being *res judicata*).

15.104 **The position of the recipient of the aid.** Note too that the General Block Exemption Regulation, Regulation 800/2008 does not benefit ad hoc aid in favour of an undertaking which is subject to an outstanding recovery order following a previous Commission decision declaring an aid incompatible with the common market or aid schemes which do not explicitly exclude the payment of individual aid in favour of an undertaking which is subject to such an order.

15.105 **Legitimate expectation as a defence.** In Case C-199/06 *CELF v SIDE* [2008] ECR I-469, [2008] 2 CMLR 561, the CJ considered a question referred by the French court as to the application of Article 108(3) TFEU to the period between the Commission adopting a decision approving an aid, and the annulment of that decision by the GC. The CJ noted that this question juxtaposed, on the one hand, the principle that acts of the Union institutions are presumed to be lawful and, on the other, the rule laid down by the first para of Article 264 TFEU (formerly Article 231 EC), namely that annulment of a decision leads to the disappearance retroactively of the contested act with regard to all persons. The Court held that although a recipient of unlawfully implemented aid is not precluded from relying on exceptional circumstances on the basis of which it had legitimately assumed the aid to be lawful, where an appeal is brought against the approval decision and that appeal is pending, the recipient 'is not entitled to harbour such assurance so long as the Community court has not delivered a definitive ruling': para 68.

Fn 533. See also Cases C-471/09P, etc, *Territorio Histórico de Vizcaya—Diputación Foral de Vizcaya v Commission*, judgment of 28 July 2011.

Fn 536. See also Case T-62/08 *ThyssenKrupp Acciai Speciali Terni v Commission*, judgment of 1 July 2010 (legitimate expectation defence rejected); Case T-177/07 *Mediaset v Commission*, judgment of 15 June 2010, paras 176 *et seq* (Commission Communication on interoperability of digital interactive TV services could not have created a legitimate expectation that a scheme which was not technologically neutral would be compatible, nor did the fact that Mediaset was the indirect rather than direct beneficiary of the aid amount to exceptional circumstances (appeal dismissed: Case C-403/10P *Mediaset v Commission*, judgment of 28 July 2011)).

Legitimate expectation: existing aids. For subsequent proceedings relating to **15.106** transitional measures considered in the *Belgian Coordination Centres* case, see Case T-189/08 *Forum 187 v Commission*, judgment of 18 March 2010 (applicant trade association did not have standing to challenge Commission decision); and Case T-94/08 *Centre de coordination Carrefour v Commission*, judgment of 18 March 2010 (individual centre did not have standing to challenge the decision since it could not benefit from any transitional provisions).

See also the discussion of the *Belgian Coordination Centres* judgment in Case C-519/07P *Commission v Koninklijke FrieslandCampina NV*, judgment of 17 September 2009. The CJ overturned the earlier judgment of the GC (Case T-348/03) and distinguished between undertakings which were already beneficiaries of the scheme now declared incompatible and undertakings who had merely submitted a request for authorisation under the scheme. The latter did not have a legitimate expectation which entitled them to transitional measures.

Fn 545. This case was distinguished by the CJ in Case C-67/09P *Nuova Agricast v Commission*, judgment of 14 October 2010 on the basis that a prudent and alert economic operator, who is deemed to be familiar with the wording of the decision approving an aid including the statement in the decision that the approval only lasted until a certain date, could have inferred from that statement that the possibility of submitting an application for aid was limited by the duration of the authorisation granted for the scheme. It could not be argued that the appellants were given a specific assurance by the Commission that they could submit their reformulated aid application after that date and nor could they legitimately expect that the Commission would, after that date, grant a fresh authorisation for a similar State aid scheme.

15.107   **Right to repayment of unlawfully levied charges.**   Fn 548. See also Case C-333/07 *Société Régie Networks v Direction de contrôle fiscal Rhône-Alpes Bourgogne* [2008] ECR I-10807 where the CJ held that the net revenue from the charge on advertising companies was used wholly and exclusively to finance the challenged radio broadcasting aid and therefore had a direct impact on the amount of that aid. However, the French Government had asked the Court, in the event that the Commission's decision approving the aid was declared invalid, to limit the temporal effects of its judgment, so that neither the levying of the charges nor the allocation of the aid would be affected. The CJ noted that the aid scheme had applied for five years and that a great deal of aid was paid under the scheme, affecting a large number of operators. Secondly, the overriding considerations of legal certainty were capable of justifying the imposition of a limitation on the temporal effects of the invalidity of the decision. The effects of the Court's declaration that the decision was invalid were therefore suspended for a period not exceeding two months from the date of delivery of the judgment if the Commission decided to adopt such a new decision under Article 108(3) TFEU, and for a reasonable further period if the Commission decided to initiate the procedure under Article 108(2). Only undertakings which, prior to the date of delivery of the judgment, brought legal proceedings or made an equivalent complaint regarding the levying of the charge on advertising companies established by the aid in question were excluded from the temporal limitation of the effects of this judgment.

8. Judicial Remedies

(a) National courts

15.109   **New aids (including alterations to existing aids).**   In Case C-333/07 *Société Régie Networks v Direction de contrôle fiscal Rhône-Alpes Bourgogne* [2008] ECR I-10807 the CJ considered a reference under Article 267 TFEU from a court before which the applicant was seeking reimbursement of a tax levied to pay for an aid scheme which the Commission had approved. The applicant argued that the Commission's approval decision was inadequately reasoned. The CJ held that the claim was admissible given that, if the decision were annulled for lack of reasoning, there was a possibility, though not a certainty, that the Commission would in the end find that the aid was incompatible so that the tax levied would have to be reimbursed. The reference under Article 267 was therefore admissible.

As regards the obligations on the national court under the final sentence of Article 108(3) TFEU when an aid is subsequently found to be compatible with the common market, see Case C-199/06 *CELF v SIDE* [2008] ECR I-469, [2008] 2 CMLR 561 and Case C-384/07 *Wienstrom v Bundesminister für Wirtschaft und Arbeit* [2008] ECR I-10393. The position now appears to be as follows. The CJ noted (i) that a positive Commission decision puts an end to the prohibition on putting advance aid into effect; (ii) where planned aid was properly notified to the Commission and was not put into effect prior to that decision, it can be put into effect as from the moment at which the decision is adopted, including, where relevant, in respect of a period predating the decision which is covered by the measure that has been declared compatible; (iii) where aid has been granted to a recipient in disregard of the last sentence of Article 108(3) TFEU, the national court may be required, upon application by another operator and even after the Commission has adopted a positive decision, to rule on the validity of the implementing measures and the recovery of the financial support granted. In this last situation EU law requires the national court to order the measures 'appropriate effectively to remedy the consequences of the unlawfulness'. However, even in the absence of exceptional circumstances, EU law does not impose an obligation of full recovery of the unlawful aid. EU law does require that the national court order the aid recipient to pay interest in respect of the period of unlawfulness. Within the framework of its domestic law, it may, if appropriate, also order the recovery of the unlawful aid, without prejudice to the Member State's right to re-implement it, subsequently. It may also be required to uphold claims for compensation for damage caused by reason of the unlawful nature of the aid. Therefore, in a situation where the unlawful putting into effect of aid is followed by a positive Commission decision, EU law does not appear to preclude the recipient from, on the one hand, demanding the disbursement of aid payable for the future and, on the other hand, keeping aid received that was granted prior to the positive decision, subject always to the consequences arising from unlawfulness of aid disbursed prematurely. The criterion that determines whether aid can be disbursed to a recipient in relation to a period predating a positive decision, or whether that recipient can keep aid already disbursed is therefore the finding, by the Commission, that the aid is compatible with the common market. In the *CELF v SIDE* case, the CJ also dealt with a question referred by the French court as to the application of Article 108(3) to the period between the Commission adopting a decision approving an aid, and the annulment of that decision by the GC. The CJ noted that the question referred juxtaposed, on the one hand, the principle that acts of the EU institutions are presumed to be lawful and, on the other, the rule laid down by the first para of Article 264 TFEU (formerly Article 231 EC), namely that annulment of a decision leads to the disappearance retroactively of the contested act with regard to all persons. The Court held that although a recipient of unlawfully implemented aid is not precluded from relying on exceptional circumstances on the basis of which it had legitimately assumed the aid to be lawful, where an appeal is brought against the approval decision and that appeal is pending, the recipient 'is not entitled to harbour such assurance so long as the [Court of Justice of the EU] has not delivered a definitive ruling': para 68. Note that in the French national proceedings, the Conseil d'État annulled the earlier decision of the Administrative Court which had ordered the recovery of the aid: decn of 19 December 2008 *CELF v Ministre de la culture et de la communication*. The Conseil ordered that further questions be referred to the CJ concerning first, whether the national judge could stay the proceedings brought for the recovery of the aid until the issue of compatibility of the aid was final; and secondly, whether the fact that the aid had been found by the Commission, on three occasions, to be compatible with the common market could (even though each of those decisions had been annulled by the GC) constitute exceptional circumstances likely to enable the national judge to limit the obligation to recover the aid. In the meantime the Conseil d'État ordered the French Ministry of Culture to recover the interest on the sums illegally granted to CELF from 1980 including during the periods between the European Commission adopting the decision declaring the aid to be compatible and the annulment of those decisions by the GC.

Fn 563. Accordingly, as the French Conseil d'État has observed, national courts have to determine whether or not a national decision constitutes a State aid within Article 107(1) TFEU. See *Chambre de commerce et d'industrie de Strasbourg v Brit Air*, judgment of 27 February 2006, upholding the lower courts' decisions that the agreements made by the Strasbourg Chamber of Commerce with Ryanair in connection with the opening of its new Strasbourg-London route constituted State aid since the financial commitments undertaken in favour of Ryanair greatly exceeded the cost of tourist promotion promised by Ryanair, and no private investor would have granted such advantages in view of the limited services offered in return. But cf Case T-196/04 *Ryanair v Commission* [2008] ECR II-3643, discussed in the update to paragraph 15.013, above.

Fn 568. See, eg *Skyways v Kristianstad Airport* Case No. Ö 916-08, judgment of the Court of Appeal of Skåne and Blekinge, 7 May 2007, where a Swedish airline claimed damages against a publicly owned airport for aid granted to a competitor that had not been notified to the Commission and the Swedish courts granted interim relief prohibiting the application of the relevant agreement. The damages claim was subsequently settled.

15.110 **Enforcement of Commission decisions.** The risk of inconsistent decisions between national courts and the EU institutions is illustrated by the proceedings concerning the sale of land for construction of a supermarket by the Municipality of Åre in Sweden. The decision by the Municipality to sell the site to a cooperative society selling consumer goods, at a price significantly below a rival bid by a competing, large retailer, was challenged as constituting unlawful State aid that had not been notified to the EU Commission. The first instance administrative court held on the facts that the sale would not involve State aid, but subsequently the EU Commission adopted a decision that the sale was State aid: Case C35/06 (ex NN 37/06) *Konsum Jämtland Ekonomisk Förening*, OJ 2008 L126/3. On that basis, the

Sundsvall Administrative Court of Appeal reversed the lower court and annulled the Municipality's decision on the ground that it involved a State aid that had not been notified in breach of Article 108(3) TFEU: Case No. 1715-06 *Andersson v Åre Municipality*, judgment of 9 April 2008. However, the Commission's decision has in turn been appealed to the GC: Case T-244/08 *Konsum Nord v Commission*, not yet decided.

National courts must ensure that the decision ordering the recovery of the unlawful aid is fully effective and achieves an outcome consistent with the objective pursued by that decision such that the annulment by a national court of a national measure implementing a Commission decision ordering recovery of unlawful aid is irreconcilable with the Member State's obligations: Case C-305/09 *Commission v Italy*, judgment of 5 May 2011. Similarly in Case C-210/09 *Scott v Ville d'Orléans*, judgment of 20 May 2010 the CJ held in a preliminary ruling that where domestic law would lead to an assessment issued in order to recover the unlawful State aid being declared void for procedural defect, the Member State's obligation to recover aid did not prevent the national court from applying that law in circumstances where the recipient of the unlawful aid had in fact already paid back the aid and where national law also allows the State authority to rectify the procedural defect. However, the annulment of the assessment must not lead to the repayment of the unlawful aid to the recipient, even on a provisional basis.

The Commission has issued a Notice towards an effective implementation of Commission decisions ordering Member States to recover unlawful and incompatible State aid, OJ 2007 C272/4: Vol II, App G8A, to explain the Commission's policy towards the implementation of recovery decisions, see update to paragraph 15.102, above.

Notice on cooperation between national courts and the Commission in the State aid field.   **15.111** The 1995 Notice referred to in this paragraph has now been replaced by the Commission notice on the enforcement of State aid law by national courts, OJ 2009 C85/1: Vol II, App G8B. The new Notice gives guidance on general issues such as identifying State aids; the 'standstill obligation'; the role of the national court in stopping the payment of illegal aid and in ensuring the recovery of illegal aid and interest. The Notice contains guidance on damages claims by competitors of the beneficiary brought either against the State or against the beneficiary itself. It provides guidance on procedural issues such as standing to bring an action and contains a section on what support the court can request from the Commission in terms of transmission of information or the giving of an opinion on aspects of the State aid rules. As with the earlier Notice, the Commission will publish a summary concerning its cooperation with national courts in its annual Report on Competition Policy. It may also make its opinions and observations available on its website. The Commission has also issued a Notice towards an effective implementation of Commission decisions ordering Member States to recover unlawful and incompatible State aid, OJ 2007 C272/4: Vol II, App G8A, to explain the Commission's policy towards the implementation of recovery decisions. This Notice contains a section concerning litigation before national courts relating to the recovery of aid: see paras 55 *et seq.*

(b) The Community Courts

(i) *Reviewable acts*

15.112 **Generally.** In Case T-152/06 *NDSHT v Commission* [2009] ECR II-1517 the GC examined in detail the text of a letter sent by a Commission official to the complainant in which the official stated that DG Comp had decided not to pursue the complaint because an initial investigation indicated that the aid challenged was an existing aid. The GC considered whether it was apparent from the substance of the contested letters that 'they may be deemed to constitute a decision under Article 4 of Reg No 659/1999, whose true addressee is the Member State concerned and which affects the interests of the applicant by bringing about a distinct change in its legal position'. The GC concluded that they were not, and that there was no reviewable act.

Cf Case C-521/06P *Athinaïki Teckniki v Commission* [2008] ECR I-5829, [2008] 3 CMLR 979 where the CJ held that a letter in which the Commission informed the complainant that it was closing the file because on the basis of information available there were no grounds to justify an investigation, was in fact a statement by the Commission that the review initiated had not enabled it to establish the existence of State aid within the meaning of Article 107 and it implicitly refused to initiate the formal investigation procedure provided for in Article 108(2). The informal nature of the decision and the fact that it left it open for the complainant to provide more information did not change its nature and it was a reviewable act. The CJ therefore referred the matter back to the GC. The Commission then purported to withdraw the letter and reopen its examination of the complaint, leading the GC to dismiss the appeal asserting that since the contested act (ie the letter) had been withdrawn the appeal was devoid of purpose (Case T-94/05 *Athinaïki Techniki v Commission*, Order of 29 June 2009). In a sharply worded judgment, the CJ annulled the GC's Order: Case C-362/09P *Athinaïki Techniki v Commission*, judgment of 16 December 2010. The Court stated that if the Commission were entitled to withdraw its act in those circumstances, it could perpetuate a state of inaction during the preliminary examination stage and avoid any judicial review. If that were the position, it would be sufficient for the Commission to decide to take no further action on a complaint lodged by an interested party and then, after that party brought an action, to reopen the preliminary examination stage and repeat those operations as many times as are necessary in order to avoid any judicial review of its actions: 'Having regard to the requirements of good administration and legal certainty and the principle of effective legal protection, it must be considered, on the one hand, that the Commission may only withdraw a decision to take no further action on a complaint regarding alleged unlawful aid in order to remedy illegality affecting that decision, and on the other hand, that the Commission cannot, after such withdrawal, pick up the procedure again at a stage earlier than the exact point at which the illegality found had occurred.': para 70. The Court annulled the order and referred the matter back again to the GC.

A letter setting out the opinion of the Commission on the proper interpretation of a exemption from the State aid rules contained in the Act of Accession of 10 Member States who joined the EU in 2004 is not a reviewable act: Case T-22/07 *US Steel Košice s.r.o. v Commission*, judgment of 14 May 2009.

A recommendation in relation to an existing aid made by the Commission under Article 18 of the Procedural Regulation and accepted by the Member State is an act capable of legal challenge: Case T-354/05 *TF1 v Commission*, judgment of 11 March 2009.

Fn 581. See also Case T-332/06 *Alcoa Trasformazioni v Commission*, judgment of 25 March 2009, paras 38 *et seq*. In that case the GC went on to point out that since the classification of a measure as State aid in a decision to initiate the formal investigation procedure is merely provisional, review by the European Courts when such a decision is challenged is limited to ascertaining whether or not the Commission has made a manifest error of assessment in forming the view that it was unable to resolve all the difficulties on that point during its initial examination of the measure concerned. To avoid confusion between the administrative and judicial proceedings, and to preserve the division of powers between the Commission and the Courts, the Courts must avoid giving a final ruling on questions on which the Commission has merely formed a provisional view: para 61.

(ii) Applicants before the Community Courts

Actions by the Commission. See, eg the actions brought by the Commission in respect of Greece's non-compliance with its obligation to recover illegal State aid granted to Olympic Airways: Case C-369/07 *Commission v Greece (Olympic Airways)*, judgment of 7 July 2009. **15.113**

The Member State cannot challenge the correctness of the Commission's decision as a defence to an action enforcing that decision under Article 258 TFEU (formerly Article 226 EC), unless it alleges that the decision was so defective as to be non-existent: Case C-177/06 *Commission v Spain* [2007] ECR I-7689.

Actions by Member States and regional bodies. A Member State can challenge a decision approving an aid if it argues that the measure does not constitute State aid at all: Case T-233/04 *Netherlands v Commission (emission trading scheme)* [2008] ECR II-591. The judgment is on appeal: Case C-279/08, not yet decided. **15.114**

Actions by private parties against decisions prohibiting aid. Note that the wording of Article 263 TFEU is different from that of Article 230 EC which it replaces. **15.115**

Article 230 EC provided that a third party could challenge a decision 'which, although in the form of a regulation or a decision addressed to another person, is of direct and individual concern to the former'. Article 263 TFEU provides that individuals may institute proceedings against an act which is of direct and individual concern to them and 'against a regulatory act which is of direct concern to them and does not entail implementing measures'. It appears therefore that, as regards regulatory acts which do not entail implementing measures, the test for standing has been relaxed by the removal of the requirement that the act be of individual concern. However, since the term 'regulatory acts' is not defined, it is not clear whether this will affect the issue of standing discussed in this paragraph.

A company mentioned in the Commission's decision as being under an obligation to reimburse the aid in question is individually affected and hence the parent company of that company is also individually affected: Case T-112/97 *Monsanto v Commission* [1999] ECR II-1277, para 58; Cases T-273&297/06 *ISD Polska v Commission*, judgment of 1 July 2009, para 43. A company which was not only active in the sector covered by a sectoral aid scheme which has been declared illegal but was also the actual recipient of aid which the Commission has ordered the Member State to recover does have standing to challenge the prohibition decision: Case T-189/03 *ASM Brescia SpA v Commission* [2009] ECR II-1831, paras 41 and 42; see similarly Case T-445/05 *Associazione italiana del risparmio gestito v Commission* [2009] ECR II-289, para 51.

In Cases C-71/09P, etc, *Comitato 'Venezia vuole vivere' v Commission*, judgment of 9 June 2011 (on appeal from Cases T-254/00, etc, *Hotel Cipriani and Others v Commission* [2008] ECR II-3269) the CJ considered the standing of individual recipients of an aid where a scheme allowing deductions from social security contributions had been prohibited by the Commission. Since the prohibition decision had ordered Italy to recover the aid, the Court held that the actual beneficiaries of individual aids granted under the scheme are, by that fact, 'individually concerned'. All the beneficiaries of the system in question are exposed, as from the time of the adoption of the Commission's decision, to the risk that the advantages which they have received will be recovered, and thus their legal position affected. Those beneficiaries form part of a restricted circle and the possibility that the sums may not ultimately be recovered does not exclude them from being regarded as individually concerned. The Court held that it was not necessary in this case to consider the situation where the Commission's decision is not accompanied by a recovery order. The Court disagreed with one aspect of the reasoning of the GC, namely where the GC had stated that it was wrong to suggest that in implementing a recovery decision, a Member State would need to verify in relation to each individual recipient whether the conditions for recovery were met. The Court noted that the Commission's prohibition decision is 'general and abstract' so that a Member State does need to verify the individual situation of each recipient of aid. But this fact does not prevent the recipients from being individually concerned for the purpose of challenging the decision.

If an aid is declared compatible with the common market then a challenge by the recipient (eg to the fact that it was classified as an aid) is inadmissible: Case T-212/00 *Nuove Industrie Molisane v Commission* [2002] ECR II-347, [2003] 1 CMLR 257; and Case T-141/03 *Sniace v Commission* [2005] ECR II-1197, [2006] 2 CMLR 621; Cases T-443&455/08 *Freistaat Sachsen and Land Sachsen-Anhalt v Commission*, judgment of 24 March 2011. But where the Commission finds that an aid is partly compatible and partly incompatible with the common market (without clearly distinguishing between the different elements) the recipient has locus to challenge the whole decision even if it could be said that the decision was, overall, favourable to the applicant: Cases T-309/04, etc, *TV2/Danmark v Commission* [2008] ECR II-2935, para 72. Further, the GC found in that case that TV2 had sufficiently demonstrated that the risk of legal proceedings at national level at the date on which TV2 initiated its challenge 'was vested and present' since, far from remaining hypothetical, that risk actually materialised in the form of the legal proceedings brought by Viasat after TV2 lodged its challenge and those proceedings were pending before the national court and had been stayed specifically to await the GC's judgment. Accordingly, TV2 had sufficient legal interest in bringing an action for annulment of the contested decision in its entirety, even insofar as that decision classified the contested measures as State aid which is partly compatible with the common market.

Note that in Case T-136/05 *EARL Salvat père & fils v Commission* [2007] ECR II-4063 the GC held that the appellants had standing to challenge those parts of the Commission's decision which prohibit aspects of the aid scheme as incompatible but did not have standing to challenge the part of the decision approving an aspect of the aid scheme.

As to the standing of a trade association to bring an appeal, see Cases T-254/05&T-375/03 *Fachvereinigung Mineralfaserindustrie v Commission*, judgment of 20 September 2007, [2007] ECR II-124*, where the GC reviewed the case law and found that the claim was inadmissible. See also Case C-319/07P *3F v Commission*, judgment of 9 July 2009 (CJ overturned judgment of the GC and held that trade union's challenge to the Commission's rejection of a complaint was admissible). See also Case T-189/08 *Forum 187 v Commission*, judgment of 18 March 2010 where the GC stated that actions brought by associations, whose function it is to defend the collective interests of the certain undertakings, are admissible in three situations: where they represent the interests of undertakings which themselves have standing to bring proceedings; where they are distinguished individually because of the impact on their own interests as associations, in particular because their position as a negotiator has been affected by the measure sought to be annulled; and where a legal provision expressly confers on them a number of rights of a procedural nature: para 58. The GC went on to hold that none of the members had standing so that the action was inadmissible.

Fn 608. See also Case T-335/08 *BNP Paribas v Commission*, judgment of 1 July 2010.

15.116   **Challenge by complainants to refusal to open formal procedure.**   In an appeal to the CJ against the GC's judgment in *British Aggregates* the CJ upheld the finding of admissibility: Case C-487/06P *British Aggregates Association v Commission* [2008] ECR I-10505. The CJ held that an action brought by an association acting in place of one or more of its members who could themselves have brought an admissible action will itself be admissible (para 39). The CJ rejected the Commission's arguments that in order for a competitor to show that it is individually concerned by a decision approving a general aid scheme it was necessary to show factors such as a significant decline in turnover, appreciable financial losses or a significant reduction in market share following the grant of the aid in question. In this case the aid challenged was specifically designed to have an effect on the structure of the market in question by transferring some of the demand for aggregates from virgin aggregates to alternative products, with the result that that levy was specifically intended to affect the competitive position of undertakings active on the market. In the subsequent proceedings the Commission did not challenge standing: Case T-359/04 *British Aggregates Association v Commission*, judgment of 9 September 2010.

In Case T-289/03 *BUPA v Commission* [2008] ECR II-81 the GC found first that BUPA had standing to challenge the Commission's refusal to open a formal investigation into the alleged aid under Article 108(2) TFEU (para 73) and then went on to consider whether BUPA also had standing to challenge the Commission's substantive conclusion that the aid was compatible. The GC held that it did because its competitive position in the market was substantially affected and it was in fact the only net contributor to the fund which was under challenge. See also Case C-176/06P *Stadtwerke Schwäbisch Hall v Commission*, judgment of 29 November 2007, [2007] ECR I-170*; Case T-388/02 *Kronoply and Kronotex v Commission*, judgment of 10 December 2008 (applicants failed to establish that they were individually affected for the purpose of challenging the substance of the Commission's decision but did have standing to challenge the failure to open the formal procedure).

In Case E-5/07 *Private Barnehagers Landsforbund v EFTA Surveillance Authority*, decn of the EFTA Court 8 February 2008, [2008] 2 CMLR 818, the EFTA Court held that the test for locus was the same whether the alleged aid concerned was a new or an existing aid: para 64.

In Case C-319/07 P *3F v Commission*, judgment of 9 July 2009 the CJ, applying the test set out in *Sytraval* and *ARE*, noted that a trade union may be regarded as 'concerned' within the meaning of Article 108(2) TFEU if it shows that its interests or those of its members might be affected by the granting of aid. The trade union must, however, show to the requisite legal standard that the aid is likely to have a real effect on its situation or that of the workers it represents: para 33. The CJ held that the GC had been wrong to interpret Case C-67/96 *Albany* [1999] ECR I-5751, [2000] 4 CMLR 446 (which held that Article 101(1) does not apply to collective labour agreements: see paragraph 2.034 in the main work) as meaning that the union could not rely on its interest in competing with other unions as the basis for its locus. It cannot be deduced from the fact that an agreement could be excluded, by reason of its nature and purpose and the social policy objectives pursued by it, from the scope of the provisions of Article 101(1) TFEU that collective negotiations or the parties involved in them are likewise, entirely and automatically, excluded from the Treaty rules on State aid, or that an action for annulment which might be brought by those parties would, almost automatically, be regarded as inadmissible because of their involvement in those negotiations.

The proceedings brought by a complainant may be protracted: see the procedural history recounted in Case T-442/03 *SIC v Commission* [2008] ECR II-1161, paras 6 *et seq.*

In Case T-423/07 *Ryanair v Commission*, judgment of 19 May 2011 the GC dismissed a claim that the Commission had failed to adopt a position in respect of a complaint lodged by Ryanair alleging that the exclusive use of Munich airport terminal facilities to Lufthansa was a State aid. Following the launch of the proceedings, the Commission opened an investigation, rendering the appeal devoid of purpose. The GC therefore dismissed the appeal without having to decide whether the Commission had been under any obligation to act.

Where none of the pleas for annulment relied on by the applicant seeks to establish the existence of serious difficulties or pleads infringement of the applicant's procedural rights, the fact that the applicant may be a person 'concerned' within the meaning of Article 108(2) is not enough to make the appeal admissible—the applicant must show that it has a particular status within the meaning of the *Plaumann* case law, *inter alia* on the ground that its market position is substantially affected by the measures covered by the decision: Case T-193/06 *Télévision française 1 SA (TF1) v Commission*, judgment of 13 September 2010.

The fact that the Commission's initial investigation is prolonged and involves sending information requests to the State alleged to have granted the aid is not enough to show that there were serious difficulties which precluded it from deciding that the investment was not an aid: Case T-36/06 *Bundesverband deutscher Banken v Commission*, judgment of 3 March 2010: 'the question whether the Commission misapplied the private investor test is not to be confused with the question whether there are serious difficulties which require the formal investigation procedure to be initiated. Consideration of whether serious difficulties exist is not aimed at establishing whether the Commission applied [Article 107 TFEU] correctly, but whether,

at the time of its adoption of the contested decision, there was sufficiently comprehensive information available to it to enable it to assess the compatibility of the
disputed measure with the common market' (para 129).

15.117   **Challenge by complainants to decision following formal investigation.**   See also
Case T-388/03 *Deutsche Post et DHL International v Commission* [2009] ECR
II-199 where the GC held that the applicants did not have sufficient standing to
challenge the substance of the Commission's decision that the notified measure was
not State aid, but that they did have standing to challenge the Commission's decision not to open the formal procedure. The role of the Court's review in such a case
was to consider any grounds which are directed at the annulment of the contested
decision and, in any event, the initiation by the Commission of the procedure
referred to in Article 108(2); it is not for the General Court to rule at that stage on
whether aid exists or whether it is compatible with the common market. Only pleas
which seek to establish that the examination by the Commission during the preliminary examination stage was insufficient or incomplete, may be examined by the
Court. These included in this case a plea that the examination carried out by the
Commission was insufficient in the light of the criteria laid down in *Altmark*. The
Court found that there was a body of objective and consistent evidence—deriving
from the excessive length of the preliminary examination procedure, from the
documents which reveal the scope and complexity of the examination to be carried
out and from the partially incomplete and insufficient content of the contested
decision—which showed that the Commission adopted the contested decision in
spite of the existence of serious difficulties. The GC held that there were serious
difficulties which should have led the Commission to initiate the procedure referred
to in Article 108(2) TFEU. The case is on appeal Case C-148/09, not yet decided.

In Case C-260/05P *Sniace v Commission* [2007] ECR I-10005, [2008] 1 CMLR
1035, the CJ dismissed the appeal from the GC judgment referred to in fn 621. The
CJ confirmed the *COFAZ* test but said that the GC was wrong if, in its *Sniace* judgment, it had treated active participation by the applicant in the formal examination
procedure as a necessary condition for it to be regarded as individually concerned
by the contested decision: para 59. But the GC had found as a fact that Sniace had
failed to show that the decision was likely to harm its legitimate interests by substantially affecting its position on the market and that finding could not be
challenged before the CJ. The appeal was dismissed. See also Case C-525/04P *Spain
v Lenzing* [2007] ECR I-9947, [2008] 1 CMLR 1068 where the CJ confirmed that
it is not sufficient for the challenger simply to show that it competes with the recipient of the aid. But in that case the CJ noted that the GC had stressed the distinctiveness
of the competitive situation of the viscose fibres market, which was characterised by
a very small number of producers and by serious production overcapacity, the significance of the distortion created by the grant of aid to an undertaking operating
in such a market, and the effect of that aid on the prices applied by a competitor.
The case was therefore distinguishable from *ARE*.

The stricter test for individual concern set out in *ARE* and *Sniace* was applied by the EFTA Court in Case E-5/07 *Private Barnehagers Landsforbund v EFTA Surveillance Authority*, decn of the EFTA Court 8 February 2008, [2008] 2 CMLR 818 (association of privately run kindergartens did not have locus to challenge a finding that public funding in Norway of municipal kindergartens was not a State aid). However, the Court went on to hold that the applicant did have locus to challenge the ESA's failure to open a formal investigation.

Fn 621. An appeal against the GC's ruling on admissibility in Case T-88/01 was dismissed by the CJ: Case C-260/05P *Sniace v Commission* [2007] ECR I-10005, [2008] 1 CMLR 1035. The CJ held that participation in the Commission's formal procedure is not a necessary condition for the finding that a decision is of individual concern. But on the facts, the GC's decision was upheld.

(iii) The grounds of annulment

Procedural irregularities. **Fn 631.** The GC's judgment in Case T-366/00 *Scott* **15.119** was overturned by the CJ: Case C-290/07P *Commission v Scott*, judgment of 2 September 2010. The CJ held, *inter alia*, that the GC had erred in holding that the Commission had acted in breach of its duty to exercise due diligence by failing to request either Scott or the French authorities to produce the valuations of the land at issue to which they referred merely in order to call in question the valuation used by the Commission: para 98. The case has been referred back to the GC.

Lack of reasoning. For a robust judgment of the GC annulling a decision on **15.120** this ground see Cases T-309/04, etc, *TV2/Danmark v Commission* [2008] ECR II-2935 where the GC found that 'the lack of a serious and detailed examination, in the contested decision, of the conditions under which TV2 was financed during the period under investigation is in turn reflected in the peremptory tone of the Commission's assertions in recital 71 of the contested decision'.

In Case C-333/07 *Société Régie Networks v Direction de contrôle fiscal Rhône-Alpes Bourgogne* [2008] ECR I-10807 the CJ held (in an Article 267 TFEU reference) that while it would have been preferable for the Commission in the contested decision expressly to have identified which of the categories of exception set out in Article 108(3) applied, the contested decision was not unlawful simply on the ground that no specific reasons were given which addressed those points: para 72. In Case T-268/06 *Olympiaki Aeroporia Ypiresies v Commission* [2008] ECR II-1091, part of the Commission's decision, concerning aid granted to an airline for losses incurred in the immediate aftermath of the terrorist attacks of 11 September 2001, was annulled for lack of reasoning. A challenge based on lack of reasoning was rejected by the GC in Case T-301/01 *Alitalia v Commission* [2008] ECR II-1753.

In Cases T-265/04, etc, *Tirrenia di Navigazione v Commission*, judgment of 4 March 2009 a Commission decision was annulled for inadequate reasoning as regards whether the aid was an existing or a new aid.

Fn 638. The appeal in Cases T-304&316/04 was dismissed: Case C-494/06P *Commission v Italy and WAM* [2009] ECR I-3639.

Fn 639. In Cases T-50/06, etc, *Ireland v Commission*, judgment of 12 December 2007, [2007] ECR II-172*, the GC noted that the appellants had raised a total of 23 pleas challenging an approval decision but decided the case on the ground of lack of adequate reasoning which it raised of its own motion. The case is on appeal: Case C-89/08P, not yet decided. See also Case T-177/07 *Mediaset v Commission*, judgment of 15 June 2010, para 140, distinguishing lack of reasoning from manifest error of assessment which can be examined by the court only if raised by the applicant (appeal dismissed: Case C-403/10P *Mediaset v Commission*, judgment of 28 July 2011); Case T-1/08 *Buczek Automotive v Commission*, judgment of 17 May 2011 (decn annulled because the Commission had not explained why trade between Member States was affected or competition distorted but had simply set out the terms of Article 107); Cases T-415/05, etc, *Greece v Commission*, judgment of 13 September 2010 (decn that an over-valuation of assets amounted to aid annulled because the Commission failed to state reasons why it had taken account only of the net book value of certain assets rather than their current market value).

Fn 640. In Cases C-341&342/06P *Chronopost and La Poste v UFEX* [2008] ECR I-4777, [2008] 3 CMLR 568 the CJ overturned the GC's judgment in Case T-613/97 *UFEX v Commission*, holding that since the contested decision clearly disclosed the Commission's reasoning, enabling the substance of that decision to be challenged subsequently before the competent court, it would be excessive to require a specific statement of reasons for each of the technical choices or each of the figures on which that reasoning is based. Neither the fact that this was the first decision dealing with the complex issue of how to calculate the aid in particular circumstances nor the fact that the Commission's decision was taken after it had withdrawn an earlier decision rejecting the complaint, increased the obligation on the Commission to state reasons.

15.121 **Rejection of complaint.** See the discussion of the appeals arising from the Commission's rejection of a complaint by Athinaïki Techniki concerning alleged State aid: Case C-362/09P *Athinaïki Techniki v Commission*, judgment of 16 December 2010, discussed in the update to paragraph 15.112, above.

15.122 **Review of the exercise of the Commission's discretion.** In adopting rules of conduct such as guidelines and notices, and announcing by publishing them that they will henceforth apply to the cases to which they relate, the Commission imposes a limit on the exercise of its discretion inasmuch as the guidelines and notices do not depart from the rules in the Treaty and are accepted by the Member States: see Cases C-75&80/05P *Germany and Glunz v Kronofrance SA* [2008] ECR I-6619, para 61.

Note that in Case C-290/07P *Commission v Scott*, judgment of 2 September 2010 the CJ overturned a ruling by the GC which had annulled a Commission decision on the grounds that the GC had exceeded its review jurisdiction. The GC had also failed to identify any manifest error of assessment on the part of the Commission in the choice of method and its application as regards a valuation exercise that constituted a complex economic assessment. The CJ remitted the case back to the GC. cf Case C-525/04P *Spain v Lenzing* [2007] ECR I-9947, [2008] 1 CMLR 1068 where the CJ rejected an argument that the GC had gone beyond the scope of proper review of the Commission's decision.

In Case T-301/01 *Alitalia v Commission* [2008] ECR II-1753, the GC noted that the Commission's assessment of whether an investment satisfies the private investor test is a complex economic matter so that judicial review of such a measure was limited.

Fn 653. In Case C-487/06P *British Aggregates Association v Commission* [2008] ECR I-10505, the CJ held that the GC erred in conducting only a limited review of the Commission's decision that the levy challenged was not a State aid. For subsequent proceedings see Case T-359/04 *British Aggregates Association v Commission*, judgment of 9 September 2010 (Commission decision to approve the aid without opening a full investigation procedure annulled).

But see Case T-163/05 *Bundesverband deutscher Banken v Commission*, judgment of 3 March 2010, para 38 where the GC held that the question of whether an investment secured an advantage which the undertaking would not have been able to obtain on the market was a matter of complex economic assessment and thus subject to the more limited standard of review.

Fn 654. In Case T-68/05 *Aker Warnow Werft GmbH, & Kvaerner ASA v Commission* [2009] ECR II-355 the GC annulled the Commission's decision on the ground that there had been a manifest error of assessment.

Fn 656. See also Case T-11/07 *Frucona Košice v Commission*, judgment of 7 December 2010, para 48.

Fn 659. See also Case T-332/06 *Alcoa Trasformazioni v Commission*, judgment of 25 March 2009 (extension of preferential electricity tariff to cover subsequent years was a new aid not an existing aid) where the GC stressed that to avoid confusion between the administrative and judicial proceedings, and to preserve the division of powers between the Commission and the European Courts, the Courts must avoid giving a final ruling on questions on which the Commission has merely formed a provisional view: para 61.

Infringement of the Treaty or of any rule of law.   **Fn 664.** See also Case T-332/06   **15.123**
Alcoa Trasformazioni v Commission, judgment of 25 March 2009 (extension of

preferential electricity tariff to cover subsequent years was a new aid not an existing aid).

9. The Relationship between Articles 87–89 and other Provisions of the Treaty

15.135   **Article 90.**   Article 90 EC is now Article 110 TFEU. In Case C-206/06 *Essent Netwerk Noord v Aluminium Delfzijl* [2008] ECR I-5497, [2008] 3 CMLR 895 the CJ held that a levy imposed on suppliers of domestic and imported electricity could be both contrary to Article 110 TFEU and a State aid because the levy was used to benefit domestic producers of electricity: 'A measure carried out by means of a discriminatory taxation and which is liable at the same time to be considered as forming part of an aid within the meaning of Article [107 TFEU], is governed both by the provisions of Articles [30 TFEU] or [110 TFEU] and by those applicable to State aid': para 59.